Linux® Bible

2008 Edition

Linux® Bible

2008 Edition

Boot Up to Ubuntu®, Fedora®, KNOPPIX, Debian®, openSUSE®, and 11 Other Distributions

Christopher Negus

WILEY

Wiley Publishing, Inc.

Linux® Bible 2008 Edition: Boot Up to Ubuntu®, Fedora®, KNOPPIX, Debian®, openSUSE®, and 11 Other Distributions

Published by
Wiley Publishing, Inc.
10475 Crosspoint Boulevard
Indianapolis, IN 46256
www.wiley.com

Copyright © 2008 by Wiley Publishing, Inc., Indianapolis, Indiana

Published simultaneously in Canada

ISBN: 978-0-470-23019-0

Manufactured in the United States of America

10 9 8 7 6 5 4 3 2 1

Library of Congress Cataloging-in-Publication Data is available from the publisher.

As always, I dedicate this book to my wife, Sheree.

About the Authors

Chris Negus has written or co-written dozens of books on Linux and UNIX, including *Red Hat Linux Bible* (all editions), *Fedora and Red Hat Enterprise Linux Bible*, *Linux Troubleshooting Bible*, *Linux Toys*, and *Linux Toys II*. In late 2007, Chris co-authored three books for the new Linux Toolbox series for power users: *Fedora Linux Toolbox*, *SUSE Linux Toolbox*, and *Ubuntu Linux Toolbox*. For eight years, he worked with the organization at AT&T that developed UNIX before moving to Utah to contribute to Novell's short-lived UnixWare project in the early 1990s. When not writing about Linux, Chris enjoys playing soccer and just hanging out with his family.

Emmett Dulaney is the author of several books on operating systems, networking, and certification. An assistant professor at Anderson University, he is also a columnist for *CertCities* and a frequent contributor to a number of other magazines.

Credits

Acquisitions Editor
Jenny Watson

Development Editor
Sara Shlaer

Technical Editor
Emmett Dulaney

Copy Editor
Nancy Rapoport

Editorial Manager
Mary Beth Wakefield

Production Manager
Tim Tate

**Vice President and
Executive Group Publisher**
Richard Swadley

Vice President and Executive Publisher
Joseph B. Wikert

Project Coordinator, Cover
Lynsey Stanford

Media Associate Project Manager
Laura Atkinson

Media Assistant Producer
Josh Frank

Media Quality Control
Kit Malone

Compositor
Kate Kaminski, Happenstance Type-O-Rama

Proofreader
Kathryn Duggan

Indexer
Johnna VanHoose Dinse

Acknowledgments

I consider anyone who has contributed to the free and open source software community to be a contributor to the book you are holding. The backbone of any Linux distribution is formed by the organizations that produce the distributions, the major projects included in Linux, and the thousands of people who give their time and code to support Linux. So, thanks to you all!

For *Linux Bible 2008 Edition*, Emmett Dulaney did most of the heavy lifting. Emmett's thorough technical edit of the entire book and updates to several critical sections made it possible for us to bring the book to market on schedule.

I'd like to acknowledge several contributors for their participation in previous editions. Wayne Tucker wrote and then updated the chapters on Debian, LAMP servers, and mail servers. Bill von Hagen contributed updates to the SUSE, Yellow Dog, and Ubuntu chapters. Jaldhar Vyas updated the Linspire chapter.

Thanks to the folks at Wiley for helping me press through the project. Jenny Watson did a wonderful job putting together the personnel needed to complete this book, in the face of my having five books scheduled to complete within a two-month period. Sara Shlaer did her usual great job keeping the project moving under a very challenging schedule. Thanks to Margot Maley Hutchison and Maureen Maloney from Waterside Productions for contracting the book for me with Wiley.

And finally, special thanks to my wife, Sheree. There's no way I could do the work I do without the solid support I get on the home front. I love you, and thanks for taking such good care of Seth, Caleb, and me.

Contents at a Glance

Part V: Running Servers

Part VI: Programming in Linux

Contents

Contents

Contents

Contents

Contents

Part III: Choosing and Installing a Linux Distribution

Contents

Contents

Part IV: Running Applications

Contents

Contents

Contents

Introduction

Insert the DVD or CD that comes with this book into a PC. Within five minutes, you'll be able to try out Linux with a full range of desktop applications. Within an hour, you can have a full-blown Linux desktop or server system installed on your computer. If you are like most of us who have been bitten by the Linux bug, you won't ever look back.

Linux Bible 2008 Edition is here to open your eyes to what Linux is, where it came from, and where it's going. But, most of all, the book is here to hand you Linux and help you get started. Because Linux is the operating system of free speech and free choice, *Linux Bible* gives you choices in selecting the Linux that is right for you.

On the DVD and CD that come with this book are 16 different Linux distributions that you are free to install, try out, and keep. You learn how those distributions are alike or different, and the book leads you through the basics of installing and setting up your Linux system as:

- **A desktop computer** — You have a full range of office, music, gaming, graphics, and other applications to use.
- **A server computer** — Using some of the world's best server software, you can set up your computer to be a Web server, file server, mail server, or print server.
- **A workstation** — You can draw on thousands of open source programming tools to develop your own software applications.

The Linux systems you have in your hand don't contain trialware or otherwise hobbled software. On the contrary, they feature software created by world-class development projects, the same teams that build the software that powers many professional businesses, schools, home desktops, and Internet service providers. In other words, this is truly first-rate software from developers who have made a commitment to producing software that can be used in the ways that you choose to use it.

Several of the Linux distributions offered on the DVD and CD that come with this book are live CDs that let you try a Linux distribution without installing. Some of those live CDs include features that let you install the contents of those live CDs to your hard disk. For example, you can try out Gentoo, Ubuntu, and Mandriva as live CDs, and then install those distributions permanently to your hard drive from icons on the desktops of those live CDs.

Unlike some other books on Linux, this book doesn't tie you to one Linux distribution. The book teaches you the essentials of Linux graphical interfaces, shell commands, and basic system administration. Separate chapters break down many of the major Linux distributions available today. Then descriptions of the major software projects in most Linux distributions (KDE and GNOME desktops, Apache Web servers, Samba file and printer sharing, and so on) guide you in setting up and using those features, regardless of which Linux you choose.

Understanding the Linux Mystique

To calm your fears that "free" software can't be that good, this book guides you through the strange and circuitous path of open source software development that led to the Linux phenomenon. It also details the major companies and organizations that are behind Linux and the open source movement today.

Along the way, you learn how you can become part of the open source and free software communities, whose stars are known by a single name (such as Linus) or a few initials (such as rms). You'll find a staggering number of open source projects, forums, and mailing lists that are thriving today (and always looking for more people to get involved).

How This Book Is Organized

Learn the basics of what goes into Linux and you will be able to use all sorts of devices and computers in the future. The book is organized in a way that enables you to start off at the very beginning with Linux, but still grow to the point where you can get going with some powerful server and programming features, if you care to.

Part I assumes that someone has set up a Linux system in front of you. So after "Starting with Linux" in Chapter 1, you learn the basics of how to

- Use the shell (Chapter 2)
- Work with your graphical desktop (Chapter 3)

In Part II, you learn how to

- Do basic administration (Chapter 4)
- Connect to the Internet (Chapter 5)
- Secure your Linux system (Chapter 6)

If you don't have Linux installed yet, this book helps you out in a big way: The companion DVD and CD include a variety of Linux distributions you can try. Part III (Chapters 7 through 19) describes each of those distributions and how to run them live or install them.

In Part IV, you learn to get some fun and useful features going in Linux so that you can

- Play music and video (Chapter 20)
- Write documents and work with graphics (Chapter 21)
- Use Web browsers and e-mail clients (Chapter 22)
- Play games (Chapter 23)

Linux creates powerful servers, and in Part V you learn to

- Set up a Web server using Apache, MySQL, and PHP in Linux (Chapter 24)
- Run a mail server (Chapter 25)
- Share printers with a CUPS print server (Chapter 26)
- Share files with a Samba or NFS file server (Chapter 27)

If you are coming to Linux for its programming environment, Part VI provides chapters that describe

- Programming environments and interfaces (Chapter 28)
- Programming tools and utilities (Chapter 29)

In addition, Appendix A tells you what's on the DVD and CD, how to install from the DVD or CD, and how to burn additional installation CDs from the software that comes with this book. Appendix B helps get you "plugged in" to the Linux community.

What You Will Get from This Book

By the time you finish this book, you'll have a good basic understanding of many of the major features in Linux and how you can use them. If you decide then that you want to go a bit deeper into any Red Hat Linux distribution, *Fedora 8 and Enterprise Linux Bible* (Wiley, 2007) is a good next step, with content that includes how to set up many different types of Linux servers.

If you are more technically oriented, *Linux Troubleshooting Bible* (Wiley, 2004) can be a good way to learn more advanced skills for securing and troubleshooting Linux systems. Or a *Linux Toolbox* book for Fedora, Ubuntu, or SUSE (Wiley, 2007) can provide you with over 1000 Linux commands to help you become a Linux power user.

If you are looking for some fun, try out some projects with an old PC and free software from *Linux Toys II* (Wiley, 2005).

Conventions Used in This Book

Throughout the book, special typography indicates code and commands. Commands and code are shown in a monospaced font:

```
This is how code looks.
```

In the event that an example includes both input and output, the monospaced font is still used, but input is presented in bold type to distinguish the two. Here's an example:

```
$ ftp ftp.handsonhistory.com
Name (home:jake): jake
Password: ******
```

The following items are used to call your attention to points that are particularly important.

NOTE Notes provide extra information to which you need to pay special attention.

TIP Tips show a special way of performing a particular task.

CAUTION Cautions alert you to take special care when executing a procedure, or damage to your computer hardware or software could result.

CROSS-REF Cross-References direct you to further information on a subject that you can find outside the current chapter.

COMING FROM WINDOWS A Coming from Windows item provides tips to help you transfer your knowledge of Windows systems to the Linux world.

The "On the CD" and "On the DVD" items point out features related to the media that accompany the book.

As for styles in the text:

- We highlight new terms and important words with italics when we introduce them.
- We show keyboard strokes like this: Ctrl+A.

We show filenames, URLs, and code within the text like so: `persistence.properties`.

Part I

Linux First Steps

Chapter 1

Starting with Linux

I n only a few years, Linux has moved from being considered a specialty operating system into the mainstream. Precompiled and configured Linux systems can be installed with no technical expertise. Versions of Linux run on all kinds of devices, from PCs to handhelds (see www.linuxdevices.com) to game consoles (such as PlayStation 3) to supercomputers. In short, Linux has become a system that can be run almost anywhere by almost anyone.

IN THIS CHAPTER

Understanding Linux

Using Linux

Linux myths, legends, and FUD

On both desktop and server computers, Linux has become a formidable operating system across a variety of business applications. Today, large enterprises can deploy thousands of systems using Linux distributions from companies such as Red Hat, Inc. and Novell, Inc. Small businesses can put together the mixture of office and Internet services they need to keep their costs down.

The free and open source software (FOSS) development model that espoused sharing, freedom, and openness is now on a trajectory to surpass the quality of other operating systems outside of the traditional Linux servers and technical workstations. What were once weak components of Linux, such as easy-to-use desktops and personal productivity applications, have improved at a rapid pace. In areas of security, usability, connectivity, and network services, Linux has continued to improve and outshine the competition.

Computer industry heavy-hitters such as Microsoft and Oracle have taken notice of Linux. Microsoft has struck agreements with Linux companies including Novell, Linspire, and Xandros to form partnerships that primarily protect those companies against threatened Microsoft lawsuits. Oracle has begun producing its own Linux system called Unbreakable Linux, to try to stem the flow of customers to Red Hat Enterprise Linux.

What does this all add up to? A growing swirl of excitement around the operating system that the big guys can't seem to get rid of. For people like you, who want the freedom to use your computer software as you like, it means great prospects for the future.

Let this book help you grab your first look at the distributions, applications, services, and community that make up the phenomenon that has become Linux.

Taking Your First Step

In your hands, you have 16 Linux distributions (on CD and DVD), thousands of applications, and descriptions for getting it all running on your own computer. For you right now, the worldwide Linux phenomenon is just a reboot away.

Linux Bible 2008 Edition brings you into the world of free and open source software that, through some strange twists and turns, has fallen most publicly under the "Linux" banner. Through descriptions and procedures, this book helps you:

- Understand what Linux is, who "owns" it, and where it comes from.
- Sort through the various distributions of Linux to choose one (or more) that is right for you. You get several Linux systems on this book's CD and DVD. (Linux is all about choice, too!)
- Try out Linux as a desktop computer, server computer, or programmer's workstation.
- Become connected to the open source software movement, as well as many separate high-quality software projects that are included with Linux.

Whether you are using Linux for the first time or just want to try out a new Linux distribution, *Linux Bible 2008 Edition* is your guide to using Linux and the latest open source technology. While different Linux distributions vary in the exact software they include, this book describes the most popular software available for Linux to:

- Manage your desktop (menus, icons, windows, and so on)
- Listen to music and watch video
- Use word processor, spreadsheet, and other office productivity applications
- Browse the Web and send e-mail
- Play games
- Find thousands of other open source software packages you can get for free

Because most Linux distributions also include features that let them act as servers (in fact, that's one of the things Linux has always been best at), you'll also learn about software available for Linux that lets you do the following:

- Connect to the Internet or other network

- Use Linux as a firewall, router, and DHCP server to protect and manage your private network

- Run a Web server (using Apache, MySQL, and PHP)

- Run a mail server (using Exim or other mail transfer agent)

- Run a print server (using Samba or CUPS)

- Run a file server (using FTP or Samba)

- Use the exact same enterprise-quality software used by major corporations (such as Google and Amazon.com), universities, and businesses of all sizes

This book guides you through the basics of getting started with the Linux features just mentioned, plus many more features that I'll get to later. You'll go through the following basic steps:

1. **Understanding Linux.** You need to know where Linux came from, how it is developed, and how it's ultimately packaged. This chapter describes the UNIX heritage on which Linux was founded, the free and open source software development efforts underway, and the organizations and individuals that package and produce Linux distributions.

2. **Trying Linux.** In the past, an impediment to trying Linux was getting it installed on a computer that was devoted solely to Microsoft Windows. With bootable Linux systems such as KNOPPIX (and others included with this book), you can boot a fully functioning Linux from DVD, CD, or floppy disk without disturbing the current contents of your computer.

3. **Installing Linux.** You can install a fully functioning Linux system permanently on your PC's hard disk. Disk space required varies from under 100 megabytes for a minimal installation to over 6 gigabytes for a full range of desktop, server, and programming features. Chapters in Part III, "Choosing and Installing a Linux Distribution," describe how to install several different Linux distributions.

4. **Using Linux.** You won't know if Linux can be used to replace your current desktop or server system until you start using it. This book helps you try OpenOffice.org software to write documents, create spreadsheets, and build presentations. It describes Rhythmbox and mplayer for playing your music and video content, respectively, and covers some of the best Linux tools available for Web browsing (for example, Firefox, Seamonkey, and Konqueror) and managing your e-mail (such as Evolution and Thunderbird).

5. **Configuring Linux.** Linux works very well as a desktop system, and it can also be configured to act as a router, a firewall, and a variety of server types. While there are some excellent graphical tools for administering Linux systems, most Linux administrators edit configuration files and run commands to configure Linux. Part II, "Running the Show," contains basic information for administering Linux, and Part V, "Running Servers," discusses procedures for setting up various types of servers.

Once you've been through the book, you should be proficient enough to track down your more advanced questions through the volumes of man pages, FAQs, HOWTOs, and forums that cover different aspects of the Linux operating system.

Starting Right Now

Now that you have read a few pages, if you are impatient to get started, insert the DVD or CD that comes with this book into the appropriate drive on your PC and reboot. When you see the boot screen, press Enter. When the DVD or CD boots, the following happens, respectively:

- **KNOPPIX starts up.** A fully functional KNOPPIX desktop Linux system will boot directly from the DVD. From that Linux system, you can do everything you'd expect to do from a modern desktop computing system: write documents, play music, communicate over the Internet, work with images, and so on. If you have a wired Ethernet connection that connects to the Internet when you start up Windows, most likely it will also connect automatically when KNOPPIX starts.

- **Damn Small Linux (DSL) starts up.** This small, amazing desktop-oriented Linux system starts up directly from the CD that comes with this book. Besides being expandable and adaptable, DSL runs on everything from low-end PCs to powerful workstation hardware while being small enough to fit on a mini CD (only about 50MB in size).

Now that you have seen some examples of what Linux can be, read on to see what Linux is and where it came from.

Understanding Linux

People who don't know what Linux is sometimes ask me if it's a program that runs on Microsoft Windows. When I tell them that Linux is, itself, an operating system like Windows and that they can remove (or never purchase) Windows, I sometimes get a surprised reaction: "A PC can run with nothing from Microsoft on it?" The answer is yes!

The next question about Linux is often: "How can Linux be free?" While the full answer to that is a bit longer (and covered later), the short answer is: "Because the people who write the code license it to be freely distributed." Keep in mind, however, that the critical issue relating to the word "free" is "freedom," meaning that you are free to rebuild, reuse, reconfigure, and otherwise do what you like with the code. The only major responsibility is that if you change the software, you pass it forward so that others may benefit from your work as well.

Linux is a full-blown operating system that is a free clone of the powerful and stable UNIX operating system. Start your computer with Linux, and Linux takes care of the operation of your PC and manages the following aspects of your computer:

- **Processor** — Because Linux can run many processes from many different users at the same time (even with multiple CPUs on the same machine), Linux needs to be able to manage those processes. The Linux scheduler sets the priorities for running tasks and manages which processes run on which CPUs (if multiple processors are present). The scheduler can be tuned differently for different types of Linux systems. If it's tuned properly, the most important processes get the quickest responses from the processor. For example, a Linux scheduler on a desktop system gives higher priority to things such as moving a window on the desktop than it does to a background file transfer.

- **Memory** — Linux tries to keep processes with the most immediate need in RAM, while managing how processes that exceed the available memory are moved to swap space. *Swap space* is a defined area on your hard disk that's used to handle the overflow of running processes and data. When RAM is full, processes are placed in swap space. When swap space is full (something that you don't want to happen), new processes can't start up.

- **Devices** — Linux supports thousands of hardware devices, yet keeps the kernel a manageable size by including only a small set of drivers in the active kernel. Using loadable modules, the kernel can add support for other hardware as needed. Modules can be loaded and unloaded on demand, as hardware is added and removed. (The kernel, described in detail a bit later on, is the heart of a Linux operating system.)

- **File systems** — File systems provide the structure in which files are stored on hard disk, CD, DVD, floppy disks, or other media. Linux knows about different file system types (such as Linux ext3 and reiserfs file systems, or VFAT and NTFS from Windows systems) and how to manage them.

- **Security** — Like UNIX, Linux was built from the ground up to enable multiple users to access the system simultaneously. To protect each user's resources, every file, directory, and application is assigned sets of read, write, and execute permissions that define who can access them. In a standard Linux system, the root user has access to the entire system, some special logins have access to control particular services (such as Apache for Web services), and users can be assigned permission individually or in groups. Recent features such as Security Enhanced Linux and AppArmor enable more refined tuning and protection in highly secure computing environments.

What I have just described are components that are primarily managed by what is referred to as the Linux *kernel*. In fact, the Linux kernel (which was created and is still maintained by Linus Torvalds) is what gives Linux its name. The kernel is the software that starts up when you boot your computer and interfaces with the programs you use so they can communicate effectively and simply with your computer hardware.

Components such as administrative commands and applications from other free and open source software projects work with the kernel to make Linux a complete operating system. The GNU Project, in particular, contributed many implementations of standard UNIX components that are now in Linux. Apache, KDE, GNOME, and other major open source projects in Linux, discussed a bit later, have also contributed to the success of Linux. Those other projects added such things as:

- **Graphical user interfaces (GUIs)** — Consisting of a graphical framework (typically the X Window System), window managers, panels, icons, and menus. GUIs enable you to use Linux with a keyboard and mouse combination, instead of just typing commands (as was done in the old days).

- **Administrative utilities** — Including hundreds (perhaps thousands) of commands and graphical windows to do such things as add users, manage disks, monitor the network, install software, and generally secure and manage your computer.

- **Applications** — Although no Linux distribution includes all of them, there are literally thousands of games, office productivity tools, Web browsers, chat windows, multimedia players, and other applications available for Linux.

- **Programming tools** — Including programming utilities for creating applications and libraries for implementing specialty interfaces.

- **Server features** — Enabling you to offer services from your Linux computer to another computer on the network. In other words, while Linux includes Web browsers to view Web pages, it can also be the computer that serves up Web pages to others. Popular server features include Web, mail, database, printer, file, DNS, and DHCP servers.

Once Linus Torvalds and friends had a working Linux kernel, pulling together a complete open source operating system was possible because so much of the available "free" software was:

- **Covered by the GNU Public License (GPL) or similar license** — That allowed the entire operating system to be freely distributed, provided guidelines were followed relating to how the source code for that software was made available going forward (see `www.gnu.org/licenses/gpl.html`).

- **Based on UNIX-like systems** — Clones of virtually all the other user-level components of a UNIX system had been created. Those and other utilities and applications were built to run on UNIX or other UNIX-like systems.

Linux has become one of the most popular culminations of the open source software movement. But the traditions of sharing code and building communities that made Linux possible started years before Linux was born. You could argue that it began in a comfortable think tank known as Bell Laboratories.

Exploring Linux History

Some histories of Linux begin with this message posted by Linus Torvalds to the `comp.os.minix` newsgroup on August 25, 1991:

> Hello everybody out there using minix -
>
> I'm doing a (free) operating system (just a hobby, won't be big and professional like gnu) for 386(486) AT clones. This has been brewing since april, and is starting to get ready. I'd like any feedback on things people like/dislike in minix, as my OS resembles it somewhat (same physical layout of the file-system (due to practical reasons) among other things) . . . Any suggestions are welcome, but I won't promise I'll implement them :-)
>
> Linus (torvalds@kruuna.helsinki.fi)

PS. Yes — it's free of any minix code, and it has a multi-threaded fs. It is NOT protable [sic] (uses 386 task switching etc), and it probably never will support anything other than AT-harddisks, as that's all I have :-(.

Reprinted from Linux International Web site
(www.li.org/linuxhistory.php)

Minix was a UNIX-like operating system that ran on PCs in the early 1990s. Like Minix, Linux was also a clone of the UNIX operating system.

> **NOTE** For a good way to learn more about how Linux was created, pick up the book *Just For Fun: The Story of an Accidental Revolutionary* by Linus Torvalds (2001, HarperCollins).

To truly appreciate how a free operating system could have been modeled after a proprietary system from AT&T Bell Laboratories, it helps to understand the culture in which UNIX was created and the chain of events that made the essence of UNIX possible to reproduce freely.

From a Free-Flowing UNIX Culture at Bell Labs

From the very beginning, the UNIX operating system was created and nurtured in a communal environment. Its creation was not driven by market needs, but by a desire to overcome impediments to producing programs. AT&T, which owned the UNIX trademark originally, eventually made UNIX into a commercial product, but by that time, many of the concepts (and even much of the early code) that made UNIX special had fallen into the public domain.

If you are under 30 years old, you may not remember a time when AT&T was "the" phone company. Up until the early 1980s, AT&T didn't have to think much about competition because if you wanted a phone in the United States, you had to go to AT&T. It had the luxury of funding pure research projects. The mecca for such projects was the Bell Laboratories site in Murray Hill, New Jersey.

After the failure of a project called Multics in 1969, Bell Labs employees Ken Thompson and Dennis Ritchie set off on their own to create an operating system that would offer an improved environment for developing software. Up to that time, most programs were written on punch cards that had to be fed in batches to mainframe computers. In a 1980 lecture on "The Evolution of the UNIX Time-sharing System," Dennis Ritchie summed up the spirit that started UNIX:

> What we wanted to preserve was not just a good environment in which to do programming, but a system around which a fellowship could form. We knew from experience that the essence of communal computing as supplied by remote-access, time-shared machines is not just to type programs into a terminal instead of a keypunch, but to encourage close communication.

The simplicity and power of the UNIX design began breaking down barriers that impeded software developers. The foundation of UNIX was set with several key elements:

- **The UNIX file system** — After creating the structure that allowed levels of subdirectories (which, for today's desktop users, looks like folders inside of folders), UNIX could be used to organize the files and directories in intuitive ways. Furthermore, complex methods of accessing disks, tapes, and other devices were greatly simplified by representing those devices as individual device files that you could also access as items in a directory.

- **Input/output redirection** — Early UNIX systems also included input redirection and pipes. From a command line, UNIX users could direct the output of a command to a file using a right arrow key (>). Later, the concept of pipes (|) was added where the output of one command could be directed to the input of another command. For example, the command line

```
$ cat file1 file2 | sort | pr | lpr
```

concatenates (cat) file1 and file2, sorts (sort) the lines in those files alphabetically, paginates the sorted text for printing (pr), and directs the output to the computer's default printer (lpr). This method of directing input and output enabled developers to create their own specialized utilities that could be joined with existing utilities. This modularity made it possible for lots of code to be developed by lots of different people.

- **Portability** — Much of the early work in simplifying the experience of using UNIX led to its also becoming extraordinarily portable to run on different computers. By having device drivers (represented by files in the file system tree), UNIX could present an interface to applications in such a way that the programs didn't have to know about the details of the underlying hardware. To later port UNIX to another system, developers had only to change the drivers. The applications didn't have to change for different hardware!

  To make the concept of portability a reality, however, a high-level programming language was needed to implement the software. To that end, Brian Kernighan and Dennis Ritchie created the C programming language. In 1973, UNIX was rewritten in C. Today, C is still the primary language used to create the UNIX (and Linux) operating system kernels.

As Ritchie went on to say in his 1980 lecture:

> Today, the only important UNIX program still written in assembler is the assembler itself; virtually all the utility programs are in C, and so are most of the applications programs, although there are sites with many in Fortran, Pascal, and Algol 68 as well. It seems certain that much of the success of UNIX follows from the readability, modifiability, and portability of its software that in turn follows from its expression in high-level languages.

If you are a Linux enthusiast and are interested in what features from the early days of Linux have survived, an interesting read is Dennis Ritchie's reprint of the first UNIX programmer's manual (dated November 3, 1971). You can find it at Dennis Ritchie's Web site: http://cm .bell-labs.com/cm/cs/who/dmr/1stEdman.html. The form of this documentation is UNIX man pages — which is still the primary format for documenting UNIX and Linux operating system commands and programming tools today.

What's clear as you read through the early documentation and accounts of the UNIX system is that the development was a free-flowing process, lacked ego, and was dedicated to making UNIX excellent. This process led to a sharing of code (both inside and outside of Bell Labs) that allowed rapid development of a high-quality UNIX operating system. It also led to an operating system that AT&T would find difficult to reel back in later.

To a Commercialized UNIX

Before the AT&T divestiture in 1984, when it was split up into AT&T and seven "baby Bell" companies, AT&T was forbidden to sell computer systems. Companies you now know by names such as Verizon, Qwest, and Lucent Technologies were all part of AT&T. As a result of AT&T's monopoly of the telephone system, the U.S. government was concerned that an unrestricted AT&T might dominate the fledgling computer industry.

Because AT&T was restricted from selling computers directly to customers before its divestiture, UNIX source code was licensed to universities for a nominal fee. There was no UNIX operating system for sale from AT&T that you didn't have to compile yourself.

BSD Arrives

In 1975, UNIX V6 became the first version of UNIX available for widespread use outside of Bell Laboratories. From this early UNIX source code, the first major variant of UNIX was created at University of California at Berkeley. It was named the Berkeley Software Distribution (BSD).

For most of the next decade, the BSD and Bell Labs versions of UNIX headed off in separate directions. BSD continued forward in the free-flowing, share-the-code manner that was the hallmark of the early Bell Labs UNIX, while AT&T started steering UNIX toward commercialization. With the formation of a separate UNIX Laboratory, which moved out of Murray Hill and down the road to Summit, New Jersey, AT&T began its attempts to commercialize UNIX. By 1984, divestiture was behind AT&T and it was ready to really start selling UNIX.

UNIX Laboratory and Commercialization

The UNIX Laboratory was considered a jewel that couldn't quite find a home or a way to make a profit. As it moved between Bell Laboratories and other areas of AT&T, its name changed several times. It is probably best remembered by its last name, which it had as it began its spin-off from AT&T: UNIX System Laboratories (USL).

The UNIX source code that came out of USL, the legacy of which is now owned in part by Santa Cruz Operation (SCO), has been used as the basis for ever-dwindling lawsuits by SCO against major Linux vendors (such as IBM and Red Hat, Inc.). Because of that, I think the efforts from USL that have contributed to the success of Linux are sometimes disrespected.

You have to remember that, during the 1980s, many computer companies were afraid that a newly divested AT&T would pose more of a threat to controlling the computer industry than would an upstart company in Redmond, Washington. To calm the fears of IBM, Intel, DEC, and other computer companies, the UNIX Lab made the following commitments to ensure a level playing field:

- **Source code only** — Instead of producing its own boxed set of UNIX, AT&T continued to sell only source code and to make it available equally to all licensees. Each company would then port UNIX to its own equipment. It wasn't until about 1992, when the lab was spun off as a joint venture with Novell (called Univel), and then eventually sold to Novell, that a commercial boxed set of UNIX (called UnixWare) was produced directly from that source code.

- **Published interfaces** — To create an environment of fairness and community to its OEMs (original equipment manufacturers), AT&T began standardizing what different ports of UNIX had to be able to do to still be called UNIX. To that end, Portable Operating System Interface (POSIX) standards and the AT&T UNIX System V Interface Definition (SVID) were specifications UNIX vendors could use to create compliant UNIX systems. Those same documents also served as road maps for the creation of Linux.

> **NOTE** In an early e-mail newsgroup post, Linus Torvalds made a request for a copy, preferably online, of the POSIX standard. I think that nobody from AT&T expected someone to actually be able to write their own clone of UNIX from those interfaces, without using any of its UNIX source code.

- **Technical approach** — Again, until the very end of USL, most decisions on the direction of UNIX were made based on technical considerations. Management was promoted up through the technical ranks and to my knowledge there was never any talk of writing software to break other companies' software or otherwise restrict the success of USL's partners.

When USL eventually started taking on marketing experts and creating a desktop UNIX product for end users, Microsoft Windows already had a firm grasp on the desktop market. Also, because the direction of UNIX had always been toward source-code licensing destined for large computing systems, USL had pricing difficulties for its products. For example, on software it was including with UNIX, USL found itself having to pay out per-computer licensing fees that were based on $100,000 mainframes instead of $2,000 PCs. Add to that the fact that no application programs were available with UnixWare, and you can see why the endeavor failed.

Successful marketing of UNIX systems at the time, however, was happening with other computer companies. SCO had found a niche market, primarily selling PC versions of UNIX running dumb terminals in small offices. Sun Microsystems was selling lots of UNIX workstations (originally based on BSD but merged with UNIX in SVR4) for programmers and high-end technology applications (such as stock trading).

Other commercial UNIXes were also emerging by the 1980s. This new ownership assertion of UNIX was beginning to take its toll on the spirit of open contributions. Lawsuits were being initiated to protect UNIX source code and trademarks. In 1984, this new, restrictive UNIX gave rise to an organization that eventually led a path to Linux: the Free Software Foundation.

To a GNU Free-Flowing (not) UNIX

In 1984, Richard M. Stallman started the GNU Project (www.gnu.org), recursively named by the phrase GNU's Not UNIX. As a project of the Free Software Foundation (FSF), GNU was intended to become a recoding of the entire UNIX operating system that could be freely distributed. The GNU Project page (www.gnu.org/gnu/thegnuproject.html) tells the story of how the project came about in Stallman's own words.

While rewriting millions of lines of code might seem daunting for one or two people, spreading the effort across dozens or even hundreds of programmers made the project possible. It turned out that not only could the same results be gained by all new code, but in some cases, that code was better than the original UNIX versions. Because everyone could see the code being produced for the project, poorly written code could be corrected quickly or replaced over time.

If you are familiar with UNIX, try searching the more than 3,400 GNU software packages for your favorite UNIX command from the Free Software Directory (http://directory.fsf.org/GNU). Chances are you will find it there, along with many, many other software projects available as add-ons.

Over time, the term *free software* has been mostly replaced by the term *open source software*. As a nod to both the two camps, however, some people use the term Free and Open Source Software (FOSS) instead. An underlying principle of FOSS, however, is that, while you are free to use the software as you like, you have some responsibility to make your improvements to the code available to others. In that way, everyone in the community can benefit from your work as you have benefited from the work of others.

To clearly define how open source software should be handled, the GNU software project created the GNU Public License (you can read the GPL in its entirety at the end of this book). While many other software licenses cover slightly different approaches to protecting free software, the GPL is perhaps the most well known — and it's the one that covers the Linux kernel itself. Basic features of the GNU Public License include:

- **Author rights** — The original author retains the rights to his or her software.
- **Free distribution** — People can use the GNU software in their own software, changing and redistributing it as they please. They do, however, have to include the source code with their distribution (or make it easily available).
- **Copyright maintained** — Even if you were to repackage and resell the software, the original GNU agreement must be maintained with the software, which means all future recipients of the software have the opportunity to change the source code, just as you did.

There is no warranty on GNU software. If something goes wrong, the original developer of the software has no obligation to fix the problem. However, there are many organizations, big and small, that offer paid support packages for the software when it is included in their Linux or other open source software distribution. (See the "OSI Open Source Definition" section later in this chapter for a more detailed definition of open source software.)

Despite its success producing thousands of UNIX utilities, the GNU Project itself failed to produce one critical piece of code: the kernel. Its attempts to build an open source kernel with the GNU Hurd project (`www.gnu.org/software/hurd`) were unsuccessful.

BSD Loses Some Steam

The one software project that had a chance of beating out Linux to be the premier open source software project was the venerable old BSD project. By the late 1980s, BSD developers at UC Berkeley realized that they had already rewritten most of the UNIX source code they had received a decade earlier.

In 1989, University of California (UC) Berkeley distributed its own UNIX-like code as Net/1 and later (in 1991) as Net/2. Just as UC Berkeley was preparing a complete, UNIX-like operating system that was free from all AT&T code, AT&T hit them with a lawsuit in 1992. The suit claimed that the software was written using trade secrets taken from AT&T's UNIX system.

It's important to note here that BSD developers had completely rewritten the copyright-protected code from AT&T. Copyright was the primary means AT&T used to protect its rights to the UNIX code. Some believe that if AT&T had patented the concepts covered in that code, there might not be a Linux (or any UNIX clone) operating system today.

The lawsuit was dropped when Novell bought UNIX System Laboratories from AT&T in 1994. But, during that critical time period, there was enough fear and doubt about the legality of the BSD code that the momentum BSD had gained to that point in the fledgling open source community was lost. Many people started looking for another open source alternative. The time was ripe for a college student from Finland who was working on his own kernel.

NOTE   Today, BSD versions are available from three projects: FreeBSD, NetBSD, and OpenBSD. People generally characterize FreeBSD as the easiest to use, NetBSD as available on the most computer hardware platforms, and OpenBSD as fanatically secure. Many security-minded individuals still prefer BSD over Linux.

Linus Builds the Missing Piece

Linus Torvalds started work on Linux in 1991, while he was a student at the University of Helsinki, Finland. He wanted to create a UNIX-like kernel so that he could use the same kind of operating system on his home PC that he used at school. At the time, Linus was using Minix, but he wanted to go beyond what the Minix standards permitted.

As noted earlier, Linus announced the first public version of the Linux kernel to the comp.os.minix newsgroup on August 25, 1991, although Linus guesses that the first version didn't actually come out until mid-September of that year.

Although Torvalds stated that Linux was written for the 386 processor and probably wasn't portable, others persisted in encouraging (and contributing to) a more portable approach in the early versions of Linux. By October 5, Linux 0.02 was released with much of the original assembly code rewritten in the C programming language, which made it possible to start porting it to other machines.

The Linux kernel was the last — and the most important — piece of code that was needed to complete a whole UNIX-like operating system under the GPL. So, when people started putting together distributions, the name Linux and not GNU is what stuck. Some distributions such as Debian, however, refer to themselves as GNU/Linux distributions. (Not including GNU in the title or subtitle of a Linux operating system is also a matter of much public grumbling of some members of the GNU Project. See `www.gnu.org`.)

Within the next few years, commercial and non-commercial Linux distributions began to emerge. MCC Interim Linux (`www.ibiblio.org/pub/historic-linux/distributions/MCC/`) was released in the U.K. in February 1992. Slackware Linux (described in Chapter 14), which was first released in April 1993, is one of the oldest surviving Linux distributions.

Today, Linux can be described as an open source UNIX-like operating system that reflects a combination of SVID, POSIX, and BSD compliance. Linux continues to aim toward compliance with POSIX as well as with standards set by the new owner of the UNIX trademark, The Open Group (`www.unix-systems.org`).

The non-profit Open Source Development Labs, renamed the Linux Foundation after merging with the Free Standards Group (`www.linux-foundation.org`), which employs Linus Torvalds, manages the direction today of Linux development efforts. Its sponsors list is like a Who's Who of commercial Linux vendors, including IBM, Red Hat, SUSE (Novell), VA Software, HP, Dell, Computer Associates, Intel, Cisco Systems, and others. The Linux Foundation's primary charter is to protect and accelerate the growth of Linux by providing legal protection and software development standards for Linux developers.

Although much of the thrust of corporate Linux efforts is on corporate, enterprise computing, huge improvements are continuing in the desktop arena as well. The KDE and GNOME desktop environments continuously improve the Linux experience for casual users. Major efforts are underway to offer critical pieces of desktop components that are still not available in open source versions, including multimedia software and office productivity applications.

Linus continues to maintain and improve the Linux kernel.

NOTE To get more detailed histories of Linux, I recommend visiting the LWN.net site. LWN.net has kept a detailed Linux timeline from 1998 to the present day. For example, the 2006 timeline is available at `http://lwn.net/Articles/Timeline2006`. Another good resource is the book *Open Sources: Voices from the Open Source Revolution* (O'Reilly). The whole first edition (published in 1999) is available online (`www.oreilly.com/catalog/opensources/book/toc.html`).

What's So Great About Linux?

Leveraging work done on UNIX and GNU projects helped to get Linux up and running quickly. The culture of sharing in the open source community and adoption of a wide array of tools for communicating on the Internet have helped Linux move quickly through infancy and adolescence to become a mature operating system.

The simple commitment to share code is probably the single most powerful contributor to the growth of the open source software movement in general, and Linux in particular. That commitment has also encouraged involvement from the kind of people who are willing to contribute back to that community in all kinds of ways. The willingness of Linus to incorporate code from others in the Linux kernel has also been critical to the success of Linux.

The following sections characterize Linux and the communities that support it.

Features in Linux

If you have not used Linux before, you should expect a few things to be different from using other operating systems. Here is a brief list of some Linux features that you might find cool:

- **No constant rebooting** — Uptime is valued as a matter of pride (remember, Linux and other UNIX systems are most often used as servers, which are expected to, and do, stay up 24/7/365). After the original installation, you can install or remove most software without having to reboot your computer.

- **Start/stop services without interrupting others** — You can start and stop individual services (such as Web, file, and e-mail services) without rebooting or even interrupting the work of any other users or features of the computer. In other words, you should not have to reboot your computer every time someone sneezes. (Installing a new kernel is just about the only reason you need to reboot.)

- **Portable software** — You can usually change to another Linux, UNIX, or BSD system and still use the exact same software! Most open source software projects were created to run on any UNIX-like system and many also run on Windows systems, if you need them to. If it won't run where you want it to, chances are that you, or someone you hire, can port it to the computer you want. (*Porting* refers to modifying an application or driver so it works in a different computer architecture or operating system.)

- **Downloadable applications** — If the applications you want are not delivered with your version of Linux, you can often download and install them with a single command, using tools such as apt, urpmi, and yum.

- **No settings hidden in code or registries** — Once you learn your way around Linux, you'll find that (given the right permissions on your computer) most configuration is done in plain text files that are easy to find and change. Because Linux is based on openness, nothing is hidden from you. Even the source code, for GPL-covered software, is available for your review.

- **Mature desktop** — The X Window System (providing the framework for your Linux desktop) has been around longer than Microsoft Windows. The KDE and GNOME desktop environments provide graphical interfaces (windows, menus, icons, and so forth) that rival those on Microsoft systems. Ease-of-use problems with Linux systems are rapidly evaporating.

- **Freedom** — Linux, in its most basic form, has no corporate agenda or bottom line to meet. You are free to choose the Linux distribution that suits you, look at the code that runs the system, add and remove any software you like, and make your computer do what you want it to do. Linux runs on everything from supercomputers to cell phones and everything in between. Many countries are rediscovering their freedom of choice and making the switch at government and educational levels. France, Germany, Korea, and India are just a few that have taken notice of Linux. The list continues to grow.

There are some aspects of Linux that make it hard for some new users to get started. One is that Linux is typically set up to be secure by default, so you need to adjust to using an administrative login (root) to make most changes that affect the whole computer system. Although this can be a bit inconvenient, trust me, it makes your computer safer than just letting anyone do anything. This model was built around a true multiuser system. You can set up logins for everyone who uses your Linux computer, and you (and others) can customize your environment however you see fit without affecting anyone else's settings.

For the same reason, many services are off by default, so you need to turn them on and do at least minimal configuration to get them going. For someone who is used to Windows, Linux can be difficult just because it is different from Windows. But because you're reading this book, I assume you want to learn about those differences.

OSI Open Source Definition

For software developers, Linux provides a platform that lets them change the operating system as they like and get a wide range of help creating the applications they need. One of the watchdogs of the open source movement is the Open Source Initiative (`www.opensource.org`). This is how the OSI Web site describes open source software:

> The basic idea behind open source is very simple: When programmers can read, redistribute, and modify the source code for a piece of software, the software evolves. People improve it, people adapt it, people fix bugs. And this can happen at a speed that, if one is used to the slow pace of conventional software development, seems astonishing.

> We in the open source community have learned that this rapid evolutionary process produces better software than the traditional closed model, in which only a very few programmers can see the source and everybody else must blindly use an opaque block of bits.

While the primary goal of open source software is to make source code available, other goals are also defined by OSI in its Open Source Definition. Most of the following rules for acceptable open source licenses are to protect the freedom and integrity of the open source code:

- **Free distribution** — An open source license can't require a fee from anyone who resells the software.
- **Source code** — The source code has to be included with the software and not be restricted from being redistributed.
- **Derived works** — The license must allow modification and redistribution of the code under the same terms.
- **Integrity of the author's source code** — The license may require that those who use the source code remove the original project's name or version if they change the source code.

- **No discrimination against persons or groups** — The license must allow all people to be equally eligible to use the source code.

- **No discrimination against fields of endeavor** — The license can't restrict a project from using the source code because it is commercial or because it is associated with a field of endeavor that the software provider doesn't like.

- **Distribution of license** — No additional license should be needed to use and redistribute the software.

- **License must not be specific to a product** — The license can't restrict the source code to a particular software distribution.

- **License must not restrict other software** — The license can't prevent someone from including the open source software on the same medium as non–open source software.

- **License must be technology-neutral** — The license can't restrict methods in which the source code can be redistributed.

Open source licenses used by software development projects must meet these criteria to be accepted as open source software by OSI. More than 40 different licenses are accepted by OSI to be used to label software as "OSI Certified Open Source Software." In addition to the GPL, other popular OSI-approved licenses include:

- **LGPL** — The GNU Lesser General Public License (LGPL) is a license that is often used for distributing libraries that other application programs depend upon.

- **BSD** — The Berkeley Software Distribution License allows redistribution of source code, with the requirement that the source code keep the BSD copyright notice and not use the names of contributors to endorse or promote derived software without written permission.

- **MIT** — The MIT license is like the BSD license, except that it doesn't include the endorsement and promotion requirement.

- **Mozilla** — The Mozilla license covers use and redistribution of source code associated with the Mozilla Web browser and related software. It is a much longer license than the others just mentioned because it contains more definitions of how contributors and those reusing the source code should behave. This includes submitting a file of changes when submitting modifications and that those making their own additions to the code for redistribution should be aware of patent issues or other restrictions associated with their code.

The end result of open source code is software that has more flexibility to grow and fewer boundaries in how it can be used. Many believe that the fact that many people look over the source code for a project will result in higher quality software for everyone. As open source advocate Eric S. Raymond says in an often-quoted line, "Many eyes make all bugs shallow."

Vibrant Communities

Communities of professionals and enthusiasts have grown around Linux and its related open source projects. Many have shown themselves willing to devote their time, knowledge, and skills on public mailing lists, forums, wikis, and other Internet venues (provided you ask politely and aren't too annoying).

Linux User Groups (LUGs) have sprung up all over the world. Many LUGs sponsor Linux installfests (where members help you install the Linux of your choice on your computer) or help nonprofit groups and schools use Linux on older computers that will no longer support the latest Microsoft Windows software. The LUG I'm a member of holds monthly meetings with talks on Linux topics and has an active Web site, mailing list, and chat server where members can help one another with Linux questions that come up.

Free online bulletin board services have sprung up to get information on specific Linux topics. Popular general Linux forums are available from `www.LinuxQuestions.org`, `www.LinuxForums.org`, and `www.LinuxHelp.net`.

Communities also gather around specific software projects and Linux distributions. SourceForge (`http://sourceforge.net/`) is home to thousands of open source software projects. Go to the SourceForge.net site and try keyword searches for topics that interest you (for example, image gallery or video editing). Each project provides links to project home pages, forums, and software download sites. There are always projects looking for people to help write code or documentation or just participate in discussions.

You'll find that most major Linux distributions have associated mailing lists and forums. You can go directly to the Web sites for the Red Hat-sponsored Fedora Linux (`http://fedoraproject.org/`), Debian (`www.debian.com`), Ubuntu (`http://ubuntuforums.org`), Gentoo (`www.gentoo.org`), and others to learn how to participate in forums and contribute to those projects.

Major Software Projects

Some software projects have grown beyond the status of being simply a component of Linux or some other UNIX derivative. Some of these projects are sponsored and maintained by organizations that oversee multiple open source projects. The most popular open source projects and organizations include the following:

- **The Apache Software Foundation** (`www.apache.org`) is not only the world's most popular open source Web server software, it's the most popular of all Web server software. Most Linux distributions that contain server software include Apache. The Apache Software Foundation maintains the Apache Web (HTTP) server and about a dozen other projects, including SpamAssassin (for blocking and filtering e-mail spam), Apache Portals (to provide portal software), and a bunch of projects for producing modules to use with your Apache Web server.

- **The Internet Systems Consortium** (`www.isc.org`) supports critical Internet infrastructure projects under open source licenses. Those projects include Bind (DNS server software), DHCP (to assign IP addresses and other information to Internet clients), INN (for creating Internet news servers), and OpenReg (a tool for managing delegation of domains in a shared registry).

- **The Free Software Foundation** (www.fsf.org) is the principal sponsor of the GNU Project. Most of the UNIX commands and utilities included in Linux that were not closely associated with the kernel were produced under the umbrella of the GNU Project.

- **The Mozilla project's** (www.mozilla.org) first major Web browser product was Mozilla Navigator, which was originally based on code released to the open source community from Netscape Communicator. Other open source browsers incorporate Mozilla's engine. The Mozilla project also offered a suite of related Internet clients that included e-mail, composer, IRC Chat, and address book software. New software development from the Mozilla project focuses on the Thunderbird e-mail and news client and Firefox Web browser, which have seen enormous success on Linux, Windows, and Mac OS X platforms in the past few years. The old Mozilla suite is offered today under the name Seamonkey (www.mozilla.org/projects/seamonkey).

- **The Samba Project** (www.samba.org) provides software for sharing files and printers using CIFS and SMB clients. These protocols are the most common means of sharing files and printers with Microsoft Windows operating systems.

- **The Sendmail Consortium** (www.sendmail.org) maintains the sendmail mail transport agent, which is the world's most popular software for transporting mail across the Internet.

There are, of course, many more open source projects and organizations that provide software included in various Linux distributions, but the ones discussed here will give you a good feel for the kind of organizations that produce open source software.

Linux in the Real World

To see how Linux and related free and open source software is being used today in the real world, I've provided some short examples that relate to Linux use in schools, small business, and enterprise venues.

Linux in Schools

Cost savings, flexibility, and a huge pool of applications have made Linux a wonderful alternative to proprietary systems for many schools. One project has been particularly successful in schools: the K12 Linux Terminal Server Project (www.k12ltsp.org).

K12LTSP is based on the Linux Terminal Service Project (www.ltsp.org) and Fedora (www.fedoraproject.org), but is tuned to work particularly in schools. With K12LTSP, you centralize all your school's applications on one or more server machines. Then you can use low-end PCs (old Pentiums or thin clients) as workstations. With thin clients starting under $200 or old PCs already hanging around your school, you can service a whole class or even a whole school for little more than the cost of the servers and some networking hardware.

By centralizing all the school's software on a limited number of servers, K12LTSP can offer both security (only a few servers to watch over) and convenience (no need to reinstall hundreds of Windows machines to upgrade or enhance the software). Each client machine controls the display, mouse, and keyboard, while all of the user's applications and files are stored on and run from the server.

The K12LTSP distribution contains many battle-tested open source applications, including full GNOME and KDE desktops, Evolution e-mail, Firefox browser, OpenOffice.org office suite, and the GNU Image Manipulation Program (GIMP) image application. It also adds DansGuardian (open source Web content filtering) and educational software (such as Gcompris). Applications that are not available in Linux can often be replaced with similar Linux applications or may be run from a Web browser.

Many schools in Oregon have adopted K12LTSP, including those attended by Linus Torvalds' children in Portland, Oregon. Adoption of K12LTSP has also begun in Atlanta, Georgia and many other cities across the United States.

Linux in Small Business

Often a small business can consolidate the Web services it needs into one or two Linux servers. It can meet its basic office computing needs with mature open source applications such as OpenOffice.org, GIMP, and a Firefox browser. But can a small business run entirely on open source software alone?

When Jim Nanney started his Coast Grocery business (www.coastgrocery.com), where residents of the Mississippi Gulf Coast can order groceries online for delivery, he set out to do just that. In part, he just wanted to see if he could rely solely on open source software. But he also figured that cost savings of at least $10,000 by not buying commercial software could help make his small business profitable a lot faster.

To allow customers to order groceries online, Jim selected the open source e-commerce software called osCommerce (www.oscommerce.com). The osCommerce software is built with the PHP Web scripting language and uses a MySQL database. Jim runs the software from a Linux system with an Apache Web server.

On the office side of the business, Jim relies entirely on Fedora Linux systems. He uses OpenOffice.org Writer for documents, GIMP and Inkscape for logos and other artwork, and GnuCash for accounting. For Web browsing, Firefox is used. So far, there has been no need to purchase any commercial software.

Here are some of the advantages that Jim has derived from his all–open source business:

- **Community support** — The communities surrounding osCommerce and Fedora have been very helpful. With active forums and 24-hour IRC channels, it has been easier to get help with those projects than with any proprietary software. Also unlike proprietary software, participants are generally quite knowledgeable and often include the developers of the software themselves.

- **Long-term security** — Jim disputes conventional wisdom that betting your business on proprietary software is safer than relying on open source. If a software company goes out of business, the small business could go down, too. But with open source, you have the code, so you could always pay someone to update the code when necessary or fix it yourself.

- **Easier improvements** — By doing some of his own PHP programming, Jim had a lot of flexibility related to adding features. In some cases, he could take existing code and modify it to suit his needs. To create a special shopping list feature, he found it easiest to write code from scratch. In the process of using the software, when he found exploitable bugs, he submitted the code fixes back to the project.

- **No compatibility problems** — On those occasions where he needed to provide information to others, compatibility has not been a problem. When he makes business cards, door hangers, or other printed material, he saves his artwork to PDF or SVG formats to send to a commercial printer. Regular documents can be exported to Word, Excel, or other common formats.

For businesses starting on a shoestring, in many cases open source software can offer both the cost savings and flexibility needed to help the business survive during the difficult start-up period. Later, it can help those same businesses thrive, because open source solutions can often be easily scaled up as the business grows.

Linux in the Enterprise

Building a company's computer infrastructure on open source software represents a huge amount of confidence that it will provide the level of reliability, security, and features that a company needs. That's why most large companies converting to open source infrastructures have gone with products from enterprise Linux providers, such as Red Hat, Inc. (Red Hat Enterprise Linux) and Novell, Inc. (SUSE Linux Enterprise).

Built into Red Hat's open source enterprise products are features such as Red Hat Directory Server, Global File System (GFS), and Cluster Suite. Directory Server can scale up to handle millions of identities, representing settings for applications, user profiles, access control, and policies across thousands of machines and users. Using GFS and Cluster Suite, an enterprise can treat its entire storage infrastructure as a common pool to minimize data duplication and simplify backups, system recovery, and adding storage and servers.

Companies moving their infrastructures to Linux include Apoteket (Sweden's government-run pharmacy), which is moving more than 900 pharmacies to Red Hat Enterprise Linux (RHEL) on Intel servers. Governments that are migrating to RHEL include cities such as Chicago and Bloomington, Illinois. You can read about other organizations migrating to RHEL on Red Hat's Success Stories page (`www.redhat.com/solutions/info/casestudies`).

Linux Myths, Legends, and FUD

The rise in the popularity of Linux has led to rampant (and sometimes strange) speculation about all the terrible things it could lead to or, conversely, to almost manic declarations of how Linux will solve all the problems of the world. I'll try as best I can (with my own admitted bias toward Linux) to present facts to address beliefs about Linux and to combat some of the unrealistic fear, uncertainty, and doubt (FUD) being spread by those with a vested interest in seeing Linux not succeed.

Can You Stop Worrying About Viruses?

Well, you can (and should) always worry about the security of any computer connected to the Internet. At the moment, however, you are probably less likely to get a virus from infected e-mail or untrusted Web sites with standard e-mail clients and Web browsers that come with Linux systems than you would with those that come with the average Microsoft Windows system.

The most commonly cited warnings to back up that statement come in a report from the United States Computer Emergency Readiness Team (CERT) regarding a vulnerability in Microsoft Internet Explorer (`www.kb.cert.org/vuls/id/713878`):

> There are a number of significant vulnerabilities in technologies relating to the IE domain/zone security model, the DHTML object model, MIME type determination, and ActiveX. It is possible to reduce exposure to these vulnerabilities by using a different Web browser, especially when browsing untrusted sites. Such a decision may, however, reduce the functionality of sites that require IE-specific features such as DHTML, VBScript, and ActiveX. Note that using a different Web browser will not remove IE from a Windows system, and other programs may invoke IE, the WebBrowser ActiveX control, or the HTML rendering engine (MSHTML).
>
> *US-CERT Vulnerability Note VU#713878*

While the note also recommends keeping up with patches from Microsoft to reduce your risks, it seems that the only real solutions are to disable Active scripting and ActiveX, use plain text e-mail, and don't visit sites you don't trust with Internet Explorer. In other words, use a browser that disables insecure features included in Microsoft products.

This announcement apparently caused quite a run on the Mozilla.org site to download a Firefox browser and related e-mail client (described in Chapter 22 of this book). Versions of those software projects run on Windows and Mac OS X, as well as on Linux. Many believe that browsers such as Firefox are inherently more secure because they don't allow nonstandard Web features that might do such things as automatically download unrequested software without your knowledge.

Research into hijacked computers being taken over, by the thousands, to be used as botnets has shown a very high percentage to be Microsoft Windows systems. The disturbing thing about the statistics, however, is that many of these systems have been upgraded with Microsoft Service Pack 2 (SP2) or other patches that were supposed to protect from those types of infections. A type of trojan referred to as SpamThru (resulting in botnets that turn out thousands of spam messages) infected a high-percentage of Windows XP systems that have been upgraded to SP2 (see www.secureworks.com/analysis/spamthru-stats).

Of course, no matter what browser or e-mail client you are using, you need to follow good security practices (such as not opening attachments or downloading files you don't trust). Also, as open source browsers and e-mail clients, such as those from Mozilla.org, become more popular, the number of possible machines to infect through those applications will make it more tempting to virus writers. (At the moment, most viruses and worms are created specifically to attack Microsoft software.)

Will You Be Sued for Using Linux?

There have been some well-financed lawsuits against Linux providers. Those with litigation against Linux have gone primarily after big companies, such as IBM, Novell, and Red Hat, Inc. Linus Torvalds himself is the rare individual who has been named in lawsuits. Most threats to individuals have been vague, general declarations from proprietary software companies that claim some infringement of their property, without being specific about what the exact infringement is.

For the past year, most vocal threats to those using Linux systems have come from Microsoft (and companies coincidentally run by ex-Microsoft employees). Before that time, the SCO Group, Inc. spent several years in litigation against major Linux players. Both of those initiatives seem to have more to do with fear mongering than they do with reality.

Microsoft Versus Linux

As of this writing, Microsoft has announced that Linux has infringed on 235 patents that Microsoft holds relating to the desktop. What it has not told us are the features that infringe on Microsoft patents and the identity of the patents. Here are some speculations about why Microsoft has not made that information public:

- **Fear is the intent** — The strategy by Microsoft is to get people and companies to pay Microsoft for their use of Linux, without actually telling them specifically what they are paying for. The Linux community has always said that they would replace any code that was shown to impinge on someone else's rights. But if Microsoft doesn't say what their property is, the problem can't ever be corrected and the fear of lawsuits can remain.

- **Too many patents** — There are literally thousands of patents relating to computer operating systems. Many of those patents are held by companies such as IBM, as well as by some open source providers, such as Red Hat, Inc. Opening that can of worms in the courtroom could mean as much trouble for Microsoft as it does for anyone else.

Few individuals have been sued because of an association with Linux. However, the level of rhetoric surrounding who *might* be sued has been raised substantially. In the alliance between Microsoft and Novell (see Chapter 10 for details), the two companies agree not to sue each other's customers for intellectual property rights violations. However, Microsoft lawyer Brad Smith had this to say about how open source developers can avoid being sued by Microsoft:

So Microsoft today is making two, I think, important commitments, or promises to different groups of developers in the open source community. The first is a promise that we won't assert our patents against individual, non-commercial, open source developers. Who are these? These are individuals who are creating code, contributing code, they're not being paid for that code, they're often working in the evenings or at home. They're not creating it as part of their job, but they're acting in an individual non-commercial way. The promise doesn't run to anybody who employs them, because after all, they're not acting in the course of their employment. But, it gives those folks a new commitment from Microsoft.

The second thing we did in this area was add a promise that goes to developers, even developers who are getting paid to create code to OpenSUSE.org, code that Novell then takes and incorporates into its distribution, and that is then covered under the patent cooperation agreement between us, because after all Novell is ensuring that our patent rights are respected in an appropriate way, and that gives us the ability to address the needs and interests of those individuals.

> www.microsoft.com/presspass/exec/steve/2006/
> 11-02NovellInterop.mspx

The actual liability to individual open source software developers, based on statements such as these from Microsoft, is still unclear. That's because there have still been no specific patent claims in connection with Linux from Microsoft. That said, because I am not a lawyer, my opinions on the subject should not be taken as legal advice. However, if you want opinions from lawyers on open source software legality, refer to the Groklaw site (`www.groklaw.net`). Likewise, here is a response from Eben Moglen of the Software Freedom Law Center:

> I and my firm don't take comfort from statement [sic] from Microsoft that they won't sue programmers as long as they don't get paid. We represent developers of free and open-source software. If Microsoft or anyone else attempts to sue our clients for doing what they do to create software, because they're being paid for it, then the people doing that will be sorry. We protect our clients.

> http://news.com.com/2061-10795_3-6132156.html

> **NOTE** A few days after Microsoft's Steve Ballmer suggested that companies would want Red Hat and others to begin paying for use of their patents, a company called IP Innovation LLC filed a patent claim against Red Hat and Novell. IP Innovation is a subsidiary of Acacia, which recently added Jonathan Taub and Brad Brunell as Vice Presidents. Taub and Brunell were highly regarded executives at Microsoft, with the latter serving as a General Manager of Intellectual Property Licensing. Check out the story here: `www.groklaw.net/article.php?story=20071011205044141`.

The SCO Lawsuits

The Linux lawsuits that got the most press a few years ago are the ones involving Santa Cruz Operation (SCO). SCO is the current owner of the UNIX source code that passed from AT&T Bell Labs to UNIX System Laboratories to Univel (a lot of people don't know that one), to Novell, and eventually to the company formed by joining SCO and Caldera Systems. Although the particulars of the claims seem to change daily, and one-by-one the claims have been shot down, SCO's basic assertion in lawsuits against IBM and others is that Linux contains UNIX System V source code that is owned by SCO. So those who sell or use Linux owe licensing fees to SCO.

As of this writing, many of the charges brought by SCO have been dismissed by the judge in the case. SCO, however, is currently stating that it may appeal and believes that there is still a foundation to its charges. A recent wrinkle in SCO's case, however, has thrown into doubt how much right SCO even has to the UNIX source code it purchased from Novell.

To a layman (I am not a lawyer!), the assertions seem weak based on the following facts:

- There seems to be no original UNIX code in Linux. And, even if a small amount of code that could be proved to be owned by SCO had made it in there by mistake, that code could be easily dropped and rewritten.

- Concepts that created UNIX all seem to be in the public domain, with public specifications of UNIX interfaces blessed by AT&T itself in the form of published POSIX and System V Interface Definition standards. While the AT&T UNIX code was covered by copyright, the *concepts* that went into that code were never patented.

- AT&T dropped a similar lawsuit in 1994 against BSD, which had actually started with UNIX source code, but had rewritten it completely over the years.

- Exactly what SCO owns has been called into question because Novell still claims some rights to the UNIX code it sold to SCO. (In fact, SCO doesn't even own the UNIX trademark, which Novell gave away to the Open Group before it sold the source code to SCO. Attempts were underway in 2004 by SCO to trademark the name UNIX System Laboratories.)

Responses to SCO's lawsuits (which certainly hold more weight than any explanations I could offer) are available from Open Group (www.opengroup.org), The Linux Foundation (formerly OSDL) (www.linux-foundation.org), IBM (ibm.com/linux), and Red Hat (www.redhat.com). The Groklaw site (www.groklaw.net) is another good spot to learn about SCO lawsuits against Linux. If you are interested in the paper trail relating SCO's ownership of UNIX, I recommend the Novell's Unique Legal Rights page (www.novell.com/licensing/indemnity/legal.html).

Software Patents

Most agree that it is illegal for someone to copy a software company's code and redistribute it without permission. However, the concept of being able to patent an *idea* that a company might incorporate in its code has become a major point of contention in recent years. Can someone patent the idea of clicking an icon to open a window?

Software companies are scrambling to file thousands of patents related to how software is used. While those companies may never create products based on those patents, the restrictions those patents might place on other software companies or open source software development is a major issue.

In the alliance between Microsoft and Novell, both companies' large patent portfolios have become a major issue of concern among the free and open source community. The fear is that those patents (in other words, the idea represented by code and not the code itself) could be used to claim a tax on every piece of open source software that is freely distributed today.

To deal with the patent issue, the recently released GNU General Public License 3 (GPLv3) includes wording that restricts anyone who delivers software covered under the GPL to exercise their patent rights against those who use or redistribute that software. The hope of the Free Software Foundation (http://gplv3.fsf.org) is that this will definitively answer the patent issues that might restrict free redistribution of GPL code.

On another front in the patent wars, the Foundation for a Free Information Infrastructure (www.ffii.org) is a group "dedicated to establishing a free market in information technology, by the removal of barriers to competition." The FFII maintains an excellent FAQ page to answer questions surrounding software patents and how they threaten innovation:

> www.ffii.org/Frequently_Asked_Questions_about_software_patents

Other Potentially Litigious Issues

Particularly contentious legal issues surround audio and video software. In Red Hat Linux 8, Red Hat, Inc. removed support for MP3 and DVD players because of questions about licensing associated with those music and movie formats. Red Hat's advice at the time was to download and install the players yourself for personal use. Red Hat didn't want to distribute those players because companies owning patents related to certain audio and video encoders might ask Red Hat to pay licensing fees for distributing those players (see www.redhat.com/advice/speaks_80mm.html).

To deal with the issue of running proprietary codecs in Linux, Linux distributions such as Fedora, Ubuntu, and others are offering tools to connect their users to sites where they can find legal codecs to use with Linux. See Chapter 8 for information on getting legal software for playing proprietary music, video, and other multimedia content.

Can Linux Really Run on Everything from Handhelds to Supercomputers?

Linux is extraordinarily scalable and runs on everything from handhelds to supercomputers. Features in the Linux 2.6 kernel have been particularly aimed at making the kernel easier to port to embedded Linux systems, as well as large multiprocessor, enterprise-quality servers. Yellow Dog Linux even offers a port of its Linux distribution that runs on Sony PlayStation 3 gaming consoles.

Will Microsoft Crush Linux?

As noted earlier, Microsoft has shifted its fear, uncertainty, and doubt (FUD) rhetoric against using Linux to FUD about using any Linux other than Novell's SUSE. Any Linux user or developer who doesn't make an agreement with Microsoft to use Microsoft's as-yet-unnamed intellectual property that is in Linux has, in the words of Microsoft President Steve Ballmer, "an undisclosed balance sheet liability."

In 1998, a series of memos were leaked from Microsoft that became known as the Halloween Documents (www.catb.org/~esr/halloween/). The sudden publication of these memos forced Microsoft to acknowledge their authenticity. The documents fueled animosity and suspicion about the intentions of Microsoft regarding Linux. In that light, you can see how some regard the recent Novell and Microsoft Patent news as simply fear, uncertainty, and doubt (FUD). As of September 2007, no specific patent infringements have been pointed out by anyone.

To many in the Linux community, statements from Microsoft in which Microsoft threatened to sue Linux developers, users, and customers who don't pay a fee to Microsoft (for code that Microsoft had no part in creating) are viewed as extortion. The result has been to divide open source proponents into either the camp for the Novell/Microsoft deal or against it. However you look at it, the battle lines have been clearly drawn.

The U.S. Justice department claimed that Microsoft used the phrase "Embrace, extend, and extinguish" as its policy toward dealing with companies or technologies that it saw as a threat (http://en.wikipedia.org/wiki/Embrace,_extend_and_extinguish). By embracing SUSE Linux, Microsoft has already divided the Linux community. It has announced plans to extend SUSE Linux to better interoperate with Windows. You can only guess what might happen to SUSE when Microsoft's five-year deal with Novell is up and much of the open source community isn't working with Novell anymore.

But it's not all gloom and doom for Linux. Major Linux vendors such as Red Hat, Inc. and the Free Software Foundation have been gearing up for this fight for years. At the time of this writing, it looks like they have a couple of aces up their sleeves as well:

- **GPLv3** — As of the end of 2007, the final text of GPLv3 was released. Most of the free and open source software community (including the Linux kernel developers) license their software using GPL.

- **Open Invention Network** (www.openinventionnetwork.com) — With sponsors such as Red Hat, IBM, Novell, Philips, Sony, and NEC, the Open Invention Network was formed as an organization for gathering patents to protect open source software. Instead of using those patents as a royalty stream, however, those patents are seen as a defense against someone who might seek to assert patent rights against open source software. It seems to be like an arms race, where it is hoped that no country will attack another since both have ammunition that could inflict damage.

- **Open source community** — So far, there have simply been pleas from the open source community to Novell to abandon the patent portion of its agreement with Microsoft. Projects such as the Samba project have come out publicly against the agreement, but so far no one has taken action. Some believe, however, that many open source projects will not be willing to work with Novell, given the aspects of the alliance with Microsoft that seem ready to punish open source developers who do paid work for anyone other than Novell.

  It's hard to imagine how any major Linux distribution could survive without assistance from the upstream projects that feed it. So, being set adrift from the open source community is surely not something Novell wants to have happen.

So, the bottom line about whether or not Microsoft will crush Linux is that a fight is brewing, but the jury is still out. It seems, however, that the free and open source community is ready to protect its rights and values.

Are You on Your Own If You Use Linux?

If you are new to Linux and are concerned about support, several companies are offering well-supported versions of Linux, such as Red Hat Enterprise Linux (from Red Hat, Inc.) and Ubuntu Linux (from Canonical Global Support Services), as well as a number of other smaller players. In the corporate arena, add IBM to that list.

As noted earlier, there are also many community sites on the Internet that offer forums, mailing lists, and other venues for getting help if you get stuck.

Is Linux Only for Geeks?

It doesn't hurt to be a geek if you want to fully explore all the potential of your Linux system. However, with a good desktop Linux distribution, tremendous improvements over the past few years relating to ease-of-use and features have made it possible to do most things you would do on any Macintosh or Windows system without being a Linux expert. The great thing is that, if you ever want to dig deeper, the opportunity is there and the education is free.

Start with a Linux system that uses the KDE or GNOME desktop. Simple menus enable you to select word processors, Web browsers, games, and dozens of other applications you commonly use on other operating systems. In most cases, you'll get along fine just using your mouse to work with windows, menus, and forms.

With Linux distributions that offer graphical tools for basic system administration (such as configuring a printer or network connection), you can be led through most tasks you need to do. Fedora, Red Hat Enterprise Linux, and Mandriva are good examples of Linux distributions that offer simplified administration tools. With a basic understanding of the Linux shell (see Chapter 2) and some help from a Linux forum, you should be able to troubleshoot most anything that goes wrong.

How Do Companies Make Money with Linux?

Open source enthusiasts believe that better software can result from an open source software development model than from proprietary development models. So in theory, any company creating software for its own use can save money by adding its software contributions to those of others to gain a much better end product for themselves.

Companies that want to make money selling software need to be more creative than they did in the old days. While you can sell the software you create that includes GPL software, you must pass the source code of that software forward. Of course, others can then recompile that product, basically using your product without charge. Here are a few ways that companies are dealing with that issue:

- **Software subscriptions** — Red Hat, Inc. sells its Red Hat Enterprise Linux products on a subscription basis. For a certain amount of money per year, you get binary code to run

Linux (so you don't have to compile it yourself), guaranteed support, tools for tracking the hardware and software on your computer, and access to the company's knowledge base.

While Red Hat's Fedora project includes much of the same software and is also available in binary form, there are no guarantees associated with the software or future updates of that software. A small office or personal user might take the risk on Fedora (which is itself an excellent operating system), but a big company that's running mission-critical applications will probably put down a few dollars for RHEL.

- **Donations** — Many open source projects accept donations from individuals or open source companies that use code from their projects. Amazingly, many open source projects support one or two developers and run exclusively on donations.

- **Bounties** — Software bounties are a fascinating way for open source software companies to make money. Let's say that you are using XYZ software package and you need a new feature right away. By paying a software bounty to the project itself, or to other software developers, you can have your needed improvements moved to the head of the queue. The software you pay for will remain covered by its open source license, but you will have the features you need, at probably a fraction of the cost of building the project from scratch.

- **Boxed sets, mugs, and T-shirts** — Many open source projects have online stores where you can buy boxed sets (some people still like physical CDs and hard copies of documentation) and a variety of mugs, T-shirts, mouse pads, and other items. If you really love a project, for goodness sake, buy a T-shirt!

This is in no way an exhaustive list, because more creative ways are being invented every day to support those who create open source software. Remember that many people have become contributors to and maintainers of open source software because they needed or wanted the software themselves. The contributions they make for free are worth the return they get from others who do the same.

How Different Are Linux Distributions from One Another?

While different Linux systems will add different logos, choose some different software components to include, and have different ways of installing and configuring Linux, most people who become used to Linux can move pretty easily from one Linux to another. There are a few reasons for this:

- **Linux Standard Base** — There is an effort called the Linux Standard Base (`www .linuxbase.org`) to which most major Linux systems subscribe. The Linux Standard Base Specification (available from this site) has as one of its primary goals to ensure that applications written for one Linux system will work on other systems. To that end, the LSB will define what libraries need to be available, how software packages can be formatted, commands and utilities that must be available, and, to some extent, how the file system should be arranged. In other words, you can rely on many components of Linux being in the same place on LSB-certified Linux systems.

■ **Open source projects** — Many Linux distributions include the same open source projects. So, for example, the most basic command and configuration files for an Apache Web server, Samba file/print server, and sendmail mail server will be the same whether you use Red Hat, Debian, or many other Linux systems. And although they can change backgrounds, colors, and other elements of your desktop, most of the ways of navigating a KDE or GNOME desktop stay the same, regardless of which Linux you use.

■ **A shell is a shell** — Although you can put different pretty faces on it, once you open a shell command-line interpreter (such as bash or sh) in Linux, most experienced Linux or UNIX users find it pretty easy to get around on most any Linux system. For that reason, I recommend that if you are serious about using Linux, you take some time to try the shell (as described in Chapter 2). Additionally, Chapters 24–27 focus on command-line and configuration file interfaces for setting up servers, because learning those ways of configuring servers will make your skills most portable across different Linux systems.

Some of the ways that Linux distributions distinguish themselves, however, are with the installers they use, their package management tools, and system administration tools. Also, distributions such as those sponsored by Red Hat will include new features developed by its sponsors to meet its commercial needs. For example, Red Hat has done a lot of work that is useful for enterprise computing environments, such as virtualization, global file systems, and software distribution tools.

Is the Linux Mascot Really a Penguin?

Figure 1-1 shows the penguin logo that Linus Torvalds approved as the official Linux mascot. His name is Tux. Use of this logo is freely available, and you find it everywhere on Linux Web sites, magazines, and other Linux venues. (I used it in my book *Linux Toys II* and on the Linuxtoys.net Web site, for example.)

FIGURE 1-1

Tux, a gentle and pleasant penguin, is the official Linux mascot.

Tux was created by Larry Ewing. Find out more about Tux from the Linux Online Logos and Mascots page (www.linux.org/info/logos.html). Refer to the Why Linux Chose a Penguin page (www.linux.org/info/penguin.html) if you would like Linus's take on the penguin mascot.

Getting Started with Linux

Although I've gone on a bit about Linux history and what Linux does, the primary goal of this book is to get you using it. To that end, I'd like to describe some things that might help you get started with Linux.

While Linux will run great on many low-end computers (even some old 486s and early Pentiums), if you are completely new to Linux, I recommend that you start with a PC that has a little more muscle. Here's why:

- Full-blown Linux operating systems with complete GNOME or KDE desktop environments perform poorly on slow CPUs and less than the recommended amount of RAM. The bells and whistles come at the price of processing power. Lighter-weight options do exist if you have limited resources.

- You can use streamlined graphical Linux installations that will fit on small hard disks (as small as 100MB) and run fairly well on slow processors. Also, there are small live CD Linux distributions, such as Damn Small Linux (DSL), that can be copied to hard disk and run from there. The 50MB DSL desktop system will run fine on old Pentium machines with little RAM. But if you want to add some of the more demanding applications to DSL, such as OpenOffice.org office applications, you will find you need more than minimal computer hardware.

If you are starting with a Pentium II, 400 MHz, your desktop will run slowly in default KDE or GNOME configurations with less than 128MB of RAM. A simpler desktop system, with just X and a window manager, will work, but won't give you the full flavor of a Linux desktop. (See Chapter 3 for information about different desktop choices and features.)

The good news is that cheap computers that you can buy from Wal-Mart or other retailers start at less than $300. Those systems will perform better than most PCs you have laying around that are more than a few years old and will come with Linux (usually Linspire) pre-installed. The bottom line is that the less you know about Linux, the more you should try to have computer hardware that is up to spec to have a pleasant experience.

If you already have a Linux system sitting in front of you, Chapters 2 through 6 will walk you through the Linux shell, desktop usage, and some basic system administration. If you don't have a Linux system running on your computer yet, you have a couple of choices:

- **Try a bootable Linux** — If you have another OS on your machine and are reluctant to disturb the contents of your computer, a bootable Linux enables you to run Linux directly from a removable medium (DVD, CD, or even a floppy disk in some cases). You'll be able to try Linux without even touching the contents of your hard disk. As noted earlier, distributions such as Damn Small Linux will run well even on less powerful machines.

- **Install Linux on your hard disk** — If you have available disk space that's not already assigned to Windows or another system, you can install Linux on your hard disk and have a more permanent operating system. Some Linux distributions, such as SUSE and Mandriva, enable you to resize your Windows hard disk to make room to install Linux. Other Linux distributions, such as Ubuntu and Gentoo, enable you to try them out from a live CD, and then install them to your hard disk from that running live CD.

Linux itself is just a kernel (like the engine of a car), so to use Linux you need to select a Linux distribution. Because the distribution you choose is so critical to your Linux experience, Part III of this book is devoted to understanding, choosing, and installing the most popular Linux distributions. Several of these distributions are included with this book, along with several useful bootable Linux distributions. If you don't already have a Linux system in front of you, refer to Chapter 7 to get started getting the Linux you want.

Summary

Linux is the most popular representation of the open source software model today and reflects a rich history of shared software development techniques that date back to the first UNIX systems of three decades ago. Today's Linux computer systems form the backbone of many major computing centers around the world.

In recent years, Linux has become a great choice as a desktop system as well. You will find many open source applications available for any type of application you can imagine (word processing, music playing, e-mail, games, and so on). With its powerful networking and built-in security features, Linux can provide a much safer computing environment than other desktop computing systems.

Linux gives you the freedom to create the kind of computer system you need.

Chapter 2

Running Commands from the Shell

Before icons and windows took over computer screens, you typed commands to interact with most computers. On UNIX systems, from which Linux was derived, the program used to interpret and manage commands was referred to as the *shell*.

No matter which Linux distribution you are using, you can always count on one thing being available to you: the shell. It provides a way to create executable script files, run programs, work with file systems, compile computer code, operate a system, and manage the computer. Although the shell is less intuitive than common graphic user interfaces (GUIs), most Linux experts consider the shell to be much more powerful than GUIs. Shells have been around a long time, and many advanced features have been built into them.

The Linux shell illustrated in this chapter is called the *bash shell*, which stands for Bourne Again Shell. The name is derived from the fact that bash is compatible with the first UNIX shell: the Bourne shell (named after its creator, and represented by the sh command). While bash is included with most distributions, and considered a standard, other shells are available. Other popular shells include the C shell (csh), which is popular among BSD UNIX users, and the Korn shell (ksh), which is popular among UNIX System V users. Linux also has a tcsh shell (a C shell look-alike) and an ash shell (another Bourne shell look-alike). Several different shells are introduced in this chapter.

> **TIP** The odds are strong that the Linux distribution you are using has more than one shell installed by default and available for your use.

Several major reasons for learning how to use the shell are:

- You will know how to get around any Linux or other UNIX-like system. For example, I can log in to my Red Hat Enterprise Linux

MySQL server, my bootable floppy router/firewall, or my wife's iMac and explore and use any of those computer systems from a shell.

■ Special shell features enable you to gather data input and direct data output between commands and the Linux file system. To save on typing, you can find, edit, and repeat commands from your shell history. Many power users hardly touch a graphical interface, doing most of their work from a shell.

■ You can gather commands into a file using programming constructs such as conditional checks, loops, and case statements to quickly do complex operations that would be difficult to retype over and over. Programs consisting of commands that are stored and run from a file are referred to as *shell scripts*. Most Linux system administrators use shell scripts to automate tasks such as backing up data, monitoring log files, or checking system health.

The shell is a command language interpreter. If you have used Microsoft operating systems, you'll see that using a shell in Linux is similar to — but generally much more powerful than — the interpreter used to run commands in DOS or in the CMD command interface. You can happily use Linux from a graphical desktop interface, but as you grow into Linux you will surely need to use the shell at some point to track down a problem or administer some features.

How to use the shell isn't obvious at first, but with the right help you can quickly learn many of the most important shell features. This chapter is your guide to working with the Linux system commands, processes, and file system from the shell. It describes the shell environment and helps you tailor it to your needs. It also explains how to use and move around the file system.

Starting a Shell

There are several ways to get to a shell interface in Linux. Three of the most common are the shell prompt, Terminal window, and virtual terminal. They're discussed in the following sections.

Using the Shell Prompt

If your Linux system has no graphical user interface (or one that isn't working at the moment), you will most likely see a shell prompt after you log in. Typing commands from the shell will probably be your primary means of using the Linux system.

The default prompt for a regular user is simply a dollar sign:

    $

The default prompt for the root user is a pound sign (also called a *hash mark*):

    #

In most Linux systems, the $ and # prompts are preceded by your username, system name, and current directory name. For example, a login prompt for the user named jake on a computer named pine with /tmp as the current directory would appear as:

```
[jake@pine tmp]$
```

You can change the prompt to display any characters you like — you can use the current directory, the date, the local computer name, or any string of characters as your prompt, for example. To configure your prompt, see the "Setting Your Prompt" section later in this chapter.

Although a tremendous number of features are available with the shell, it's easy to begin by just typing a few commands. Try some of the commands shown in the remainder of this section to become familiar with your current shell environment.

In the examples that follow, the dollar ($) and pound (#) symbols indicate a prompt. While a $ indicates that the command can be run by any user, a # typically means you should run the command as the root user — many administrative tools require root permission to be able to run them. The prompt is followed by the command that you type (and then you press Enter or Return, depending on your keyboard). The lines that follow show the output resulting from the command.

Using a Terminal Window

With the desktop GUI running, you can open a terminal emulator program (sometimes referred to as a Terminal window) to start a shell. Most Linux distributions make it easy for you to get to a shell from the GUI. Here are two common ways to launch a Terminal window from a Linux desktop:

- **Right-click the desktop.** In the context menu that appears, look for Shells, New Terminal, Terminal Window, Xterm, or some similar item and select it. In Fedora, right-click on the desktop and click Open Terminal.

- **Click on the panel menu.** Many Linux desktops include a panel at the bottom of the screen from which you can launch applications. For example, in systems that use the GNOME desktop, you can select Applications ➪ Accessories ➪ Terminal to open a Terminal window. For Mandriva, select System ➪ Terminals.

In all cases, you should just be able to type a command as you would from a shell with no GUI. Different terminal emulators are available with Linux. One of the following is likely to be the default used with your Linux system:

- **xterm** — A common terminal emulator for the X Window System. (In fact, I've never seen an X Window System for a major Linux distribution that didn't include xterm.) Although it doesn't provide menus or many special features, it is available with most Linux distributions that support a GUI.

- **gnome-terminal** — The default Terminal emulator window that comes with GNOME. It consumes more system resources than xterm does, and it has useful menus for cutting and pasting, opening new Terminal tabs or windows, and setting terminal profiles.

- **konsole** — The konsole terminal emulator that comes with the KDE desktop environment. With konsole, you can display multi-language text encoding and text in different colors.

The differences in running commands within a Terminal window have more to do with the shell you are running than the type of Terminal window you are using. Differences in Terminal windows have more to do with the features each supports — for example, how much output is saved that can be scrolled back to, whether you can change font types and sizes, and whether the Terminal window supports features such as transparency.

Using Virtual Terminals

Most Linux systems that include a desktop interface start multiple virtual terminals running on the computer. Virtual terminals are a way to have multiple shell sessions open at once outside of the graphical interface you are using.

You can switch between virtual terminals much the same way that you would switch between workspaces on a GUI. Press Ctrl+Alt+F1 (or F2, F3, F4, and so on up to F6 on Fedora and other Linux systems) to display one of six virtual terminals. The next virtual workspace after the virtual terminals is where the GUI is, so if there are six virtual terminals, you can return to the GUI (if one is running) by pressing Ctrl+Alt+F7. (For a system with four virtual terminals, you return to the GUI by pressing Ctrl+Alt+F5.)

Choosing Your Shell

In most Linux systems, your default shell is the bash shell. To find out what your current login shell is, type the following command:

```
$ echo $SHELL
/bin/bash
```

In this example, it's the bash shell. There are many other shells, and you can activate a different one by simply typing the new shell's command (ksh, tcsh, csh, sh, bash, and so forth) from the current shell. For example, to change temporarily to the C shell, type the following command:

```
$ csh
```

NOTE   Most full Linux systems include all of the shells described in this section. However, some smaller Linux distributions may include only one or two shells. The best way to find out if a particular shell is available is to type the command and see if the shell starts.

You might want to choose a different shell to use because:

- You are used to using UNIX System V systems (often ksh by default) or Sun Microsystems and other Berkeley UNIX–based distributions (frequently csh by default), and you are more comfortable using default shells from those environments.
- You want to run shell scripts that were created for a particular shell environment, and you need to run the shell for which they were made so you can test or use those scripts.
- You might simply prefer features in one shell over those in another. For example, a member of my Linux Users Group prefers ksh over bash because he doesn't like the way aliases are always set up with bash.

Although most Linux users have a preference for one shell or another, when you know how to use one shell, you can quickly learn any of the others by occasionally referring to the shell's man page (for example, type **man bash**). Most people use bash just because they don't have a particular reason for using a different shell. In Chapter 4, you learn how to assign a different default shell for a user. The following sections introduce several of the most common shells available with Linux.

Using bash (and Earlier sh) Shells

As mentioned earlier, the name *bash* is an acronym for Bourne Again Shell, acknowledging the roots of bash coming from the Bourne shell (sh command) created by Steve Bourne at AT&T Bell Labs. Brian Fox of the Free Software Foundation created bash, under the auspices of the GNU Project. Development was later taken over by Chet Ramey at Case Western Reserve University.

Bash includes features originally developed for sh and ksh shells in early UNIX systems, as well as some csh features. Expect bash to be the default shell in whatever Linux system you are using, with the exception of some specialized Linux systems (such as those run on embedded devices or run from a floppy disk) that may require a smaller shell that needs less memory and entails fewer features. Most of the examples in this chapter are based on the bash shell.

 The bash shell is worth knowing not only because it is the default in most installations, but because it is the one tested in most Linux certification exams.

Bash can be run in various compatibility modes so that it behaves like different shells. It can be run to behave as a Bourne shell (bash +B) or as a POSIX-compliant shell (type bash --posix), for example, enabling it to read configuration files that are specific to those shells and run initialization shell scripts written directly for those shells, with a greater chance of success.

All of the Linux distributions included with this book use bash as the default shell, with the exception of some bootable Linux distributions, which use the ash shell instead.

Using tcsh (and Earlier csh) Shells

The tcsh shell is the open source version of the C shell (csh). The csh shell was created by Bill Joy and used with most Berkeley UNIX systems (such as those produced by Sun Microsystems) as the default shell. Features from the TENEX and TOPS-20 operating systems (used on PDP-11s in the 1970s) that are included in this shell are responsible for the T in tcsh.

Many features of the original csh shell, such as command-line editing and its history mechanism, are included in tcsh as well as in other shells. While you can run both csh and tcsh on most Linux systems, both commands actually point to the same executable file. In other words, starting csh actually runs the tcsh shell in csh compatibility mode.

Using ash

The ash shell is a lightweight version of the Berkeley UNIX sh shell. It doesn't include many of the sh shell's basic features, and is missing such features as command histories. Kenneth Almquist created the ash shell.

The ash shell is a good shell for embedded systems that have fewer system resources available. The ash shell is about one-seventh the size of bash (about 100K versus 712K for bash). Because of cheaper memory prices these days, however, many embedded and small bootable Linux systems have enough space to include the full bash shell.

Using ksh

The ksh shell was created by David Korn at AT&T Bell Labs and is the successor to the sh shell. It became the default and most commonly used shell with UNIX System V systems. The open source version of ksh was originally available in many rpm-based systems (such as Fedora and Red Hat Enterprise Linux) as part of the pdksh package. Now, however, David Korn has released the original ksh shell as open source, so you can look for it as part of a ksh software package in most Linux systems (see www.kornshell.com).

Using zsh

The zsh shell is another clone of the sh shell. It is POSIX-compliant (as is bash), but includes some different features, such as spell checking and a different approach to command editing. The first Mac OS X systems used zsh as the default shell, although now bash is used by default.

Exploring the Shell

Once you have access to a shell in Linux, you can begin by typing some simple commands. The section "Using the Shell in Linux" later in this chapter provides more details about options, arguments, and environment variables. For the time being, the following sections will help you poke around the shell a bit.

 If you don't like your default shell, simply type the name of the shell you want to try out temporarily. To change your shell permanently, use the `usermod` command. For example, to change to the csh shell for the user named chris, type the following as root user from a shell:

```
# usermod -s /bin/csh chris
```

Checking Your Login Session

When you log in to a Linux system, Linux views you as having a particular identity, which includes your username, group name, user ID, and group ID. Linux also keeps track of your login session: it knows when you logged in, how long you have been idle, and where you logged in from.

To find out information about your identity, use the `id` command as follows:

```
$ id
uid=501(chris) gid=105(sales) groups=105(sales),4(adm),7(lp)
```

In this example, the username is `chris`, which is represented by the numeric user ID (uid) 501. The primary group for chris is called `sales`, which has a group ID (gid) of 105. The user chris also belongs to other groups called `adm` (gid 4) and `lp` (gid 7). These names and numbers represent the permissions that `chris` has to access computer resources. (Permissions are described in the section "Understanding File Permissions" later in this chapter.)

NOTE Based on the distribution you are using, the uid numbering may be in the thousands.

You can see information about your current login session by using the `who` command. In the following example, the `-u` option says to add information about idle time and the process ID, and `-H` asks that a header be printed:

```
$ who -uH
NAME       LINE     TIME             IDLE      PID    COMMENT
chris      tty1     Jan 13 20:57     .         2013
```

The output from this `who` command shows that the user chris is logged in on `tty1` (which is the monitor connected to the computer), and his login session began at 20:57 on January 13. The `IDLE` time shows how long the shell has been open without any command being typed (the dot indicates that it is currently active). PID shows the process ID of the user's login shell. `COMMENT` would show the name of the remote computer the user had logged in from, if that user had logged in from another computer on the network, or the name of the local X display if you were using a Terminal window (such as :0.0).

Checking Directories and Permissions

Associated with each shell is a location in the Linux file system known as the *current* or *working directory*. Each user has a directory that is identified as the user's home directory. When you first log in to Linux, you begin with your home directory as the current directory.

When you request to open or save a file, your shell uses the current directory as the point of reference. Simply provide a filename when you save a file, and it is placed in the current directory. Alternatively, you can identify a file by its relation to the current directory (relative path), or you can ignore the current directory and identify a file by the full directory hierarchy that locates it (absolute path). The structure and use of the file system is described in detail later in this chapter.

To find out what your current directory (the *present working directory*) is, type the pwd command:

```
$ pwd
/usr/bin
```

In this example, the current/working directory is /usr/bin. To find out the name of your home directory, type the echo command, followed by the $HOME variable:

```
$ echo $HOME
/home/chris
```

Here, the home directory is /home/chris. To get back to your home directory, just type the change directory (cd) command. (Although cd followed by a directory name changes the current directory to the directory that you choose, simply typing cd with no directory name takes you to your home directory.)

```
$ cd
```

 Instead of typing $HOME, you can use the tilde (~) to refer to your home directory. So, to see your home directory, you could simply type echo ~.

To list the contents of your home directory, either type the full path to your home directory, or use the ls command without a directory name. Using the -a option to ls enables you to view the hidden files (known as *dot files* because they start with that character) as well as all other files. With the -l option, you can see a long, detailed list of information on each file. (You can put multiple single-letter options together after a single dash — for example, -la.)

```
$ ls -la /home/chris
total 158
drwxrwxrwx   2 chris sales   4096    May 12 13:55  .
drwxr-xr-x   3 root  root    4096    May 10 01:49  ..
-rw-------   1 chris sales   2204    May 18 21:30  .bash_history
-rw-r--r--   1 chris sales     24    May 10 01:50  .bash_logout
-rw-r--r--   1 chris sales    230    May 10 01:50  .bash_profile
-rw-r--r--   1 chris sales    124    May 10 01:50  .bashrc
drw-r--r--   1 chris sales   4096    May 10 01:50 .kde
-rw-rw-r--   1 chris sales 149872    May 11 22:49 letter


   ^            ^ ^       ^              ^  ^             ^
  col 1      col 2 col 3 col 4    col 5  col 6         col 7
```

Displaying a long list (-l option) of the contents of your home directory shows you more about file sizes and directories. The total line shows the total amount of disk space used by the files in the list (158 kilobytes in this example). Directories such as the current directory (.) and the parent directory (..) — the directory above the current directory — are noted as directories by the letter d at the beginning of each entry (each directory begins with a d, and each file begins with a -).

The file and directory names are shown in column 7. In this example, a dot (.) represents /home/chris and two dots (..) represents /home — the parent directory of /chris. Most of the files in this example are dot (.) files that are used to store GUI properties (.kde directory) or shell properties (.bash files). The only non-dot file in this list is the one named letter. Column 3 shows the directory or file owner. The /home directory is owned by root, and everything else is owned by the user chris, who belongs to the sales group (groups are listed in column 4).

In addition to the d or -, column 1 on each line contains the permissions set for that file or directory. (Permissions and configuring shell property files are described later in this chapter.) Other information in the listing includes the number of links to the item (column 2), the size of each file in bytes (column 5), and the date and time each file was most recently modified (column 6).

NOTE The number of characters shown for a directory (4096 bytes in these examples) reflects the size of the file containing information about the directory. While this number can grow to more than 4096 bytes for a directory that contains a lot of files, this number doesn't reflect the size of files contained in that directory.

NOTE The format of the time and date column can vary. Instead of displaying May 12, the display can be 2008-05-12 depending upon the distribution.

Checking System Activity

In addition to being a multiuser operating system, Linux is a multitasking system. *Multitasking* means that many programs can be running at the same time. An instance of a running program is referred to as a *process*. Linux provides tools for listing running processes, monitoring system usage, and stopping (or killing) processes when necessary.

The most common utility for checking running processes is the ps command. Use it to see which programs are running, the resources they are using, and who is running them. Here's an example of the ps command:

```
$ ps au
USER   PID %CPU %MEM  VSZ   RSS  TTY    STAT START TIME COMMAND
root  2146 0.0  0.8 1908  1100  ttyp0  S    14:50 0:00 login --jake
jake  2147 0.0  0.7 1836  1020  ttyp0  S    14:50 0:00 -bash
jake  2310 0.0  0.7 2592   912  ttyp0  R    18:22 0:00 ps au
```

In this example, the -a option asks to show processes of all users who are associated with your current terminal, and the -u option asks that usernames be shown, as well as other information such as the time the process started and memory and CPU usage. The concept of a terminal comes from the old days, when people worked exclusively from character terminals, so a terminal typically represented a single person at a single screen. Now you can have many "terminals" on one screen by opening multiple Terminal windows.

On this shell session, there isn't much happening. The first process shows that the user named jake logged in to the login process (which is controlled by the root user). The next process shows that jake is using a bash shell and has just run the ps au command. The terminal device ttyp0 is being used for the login session. The STAT column represents the state of the process, with R indicating a currently running process and S representing a sleeping process.

> **NOTE** Several other values can appear under the STAT column. For example, a plus sign (+) indicates that the process is associated with the foreground operations.

The USER column shows the name of the user who started the process. Each process is represented by a unique ID number referred to as a process ID (PID). (You can use the PID if you ever need to kill a runaway process.) The %CPU and %MEM columns show the percentages of the processor and random access memory, respectively, that the process is consuming. VSZ (virtual set size) shows the size of the image process (in kilobytes), and RSS (resident set size) shows the size of the program in memory. START shows the time the process began running, and TIME shows the cumulative system time used. (Many commands consume very little CPU time, as reflected by 0:00 for processes that haven't even used a whole second of CPU time.)

Many processes running on a computer are not associated with a terminal. A normal Linux system has many processes running in the background. Background system processes perform such tasks as logging system activity or listening for data coming in from the network. They are often started when Linux boots up and run continuously until it shuts down. To page through all the processes running on your Linux system, add the pipe (|) and the less command to ps aux, like this:

```
$ ps aux | less
```

A pipe (above the backslash character on the keyboard) enables you to direct the output of one command to be the input of the next command. In this example, the output of the ps command (a list of processes) is directed to the less command, which lets you page through that information. Use the spacebar to page through, and type **q** to end the list. You can also use the arrow keys to move one line at a time through the output.

Exiting the Shell

To exit the shell when you are done, type **exit** or press Ctrl+D.

You've just seen a few commands that can help you quickly familiarize yourself with your Linux system. There are hundreds of other commands that you can try. You'll find many in the /bin and /usr/bin directories, and you can use ls to see a directory's command list: ls /bin, for example, results in a list of commands in the /bin. Then use the man command (for example, man hostname) to see what each command does. Administrative commands are also in /sbin or /usr/sbin directory.

Using the Shell in Linux

When you type a command in a shell, you can include other characters that change or add to how the command works. In addition to the command itself, these are some of the other items that you can type on a shell command line:

■ **Options** — Most commands have one or more options you can add to change their behavior. Options typically consist of a single letter, preceded by a dash. You can also often combine several options after a single dash. For example, the command `ls -la` lists the contents of the current directory. The `-l` asks for a detailed (long) list of information, and the `-a` asks that files beginning with a dot (.) also be listed. When a single option consists of a word, it is usually preceded by a double dash (`--`). For example, to use the help option on many commands, you enter `--help` on the command line.

> **NOTE** You can use the `--help` option with most commands to see the options and arguments that they support — for example, `hostname --help`.

■ **Arguments** — Many commands also accept *arguments* after certain options are entered or at the end of the entire command line. An argument is an extra piece of information, such as a filename, that can be used by the command. For example, `cat /etc/passwd` displays the contents of the `/etc/passwd` file on your screen. In this case, `/etc/passwd` is the argument.

■ **Environment variables** — The shell itself stores information that may be useful to the user's shell session in what are called *environment variables*. Examples of environment variables include `$SHELL` (which identifies the shell you are using), `$PS1` (which defines your shell prompt), and `$MAIL` (which identifies the location of your mailbox). See the section "Using Shell Environment Variables" later in this chapter for more information.

> **TIP** You can check your environment variables at any time. Type `declare` to list the current environment variables. Or you can type `echo $VALUE`, where *VALUE* is replaced by the name of a particular environment variable you want to list. And because there are always multiple ways to do anything in Linux, you can also type `env` to get a succinct list of the current environment variables and their values.

■ **Metacharacters** — These are characters that have special meaning to the shell. They can be used to direct the output of a command to a file (>), pipe the output to another command (|), and run a command in the background (&), to name a few. Metacharacters are discussed later in this chapter.

To save you some typing, there are shell features that store commands you want to reuse, recall previous commands, and edit commands. You can create aliases that enable you to type a short command to run a longer one. The shell stores previously entered commands in a history list, which you can display and from which you can recall commands. You'll see how this works a little later in the chapter.

Unless you specifically change to another shell, the bash shell is the one you use with most Linux systems. The bash shell contains most of the powerful features available in other shells. Although the description in this chapter steps you through many bash shell features, you can learn more about the bash shell by typing **man bash**. The sidebar "Getting Help Using the Shell" shows you a few other ways to learn about using the shell.

Locating Commands

If you know the directory that contains the command you want to run, one way to run it is to type the full, or absolute, path to that command. For example, you run the `date` command from the `/bin` directory by typing:

```
$ /bin/date
```

Of course, this can be inconvenient, especially if the command resides in a directory with a long path name. The better way is to have commands stored in well-known directories, and then add those directories to your shell's PATH environment variable. The path consists of a list of directories that are checked sequentially for the commands you enter. To see your current path, type the following:

```
$ echo $PATH
/bin:/usr/bin:/usr/local/bin:/usr/bin/X11:/usr/X11R6/bin:/home/chris/bin
```

The results show the default path for a regular Linux user. Directories in the path list are separated by colons. Most user commands that come with Linux are stored in the `/bin`, `/usr/bin`, or `/usr/local/bin` directory. Although many graphical commands (that are used with GUIs) are contained in `/usr/bin`, there are some special X commands that are in `/usr/bin/X11` and `/usr/X11R6/bin` directories. The last directory shown is the `bin` directory in the user's `home` directory.

TIP If you want to add your own commands or shell scripts, place them in the `bin` directory in your home directory (such as `/home/chris/bin` for the user named chris). **This directory is automatically added to your path in some Linux systems, although you may need to create that directory or add it to your PATH on other Linux systems. So as long as you add the command to your bin with execute permission (described in the section "Understanding File Permissions" later in this chapter), you can immediately begin using the command by simply typing the command name at your shell prompt.**

Unlike some other operating systems, Linux does not, by default, check the current directory for an executable before searching the path. It immediately begins searching the path, and executables in the current directory are run only if they are in the PATH variable or you give their absolute address.

If you are the root user, directories containing administrative commands are typically in your path. These directories include `/sbin` and `/usr/sbin`. (You may need to start your shell with a `-l` or `-login` option to have `/sbin` and `/usr/sbin` added to your PATH.)

Getting Help Using the Shell

When you first start using the shell, it can be intimidating. All you see is a prompt. How do you know which commands are available, which options they use, or how to use advanced features? Fortunately, lots of help is available. Here are some places you can look to supplement what you learn in this chapter:

- Check the PATH — Type **echo $PATH**. You see a list of the directories containing commands that are immediately accessible to you. Listing the contents of those directories displays most standard Linux commands.

- Use the `help` command — Some commands are built into the shell, so they do not appear in a directory. The `help` command lists those commands and shows options available with each of them. (Type **help | less** to page through the list.) For help with a particular built-in command, type **help** *command*, replacing *command* with the name that interests you. The `help` command works with the bash shell only.

- Use `--help` with the command — Many commands include a `--help` option that you can use to get information about how the command is used. For example, type **date --help | less**. The output shows not only options, but also time formats you can use with the date command.

- Use the `man` command — To learn more about a particular command, type **man** *command*. (Replace *command* with the command name you want.) A description of the command and its options appears on the screen.

- Use the `info` command — The `info` command is another tool for displaying information about commands from the shell. The `info` command can move among a hierarchy of nodes to find information about commands and other items. Not all commands have information available in the info database, but sometimes more information can be found there than on a man page.

The path directory order is important. Directories are checked from left to right. So, in this example, if there is a command called `foo` located in both the `/bin` and `/usr/bin` directories, the one in `/bin` is executed. To have the other `foo` command run, you either type the full path to the command or change your PATH variable. (Changing your PATH and adding directories to it are described later in this chapter.)

Not all the commands that you run are located in directories in your PATH variable. Some commands are built into the shell. Other commands can be overridden by creating aliases that define any commands and options that you want the command to run. There are also ways of defining a function that consists of a stored series of commands. Here is the order in which the shell checks for the commands you type:

1. **Aliases** — Names set by the `alias` command that represent a particular command and a set of options. (Type **alias** to see what aliases are set.) Often, aliases enable you to define a short name for a long, complicated command.

2. **Shell reserved word** — Words reserved by the shell for special use. Many of these are words that you would use in programming-type functions, such as do, while, case, and else.

3. **Function** — A set of commands that are executed together within the current shell.

4. **Built-in command** — A command built into the shell. As a result, there is no representation of the command in the file system. Some of the most common commands you will use are shell built-in commands, such as cd (to change directories), echo (to echo text to the screen), exit (to exit from a shell), fg (to bring a command running in the background to the foreground), history (to see a list of commands that were previously run), pwd (to list the present working directory), set (to set shell options), and type (to show the location of a command).

5. **File system command** — A command that is stored in and executed from the computer's file system. (These are the commands that are indicated by the value of the PATH variable.)

To find out where a particular command is taken from, you can use the type command. (If you are using a shell other than bash, use the which command instead.) For example, to find out where the bash shell command is located, type the following:

```
$ type bash
bash is /bin/bash
```

Try these few words with the type command to see other locations of commands: which, case, and return. If a command resides in several locations, you can add the -a option to have all the known locations of the command printed.

> **TIP** Sometimes you run a command and receive an error message that the command was not found or that permission to run the command was denied. In the first case, check that you spelled the command correctly and that it is located in your PATH variable. In the second case, the command may be in the PATH variable, but may not be executable. Adding execute permissions to a command is described later in this chapter.

Rerunning Commands

After typing a long or complex command line, it's annoying to learn that you mistyped something. Fortunately, some shell features let you recall previous command lines, edit those lines, or complete a partially typed command line.

The *shell history* is a list of the commands that you have entered before. Using the history command in a bash shell, you can view your previous commands. Then, using various shell features, you can recall individual command lines from that list and change them however you please.

The rest of this section describes how to do command-line editing, how to complete parts of command lines, and how to recall and work with the history list.

Command-Line Editing

If you type something wrong on a command line, the bash shell ensures that you don't have to delete the entire line and start over. Likewise, you can recall a previous command line and change the elements to make a new command.

By default, the bash shell uses command-line editing that is based on the emacs text editor. (Type **man emacs** to read about it, if you care to.) If you are familiar with emacs, you probably already know most of the keystrokes described here.

 If you prefer the vi command for editing shell command lines, you can easily make that happen. Add the line:

```
set -o vi
```

to the .bashrc file in your home directory. The next time you open a shell, you can use vi commands (as described in the tutorial later in this chapter) to edit your command lines.

To do the editing, you can use a combination of control keys, meta keys, and arrow keys. For example, Ctrl+F means to hold the Ctrl key and type **f**. Alt+F means to hold the Alt key and type **f**. (Instead of the Alt key, your keyboard may use a Meta key or the Esc key. On a Windows keyboard, you can use the Windows key.)

To try out a bit of command-line editing, type the following:

```
$ ls /usr/bin | sort -f | less
```

This command lists the contents of the /usr/bin directory, sorts the contents in alphabetical order (regardless of case), and pipes the output to less. The less command displays the first page of output, after which you can go through the rest of the output a line (press Enter) or a page (press the spacebar) at a time (type **q** when you are done). Now, suppose you want to change /usr/bin to /bin. You can use the following steps to change the command:

1. Press the up arrow to recall the line.
2. Press Ctrl+A. This moves the cursor to the beginning of the command line.
3. Press Ctrl+F or the right arrow (→) key. Repeat this command a few times to position the cursor under the first slash (/).
4. Press Ctrl+D. Type this command four times to delete /usr from the line.
5. Press Enter. This executes the command line.

As you edit a command line, at any point you can type regular characters to add those characters to the command line. The characters appear at the location of your cursor. You can use right (→) and left (←) arrow keys to move the cursor from one end to the other on the command line. You can also press the up (↑) and down (↓) arrow keys to step through previous commands in the history list to select a command line for editing. (See the discussion on command recall for details on how to recall commands from the history list.)

There are many keystrokes you can use to edit your command lines. Table 2-1 lists the keystrokes that you can use to move around the command line.

TABLE 2-1

Keystrokes for Navigating Command Lines

Keystroke	Full Name	Meaning
Ctrl+F	Character forward	Go forward one character.
Ctrl+B	Character backward	Go backward one character.
Alt+F	Word forward	Go forward one word.
Alt+B	Word backward	Go backward one word.
Ctrl+A	Beginning of line	Go to the beginning of the current line.
Ctrl+E	End of line	Go to the end of the line.
Ctrl+L	Clear screen	Clear the screen and leave line at the top of the screen.

The keystrokes in Table 2-2 can be used to edit command lines.

TABLE 2-2

Keystrokes for Editing Command Lines

Keystroke	Full Name	Meaning
Ctrl+D	Delete current	Delete the current character.
Backspace	Delete previous	Delete the previous character.
Ctrl+T	Transpose character	Switch positions of the current and previous characters.
Alt+T	Transpose words	Switch positions of the current and previous characters.
Alt+U	Uppercase word	Change the current word to uppercase.
Alt+L	Lowercase word	Change the current word to lowercase.
Alt+C	Capitalize word	Change the current word to an initial capital letter.
Ctrl+V	Insert special character	Add a special character. For example, to add a Tab character, press Ctrl+V+Tab.

Use the keystrokes in Table 2-3 to cut and paste text on a command line.

TABLE 2-3

Keystrokes for Cutting and Pasting Text in Command Lines

Keystroke	Full Name	Meaning
Ctrl+K	Cut end of line	Cut text to the end of the line.
Ctrl+U	Cut beginning of line	Cut text to the beginning of the line.
Ctrl+W	Cut previous word	Cut the word located behind the cursor.
Alt+D	Cut next word	Cut the word following the cursor.
Ctrl+Y	Paste recent text	Paste most recently cut text.
Alt+Y	Paste earlier text	Rotate back to previously cut text and paste it.
Ctrl+C	Delete whole line	Delete the entire line.

Command-Line Completion

To save you a few keystrokes, the bash shell offers several different ways of completing partially typed values. To attempt to complete a value, type the first few characters, and then press Tab. Here are some of the values you can type partially:

■ **Environment variable** — If the text you type begins with a dollar sign ($), the shell completes the text with an environment variable from the current shell.

■ **Username** — If the text you type begins with a tilde (~), the shell completes the text with a username.

■ **Command, alias, or function** — If the text you type begins with regular characters, the shell tries to complete the text with a command, alias, or function name.

■ **Hostname** — If the text you type begins with an at (@) sign, the shell completes the text with a hostname taken from the /etc/hosts file.

 To add hostnames from an additional file, you can set the HOSTFILE variable to the name of that file. The file must be in the same format as /etc/hosts.

Here are a few examples of command completion. (When you see **<Tab>**, it means to press the Tab key on your keyboard.) Type the following:

```
$ echo $OS<Tab>
$ cd ~ro<Tab>
$ fing<Tab>
```

The first example causes $OS to expand to the $OSTYPE variable. In the next example, ~ro expands to the root user's home directory (~root/). Next, fing expands to the finger command.

Of course, there will be times when there are several possible completions for the string of characters you have entered. In that case, you can check the possible ways text can be expanded by pressing Esc+? (or by pressing Tab twice) at the point where you want to do completion. This shows the result you would get if you checked for possible completions on $P.

```
$ echo $P<Esc+?>
$PATH $PPID $PS1 $PS2 $PS4 $PWD
$ echo $P
```

In this case, there are six possible variables that begin with $P. After possibilities are displayed, the original command line returns, ready for you to complete it as you choose.

Command-Line Recall

After you type a command line, that entire command line is saved in your shell's history list. The list is stored in a history file, from which any command can be recalled to run again. After it is recalled, you can modify the command line, as described earlier.

To view your history list, use the history command. Type the command without options or followed by a number to list that many of the most recent commands. For example:

```
$ history 8
 382 date
 383 ls /usr/bin | sort -a | more
 384 man sort
 385 cd /usr/local/bin
 386 man more
 387 useradd -m /home/chris -u 101 chris
 388 passwd chris
 389 history 8
```

A number precedes each command line in the list. You can recall one of those commands using an exclamation point (!). Keep in mind that when using an exclamation point, the command runs blind, without presenting an opportunity to confirm the command you're referencing. There are several ways to run a command immediately from this list, including:

- *!n*—Run command number. Replace the *n* with the number of the command line, and that line is run. For example, here's how to repeat the date command shown as command number 382 in the preceding history listing:

```
$ !382
date
Thu Oct 26 21:30:06 PDT 2008
```

- *!!*—Run previous command. Runs the previous command line. Here's how you'd immediately run that same date command:

```
$ !!
date
Thu Oct 26 21:30:39 PDT 2008
```

■ `!?string?` — Run command containing string. This runs the most recent command that contains a particular *string* of characters. For example, you can run the `date` command again by just searching for part of that command line as follows:

```
$ !?dat?
date
Thu Oct 26 21:32:41 PDT 2008
```

Instead of just running a `history` command line immediately, you can recall a particular line and edit it. You can use the following keys or key combinations to do that, as shown in Table 2-4.

TABLE 2-4

Keystrokes for Using Command History

Key(s)	Function Name	Description
Arrow Keys (↑ and ↓)	Step	Press the up and down arrow keys to step through each command line in your history list to arrive at the one you want. (Ctrl+P and Ctrl+N do the same functions, respectively.)
Ctrl+R	Reverse Incremental Search	After you press these keys, you enter a search string to do a reverse search. As you type the string, a matching command line appears that you can run or edit.
Ctrl+S	Forward Incremental Search	Same as the preceding function but for a forward search.
Alt+P	Reverse Search	After you press these keys, you enter a string to do a reverse search. Type a string and press Enter to see the most recent command line that includes that string.
Alt+N	Forward Search	Same as the preceding function but for a forward search.

Another way to work with your history list is to use the `fc` command. Type **fc** followed by a history line number, and that command line is opened in a text editor. Make the changes that you want. When you exit the editor, the command runs. You can also give a range of line numbers (for example, `fc 100 105`). All the commands open in your text editor, and then run one after the other when you exit the editor.

The history list is stored in the `.bash_history` file in your home directory. Up to 1,000 history commands are stored for you by default.

NOTE Some people disable the history feature for the root user by setting the `HISTFILE` to `/dev/null` or simply leaving `HISTSIZE` blank. This prevents information about the root user's activities from potentially being exploited. If you are an administrative user with root privileges, you may want to consider emptying your file upon exiting as well, for the same reasons.

Connecting and Expanding Commands

A truly powerful feature of the shell is the capability to redirect the input and output of commands to and from other commands and files. To allow commands to be strung together, the shell uses metacharacters. As noted earlier, a metacharacter is a typed character that has special meaning to the shell for connecting commands or requesting expansion.

Piping Commands

The pipe (`|`) metacharacter connects the output from one command to the input of another command. This lets you have one command work on some data, and then have the next command deal with the results. Here is an example of a command line that includes pipes:

```
$ cat /etc/password | sort | less
```

This command lists the contents of the `/etc/password` file and pipes the output to the `sort` command. The `sort` command takes the usernames that begin each line of the `/etc/password` file, sorts them alphabetically, and pipes the output to the `less` command (to page through the output).

Pipes are an excellent illustration of how UNIX, the predecessor of Linux, was created as an operating system made up of building blocks. A standard practice in UNIX was to connect utilities in different ways to get different jobs done. For example, before the days of graphical word processors, users created plain-text files that included macros to indicate formatting. To see how the document really appeared, they would use a command such as the following:

```
$ gunzip < /usr/share/man/man1/grep.1.gz | nroff -c -man | less
```

In this example, the contents of the `grep` man page (`grep.1.gz`) are directed to the `gunzip` command to be unzipped. The output from `gunzip` is piped to the `nroff` command to format the man page using the manual macro (`-man`). The output is piped to the `less` command to display the output. Because the file being displayed is in plain text, you could have substituted any number of options to work with the text before displaying it. You could sort the contents, change or delete some of the content, or bring in text from other documents. The key is that, instead of all those features being in one program, you get results from piping and redirecting input and output between multiple commands.

Sequential Commands

Sometimes you may want a sequence of commands to run, with one command completing before the next command begins. You can do this by typing several commands on the same command line and separating them with semicolons (`;`):

```
$ date ; troff -me verylargedocument | lpr ; date
```

In this example, I was formatting a huge document and wanted to know how long it would take. The first command (`date`) showed the date and time before the formatting started. The `troff` command formatted the document and then piped the output to the printer. When the formatting was done, the date and time was printed again (so I knew how long the `troff` command took to complete).

Another useful command to add to the end of a long command line is the `mail` command. You could add `mail -s "Finished the long command" chris@example.com` to the end of a command line. Then, for example, a mail message is sent to the user you choose after the command completes.

Background Commands

Some commands can take a while to complete. Sometimes you may not want to tie up your shell waiting for a command to finish. In those cases, you can have the commands run in the background by using the ampersand (&).

Text formatting commands (such as `nroff` and `troff`, described earlier) are examples of commands that are often run in the background to format a large document. You also might want to create your own shell scripts that run in the background to check continuously for certain events to occur, such as the hard disk filling up or particular users logging in.

Here is an example of a command being run in the background:

```
$ troff -me verylargedocument | lpr &
```

Other ways to manage background and foreground processes are described in the section "Managing Background and Foreground Processes" later in this chapter.

Expanding Commands

With command substitution, you can have the output of a command interpreted by the shell instead of by the command itself. In this way, you can have the standard output of a command become an argument for another command. The two forms of command substitution are `$(command)` and `` `command` `` (backticks, not single quotes).

The command in this case can include options, metacharacters, and arguments. Here is an example of using command substitution:

```
$ vi $(find /home | grep xyzzy)
```

In this example, the command substitution is done before the `vi` command is run. First, the `find` command starts at the `/home` directory and prints out all files and directories below that point in the file system. The output is piped to the `grep` command, which filters out all files except for those that include the string `xyzzy` in the filename. Finally, the `vi` command opens all filenames for editing (one at a time) that include `xyzzy`.

This particular example is useful if you want to edit a file for which you know the name but not the location. As long as the string is uncommon, you can find and open every instance of a filename existing beneath a point you choose in the file system. (In other words, don't use grep a from the root file system or you'll match and try to edit several thousand files.)

Expanding Arithmetic Expressions

There may be times when you want to pass arithmetic results to a command. There are two forms you can use to expand an arithmetic expression and pass it to the shell: $[expression] and $(expression). Here is an example:

```
$ echo "I am $[2008 - 1957] years old."
I am 51 years old.
```

The shell interprets the arithmetic expression first (2008 - 1957), and then passes that information to the echo command. The echo command displays the text, with the results of the arithmetic (51) inserted.

Here's an example of the other form:

```
$ echo "There are $(ls | wc -w) files in this directory."
There are 14 files in this directory.
```

This lists the contents of the current directory (ls) and runs the word count command to count the number of files found (wc -w). The resulting number (14 in this case) is echoed back with the rest of the sentence shown.

Expanding Environment Variables

Environment variables that store information within the shell can be expanded using the dollar sign ($) metacharacter. When you expand an environment variable on a command line, the value of the variable is printed instead of the variable name itself, as follows:

```
$ ls -l $BASH
-rwxr-xr-x 1 root  root  625516 Dec 5 11:13 /bin/bash
```

Using $BASH as an argument to ls -l causes a long listing of the bash command to be printed. The following section discusses shell environment variables.

Creating Your Shell Environment

You can tune your shell to help you work more efficiently. Your prompt can provide pertinent information each time you press Enter. You can set aliases to save your keystrokes and permanently set environment variables to suit your needs. To make each change occur when you start a shell, add this information to your shell configuration files.

Configuring Your Shell

Several configuration files support how your shell behaves. Some of the files are executed for every user and every shell, while others are specific to the user who creates the configuration file. Table 2-5 shows the files that are of interest to anyone using the bash shell in Linux.

TABLE 2-5

Bash Configuration Files

File	Description
/etc/profile	Sets up user environment information for every user. It is executed when you first log in. This file provides values for your path, as well as setting environment variables for such things as the location of your mailbox and the size of your history files. Finally, /etc/profile gathers shell settings from configuration files in the /etc/profile.d directory.
/etc/bashrc	Executes for every user who runs the bash shell, each time a bash shell is opened. It sets the default prompt and may add one or more aliases. Values in this file can be overridden by information in each user's ~/.bashrc file.
~/.bash_profile	Used by each user to enter information that is specific to his or her own use of the shell. It is executed only once, when the user logs in. By default it sets a few environment variables and executes the user's .bashrc file.
~/.bashrc	Contains the information that is specific to your bash shells. It is read when you log in and also each time you open a new bash shell. This is the best location to add environment variables and aliases so that your shell picks them up.
~/.bash_logout	Executes each time you log out (exit the last bash shell). By default, it simply clears your screen.

To change the /etc/profile or /etc/bashrc files, you must be the root user. Users can change the information in the $HOME/.bash_profile, $HOME/.bashrc, and $HOME/.bash_logout files in their own home directories.

The following sections provide ideas about items to add to your shell configuration files. In most cases, you add these values to the .bashrc file in your home directory. However, if you administer a system, you may want to set some of these values as defaults for all of your Linux system's users.

Setting Your Prompt

Your prompt consists of a set of characters that appear each time the shell is ready to accept a command. The PS1 environment variable sets what the prompt contains and is what you interact with most of the time. If your shell requires additional input, it uses the values of PS2, PS3, and PS4.

When your Linux system is installed, often a prompt is set to contain more than just a dollar sign or pound sign. For example, in Fedora or Red Hat Enterprise Linux, your prompt is set to include the following information: your username, your hostname, and the base name of your current working directory. That information is surrounded by brackets and followed by a dollar sign (for regular users) or a pound sign (for the root user). Here is an example of that prompt:

```
[chris@myhost bin]$
```

If you change directories, the bin name would change to the name of the new directory. Likewise, if you were to log in as a different user or to a different host, that information would change.

You can use several special characters (indicated by adding a backslash to a variety of letters) to include different information in your prompt. These can include your terminal number, the date, and the time, as well as other pieces of information. Table 2-6 provides some examples (you can find more on the bash man page).

TABLE 2-6

Characters to Add Information to the bash Prompt

Special Character	Description
\!	Shows the current command history number. This includes all previous commands stored for your username.
\#	Shows the command number of the current command. This includes only the commands for the active shell.
\$	Shows the user prompt ($) or root prompt (#), depending on which user you are.
\W	Shows only the current working directory base name. For example, if the current working directory was /var/spool/mail, this value simply appears as mail.
\[	Precedes a sequence of nonprinting characters. This can be used to add a terminal control sequence into the prompt for such things as changing colors, adding blink effects, or making characters bold. (Your terminal determines the exact sequences available.)
\]	Follows a sequence of nonprinting characters.
\\	Shows a backslash.
\d	Displays the day name, month, and day number of the current date. For example: Sat Jan 23.
\h	Shows the hostname of the computer running the shell.
\n	Causes a newline to occur.
\nnn	Shows the character that relates to the octal number replacing *nnn*.
\s	Displays the current shell name. For the bash shell, the value would be bash.
\t	Prints the current time in hours, minutes, and seconds (for example, 10:14:39).
\u	Prints your current username.
\w	Displays the full path to the current working directory.

TIP If you are setting your prompt temporarily by typing at the shell, you should put the value of PS1 in quotes. For example, you could type export PS1="[\t \w]\$ " to see a prompt that looks like this: [20:26:32 /var/spool]$.

To make a change to your prompt permanent, add the value of PS1 to your .bashrc file in your home directory (assuming that you are using the bash shell). There may already be a PS1 value in that file that you can modify. Refer to the Bash Prompt HOWTO (`www.tldp.org/HOWTO/Bash-Prompt-HOWTO`) for information on changing colors, commands, and other features of your bash shell prompt.

Adding Environment Variables

You may consider adding a few environment variables to your `.bashrc` file. These can help make working with the shell more efficient and effective:

- `TMOUT` — Sets how long the shell can be inactive before bash automatically exits. The value is the number of seconds for which the shell has not received input. This can be a nice security feature, in case you leave your desk while you are still logged in to Linux. So as not to be logged off while you are working, you may want to set the value to something like TMOUT=1800 (to allow 30 minutes of idle time). You can use any terminal session to close the current shell after a set number of seconds — for example, TMOUT=30.

- `PATH` — As described earlier, the `PATH` variable sets the directories that are searched for commands you use. If you often use directories of commands that are not in your PATH, you can permanently add them. To do this, add a PATH variable to your `.bashrc` file. For example, to add a directory called `/getstuff/bin`, type the following:

```
PATH=$PATH:/getstuff/bin ; export PATH
```

This example first reads all the current path directories into the new PATH ($PATH), adds the `/getstuff/bin` directory, and then exports the new PATH.

CAUTION Some people add the current directory to their PATH by adding a directory identified simply as a dot (.), as follows:

```
PATH=.:$PATH ; export PATH
```

This enables you always to run commands in your current directory before evaluating any other command in the path (which people may be used to if they have used DOS). However, the security risk with this procedure is that you could be in a directory that contains a command that you don't intend to run from that directory. For example, a malicious person could put an `ls` command in a directory that, instead of listing the content of your directory, does something devious. Because of this, the practice of adding the dot to your path is highly discouraged.

- `WHATEVER` — You can create your own environment variables to provide shortcuts in your work. Choose any name that is not being used and assign a useful value to it. For example, if you do a lot of work with files in the `/work/time/files/info/memos` directory, you could set the following variable:

```
M=/work/time/files/info/memos ; export M
```

You could make that your current directory by typing cd $M. You could run a program from that directory called `hotdog` by typing $M/hotdog. You could edit a file from there called `bun` by typing vi $M/bun.

Adding Aliases

Setting aliases can save you even more typing than setting environment variables. With aliases, you can have a string of characters execute an entire command line. You can add and list aliases with the alias command. Here are some examples of using alias from a bash shell:

```
alias p='pwd ; ls -CF'
alias rm='rm -i'
```

In the first example, the letter p is assigned to run the command pwd, and then to run ls -CF to print the current working directory and list its contents in column form. The second runs the rm command with the -i option each time you simply type rm. (This is an alias that is often set automatically for the root user, so that instead of just removing files, you are prompted for each individual file removal. This prevents you from automatically removing all the files in a directory by mistakenly typing something such as rm *.)

While you are in the shell, you can check which aliases are set by typing the alias command. If you want to remove an alias, type **unalias**. (Remember that if the alias is set in a configuration file, it will be set again when you open another shell.)

Using Shell Environment Variables

Every active shell stores pieces of information that it needs to use in what are called *environment variables*. An environment variable can store things such as locations of configuration files, mailboxes, and path directories. They can also store values for your shell prompts, the size of your history list, and type of operating system.

To see the environment variables currently assigned to your shell, type the declare command. (It will probably fill more than one screen, so type **declare | more**. The declare command also shows functions as well as environment variables.) You can refer to the value of any of those variables by preceding it with a dollar sign ($) and placing it anywhere on a command line. For example:

```
$ echo $USER
chris
```

This command prints the value of the USER variable, which holds your username (chris). Substitute any other value for USER to print its value instead.

Common Shell Environment Variables

When you start a shell (by logging in or opening a Terminal window), a lot of environment variables are already set. Table 2-7 shows some variables that are either set when you use a bash shell or that can be set by you to use with different features.

TABLE 2-7

Common Shell Environment Variables

Variable	Description
BASH	Contains the full path name of the bash command. This is usually /bin/bash.
BASH_VERSION	A number representing the current version of the bash command.
EUID	This is the effective user ID number of the current user. It is assigned when the shell starts, based on the user's entry in the /etc/passwd file.
FCEDIT	If set, this variable indicates the text editor used by the fc command to edit history commands. If this variable isn't set, the vi command is used.
HISTFILE	The location of your history file. It is typically located at $HOME/.bash_history.
HISTFILESIZE	The number of history entries that can be stored. After this number is reached, the oldest commands are discarded. The default value is 1000.
HISTCMD	This returns the number of the current command in the history list.
HOME	This is your home directory. It is your current working directory each time you log in or type the cd command with any options.
HOSTTYPE	A value that describes the computer architecture on which the Linux system is running. For Intel-compatible PCs, the value is i386, i486, i586, i686, or something like i386-linux. For AMD 64-bit machines, the value is x86_64.
MAIL	This is the location of your mailbox file. The file is typically your username in the /var/spool/mail directory.
OLDPWD	The directory that was the working directory before you changed to the current working directory.
OSTYPE	A name identifying the current operating system. For Fedora Linux, the OSTYPE value is either linux or linux-gnu, depending on the type of shell you are using. (Bash can run on other operating systems as well.)
PATH	The colon-separated list of directories used to find commands that you type. The default value for regular users is /bin:/usr/bin:/usr/local/bin:/usr/bin/X11:/usr/X11R6/bin:~/bin. You need to type the full path or a relative path to a command you want to run that is not in your PATH. For the root user, the value also includes /sbin, /usr/sbin, and /usr/local/sbin.
PPID	The process ID of the command that started the current shell (for example, its parent process).
PROMPT_COMMAND	Can be set to a command name that is run each time before your shell prompt is displayed. Setting PROMPT_COMMAND=date lists the current date/time before the prompt appears.
PS1	Sets the value of your shell prompt. There are many items that you can read into your prompt (date, time, username, hostname, and so on). Sometimes a command requires additional prompts, which you can set with the variables PS2, PS3, and so on.

continued

61

Variable	Description
TABLE 2-7	*(continued)*
PWD	This is the directory that is assigned as your current directory. This value changes each time you change directories using the cd command.
RANDOM	Accessing this variable causes a random number to be generated. The number is between 0 and 99999.
SECONDS	The number of seconds since the time the shell was started.
SHLVL	The number of shell levels associated with the current shell session. When you log in to the shell, the SHLVL is 1. Each time you start a new bash command (by, for example, using su to become a new user, or by simply typing bash), this number is incremented.
TMOUT	Can be set to a number representing the number of seconds the shell can be idle without receiving input. After the number of seconds is reached, the shell exits. This is a security feature that makes it less likely for unattended shells to be accessed by unauthorized people. (This must be set in the login shell for it to actually cause the shell to log out the user.)
UID	The user ID number assigned to your username. The user ID number is stored in the /etc/password file.

Setting Your Own Environment Variables

Environment variables can provide a handy way to store bits of information that you use often from the shell. You can create any variables that you want (avoiding those that are already in use) so that you can read in the values of those variables as you use the shell. (The bash man page lists variables already in use.)

To set an environment variable temporarily, you can simply type a variable name and assign it to a value. Here's an example:

```
$ AB=/usr/dog/contagious/ringbearer/grind ; export AB
```

This example causes a long directory path to be assigned to the AB variable. The export AB command says to export the value to the shell so that it can be propagated to other shells you may open. With AB set, you go to the directory by typing the following:

```
$ cd $AB
```

The problem with setting environment variables in this way is that as soon as you exit the shell in which you set the variable, the setting is lost. To set variables permanently, add variable settings to a bash configuration file, as described later in this section.

NOTE Another option to add the settings to the bash configuration file is to create an executable script file that contains these settings. This is useful when you don't use the settings all the time, but need to use them occasionally. They are there only for the life of the session after the script file has run.

If you want to have other text right up against the output from an environment variable, you can surround the variable in braces. This protects the variable name from being misunderstood. For example, if you want to add a command name to the AB variable shown earlier, you can type the following:

```
$ echo ${AB}/adventure
/usr/dog/contagious/ringbearer/grind/adventure
```

Remember that you must export the variable so that it can be picked up by other shell commands. You must add the export line to a shell configuration file for it to take effect the next time you log in. The export command is fairly flexible. Instead of running the export command after you set the variable, you can do it all in one step, as follows:

```
$ export XYZ=/home/xyz/bin
```

You can override the value of any environment variable. This can be temporary, by simply typing the new value, or you can add the new export line to your $HOME/.bashrc file. One useful variable to update is PATH:

```
$ export PATH=$PATH:/home/xyz/bin
```

In this example, the /home/xyz/bin directory is added to the PATH, a useful technique if you want to run a bunch of commands from a directory that is not normally in your PATH, without typing the full or relative path each time.

If you decide that you no longer want a variable to be set, you can use the unset command to erase its value. For example, you can type **unset XYZ**, which causes XYZ to have no value set. (Remember to remove the export from the $HOME/.bashrc file — if you added it there   or it will return the next time you open a shell.)

Managing Background and Foreground Processes

If you are using Linux over a network or from a *dumb* terminal (a monitor that allows only text input with no GUI support), your shell may be all that you have. You may be used to a graphical environment where you have a lot of programs active at the same time so that you can switch among them as needed. This shell thing can seem pretty limited.

Although the bash shell doesn't include a GUI for running many programs, it does let you move active programs between the background and foreground. In this way, you can have a lot of stuff running, while selectively choosing the program you want to deal with at the moment.

There are several ways to place an active program in the background. One mentioned earlier is to add an ampersand (&) to the end of a command line. Another way is to use the at command to run commands in a way in which they are not connected to the shell.

To stop a running command and put it in the background, press Ctrl+Z. After the command is stopped, you can either bring it back into the foreground to run (the fg command) or start it running in the background (the bg command). Keep in mind that any command running in the background might spew output during commands that you run subsequently from that shell. For example, if output appears from a backgrounded command during a vi session, simply press Ctrl+L to redraw the screen to get rid of the output.

 To avoid having the output appear, you should have any process running in the background send its output to a file or to null.

Starting Background Processes

If you have programs that you want to run while you continue to work in the shell, you can place the programs in the background. To place a program in the background at the time you run the program, type an ampersand (&) at the end of the command line, like this:

```
$ find /usr > /tmp/allusrfiles &
```

This example command finds all files on your Linux system (starting from /usr), prints those filenames, and puts those names in the file /tmp/allusrfiles. The ampersand (&) runs that command line in the background. To check which commands you have running in the background, use the jobs command, as follows:

```
$ jobs
[1]  Stopped (tty output)  vi /tmp/myfile
[2]  Running          find /usr -print > /tmp/allusrfiles &
[3]  Running          nroff -man /usr/man2/* >/tmp/man2 &
[4]- Running          nroff -man /usr/man3/* >/tmp/man3 &
[5]+ Stopped          nroff -man /usr/man4/* >/tmp/man4
```

The first job shows a text-editing command (vi) that I placed in the background and stopped by pressing Ctrl+Z while I was editing. Job 2 shows the find command I just ran. Jobs 3 and 4 show nroff commands currently running in the background. Job 5 had been running in the shell (foreground) until I decided too many processes were running and pressed Ctrl+Z to stop job 5 until a few processes had completed.

The plus sign (+) next to number 5 shows that it was most recently placed in the background. The minus sign (-) next to number 4 shows that it was placed in the background just before the most recent background job. Because job 1 requires terminal input, it cannot run in the background. As a result, it is Stopped until it is brought to the foreground again.

 To see the process ID for the background job, add a -l (the lowercase letter L) option to the jobs command. If you type ps, you can use the process ID to figure out which command is for a particular background job.

Using Foreground and Background Commands

Continuing with the example, you can bring any of the commands on the jobs list to the foreground. For example, to edit myfile again, type:

```
$ fg %1
```

As a result, the vi command opens again, with all text as it was when you stopped the vi job.

CAUTION Before you put a text processor, word processor, or similar program in the background, make sure you save your file. It's easy to forget you have a program in the background, and you will lose your data if you log out or the computer reboots later on.

To refer to a background job (to cancel it or bring it to the foreground), use a percent sign (%) followed by the job number. You can also use the following to refer to a background job:

- % — Refers to the most recent command put into the background (indicated by the plus sign when you type the jobs command). This action brings the command to the foreground.

- %string — Refers to a job where the command begins with a particular string of characters. The string must be unambiguous. (In other words, typing %vi when there are two vi commands in the background results in an error message.)

- %?string — Refers to a job where the command line contains a string at any point. The string must be unambiguous or the match will fail.

- %-- — Refers to the previous job stopped before the one most recently stopped.

If a command is stopped, you can start it running again in the background using the bg command. For example, take job 5 from the jobs list in the previous example:

```
[5]+ Stopped          nroff -man man4/* >/tmp/man4
```

Type the following:

```
$ bg %5
```

After that, the job runs in the background. Its jobs entry appears as follows:

```
[5]  Running          nroff -man man4/* >/tmp/man4 &
```

Working with the Linux File System

The Linux file system is the structure in which all the information on your computer is stored. Files are organized within a hierarchy of directories. Each directory can contain files, as well as other directories.

If you were to map out the files and directories in Linux, it would look like an upside-down tree. At the top is the root directory, which is represented by a single slash (/). Below that is a set of common directories in the Linux system, such as bin, dev, home, lib, and tmp, to name a few. Each of those directories, as well as directories added to the root, can contain subdirectories.

Figure 2-1 illustrates how the Linux file system is organized as a hierarchy. To demonstrate how directories are connected, the figure shows a /home directory that contains subdirectories for three users: chris, mary, and tom. Within the chris directory are subdirectories: briefs, memos, and personal. To refer to a file called inventory in the chris/memos directory, you can type the full path of /home/chris/memos/inventory. If your current directory is /home/chris/memos, you can refer to the file as simply inventory.

The Linux file system is organized as a hierarchy of directories.

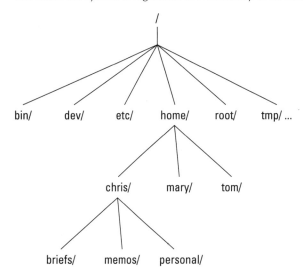

Some of the Linux directories that may interest you include the following:

- /bin — Contains common Linux user commands, such as ls, sort, date, and chmod.
- /boot — Has the bootable Linux kernel and boot loader configuration files (GRUB).
- /dev — Contains files representing access points to devices on your systems. These include terminal devices (tty*), floppy disks (fd*), hard disks (hd*), RAM (ram*), and CD-ROM (cd*). (Users normally access these devices directly through the device files.)
- /etc — Contains administrative configuration files.
- /home — Contains directories assigned to each user with a login account (with the exception of root).
- /media — Provides a standard location for mounting and automounting devices, such as remote file systems and removable media (with directory names of cdrecorder, floppy, and so on).
- /mnt — A common mount point for many devices before it was supplanted by the standard /media directory. Some bootable Linux systems still used this directory to mount hard disk partitions and remote file systems.
- /proc — Contains information about system resources.

- `/root` — Represents the root user's home directory. The home directory for root does not reside beneath `/home` for security reasons.

- `/sbin` — Contains administrative commands and daemon processes.

- `/sys` — A `/proc`-like file system, new in the Linux 2.6 kernel and intended to contain files for getting hardware status and reflecting the system's device tree as it is seen by the kernel. It pulls many of its functions from `/proc`.

- `/tmp` — Contains temporary files used by applications.

- `/usr` — Contains user documentation, games, graphical files (X11), libraries (lib), and a variety of other user and administrative commands and files.

- `/var` — Contains directories of data used by various applications. In particular, this is where you would place files that you share as an FTP server (`/var/ftp`) or a Web server (`/var/www`). It also contains all system log files (`/var/log`) and spool files in `/var/spool` (such as `mail`, `cups`, and `news`).

The file systems in the DOS or Microsoft Windows operating systems differ from Linux's file structure, as the sidebar "Linux File Systems Versus Windows-Based File Systems" explains.

Linux File Systems Versus Windows-Based File Systems

Although similar in many ways, the Linux file system has some striking differences from file systems used in MS-DOS and Windows operating systems. Here are a few:

- In MS-DOS and Windows file systems, drive letters represent different storage devices (for example, A: is a floppy drive and C: is a hard disk). In Linux, all storage devices are fit into the file system hierarchy. So, the fact that all of `/usr` may be on a separate hard disk or that `/mnt/rem1` is a file system from another computer is invisible to the user.

- Slashes, rather than backslashes, are used to separate directory names in Linux. So, `C:\home\chris` in an MS system is `/home/chris` in a Linux system.

- Filenames almost always have suffixes in DOS (such as .txt for text files or .doc for word-processing files). Although at times you can use that convention in Linux, three-character suffixes have no required meaning in Linux. They can be useful for identifying a file type. Many Linux applications and desktop environments use file suffixes to determine the contents of a file. In Linux, however, DOS command extensions such as .com, .exe, and .bat don't necessarily signify an executable (permission flags make Linux files executable).

- Every file and directory in a Linux system has permissions and ownership associated with it. Security varies among Microsoft systems. Because DOS and MS Windows began as single-user systems, file ownership was not built into those systems when they were designed. Later releases added features such as file and folder attributes to address this problem.

Creating Files and Directories

As a Linux user, most of the files you save and work with will probably be in your home directory. Table 2-8 shows commands to create and use files and directories.

TABLE 2-8

Commands to Create and Use Files

Command	Result
cd	Change to another directory.
pwd	Print the name of the current (or present) working directory.
mkdir	Create a directory.
chmod	Change the permissions on a file or directory.
ls	List the contents of a directory.

The following steps lead you through creating directories within your home directory and moving among your directories, with a mention of setting appropriate file permissions:

1. Go to your home directory. To do this, simply type **cd**. (For other ways of referring to your home directory, see the sidebar "Identifying Directories".)

2. To make sure that you're in your home directory, type **pwd**. When I do this, I get the following response (yours will reflect your home directory):

```
$ pwd
/home/chris
```

3. Create a new directory called test in your home directory, as follows:

```
$ mkdir test
```

4. Check the permissions of the directory:

```
$ ls -ld test
drwxr-xr-x  2 chris  sales  1024  Jan 24 12:17 test
```

This listing shows that test is a directory (d). The d is followed by the permissions (rwxr-xr-x), which are explained later in the section "Understanding File Permissions." The rest of the information indicates the owner (chris), the group (sales), and the date that the files in the directory were most recently modified (Jan. 24 at 12:17 p.m.).

In some Linux systems, such as Fedora, when you add a new user, the user is assigned to a group of the same name by default. For example, in the preceding text, the user chris would be assigned to the group chris. This approach to assigning groups is referred to as the user private group scheme.

For now, type the following:

```
$ chmod 700 test
```

This step changes the permissions of the directory to give you complete access and everyone else no access at all. (The new permissions should read as follows: rwx------.)

5. Make the test directory your current directory as follows:

```
$ cd test
```

Identifying Directories

When you need to identify your home directory on a shell command line, you can use the following:

- $HOME — This environment variable stores your home directory name.
- ~ — The tilde (~) represents your home directory on the command line.

You can also use the tilde to identify someone else's home directory. For example, ~chris would be expanded to the chris home directory (probably /home/chris).

Other special ways of identifying directories in the shell include the following:

- . — A single dot (.) refers to the current directory.
- .. — Two dots (..) refer to a directory directly above the current directory.
- $PWD — This environment variable refers to the current working directory.
- $OLDPWD — This environment variable refers to the previous working directory before you changed to the current one.

Using Metacharacters and Operators

To make efficient use of your shell, the bash shell lets you use certain special characters, referred to as metacharacters and operators. Metacharacters can help you match one or more files without typing each file completely. Operators enable you to direct information from one command or file to another command or file.

Using File-Matching Metacharacters

To save you some keystrokes and to be able to refer easily to a group of files, the bash shell lets you use metacharacters. Anytime you need to refer to a file or directory, such as to list it, open it, or remove it, you can use metacharacters to match the files you want. Here are some useful metacharacters for matching filenames:

- ■ `*` — Matches any number of characters.
- ■ `?` — Matches any one character.
- ■ `[...]` — Matches any one of the characters between the brackets, which can include a dash-separated range of letters or numbers.

Try out some of these file-matching metacharacters by first going to an empty directory (such as the `test` directory described in the previous section) and creating some empty files:

```
$ touch apple banana grape grapefruit watermelon
```

The `touch` command creates empty files. The next few commands show you how to use shell metacharacters with the `ls` command to match filenames. Try the following commands to see if you get the same responses:

```
$ ls a*
apple
$ ls g*
grape
grapefruit
$ ls g*t
grapefruit
$ ls *e*
apple grape grapefruit watermelon
$ ls *n*
banana watermelon
```

The first example matches any file that begins with an a (`apple`). The next example matches any files that begin with g (`grape`, `grapefruit`). Next, files beginning with g and ending in t are matched (`grapefruit`). Next, any file that contains an e in the name is matched (`apple`, `grape`, `grapefruit`, `watermelon`). Finally, any file that contains an n is matched (`banana`, `watermelon`).

Here are a few examples of pattern matching with the question mark (?):

```
$ ls ????e
apple grape
$ ls g???e*
grape grapefruit
```

The first example matches any five-character file that ends in e (`apple`, `grape`). The second matches any file that begins with g and has e as its fifth character (`grape`, `grapefruit`).

Here are a couple of examples using braces to do pattern matching:

```
$ ls [abw]*
apple banana watermelon
$ ls [agw]*[ne]
apple grape watermelon
```

In the first example, any file beginning with a, b, or w is matched. In the second, any file that begins with a, g, or w and also ends with either n or e is matched. You can also include ranges within brackets. For example:

```
$ ls [a-g]*
apple banana grape grapefruit
```

Here, any filenames beginning with a letter from a through g are matched.

Using File-Redirection Metacharacters

Commands receive data from standard input and send it to standard output. Using pipes (described earlier), you can direct standard output from one command to the standard input of another. With files, you can use less than (<) and greater than (>) signs to direct data to and from files. Here are the file-redirection characters:

- < — Directs the contents of a file to the command. In most cases, this is the default action expected by the command and the use of the character is optional; using more bigfile is the same as more < bigfile.
- > — Directs the output of a command to a file, deleting the existing file.
- >> — Directs the output of a command to a file, adding the output to the end of the existing file.

Here are some examples of command lines where information is directed to and from files:

```
$ mail root < ~/.bashrc
$ man chmod | col -b > /tmp/chmod
$ echo "I finished the project on $(date)" >> ~/projects
```

In the first example, the contents of the .bashrc file in the home directory are sent in a mail message to the computer's root user. The second command line formats the chmod man page (using the man command), removes extra back spaces (col -b), and sends the output to the file /tmp/chmod (erasing the previous /tmp/chmod file, if it exists). The final command results in the following text being added to the user's project file:

```
I finished the project on Sat Jan 27 13:46:49 PST 2008
```

Understanding File Permissions

After you've worked with Linux for a while, you are almost sure to get a Permission denied message. Permissions associated with files and directories in Linux were designed to keep users from accessing other users' private files and to protect important system files.

The nine bits assigned to each file for permissions define the access that you and others have to your file. Permission bits for a regular file appear as `-rwxrwxrwx`.

NOTE For a regular file, a dash appears in front of the nine-bit permissions indicator. Instead of a dash, you might see a `d` (for a directory), `l` (for a link), `b` (for a character device), or `c` (for a character device).

Of the nine-bit permissions, the first three bits apply to the owner's permission, the next three apply to the group assigned to the file, and the last three apply to all others. The `r` stands for read, the `w` stands for write, and the `x` stands for execute permissions. If a dash appears instead of the letter, it means that permission is turned off for that associated read, write, or execute.

Because files and directories are different types of elements, read, write, and execute permissions on files and directories mean different things. Table 2-9 explains what you can do with each of them.

TABLE 2-9

Setting Read, Write, and Execute Permissions

Permission	File	Directory
Read	View what's in the file.	See what files and subdirectories it contains.
Write	Change the file's content, rename it, or delete it.	Add files or subdirectories to the directory.
Execute	Run the file as a program.	Change to that directory as the current directory, search through the directory, or execute a program from the directory.

You can see the permission for any file or directory by typing the `ls -ld` command. The named file or directory appears as those shown in this example:

```
$ ls -ld ch3 test
-rw-rw-r--  1 chris  sales  4983  Jan 18 22:13 ch3
drwxr-xr-x  2 chris  sales  1024  Jan 24 13:47 test
```

The first line shows that the `ch3` file has read and write permission for the owner and the group. All other users have read permission, which means they can view the file but cannot change its contents or remove it. The second line shows the `test` directory (indicated by the letter d before the permission bits). The owner has read, write, and execute permission, while the group and other users have only read and execute permissions. As a result, the owner can add, change, or delete files in that directory, and everyone else can only read the contents, change to that directory, and list the contents of the directory.

If you own a file, you can use the `chmod` command to change the permission on it as you please. In one method of doing this, each permission (read, write, and execute) is assigned a number — r=4, w=2, and x=1 — and you use each set's total number to establish the permission. For example, to make permissions wide open for yourself as owner, you'd set the first number to 7 (4+2+1), and then you'd give the group and others read-only permission by setting both the second and third numbers to 4 (4+0+0), so that the final number is 744. Any combination of permissions can result from 0 (no permission) through 7 (full permission).

Here are some examples of how to change permissions on a file (named file) and what the resulting permission would be:

```
# chmod 777 file       rwxrwxrwx
# chmod 755 file       rwxr-xr-x
# chmod 644 file       rw-r--r-
# chmod 000 file       ---------
```

You can also turn file permissions on and off using plus (+) and minus (-) signs, respectively. This can be done for the owner user (u), owner group (g), others (o), and all users (a). For example, start with a file that has all permissions open (rwxrwxrwx). Run the following chmod commands using minus sign options. The resulting permissions are shown to the right of each command:

```
chmod a-w file        r-xr-xr-x
chmod o-x file        rwsrwsrw-
chmod go-rwx file     rwx------
```

Likewise, here are some examples, starting with all permissions closed (---------), where the plus sign is used with chmod to turn permissions on:

```
chmod u+rw files      rw-------
chmod a+x files       --x--x--x
chmod ug+rx files     r-xr-x---
```

When you create a file, it's given the permission rw-r--r-- by default. A directory is given the permission rwxr-xr-x. These default values are determined by the value of umask. Type **umask** to see what your umask value is. For example:

```
$ umask
022
```

The umask value masks the permissions value of 666 for a file and 777 for a directory. The umask value of 022 results in permission for a directory of 755 (rwxr-xr-x). That same umask results in a file permission of 644 (rw-r--r--). (Execute permissions are off by default for regular files.)

> **TIP** Time saver: Use the -R options of chmod, to change the permission for all of the files and directories within a directory structure at once. For example, if you wanted to open permissions completely to all files and directories in the /tmp/test directory, you could type the following:
>
> ```
> $ chmod -R 777 /tmp/test
> ```
>
> This command line runs chmod recursively (-R) for the /tmp/test directory, as well as any files or directories that exist below that point in the file system (for example, /tmp/test/hat, /tmp/test/hat/caps, and so on). All would be set to 777 (full read/write/execute permissions). This is not something you would do on an important directory on a read/write file system. However, you might do this before you create a directory structure on a CD-ROM that you want to be fully readable and executable to someone using the CD-ROM later.

CAUTION The -R option of chmod works best if you are opening permissions completely or adding execute permission (as well as the appropriate read/write permission). The reason is that if you turn off execute permission recursively, you close off your capability to change to any directory in that structure. For example, chmod -R 644 /tmp/test turns off execute permission for the /tmp/test directory, and then fails to change any files or directories below that point. Execute permissions must be on for a directory to be able to change to that directory.

Moving, Copying, and Deleting Files

Commands for moving, copying, and deleting files are fairly straightforward. To change the location of a file, use the mv command. To copy a file from one location to another, use the cp command. To remove a file, use the rm command. Here are some examples:

```
$ mv abc def
$ mv abc ~
$ cp abc def
$ cp abc ~
$ rm abc
$ rm *
```

Of the two move (mv) commands, the first moves the file abc to the file def in the same directory (essentially renaming it), whereas the second moves the file abc to your home directory (~). The first copy command (cp) copies abc to the file def in the same directory, whereas the second copies abc to your home directory (~). The first remove command (rm) deletes the abc file; the second removes all the files in the current directory (except those that start with a dot).

NOTE For the root user, the mv, cp, and rm commands are aliased to each be run with the -i option. This causes a prompt to appear asking you to confirm each move, copy, and removal, one file at a time, and is done to prevent the root user from messing up a large group of files by mistake.

Another alternative with mv is to use the -b option. With -b, if a file of the same name exists at the destination, a backup copy of the old file is made before the new file is moved there.

Using the vi Text Editor

It's almost impossible to use Linux for any period of time and not need to use a text editor. This is because most Linux configuration files are plain text files that you will almost certainly need to change manually at some point.

If you are using a GUI, you can run gedit, which is fairly intuitive for editing text. There's also a simple text editor you can run from the shell called nano. However, most Linux shell users will use either vi or emacs to edit text files. The advantage of vi or emacs over a graphical editor is that you can use it from any shell, a character terminal, or a character-based connection over a network (using telnet or ssh, for example) — no GUI is required. They also each contain tons of features, so you can continue to grow with them.

This section provides a brief tutorial on the vi text editor, which you can use to manually edit a configuration file from any shell. (If vi doesn't suit you, see the sidebar "Exploring Other Text Editors" for other options.)

The vi editor is difficult to learn at first, but once you know it, you never have to use a mouse or a function key — you can edit and move around quickly and efficiently within files just by using the keyboard.

Exploring Other Text Editors

Dozens of text editors are available for use with Linux. Here are a few that might be in your Linux distribution, which you can try out if you find vi to be too taxing.

Text Editor	Description
nano	A popular, streamlined text editor that is used with many bootable Linuxes and other limited-space Linux environments. For example, nano is often available to edit text files during a Linux install process.
gedit	The GNOME text editor that runs in the GUI.
jed	This screen-oriented editor was made for programmers. Using colors, jed can highlight code you create so you can easily read the code and spot syntax errors. Use the Alt key to select menus to manipulate your text.
joe	The joe editor is similar to many PC text editors. Use control and arrow keys to move around. Press Ctrl+C to exit with no save or Ctrl+X to save and exit.
kate	A nice-looking editor that comes in the kdebase package. It has lots of bells and whistles, such as highlighting for different types of programming languages and controls for managing word wrap.
kedit	A GUI-based text editor that comes with the KDE desktop.
mcedit	With mcedit, function keys help you get around and save, copy, move, and delete text. Like jed and joe, mcedit is screen-oriented.
nedit	An excellent programmer's editor. You need to install the optional nedit package to get this editor.

If you use ssh to log in to other Linux computers on your network, you can use any editor to edit files. A GUI-based editor will pop up on your screen. When no GUI is available, you will need a text editor that runs in the shell, such as vi, jed, or joe.

Starting with vi

Most often, you start vi to open a particular file. For example, to open a file called /tmp/test, type the following command:

```
$ vi /tmp/test
```

If this is a new file, you should see something similar to the following:

```
~
~
~
~
~
"/tmp/test" [New File]
```

The box at the top represents where your cursor is. The bottom line keeps you informed about what is going on with your editing (here you just opened a new file). In between, there are tildes (~) as filler because there is no text in the file yet. Now here's the intimidating part: There are no hints, menus, or icons to tell you what to do. On top of that, you can't just start typing. If you do, the computer is likely to beep at you. And some people complain that Linux isn't friendly.

The first things you need to know are the different operating modes: command and input. The vi editor always starts in command mode. Before you can add or change text in the file, you have to type a command (one or two letters and an optional number) to tell vi what you want to do. Case is important, so use uppercase and lowercase exactly as shown in the examples! To get into input mode, type an input command. To start out, type either of the following:

- **a** — The add command. After it, you can input text that starts to the *right* of the cursor.
- **i** — The insert command. After it, you can input text that starts to the *left* of the cursor.

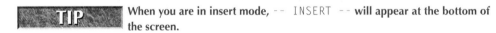 **When you are in insert mode,** -- INSERT -- **will appear at the bottom of the screen.**

Type a few words and then press Enter. Repeat that a few times until you have a few lines of text. When you're finished typing, press Esc to return to command mode. Now that you have a file with some text in it, try moving around in your text with the following keys or letters:

- **Arrow keys** — Move the cursor up, down, left, or right in the file one character at a time. To move left and right, you can also use Backspace and the spacebar, respectively. If you prefer to keep your fingers on the keyboard, move the cursor with h (left), l (right), j (down), or k (up).
- **w** — Moves the cursor to the beginning of the next word.
- **b** — Moves the cursor to the beginning of the previous word.
- **0** (*zero*) — Moves the cursor to the beginning of the current line.
- **$** — Moves the cursor to the end of the current line.
- **H** — Moves the cursor to the upper-left corner of the screen (first line on the screen).

- **M** — Moves the cursor to the first character of the middle line on the screen.
- **L** — Moves the cursor to the lower-left corner of the screen (last line on the screen).

The only other editing you need to know is how to delete text. Here are a few vi commands for deleting text:

- **x** — Deletes the character under the cursor.
- **X** — Deletes the character directly before the cursor.
- **dw** — Deletes from the current character to the end of the current word.
- **d$** — Deletes from the current character to the end of the current line.
- **d0** — Deletes from the previous character to the beginning of the current line.

To wrap things up, use the following keystrokes for saving and quitting the file:

- **ZZ** — Save the current changes to the file and exit from vi.
- **:w** — Save the current file but continue editing.
- **:wq** — Same as ZZ.
- **:q** — Quit the current file. This works only if you don't have any unsaved changes.
- **:q!** — Quit the current file and *don't* save the changes you just made to the file.

> **TIP** If you've really trashed the file by mistake, the :q! command is the best way to exit and abandon your changes. The file reverts to the most recently changed version. So, if you just did a :w, you are stuck with the changes up to that point. If you just want to undo a few bad edits, type **u** to back out of your changes.

You have learned a few vi editing commands. I describe more commands in the following sections. First, however, here are a few tips to smooth out your first trials with vi:

- **Esc** — Remember that Esc gets you back to command mode. (I've watched people press every key on the keyboard trying to get out of a file.) Esc followed by **ZZ** gets you out of command mode, saves the file, and exits.
- **u** — Type **u** to undo the previous change you made. Continue to type **u** to undo the change before that, and the one before that.
- **Ctrl+R** — If you decide you didn't want to undo the previous command, use Ctrl+R for Redo. Essentially, this command undoes your undo.
- **Caps Lock** — Beware of hitting Caps Lock by mistake. Everything you type in vi has a different meaning when the letters are capitalized. You don't get a warning that you are typing capitals — things just start acting weird.
- **:!** *command* — You can run a command while you are in vi using : ! followed by a command name. For example, type **:!date** to see the current date and time, type **:!pwd** to see what your current directory is, or type **:!jobs** to see if you have any jobs running in the background. When the command completes, press Enter and you are back to editing the

file. You could even use this technique to launch a shell (`:!bash`) from vi, run a few commands from that shell, and then type **exit** to return to vi. (I recommend doing a save before escaping to the shell, just in case you forget to go back to vi.)

- **Ctrl+G** — If you forget what you are editing, pressing these keys displays the name of the file that you are editing and the current line that you are on at the bottom of the screen. It also displays the total number of lines in the file, the percentage of how far you are through the file, and the column number the cursor is on. This just helps you get your bearings after you've stopped for a cup of coffee at 3 a.m.

Moving Around the File

Besides the few movement commands described earlier, there are other ways of moving around a vi file. To try these out, open a large file that you can't do much damage to. (Try copying `/var/log/messages` to `/tmp` and opening it in vi.) Here are some movement commands you can use:

- **Ctrl+F** — Page ahead, one page at a time.
- **Ctrl+B** — Page back, one page at a time.
- **Ctrl+D** — Page ahead one-half page at a time.
- **Ctrl+U** — Page back one-half page at a time.
- **G** — Go to the last line of the file.
- **1G** — Go to the first line of the file. (Use any number to go to that line in the file.)

Searching for Text

To search for the next occurrence of text in the file, use either the slash (/) or the question mark (?) character. Follow the slash or question mark with a pattern (string of text) to search forward or backward, respectively, for that pattern. Within the search, you can also use metacharacters. Here are some examples:

- `/hello` — Searches forward for the word `hello`.
- `?goodbye` — Searches backward for the word `goodbye`.
- `/The.*foot` — Searches forward for a line that has the word `The` in it and also, after that at some point, the word `foot`.
- `?[pP]rint` — Searches backward for either `print` or `Print`. Remember that case matters in Linux, so make use of brackets to search for words that could have different capitalization.

The vi editor was originally based on the ex editor, which didn't let you work in full-screen mode. However, it did enable you to run commands that let you find and change text on one or more lines at a time. When you type a colon and the cursor goes to the bottom of the screen, you are essentially in ex mode. Here is an example of some of those ex commands for searching for and changing text. (I chose the words `Local` and `Remote` to search for, but you can use any appropriate words.)

- `:g/Local` — Searches for the word `Local` and prints every occurrence of that line from the file. (If there is more than a screenful, the output is piped to the `more` command.)

- `:s/Local/Remote` — Substitutes `Remote` for the word `Local` on the current line.

- `:g/Local/s//Remote` — Substitutes the first occurrence of the word `Local` on every line of the file with the word `Remote`.

- `:g/Local/s//Remote/g` — Substitutes every occurrence of the word `Local` with the word `Remote` in the entire file.

- `:g/Local/s//Remote/gp` — Substitutes every occurrence of the word `Local` with the word `Remote` in the entire file, and then prints each line so that you can see the changes (piping it through `more` if output fills more than one page).

Using Numbers with Commands

You can precede most vi commands with numbers to have the command repeated that number of times. This is a handy way to deal with several lines, words, or characters at a time. Here are some examples:

- `3dw` — Deletes the next three words.

- `5cl` — Changes the next five letters (that is, it removes the letters and enters input mode).

- `12j` — Moves down 12 lines.

Putting a number in front of most commands just repeats those commands. At this point, you should be fairly proficient at using the `vi` command. Once you get used to using vi, you will probably find other text editors less efficient to use.

> **NOTE** When you invoke vi in many Linux systems, you're actually invoking the vim text editor, which runs in vi compatibility mode. Those who do a lot of programming might prefer vim because it shows different levels of code in different colors. vim has other useful features, such as the capability to open a document with the cursor at the same place as it was when you last exited that file.

Summary

Working from a shell command line within Linux may not be as simple as using a GUI, but it offers many powerful and flexible features. This chapter explains how to find your way around the shell in Linux and provides examples of running commands, including recalling commands from a history list, completing commands, and joining commands.

The chapter describes how shell environment variables can be used to store and recall important pieces of information. It also teaches you how to modify shell configuration files to tailor the shell to suit your needs. Finally, this chapter shows you how to use the Linux file system to create files and directories, use permissions, work with files (moving, copying, and removing them), and how to edit text files from the shell using the vi command.

Chapter 3

Getting into the Desktop

I n the past few years, graphical user interfaces (GUIs) available for Linux have become as easy to use as those on the Apple Mac or Microsoft Windows systems. With these improvements, even a novice computer user can start using Linux without needing to have an expert standing by.

You don't need to understand the underlying framework of the X Window System, window managers, widgets, and whatnots to get going with a Linux desktop system. That's why I start by explaining how to use the two most popular desktop environments: KDE (K desktop environment) and GNOME. After that, if you want to dig deeper, I tell you how you can put together your own desktop by discussing how to choose your own X-based window manager to run in Linux.

IN THIS CHAPTER

Understanding your desktop

Using the K desktop environment

Using the GNOME desktop environment

Configuring your own desktop

Playing with desktop eye candy using AIGLX

Understanding Your Desktop

When you install Linux distributions such as Fedora, SUSE, Mandriva, and Ubuntu, you have the option to choose a desktop environment. Distributions such as Gentoo and Debian GNU/Linux give you the option to go out and get whatever desktop environment you want (without particularly prompting you for it). When you are given the opportunity to select a desktop during installation, your choices usually include one or more of the following:

- **K desktop environment** (www.kde.org) — In addition to all the features you would expect to find in a complete desktop environment (window managers, toolbars, panels, menus, keybindings, icons, and so on), KDE has many bells and whistles available.

Applications for graphics, multimedia, office productivity, games, system administration, and many other uses have been integrated to work smoothly with KDE, which is the default desktop environment for SUSE, KNOPPIX, and various other Linux distributions.

- **GNOME desktop environment** (`www.gnome.org`) — GNOME is a more streamlined desktop environment. It includes a smaller feature set than KDE and runs faster in many lower-memory systems. Some think of GNOME as a more business-oriented desktop. It's the default desktop for Red Hat–sponsored systems such as Fedora and RHEL, Ubuntu, and others.

NOTE The KDE Desktop is based on the Qt 3 graphical toolkit. GNOME is based on GTK+ 2. Although graphical applications are usually written to either QT 3 or GTK+ 2, by installing both desktops you will have the libraries needed to run applications written for both toolkits from either environment.

- **X and a window manager** (`X.org` or `XFree86.org` + WM) — You don't need a full-blown desktop environment to operate Linux from a GUI. The most basic, reasonable way of using Linux is to simply start the X Window System server and a window manager of your choice (there are dozens to choose from). Many advanced users go this route because it can offer more flexibility in how they set up their desktops.

The truth is that most X applications run in any of the desktop environments just described (provided that proper libraries are included with your Linux distribution as noted earlier). So you can choose a Linux desktop based on the performance, customization tools, and controls that best suit you. Each of these three types of desktop environments is described in this chapter.

Starting the Desktop

Because the way that you start a desktop in Linux is completely configurable, different distributions offer different ways of starting up the desktop. Once your Linux distribution is installed, it may just boot to the desktop, offer a graphical login, or offer a text-based login. Bootable Linux systems (which don't have to be installed at all) typically just boot to the desktop.

Boot to the Desktop

Some bootable Linux systems boot right to a desktop without requiring you to log in so you can immediately start working with Linux. KNOPPIX is an example of a distribution that boots straight to a Linux desktop from a CD. That desktop system usually runs as a particular username (such as knoppix, in the case of the KNOPPIX distribution). To perform system administration, you have to switch to the administrator's account temporarily (using the `su` or `sudo` command).

Boot to a Graphical Login

Most desktop Linux systems that are installed on your hard disk boot up to a graphical login screen. Although the X display manager (xdm) is the basic display manager that comes with the X Window System, KDE and GNOME each have their own graphical display managers that are used as login screens (kdm and gdm, respectively). So chances are that you will see the login screen associated with KDE or GNOME (depending on which is the default on your Linux system).

NOTE When Linux starts up, it enters into what is referred to as a run level or system state. Typically, a system set to start at run level 5 boots to a graphical login prompt. A system set to run level 3 boots to a text prompt. The run level is set by the `initdefault` line in the `/etc/inittab` file. Change the number on the `initdefault` line as you please between 3 and 5. Don't use any other number unless you know what you are doing. Never use 0 or 6, because those numbers are used to shut down and reboot the system, respectively.

Because graphical login screens are designed to be configurable, you often find that the distribution has its own logo or other graphical elements on the login screen. For example, Figure 3-1 shows a basic graphical login panel displayed by the kdm graphical display manager.

FIGURE 3-1

A simple KDE display manager (kdm) login screen includes a clock, login name list, and a few menu selections.

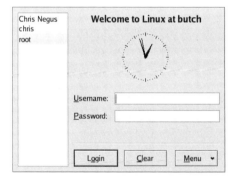

With Fedora Linux, the default login screen is based on the GNOME display manager (gdm). To begin a session, you can just enter your login (username) and password to start up your personal desktop environment. Your selected desktop environment — KDE or GNOME — comes up ready for you to use. Although the system defines a desktop environment by default, you can typically change desktop environments on those Linux systems, such as Fedora, that offer both KDE and GNOME.

To end a session, you can choose to log out. Figure 3-2 shows the graphical menu for ending a session or changing the computer state.

FIGURE 3-2

The Session menu in Fedora

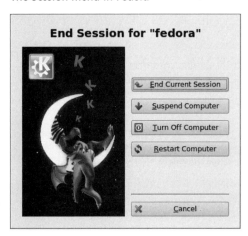

X display managers can enable you to do a lot more than just get to your desktop. Although different graphical login screens offer different options, here are some you may encounter:

- **Session/Options** — Look for a Session or Options button on the login screen. From there, you can choose to start your login session with a GNOME, KDE, or Failsafe Terminal environment. (Failsafe Terminal simply opens a Terminal window so, presumably, you can make a quick fix to the system without starting up a whole desktop environment.)

- **Language** — Linux systems that are configured to start multiple languages may give you the opportunity to choose a language (other than the default language) to boot into. For this to work, however, you must have installed support for the language you choose.

- **Reboot or Shutdown** — There's no need to log in if all you want to do is turn off or restart your computer. Most graphical login screens offer you the option of rebooting or shutting down the machine from that screen.

If you don't like the way the graphical login screen looks, or you just want to assert greater control over how it works, there are many ways to configure and secure X graphical login screens. Later, after you are logged in, you can use the following tools (as root user) to configure the login screen:

- **KDE login manager** — From the KDE Control Center, you can modify your KDE display manager using the Login Manager screen (from KDE Control Center, select System Administration ➪ Login Manager). You can change logos, backgrounds, color schemes, and other features related to the look-and-feel of the login screen.

- **GNOME login manager** — The GNOME display manager (gdm) comes with a Login Window Preferences utility (from the desktop, run the gdmsetup command as root user). From the Login Window Preferences window, you can select the Local tab and choose a whole different theme for the login manager. On the Security tab, you may notice that all TCP connections to the X server are disallowed. Don't change this selection because no processes other than those handled directly by your display manager should be allowed to connect to the login screen.

After your login and password have been accepted, the desktop environment configured for your user account starts up. Users can modify their desktop environments to suit their tastes (even to the point of changing the entire desktop environment used).

Boot to a Text Prompt

Instead of a nice graphical screen with pictures and colors, you might see a login prompt that looks like this:

```
Welcome to XYZ Linux
yourcomputer login:
```

This is the way all UNIX and older Linux systems used to appear on the screen when they booted up. Now this is the login prompt that is typical for a system that is installed as a server or, for some reason, was configured not to start an X display manager for you to log in. Run level 3 boots to a plain-text login prompt in multiuser mode.

Just because you have a text prompt doesn't necessarily mean you can start a desktop environment. Many Linux experts boot to a text prompt because they want to bypass the graphical login screen or use the GUI only occasionally. However, if X and the necessary other desktop components are installed on your computer, you can typically start the desktop after you log in by typing the following command:

```
$ startx
```

The default desktop environment starts up, and you should be ready to go. What you do next depends on whether you have a KDE, GNOME, or some sort of homespun desktop environment.

NOTE In most cases, the GUI configuration you set up during installation for your video card and monitor gets you to a working desktop environment. If, for some reason, the screen is unusable when you start the desktop, you need to do some additional configuration. The section "Configuring Your Own Desktop" later in this chapter describes some tools you can use to get your desktop working.

K Desktop Environment

The KDE was created to bring a high-quality desktop environment to UNIX (and now Linux) workstations. Integrated within KDE are tools for managing files, windows, multiple desktops, and applications. If you can work a mouse, you can learn to navigate the KDE desktop.

The lack of an integrated, standardized desktop environment once held back Linux and other UNIX systems from acceptance on the desktop. While individual applications ran well, you mostly could not drag-and-drop files or other items between applications. Likewise, you couldn't open a file and expect the machine to launch the correct application to deal with it or save your windows from one login session to the next. With KDE, you can do all those things and much more. For example, you can:

- Drag-and-drop a document from a folder window (Konqueror) to the Trash icon (to get rid of it) or on an OpenOffice.org Writer icon (to open it for editing).
- Right-click an image file (JPEG, PNG, and so on), and the OpenWith menu lets you choose to open the file using an image viewer (KView), editor (The GIMP), slide show viewer (KuickShow), or other application.

To make more applications available to you in the future, KDE provides a platform for developers to create programs that easily share information and detect how to deal with different data types. The things you can do with KDE increase in number every day.

KDE is the default desktop environment for Mandriva, KNOPPIX, and several other Linux systems. SUSE, openSUSE, and related distributions moved from KDE to GNOME as the default desktop, but still make KDE available. KDE is also available with Red Hat Enterprise Linux and Fedora but is not installed by default when they are installed as desktop systems (you need to specifically request KDE during installation).

The following section describes how to get started with KDE. This includes using the KDE Setup Wizard, maneuvering around the desktop, managing files, and adding application launchers.

Using the KDE Desktop

KDE uses a lot of the design elements that come from the KDE project, so it's pretty easy to distinguish from other desktop environments. The look-and-feel has similarities to both Windows and Macintosh systems. Figure 3-3 shows an example of the KDE desktop.

Some of the key elements of the KDE desktop include:

- **Desktop icons** — The desktop may start out with only a Trash icon on the screen, or include those that enable you to access removable media (CD, floppy disk, and so on). You can add as many icons as you like and are comfortable with.
- **Panel** — The KDE panel (shown along the bottom of the screen) includes items that enable you to launch applications and to see minimized representations of active windows, applets, and virtual desktops. An icon on the left side of the panel is used to represent the main menu on a KDE desktop: this may be a "K" for KDE, an "F" for Fedora, or almost any other value.

FIGURE 3-3

The KDE desktop includes a panel, desktop icons, and much more.

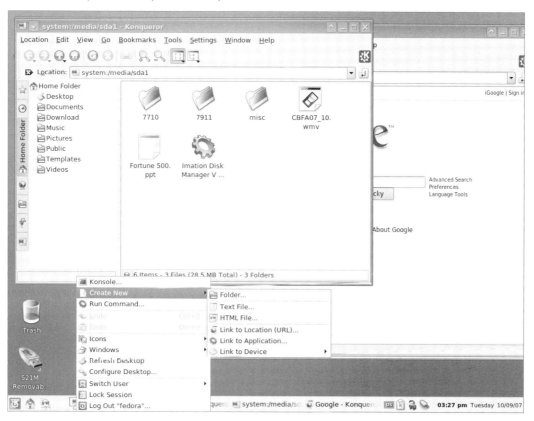

- **Konqueror file manager** — Konqueror is the file manager window used with KDE desktops. It can be used not only to manage files but also to display Web pages. Konqueror is described in detail later in this chapter.

- **Desktop menu** — Right-click the desktop to see a menu of common tasks. The menu provides a quick way to access your bookmarks; create new folders, files, or devices (with devices, you're actually choosing to mount a device on a particular part of the file system); straighten up your windows or icons; configure the desktop; and log out of your KDE session.

To navigate the KDE desktop, you can use the mouse or key combinations. The responses from the desktop to your mouse depend on which button you click and where the mouse pointer is located.

Table 3-1 describes the results of clicking each mouse button with the mouse pointer placed in different locations. (You can change any of these behaviors from the Windows Behavior panel on the KDE Control Center. From the KDE menu, select Control Center, and then choose the Window Behavior selection under the Desktop heading.)

TABLE 3-1

Single-Click Mouse Actions

Pointer Position	Mouse Button	Result
Window title bar or frame (current window active)	Left	Raises current window
Window title bar or frame (current window active)	Middle	Lowers current window
Window title bar or frame (current window active)	Right	Opens operations menu
Window title bar or frame (current window not active)	Left	Activates current window and raises it to the top
Window title bar or frame (current window not active)	Middle	Activates current window and lowers it
Window title bar or frame (current window not active)	Right	Opens operations menu without changing position
Inner window (current window not active)	Left	Activates current window, raises it to the top, and passes the click to the window
Inner window (current window not active)	Middle or Right	Activates current window and passes the click to the window
Any part of a window	Middle (plus hold Alt key)	Toggles between raising and lowering the window
Any part of a window	Right (plus hold Alt key)	Resizes the window
On the desktop area	Left (hold and drag)	Selects a group of icons
On the desktop area	Right	Opens system pop-up menu

Click a desktop icon to open it. Double-clicking a window title bar results in a window-shade action, where the window scrolls up and down into the title bar.

If you don't happen to have a mouse or you just like to keep your hands on the keyboard, there are several keystroke sequences you can use to navigate the desktop. Table 3-2 lists some examples.

TABLE 3-2

Keystrokes

Key Combination	Result	Directions
Ctrl+Tab	Step through the virtual desktops	To go from one virtual desktop to the next, hold down the Ctrl key and press the Tab key until you see the desktop that you want to make current. Then release the Ctrl key to select that desktop.
Alt+Tab	Step through windows	To step through each of the windows that are running on the current desktop, hold down the Alt key and press the Tab key until you see the one you want. Then release the Alt key to select it.
Alt+F2	Open Run Command box	To open a box on the desktop that lets you type in a command and run it, hold the Alt key and press F2. Next, type the command in the box and press Enter to run it. You can also type a URL into this box to view a Web page.
Alt+F4	Close current window	To close the current window, press Alt+F4.
Ctrl+Alt+Esc	Close another window	To close an open window on the desktop, press Ctrl+Alt+Esc. When a skull and crossbones appear as the pointer, move the pointer over the window you want to close and click the left mouse button. (This is a good technique for killing a window that has no borders or menu.)
Ctrl+F1, F2, F3, or F4 key	Switch virtual desktops	Go directly to a particular virtual desktop by pressing and holding the Ctrl key and pressing one of the following: F1, F2, F3, or F4. These actions take you directly to desktops one, two, three, and four, respectively. You could do this for up to eight desktops, if you have that many configured.
Alt+F3	Open window operation menu	To open the operations menu for the active window, press Alt+F3. When the menu appears, move the arrow keys to select an action (Move, Size, Minimize, Maximize, and so on), and then press Enter to select it.

Managing Files with the Konqueror File Manager

The Konqueror file manager helps elevate the KDE environment from just another X window manager to an integrated desktop that competes with GUIs from Apple Computing or Microsoft. The features in Konqueror rival those offered by those user-friendly desktop systems. Figure 3-4 shows an example of the Konqueror file manager window in KNOPPIX.

FIGURE 3-4

Konqueror provides a network-ready tool for managing files.

Konqueror's greatest strengths over earlier file managers include the following:

- **Network desktop** — If your computer is connected to the Internet or a LAN, features built into Konqueror enable you to create links to files (using FTP) and Web pages (using HTTP) on the network and open them in the Konqueror window. Those links can appear as file icons in a Konqueror window or on the desktop. Konqueror also supports WebDAV, which can be configured to allow local read and write access to remote folders (which is a great tool if you are maintaining a Web server).

- **Web browser interface** — The Konqueror interface works like Firefox, Internet Explorer, and most other Web browsers in the way you select files, directories, and Web content. Because Konqueror is based on a browser model, a single click opens a file, a link to a network resource, or an application program. You can also open content by typing Web-style addresses in the Location box. The rendering engine used by Konqueror, called KHTML, is also used by Safari (the popular Web browser for Apple Mac OS X systems).

TIP Web pages that contain Java and JavaScript content run by default in Konqueror. To check that Java and JavaScript support are turned on, choose Settings ➪ Configure Konqueror. From the Settings window, click Java & JavaScript and select the Java tab. To enable Java, click the Enable Java Globally box and click Apply. Repeat for the JavaScript tab.

- **File types and MIME types** — If you want a particular type of file to always be launched by a particular application, you can configure that file yourself. KDE already has dozens of MIME types defined so that particular file and data types can be automatically detected and opened in the correct application. There are MIME types defined for audio, image, text, video, and a variety of other content.

Of course, you can also perform many standard file manager functions with Konqueror. For example, you can manipulate files by using features such as select, move, cut, paste, and delete; search directories for files; create new items (files, folders, and links, to name a few); view histories of the files and Web sites you have opened; and create bookmarks.

Working with Files

Because most of the ways of working with files in Konqueror are quite intuitive (by intention), Table 3-3 provides a quick rundown of how to do basic file manipulation.

TABLE 3-3

Working with Files in Konqueror

Task	Action
Open a file	Left-click the file. It will open right in the Konqueror window, if possible, or in the default application set for the file type. You also can open directories, applications, and links by left-clicking them.
Open a file with a specific application	Right-click a data file, choose Open With from the pop-up menu, and then select one of the available applications to open the file. The applications listed are those that are set up to open the file. Select Other to choose a different application.
Delete a file	Right-click the file and select Delete. You are asked if you really want to delete the file. Click Yes to permanently delete it. (As an alternative, you can select Move to Trash, which results in the file being moved to the trash can you can access from the desktop.)
Copy a file	Right-click the file and select Copy. This copies the file to your clipboard. After that, you can paste it to another folder. Click the Klipper (clipboard) icon in the panel to see a list of copied files. Klipper holds the seven most recently copied files, by default. Click the Klipper icon and select Configure Klipper to change the number of copied files Klipper will remember.

continued

TABLE 3-3 (continued)	
Task	**Action**
Paste a file	Right-click (an open area of a folder) and select Paste. A copy of the file you copied previously is pasted in the current folder.
Link a file	Drag-and-drop a file from one folder to another. When the menu appears, click Link Here. (A linked file lets you access a file from a new location without having to make a copy of the original file. When you open the link, a pointer to the original file causes it to open.)
Move a file Copy a file Create a link to a file	With the original folder and target folder both open on the desktop, click and hold the left mouse button on the file you want to move, drag the file to an open area of the new folder, and release the mouse button. From the menu that appears, click Move. (You also can use this menu to copy or create a link to the file.)

There are also several features for viewing information about the files and folders in your Konqueror windows:

- **View quick file information** — Positioning the mouse pointer over the file displays information such as its filename, size, and type in the window footer.

- **View hidden files** — Selecting View ⇨ Show Hidden Files enables you to see files that begin with a dot (.). Dot files tend to be used for configuration and don't generally need to be viewed in your daily work.

- **View file system tree** — Selecting View ⇨ View Mode ⇨ Tree View provides a tree view of your folder, displaying folders above the current folder in the file system. You can click a folder in the tree view to jump directly to that folder. Multicolumn, Detailed List, and Text views are also available.

- **Change icon view** — Select View ⇨ Icon Size, and then choose Large, Medium, or Small to set the size of the icons that are displayed in the window. You can also choose Default Size to return to the default icon size (which is medium, unless you have changed the default through the Configure Konqueror window).

To act on a group of files at the same time, you can take a couple of actions. Choose Edit ⇨ Selection ⇨ Select. A pop-up window lets you match all (*) or any group of documents indicated by typing letters, numbers, and wildcard characters. Or, you can select a group of files by clicking in an open area of the folder and dragging the pointer across the files you want to select. All files within the box will be highlighted. When files are highlighted, you can move, copy, or delete the files as described earlier.

Searching for Files

If you are looking for a particular file or folder, you can use the Konqueror Find feature. To open a Find window to search for a file, open a local folder (such as /home/chris) and choose Tools ⇨

Find File; the Find box appears in your Konqueror window. You can also start the kfind window by typing **kfind** from a Terminal window.

Figure 3-5 shows the kfind window in Konqueror.

Search for files and folders from the kfind window.

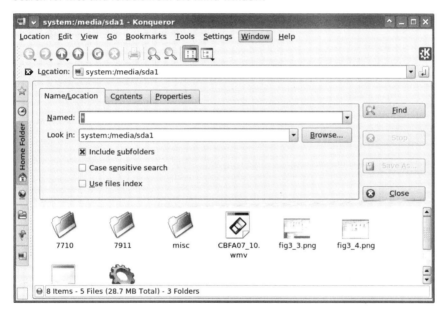

Simply type the name of the file you want to search for (in the Named text box) and the folder, including all subfolders, you want to search in (in the Look in text box). Then click the Find button. Use metacharacters, if you like, with your search. For example, search for `*.rpm` to find all files that end in `.rpm`, or `z*.doc` to find all files that begin with z and end with `.doc`. You can also select to have the search be case-sensitive or click the Help button to get more information on searching.

To further limit your search, you can click the Date Range tab and then enter a date range (between), a number of months before today (during the previous x months), or the number of days before today (during the previous x days). Select the Advanced tab to choose to limit the search to files of a particular type (of Type), files that include text that you enter (Containing Text), or that are of a certain size (Size is) in kilobytes.

Creating New Files and Folders

You can create a variety of file types when using the Konqueror window. Choose Edit ⇨ Create New, and select Folder (to create a new folder) or one of several different types under the File or

Device submenu. Depending on which version of Konqueror you are using, you might be able to create some or all of the file types that follow:

- **HTML File** — Opens a dialog box that lets you type the name of an HTML file to create.

- **Link to Application** — Opens a window that lets you type the name of an application. Click the Permissions tab to set file permissions (Exec must be on if you want to run the file as an application). Click the Execute tab and type the name of the program to run (in the field Execute on click) and a title to appear in the title bar of the application (in the field Window Title). If it is a text-based command, select the Run in terminal check box. Select the check box to Run as a different user and add the username. Click the Application tab to assign the application to handle files of particular MIME types. Click OK.

- **Link to Location (URL)** — Selecting this menu item opens a dialog box that lets you create a link to a Web address. Type a name to represent the address and type the name of the URL (Web address) for the site. (Be sure to add the `http://`, `ftp://`, or other prefix.)

- **Text File** — Opens a dialog box that lets you create a document in text format and place it in the Konqueror window. Type the name of the text document to create and click OK.

Under the Device submenu, you can make the following selections:

- **CD-ROM Device** — Opens a dialog box that lets you type a new CD-ROM device name. Click the Device tab and type the device name (`/dev/cdrom`), the mount point (such as `/mnt/cdrom`), and the file system type (you can use iso9660 for the standard CD-ROM file system, ext2 for Linux, or msdos for DOS). When the icon appears, you can open it to mount the CD-ROM and display its contents.

- **CDWRITER Device** — From the window that opens, enter the device name of your CD writer.

- **DVD-ROM Device** — Opens a dialog box that lets you type a new CD-ROM or DVD-ROM device name. Click the Device tab and type the device name (such as `/dev/cdrom`), the mount point (such as `/mnt/cdrom`), and the file system type (you can use iso9660 for the standard CD-ROM file system, ext2 for Linux, or msdos for DOS). When the icon appears, you can open it to mount the CD-ROM or DVD-ROM and display its contents.

- **Camera Device** — In the dialog box that opens, identify the device name for the camera devices that provides access to your digital camera.

- **Floppy Device** — Opens a dialog box in which you type a new floppy name. Click the Device tab and type the device name (`/dev/fd0`), the mount point (such as `/mnt/floppy`), and the file system type (you can use auto to autodetect the contents, ext2 for Linux, or msdos for DOS). When the icon appears, open it to mount the floppy and display its contents.

- **Hard Disc Device** — Opens a dialog box that lets you type the name of a new hard disk or hard-disk partition. Click the Device tab and type the device name (`/dev/hda1`), the mount point (such as `/mnt/win`), and the file system type (you can use auto to autodetect the contents, ext2 or ext3 for Linux, or vfat for a Windows file system). When the icon appears, you can open it to mount the file system and display its contents.

Creating MIME types and applications is described later in this chapter.

Using Other Browser Features

Because Konqueror performs like a Web browser as well as a file manager, it includes several other browser features. For example, the bookmarks feature enables you to keep a bookmark list of Web sites you have visited. Click Bookmarks, and a drop-down menu of the sites you have bookmarked appears. Select from that list to return to a site. There are several ways to add and change your bookmarks list:

- **Add Bookmark** — To add the address of the page currently being displayed to your bookmark list, choose Bookmarks ⇨ Add Bookmark. The next time you click Bookmarks, you will see the bookmark you just added on the Bookmarks menu. In addition to Web addresses, you can also bookmark any file or folder.

- **Edit Bookmarks** — Select Bookmarks ⇨ Edit Bookmarks to open a tree view of your bookmarks. From the Bookmark Editor window that appears, you can change the URLs, the icon, or other features of the bookmark. There is also a nice feature that lets you check the status of the bookmark (that is, the address available).

- **New Bookmark Folder** — You can add a new folder of bookmarks to your Konqueror bookmarks list. To create a bookmarks folder, choose Bookmarks ⇨ New Folder. Then type a name for the new Bookmarks folder, and click OK. The new bookmark folder appears on your bookmarks menu. You can add the current location to that folder by clicking on the folder name and selecting Add Bookmark.

Configuring Konqueror Options

You can change many of the visual attributes of the Konqueror window, including which menu bars and toolbars appear. You can have any of the following bars appear on the Konqueror window: Menubar, Toolbar, Extra Toolbar, Location Toolbar, and Bookmark Toolbar. Select Settings, and then click the bar you want to have appear (or not appear). The bar appears when a check mark is shown next to it.

You can modify a variety of options for Konqueror by choosing Settings ⇨ Configure Konqueror. The Konqueror Settings window appears, offering the following options:

- **Behavior (File)** — Change file manager behavior.

- **Appearance** — Change file manager fonts and colors.

- **Previews & Meta-Data** — An icon in a Konqueror folder can be made to resemble the contents of the file it represents. For example, if the file is a JPEG image, the icon representing the file could be a small version of that image. Using the Previews features, you can limit the size of the file used (1MB is the default) because many massive files could take too long to refresh on the screen. You can also choose to have any thumbnail embedded in a file to be used as the icon or have the size of the icon reflect the shape of the image used.

- **File Associations** — Describes which programs to launch for each file type.

- **Web Behavior** — Click the Behavior (Browser) button to open a window to configure the Web browser features of Konqueror. By enabling Form Completion, Konqueror can save form data you type and, at a later time, fill that information into other forms. If your computer has limited resources, you can speed up the page display by clearing the Automatically Load Images check box or by disabling animations.

- **Java and JavaScript** — Enable or disable Java and JavaScript content contained in Web pages in your Konqueror window.

- **AdBlock Filters** — Click here to create a list of URLs that are filtered as you browse the Web. Filtering is based on frame and image names. Filtered URLs can be either thrown away or replaced with an image. You can also import and export lists of filters here.

- **Fonts** — Choose which fonts to use, by default, for various fonts needed on Web pages (standard font, fixed font, serif font, sans serif font, cursive font, and fantasy font). The serif fonts are typically used in body text, while sans serif fonts are often used in headlines. You can also set the Minimum and Medium font sizes.

- **Web Shortcuts** — Display a list of keyword shortcuts you can use to go to different Internet sites. For example, follow the word "ask" with a search string to search the Ask Jeeves (`www.ask.com`) Web site.

- **History Sidebar** — Modify the behavior of the list of sites you have visited (the history). By default, the most recent 500 URLs are stored, and after 500 days (KNOPPIX) or 90 days (Fedora), a URL is dropped from the list. There's also a button to clear your history. (To view your history list in Konqueror, open the left side panel, and then click the tiny scroll icon.)

- **Cookies** — Choose whether cookies are enabled in Konqueror. By default, you are asked to confirm that it is okay each time a Web site tries to create or modify a cookie. You can change that to either accept or reject all cookies. You can also set policies for acceptance or rejection of cookies based on host and domain names.

- **Cache** — Indicate how much space on your hard disk can be used to store the sites you have visited (based on the value in the Disk Cache Size field).

- **Proxy** — Click Proxy to configure Konqueror to access the Internet through a proxy server (by default, Konqueror tries to connect there directly). You need to enter the address and port number of the computer providing HTTP and/or FTP proxy services. Alternatively, you can have Konqueror try to automatically detect the proxy configuration.

- **Stylesheets** — Choose whether to use the default stylesheet, a user-defined stylesheet, or a custom stylesheet. The stylesheet sets the font family, font sizes, and colors that are applied to Web pages. (This won't change particular font requests made by the Web page.) If you select a custom stylesheet, click the Customize tab to customize your own fonts and colors.

- **Crypto** — Display a list of secure certificates that can be accepted by the Konqueror browser. By default, Secure Socket Layer (SSL) versions 2 and 3 certificates are accepted, as is TLS support (if supported by the server). You can also choose to be notified when you are entering or leaving a secure Web site.

- **Browser Identification** — Set how Konqueror identifies itself when it accesses a Web site. By default, Konqueror tells the Web site that it is the Mozilla Web browser. You can select Konqueror to appear as different Web browsers to specific sites. You must sometimes do this when a site denies you access because you do not have a specific type of browser (even though Konqueror may be fully capable of displaying the content).

- **Plugins** — Display a list of directories that Konqueror will search to find plug-ins. Konqueror can also scan your computer to find plug-ins that are installed for other browsers in other locations.

- **Performance** — Display configuration settings that can be used to improve Konqueror performance. You can preload an instance after KDE startup or minimize memory usage.

Managing Windows

If you have a lot of icons on the desktop and windows open at the same time, organizing those items can make it much easier to manage your desktop. KDE helps you out by maintaining window lists you can work with and shortcuts for keeping the windows and icons in order.

Using the Taskbar

When you open a window, a button representing the window appears in the taskbar at the bottom of the screen. Here is how you can manage windows from the taskbar.

- **Toggle windows** — Left-click any running task in the taskbar to toggle between opening the window and minimizing it.

- **Position windows** — You can choose to have the selected window be above or below other windows or displayed in full screen. Right-click the running task in the taskbar and select Advanced. Then choose Keep Above Others, Keep Below Others, or Fullscreen.

- **Move windows** — Move a window from the current desktop to any other virtual desktop. Right-click any task in the taskbar, select To Desktop, and then select any desktop number. The window moves to that desktop.

All the windows that are running, regardless of which virtual desktop you are on, appear in the taskbar. If there are multiple windows of the same type shown as a single task, you can right-click that task; then, select All to Desktop to move all related windows to the desktop you pick.

Creating an Image Gallery with Konqueror

There's a neat feature in Konqueror that lets you create a quick image gallery. The feature takes a directory of images, creates thumbnails for each one, and generates an HTML (Web) page. The HTML page includes a title you choose, all image thumbnails arranged on a page, and links to the larger images. Here's how you do it:

1. Add images you want in your gallery to any folder (for example, /home/chris/Pictures). Make sure they are sized, rotated, and cropped the way you like before beginning. (Try The GIMP for manipulating your images by typing **gimp&** from a Terminal.)

2. Open the folder in Konqueror (for example, type **/home/chris/Pictures** in the Location box).

3. Click Tools ⇨ Create Image Gallery. The Create Image Gallery window appears.

4. Type a title for the image gallery into the Page Title box. You can also select other attributes of the gallery, such as the number of rows, information about the image to appear on the page (name, size, and dimension), the fonts, and the colors to use.

5. Click OK.

Konqueror generates the thumbnails and adds them to the thumbs directory. The image gallery page itself opens and is saved to the images.html file. (Select the Folders button to save the gallery under a different name. You can also have Konqueror create galleries in recursive subfolders to a depth you choose.) You can now copy the entire contents of this directory to a Web server and publish your pictures on the Internet. Here's an example of a Konqueror image gallery.

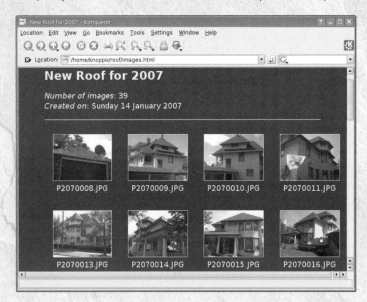

Uncluttering the Desktop

If your windows are scattered willy-nilly all over the desktop, here are a couple of ways you can make your desktop's appearance a little neater:

- **Unclutter windows** — Right-click the desktop, and then click Windows ⇨ Unclutter Windows on the menu. All windows that are currently displayed on the desktop are lined up along the left side of the screen (or aligned with other windows), from the top down.

- **Cascade windows** — Right-click the desktop, and then click Windows ⇨ Cascade windows on the menu. The windows are aligned as they are with the Unclutter selection, except that the windows are each indented starting from the upper-left corner.

If you find yourself with icons all over the desktop, you can organize them from the desktop menu. Right-click the desktop, and then select Icons ⇨ Sort Icon. From the menu that appears, select to sort icons by name, size, type, or date. You can also choose to simply line up all icons vertically or horizontally.

Moving Windows

The easiest way to move a window from one location to another is to place the cursor on the window's title bar, hold down the mouse button and drag the window to a new location, and release the mouse button to drop the window. Another way to do it is to click the window menu button (top-left corner of the title bar), select Move, move the mouse to relocate the window, and then click again to place it.

> **TIP** If somehow the window gets stuck in a location where the title bar is off the screen, you can move it back to where you want it by holding down the Alt key and clicking the left mouse button in the inner window. Then move the window where you want it and release.

Resizing Windows

To resize a window, grab anywhere on the outer edge of the window border, and then move the mouse until the window is the size you want. Grab a corner to resize vertically and horizontally at the same time. Grab a side to resize in only one direction.

You can also resize a window by clicking the window menu button (top-left corner of the title bar) and selecting Resize. Move the mouse until the window is resized and click to leave it there.

Pinning Windows on the Top or Bottom

You can set a window to always stay on top of all other windows or always stay under them. Keeping a window on top can be useful for a small window that you want to always refer to (such as a clock or a small TV viewing window). To pin a window on top of the desktop, click in the window title bar. From the menu that appears, select Advanced ⇨ Keep Above Others. Likewise, to keep the window on the bottom, select Advanced ⇨ Keep Below Others.

Using Virtual Desktops

To give you more space to run applications than will fit on your physical screen, KDE gives you access to several virtual desktops at the same time. Using the 1, 2, 3, and 4 buttons on the panel, you can easily move between the different desktops. Just click the one you want.

If you want to move an application from one desktop to another, you can do so from the window menu. Click the window menu button for the window you want to move, click To Desktop, and then select Desktop 1, 2, 3, or 4. The window will disappear from the current desktop and move to the one you selected.

Configuring the Desktop

If you want to change the look, feel, or behavior of your KDE desktop, the best place to start is the KDE Control Center. The Control Center window (see Figure 3-6) lets you configure dozens of attributes associated with colors, fonts, backgrounds, and screen savers. You can also change attributes relating to how you work with windows and files.

To open the KDE Control Center from the desktop, select Control Center from the K menu or open a Terminal window and type `sudo kcontrol`.

FIGURE 3-6

Manage your KDE desktop from the KDE Control Center.

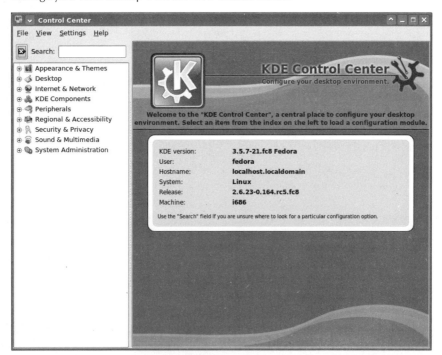

Click the plus (+) sign next to the topic you want to configure, and then select the particular item you want to configure. The following sections describe some of the features you can configure from the Control Center.

Changing the Display

You can change a lot of the look-and-feel of your desktop display. Under the Appearance & Themes topic (click the plus sign), you can change Background, Colors, Fonts, Icons, Launch Feedback, Panel, Screen Saver, Style, Theme Manager, and Window Decoration.

Here are a few of the desktop features you may want to change:

- **Background** — Under the Appearance & Themes heading in the KDE Control Center, select Background. By default, all of your virtual desktops use the same background. To have different backgrounds for each virtual desktop, select the box next to the Setting for Desktop heading, choose any of the four desktops, and then choose the background you want for the current desktop.

  For each desktop, select Picture, Slideshow, or No Picture. For a Picture, there are several backgrounds you can choose from the pull-down menu, or you can browse your file system for a picture. To do a slide show, click Slideshow and select Setup (to choose your pictures and define how often they change).

  Click Apply to apply your selections.

- **Screen Saver** — Under the Appearance & Themes heading, select Screen Saver. From the window that appears, select from a list of screen savers. KNOPPIX includes only a blank screen saver. However, Fedora comes with about 160 different screen savers My favorite is Slideshow, where you can have a slide show of images for your screen saver. Click Setup to identify an image directory or otherwise modify the behavior of the screen saver. Under settings, select how many minutes of inactivity before the screen saver turns on. You can also choose Require Password to require that a password be entered before you can access your display after the screen saver has come on.

TIP If you are working in a place where you want your desktop to be secure, be sure to turn on the Require Password feature. This prevents others from gaining access to your computer when you forget to lock it or shut it off. If you have any virtual terminals open, switch to them and type **vlock** to lock each of them as well. (You need to install the vlock package if the vlock command isn't available.)

- **Fonts** — You can assign different fonts to different places in which fonts appear on the desktop. Under the Appearance & Themes heading, select Fonts. Select one of the categories of fonts (General, Fixed width, Toolbar, Menu, Window title, Taskbar, or Desktop fonts). Then click the Choose check box to select a font from the Select Font list box that you want to assign to that category. If the font is available, an example of the text appears in the Sample text box.

 **TIP**   To use 100 dpi fonts, you need to add an entry for 100 dpi fonts to the `/etc/X11/` `xorg.conf` file. After you make that change, you need to restart the X server for it to take effect.

Other attributes you can change for the selected fonts are size (in points) and character set (to select an ISO standard character set). Select Apply to apply the changes.

- **Colors** — Under the Appearance & Themes heading, select Colors. The window that appears lets you change the color of selected items on the desktop. Select a whole color scheme from the Color Scheme list box. Or select an item from the Widget color box to change a particular item. Items you can change include text, backgrounds, links, buttons, and title bars.

Changing Panel Attributes

For most people, the panel is the place where they select which desktop is active and which applications are run. You can change panel behavior from the Configure Panel window. Right-click any empty space on your panel, and then select Configure Panel. You can change these features from the Settings window that appears:

- **Arrangement** — Change the location of the panel by clicking Top, Left, Bottom, or Right in the Panel Location list box. The Panel Style selection lets you change the size of the Panel from Medium to Tiny, Small, or Large.

- **Hiding** — Certain selections enable you to autohide the panel or use hide buttons. Under the Hide Mode heading, choose whether to hide the panel only when a panel hiding button is clicked or to hide it automatically after a set number of seconds when the cursor is not in the panel area. You can also show or not show hiding buttons. Sliders let you select the delay and speed at which panels and buttons are hidden.

- **Menus** — Unlike with the GNOME main menu, with KDE you have the capability to manipulate the main menu from the GUI. Click the Edit K Menu button. The KDE Menu editor that appears lets you cut, copy, paste, remove, and modify submenus and applications from your main menu.

- **Appearance** — You can change the panel background (transparency or background image) or button backgrounds (using colors or patterns). You can also change whether or not tooltips appear when you move your mouse over a desktop item.

- **Taskbar** — Change how the taskbar looks and behaves. From the Actions box, choose what action occurs from clicking each mouse button on the taskbar. You can also choose how windows are sorted and displayed on the taskbar.

Adding Application Launchers and MIME Types

You want to be able to quickly access the applications that you use most often. One of the best ways to make that possible is to add icons to the panel or the desktop that can launch the applications you need with a single click. Procedures for adding applications to the panel and desktop are described in the following sections.

Adding Applications to the Panel

You can add any KDE application to the KDE panel quite easily. Here's how:

1. Right-click an open space on the panel.

2. Choose Add Application to Panel.

3. Select one of the categories of applications.

4. Select any application from that category (or select Add This Menu to add the whole menu of applications).

An icon representing the application immediately appears on the panel. (If the panel seems a bit crowded, you might want to remove applications you don't use.)

If you decide later that you no longer want this application to be available on the panel, right-click the edge of the icon and click the Remove button. To move it to a different location on the panel, right-click it, click Move, move it to where you want it on the panel, and click again.

Adding Applications to the Desktop

To add an application to the desktop, use the desktop menu. Here's how:

1. Right-click an open area of the desktop.

2. Select Create New ➪ Link to Application from the menu.

3. On the Properties window that appears, click the General tab and replace Link to Application with the name you want to appear for the application on the desktop. On that same tab, click the gear icon and select one icon from the list to represent your application.

4. Click the Application tab and add a description of the application and a comment. Then in the Command box, type the command you want to run or browse your file system (click the Browse button) to find the command to run.

5. Click OK, and the icon for the new application launcher appears on the desktop.

If you decide later that you no longer want this application to be available on the desktop, right-click the icon and click Delete or Move to Trash.

The GNOME Desktop

GNOME (pronounced *guh-nome*) provides the desktop environment that you get by default when you install Fedora, Ubuntu, or another Linux system. This desktop environment provides the software that is between your X Window System framework and the look-and-feel provided by the window manager. GNOME is a stable and reliable desktop environment, with a few cool features.

The GNOME 2.18 desktop comes with the most recent version of Fedora. Recent GNOME improvements include advancements in 3D effects (see "3D Effects with AIGLX" later in this chapter), improved usability features, and applications for power management and note taking.

NOTE   The Online Desktop is new with Fedora and intended to provide a bare interface that acts as a platform for running only online applications (such as Facebook, GMail, and so on). See the section "Configuring a GNOME Online Desktop" later in this chapter for more information.

To use your GNOME desktop, you should become familiar with the following components:

- **Metacity (window manager)** — The default window manager for GNOME in Fedora and RHEL is Metacity. Metacity configuration options let you control such things as themes, window borders, and controls used on your desktop.

- **Nautilus (file manager/graphical shell)** — When you open a folder (by double-clicking the Home icon on your desktop, for example), the Nautilus window opens and displays the contents of the selected folder. Nautilus can also display other types of content, such as shared folders from Windows computers on the network (using SMB).

- **GNOME panels (application/task launcher)** — These panels, which line the top and bottom of your screen, are designed to make it convenient for you to launch the applications you use, manage running applications, and work with multiple virtual desktops. By default, the top panel contains menu buttons (Applications, Places, and Desktop), desktop application launchers (Evolution e-mail and a set of OpenOffice.org applications), a workspace switcher (for managing four virtual desktops), and a clock. It also has an icon to alert you when you need software updates. The bottom panel contains window lists and the workspace switcher.

- **Desktop area** — The windows and icons you use are arranged on the desktop area, which supports drag-and-drop between applications, a desktop menu (right-click to see it), and icons for launching applications. There is a Computer icon that consolidates CD drives, floppy drives, the file system, and shared network resources in one place.

If you have used earlier versions of GNOME, here are some feature additions you will find useful in the most recent versions of GNOME:

- **XSPF playlists in Totem** — The Totem video/audio player now includes support for open standard XSPF playlists (`www.xspf.org`). Other improvements to Totem allow it to interact with content from Web sites.

- **Screensaver previews** — Previewing screen savers in full-screen mode is now supported.

- **Direct DVD burning** — Use the Nautilus CD burner feature to burn DVDs directly, without needing to first create an ISO image.

- **Drag from taskbar** — Drag an application from the taskbar to workspaces represented in the Workspace Switcher panel to move the application to a new workspace.

- **Nautilus text or button browsing** — When saving or opening files or folders in Nautilus, a new toggle button enables you to choose between browsing by clicking on buttons or by typing full path names.

GNOME also includes a set of Preferences windows that enable you to configure different aspects of your desktop. You can change backgrounds, colors, fonts, keyboard shortcuts, and other features related to the look and behavior of the desktop. Figure 3-7 shows how the GNOME desktop environment appears the first time you log in, with a few windows added to the screen.

The GNOME desktop environment

The desktop shown in Figure 3-7 is for Fedora. The following sections provide details on using the GNOME desktop.

Using the Metacity Window Manager

The Metacity window manager seems to have been chosen as the default window manager for GNOME in Red Hat Linux because of its simplicity. The creator of Metacity refers to it as a "boring window manager for the adult in you" — and then goes on to compare other window managers to colorful, sugary cereal, while Metacity is characterized as Cheerios.

To use 3D effects in Fedora, your best solution is to use the Compiz window manager, as described later in this chapter.

There really isn't much you can do with Metacity (except get your work done efficiently). Assigning new themes to Metacity and changing colors and window decorations are done through the GNOME preferences (and are described later). A few Metacity themes exist, but expect the number to grow.

Basic Metacity functions that might interest you are keyboard shortcuts and the workspace switcher. Table 3-4 shows keyboard shortcuts to get around the Metacity window manager.

TABLE 3-4

Metacity Keyboard Shortcuts

Actions		Keystrokes
Window focus	Cycle forward, with pop-up icons	Alt+Tab
	Cycle backward, with pop-up icons	Alt+Shift+Tab
	Cycle forward, without pop-up icons	Alt+Esc
	Cycle backward, without pop-up icons	Alt+Shift+Esc
Panel focus	Cycle forward among panels	Alt+Ctrl+Tab
	Cycle backward among panels	Alt+Ctrl+Shift+Tab
Workspace focus	Move to workspace to the right	Ctrl+Alt+right arrow
	Move to workspace to the left	Ctrl+Alt+left arrow
	Move to upper workspace	Ctrl+Alt+up arrow
	Move to lower workspace	Ctrl+Alt+down arrow
Minimize/maximize all windows		Ctrl+Alt+D
Show window menu		Alt+Spacebar
Close menu		Esc

Another Metacity feature of interest is the workspace switcher. Four virtual workspaces appear in the Workspace Switcher on the GNOME panel. You can do the following with the Workspace Switcher:

- **Choose current workspace** — Four virtual workspaces appear in the Workspace Switcher. Click any of the four virtual workspaces to make it your current workspace.

- **Move windows to other workspaces** — Click any window, each represented by a tiny rectangle in a workspace, to drag-and-drop it to another workspace. Likewise, you can drag an application from the Window List to move that application to another workspace.

- **Add more workspaces** — Right-click the Workspace Switcher, and select Preferences. You can add workspaces (up to 32).

- **Name workspaces** — Right-click the Workspace Switcher and select Preferences. Click in the Workspaces pane to change names of workspaces to any names you choose.

You can view and change information about Metacity controls and settings using the gconf-editor window (type **gconf-editor** from a Terminal window). As the window says, it is not the recommended way of changing preferences, so when possible, you should change the desktop through GNOME preferences. However, gconf-editor is a good way to see descriptions of each Metacity feature.

From the gconf-editor window, select apps ⇨ metacity, and then choose from general, global_ keybindings, keybindings_commands, window_keybindings, and workspace_names. Click each key to see its value, along with short and long descriptions of the key.

Using the GNOME Panels

The GNOME panels are placed on the top and bottom of the GNOME desktop. From those panels you can start applications (from buttons or menus), see what programs are active, and monitor how your system is running. There are also many ways to change the top and bottom panels — by adding applications or monitors or by changing the placement or behavior of the panel, for example.

Right-click any open space on either panel to see the Panel menu. Figure 3-8 shows the Panel menu on the top.

FIGURE 3-8

The GNOME panel menu

From GNOME's Panel menu, you can choose from a variety of functions, including:

- **Add to Panel** — Add an applet, menu, launcher, drawer, or button.

- **Properties** — Change the panel's position, size, and background properties.

- **Delete This Panel** — Delete the current panel.

- **New Panel** — Add panels to your desktop in different styles and locations.

You can also work with items on a panel. For example, you can:

- **Move items** — To move an item on a panel, right-click it, select move, and then drag and drop it to a new position.

- **Resize items** — Some elements, such as the Window List, can be resized by clicking an edge and dragging it to the new size.

- **Use the Window List** — Tasks running on the desktop appear in the Window List area. Click a task to minimize or maximize it.

The following sections describe some things you can do with the GNOME panel.

Using the Applications, Places, and System Menus

The Applications menu displays most of the applications and system tools you will use from the desktop. The Places menu lets you select places to go, such as the Desktop folder, home folder, removable media, or network locations. The System menu lets you change preferences and system settings, as well as get other information about GNOME.

Click Applications on the panel, and you see categories of applications and system tools that you can select. Click the application you want to launch. To add an item from a menu so that it can launch from the panel, drag-and-drop the item you want to the panel. You can manually add items to your GNOME menus.

To add to the main menu, create a .desktop file in the /usr/share/applications directory. The easiest way to do that is to copy an existing .desktop file that is on the menu you want and modify it. For example, to add a video player to the Sound & Video menu, you can do the following (as root user):

```
# cd /usr/share/applications
# cp gnome-cd.desktop vidplay.desktop
```

Next, use any text editor to change the contents of the vidplay.desktop file you created by adding a comment, a file to execute, an icon to display, and an application name. After you save the changes, the new item immediately appears on the menu (no need to restart anything). The following is an example of what the vidplay.desktop entry just created might look like:

```
[Desktop Entry]
Encoding=UTF-8
Name=My Video Player
Comment=Play Videos
Exec=myplayer
Icon=redhat-sound_video.png
StartupNotify=true
Terminal=false
Type=Application
Categories=GNOME;GTK;AudioVideo;Audio;Player;
OnlyShowIn=GNOME;
```

From the previous example, My Video Player appears on the Sound and Video menu along with an icon (`redhat-sound_video.png` from the `/usr/share/pixmaps` directory). The words Play Videos appear when the mouse pointer hovers over the menu entry. When launched from the menu, the `myplayer` command is run.

Adding an Applet

There are several small applications, called *applets,* that you can run directly on the GNOME panel. These applications can show information you may want to see on an ongoing basis or may just provide some amusement. To see what applets are available and to add applets that you want to your panel, perform the following steps:

1. Right-click an open space in the panel so that the panel menu appears.

2. Select Add to Panel. An Add to Panel window appears.

3. Select from among several dozen applets, including a clock, dictionary lookup, stock ticker, and weather report. The applet you select appears on the panel, ready for you to use.

Figure 3-9 shows (from left to right) eyes, system monitor, CD player, stock ticker, e-mail Inbox monitor, and dictionary lookup applets.

FIGURE 3-9

Placing applets on the panel makes it easy to access them.

After an applet is installed, right-click it on the panel to see what options are available. For example, select Preferences for the stock ticker, and you can add or delete stocks whose prices you want to monitor. If you don't like the applet's location, right-click it, click Move, slide the mouse until the applet is where you want it (even to another panel), and click to set its location.

If you no longer want an applet to appear on the panel, right-click it, and then click Remove From Panel. The icon representing the applet disappears. If you find that you have run out of room on your panel, you can add a new panel to another part of the screen, as described in the next section.

Adding Another Panel

You can have several panels on your GNOME desktop. You can add panels that run along the entire bottom, top, or side of the screen. To add a panel, do the following:

1. Right-click an open space in the panel so that the Panel menu appears.

2. Select New Panel. A new panel appears on the side of the screen.

3. Right-click an open space in the new panel and select Properties.

4. From the Panel Properties, select where you want the panel from the Orientation box (Top, Bottom, Left, or Right).

After you've added a panel, you can add applets or application launchers to it as you did to the default panel. To remove a panel, right-click it and select Delete This Panel.

Adding an Application Launcher

Icons on your panel represent a Web browser and several office productivity applications. You can add your own icons to launch applications from the panel as well. To add a new application launcher to the panel, do the following:

1. Right-click in an open space on the panel.

2. Select Add to Panel ⇨ Application Launcher from the menu. All application categories from your Applications and System menus appear.

3. Select the arrow next to the category of application you want, and then select Add. An icon representing the application appears on the panel.

To launch the application you just added, simply click the icon on the panel.

If the application you want to launch is not on one of your menus, you can build a launcher yourself as follows:

1. Right-click in an open space on the panel.

2. Select Add to Panel ⇨ Custom Application Launcher ⇨ Add. The Create Launcher window appears.

3. Provide the following information for the application that you want to add:

   - **Type** — Select Application (to launch a regular GUI application) or Application in Terminal. Use Application in Terminal if the application is a character-based or ncurses application. (Applications written using the ncurses library run in a Terminal window but offer screen-oriented mouse and keyboard controls.)

   - **Name** — A name to identify the application (this appears in the tooltip when your mouse is over the icon).

   - **Command** — The command line that is run when the application is launched. Use the full path name, plus any required options.

   - **Comment** — A comment describing the application. It also appears when you later move your mouse over the launcher.

4. Click the Icon box (it might say No Icon). Select one of the icons shown and click OK. Alternatively, you can browse the Linux file system to choose an icon.

> **NOTE** Icons available to represent your application are contained in the /usr/share/ pixmaps directory. These icons are either in .png or .xpm format. If there isn't an icon in the directory you want to use, create your own (in one of those two formats) and assign it to the application.

5. Click OK.

The application should now appear in the panel. Click it to start the application.

Adding a Drawer

A drawer is an icon that you can click to display other icons representing menus, applets, and launchers; it behaves just like a panel. Essentially, any item you can add to a panel you can add to a drawer. By adding a drawer to your GNOME panel, you can include several applets and launchers that together take up the space of only one icon. Click on the drawer to show the applets and launchers as though they were being pulled out of a drawer icon on the panel.

To add a drawer to your panel, right-click the panel and select Add to Panel ⇨ Drawer. A drawer appears on the panel. Right-click it, and add applets or launchers to it as you would to a panel. Click the icon again to retract the drawer.

Figure 3-10 shows a portion of the panel with an open drawer that includes xeyes (an applet which features eyes that follow your mouse pointer around the desktop), an icon for running GIMP, and an icon for launching a Terminal window.

FIGURE 3-10

Add launchers or applets to a drawer on your GNOME panel.

Changing Panel Properties

Those panel properties you can change are limited to the orientation, size, hiding policy, and background. To open the Panel Properties window that applies to a specific panel, right-click on an open space on the panel and choose Properties. The Panel Properties window that appears includes the following values:

- **Orientation** — Move the panel to different locations on the screen by clicking on a new position.
- **Size** — Select the size of your panel by choosing its height in pixels (48 pixels by default).
- **Expand** — Select this check box to have the panel expand to fill the entire side, or clear the check box to make the panel only as wide as the applets it contains.
- **AutoHide** — Select whether a panel is automatically hidden (appearing only when the mouse pointer is in the area).
- **Show Hide buttons** — Choose whether the Hide/Unhide buttons (with pixmap arrows on them) appear on the edges of the panel.

- **Arrows on hide buttons** — If you select Show Hide Buttons, you can choose to have arrows on those buttons.

- **Background** — From the Background tab, you can assign a color to the background of the panel, assign a pixmap image, or just leave the default (which is based on the current system theme). Click the Background Image check box if you want to select an Image for the background, and then select an image, such as a tile from /usr/share/backgrounds/tiles or another directory.

> **TIP** I usually turn on the AutoHide feature and turn off the Hide buttons. Using AutoHide gives you more desktop space to work with. When you move your mouse to the edge where the panel is, the panel pops up — so you don't need Hide buttons.

Using the Nautilus File Manager

At one time, file managers did little more than let you run applications, create data files, and open folders. These days, as the information a user needs expands beyond the local system, file managers are expected to also display Web pages, access FTP sites, and play multimedia content. The Nautilus file manager, which is the default GNOME file manager, is an example of just such a file manager.

When you open the Nautilus file manager window (for example, by opening the Home icon or another folder on your desktop), you see the name of the location you are viewing (such as the folder name) and what that location contains (files, folders, and applications). Figure 3-11 is an example of the file manager window displaying the home directory of the guest user.

FIGURE 3-11

The Nautilus file manager enables you to move around the file system, open directories, launch applications, and open Samba folders.

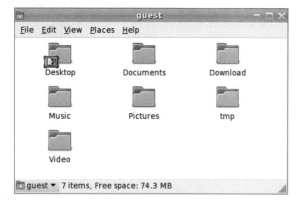

Beginning with GNOME 2.16, the default Nautilus window has been greatly simplified to show fewer controls and provide more space for file and directory icons. Double-click a folder to open that folder in a new window. Select your folder name in the lower-left corner of the window to see the file system hierarchy above the current folder. GNOME remembers whatever size, location, and other setting you had for the folder the last time you closed it and returns it to that state the next time you open it.

To see more controls, right-click a folder and select Browse Folder to open it. Icons on the toolbar of the Nautilus window let you move forward and back among the directories and Web sites you visit. To move up the directory structure, click the up arrow. If you prefer to type the path to the folder you want, instead of clicking icons, you can toggle between button- and text-based location bars (click the paper and pencil icon next to the location buttons to change the view).

To refresh the view of the folder, click the Reload button. The Home button takes you to your home page, and the Computer button lets you see the same type of information you would see from a My Computer icon on a Windows system (CD drive, floppy drive, hard disk file systems, and network folders).

Icons in Nautilus often indicate the type of data that a particular file contains. The contents or file extension of each file can determine which application is used to work with the file, or you can right-click an icon to open the file it represents with a particular application or viewer.

Here are some of the more interesting features of Nautilus:

- **Sidebar** — From the Browse Folder view described previously, select View ➪ Side Pane to have a sidebar appear in the left column of the screen. From the sidebar, you can click a pull-down menu that represents different types of information you can select one at a time.

    The Tree tab, for example, shows a tree view of the directory structure, so you can easily traverse your directories. The Notes tab lets you add notes that become associated with the current Directory or Web page, and the History tab displays a history of directories you have visited, enabling you to click those items to return to the sites they represent. There is also an Emblems tab that lets you drag-and-drop emblems on files or folders to indicate something about the file or folder (emblems include icons representing drafts, urgent, bug, and multimedia).

- **Windows file and printer sharing** — If your computer is connected to a LAN on which Windows computers are sharing files and printers, you can view those resources from Nautilus. Type **smb:** in the Open Location box (select File ➪ Open Location to get there) to see available workgroups. Click a workgroup to see computers from that workgroup that are sharing files and printers. Figure 3-12 shows an example of Nautilus displaying icons representing Windows computers in a workgroup called estreet (`smb://estreet`).

FIGURE 3-12

Display shared Windows file and printer servers (SMB) in Nautilus.

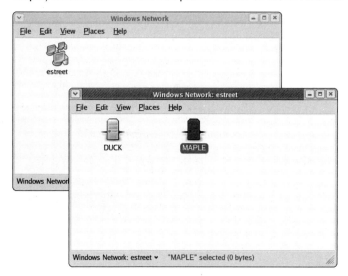

- **MIME types and file types** — To handle different types of content that may be encountered in the Nautilus window, you can set applications to respond based on MIME type and file type. With a folder displayed, right-click a file for which you want to assign an application. Click either Open With an Application or Open With a Viewer. If no application or viewer has been assigned for the file type, click Associate Application to be able to select an application. From the Add File Types window, you can add an application based on the file extension and MIME type representing the file.

- **Drag-and-drop** — You can use drag-and-drop within the Nautilus window, between the Nautilus and the desktop, or among multiple Nautilus windows. As other GNOME-compliant applications become available, they are expected to also support the drag-and-drop feature.

If you would like more information on the Nautilus file manager, visit the GNOME Web site (`www.gnome.org/nautilus`).

3D Effects with AIGLX

Several different initiatives have made strides in recent years to bring 3D desktop effects to Linux. openSUSE has the Xgl project (`http://en.opensuse.org/Xgl`), while Fedora has AIGLX (`http://fedoraproject.org/wiki/RenderingProject/aiglx`).

The goal of the Accelerated Indirect GLX project (AIGLX) is to add 3D effects to everyday desktop systems. It does this by implementing OpenGL (`http://opengl.org`) accelerated effects using the Mesa (`www.mesa3d.org`) open source OpenGL implementation.

Currently, AIGLX supports a limited set of video cards and implements only a few 3D effects, but it does offer some insight into the eye candy that is in the works.

Because direct rendering infrastructure (DRI) is required for AIGLX, cards that don't support that feature cannot be used. For example, NVidia cards are not currently supported and so cannot be used, although you can expect NVidia support to be added soon. The cards that are known to *not* work with AIGLX also include ATI Rage 128 and Mach 64, Matrox G200 through G550, and 3DFX Voodoo 1 and 2.

If your video card was properly detected and configured, you may be able to simply turn on the Desktop Effects feature to see the effects that have been implemented so far. To turn on Desktop Effects, select System ⇨ Preferences ⇨ Desktop Effects. When the Desktop Effects pop-up window appears, select Enable Desktop Effects, which does the following:

- Stops the current window manager and starts the Compiz window manager.

- Enables the Windows Wobble When Moved effect. With this effect on, when you grab the title bar of the window to move it, the window will wobble as it moves. Menus and other items that open on the desktop also wobble.

- Enables the Workspaces on a Cube effect. Drag a window from the desktop to the right or the left, and the desktop will rotate like a cube, with each of your desktop workspaces appearing as a side of that cube. Drop the window on the workspace where you want it to go. You can also click on the Workspace Switcher applet in the bottom panel to rotate the cube to display different workspaces.

Other nice desktop effects result from using the Alt+Tab key combination to tab among different running windows. As you press Alt+Tab, a thumbnail of each window scrolls across the screen and the window it represents is highlighted.

Figure 3-13 shows an example of a Compiz desktop with AIGLX enabled. With Alt+Tab pressed, thumbnails of several GIMP windows (containing house pictures) scroll from right to left. The middle, highlighted thumbnail represents the window that is currently selected.

If you get tired of wobbling windows and spinning cubes, you can easily turn off the AIGLX 3D effects and return Metacity as the window manager. Just select System ⇨ Preferences ⇨ Desktop Effects again and toggle off the Enable Desktop Effects button to turn off the feature.

If you have a supported video card, but find that you are not able to turn on the Desktop Effects, check that your X server started properly. In particular, make sure that your `/etc/X11/xorg.conf` file is properly configured. Make sure that DRI and GLX are loaded in the Module section. Also, add an extensions section anywhere in the file (typically at the end of the file) that appears as follows:

```
Section "extensions"
 Option "Composite"
EndSection
```

FIGURE 3-13

Alt+Tab through thumbnails of active windows with AIGLX desktop effects enabled.

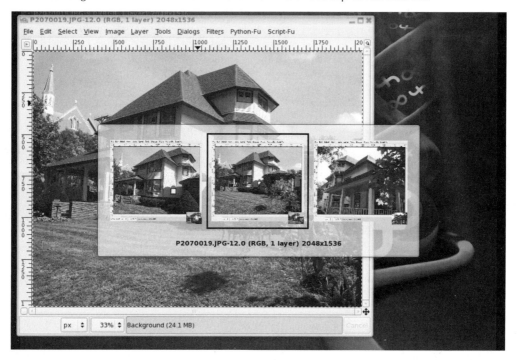

Another option is to add the following line to the /etc/X11/xorg.conf file in the Device section:

```
Option "XAANoOffscreenPixmaps"
```

The XAANoOffscreenPixmaps option will improve performance. Check your /var/log/Xorg.log file to make sure that DRI and AIGLX features were started correctly. The messages in that file can help you debug other problems as well.

Changing GNOME Preferences

There are many ways to change the behavior, look, and feel of your GNOME desktop. Most GNOME preferences can be modified from selections on the Preferences menu (select System ➪ Preferences).

Unlike earlier versions of GNOME for Fedora, boundaries between preferences related to the window manager (Metacity), file manager (Nautilus), and the GNOME desktop itself have been blurred. Preferences for all of these features are available from the Preferences menu.

The following items highlight some of the preferences you might want to change:

- **Accessibility** — If you have difficulty operating a mouse or keyboard, the Keyboard Accessibility Preferences (AccessX) window lets you adapt mouse and keyboard settings to make it easier for you to operate your computer. From the Preferences window, open Accessibility.

- **Desktop Background** — From Desktop Background Preferences, you can choose a solid color or an image to use as wallpaper. If you choose to use a solid color (by selecting No Wallpaper), click the Color box, select a color from the palette, and click OK.

  To use wallpaper for your background, open the folder containing the image you want to use, and then drag the image into the Desktop Wallpaper pane on the Desktop Preferences window. You can choose from a variety of images in the /usr/share/nautilus/patterns and /usr/share/backgrounds/tiles directories. Then choose to have the wallpaper image tiled (repeated pattern), centered, scaled (in proportion), or stretched (using any proportion to fill the screen).

- **Screensaver** — Choose from dozens of screen savers from the Screensaver window. Select Random to have your screen saver chosen randomly from those you mark with a check, or select one that you like from the list to use all the time. Next, choose how long your screen must be idle before the screen saver starts (the default is 10 minutes). You can also choose to lock the screen when the screen saver is active, so a password is required to return to the desktop.

- **Theme** — Choose an entire theme of elements to be used on your desktop, if you like. A desktop theme affects not only the background but also the way that many buttons and menu selections appear. Only a few themes are available for the window manager (Metacity) in the Fedora distribution, but you can get a bunch of other themes from themes.freshmeat.net (click Metacity).

  Click Theme Details, and then click the Controls tab to choose the type of controls to use on your desktop. Click the Window Border tab to select from different themes that change the title bar and other borders of your windows. Click the Icons tab to choose different icons to represent items on your desktop. Themes change immediately as you click or when you drag a theme name on the desktop.

Exiting GNOME

When you are done with your work, you can either log out from your current session or shut down your computer completely. To exit from GNOME, do the following:

1. Click the System button from the panel.
2. Select Log Out from the menu. A pop-up window appears, asking if you want to Log Out. Some versions will also ask if you want to Shut Down or Restart the computer.

3. Select OK from the pop-up menu. This logs you out and returns you to either the graphical login screen or to your shell login prompt. (If you select Shut Down, the system shuts down, and if you select Reboot, the system restarts.)

4. Select OK to finish exiting from GNOME.

If you are unable to get to the Log Out button (if, for example, your panel crashed), there are two other exit methods. Try one of these ways, depending on how you started the desktop:

- If you started the desktop by typing startx from your login shell, press Ctrl+Backspace to end your GNOME session. Or you could press Ctrl+Alt+F1 to return to your login shell. Then press Ctrl+C to kill the desktop.

- If you started the desktop from a graphical login screen, first open a Terminal window (right-click the desktop and select New Terminal). In the Terminal window, type **ps x | grep gnome-session** to determine the process number (PID) shown in the left column. Then type **kill -9** *PID*, where *PID* is replaced by the PID number. You should see the graphical login screen.

Although these are not the most graceful ways to exit the desktop, they work. You should be able to log in again and restart the desktop.

Configuring a GNOME Online Desktop

The GNOME Online Desktop project (`http://live.gnome.org/OnlineDesktop`) represents a new way of approaching desktop computing. It acknowledges that peoples' stuff (documents, digital images, videos, and so on) and activities (searches, blogging, e-mail, instant messaging, news feeds, and so on) are moving from the local hard disk to the Internet.

The first experimental release of the GNOME Online Desktop was distributed with Fedora 8 near the end of 2007. However, because it is part of the GNOME project, you can expect to see it with every major Linux distribution before the end of 2008.

The centerpiece of the GNOME Online Desktop project is the sidebar referred to as BigBoard (`http://live.gnome.org/BigBoard`). From BigBoard, you consolidate icons and menus to connect to your online photo services (such as Flickr), retail accounts (such as Amazon), movie rentals (such as Netflix), and others. It also, however, keeps track of the files and applications you use locally.

The settings that drive your personal Online Desktop are themselves stored online. A GNOME.org account can store information about your desktop applications. A Mugshot (`www.mugshot.org`) account lets you tie together connections to your online friends and activities. The information is downloaded to your desktop when you log in to the Online Desktop. That allows the Online Desktop concept to move away from a single computer, so you someday can have your whole desktop setup available from any computer with an Internet connection.

To get started with Online Desktop in Fedora 8, select Session ⇨ Online Desktop from the login screen. Then log in to Fedora. Create a user account at GNOME.org and Mugshot.org. Then configure your Mugshot account to connect to your accounts at popular sites such as Amazon.com, Flickr.com, Netflix.com, and others.

From your Online Desktop sidebar, log in to your Mugshot account. Your Online Desktop sidebar will become populated with your configured online accounts, popular applications, links to friends' accounts, and other items. Figure 3-14 shows an example of an Online Desktop in Fedora 8 Linux.

FIGURE 3-14

Use Online Desktop and Mugshot to connect to online services and friends.

Small icons beneath your user name represent the configured online services. A search box lets you select from a half dozen different search engines. Popular applications and files you have opened recently appear on the sidebar. You can also see your Google calendar and the people you have invited to be your friends.

Mugshot provides the site for configuring many Online Desktop features. You can see the same information from your Mugshot site that appears on your Online Desktop. The Mugshot icon in the bottom panel displays stacks of activities you and your other Mugshot friends.

Because Online Desktop is still under development, expect to have many more features and services available by the time you read this text. In particular, work is being done to integrate online applications, so you will be able to work with Web applications to use your documents, spreadsheets, and other important information.

Configuring Your Own Desktop

Today's modern desktop computer systems are made to spoon-feed you your operating system. In the name of ease of use, some desktop environments spend a lot of resources on fancy panels, complex control centers, and busy applets. In short, they can become bloated.

Many technically inclined people want a more streamlined desktop — or at least want to choose their own bells and whistles. They don't want to have to wait for windows to redraw or menus to come up. Linux enables those people to forget the complete desktop environments and configure:

- **X** — The X Window System provides the framework of choice for Linux and most UNIX systems. When you configure X yourself, you can choose the video driver, monitor settings, mouse configuration, and other basic features needed to get your display working properly.

- **Window manager** — Dozens of window managers are available to use with X on a Linux system. Window managers add borders and buttons to otherwise bare X windows. They add colors and graphics to backgrounds, menus, and windows. Window managers also define how you can use keyboard and mouse combinations to operate your desktop.

You need to configure X directly only if your desktop isn't working (the desktop may appear scrambled or may just plain crash). You may choose to configure X if you want to tune it to give you higher resolutions or more colors than you get by default.

Still to come in this chapter: examining tools for tuning X and, in particular, working with the xorg.conf file. You'll also explore a few popular window managers that you might want to try out. Slackware Linux is used to illustrate how to choose and configure a window manager because Slackware users tend to like simple, direct ways of working with the desktop (when they need a desktop at all).

Configuring X

Before 2004, most Linux distributions used the X server from the XFree86 project (www.xfree86 .org). Because of licensing issues, many of the major Linux vendors (including Red Hat, SUSE, and Slackware) changed to the X server from X.Org (www.X.org). The descriptions of how to get X going on your machine assume you are using the X.Org X server.

NOTE To determine which X server is installed on your system, from a Terminal window type **man Xorg** and man **XFree86**. If you have only one X server installed on your computer (which you probably do), only the one installed will show a man page. While you are there, press the spacebar to page through the features of your X server.

It's possible that you already did some configuration when you installed Linux. If you are able to start a desktop successfully and your mouse, keyboard, and screen all seem to be behaving, you may not have to do anything more to configure X.

However, if you can't start the desktop or you want to adjust some basic features (such as screen resolution or number of colors supported), the following sections offer some ideas on how to go about doing those things.

Creating a Working X Configuration File

If your desktop crashes immediately or shows only garbled text, try to create a new X configuration file. With the X.Org X server, that file is `/etc/X11/xorg.conf`.

NOTE In XFree86, the configuration file, which has basically the same format, is `/etc/X11/XF86Config`.

To have X try to create a working `xorg.conf` file for you to use, do the following from a Terminal window as root user:

1. If Linux booted to a command prompt, go to the next step. However, if it tried to start X automatically, you might have an illegible screen. In that case, press these keys together: Ctrl+Alt+Backspace. It should kill your X server and get you back to a command prompt. If X tries to restart (and is still messed up), press Ctrl+Alt+F2. When you see the command prompt, log in as root and type **init 3**. This will temporarily bring you down to a nongraphical state.

2. To have X probe your video hardware and create a new configuration file, type:

```
# Xorg -configure
```

3. The file `x.org.conf.new` should appear in your home directory. To test if this new configuration file works, type the following to start the X server:

```
# X -xf86config /root/xorg.conf.new
```

   A gray background with an X in the middle should appear. Move the mouse to move the X pointer. If that succeeds, you have a working `xorg.conf` file to use.

4. Press Ctrl+Alt+Backspace to exit the X server.

5. Copy the new configuration file to where it is picked up the next time X starts.

```
# cp /root/xorg.conf.new /etc/X11/xorg.conf
```

Chances are that you have a very basic X configuration that you may want to tune further.

Getting New X Drivers

Working video drivers in Linux are available with most video cards you can purchase today. However, to get some advanced features from your video cards (such as 3D acceleration) you may need to get proprietary drivers directly from the video manufacturers. In particular, you may want to get drivers from NVidia and ATI.

To get new drivers for video cards or chipsets from NVidia, go to the NVidia site (www.nvidia.com) and select the Download Drivers button. Follow the link to Linux and FreeBSD drivers. Links from the page that appears will take you to a Web page from which you can download the new driver and get instructions for installing it.

For ATI video cards and chipsets, go to www.ati.com and select Drivers & Software. Follow the links to Linux drivers and related installation instructions.

There are NVidia and ATI drivers that have been packaged for the particular kernel you are running for many of the popular Linux distributions. Because these drivers are not open source, however, you typically have to enable third-party software repositories to get them to work.

Tuning Up Your X Configuration File

The xorg.conf file might look a bit complicated when you first start working with it. However, chances are that you will need to change only a few key elements in it. As root user, open the /etc/X11/xorg.conf file in any text editor. Here are some things you can look for:

- **Mouse** — Look for an InputDevice section with a Mouse0 or Mouse1 identifier. That section for a simple two-button, PS2 mouse might look as follows:

```
Section "InputDevice"
    Identifier    "Mouse0"
    Driver        "mouse"
    Option        "Protocol" "PS/2"
    Option        "Device" "/dev/psaux"
EndSection
```

If you are unable to use some feature of the mouse, such as a middle wheel, you might be able to get it working with an entry that looks more like the following:

```
Section "InputDevice"
    Identifier    "Mouse0"
    Driver        "mouse"
    Option        "Protocol" "IMPS/2"
    Option        "Device" "/dev/psaux"
    Option        "ZAxisMapping" "4 5"
EndSection
```

Don't change the mouse identifier, but you can change the protocol and add the ZAxisMapping line to enable your wheel mouse. Try restarting X and trying your mouse wheel on something like a Web page to see if you can scroll up and down with it.

Your mouse might be connected in a different way (such as a bus or serial mouse) or may have different buttons to enable. Tools for configuring your mouse are distribution-specific. Try mouseconfig, mouseadmin, or system-config-mouse to reconfigure your mouse from the command line.

- **Monitor** — The monitor section defines attributes of your monitor. There are generic settings you can use if you don't exactly know the model of your monitor. Changing the Horizontal Sync and Vertical Refresh rates without checking your monitor's technical specifications is not recommended; you could damage the monitor. Here's an example of an entry that will work on many LCD panels:

```
Section "Monitor"
    Identifier    "Monitor0"
    VendorName    "Monitor Vendor"
    ModelName     "LCD Panel 1024x768"
    HorizSync     31.5 - 48.5
    VertRefresh   40.0 - 70.0
EndSection
```

Here's an entry for a generic CRT monitor that will work on many CRTs:

```
Section "Monitor"
    Identifier    "Monitor0"
    VendorName    "Monitor Vendor"
    ModelName     "Generic Monitor, 1280x1024 @ 74 Hz"
    HorizSync     31.5 - 79.0
    VertRefresh   50.0 - 90.0
EndSection
```

If a tool is available to select your monitor model directly, that would be the best way to go. For example, in Red Hat systems, you would run system-config-xfree86 to change monitor settings.

- **Video device** — The Device section is where you identify the driver to use with your video device and any options to use with it. It's important to get this section right. The Xorg command described earlier usually does a good job detecting the driver. If you want to change to a different one, this is where to do so. Here's an example of the Device section after I added a video driver from NVIDIA to my system (the driver name is nv):

```
Section "Device"
    Identifier    "Card0"
    Driver        "nv"
```

```
        VendorName    "nVidia Corporation"
        BoardName     "Unknown Board"
        BusID         "PCI:1:0:0"
   EndSection
```

- **Screen resolution** — The last major piece of information you may want to add is the screen resolution and color depth. There will be a screen resolution associated with each video card installed on your computer. The `Screen` section defines default color depths (such as 8, 16, or 24) and modes (such as 1024 × 768, 800 × 600, or 640 × 480). Set the `DefaultDepth` to the number of bits representing color depth for your system, and then add a `Modes` line to set the screen resolution.

To read more about how to set options in your `xorg.conf` file, type **man xorg.conf**. If your X server is XFree86, type **man XF86Config**.

Choosing a Window Manager

Fully integrated desktop environments have become somewhat unfriendly to changing out window managers. However, you can completely bypass KDE or GNOME, if you like, and start your desktop simply with X and a window manager of your choice.

Although I'm using Slackware as the reference distribution for describing how to change window managers, the concept is the same on other Linux systems. In general, if no desktop environment is running in Linux, you can start it by typing the following:

```
$ startx
```

This command starts up your desktop environment or window manager, depending on how your system is configured. Although a variety of configuration files are read and commands are run, essentially which desktop you get depends on the contents of two files:

- `/etc/X11/xinit/xinitrc` — If a user doesn't specifically request a particular desktop environment or window manager, the default desktop settings will come from the contents of this file. The `xinitrc` file is the system-wide X configuration file. Different Linux systems use different `xinitrc` files.

- `$HOME/.xinitrc` — The `.xinitrc` file is used to let individual users set up their own desktop startup information. Any user can add a `.xinitrc` file to his or her own home directory. The result is that the contents of that file will override any system-wide settings. If you do create your own `.xinitrc` file, it should have as its last line `exec windowmanager`, where *windowmanager* is the name of your window manager; for example:

```
exec /usr/X1R6/bin/blackbox
```

Slackware has at least seven different window managers from which you can choose, making it a good place to try out a few. It also includes a tool called `xwmconfig`, which lets you change the window manager system-wide (in the /etc/X11/xinit/xinitrc file). To use that tool, as the root user simply type **xwmconfig** from any shell on a Slackware system. Figure 3-15 shows an example of that screen.

FIGURE 3-15

In Slackware, you can change window managers using the xwmconfig command.

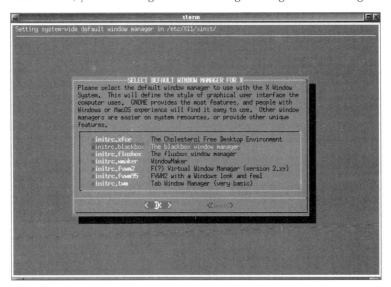

Select the window manager you want to try from that screen and select OK. That window manager will start the next time you run startx (provided you don't override it by creating your own .xinitrc file). Here are your choices:

- **Xfce** (www.xfce.org) — The xfce window manager is designed to be lightweight and fast.

- **Blackbox** (www.blackboxwm.sourceforge.net) — Another lightweight window manager that strives to require few library dependencies so it can run in many environments. It offers many features for setting colors and styles.

- **FluxBox** (http://fluxbox.sourceforge.net) — Based on Blackbox (0.61.1), FluxBox adds nice features such as window tabs (where you can join multiple windows so they appear as multiple tabs on a single window). It also includes an icon bar and adds some useful mouse features (such as using your mouse wheel to change workspaces).

- **Window Maker** (www.windowmaker.org) — Window Maker is a clone of the NEXTSTEP graphical interface, a popular UNIX workstation of the 1980s and 1990s. It is a particularly attractive window manager, with support for themes, various window decorations, and features for changing backgrounds and animations, and adding applets (called docapps).

- **FVWM** (www.fvwm.org) — This window manager supports full internationalization, window manager hints, and improved font features. Interesting features include window shading in all directions (even diagonal) and side titles (including text displayed vertically).

- **FVWM-95** (http://fvwm95.sourceforge.net) — A version of FVWM that was created to look and feel like Windows 95.

- **Twm (Tabbed Window Manager)** — Although no longer actively maintained, some people still use twm when they want a truly bare-bones desktop. Until you click the left mouse button in twm, there's nothing on the screen. Use the menu that pops up to open and close windows.

Many other window managers are available for Linux as well. To check out some more, visit the Xwinman Web site (www.plig.org/xwinman).

Once the system default is set for your window manager, users can set their own window manager to override that decision. The following section describes how to do that.

Choosing Your Personal Window Manager

Simply adding an exec line with the name of the window manager you want to use to your own .xinitrc file in your home directory causes startx to start that window manager for you. Here is an example of the contents of a .xinitrc to start the Window Maker window manager:

```
exec /usr/bin/wmaker
```

Make sure that the file is executable (chmod 755 $HOME/.xinitrc). The Window Maker window manager should start the next time you start your desktop. Other window managers you can choose include Blackbox (/usr/X11R6/bin/blackbox), FluxBox (/usr/X11R6/bin/fluxbox), FVWM (/usr/X11R6/bin/fluxbox), FVWM-95 (/usr/X11R6/bin/fvwm95), and twm (/usr/X11R6/bin/twm).

Getting More Information

If you tried configuring X and you still have a server that crashes or has a garbled display, your video card may either be unsupported or require special configuration. Here are a couple of locations you can check for further information:

- **X.Org** (www.x.org) — The latest information about the X servers that come with Fedora is available from the X.Org Web site. X.Org is the freeware version of X recently used by many major Linux distributions to replace the XFree86 X server.

- **X documentation** — README files specific to different types of video cards are delivered with the X.Org X server. Visit the X doc directory (/usr/X11R6/lib/X11/doc) for a README file specific to the type of video card (or more specifically, the video chipset) you are using. A lot of good information can also be found on the xorg.conf man page (type **man xorg.conf**).

Summary

Complete desktop environments that run in Linux can rival desktop systems from any operating system. KDE and GNOME are the most popular desktop environments available today for Linux. For people who want a sleeker, more lightweight desktop environment, a variety of simple window managers (Blackbox, FVWM, twm, FluxBox, and many others) are available to use in Linux as well.

The KDE desktop is well known for its large set of integrated applications (office productivity tools, games, multimedia, and other applications). GNOME has the reputation of being a more basic, business-oriented desktop. Most Linux distributions such as Slackware and Gentoo offer GNOME and KDE desktops that aren't changed much from how they are delivered from those desktop projects. Other Linux systems (such as Fedora) put their own look-and-feel over GNOME and KDE desktops.

While the latest Windows systems won't run on many older 486 and Pentium machines, you can use an efficient Linux system such as Slackware, add a lightweight window manager, and get reasonably good performance with your desktop system on those machines.

Part II

Running the Show

Chapter 4

Learning Basic Administration

L inux, like other UNIX-based systems, was intended for use by more than one person at a time. *Multiuser* features enable many people to have accounts on a single Linux system, with their data kept secure from others. *Multitasking* enables many people to run programs on the computer at the same time, with each person running more than one program. Sophisticated networking protocols and applications make it possible for a Linux system to extend its capabilities to network users and computers around the world. The person assigned to manage all of this stuff is called the *system administrator.*

Even if you are the only person using a Linux system, system administration is still set up to be separate from other computer use. To do most administrative tasks, you need to be logged in as the root user (also called the *superuser*) or temporarily get root permission. Users other than root cannot change, or in some cases even see, some of the configuration information for a Linux system. In particular, security features such as stored passwords are protected from general view.

Because Linux system administration is such a huge topic, this chapter focuses on the general principles of Linux system administration. In particular, it examines some of the basic tools you need to administer a Linux system for a personal desktop or on a small LAN. Beyond the basics, this chapter also teaches you how to work with file systems and monitor the setup and performance of your Linux system.

Graphical Administration Tools

Many Linux systems come with simplified graphical tools for administering Linux. If you are a casual user, these tools often let you do everything you need to administer your system without editing configuration files or running shell commands.

Let's examine some of the Web-based administration tools available to use with most Linux systems.

Using Web-Based Administration

Web-based administration tools are available with many open source projects to make those projects more accessible to casual users. Often all you need to use those tools is a Web browser (such as Firefox), the port number of the service, and the root password. Projects such as Samba and CUPS come with their own Web administration tools. Webmin is a general-purpose tool for administering a variety of Linux system services from your Web browser.

The advantages of Web-based administration tools are that you can operate them from a familiar interface (your Web browser) and you can access them remotely.

 Some Linux distributions come with their own set of graphical administration tools (such as SUSE's YaST or Red Hat's system-config tools). You should generally use those instead of any Web-based interface that comes with a project because a distribution's own tools are usually better integrated with its tools for starting and stopping services.

Open Source Projects Offering Web Administration

Several major open source projects come with Web-based interfaces for configuring those projects. Regardless of which Linux you are using, you can use your Web browser to configure the following projects:

- **Samba** — To set up Samba for doing file and printer sharing with Microsoft Windows systems on your LAN, use the Samba SWAT Web-based administration tools from any Web browser. With SWAT installed and running, you can access your Samba server configuration from your Web browser by typing the following URL in the location box:

```
http://localhost:901
```

NOTE If you get an `Unable to Connect` message, **Samba is not installed or running.**

The Samba project also offers other graphical tools for administering Samba. You can check them out at `http://samba.org/samba/GUI`. For descriptions of these tools, see Chapters 26 and 27.

■ **CUPS** — The Common UNIX Printing Service (CUPS) has its own Web administration tool. With CUPS installed and configured, you can typically use CUPS Web administration by typing the following URL in your Web browser's location box:

```
http://localhost:631
```

You use the CUPS administration tool to manage printers and classes and do a variety of administration tasks. CUPS is described in Chapter 26.

Samba and CUPS are included with many Linux distributions. Other projects that offer Web-based administration that may or may not be in your Linux distribution include SquirrelMail (a Webmail interface) and Mailman (a mailing list facility).

Because many Web browser administrative interfaces send data in clear text, they are most appropriate to be used on the local system. However, because they are Web-based, you can also use these interfaces from your LAN or other network. If you plan to expose these administrative interfaces to an untrusted network, however, you should consider encrypting your communications.

The Webmin Administration Tool

The Webmin facility (`www.webmin.com`) offers more complete Web-based Linux and UNIX administration features. Although Webmin isn't delivered with some Linux systems that offer their own graphical administration tools (such as Fedora and RHEL), the Webmin project has ported Webmin to run on more than 70 different operating systems. Supported Linux distributions include SUSE, Red Hat (Fedora and RHEL), Debian, Ubuntu, Gentoo, Slackware, Mandriva, Yellow Dog, and others (see `www.webmin.com/support.html` for a complete list).

Once you get Webmin from Webmin.com and install it, you can use Webmin from your Web browser. To start the Webmin interface, type the following in the Web browser's location box:

```
http://localhost:10000
```

After you log in as root user, the main Webmin page displays, as shown in Figure 4-1.

Graphical Administration with Different Distributions

Some people fear that once they've left the familiar confines of their Microsoft Windows system for Linux, they'll be stuck doing everything from a command line. To gain a wider audience, commercial Linux distributions such as Red Hat Enterprise Linux and SUSE created their own sets of graphical tools to provide an easy entry point for new Linux users. The following sections describe Red Hat's system-config and SUSE's YaST graphical administration tools.

FIGURE 4-1

Webmin offers a Web browser interface for administering Linux.

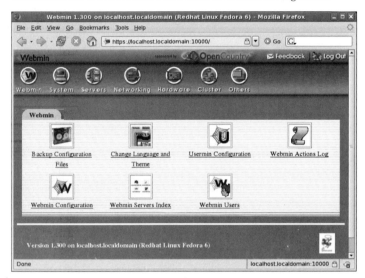

Red Hat Config Tools

A set of graphical tools that comes with Fedora and Red Hat Enterprise Linux systems can be launched from the Administration submenu of the System menu or from the command line. Most of the Fedora and RHEL tools that launch from the command line begin with the system-config string (such as system-config-network).

NOTE   **In Fedora Core 1 and previous versions of Red Hat Linux, the GUI administrations tools all began with** redhat-, **such as** redhat-config-network **and** redhat-logviewer. **Starting with Fedora Core 2, those names have all changed to** system-, **resulting in names like** system-config-network **and** system-config-display.

These administrative tasks require root permission; if you are logged in as a regular user, you must enter the root password before the GUI application's window opens. After you've entered that password, most of the system configuration tools will open without requiring you to retype the password during this login session. Look for a yellow badge icon in the upper-right corner of the panel, indicating that you have root authorization. Click the badge to open a pop-up window that enables you to remove authorization. Otherwise, authorization goes away when you close the GUI window.

The following list describes many of the graphical tools you can use to administer a Fedora or Red Hat Enterprise Linux system. Start these windows from the Administration submenu on the System menu. The name of the package that must be installed to get the feature is shown in parentheses.

NOTE The availability of the selections described below depends on which features you have installed.

- **Server Settings** — Access the following server configuration windows from this submenu:

  - **Domain Name System** (`system-config-bind`) — Create and configure zones if your computer is acting as a DNS server.

  - **HTTP** (`system-config-httpd`) — Configure your computer as an Apache Web server.

  - **NFS** (`system-config-nfs`) — Set up directories from your system to be shared with other computers on your network using the NFS service.

  - **Samba NFS** (`system-config-nfs`) — Configure Windows (SMB) file sharing. (To configure other Samba features, you can use the SWAT window.)

  - **Services** (`system-config-services`) — Display and change which services are running on your Fedora system at different run levels from the Service Configuration window.

- **Authentication** (`authconfig-gtk`) — Change how users are authenticated on your system. Usually, Shadow Passwords and MD5 Passwords are selected. However, if your network supports LDAP, Kerberos, SMB, NIS, or Hesiod authentication, you can select to use any of those authentication types.

- **Bootloader** — If you have multiple operating systems on your computer, or multiple Linux kernels available to boot in Linux, you can use the Boot Configuration screen to choose which to boot by default. For example, you might have Fedora Linux, SUSE, and Windows XP all on the same hard disk. You could choose which would start automatically (after a set number of seconds), if one wasn't selected explicitly.

- **Date & Time** (`system-config-date`) — Set the date and time or choose to have an NTP server keep system time in sync.

- **Display** (`system-config-display`) — Change the settings for your X desktop, including color depth and resolution for your display. You can also choose settings for your video card and monitor.

- **Firewall** (`system-config-firewall`) — Configure your firewall to allow or deny services to computers from the network.

- **Hardware Browser** (`hwbrowser`) — View information about your computer's hardware.

- **Keyboard** (`system-config-keyboard`) — Choose the type of keyboard you are using, based on language.

- **Language** (`system-config-language`) — Select the default language used for the system.

- **Logical Volume Management** (`system-config-lvm`) — Manage your LVM partitions.

- **Login Screen** (`gdm`) — Control how your login screen appears and behaves.

- **Network** (`system-config-network`)—Manage your current network interfaces and add interfaces.

- **Printing** (`system-config-printer`)—Configure local and network printers.

- **Root Password** (`system-config-rootpassword`)—Change the root password.

- **SELinux Management** (`system-config-selinux`)—Set SELinux enforcing modes and default policy.

- **SELinux Troubleshooter** (`setroubleshoot-server`)—Monitor and diagnose SELinux AVC denials.

- **Soundcard Detection** (`system-config-soundcard`)—Try to detect and configure your sound card.

- **System Log** (`gnome-utils`) —View system log files, and search them for keywords.

- **Users & Groups** (`system-config-users`)—Add, display, and change user and group accounts for your Fedora system.

Other administrative utilities are available from the Applications menu on the top panel. The Add/Remove Software selection lets you select software from any yum-enabled software repository available on the network. For other administrative tools, select the System Tools submenu to see some of the following options:

- **Configuration Editor (gconf-editor)**—Directly edit the GNOME configuration database.

- **Disk Usage Analyzer (gnome-utils)**—Display detailed information about your hard disks and removable storage devices.

- **Kickstart (system-config-kickstart)**—Create a kickstart configuration file that can be used to install multiple Fedora systems without user interaction.

- **Software Updater (pirut)**—Run the Package Updater utility (pup) to get updates for all system packages.

Other applications that you add to Fedora or RHEL may also include administrative utilities that will appear in the System Tools submenu.

SUSE YaST Tools

The YaST administrative interface is one of the strongest features of SUSE Linux. From a SUSE desktop, open the YaST Control Center by selecting System ⇨ YaST from the main menu. Figure 4-2 shows an example of the YaST Control Center.

YaST has some useful tools in its Hardware section that enable you to probe your computer hardware. Selecting Hardware Info on my system, for example, enabled me to see that the CD-ROM drive that YaST detected was available through device /dev/cdrom and that it supported CD-R, CD-RW, and DVD media. I could also see detailed information about my CPU, network card, PCI devices, sound card, and various storage media.

FIGURE 4-2

Use the YaST Control Center to administer SUSE systems.

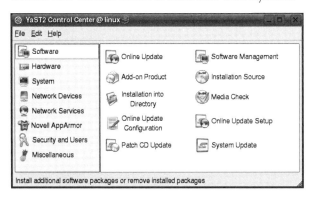

YaST also offers interfaces for configuring and starting network devices, as well as a variety of services to run on those devices. In addition, you can use YaST to configure your computer as a client for file sharing (Samba and NFS), e-mail (sendmail), and a variety of network services.

SUSE Linux Enterprise Server comes with a wider range of configuration tools that are specifically geared toward server setup, including tools for configuring a mail server, VPN tunnels, and full Samba 3. While other distributions may include proprietary tools, YaST is in a class of its own.

Using the root Login

Every Linux system starts out with at least one administrative user account (the root user) and possibly one or more regular user accounts (given a name that you choose, or a name assigned by Linux). In most cases, you log in as a regular user and become the root user to do an administrative task.

The root user has complete control of the operation of your Linux system. That user can open any file or run any program. The root user also installs software packages and adds accounts for other people who use the system.

 Think of the root user in Linux as analogous to the Administrator user in Windows.

When you first install most Linux systems, you add a password for the root user. You must remember and protect this password — you will need it to log in as root or to obtain root permission while you are logged in as some other user. Other Linux systems (such as KNOPPIX) start you without an available root password, so you may want to add one when you first start up by typing the following from a Terminal window or other shell:

```
# passwd root
Changing password for user root.
New UNIX password: ********
Retype new UNIX password: ********
```

> **NOTE** Some bootable Linux distributions give you (as a regular user) the power to run commands as root. You simply have to ask for the privilege using the sudo command. For example, from a Terminal window, to open a shell as root, type the following:

```
$ sudo su -
#
```

You'll find out more about the sudo command later in this chapter.

The home directory for the root user is typically /root. The home directory and other information associated with the root user account are located in the /etc/passwd file. Here's what the root entry looks like in the /etc/passwd file:

```
root:x:0:0:root:/root:/bin/bash
```

This shows that for the user named root the user ID is set to 0 (root user), the group ID is set to 0 (root group), the home directory is /root, and the shell for that user is /bin/bash. (We're using a shadow password file to store encrypted password data, so the password field here contains an *x*.) You can change the home directory or the shell used by editing the values in this file. A better way to change these values, however, is to use the usermod command (see the section "Modifying Users with usermod" later in this chapter).

> **NOTE** By default, the root account is disabled in Ubuntu. This means that even though the account exists, you cannot log in using it or use su to become the root user. This adds an additional level of security to Ubuntu, and requires you to use sudo before each command you want to execute at root level.

Becoming Root from the Shell (su Command)

Although you can become the superuser by logging in as root, sometimes that is not convenient. For example, you may be logged in to a regular user account and just want to make a quick administrative change to your system without having to log out and log back in. Or, you may need to log in over the network to make a change to a Linux system but find that the system doesn't allow root users in from over the network (a common practice in the days before secure shells were available).

The solution is to use the su command. From any Terminal window or shell, you can simply type the following:

```
$ su
Password: ******
#
```

When you are prompted, type in the root user's password. The prompt for the regular user ($) changes to the superuser prompt (#). At this point, you have full permission to run any command and use any file on the system. However, one thing that the su command doesn't do when used this way is read in the root user's environment. As a result, you may type a command that you know is available and get the message Command Not Found. To fix this problem, use the su command with the dash (-) option instead, like this:

```
$ su -
Password: ******
#
```

You still need to type the password, but after that, everything that normally happens at login for the root user happens after the su command is completed. Your current directory will be root's home directory (probably /root), and things such as the root user's PATH variable will be used. If you become the root user by just typing su, rather than su -, you won't change directories or the environment of the current login session.

 While becoming root is strongly discouraged with Ubuntu, you can do so if you must with the command sudo -i -1 root and giving the password.

You can also use the su command to become a user other than root. This is useful for troubleshooting a problem that is being experienced by a particular user, but not by others on the computer (such as an inability to print or send e-mail). For example, to have the permissions of a user named jsmith, you'd type the following:

```
$ su - jsmith
```

Even if you were root user before you typed this command, afterward you would have only the permissions to open files and run programs that are available to jsmith. As root user, however, after you type the su command to become another user, you don't need a password to continue. If you type that command as a regular user, you must type the new user's password.

When you are finished using superuser permissions, return to the previous shell by exiting the current shell. Do this by pressing Ctrl+D or by typing **exit**. If you are the administrator for a computer that is accessible to multiple users, don't leave a root shell open on someone else's screen (unless you want to let that person do anything he wants to the computer)!

Allowing Limited Administrative Access

As mentioned earlier, when you run GUI tools as a regular user (from Fedora, SUSE, or some other Linux systems), you are prompted for the root password before you are able to access the tool. By entering the root password, you are given root privilege for that task. In the case of Fedora, after you enter the password, a badge icon appears in the top panel, indicating that root authorization is still available for other GUI tools to run from that desktop session.

A particular user can also be given administrative permissions for particular tasks without being given the root password. For example, a system administrator can add a user to particular groups, such as modem, disk, users, cdrom, ftp, mail, or www, and then open group permission to use those services. Or, an administrator can add a user to the wheel group and add entries to the /etc/sudoers file to allow that user to use the sudo command to run individual commands as root. (See the description of sudo later in this chapter.)

> **NOTE**   The wheel group does not exist in all distributions. In Ubuntu, for example, wheel is not created automatically.

A fairly new feature being added to some Linux distributions used in highly secure environments is Security Enhanced Linux (SELinux). With SELinux, instead of one all-powerful root user account, multiple roles can be defined to protect selected files and services. In that way, for example, if someone cracks your Web server, he does not automatically have access to your mail server, user passwords, or other services running on the computer.

Exploring Administrative Commands, Configuration Files, and Log Files

You can expect to find many commands, configuration files, and log files in the same places in the file system, regardless of which Linux distribution you are using. The following sections give you some pointers on where to look for these important elements.

> **COMING FROM WINDOWS**   If GUI administrative tools for Linux have become so good, why do you need to know about administrative files? For one thing, while GUI tools differ among Linux versions, many underlying configuration files are the same. So, if you learn to work with them, you can work with almost any Linux system. Also, if a feature is broken or if you need to do something that's not supported by the GUI, when you ask for help, Linux experts almost always tell you how to change the configuration file directly.

Administrative Commands

Only the root user is intended to use many administrative commands. When you log in as root (or use su - from the shell to become root), your $PATH variable is set to include some directories that contain commands for the root user. These include the following:

- /sbin — Contains commands for modifying your disk partitions (such as fdisk), checking file systems (fsck), and changing system states (init).

- /usr/sbin — Contains commands for managing user accounts (such as useradd) and adding mount points for automounting file systems (automount). Commands that run as daemon processes are also contained in this directory. (Look for commands that end in d, such as sshd, pppd, and cupsd.)

Some administrative commands are contained in regular user directories (such as /bin and /usr/bin). This is especially true of commands that have some options available to everyone. An example is the /bin/mount command, which anyone can use to list mounted file systems, but only root can use to mount file systems. (Some desktops, however, are configured to let regular users use mount to mount CDs, DVDs, or other removable media by adding keywords to the /etc/fstab file.)

 **See the section "Mounting File Systems" later in this chapter for instructions on how to mount a file system.**

To find commands intended primarily for the system administrator, check out the section 8 manual pages (usually in /usr/share/man/man8). They contain descriptions and options for most Linux administrative commands.

Some third-party applications add administrative commands to directories that are not in your PATH. For example, an application may put commands in /usr/local/bin, /opt/bin, or /usr/local/sbin. Some Linux distributions automatically add those directories to your PATH, usually before your standard bin and sbin directories. In that way, commands installed to those directories are not only accessible, but can also override commands of the same name in other directories.

Administrative Configuration Files

Configuration files are another mainstay of Linux administration. Almost everything you set up for your particular computer — user accounts, network addresses, or GUI preferences — is stored in plain-text files. This has some advantages and some disadvantages.

The advantage of plain-text files is that it's easy to read and change them. Any text editor will do. The downside, however, is that as you edit configuration files, no error checking is going on. You have to run the program that reads these files (such as a network daemon or the X desktop) to find out whether you set up the files correctly. There are no standards for the structure of configuration files, so you need to learn the format of each file individually. A comma or a quote in the wrong place can sometimes cause a whole interface to fail.

 **Some software packages offer a command to test the sanity of the configuration file tied to a package before you start a service. For example, the** testparm **command is used with Samba to check the sanity of your** smb.conf **file. Other times, the daemon process providing a service offers an option for checking your config file. For example, run** httpd -t **to check your Apache Web server configuration before starting your Web server.**

Throughout this book you'll find descriptions of the configuration files you need to set up the different features that make up Linux systems. The two major locations of configuration files are your home directory (where your personal configuration files are kept) and the /etc directory (which holds system-wide configuration files).

Following are descriptions of directories (and subdirectories) that contain useful configuration files. (Refer to Table 4-1 for some individual configuration files in /etc that are of particular interest.) Viewing the contents of Linux configuration files can teach you a lot about administering Linux systems.

- $HOME — All users store information in their home directories that directs how their login accounts behave. Most configuration files in $HOME begin with a dot (.), so they don't appear in a user's directory when you use a standard ls command (you need to type `ls -a` to see them). There are dot files that define how each user's shell behaves, the desktop look-and-feel, and options used with your text editor. There are even files such as `.ssh/*` and `.rhosts` that configure network permissions for each user. (To see the name of your home directory, type **echo $HOME** from a shell.)

- `/etc` — This directory contains most of the basic Linux system-configuration files. Table 4-1 shows some `/etc` configuration files of interest.

- `/etc/cron*` — Directories in this set contain files that define how the crond utility runs applications on a daily (`cron.daily`), hourly (`cron.hourly`), monthly (`cron.monthly`), or weekly (`cron.weekly`) schedule.

- `/etc/cups` — Contains files used to configure the CUPS printing service.

- `/etc/default` — Contains files that set default values for various utilities. For example, the file for the `useradd` command defines the default group number, home directory, password expiration date, shell, and skeleton directory (`/etc/skel`) that are used when creating a new user account.

- `/etc/httpd` — Contains a variety of files used to configure the behavior of your Apache Web server (specifically, the httpd daemon process). (On some Linux systems, `/etc/apache` is used instead.)

- `/etc/init.d` — Contains the permanent copies of System V–style run-level scripts. These scripts are often linked from the `/etc/rc?.d` directories to have each service associated with a script started or stopped for the particular run level. The ? is replaced by the run-level number (0 through 6). (Slackware puts its run-level scripts in the `/etc/rc.d` directory.)

- `/etc/mail` — Contains files used to configure your sendmail mail service.

- `/etc/pcmcia` — Contains configuration files that allow you to have a variety of PCMCIA cards configured for your computer. (PCMCIA slots are those openings on your laptop that enable you to have credit card–sized cards attached to your computer. You can attach devices such as modems and external CD-ROMs.)

- `/etc/postfix` — Contains configuration files for the postfix mail transport agent.

- `/etc/ppp` — Contains several configuration files used to set up Point-to-Point Protocol (PPP) so that you can have your computer dial out to the Internet.

- `/etc/rc?.d` — There is a separate `rc?.d` directory for each valid system state: `rc0.d` (shutdown state), `rc1.d` (single-user state), `rc2.d` (multiuser state), `rc3.d` (multiuser plus networking state), `rc4.d` (user-defined state), `rc5.d` (multiuser, networking, plus GUI login state), and `rc6.d` (reboot state). Some Linux distros, such as Slackware, put most of the start-up scripts directly in `/etc/rc.d`, without the runlevel notation.

- `/etc/security` — Contains files that set a variety of default security conditions for your computer. These files are part of the pam (pluggable authentication modules) package.

- `/etc/skel` — Any files contained in this directory are automatically copied to a user's home directory when that user is added to the system. By default, most of these files are dot (.) files, such as `.kde` (a directory for setting KDE desktop defaults) and `.bashrc` (for setting default values used with the bash shell).

- /etc/sysconfig — Contains important system configuration files that are created and maintained by various services (including iptables, samba, and most networking services). These files are critical for Linux distributions that use GUI administration tools but are not used on other Linux systems at all.

- /etc/xinetd.d — Contains a set of files, each of which defines a network service that the xinetd daemon listens for on a particular port. When the xinetd daemon process receives a request for a service, it uses the information in these files to determine which daemon processes to start to handle the request.

TABLE 4-1

/etc Configuration Files of Interest

File	Description
aliases	Can contain distribution lists used by the Linux mail service. (This file may be located in /etc/mail.)
bashrc	Sets system-wide defaults for bash shell users. (This may be called bash.bashrc on some Linux distributions.)
crontab	Sets the cron environment and times for running automated tasks.
csh.cshrc (or cshrc)	Sets system-wide defaults for csh (C shell) users.
exports	Contains a list of local directories that are available to be shared by remote computers using the Network File System (NFS).
fstab	Identifies the devices for common storage media (hard disk, floppy, CD-ROM, and so on) and locations where they are mounted in the Linux system. This is used by the mount command to choose which file systems to mount when the system first boots.
group	Identifies group names and group IDs (GIDs) that are defined on the systems. Group permissions in Linux are defined by the second of three sets of rwx (read, write, execute) bits associated with each file and directory.
gshadow	Contains shadow passwords for groups.
host.conf	Sets the locations in which domain names (for example, redhat.com) are searched for on TCP/IP networks (such as the Internet). By default, the local hosts file is searched and then any name server entries in resolv.conf.
hosts	Contains IP addresses and hostnames that you can reach from your computer. (Usually this file is used just to store names of computers on your LAN or small private network.)
hosts.allow	Lists host computers that are allowed to use certain TCP/IP services from the local computer.
hosts.deny	Lists host computers that are *not* allowed to use certain TCP/IP services from the local computer (although this file will be used if you create it, it doesn't exist by default).

continued

143

TABLE 4-1 *(continued)*	
File	**Description**
inittab	Contains information that defines which programs start and stop when Linux boots, shuts down, or goes into different states in between. This is the most basic configuration file for starting Linux.
lilo.conf	Sets Linux boot loader (lilo) parameters to boot the computer. In particular, it lists information about bootable partitions on your computer. (If your distribution uses the GRUB boot loader, you may not see this file.)
modules.conf	Contains aliases and options related to loadable kernel modules used by your computer.
mtab	Contains a list of file systems that are currently mounted.
mtools.conf	Contains settings used by DOS tools in Linux.
named.conf	Contains DNS settings if you are running your own DNS server.
ntp.conf	Includes information needed to run the Network Time Protocol (NTP).
passwd	Stores account information for all valid users for the system. Also includes other information, such as the home directory and default shell. (Rarely includes the user passwords themselves, which are typically stored in the /etc/shadow file.)
printcap	Contains definitions for the printers configured for your computer. (If the printcap file doesn't exist, look for printer information in the /etc/cups directory.)
profile	Sets system-wide environment and startup programs for all users. This file is read when the user logs in.
protocols	Sets protocol numbers and names for a variety of Internet services.
resolv.conf	Identifies the locations of DNS name server computers that are used by TCP/IP to translate Internet *host.domain* names into IP addresses. (When a Web browser or mail client looks for an Internet site, it checks servers listed in this file to locate the site.)
rpc	Defines remote procedure call names and numbers.
services	Defines TCP/IP and UDP services and their port assignments.
shadow	Contains encrypted passwords for users who are defined in the passwd file. (This is viewed as a more secure way to store passwords than the original encrypted password in the passwd file. The passwd file needs to be publicly readable, whereas the shadow file can be unreadable by all but the root user.)
shells	Lists the shell command-line interpreters (bash, sh, csh, and so on) that are available on the system, as well as their locations.
sudoers	Sets commands that can be run by users, who may not otherwise have permission to run the command, using the sudo command. In particular, this file is used to provide selected users with root permission.

TABLE 4-1 (continued)	
File	**Description**
`syslog.conf`	Defines what logging messages are gathered by the syslogd daemon and what files they are stored in. (Typically, log messages are stored in files contained in the `/var/log` directory.)
`termcap`	Lists definitions for character terminals, so that character-based applications know what features are supported by a given terminal. Graphical terminals and applications have made this file obsolete to most people. (Termcap was the BSD UNIX way of storing terminal information; UNIX System V used definitions in `/usr/share/terminfo` files.)
`xinetd.conf`	Contains simple configuration information used by the xinetd daemon process. This file mostly points to the `/etc/xinetd.d` directory for information about individual services. (Some systems use the `inetd.conf` file and the inetd daemon instead.)

Another directory, `/etc/X11`, includes subdirectories that each contain system-wide configuration files used by X and different X window managers available for Linux. The `xorg.conf` file (which makes your computer and monitor usable with X) and configuration directories containing files used by `xdm` and `xinit` to start X are in here.

Directories relating to window managers contain files that include the default values that a user will get if that user starts one of these window managers on your system. Window managers that may have system-wide configuration files in these directories include Twm (`twm`).

 Some files and directories in `/etc/X11` are linked to locations in the `/usr/X11R6` directory.

Administrative Log Files

One of the things that Linux does well is keep track of itself. This is a good thing, when you consider how much is going on in a complex operating system. Sometimes you are trying to get a new facility to work and it fails without giving you the foggiest reason why. Other times you want to monitor your system to see if people are trying to access your computer illegally. In any of those cases, you can use log files to help track down the problem.

The main utilities for logging error and debugging messages for Linux are the syslogd and klogd daemons. General system logging is done by syslogd. Logging that is specific to kernel activity is done by klogd. Logging is done according to information in the `/etc/syslog.conf` file. Messages are typically directed to log files that are usually in the `/var/log` directory. Here are a few common log files:

- `boot.log` — Contains boot messages about services as they start up.
- `messages` — Contains many general informational messages about the system.
- `secure` — Contains security-related messages, such as login activity.
- `XFree86.0.log` or `Xorg.0.log` — Depending on which X server you are using, contains messages about your video card, mouse, and monitor configuration.

If you are using a Fedora Linux system, the System Log Viewer utility is a good way to step through your system's log files. From the System menu, select Administration ⇨ System Log. You not only can view boot, kernel, mail, security, and other system logs, but you can also use the viewing pane to select log messages from a particular date.

Using sudo and Other Administrative Logins

You don't hear much about other administrative logins (besides root) being used with Linux. It was a fairly common practice in UNIX systems to have several different administrative logins that allowed administrative tasks to be split among several users. For example, a person sitting near a printer could have lp permissions to move print jobs to another printer if he knew a printer wasn't working.

In any case, administrative logins are available with Linux, so you may want to look into using them. Here are some examples:

- **lp** — User can control some printing features. Having a separate lp administrator allows someone other than the superuser to do such things as move or remove lp logs and print spool files. The home directory for lp is /var/spool/lpd.

- **mail** — User can work with administrative e-mail features. The mail group, for many Linux systems, has group permissions to use mail files in /var/spool/mail (which is also often the mail user's home directory).

- **uucp** — User owns various uucp commands (once used as the primary method for dial-up serial communications) as well as log files in /var/log/uucp, spool files in /var/spool, administrative commands (such as uuchk, uucico, uuconv, and uuxqt) in /usr/sbin, and user commands (uucp, cu, uuname, uustat, and uux) in /usr/bin. The home directory for uucp is /var/spool/uucp.

- **bin** — User owns many commands in /bin in traditional UNIX systems. This is not the case in some Linux systems (such as Red Hat and Gentoo) because root owns most executable files. The home directory of bin is /bin.

- **news** — User could do administration of Internet news services, depending on how you set permission for /var/spool/news and other news-related resources. The home directory for news is /etc/news.

By default, the administrative logins in the preceding list are disabled. You would need to change the default shell from its current setting (usually /sbin/nologin or /bin/false) to a real shell (typically /bin/bash) to use these.

One way to give full or limited root privileges to any nonroot user is to set up the sudo facility, which simply entails adding the user to /etc/sudoers and defining what privilege you want that user to have. Then the user can run any command he or she is privileged to use by preceding that command with the sudo command.

Here's an example of how to use the sudo facility to give any users that are added to the wheel group full root privileges:

1. As the root user, edit the /etc/sudoers file by running the visudo command:

    ```
    # /usr/sbin/visudo
    ```

    By default, the file opens in vi, unless your EDITOR variable happens to be set to some other editor acceptable to visudo (for example, export EDITOR=gedit). The reason for using visudo is that the command locks the /etc/sudoers file and does some basic sanity checking of the file to ensure it has been edited correctly.

 **If you are stuck here, refer to the vi tutorial in Chapter 2 for information on using the vi editor.**

2. Uncomment the following line to allow users in the wheel group to have full root privileges on the computer:

    ```
    %wheel      ALL=(ALL)      ALL
    ```

TIP **If you look at the** sudoers **file in Ubuntu, you will see that this privilege exists, by default, for the admin group members.**

    This line causes users in the wheel group to provide a password (their own password, not the root password) in order to use administrative commands. To allow users in the wheel group to have that privilege without using a password, uncomment the following line instead:

    ```
    %wheel      ALL=(ALL)      NOPASSWD: ALL
    ```

3. Save the changes to the /etc/sudoers file (in vi, press **Esc**, and then type **ZZ**).
4. Still as root user, open the /etc/group file in any text editor and add to the wheel line any users you want to have root privilege. For example, if you were to add the users mary and jake to the wheel group, the line would appear as follows:

    ```
    wheel:x:10:root,mary,jake
    ```

Now users mary and jake can run the sudo command to run commands, or parts of commands, that are normally restricted to the root user. The following is an example of a session by the user jake after he has been assigned sudo privileges:

```
[jake]$ sudo umount /mnt/win

    We trust you have received the usual lecture
    from the local System Administrator. It usually
    boils down to these two things:

        #1) Respect the privacy of others.
        #2) Think before you type.

Password: *********
```

```
 [jake]$ umount /mnt/win
 mount: only root can mount /dev/sda1 on /mnt/win
 [jake]$ sudo umount /mnt/win
 [jake]$
```

In this session, the user jake runs the sudo command to unmount the /mnt/win file system (using the umount command). He is given a warning and asked to provide his password (this is jake's password, *not* the root password).

Even after jake has given the password, he must still use the sudo command to run subsequent administrative commands as root (the umount fails, but the sudo umount succeeds). Notice that he is not prompted for a password for the second sudo. That's because after entering his password successfully, he can enter as many sudo commands as he wants for the next 5 minutes without having to enter it again. (You can change the timeout value from 5 minutes to however long you want by setting the passwd_timeout value in the /etc/sudoers file.)

The preceding example grants a simple all-or-nothing administrative privilege to everyone you put in the wheel group. However, the /etc/sudoers file gives you an incredible amount of flexibility in permitting individual users and groups to use individual applications or groups of applications. Refer to the sudoers and sudo man pages for information about how to tune your sudo facility. Refer to the pam_wheel man page to see how the pam facility affects members of the wheel group.

Administering Your Linux System

Your system administrator duties don't end after you have installed Linux. If multiple people are using your Linux system, you, as administrator, must give each person his own login account. You'll use useradd and related commands to add, modify, and delete user accounts.

Configuring hardware is also on your duty list. When you add hardware to your Linux computer, that hardware is often detected and configured automatically. In some cases, however, the hardware may not have been set up properly, and you will use commands such as lsmod, modprobe, insmod, and rmmod to configure the right modules to get the hardware working.

> **NOTE** A *device driver* is the code permanently built into the kernel to allow application programs to talk to a particular piece of hardware. A *module* is like a driver, but it is loaded on demand. The section "Configuring Hardware" later in this chapter includes information about using these commands to configure modules.

Managing file systems and disk space is your responsibility, too. You must keep track of the disk space being consumed, especially if your Linux system is shared by multiple users. At some point, you may need to add a hard disk or track down what is eating up your disk space (you use commands such as find to do this).

Your duties also include monitoring system performance. You may have a runaway process on your system, or you may just be experiencing slow performance. Tools that come with Linux can help you determine how much of your CPU and memory is being consumed.

These tasks are explored in the rest of this chapter.

Creating User Accounts

Every person who uses your Linux system should have a separate user account. Having a user account provides each person with an area in which to securely store files, as well as a means of tailoring his or her user interface (GUI, path, environment variables, and so on) to suit the way that he or she uses the computer.

You can add user accounts to most Linux systems in several ways — Fedora and Red Hat Enterprise Linux systems use the system-config-users utility, for example, and SUSE offers a user setup module in YaST. This chapter describes how to add user accounts from the command line with useradd because most Linux systems include that command.

Adding Users with useradd

The most straightforward method for creating a new user from the shell is with the useradd command. After opening a Terminal window with root permission, you simply invoke useradd at the command prompt, with details of the new account as parameters.

The only required parameter is the login name of the user, but you probably want to include some additional information ahead of it. Each item of account information is preceded by a single letter option code with a dash in front of it. Table 4-2 lists the options available with useradd.

TABLE 4-2

useradd Command Options

Option	Description
-c comment -c "comment here"	Provide a description of the new user account. Often the person's full name. Replace comment with the name of the user account (-c jake). Use quotes to enter multiple words (-c "jake jackson").
-d home_dir	Set the home directory to use for the account. The default is to name it the same as the login name and to place it in /home. Replace home_dir with the directory name to use (for example, -d /mnt/homes/jake).
-D	Rather than create a new account, save the supplied information as the new default settings for any new accounts that are created.
-e expire_date	Assign the expiration date for the account in MM/DD/YYYY format. Replace expire_date with a date you want to use (-e 05/06/2008).
-f -1	Set the number of days after a password expires until the account is permanently disabled. The default, -1, disables the option. Setting this to 0 disables the account immediately after the password has expired. Replace -1 with the number to use.
-g group	Set the primary group (as listed in the /etc/group file) the new user will be in. Replace group with the group name (-g wheel).

continued

149

TABLE 4-2	*(continued)*
Option	**Description**
`-G grouplist`	Add the new user to the supplied comma-separated list of groups (`-G wheel,sales,tech,lunch`).
`-k skel_dir`	Set the skeleton directory containing initial configuration files and login scripts that should be copied to a new user's home directory. This parameter can be used only in conjunction with the `-m` option. Replace `skel_dir` with the directory name to use. (Without this option, the `/etc/skel` directory is used.)
`-m`	Automatically create the user's home directory and copy the files in the skeleton directory (`/etc/skel`) to it.
`-M`	Do not create the new user's home directory, even if the default behavior is set to create it.
`-n`	Turn off the default behavior of creating a new group that matches the name and user ID of the new user. This option is available with Red Hat Linux systems. Other Linux systems often assign a new user to the group named users instead.
`-o`	Use with `-u uid` to create a user account that has the same UID as another username. (This effectively lets you have two different usernames with authority over the same set of files and directories.)
`-p passwd`	Enter a password for the account you are adding. This must be an encrypted password. Instead of adding an encrypted password here, you can simply use the `passwd user` command later to add a password for `user`.
`-s shell`	Specify the command shell to use for this account. Replace `shell` with the command shell (`-s bash`).
`-u user_id`	Specify the user ID number for the account (`-u 474`). Without the `-u` option, the default behavior is to automatically assign the next available number. Replace `user_id` with the ID number (`-u`).

For example, let's create an account for a new user named Mary Smith with a login name of mary. First, log in as root, and then type the following command:

```
# useradd -c "Mary Smith" mary
```

TIP When you choose a username, don't begin with a number (for example, 26jsmith). Also, it's best to use all lowercase letters, no control characters or spaces, and a maximum of 8 characters. The `useradd` command allows up to 32 characters, but some applications can't deal with usernames that long. Tools such as `ps` display UIDs instead of names if names are too long. Having users named Jsmith and jsmith can cause confusion with programs (such as sendmail) that don't distinguish case.

Next, set mary's initial password using the `passwd` command. You're prompted to type the password twice:

```
# passwd mary
Changing password for user mary.
New password: *******
Retype new password: *******
```

Asterisks in this example represent the password you type. Nothing is actually displayed when you type the password. Also keep in mind that running `passwd` as root user lets you add short or blank passwords that regular users cannot add themselves.

In creating the account for mary, the `useradd` command performs several actions:

- Reads the `/etc/login.defs` file to get default values to use when creating accounts.
- Checks command-line parameters to find out which default values to override.
- Creates a new user entry in the `/etc/passwd` and `/etc/shadow` files based on the default values and command-line parameters.
- Creates any new group entries in the `/etc/group` file. (Fedora creates a group using the new user's name; Gentoo adds the user to the users group; and SUSE adds it to every group you set for new users, such as dialout, audio, video, and other services.)
- Creates a home directory, based on the user's name, in the `/home` directory.
- Copies any files located within the `/etc/skel` directory to the new home directory. This usually includes login and application startup scripts.

The preceding example uses only a few of the available `useradd` options. Most account settings are assigned using default values. You can set more values explicitly, if you want to; here's an example that uses a few more options to do so:

```
# useradd -g users -G wheel,apache -s /bin/tcsh -c "Mary Smith" mary
```

In this case, `useradd` is told to make `users` the primary group mary belongs to (`-g`), add her to the wheel and apache groups, and assign tcsh as her primary command shell (`-s`). A home directory in `/home` under the user's name (`/home/mary`) is created by default. This command line results in a line similar to the following being added to the `/etc/passwd` file:

```
mary:x:502:100:Mary Smith:/home/mary:/bin/tcsh
```

Each line in the `/etc/passwd` file represents a single user account record. Each field is separated from the next by a colon (:) character. The field's position in the sequence determines what it is. As you can see, the login name is first. Again, the password field contains an x because we are using a shadow password file to store encrypted password data. The user ID selected by `useradd` is 502.

The primary group ID is 100, which corresponds to the users group in the /etc/group file. The comment field was correctly set to Mary Smith, the home directory was automatically assigned as /home/mary, and the command shell was assigned as /bin/tcsh, exactly as specified with the useradd options.

By leaving out many of the options (as I did in the first useradd example), defaults are assigned in most cases. For example, by not using -g users or -G wheel,apache, in Fedora a group named mary would have been created and assigned to the new user. Other Linux systems assign users as the group name by default. Likewise, excluding -s /bin/tcsh causes /bin/bash to be assigned as the default shell.

The /etc/group file holds information about the different groups on your Linux system and the users who belong to them. Groups are useful for enabling multiple users to share access to the same files while denying access to others. Peek at the /etc/group file, and you find something similar to this:

```
bin:x:1:root,bin,daemon
daemon:x:2:root,bin,daemon
sys:x:3:root,bin,adm
adm:x:4:root,adm,daemon
tty:x:5:
disk:x:6:root
lp:x:7:daemon,lp
mem:x:8:
kmem:x:9:
wheel:x:10:root,joe,mary
apache:x:48:mary
      .
      .
      .
nobody:x:99:
users:x:100:
chris:x:500
sheree:x:501
```

Each line in the group file contains the name of a group, the group ID number associated with it, and a list of users in that group. By default, each user is added to his or her own group, beginning with GID 500. Note that mary was added to the wheel and apache groups instead of having her own group.

It is actually rather significant that mary was added to the wheel group. By doing this, you grant her the capability to use the sudo command to run commands as the root user (provided that sudo is configured as described earlier in this chapter).

Setting User Defaults

The useradd command determines the default values for new accounts by reading the /etc/login.defs file. You can modify those defaults by either editing that file manually with a standard text editor or by running the useradd command with the -D option. Although `login.defs` is different on different Linux systems, here is an example containing many of the settings you might find in a `login.defs` file:

```
PASS_MAX_DAYS     99999
PASS_MIN_DAYS     0
PASS_MIN_LEN      5
PASS_WARN_AGE     7

UID_MIN                   500
UID_MAX                 60000
GID_MIN                   500
GID_MAX                 60000

CREATE_HOME yes
```

All uncommented lines contain keyword/value pairs. For example, the keyword `PASS_MIN_LEN` is followed by some white space and the value 5. This tells `useradd` that the user password must be at least five characters. Other lines let you customize the valid range of automatically assigned user ID numbers or group ID numbers. (Fedora starts at UID 500; other Linuxes start with UID 100.) A comment section that explains that keyword's purpose precedes each keyword (which I edited out here to save space). Altering a default value is as simple as editing the value associated with a keyword and then saving the file.

If you want to view the defaults, type the `useradd` command with the `-D` option, as follows:

```
# useradd -D
GROUP=100
HOME=/home
INACTIVE=-1
EXPIRE-
SHELL=/bin/bash
SKEL=/etc/skel
```

You can also use the `-D` option to change defaults. When run with this flag, `useradd` refrains from actually creating a new user account; instead, it saves any additionally supplied options as the new default values in `/etc/login.defs`. Not all `useradd` options can be used in conjunction with the `-D` option. You can use only the five options listed in Table 4-3.

TABLE 4-3

useradd Options for Changing User Defaults

Options	Description
`-b default_home`	Set the default directory in which user home directories are created. Replace `default_home` with the directory name to use (`-b garage`). Usually this is `/home`.
`-e default_expire_date`	Set the default expiration date on which the user account is disabled. The `default_expire_date` value should be replaced with a date in the form MM/DD/YYYY (`-e 10/15/2008`).

continued

TABLE 4-3 *(continued)*	
Option	**Description**
`-f default_inactive`	Set the number of days after a password has expired before the account is disabled. Replace `default_inactive` with a number representing the number of days (`-f 7`).
`-g default_group`	Set the default group that new users will be placed in. Typically, `useradd` creates a new group with the same name and ID number as the user. Replace `default_group` with the group name to use (`-g bears`).
`-s default_shell`	Set the default shell for new users. Normally this is `/bin/bash`. Replace `default_shell` with the full path to the shell that you want as the default for new users (`-s /bin/ash`).

To set any of the defaults, give the `-D` option first, and then add the defaults you want to set. For example, to set the default home directory location to `/home/everyone` and the default shell to `/bin/tcsh`, type the following:

```
# useradd -D -b /home/everyone -s /bin/tcsh
```

Besides setting up user defaults, an administrator can create default files that are copied to each user's home directory for use. These files can include login scripts and shell configuration files (such as `.bashrc`).

Other commands that are useful for working with user accounts include `usermod` (to modify settings for an existing account) and `userdel` (to delete an existing user account).

Modifying Users with usermod

The `usermod` command provides a simple and straightforward method for changing account parameters. Many of the options available with it mirror those found in `useradd`. Table 4-4 lists the options that can be used with this command.

TABLE 4-4	
usermod Options	
Option	**Description**
`-c username`	Change the description associated with the user account. Replace `username` with the name of the user account (`-c jake`). Use quotes to enter multiple words (`-c "jake jackson"`).
`-d home_dir`	Change the home directory to use for the account. The default is to name it the same as the login name and to place it in `/home`. Replace `home_dir` with the directory name to use (for example, `-d /mnt/homes/jake`).

TABLE 4-4	(continued)
Option	**Description**
-e *expire_date*	Assign a new expiration date for the account in MM/DD/YYYY format. Replace *expire_date* with a date you want to use (-e 05/06/2008).
-f *-1*	Change the number of days after a password expires until the account is permanently disabled. The default, -1, disables the option. Setting this to 0 disables the account immediately after the password has expired. Replace *-1* with the number to use.
-g *group*	Change the primary group (as listed in the /etc/group file) the user will be in. Replace *group* with the group name (-g wheel).
-G *grouplist*	Add the user to the supplied comma-separated list of groups (-G wheel,sales,tech,lunch).
-l *login_name*	Change the login name of the account.
-m	Available only when -d is used, this causes the contents of the user's home directory to be copied to the new directory.
-o	Use only with -u uid to remove the restriction that UIDs must be unique.
-s *shell*	Specify a different command shell to use for this account. Replace *shell* with the command shell (-s bash).
-u *user_id*	Change the user ID number for the account. Replace *user_id* with the ID number (-u 474).

As an example, to change the shell to the csh shell for the user named chris, type the following as root user from a shell:

```
# usermod -s /bin/csh chris
```

Deleting Users with userdel

Just as usermod is used to modify user settings and useradd is used to create users, userdel is used to remove users. The following command will remove the user chris:

```
# userdel chris
```

The only option available with this utility is -r, which is used to remove not only the user, but also their home directory:

```
# userdel -r chris
```

Configuring Hardware

In a perfect world, after installing and booting Linux, all of your hardware is detected and available for access. Although many Linux systems are rapidly moving closer to that world, there are times when you must take special steps to get your computer hardware working. Also, the growing use of removable USB and FireWire devices (CDs, DVDs, flash drives, digital cameras, and removable hard drives) has made it important for Linux to:

- Efficiently manage hardware that comes and goes.
- Look at the same piece of hardware in different ways (for example, be able to see a printer as a fax machine, scanner, and storage device, as well as a printer).

If you are using a Linux system that includes the 2.6 kernel (as the latest versions of most major Linux systems do), new kernel features have made it possible to change drastically the way hardware devices are detected and managed. Features in, or closely related to, the kernel include *Udev* (to dynamically name and create devices as hardware comes and goes), and *Hotplug* and *HAL* (to pass information about hardware changes to user space). Then features such as *fstab-sync* and *gnome-volume-manager* are used to react to hardware changes (for example, to mount a device or launch an application to read the device).

If all this sounds a bit confusing, don't worry. It's actually designed to make your life as a Linux user much easier. The end result of features built on the 2.6 kernel is that device handling in Linux has become:

- **More automatic** — For most common hardware, when a hardware device is connected or disconnected, it is automatically detected and identified. Interfaces to access the hardware are added, so it is accessible to Linux. Then the fact that the hardware is present (or removed) is passed to the user level, where applications listening for hardware changes are ready to mount the hardware and/or launch an application (such as an image viewer or music player).
- **More flexible** — If you don't like what happens automatically when a hardware item is connected or disconnected, you can change it. For example, features built into GNOME and KDE desktops let you choose what happens when a music CD or movie DVD is inserted, or when a digital camera is connected. If you prefer a different program be launched to handle it, you can easily make that change.

This section covers several issues relating to getting your hardware working properly in Linux. First, it describes how to configure Linux to deal with removable media. Then it tells how to use tools for manually loading and working with drivers for hardware that is not detected and loaded properly.

Managing Removable Hardware

Linux systems such as SUSE, RHEL, Fedora, and others that support full KDE and GNOME desktop environments include simple graphical tools for configuring what happens when you attach popular removable devices to the computer. So, with a KDE or GNOME desktop running, you simply plug in a USB device or insert a CD or DVD, and a window may pop up to deal with that device.

Although different desktop environments share many of the same underlying mechanisms (Udev and Hotplug) to detect and name removable hardware, they offer different tools for configuring how they are mounted or used. Udev (using the udevd daemon) creates and removes devices

(/dev directory) as hardware is added and removed from the computer. The Hardware Abstraction layer (HAL) provides the overall platform for discovering and configuring hardware. Settings that are of interest to someone using a desktop Linux system, however, can be configured with easy-to-use desktop tools.

The following sections describe how removable hardware and media are configured, using a GNOME desktop in Fedora or a KDE desktop in SUSE.

Removable Media on a GNOME Desktop

The GNOME desktop offers the Removable Drives and Media Preferences window to define what happens when you attach removable devices or insert removable media into the computer. The descriptions in this section are based on GNOME 2.16.

From a GNOME desktop, select System ➪ Preferences ➪ Removable Drives and Media to see how your system is configured to handle removable hardware and media. Figure 4-3 shows an example of that window.

FIGURE 4-3

Change removable hardware and media settings in GNOME.

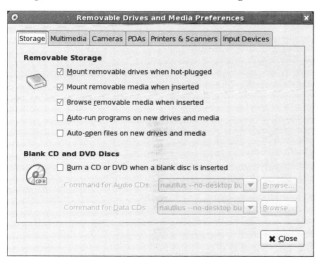

The following settings are available from the Removable Drives and Media Preferences window on the Storage tab. These settings relate to how removable media are handled when they are inserted or plugged in:

■ **Mount removable drives when hot-plugged** — When a removable drive (such as a USB hard drive) is plugged into a running system, that drive is automatically mounted in a subdirectory of /media.

■ **Mount removable media when inserted** — When a removable medium (such as a CD or DVD) is inserted into a drive, the medium is automatically mounted to a subdirectory of /media that is based on the medium's volume ID.

■ **Browse removable media when inserted** — After a removable medium is inserted and mounted, a Nautilus window opens to display the contents of that medium.

■ **Auto-run programs on new drives and media** — After a removable medium is inserted and mounted, auto-run any program in the top-level directory of the medium that is named .autorun, autorun, or autorun.sh.

■ **Auto-open files on new drives and media** — After a removable medium is inserted and mounted, open any file in the top-level directory of the medium that is named .autoopen or autoopen.

■ **Burn a CD or DVD when a blank disc is inserted** — When a blank CD or DVD is inserted, you are asked if you want to make an audio CD or data CD. Either selection opens a CD/DVD Creator Nautilus window for you to drag-and-drop files on. Click Write to Disc when you are done, and the files are burned to that medium.

Note that the settings described here are only in effect for the user that is currently logged in. So if multiple users have login accounts, each can have his or her own way of handling removable media.

The following settings are available from the Removable Drives and Media Preferences window on the Multimedia tab:

■ **Audio CD** — When an audio CD is inserted, the Totem player opens and starts playing the music found on the disk. You can change to a different audio player by changing the command, or you can clear the "Play audio CD discs when inserted" check box to not have audio play automatically. Some people prefer to use GNOME-CD as their CD player.

■ **Video DVD Discs** — The Totem player is started, by default, when you insert a commercial video DVD disk into the DVD drive.

> **NOTE** The Totem movie player will not play movie DVDs unless you add extra software to decrypt the DVD. There are legal issues and other movie player options you should look into if you want to play commercial DVD movies from Linux. See Chapter 20 for more information about video players in Linux.

■ **Portable Music Players** — A music player is started in Linux to play files from your portable iPod or other music player, if this is selected and you enter a player to use. The banshee project (http://banshee-project.org) includes software for playing music from iPods in Linux. (From Fedora, type **yum install banshee** to install the software from Fedora Extras. Then add **ipod %d** to this field to use the player.)

From the Cameras tab, the following settings are available:

■ **Digital Camera** — Connect a digital camera, and the gThumb Image Viewer (gthumb-import command) will open, ready to import digital images from your camera. You can have other commands open the folder of digital images from your camera by replacing the gthumb-import command with an image viewer or import application you prefer.

- **Digital Video Camera** — When a digital video camera is detected, you can select to have a command you choose open the contents of that camera in a digital video editor such as Kino (`www.kinodv.org`).

Although there are no other commands set to launch automatically for other types of devices, there are several types of devices you can configure. From the PDAs tab, you can select what commands to run if a Palm or PocketPC is connected to your computer. From the other tabs, you can indicate what to do when USB printers, scanners, mice, keyboards, or tablets are connected.

Removable Media on a SUSE KDE Desktop

When you insert a removable medium (CD or DVD) or plug in a removable device (digital camera or USB flash drive) from a KDE desktop in SUSE, a window opens to let you choose the type of action to take on it. If you want to add a different action, or change an existing action, click the Configure button.

Figure 4-4 shows an example of the window that appears when a 32MB USB flash drive is inserted, as well as the KDE Control Module that appears when Configure is selected.

FIGURE 4-4

Use the KDE Control Module to set how to respond to inserted media.

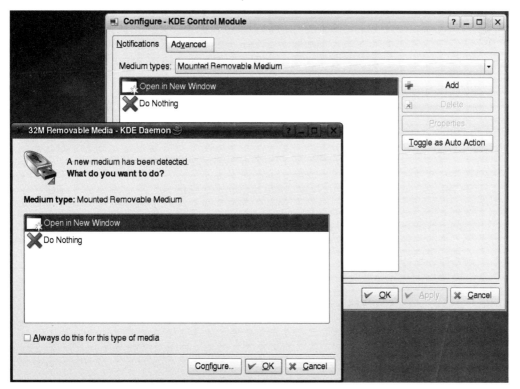

From the KDE Control Module, select the media type you want to change (in this case, Mounted Removable Medium). Click Add, and then select the type of action you would like to add as an option when that type of media is detected.

Working with Loadable Modules

If you have added hardware to your computer that isn't properly detected, you might need to manually load a module for that hardware. Linux comes with a set of commands for loading, unloading, and getting information about hardware modules.

If you have installed the Linux kernel source code, source code files for available drivers are stored in subdirectories of the /usr/src/linux*/drivers directory. You can find information about these drivers in a couple of ways:

- make xconfig — With /usr/src/linux* as your current directory, type **make xconfig** from a Terminal window on the desktop. Select the category of module you want and then click Help next to the driver that interests you. The help information that appears includes a description of the driver. (If your system is missing graphical libraries needed to run make xconfig, try make menuconfig instead.)

- **Documentation** — The /usr/src/linux*/Documentation directory contains lots of plain-text files describing different aspects of the kernel and related drivers.

After modules have been built, they are installed in the /lib/modules/ subdirectories. The name of the directory is based on the release number of the kernel that the modules were compiled for. Modules that are in that directory can then be loaded and unloaded as they are needed. Before building modules for a new kernel, or more important, a current kernel, it may be wise to add your initials to the kernel Makefile under the variable EXTRAVERSION at the top of the Makefile. This installs your new modules under /lib/modules/kernel-version with the EXTRAVERSION suffixed to the directory. If you completely wreck the module build, you haven't overwritten the current modules you may be running. It also makes it easier to identify custom kernel modules when debugging.

Listing Loaded Modules

To see which modules are currently loaded into the running kernel on your computer, use the lsmod command. Here's an example:

```
# lsmod
Module                    Size   Used by
snd_seq_oss              38912   0
snd_seq_midi_event        9344   1 snd_seq_oss
snd_seq                  67728   4
snd_seq_oss,snd_seq_midi_event
```

```
snd_seq_device         8328   2 snd_seq_oss,snd_seq
.
.
.
autofs                16512   0
ne2k_pci               9056   0
8390                  13568   1 ne2k_pci
ohci1394              41860   0
ieee1394             284464   1 ohci1394
floppy                65712   0
sg                    36120   0
scsi_mod             124600   1 sg
parport_pc            39724   0
parport               47336   1 parport_pc
ext3                 128424   2
jbd                   86040   1 ext3
```

> **NOTE** If you don't have a Linux system installed yet, try booting KNOPPIX and using lsmod to list your loaded modules. If all your hardware is working properly, write down the list of modules. Later, when you permanently install Fedora or some other Linux system, if your CD drive, modem, video card, or other hardware doesn't work properly, you can use your list of modules to determine which module should have been used and load it, as described in the next section.

This output shows a variety of modules that have been loaded on a Linux system, including several to support the ALSA sound system, some of which provide OSS compatibility (snd_seq_oss).

To find information about any of the loaded modules, use the modinfo command. For example, you could type the following:

```
# /sbin/modinfo -d snd-seq-oss
"OSS-compatible sequencer module"
```

Not all modules have descriptions available and if nothing is available, no data will be returned. In this case, however, the snd-seq-oss module is described as an OSS-compatible sequencer module. You can also use the -a option to see the author of the module, or -n to see the object file representing the module. The author information often has the e-mail address of the driver's creator, so you can contact the author if you have problems or questions about it.

Loading Modules

You can load any module that has been compiled and installed (to the /lib/modules directory) into your running kernel using the modprobe command. A common reason for loading a module is to use a feature temporarily (such as loading a module to support a special file system on a floppy you want to access). Another reason is to identify a module that will be used by a particular piece of hardware that could not be autodetected.

Here is an example of the `modprobe` command being used to load the parport module, which provides the core functions to share parallel ports with multiple devices:

```
# modprobe parport
```

After parport is loaded, you can load the parport_pc module to define the PC-style ports available through the interface. The parport_pc module lets you optionally define the addresses and IRQ numbers associated with each device sharing the parallel port. For example:

```
# modprobe parport_pc io=0x3bc irq=auto
```

In this example, a device is identified as having an address of `0x3bc`, and the IRQ for the device is autodetected.

The `modprobe` command loads modules temporarily — they disappear at the next reboot. To permanently add the module to your system, add the `modprobe` command line to one of the startup scripts run at boot time. You can also add modules to the `/etc/modules` file to have them loaded at startup.

> **NOTE** An alternative to `modprobe` is the `insmod` command. The advantage of using `modprobe`, however, is that `insmod` loads only the module you request, whereas `modprobe` tries to load other modules that the one you requested is dependent on.

Removing Modules

Use the `rmmod` command to remove a module from a running kernel. For example, to remove the module parport_pc from the current kernel, type the following:

```
# rmmod parport_pc
```

If it is not currently busy, the parport_pc module is removed from the running kernel. If it is busy, try killing any process that might be using the device. Then run `rmmod` again. Sometimes, the module you are trying to remove depends on other modules that may be loaded. For instance, the `usbcore` module cannot be unloaded while the USB printer module (`usblp`) is loaded, as shown here:

```
# rmmod usbcore
ERROR: Module usbcore is in use by wacom,usblp,ehci_hcd,ohci_hcd
```

Managing File Systems and Disk Space

File systems in Linux are organized in a hierarchy, beginning from root (/) and continuing downward in a structure of directories and subdirectories. As an administrator of a Linux system, it's your duty to make sure that all the disk drives that represent your file system are available to the users of the computer. It is also your job to make sure there is enough disk space in the right places in the file system for users to store what they need.

File systems are organized differently in Linux than they are in Microsoft Windows operating systems. Instead of drive letters (for example, A:, B:, C:) for each local disk, network file system, CD-ROM, or other type of storage medium, everything fits neatly into the directory structure.

Some drives are connected (mounted) automatically into the file system. For example, a CD might be mounted on /media/cdrom. If the drive isn't mounted automatically, it is up to an administrator to create a mount point in the file system and then connect the disk to that point.

The organization of your file system begins when you install Linux. Part of the installation process is to divide your hard disk (or disks) into partitions. Those partitions can then be assigned to:

- A part of the Linux file system
- Swap space for Linux
- Other file system types (perhaps containing other bootable operating systems)
- Free space (you can leave space unassigned so you can format it later as you need it)

This chapter focuses on partitions that are used for the Linux file system. To see what partitions are currently set up on partitions that the Linux kernel has detected, use the fdisk command:

```
# /sbin/fdisk -l

Disk /dev/sda:  40.0 GB, 40020664320 bytes
255 heads, 63 sectors/track, 4825 cylinders
Units = cylinders of 16065 * 512 bytes = 8225280 bytes

   Device Boot      Start         End      Blocks   Id  System
/dev/sda1   *           1          13         104    b  Win95 FAT32
/dev/sda2              84          89       48195   83  Linux
/dev/sda3              90         522    3478072+   83  Linux
/dev/sda4             523         554      257040    5  Extended
/dev/sda5             523         554     257008+   82  Linux swap
```

This output shows the disk partitioning for a computer capable of running both Linux and Microsoft Windows. You can see that the Linux partition on /dev/sda3 has most of the space available for data. There is a Windows partition (/dev/sda1) and a Linux swap partition (/dev/sda5). There is also a small /boot partition (46MB) on /dev/sda2. In this case, the root partition for Linux has 3.3GB of disk space and resides on /dev/sda3. Fdisk -l uses partition information found in /proc/partitions unless explicitly given on the command line.

Next use the mount command (with no options) to see what partitions are actually being used for your Linux system (which available disk partitions are actually mounted and where they are mounted):

```
# mount
/dev/sda3 on / type ext3 (rw)
/dev/sda2 on /boot type ext3 (rw)
/dev/sda1 on /mnt/win type vfat (rw)
/dev/proc on /proc type proc (rw)
/dev/sys on /sys type sysfs (rw)
/dev/devpts on /dev/pts type devpts (rw,gid=5,mode=620)
```

```
/dev/shm on /dev/shm type tmpfs (rw)
none on /proc/sys/fs/binfmt_misc type binfmt_misc (rw)
/dev/cdrom on /media/cdrecorder type iso9660 (ro,nosuid,nodev)
```

Although some of the file systems shown as mounted are for special purposes (/sys, /proc, and others), our concern here is with disk partition (/dev/hd*, /dev/sd*, and so on). The mounted Linux partitions in this case are /dev/sda2, which provides space for the /boot directory (contains data for booting Linux), and /dev/sda3, which provides space for the rest of the Linux file system beginning from the root directory (/).

This particular system also contains a Windows partition that was mounted in the /mnt/win directory and a CD that was mounted in /media/cdrecorder. (With most GUI interfaces, the CD is typically mounted automatically when you insert it. For 2.6 kernels, look in the /media directory; for 2.4 kernels the /mnt directory is often used.)

After the word type, you can see the type of file system contained on the device. (See the description of different file system types in Table 4-5.) Particularly on larger Linux systems, you may have multiple partitions for several reasons:

- **Multiple hard disks** — You may have several hard disks available to your users. In that case you would have to mount each disk (and possibly several partitions from each disk) in different locations in your file system.

- **Protecting different parts of the file system** — If the users on a system consume all of the file system space, the entire system can fail. For example, there may be no place for temporary files to be copied (so the programs writing to temporary files fail), and incoming mail may fail to be written to mail boxes. With multiple mounted partitions, if one partition runs out of space, the others can continue to work.

- **Multiple operating systems** — You can configure your disk to contain multiple partitions that can each be used to hold a different operating system type. For example, if you started with a computer that had Windows on the hard disk, you could put Linux on a separate partition, and then set up the computer to boot either operating system.

- **Backups** — Some fast ways exist to back up data from your computer that involve copying the entire image of a disk or partition. If you want to restore that partition later, you can simply copy it back (bit by bit) to a hard disk. With smaller partitions, this approach can be done fairly efficiently.

- **Protecting from disk failure** — If one disk (or part of one disk) fails, having multiple partitions mounted on your file system may let you continue working and just fix the one disk that fails. Ghost for Linux (http://freshmeat.net/projects/g4l) is an example of a tool for backing up a hard disk partition in Linux.

When a disk partition is mounted on the Linux file system, all directories and subdirectories below that mount point are stored on that partition. So, for example, if you were to mount one partition on / and one on /usr, everything below the /usr mount point would be stored on the second partition, while everything else would be stored on the first partition. If you then mounted another partition on /usr/local, everything below that mount point would be on the third partition, while everything else below /usr would be on the second partition.

What happens if a remote file system is unmounted from your computer, and you go to save a file in that mount point directory? You will write the file to that directory, and it will be stored on your local hard disk. When the remote file system is remounted, however, the file you saved will seem to disappear. To get the file back, you'll have to unmount the remote file system (causing the file to reappear), move the file to another location, remount the file system, and copy the file back there.

Mount points often mentioned as being candidates for separate partitions include /, /boot, /home, /usr, and /var. The root file system (/) is the catchall for directories that aren't in other mount points. The root file system's mount point (/) is the only one that is required. The /boot directory holds the images needed to boot the operating system. The /home file system is where all the user accounts are typically stored. Applications and documentation are stored in /usr. Below the /var mount point is where log files, temporary files, server files (Web, FTP, and so on), and lock files are stored (that is, items that need disk space for your computer's applications to keep running).

The fact that multiple partitions are mounted on your file system is invisible to people using your Linux system. It is an issue only when a partition runs out of space or if users need to save or use information from a particular device (such as a floppy disk or remote file system) that isn't mounted. Of course, any user can check this by typing the mount command.

Mounting File Systems

Most of your hard disks are mounted automatically for you. When you install Fedora, Ubuntu, SUSE, or some other Linux systems, you are asked to create partitions and indicate the mount points for those partitions. (Other Linux installation procedures will expect you to know that you have to partition before beginning.) When you boot Linux, all Linux partitions residing on hard disk that are listed in your /etc/fstab file are typically mounted. For that reason, this section focuses mostly on how to mount other types of devices so that they become part of your Linux file system.

The mount command is used not only to mount devices, but also to mount other kinds of file systems on your Linux system. This means that you can store files from other operating systems or use file systems that are appropriate for certain kinds of activities (such as writing large block sizes). The most common use of this feature for the average Linux user, however, is to enable that user to obtain and work with files from floppy disks, CD-ROMs, or other removable media.

With the addition of automatic mounting features and changes in how removable media are identified with the Linux 2.6 kernel (see descriptions of Udev and HAL earlier in this chapter), you no longer need to manually mount removable media for many Linux desktop systems. Understanding how to manually mount and unmount file systems on a Linux server, however, can be a very useful skill.

Supported File Systems

To see file system types that are currently available to be used on your system, type **cat /proc/ filesystems**. Table 4-5 shows the file system types that are supported in Linux, although they may not be in use at the moment, or they may not be built into your current kernel (so they may need to be loaded as modules).

TABLE 4-5

Supported File System Types

Type	Description
adfs	Acorn disk file system, which is the standard file system used on RiscOS operating systems.
befs	File system used by the BeOS operating system.
cifs	Common Internet File System (CIFS), the virtual file system used to access servers that comply with the SNIA CIFS specification. CIFS is an attempt to refine and standardize the SMB protocol used by Samba and Windows file sharing.
ext3	Ext file systems are the most common in Red Hat and many other Linux systems. The ext3 file system, also called the Third Extended file system, includes journaling features that, compared to ext2, improve a file system's capability to recover from crashes.
ext2	The default file system type for earlier Linux systems. Features are the same as ext3, except that ext2 doesn't include journaling features.
ext	This is the first version of ext3. It is not used very often anymore.
iso9660	Evolved from the High Sierra file system (the original standard for CD-ROMs). Extensions to the High Sierra standard (called Rock Ridge extensions) allow iso9660 file systems to support long filenames and UNIX-style information (such as file permissions, ownership, and links). Data CD-ROMs typically use this file system type.
kafs	AFS client file system. Used in distributed computing environments to share files with Linux, Windows, and Macintosh clients.
minix	Minix file system type, used originally with the Minix version of UNIX. It supports filenames of up to only 30 characters.
msdos	An MS-DOS file system. You can use this type to mount floppy disks that come from Microsoft operating systems.
vfat	Microsoft extended FAT (VFAT) file system.
umsdos	An MS-DOS file system with extensions to allow features that are similar to UNIX (including long filenames).
proc	Not a real file system, but rather a file system interface to the Linux kernel. You probably won't do anything special to set up a proc file system. However, the /proc mount point should be a proc file system. Many utilities rely on /proc to gain access to Linux kernel information.
reiserfs	ReiserFS journaled file system. ReiserFS and ext3 are the most common file system types used with Linux today.
swap	Used for swap partitions. Swap areas are used to hold data temporarily when RAM is currently used up. Data is swapped to the swap area and then returned to RAM when it is needed again.
squashfs	Compressed, read-only file system type. Squashfs is popular on live CDs, where there is limited space and a read-only medium (such as a CD or DVD).

TABLE 4-5	*(continued)*
Type	**Description**
nfs	Network File System (NFS) used to mount file systems on other Linux or UNIX computers.
hpfs	File system used to do read-only mounts of an OS/2 HPFS file system.
ncpfs	This relates to Novell NetWare file systems. NetWare file systems can be mounted over a network.
ntfs	Windows NT file system. Depending upon the distribution you have, it may be supported as a read-only file system (so that you can mount and copy files from it).
affs	File system used with Amiga computers.
ufs	File system popular on Sun Microsystems operating systems (that is, Solaris and SunOS).

If you want to use a file system type that is not currently shown as available on your system (when you type `cat /proc/filesystems`), try using `modprobe` to load the module for that file systems. For example, `modprobe ufs` adds the UFS file system type to the running kernel. Type **man fs** to see descriptions of Linux file systems.

Using the fstab File to Define Mountable File Systems

The hard disk partitions on your local computer and the remote file systems you use every day are probably set up to automatically mount when you boot Linux. The `/etc/fstab` file contains definitions for each partition, along with options describing how the partition is mounted. Here's an example of an `/etc/fstab` file:

```
LABEL=/          /                ext3           defaults             1 1
LABEL=/boot      /boot            ext3           defaults             1 2
/dev/devpts      /dev/pts         devpts         gid=5,mode=620       0 0
/dev/shm         /dev/shm         tmpfs          defaults             0 0
/dev/proc        /proc            proc           defaults             0 0
/dev/sys         /sys             sysfs          defaults             0 0
/dev/sda5        swap             swap           defaults             0 0
/dev/cdrom       /media/cdrecorder udf,iso9660   exec,noauto,managed  0 0
/dev/sda1        /mnt/win         vfat           noauto               0 0
/dev/fd0         /mnt/floppy      auto           noauto,owner         0 0
```

All partitions listed in this file are mounted at boot time, except for those set to `noauto` in the fourth field. In this example, the root (`/`) and boot (`/boot`) hard disk partitions are mounted at boot time, along with the `/dev/pts`, `/dev/shm`, `/dev/sys`, `/dev/shm`, and `/proc` file systems (which are not associated with particular storage devices). The CD drive (`/dev/cdrom`) and floppy disk (`/dev/fd0`) drives are not mounted at boot time. Definitions are put in the `fstab` file for floppy and CD drives so that they can be mounted in the future (as described later).

I also added one line for `/dev/sda1`, which enables me to mount the Windows (vfat) partition on my computer so I don't have to always boot Windows to get at the files on my Windows partition.

COMING FROM WINDOWS   Most Windows systems today use the NTFS file system. Support for this system, how-ever, is not delivered with every Linux system. NTFS support was added to the Fedora repository in Fedora 7 with the ntfs-3g package. Other NTFS support is available from the Linux-NTFS project (www.linux-ntfs.org/).

If your computer is configured to dual boot Linux and Windows, you can mount your Windows file system to make it available in Linux. To access your Windows partition, you must first create the mount point (in this example, by typing **mkdir /mnt/win**). Then you can mount it when you choose by typing (as root) **mount /mnt/win.**

Different Linux distributions will set up their fstab file differently. Some don't use labels and many others don't use a separate /boot partition by default. They will just have a swap partition and have all user data under the root partition (/).

Here is what's in each field of the fstab file:

- **Field 1** — The name of the device representing the file system. This field can include the LABEL option, with which you can indicate a universally unique identifier (UUID) or volume label instead of a device name. The advantage to this approach is that because the partition is identified by volume name, you can move a volume to a different device name and not have to change the fstab file.

- **Field 2** — The mount point in the file system. The file system contains all data from the mount point down the directory tree structure unless another file system is mounted at some point beneath it.

- **Field 3** — The file system type. Valid file system types are described in the section "Supported File Systems" earlier in this chapter.

- **Field 4** — Options to the mount command. In the preceding example, the noauto option prevents the indicated file system from being mounted at boot time, and ro says to mount the file system read-only (which is reasonable for a CD drive). Commas must separate options. See the mount command manual page (under the -o option) for information on other supported options.

TIP   Normally, only the root user is allowed to mount a file system using the mount command. However, to allow any user to mount a file system (such as a file system on a floppy disk), you could add the user option to Field 4 of /etc/fstab. In SUSE, read/write permissions are given to specific devices (such as disk or audio devices) by specific groups (such as the disk or audio group) so that users assigned to those groups can mount or otherwise access those devices. In the YaST Control Center, choose Security and Users ⇨ User Management ⇨ Expert Options ⇨ Defaults for New Users. The Secondary Groups box indicates which of these additional groups each user is assigned to.

- **Field 5** — The number in this field indicates whether the indicated file system needs to be dumped (that is, have its data backed up). A 1 means that the file system needs to be dumped, and a 2 means that it doesn't. (I don't think this field is useful anymore because many Linux systems no longer include the dump command. Most often, a 0 is used.)

■ **Field 6** — The number in this field indicates whether the indicated file system needs to be checked with fsck. 1 means it needs to be checked, and 2 means it doesn't.

If you want to add an additional local disk or partition, you can create an entry for it in the /etc/fstab file. See Chapter 27 for information on mounting Samba, NFS, and other remount file systems from /etc/fstab.

Using the mount Command to Mount File Systems

Linux systems automatically run mount -a (mount all file systems) each time you boot. For that reason, you generally use the mount command only for special situations. In particular, the average user or administrator uses mount in two ways:

■ To display the disks, partitions, and remote file systems currently mounted.

■ To temporarily mount a file system.

Any user can type mount (with no options) to see what file systems are currently mounted on the local Linux system. The following is an example of the mount command. It shows a single hard disk partition (/dev/sda1) containing the root (/) file system, and proc and devpts file system types mounted on /proc and /dev, respectively. The last entry shows a floppy disk, formatted with a standard Linux file system (ext3) mounted on the /mnt/floppy directory.

```
$ mount
/dev/sda3 on / type ext3 (rw)
/dev/sda2 on /boot type ext3 (rw)
/dev/sda1 on /mnt/win type vfat (rw)
/dev/proc on /proc type proc (rw)
/dev/sys on /sys type sysfs (rw)
/dev/devpts on /dev/pts type devpts (rw,gid=5,mode=620)
/dev/shm on /dev/shm type tmpfs (rw)
none on /proc/sys/fs/binfmt_misc type binfmt_misc (rw)
/dev/cdrom on /media/cdrecorder type iso9660 (ro,nosuid,nodev)
/dev/fd0 on /mnt/floppy type ext3 (rw)
```

Traditionally, the most common devices to mount by hand are your floppy disk and your CD drive. However, depending on the type of desktop you are using, CDs and floppy disks may be mounted for you automatically when you insert them. (In some cases, the autorun program may also run automatically. For example, autorun may start a CD music player or software package installer to handle the data on the medium.)

Mounting Removable Media

If you want to mount a file system manually, the /etc/fstab file helps make it simple to mount a floppy disk or a CD. In some cases, you can use the mount command with a single option to indicate what you want to mount, and information is taken from the /etc/fstab file to fill in the other options. There are probably already entries in your /etc/fstab file to let you do these quick mounts in the following two cases:

- **CD** — If you are mounting a CD that is in the standard ISO 9960 format (as most software CD-ROMs are), you can mount that CD by placing it in your CD-ROM drive and typing one of the following:

```
# mount /media/cd*
# mount /mnt/cdrom
```

By default, a CD is usually mounted on the /mnt/cdrom directory (Linux 2.4 kernels) or a subdirectory of /media (Linux 2.6 kernels). (The file system type, device name, and other options are filled in automatically.) To see the contents, type **cd /mnt/cdrom** or **cd /media/cd***, and then type **ls**. Files from the CD's root directory will be displayed.

- **Floppy disk** — If you want to mount a floppy in the Linux ext3 file system format (ext3), or in some cases a format that can be autodetected, mount that floppy disk by inserting it in your floppy drive and typing one of the following:

```
# mount /media/floppy*
# mount /mnt/floppy
```

The file system type (ext3), device (/dev/fd0), and mount options are filled in from the /etc/fstab file. You should be able to change to the floppy disk directory (cd /mnt/floppy or cd /media/floppy*) and list the contents of the floppy's top directory (ls).

NOTE In both of the these cases, you could give the device name (which is something like /dev/cdrom or /dev/fd0) instead of the mount point directory to get the same results.

Of course, it is possible that you may get floppy disks you want to use that are in different formats. Someone may give you a floppy containing files from an older Microsoft operating system (in MS-DOS format). Or you may get a file from another UNIX system. In those cases, you can fill in your own options instead of relying on options from the /etc/fstab file. In some cases, Linux autodetects that the floppy disk contains an MS-DOS (or Windows vfat) file system and mounts it properly without additional arguments. If it doesn't, here's an example of how to mount a floppy containing MS-DOS files:

```
# mkdir /mnt/floppy
# mount -t msdos /dev/fd0 /mnt/floppy
```

This shows the basic format of the mount command you would use to mount a floppy disk. You can change msdos to any other supported file system type (described earlier in this chapter) to mount a floppy of that type. Instead of using floppy drive A: (/dev/fd0), you could use drive B: (/dev/fd1) or any other accessible drive. Instead of mounting on /mnt/floppy, you could create any other directory and mount the floppy there.

Here are some other useful options you could add to the `mount` command:

- `-t auto` — If you aren't sure exactly what type of file system is contained on the floppy disk (or other medium you are mounting), use this option to indicate the file system type. The `mount` command will query the disk to try to ascertain what type of file system it contains.

- `-r` — If you don't want to make changes to the mounted file system (or can't because it is a read-only medium), use this option to mount it read-only.

- `-w` — This mounts the file system with read/write permission.

Mounting a Disk Image in Loopback

Another valuable way to use the `mount` command has to do with disk images. If you download a CD or floppy disk image from the Internet and you want to see what it contains, you can do so without burning it to CD or floppy. With the image on your hard disk, create a mount point and use the `-o loop` option to mount it locally. Here's an example:

```
# mkdir /mnt/mycdimage
# mount -o loop whatever-i386-disc1.iso /mnt/mycdimage
```

In this example, the `/mnt/mycdimage` directory is created, and then the disk image file (`whatever-i386-disc1.iso`) residing in the current directory is mounted on it. You can now `cd` to that directory, view the contents of it, and copy or use any of its contents. This is useful for downloaded CD images from which you want to install software without having to burn the image to CD. You could also share that mountpoint over NFS, so you could install the software from another computer. When you are done, just type **umount /mnt/cdimage** to unmount it.

Other options to `mount` are available only for specific file system types. See the `mount` manual page for those and other useful options.

Using the umount Command

When you are done using a temporary file system, or you want to unmount a permanent file system temporarily, use the `umount` command. This command detaches the file system from its mount point in your Linux file system. To use `umount`, you can give it either a directory name or a device name. For example:

```
# umount /mnt/floppy
```

This unmounts the device (probably `/dev/fd0`) from the mount point `/mnt/floppy`. You can also unmount using the form

```
# umount /dev/fd0
```

In general, it's better to use the directory name (`/mnt/floppy`) because the `umount` command will fail if the device is mounted in more than one location. (Device names all begin with `/dev`.)

If you get the message `device is busy`, the `umount` request has failed because either a process has a file open on the device or you have a shell open with a directory on the device as a current directory. Stop the processes or change to a directory outside the device you are trying to unmount for the `umount` request to succeed.

An alternative for unmounting a busy device is the `-l` option. With `umount -l` (a lazy unmount), the unmount happens as soon as the device is no longer busy. To unmount a remote NFS file system that's no longer available (for example, the server went down), you can use the `umount -f` option to forcibly unmount the NFS file system.

> **TIP**   A really useful tool for discovering what's holding open a device you want to unmount is the `lsof` command. Type **lsof** with the name of the partition you want to unmount (such as `lsof /mnt/floppy`). The output shows you what commands are holding files open on that partition.

Using the mkfs Command to Create a File System

You can create a file system for any supported file system type on a disk or partition that you choose. You do so with the `mkfs` command. While this is most useful for creating file systems on hard-disk partitions, you can create file systems on floppy disks or rewritable CDs as well.

Here is an example of using `mkfs` to create a file system on a floppy disk:

```
# mkfs -t ext3 /dev/fd0
mke2fs 1.39, (29-May-2008)
Filesystem label=
OS type: Linux
Block size=1024 (log=0)
Fragment size=1024 (log=0)
184 inodes, 1440 blocks
72 blocks (5.00%) reserved for the super user
First data block=1
1 block group
8192 blocks per group, 8192 fragments per group
184 inodes per group

Writing inode tables: done

Filesystem too small for a journal
Writing superblocks and filesystem accounting information:
done

The filesystem will be automatically checked every 32 mounts
or
180 days, whichever comes first. Use tune2fs -c or -i to override.
```

You can see the statistics that are output with the formatting done by the `mkfs` command. The number of inodes and blocks created are output, as are the number of blocks per group and fragments per group. You could now mount this file system (`mount /mnt/floppy`), change to it as your current directory (`cd /mnt/floppy`), and create files on it as you please.

Adding a Hard Disk

Adding a new hard disk to your computer so that it can be used by Linux requires a combination of steps described in previous sections. Here's the general procedure:

1. Install the new hard disk hardware.
2. Identify the partitions on the new disk.
3. Create the file systems on the new disk.
4. Mount the file systems.

The easiest way to add a hard disk to Linux is to have the entire disk devoted to a single Linux partition. You can have multiple partitions, however, and assign them each to different types of file systems and different mount points, if you like. The following process takes you through adding a hard disk containing a single Linux partition. Along the way, it also notes which steps you need to repeat to have multiple file systems with multiple mount points.

This procedure assumes that Linux is already installed and working on the computer. If this is not the case, follow the instructions for adding a hard disk on your current operating system. Later, when you install Linux, you can identify this disk when you are asked to partition your hard disk(s).

1. Follow the manufacturer's instructions for physically installing and connecting the new hard disk in your computer. If, presumably, this is a second hard disk, you may need to change jumpers on the hard disk unit itself to have it operate as a slave hard disk (if it's on the same cable as your first hard disk). You may also need to change the BIOS settings.
2. Boot your computer to Linux.
3. Determine the device name for the hard disk. As root user from a shell, type:

```
# dmesg | less
```

4. From the output, look for an indication that the new disk was found. For example, if it's a second IDE hard disk, you should see hdb: in the output. For a second SCSI drive, you should see sdb: instead. (The hd? and sd? drive letters are incremented as they are found by the kernel.) Be sure you identify the correct disk, or you will erase all the data from disks you probably want to keep!
5. Use the fdisk command to create partitions on the new disk. For example, if you are formatting the second IDE disk (hdb), you can type the following:

```
# fdisk /dev/hdb
```

Now you are in fdisk command mode, where you can use the fdisk single-letter command set to work with your partitions. If the disk had existing partitions on it, you can change or delete those partitions now. Or, you can simply reformat the whole disk to blow everything away. Use p to view all partitions and d to delete a partition.

6. To create a new partition, type the following:

n

7. Choose an extended (e) or primary (p) partition. To choose a primary partition, type the following:

p

8. Type in the partition number. If you are creating the first partition (or for only one partition), type the number one:

1

Enter the first cylinder number (1 is the default). A range of cylinder numbers is displayed (for example, 1-4865 is the number of cylinders that appears for my 40GB hard drive).

9. To assign the new partition to begin at the first cylinder on the new hard disk, type the number **1**.

10. Enter the last cylinder number. If you are using the entire hard disk, use the last cylinder number shown. Otherwise, choose the ending cylinder number or indicate how many megabytes the partition should have.

11. To create more partitions on the hard disk, repeat steps 6 through 10 for each partition (possibly changing the file system types as needed).

12. Type **w** to write changes to the hard disk and exit from the `fdisk` command. At this point, you should be back at the shell.

13. To create a file system on the new disk partition, use the `mkfs` command. By default, this command creates an ext2 file system, which is usable by Linux. However, in most cases you will want to use a journaling file system (such as ext3 or reiserfs). To create an ext3 file system on the first partition of the second hard disk, type the following:

```
# mkfs -t ext3 /dev/hdb1
```

If you created multiple partitions, repeat this step for each partition (such as `/dev/hdb2`, `/dev/hdb3`, and so on).

TIP If you don't use `-t ext3`, an ext2 file system is created by default. Use other commands, or options to this command, to create other file system types. For example, use `mkfs.vfat` **to create a VFAT file system,** `mkfs.msdos` **for DOS, or** `mkfs.reiserfs` **for a Reiser file system type. The** `tune2fs` **command, described later in this section, can be used to change an ext2 file system to an ext3 file system.**

14. After the file system is created, you can have the partition permanently mounted by editing `/etc/fstab` and adding the new partition. Here is an example of a line you might add to that file:

```
/dev/hdb1     /abc          ext3      defaults      1 1
```

In this example, the partition (/dev/hdb1) is mounted on the /abc directory as an ext3 file system. The `defaults` keyword causes the partition to be mounted at boot time. The numbers 1 1 cause the disk to be checked for errors. Add one line like this example for each partition you created.

15. Create the mount point. For example, to mount the partition on /abc (as shown in the previous step), type the following:

```
# mkdir /abc
```

16. Create your other mount points if you created multiple partitions. The next time you boot Linux, the new partition(s) will be automatically mounted on the abc directory.

After you have created the file systems on your partitions, a nice tool for adjusting those file systems is the `tune2fs` command. You can use it to change volume labels, how often the file system is checked, and error behavior. You can also use it to change an ext2 file system to an ext3 file system so the file system can use journaling. For example:

```
# tune2fs -j /dev/hdb1
tune2fs 1.39 (29-May-2008)
Creating journal inode: done
This filesystem will be automatically checked every 38 mounts or
180 days, whichever comes first. Use tune2fs -c or -i to override.
```

By adding the -j option to `tune2fs`, you can either change the journal size or attach the file system to an external journal block device (essentially turning a nonjournaling ext2 file system into a journaling ext3 file system). After you use `tune2fs` to change your file system type, you probably need to correct your /etc/fstab file to include the file type change (from ext2 to ext3).

Checking System Space

Running out of disk space on your computer is not a happy situation. You can use tools that come with Linux to keep track of how much disk space has been used on your computer, and you can keep an eye on users who consume a lot of disk space.

Displaying System Space with df

You can display the space available in your file systems using the df command. To see the amount of space available on all the mounted file systems on your Linux computer, type **df** with no options:

```
$ df
Filesystem     1k-blocks      Used  Available  Use%  Mounted on
/dev/sda3       30645460   2958356   26130408   11%  /
/dev/sda2          46668      8340      35919   19%  /boot
/dev/fd0            1412        13       1327    1%  /mnt/floppy
```

This example output shows the space available on the hard disk partition mounted on the / (root) partition (/dev/sda1) and /boot partition (/dev/sda2), and the floppy disk mounted on the

/mnt/floppy directory (/dev/fd0). Disk space is shown in 1K blocks. To produce output in a more human-readable form, use the -h option:

```
$ df -h
Filesystem          Size  Used  Avail  Use%  Mounted on
/dev/sda3            29G   2.9G   24G   11%   /
/dev/sda2            46M   8.2M   25M   19%   /boot
/dev/fd0            1.4M    13k  1.2M    1%   /mnt/floppy
```

With the df -h option, output appears in a friendlier megabyte or gigabyte listing. Other options with df enable you to do the following:

- Print only file systems of a particular type (-t type)
- Exclude file systems of a particular type (-x type)
- Include file systems that have no space, such as /proc and /dev/pts (-a)
- List only available and used inodes (-i)
- Display disk space in certain block sizes (--block-size=#)

Checking Disk Usage with du

To find out how much space is being consumed by a particular directory (and its subdirectories), use the du command. With no options, du lists all directories below the current directory, along with the space consumed by each directory. At the end, du calculates total disk space used within that directory structure.

The du command is a good way to check how much space is being used by a particular user (du /home/user1) or in a particular file system partition (du /var). By default, disk space is displayed in 1K block sizes. To make the output friendlier (in kilobytes, megabytes, and gigabytes), use the -h option as follows:

```
$ du -h /home/jake
114k    /home/jake/httpd/stuff
234k    /home/jake/httpd
137k    /home/jake/uucp/data
701k    /home/jake/uucp
1.0M    /home/jake
```

The output shows the disk space used in each directory under the home directory of the user named jake (/home/jake). Disk space consumed is shown in kilobytes (k) and megabytes (M). The total space consumed by /home/jake is shown on the last line.

Finding Disk Consumption with find

The find command is a great way to find file consumption of your hard disk using a variety of criteria. You can get a good idea of where disk space can be recovered by finding files that are over a certain size or were created by a particular person.

NOTE   You must be the root user to run this command effectively, unless you are just checking your personal files. If you are not the root user, there will be many places in the file system that you will not have permission to check. Regular users can usually check their own home directories but not those of others.

In the following example, the find command searches the root file system (/) for any files owned by the user named jake (-user jake) and prints the filenames. The output of the find command is organized in a long listing in size order (ls -ldS). Finally, that output is sent to the file /tmp/jake. When you view the file /tmp/jake (for example, less /tmp/jake), you will find all of the files that are owned by the user jake listed in size order. Here is the command line:

```
# find / -xdev -user jake -print | xargs ls -ldS > /tmp/jake
```

TIP   The -xdev option prevents file systems other than the selected file system from being searched. This is a good way to cut out a lot of junk that may be output from the /proc file system. It can also keep large remotely mounted file systems from being searched.

Here's another example, except that instead of looking for a user's files, we're looking for files larger than 100 kilobytes (-size +100k):

```
# find / -xdev -size +100k -print | xargs ls -ldS > /tmp/size
```

You can save yourself a lot of disk space by just removing some of the largest files that are no longer needed. In this example, you can see large files are sorted by size in the /tmp/size file.

Monitoring System Performance

If your Linux system is a multiuser computer, sharing the processing power of that computer can be a major issue. Likewise, any time you can stop a runaway process or reduce the overhead of an unnecessary program running, your Linux server can do a better job serving files, Web pages, or e-mail to the people who rely on it.

Some distributions of Linux include graphical utilities to simplify administration, such as System Monitor in Ubuntu (shown in Figure 4-5).

All Linux distributions include utilities that can help you monitor the performance of your Linux system. The kinds of features you want to monitor in Linux include CPU usage, memory usage (RAM and swap space), and overall load on the system. A popular tool for monitoring that information in Linux is the top command.

To start the top utility in a Terminal window, type **top**. The top command determines the largest CPU-consuming processes on your computer, displays them in descending order on your screen, and updates the list every five seconds.

By adding the -S option to top, the display shows you the cumulative CPU time for each process, as well as any child processes that may already have exited. If you want to change how often the screen is updated, you can add the -d secs option, where secs is replaced by the number of seconds between updates.

FIGURE 4-5

FIGURE 4-5

System Monitor, in Ubuntu, allows you to view processes, resources, and devices.

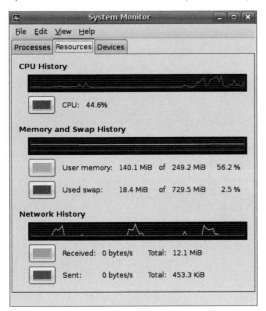

By default, processes are sorted by CPU usage. You can sort processes numerically by PID (type **N**), by age (type **A**), by resident memory usage (type **M**), or by time (type **T**). To return to CPU usage, type **P**. To terminate a process, type **k** and enter the PID of the process you want to kill (listed in the left column). Be careful to kill only processes you are sure you don't need or want.

Summary

Although you may be using Linux as a single-user system, many of the tasks you must perform to keep your computer running are defined as administrator tasks. A special user account called the root user is needed to do many of the things necessary to keep Linux working as you would like it to. If you are administering a Linux system used by lots of people, the task of administration becomes even larger. You must be able to add and support users, maintain the file systems, and ensure that system performance serves your users well.

To help the administrator, Linux comes with a variety of command-line utilities and graphical windows for configuring and maintaining your system. Commands such as `mkfs` and `mount` let you create and mount file systems, respectively. Tools such as `top` let you monitor system performance.

Chapter 5

Getting on the Internet

You won't tap into the real power of Linux until you have connected it to a network — in particular, the Internet. Your computer probably has an Ethernet interface built in, so you can just plug a LAN (local area network) cable into it to connect to a LAN (hub or switch), DSL bridge or router, or cable modem. Some computers, particularly laptops, may have wireless Ethernet hardware built in.

Your computer also may have a dial-up modem. If you have an older computer that has no Ethernet card or you are in a situation in which you need to dial out over regular phone lines to reach your Internet service provider (ISP), you use this modem to get on the Internet.

This chapter describes how to connect your Linux system to the Internet. With broadband and wireless networks becoming more prevalent, Ethernet connections are becoming the most common means of connecting to the Internet. For dial-up connections, you'll see how to use kppp (a dialer GUI that is often packaged with KDE desktops).

Sharing Internet connections with multiple desktop systems or even your own mail or Web server is not that difficult to do from a hardware perspective. However, there are some security and configuration issues to consider when you set out to expand how you use your Internet connection. A Linux system includes software that lets you configure it as a firewall, router, and a variety of server types to help you get this done.

179

Connecting to the Network

Linux supports a wide range of wired and wireless network devices, as well as a dizzying array of network protocols to communicate over that media. As a home or small office Linux user, you can start evaluating how to configure your connection to the Internet from Linux by considering:

- The type of Internet account you have with your ISP (dial-up or broadband)
- Whether or not you are connecting a single computer, a bunch of desktops, and/or one or more server machines to the Internet

Connecting via Dial-Up Service

Until a few years ago, dial-up was the most common method for an individual to get on to the Internet. Many computers had dial-up modems built into the motherboard or had serial ports where a modem could easily be connected. Many computers today do not include modems, but serial or USB modems can be purchased for just a few dollars if you need to use dial-up.

Once you have a modem (56 Kbps speed is the standard today), the only other equipment you need is a regular telephone line. Essentially, you can use a dial-up modem anywhere you can connect to a phone line. Linux contains the tools you need to configure and complete a dial-up connection. Figure 5-1 shows the setup for the connection.

FIGURE 5-1

Connect a modem to a serial or USB port and dial out over regular phone lines.

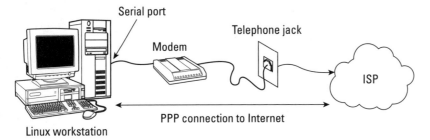

One difficulty with using modems in Linux is that many computers with built-in modems (especially laptops) come with what are referred to as *Winmodems*. With Winmodems, some of the processing normally done on the modem is actually implemented within the Windows system. Winmodems don't always look like real modems to Linux systems because, without the code that's inside Windows, they don't behave like real modems when they are connected to Linux systems.

Some Winmodems are supported in Linux, and those are sometimes referred to as *Linmodems*. If you find that Linux fails to detect your modem, check out the Linmodems Support Page (http://linmodems.technion.ac.il) or the LinModems.org page (www.linmodems.org). It can help you determine if you have a Winmodem and, if so, help you find the right Linmodem driver (if one is available).

> **TIP**   If you find that you have a Winmodem, you are usually better off getting a real modem instead. An inexpensive external serial modem can save you the trouble of getting and loading a Linmodem driver that may or may not work. Most external modems or internal PCI modems described as being "controller-based" work well in Linux.

Connecting a Single Computer to Broadband

Increasingly, individuals have the option of signing up for broadband Internet service with cable television providers or local telephone companies. These connections typically provide transmission speeds rated at least five times greater than you can get with a dial-up connection.

To make broadband connections from your home or small office, you typically need a cable modem or Digital Subscriber Line (DSL) modem. Cable modems share the bandwidth of the cable television line coming into your location. DSL uses existing house or office phone wires to connect to the Internet, sharing the wires with your phone service.

Because there are many ways that your ISP may be providing your Internet service, you should check with it to get the right hardware you need to connect. In particular, you should know that there are several incompatible DSL standards (ADSL, CDSL, HDSL, SDSL, and so on), so you can't just go out and buy DSL equipment without some guidance.

If you are using an external DSL or cable modem, chances are that a single connection from your Linux machine to that equipment requires only:

- An Ethernet port on your computer
- A LAN cable (often provided with the ISP equipment)
- The DSL router/bridge or cable modem (often provided by ISP)

Figure 5-2 illustrates a Linux computer connected to a broadband cable modem.

Broadband equipment often supplies a service called Dynamic Host Configuration Protocol (DHCP). DHCP provides the Internet addresses and other information that a client computer needs to connect to the network. With the cable/DSL modem acting as a DHCP server, you can literally start using the Internet without doing any special configuration in Linux. Just plug in, boot Linux, and start browsing the Web.

> **NOTE**   The DSL or cable modem often acts as a router between the ISP and your computer. Usually that device will also include a firewall configured to do network address translation. Alternatively, some broadband equipment operates in a "bridging mode," in which it doesn't do routing, but simply passes data through as though your computer were on the same LAN as that of the ISP. In this setup, the public IP address is assigned to your computer instead of the DSL or cable modem.

FIGURE 5-2

Connect an Ethernet card to broadband and start surfing.

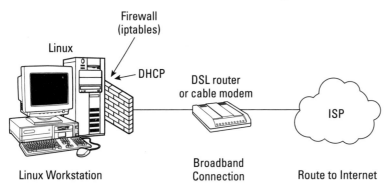

Connecting Multiple Computers to Broadband

Instead of connecting your Linux computer directly to the cable modem or DSL equipment, you can join your machines together on a LAN, and then connect the LAN to your ISP equipment so that everyone in the house or office can share the broadband connection. It's fairly simple; you just connect your cable/DSL modem to your LAN instead of directly to your Linux box. In this configuration, however, you should consider adding a firewall/router as a buffer between your LAN and the outside world. That machine would perform such duties as:

- **Blocking access** — A well-configured firewall blocks access to all ports except those that you need to access the Internet the way you want, thereby minimizing the risks of intruders getting into your LAN.

- **NAT or IP Masquerading** — For the most part, you want the computers behind your firewall that are simply desktop systems to not be accessible to others from the Internet. By configuring your firewall to do NAT or IP Masquerading, your computers can be assigned private IP addresses. Your firewall then handles forwarding of messages between your LAN and the Internet. This is a good arrangement for several reasons. For one thing, the IP addresses of your private computers are not exposed to the outside world. Also, you can save the cost of paying your ISP for permanent IP addresses.

- **DHCP service** — Many firewall systems can act as a DHCP server. Those private IP addresses you can use with a NAT firewall can be assigned from the DHCP service running on your firewall system. When the client computer on your LAN starts up, besides its IP address, your DHCP service can tell the client the location of its DNS server, gateway to the Internet, or other information.

■ **Routing** — In the home and small-office LAN environment illustrated in Figure 5-3, the firewall computer often has two Ethernet interfaces: one connected to the LAN and the other to the DSL or cable modem that leads to the ISP. Because the Ethernet interfaces are viewed as being on separate subnetworks, the firewall/router must be configured to forward packets across the two interfaces. It's not a big deal, but it does require a separate step to tell the firewall system that you want it to forward packets between the two subnetworks.

CROSS-REF Chapter 18 discusses setting up a firewall/router, using a Linux distribution designed specifically for the task.

FIGURE 5-3

A firewall provides a safeguard between your LAN and the Internet.

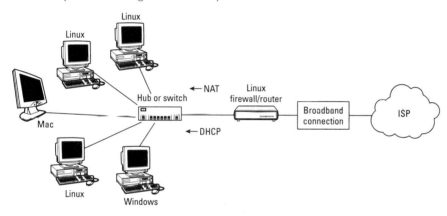

In this example, the equipment you need includes:

■ An Ethernet port on each computer plus an extra port for the firewall/router

■ A LAN cable for each computer

■ A hub or a switch

■ A low-end PC (a PC with as little power as a 486 might do) running as a Linux firewall/router

■ The DSL or cable modem

An alternative to this wired configuration is to replace the hub or switch with a wireless access point. Then each computer equipped with a wireless LAN card can get on the network without wires.

Connecting Servers

So far you've seen configurations that let one or more computers from your home or small business browse the Web. Allowing someone from the Internet to request services (Web pages, file transfers, and so forth) from your computers requires some extra thought.

After you have TCP/IP (the primary set of protocols used on the Internet) configured to connect to your ISP, requests for data can pass in either direction between your computers and the Internet unless you use a firewall to restrict traffic. So the same connection you use for Internet browsing can be used to offer services to the Internet, with a few caveats:

- **Permanent IP address** — Each time you reboot your computer, your ISP's DHCP server dynamically assigns your DSL/cable modem's IP address. For that reason, your IP address could change at each reboot. If you want your servers to be reachable on a permanent basis, you usually need at least one permanent IP address at which people can reach your servers. You will have to ask your ISP about a permanent IP address, and it might cost you extra money to have one.

NOTE A service called Dynamic DNS can be used in place of paying for a permanent IP address. With Dynamic DNS, you hire a service to constantly check whether your IP address has changed and assign your DNS hostname to the new address if it does. You can search the Web for "Dynamic DNS" to find companies that offer that service.

- **ISP acceptable use policy** — Check that you are allowed to have incoming connections. Some ISPs, especially for inexpensive, home-use broadband service, will block incoming connections to Web servers or mail servers.

- **DNS hostname** — Although typing an IP address into a browser location box works just fine, most people prefer to use names (such as www.linuxtoys.net) to reach a server. That requires you to purchase a DNS domain name and have an entry set up in a DNS server to resolve the name to the IP address of your server.

Although there is nothing magical about setting up an Internet server, given the few issues just mentioned, creating a public server can be a lot like opening up the doors of your house so that strangers can wander in. You want some policies in place to restrict where the strangers can go and what they can do.

For home or small-office locations that have a single Internet connection (represented by one public IP address), servers can be more exposed to the Internet than desktop systems by keeping them in one area that's referred to as the DMZ (demilitarized zone). In this configuration (illustrated in Figure 5-4), servers are directly behind the outside firewall. Desktop systems (that aren't to be accessible by people from the Internet) are behind a second, more restrictive firewall.

Whether you use Linux or dedicated firewall devices to provide firewall service, the outside firewall allows requests in for Web services (port 80), FTP services (ports 20 and 21), simple mail transfer protocol (port 25), and possibly other services. The internal firewall blocks any requests for services from the outside and allows only Internet communications that were initiated from computers behind the inside firewall.

FIGURE 5-4

Add servers to a DMZ where they can be more publicly accessible than your desktop systems.

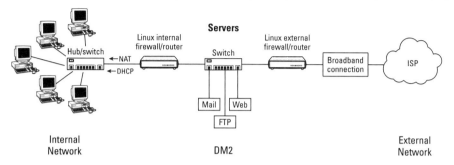

CROSS-REF **Chapters 24 though 27 explain how to configure different server types, and Chapter 18 describes how to set up Linux as a router/firewall. Chapter 18 includes details on how to configure features such as IP Masquerading, NAT, and packet forwarding.**

Connecting Other Equipment

Although I've focused on basic Ethernet equipment and dial-up modems for configuring network connections, Linux supports many, many other types of network equipment as well as different protocols for communicating over that equipment. Here are a few examples:

- **ISDN** — Integrated Services Digital Network (ISDN) lines were the preferred method of high-speed data lines to small businesses in the United States before DSL became widespread. It is still popular in Europe, but is being supplanted by more affordable DSL equipment. ISDN4Linux drivers and tools are available in many Linux systems for connecting to ISDN networks.

- **USB cable modem** — Most cable modems offer an Ethernet port that you can connect to directly from your computer's own Ethernet port. However, if you don't have an Ethernet port, often you can connect to the cable modem through one of your USB ports. (You may need to manually load a usbnet or cdc_ether driver to get this to work.)

- **Token ring** — Although rarely used now, token ring network cards are still supported. Support for token ring network cards is included in most Linux systems, although token rings are rarely used now. They were once popular at locations that had many IBM systems.

- **PLIP** — It's possible to connect two computers together from their parallel ports so that they can communicate using TCP/IP protocols. Parallel Line Internet Protocol (PLIP) requires only a special type of null modem cable (for the specs for that cable, refer to `http://tldp.org/HOWTO/NET3-4-HOWTO-9.html`). Most Linux systems have built-in software that enables you to log in, transfer files, and perform other activities over that connection.

If your system has Linux source code installed, you can read about supported hardware devices in the documentation that comes with that source code. On Fedora and some other Linux systems, the location of kernel documentation for various networking hardware is `/usr/src/linux*/Documentation/networking`.

Using Ethernet Connections to the Internet

Most Linux systems today will either automatically detect or allow you to set up your Internet connection when you install Linux. Here's the general (default) way that a network connection on a desktop system, with Linux installed, is started up:

1. Check whether you have an Ethernet port on your computer (most recent computers have one). If so, connect your Ethernet card to the equipment that gets you to the Internet (cable modem, DSL router/bridge, or network hub/switch). If not, you can purchase an Ethernet card at any retailer that sells computer hardware.

2. Ensure that appropriate drivers are available for the card and bring up the interface (typically, the first wired Ethernet card is assigned to the eth0 interface). Usually, simply starting the computer causes the card to be detected and the appropriate driver to be loaded.

3. Get an IP address using DHCP if there is a DHCP server available through the interface. Most ISPs and businesses expect you to connect to their networks using DHCP, so they will have provided a DHCP server to the equipment where you connect your computer to the network.

As long as your desktop system is connected to a network that has a DHCP server willing to give it an IP address, you can be up and browsing the Web in no time.

If you find that the automatic method (DHCP) of connecting to your network doesn't work, it gets a bit trickier to connect to the Internet. Different Linux distributions offer different tools for manually configuring your Internet connection. The following sections describe a few graphical tools and some command-line and configuration-file approaches to configuring wired and wireless network connections.

Configuring Ethernet During Installation

Many Linux install processes ask you if you want to configure your network connection for your Ethernet cards. This is typically just for your Ethernet cards and not for dial-up modems or other networking equipment. Information you'll need for that process (IP address, gateway, DNS server, and so on) is explained in Chapter 7.

When you boot Linux, you can check whether you have access to the Internet by opening a Web browser (such as Firefox or Konqueror) and typing in a Web address. If the Web site doesn't appear in your browser, you'll need to do some troubleshooting. The section "Understanding Your Internet Connection" later in this chapter provides information on how to track down problems with your Internet connection.

Configuring Ethernet from the Desktop

Most major Linux distributions offer graphical tools for configuring network interfaces. These tools step you through the information you need to enter, and then start up the network interface (if you choose) to begin browsing the Web.

Here is a list of tools for configuring network interfaces in a few different Linux distributions. Some of these are graphical tools, and some are menu-based:

- **Red Hat Enterprise/Fedora Linux** — The Network Configuration window lets you configure a network connection using Ethernet, ISDN, modem, token ring, wireless, and xDSL hardware. Start the Network Configuration window from the System menu by selecting Administration ⇨ Network or by typing **system-config-network** and entering the root password when prompted. (On older Red Hat Linux systems, the command was `redhat-config-network`.)

- **SUSE Linux** — The YaST Control Center that comes with SUSE contains features for configuring your network. From the SUSE menu on the panel, select Administrator Settings (YaST), and then choose Network Devices. The YaST Control Center lets you configure a DSL, ISDN, Modem, or Network Card interface to the network. Select Network Card to configure your wired Ethernet interface to the Internet.

- **Gentoo Linux** — From a shell (as root user), type **net-setup eth0** to start a menu-driven interface to configure the network connection from your first Ethernet card (eth0). The tool lets you have the interface try to start using DHCP or use static address information that you provide.

- **Ubuntu Linux** — Select System ⇨ Administration ⇨ Networking from the desktop. Enter the administrative password when prompted. From the Network Settings window that appears, choose the interface you want to configure and select Properties. A dialog box similar to that shown in Figure 5-5 will appear.

FIGURE 5-5

Configuring an interface in Ubuntu

■ **KNOPPIX** — Select the squished penguin icon in the panel on the KNOPPIX desktop, and choose Networking/Internet from the menu. Select the Network card configuration menu entry to configure your network card. Or select from several other network equipment types instead (ADSL, GPRS, ISDN, Modem, or Wavelan).

Using Network Configuration GUI in Fedora

An example of a graphical tool for configuring your Ethernet interface is the Network Configuration GUI that comes with Fedora and Red Hat Enterprise Linux systems. If you did not configure your LAN connection during installation of Fedora or RHEL, you can do so at any time using the Network Configuration window. The IP address and hostnames can be assigned statically to an Ethernet interface or retrieved dynamically at boot time from a DHCP server.

NOTE A computer can have more than one IP address because it can have multiple network interfaces. Each network interface must have an IP address to connect to a network (even if the address is assigned temporarily). So, if you have two Ethernet cards (eth0 and eth1), each needs its own IP address. Also, the address 127.0.0.1 represents the local host so that users on the local computer can access services in loopback.

Here's how to define the IP address for your Ethernet interface in Fedora or RHEL:

1. From the red hat menu, choose Desktop ➪ System Settings ➪ Network or, as root user from a Terminal window, type **system-config-network**. (If prompted, type the root password.) The Network Configuration window appears.

2. Click the Devices tab. A listing of your existing network interfaces appears.

3. Double-click the eth0 interface (representing your first Ethernet card). A pop-up window titled Ethernet Device appears (see Figure 5-6), enabling you to configure your eth0 interface.

4. Select your preferences:

   ■ **Activate device when computer starts** — Check here to have eth0 start at boot time.

   ■ **Allow all users to enable and disable the device** — Check to let non-root users enable and disable the network interface.

   ■ **Enable IPv6 configuration for this interface** — Check here if you are connected to an IPV6 network. (Most networks are still IPV4.)

5. You also must choose whether to get your IP addresses from another computer at boot time or enter the addresses yourself:

   ■ **Automatically obtain IP address settings with** — Select this box if you have a DHCP or BOOTP server on the network from which you can obtain your computer's IP address, netmask, and gateway. DHCP is recommended if you have more than just a couple of computers on your LAN. Optionally, you can set your own hostname, which can be just a name (such as `jukebox`) or a fully qualified domain name (such as `jukebox.linuxtoys.net`).

FIGURE 5-6

Configure and activate Ethernet devices in Fedora.

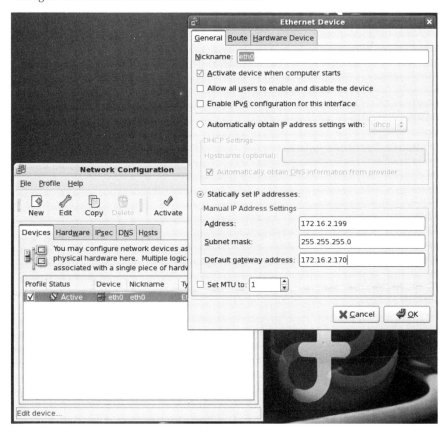

- **Statically set IP addresses** — If there is no DHCP or other boot server on your LAN, add necessary IP address information statically by selecting this option and following these steps:

  a. Type the IP address of the computer into the Address box. This number must be unique on your network. For your private LAN, you can use private IP addresses.

  b. Enter the netmask in the Subnet Mask box. The netmask indicates the part of the IP address that represents the network.

  c. Type the IP address of the computer into the Default Gateway Address box if a computer or router connected to your LAN provides routing functions to the Internet or other network. (Chapter 18 describes how to use NAT or IP Masquerading and how to use Linux as a router.)

6. Click OK in the Ethernet Device window to save the configuration and close the window.

7. Click File ⇨ Save to save the information you entered.

8. Click Activate in the Network Configuration window to start your connection to the LAN.

Identifying Other Computers (Hosts and DNS)

Each time you use a name to identify a computer, such as when browsing the Web or using an e-mail address, the computer name must be translated into an IP address. To resolve names to IP addresses, Linux goes through a search order (usually based on the contents of three files in /etc: resolv.conf, nsswitch.conf, and host.conf). By default, it checks hostnames you add yourself (which end up in the /etc/hosts file), hosts available via NIS, and hostnames available via DNS.

Again, for RHEL and Fedora systems, you can use the Network Configuration window to add the following:

- **Hostnames** — You might do this to identify hosts on your LAN that are not configured on a DNS server.

- **DNS search path** — By adding domain names to a search path (such as linuxtoys.net), you can browse to a site by its hostname (such as jukebox), and have Linux search the domains you added to the search path to find the host you are looking for (such as jukebox.linuxtoys.net).

- **DNS name servers** — A DNS server can resolve addresses for the domains it serves and contact other DNS servers to get addresses for all other DNS domains.

NOTE If you are configuring a DNS server, you can use that server to centrally store names and IP addresses for your LAN. This saves you the trouble of updating every computer's /etc/hosts file every time you add or change a computer on your LAN.

To add hostnames, IP addresses, search paths, and DNS servers in Fedora, do the following:

1. Start the Network Configuration. As root user from a Terminal window, type **system-config-network**, or from the top panel, click System ⇨ Administration ⇨ Network. The Network Configuration window appears.

2. Click the Hosts tab. A list of IP addresses, hostnames, and aliases appears.

3. Click New. An Add/Edit Hosts Entry pop-up window appears.

4. Type in the IP address number, hostname, and, optionally, the host alias.

5. Click OK.

6. Repeat this process until you have added every computer on your LAN that cannot be reached by DNS.

7. Click the DNS tab.

8. Type the IP address of the computers that serve as your Primary and Secondary DNS servers. (You get these IP addresses from your ISP or, if you created your own DNS server, you can enter that server's IP address.)

9. Type the name of the domain (probably the name of your local domain) to be searched for hostnames into the DNS Search Path box.

10. Click File ⇨ Save to save the changes.

11. Click File ⇨ Quit to exit.

Now, when you use programs such as ftp, ssh, or other TCP/IP utilities, you can use any hostname that is identified on your local computer, exists in your search path domain, or can be resolved from the public Internet DNS servers. (Strictly speaking, you don't have to set up your /etc/hosts file. You could use IP addresses as arguments to TCP/IP commands. But names are easier to work with.)

Using the Network Settings GUI in Ubuntu

In Ubuntu Linux, the Network Settings window lets you configure your network connections. Assuming your computer has an Ethernet card installed, you can follow the procedure below to create a network connection to the Internet or other TCP/IP network.

1. Start Network Settings. Click System ⇨ Administration ⇨ Networking. The Network Settings window appears.

2. Select the Ethernet connection entry on the screen for the interface you want to configure and click Properties. The first Ethernet card should be identified as eth0 (if other Ethernet cards are present, they will be identified as eth1, eth2, and so on). The Interface properties window appears, as shown in Figure 5-7.

    Figure 5-7 contains an example of an Ethernet connection configured to use DHCP to get the information it needs to start up (IP address, Subnet mask, and so on) from a DHCP server on your network. The Enable this connection check box indicates that the eth0 connection is started up automatically at boot time.

    If your cable modem, DSL equipment or other network server offers a DHCP service, the example shown in Figure 5-7 may be all you need to do. However, if no DHCP service is available or you simply want to set your connection information manually, continue to the next step.

3. If you want to manually configure your Ethernet connection, select the following from the Interface Properties pop-up window:

    ▓ **Configuration** — Select Static IP address to be able to set your address information manually, instead of getting it automatically from a DHCP service.

    ▓ **IP address** — Type the IP address you want to use for this computer into the IP address box. This number must be unique on your network. For your private LAN, you can use private IP addresses.

FIGURE 5-7

Use DHCP or static IP addresses for Ethernet connections in Ubuntu.

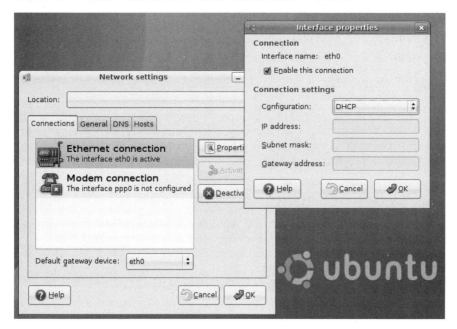

■ **Subnet mask** — Enter the netmask in the Subnet mask box. The netmask indicates the part of the IP address that represents the network. For example, a netmask of 255.255.255.0 for the IP address 10.0.0.5 indicates that the network address is 10.0.0 and the host address is 5. Other computers on the network could use the same netmask with IP addresses such as 10.0.0.1, 10.0.0.2, and so on up to 254.

■ **Gateway address** — Type the IP address of the device that is acting as a router between your computer and the Internet or other network. (See Chapter 18 for information on using NAT or IP Masquerading if you are using Linux as a router.)

Select OK when you have filled in all the necessary information.

There are other features you can set as well that relate to your network connections in Ubuntu. From the General tab, you can add the hostname and domain name assigned to your computer. The Hosts tab lets you enter the IP address and hostname for individual hosts that you want to enter manually.

From the DNS tab, you can indicate the IP addresses of the servers your computer will use to resolve names of the computers you communicate with (using e-mail, Web browsers, and so on) into IP addresses. You can also indicate the Search Domains value, so those times that you try to connect to a computer by hostname, but no domain name, your system knows which domains to search first for that host.

Understanding Your Internet Connection

If your Ethernet interface to the Internet is not working, there are ways to check what's happening that will work on many Linux distributions. Use the following procedure to find out how your network interfaces are working:

1. Open a shell (if you are using a graphical interface, open a Terminal window).

2. Type the following right after you boot your computer to verify whether Linux found your card and installed the Ethernet interface properly:

```
dmesg | grep eth | less
```

The dmesg command lists all the messages that were output by Linux at boot time. The grep eth command causes only those lines that contain the word *eth* to be printed. Here are a couple of examples:

```
eth0: VIA Rhine II at 0xee001000, 00:0d:61:25:d4:17, IRQ 185.
eth0: MII PHY found at address 1, status 0x786d advertising
01e1 Link 45e1.
eth0: link up, 100Mbps, full-duplex, lpa 0x45E1
eth0: no IPv6 routers present
```

The first message appeared on my desktop computer with a VIA Rhine Ethernet controller. It shows that a card was found at software IRQ 185 with a port address of 0xee001000 and an Ethernet hardware address (MAC address) of 00:0d:61:25:d4:17. The other lines indicate that the link is up on the eth0 interface and running at 100 Mbps in full-duplex. In this case IPv6 routing is not enabled.

NOTE If the eth0 interface is not found, but you know that you have a supported Ethernet card, type **lspci -vv | grep -i eth** to see if the Ethernet card is detected on the PCI bus. If it doesn't appear, check that your Ethernet card is properly seated in its slot. Here's what appeared for the preceding example:

```
00:12.0 Ethernet controller: VIA Technologies, Inc.
VT6102 [Rhine-II] (rev 74)
```

3. To view which network interfaces are up and running, type the following:

```
$ /sbin/ifconfig -a
eth0      Link encap:Ethernet  HWaddr 00:0D:61:25:D4:17
```

```
            inet addr:10.0.0.5  Bcast:10.0.0.255  Mask:255.255.255.0
            UP BROADCAST RUNNING MULTICAST  MTU:1500  Metric:1
            RX packets:326100 errors:0 dropped:0 overruns:0 frame:0
            TX packets:215931 errors:0 dropped:0 overruns:0 carrier:0
            collisions:5919 txqueuelen: 1000
            RX bytes:168378315 (160.5 Mb)  TX bytes:40853243 (38.9 Mb)
lo          Link encap:Local Loopback
            inet addr:127.0.0.1  Mask:255.0.0.0
            UP LOOPBACK RUNNING  MTU:16436  Metric:1
            RX packets:37435 errors:0 dropped:0 overruns:0 frame:0
            TX packets:37435 errors:0 dropped:0 overruns:0 carrier:0
            collisions:0 txqueuelen: 0
            RX bytes:2353172 (2.2 Mb)  TX bytes:2353172 (2.2 Mb)
```

The output shows a loopback interface (lo) and one Ethernet card (eth0). The Ethernet interface (eth0), is assigned the IP address of 10.0.0.5. In this example, the eth0 has an IP address of 10.0.0.5. Again, notice that the MAC address, which is a unique address related to the Ethernet card hardware, is noted after the HWaddr indicator (00:0D:61:25:D4:17).

4. Communicate with another computer on the LAN. The ping command can be used to send a packet to another computer and to ask for a packet in return. You can give ping either a hostname (butch) or an IP address (10.0.0.10). For example, to ping a computer on the network called butch, type the following command:

ping butch

If the computer can be reached, the output will look similar to the following:

```
PING butch (10.0.0.10): 56(84) data bytes
64 bytes from butch (10.0.0.10): icmp_seq=1 ttl=255 time=0.351 ms
64 bytes from butch (10.0.0.10): icmp_seq=2 ttl=255 time=0.445 ms
64 bytes from butch (10.0.0.10): icmp_seq=3 ttl=255 time=0.409 ms
64 bytes from butch (10.0.0.10): icmp_seq=4 ttl=255 time=0.457 ms
64 bytes from butch (10.0.0.10): icmp_seq=5 ttl=255 time=0.401 ms
64 bytes from butch (10.0.0.10): icmp_seq=6 ttl=255 time=0.405 ms
64 bytes from butch (10.0.0.10): icmp_seq=7 ttl=255 time=0.443 ms
64 bytes from butch (10.0.0.10): icmp_seq=8 ttl=255 time=0.384 ms
64 bytes from butch (10.0.0.10): icmp_seq=9 ttl=255 time=0.365 ms
64 bytes from butch (10.0.0.10): icmp_seq=10 ttl=255 time=0.367 ms
--- butch statistics ---
10 packets transmitted, 10 packets received, 0% packet loss, time 9011ms
rtt min/avg/max/mdev = 0.351/0.402/0.457/0.042 ms
```

A line of output is printed each time a packet is sent and received in return. It shows how much data was sent and how long it took for each package to be received. Watch this for a while, and then press Ctrl+C to stop ping. You'll see statistics on how many packets were transmitted, received, and lost.

If the output doesn't show that packets have been received, there's no contact with the other computer. Verify that the names and addresses of the computers that you want to reach are in your /etc/hosts file or that your DNS server is accessible. Next, confirm that the names and IP addresses you have for the other computers you are trying to reach are correct (the IP addresses are the most critical).

5. If you are able to reach an IP address on your LAN with ping, but are unable to ping a host computer by name, you may not be communicating with your DNS server. Repeat the ping command with the IP address of your DNS server to see if it is up and that you are able to communicate with it.

Using Dial-Up Connections to the Internet

Many individuals and even some small businesses that need to connect to the Internet still do so using modems and telephone lines. The modem connects to a serial port (COM1, COM2, and so on) on your computer and then into a telephone jack. Your computer dials a modem at your Internet service provider or business that has a connection to the Internet.

The most common protocol for making dial-up connections to the Internet (or other TCP/IP network) is Point-to-Point Protocol (PPP). Let's look at how to use PPP to connect to the Internet.

CROSS-REF See Chapter 9 for information on configuring a dial-up connection that is specific to Debian.

Getting Information

To establish a PPP connection, you need to get some information from the administrator of the network to which you are connecting. This is either your Internet service provider (ISP) when you sign up for Internet service, or the person in your workplace who walks around carrying cables, two or more cellular phones, and a couple of beepers (when a network goes down, these people are in demand!). Here is the kind of information you need to set up your PPP connection:

■ **Telephone number** — Gives you access to the modem (or pool of modems) at the ISP. If it is a national ISP, make sure that you get a local or toll-free telephone number (otherwise, you'll rack up long-distance fees on top of your ISP fees).

■ **Account name and password** — Used to verify that you have an Internet account with the ISP. This is an account name when you connect to Linux or other UNIX system, but may be referred to as a system name when you connect to an NT server.

■ **An IP number** — Most ISPs use Dynamic IP numbers, which means that you are assigned an IP number temporarily when you are connected. Your ISP assigns a permanent IP number if it uses Static IP addresses. If your computer or all the computers on your LAN need to have a more permanent presence on the network, you may be given one Static IP number or a set of Static IP addresses to use.

- **DNS server IP addresses** — Your computer translates Internet hostnames to IP addresses by querying a domain name system (DNS) server. Your ISP should give you at least one IP address for a preferred (and possibly alternate) DNS server.

- **PAP or CHAP secrets** — You may need a PAP (Password Authentication Protocol) ID or CHAP (Challenge Handshake Authentication Protocol) ID and a secret, instead of a username and password when connecting to a Windows NT system. These features are used with authentication on Microsoft and some other operating systems. Linux and other UNIX servers don't typically use this type of authentication, although they support PAP and CHAP on the client side. Your ISP will tell you if you are using PAP or CHAP.

Your ISP typically provides services such as news and mail servers for use with your Internet connection. To configure these useful services, you need the following information:

- **Mail server** — If your ISP is providing you with an e-mail account, you must know the address of the mail server, the type of mail service (such as POP3 — Post Office Protocol; or IMAP — Internet Message Access Protocol), and the authentication password for the mail server so you can get your e-mail.

- **News server** — If your ISP provides the name of a news server so that you can participate in newsgroups, the server may require you to log on, so you need a password. The ISP provides that password, if required.

After you've gathered this information, you're ready to set up your connection to the Internet. To configure Linux to connect to your ISP, read on.

Setting Up Dial-Up PPP

PPP is used to create IP connections over serial lines. Most often, the serial connection is established over a modem; however, it also works over serial cables (null modem cables) or digital lines (including ISDN and DSL).

Although one side must dial out and the other side must receive the call to create the PPP connection over a modem, after the connection is established, information can flow in both directions. For the sake of clarity, however, I refer to the computer placing the call as the client and the computer receiving the call as the server.

To simplify the process of configuring PPP (and other network interfaces), most Linux systems include graphical tools to configure dial-up. Two such tools, available with Fedora and RHEL, are:

- **Network Configuration window** — The same utility used to configure Ethernet cards can be used to configure modems. From the GNOME top panel in Fedora and RHEL systems, choose System ➪ Administration ➪ Network. When that window appears, select New. The Select Device Type pop-up that appears enables you to configure and test your modem for a dial-up PPP connection.

- **KDE PPP (KPPP) window** — From the KDE desktop, select Internet ➪ KPPP, or from a Terminal window run the kppp command. From the KPPP window, you can set up and launch a PPP dial-up connection.

Before you begin either of these procedures, physically connect your modem to your computer, plug it in, and connect it to your telephone line. If you have an internal modem, you will probably see a telephone port on the back of your computer to which you need to connect. If your modem isn't detected, you can reboot your computer or run `wvdialconf create` (as described later in this chapter) to have it detected.

Creating a Dial-Up Connection with the Internet Configuration Wizard

If you are using a Fedora or RHEL system, you can use the Internet Configuration Wizard to set up dial-up networking. Here's how:

1. Choose System ➪ Administration ➪ Network. When the window appears, select New. (Type the root password, if prompted.) An Add New Device Type window appears (see Figure 5-8).

The Internet Configuration Wizard helps you set up a PPP Internet connection.

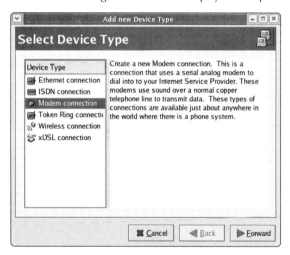

2. Select Modem connection and click Forward. The wizard searches for a modem and then the Select Modem window appears.

3. Select the following modem properties:

   ■ **Modem Device** — If the modem is connected to your first serial port (COM1) you can select `/dev/ttyS0`; for the second serial port (COM2) choose `/dev/ttyS1`. (By convention, the device is often linked to `/dev/modem`. Type **ls -l /dev/modem** to see if it is linked to `/dev/ttyS0`, `/dev/ttyS1`, or another tty device.)

   ■ **Baud Rate** — This is the rate at which the computer talks to the modem (which is typically considerably faster than the modem can talk over the phone lines). The default is 115200 bits per second, which is probably fine for dial-up connections.

- **Flow Control** — Check the modem documentation to see if the modem supports hardware flow control (CRTSCTS). If it doesn't, select software flow control (XON/XOFF). Flow control prevents more data than the modem can handle from being sent to it.

- **Modem Volume** — This is off by default because the noise can be annoying, but if you select medium while you're setting up the modem, the sound can give you a sense of where things are stopping if you can't get a connection. You can turn it off after everything's working.

- **Use Touch Tone Dialing** — Leave this check box selected in most cases. If for some reason your phone system doesn't support touch-tone dialing, you can turn it off.

4. Click Forward. The Select Provider window appears. Enter the following provider information:

   - **Internet Provider** — If you are using Internet service in any of the countries shown in the Internet Provider window, select the plus sign next to that country name. If your Internet service provider appears in the National list, select it. Information is automatically filled in for that provider. Otherwise, you need to fill in the rest of the dialog box.

   - **Phone Number** — The telephone number of the ISP you want to dial in to. (An optional prefix is available in case you need to dial 9 or some other number to get an outside dial tone.)

   - **Provider Name** — The name of the Internet service provider. If there is only one ISP, I recommend you use it as the ppp0 provider name.

   - **Login Name** — The login name assigned to you by the ISP. The ISP may have called the login name a login ID or something similar.

   - **Password** — The password associated with the login name.

5. Click Forward, and the IP Settings window appears. With a dial-up connection, you would typically select Automatically Obtain IP Address Settings. However, if the ISP has assigned a static IP address that you can use, select the Statically Set IP Addresses check box, and then enter your IP address, subnet mask, and default gateway address in the appropriate fields. Click Forward to continue.

6. The Create Dialup Connection window appears, displaying the information you just entered. If all the information looks correct, click Apply (otherwise, click the Back button, correct your information, and click Forward again to return to this window).

7. After you click Apply, the Network Configuration window appears, ideally with a new PPP connection of modem type appearing in the window. (If it doesn't appear, select System Settings ➪ Network.)

8. Select the new dial-up entry (so it is highlighted), and choose File ➪ Save to save its new configuration.

Now select the PPP device name and click the Activate button. The Internet dialer starts up and dials your ISP. (If you have sound turned on, you should hear your modem dialing out.) If everything is working properly, your login and password are accepted and the PPP connection is made.

Try opening Firefox or another Web browser to see if you can access a Web site on the Internet. If this doesn't work the first time, don't be discouraged. There are things to check to get your dial-up PPP connection working. Skip ahead to the "Checking Your PPP Connection" section.

Launching Your PPP Connection

Your dial-up connection is now configured, but it is not set to connect automatically. One way to start the connection is to set it up to launch manually from the desktop panel. Here's how:

From the GNOME desktop:

1. Right-click the panel, choose Add to Panel ➪ Modem Lights, and then select Add. A Modem Lights icon appears on the panel.

2. Select the new icon from the panel. You are asked if you want to start a connection with your modem.

3. Select Connect to start the connection.

From the KDE desktop:

1. Right-click the panel and then choose Add Application to Panel ➪ Internet ➪ KPPP.

2. Select the new icon from the panel (type the root password, if prompted). A KPPP window appears.

3. Select the dial-up interface you added (probably ppp0) and click Connect to connect.

From this point forward, icons appear on your desktop that you can select to immediately connect to your ISP over the dial-up connection you configured.

Launching Your PPP Connection on Demand

Instead of starting a dial-up PPP connection manually each time you want to contact the Internet, you can set your dial-up connection to start automatically when an application (such as a Web browser or an e-mail program) tries to use the connection. On-demand dialing is particularly useful if:

■ The dial-up connection on your Linux system is acting as the gateway for other comput-ers in your home or office. You don't have to run over to your Linux box to start the con-nection when another computer needs the dial-up connection.

■ Programs that you run during off hours, such as remote backups, require an Internet connection.

■ You don't want to be bothered clicking an extra icon when you just want to browse the Web a bit.

The risk of on-demand dialing is that because it gets going automatically, the dial-up connection can start up when you don't want it to. (Some people get worried when their computers start dial-ing by themselves in the middle of the night.)

For RHEL and Fedora systems, here is an example of settings you can add to your dial-up configuration file (probably /etc/sysconfig/network-scripts/ifcfg-ppp0) to configure on-demand dialing:

```
ONBOOT=yes
DEMAND=yes
IDLETIMEOUT=600
RETRYTIMEOUT=30
```

The ONBOOT=yes setting starts the pppd daemon (but doesn't immediately begin dialing because DEMAND is set to yes). Also, because of the setting DEMAND=yes, a dial-up connection attempt is made any time traffic tries to use your dial-up connection. With IDLETIMEOUT set to 600, the connection is dropped after 600 seconds (10 minutes) with no traffic on the connection. With RETRYTIMEOUT set to 30, a dropped connection is retried after 30 seconds (unless the connection was dropped by an idle timeout, in which case there is no retry). You can change the timeout values as it suits you.

> **NOTE** Because it can take a bit of time for dial-up connections to be established, operations may fail while dialing occurs. In particular, DNS requests can time out in 30 seconds, which may not be long enough to establish a dial-up connection. If you have three DNS servers configured for each client, you have a 90-second timeout period. As a result, the modem connection may be running before the request fails.

Checking Your PPP Connection

To debug your PPP connection or simply to better understand how it works, you can run through the steps that appear in the following sections. They will help you understand where information is being stored and how tools can be used to track this information.

Checking That Your Modem Was Detected

It is possible that your modem is not supported under Linux. If that is the case, your PPP connection might be failing because the modem was not detected at all. To scan your serial ports to see where your modem might be, type the following (as root user):

```
$ wvdialconf /etc/wvdial.conf.new
```

The wvdialconf command builds a configuration file (in this example, the /etc/wvdial .conf.new file) that is used by the dialer command (wvdial). (You need this file only if you use wvdial to do your dial-up.) Its first action, however, is to scan the serial ports on your computer and report where it finds modems. If it tells you that no modem was detected, it's likely that either your modem isn't connected properly or no driver is available to support the modem.

If the modem wasn't detected, you should determine whether it is a modem supported in Linux. You can do this by finding out what type of chip set is used in the modem. This is even more important than finding out the manufacturer of the modem because the same manufacturer can use chips from different companies. (This applies primarily to internal modems because most external serial modems and many USB modems are supported in Linux.)

After you have determined the chip set being used, check Linmodems.org's Web site (www
.linmodems.org). Search for the chip set on your modem from this site. In many cases,
the site can tell you if there is a driver available for your modem.

A nice tool for determining what type of Winmodem you have and how to get it working is
scanModem. If you have access to the Internet from another machine, you can download
scanModem from this address:

    http://linmodems.technion.ac.il/packages/scanModem.gz

Because you probably don't have a working Internet connection yet, find a way to copy
scanModem.gz to your Linux system (maybe copy it to a flash drive or burn it to a CD). As root
user from a Terminal window, type these commands, with that file in the current directory:

```
# gunzip scanModem.gz
# chmod 755 scanModem
# ./scanModem
```

The result is a Modem directory containing text files describing your modem and what you can do
to configure it.

NOTE If you are a new Linux user with a Winmodem and you are still baffled after referring to
the linmodems.org site, you might consider getting a serial or USB modem. To get
your Winmodem working, you might need to download, compile, and load a modem driver. Especially
with some older Winmodems, drivers have not all been updated to work with the latest kernels.
Picking up a cheap serial modem (under $20) from a used computer store can save hours of frustra-
tion that may still result in failure.

Connecting to the Internet with Wireless

Setting up a wireless network connection can be one of the more challenging features to get working in Linux. Despite improvements to open source drivers for many wireless devices, you can't
assume that any wireless card connected to a computer running Linux will just work.

Wireless card manufacturers have, for the most part, not released specifications for their equipment
that would allow open source developers to create Linux drivers. Most vendors simply produce
binary-only drivers for Microsoft Windows systems. As a result of this state of the wireless world,
the following wireless projects have emerged to help Linux users:

- **ndiswrappers** (http://ndiswrapper.sourceforge.net) — This project lets you
  use wireless drivers in Linux that were created to run in Windows.

- **madwifi** (http://madwifi.org) — Supports drivers for wireless chipsets from Atheros
  (www.atheros.com).

- **Intel PRO/Wireless for Linux** (http://ipw2100.sourceforge.net) — There are
  several wireless driver projects to support drivers for Intel PRO/Wireless hardware.

In some cases, you may simply want to get the wireless interface built into your laptop to work. To check the list of supported Linux wireless cards, refer to: `http://rfswitch.sourceforge.net/?page=laptop_matrix`.

Because wireless card firmware is required in order to get many wireless networking cards to work, the software you need for installing the drivers for those cards is not included in many major Linux releases. For example, if you are using Fedora, you can get ndiswrapper and madwifi RPM packages from the third-party `rpm.livna.org` site. Then, in the case of ndiswrapper, you need to install the firmware for your network card from the card manufacturer.

Once the proper driver for your wireless card is installed and activated, there are different tools available for configuring your wireless cards in different Linux releases. Here are examples:

- **Wireless in Fedora** — In Fedora, use the Network Manager to configure your wireless network cards (as root, type **service NetworkManager on**). Then configure your wireless connection from a network icon that appears in the panel.

- **Wireless in KNOPPIX** — In KNOPPIX, try KWiFiManager. From the KDE menu, select KNOPPIX ➪ Network/Internet ➪ KWiFiManager.

For further information on configuring wireless devices in Linux, refer to the Wireless LAN resources for Linux page:

`http://hpl.hp.com/personal/Jean_Tourrilhes/Linux/Wireless.html`

If you find that you are unable to get the driver for your particular wireless card working at all, determine the type of card you have, using one of the following commands:

```
# dmesg |grep -i wireless
# lspci -vv |grep -i wireless
```

Then use some search tool, such as Google, to search for the name and model of your wireless card, along with the word "Linux" or the particular distribution of Linux you are using. Chances are, if your wireless device is at all popular, someone else has tried to get it working in Linux and has probably shared their experiences somewhere online.

Summary

There are many different tools for configuring network connections in the various Linux distributions. Fedora and other Red Hat Enterprise Linux systems use a graphical Network Configuration. SUSE Linux uses its YaST administrative interface to configure network equipment. For dial-up networks, the KDE desktop includes the kppp GUI tool for configuring modems. If your network connection doesn't start up automatically (as it does in many cases), this chapter explains how to use some of these network configuration tools to configure it manually.

By adding your computer to a public network, such as the Internet, you open it to possible intruders. The next chapter describes ways in which you can secure your computer from unwanted access.

Chapter 6

Securing Linux

Since the dawn of interconnected networks, some users have been trying to break into other users' systems. As the Internet has grown and broadband Internet access has spread, the problem has become more severe. A home computer running an insecure configuration can be used as a powerful mail relay, provide storage for traffic in pirated data, allow the user's personal information to become compromised, or any number of other such horrors.

Once upon a time, network attacks required some effort and skill on the part of the attacker. Today, automated tools can get even the most novice user up and running trying to compromise network attached systems in an alarmingly short time. Additionally, worms have the capability to turn large numbers of insecure systems into an army of "zombies" usable for massive, coordinated, distributed Denial of Service (DDOS) attacks.

Why should you care about security? According to the Internet Storm Center (`http://isc.sans.org`), a computer connected to the Internet has an average of 16 minutes before it falls under some form of attack. Securing any computer system is not hugely difficult; it simply requires some common sense and careful application of good security practices.

In many cases, good practices for setting and protecting passwords, monitoring log files, and creating good firewalls will keep out many would-be intruders. Sometimes, more proactive approaches are needed to respond to break-ins.

Many tasks associated with securing your Linux system are common to desktop and server systems. However, because servers allow some level of access by outside clients, there are special considerations for protecting servers.

This chapter describes general tasks for securing Linux systems and techniques for securing desktop and server systems. It then describes some tools you can try out from a bootable Linux system to troubleshoot your computer and network.

Linux Security Checklist

While most Linux systems offer all the tools you need to secure your computer, if you are reckless, someone can (and probably will) harm your system, take it over, or try to steal your data. Keep in mind that no security measures are 100 percent reliable and that, given physical access to a computer or an unlimited amount of time to try to break in, a skilled and determined cracker can break into any computer.

That said, however, there are many safeguards you can take to improve your chances of keeping your Linux system safe. The following checklist covers a range of security features to protect your Linux desktop or server.

- **Control physical access.** Keeping your computer behind locked doors is a good idea, especially if your computer contains critical data. You can limit what a person can do to your computer with physical access by enabling passwords in the BIOS (to prevent the computer from booting at all) and in the GRUB or LILO boot loader. You can also limit which devices can be booted in the BIOS.

- **Add users and passwords.** Creating separate user accounts (each with a good password) is your first line of defense in keeping your data secure. Users are protected from each other, as well as from an outsider who takes over one user account. Setting up group accounts can extend the concept of ownership to multiple users. See Chapter 4 for more on setting up user accounts and also see "Using Password Protection" later in this chapter.

- **Set read, write, and execute permissions.** Every item in a Linux system (including files, directories, applications, and devices) can be restricted by read, write, and execute permissions for that item's owner and group, as well as for all others. In this way, for example, you can let other users run a command or open a file, without allowing them to change it. See Chapter 2 for information on setting file and directory permissions.

- **Protect the root user.** In standard Linux systems, the root user (as well as other administrative user accounts such as apache) has special abilities to use and change your Linux system. Protect the root account's password and don't use the root account when you don't need to. An open shell or desktop owned by the root user can be a target for attack. Running graphical administration windows as a regular user (entering the root password as prompted) and running administrative commands using `sudo` can reduce exposure to attacks on your root account. See Chapter 4 for information on handling the root user account.

> **NOTE** Some distributions, such as Ubuntu, simplify the protection of the root account by automatically disabling it.

■ **Use trusted software.** While there are no guarantees with open source software, you have a better chance of avoiding compromised software by using an established Linux distribution (such as Fedora, Debian, or SUSE). Software repositories where you get add-on packages or updates should likewise be scrutinized. Using valid GPG public keys can help ensure that the software you install comes from a valid vendor. And, of course, always be sure of the source of data files you receive before opening them in a Linux application. If you download full ISO images of a distribution, check their integrity using MD5 or SHA1 checksums provided from their creator.

■ **Get software updates.** As vulnerabilities and bugs are discovered in software packages, every major Linux distribution (including Debian, SUSE, Gentoo, and Red Hat distributions) offers tools for getting and installing those updates. Be sure to get those updates, especially if you are using Linux as a server. These tools include apt, yum, and emerge.

■ **Use secure applications.** Even with software that is valid and working, some applications offer better protection from attack or invasion than others. For example, if you want to log in to a computer over the Internet, the Secure Shell service (ssh) is considered more secure than rlogin or telnet services (which pass clear-text passwords). Also, some services that are thought to be insecure if you expose them on the Internet (such as Samba and NFS) can be used more securely over the Internet through VPN tunnels (such as IPSec or CIPE).

■ **Use restrictive firewalls.** A primary job of a firewall is to accept requests for services from a network that you want to allow and turn away requests that you don't (based primarily on port numbers requested). A desktop system should refuse requests that come in on most ports. A server system should allow requests for a controlled set of ports. See Chapter 18 for information on how to set up a firewall using iptables.

■ **Enable only services you need.** To offer services in Linux (such as Web, file, or mail services), a daemon process will listen on a particular port number. Don't enable services you don't need. In fact, don't even install server software you don't need.

NOTE A program that runs quietly in the background handling service requests (such as sendmail) is called a *daemon*. Usually, daemons are started automatically when your system boots up, and they keep running until your system is shut down. Daemons may also be started on an as-needed basis by xinetd, a special daemon that listens on a large number of port numbers and then launches the requested process.

■ **Limit access to services.** You can restrict access to a service you want to have on by allowing access only from a particular host computer, domain, or network interface. For example, a computer with interfaces to both the Internet and a local LAN might limit access to a service such as NFS to computers on the LAN, but not offer those same services to the Internet. Services may limit access in their own configuration files or using TCP/IP wrappers (described later in this chapter).

■ **Check your system.** Linux has tons of tools available for checking the security of your system. After you install Linux, you can check access to its ports using nmap or watch network traffic using Ethereal. You can also add popular security tools such as Nessus, to get a more complete view of your system security. Security tools included on the CD and DVD with this book are described in this chapter.

■ **Monitor your system.** You can log almost every type of activity on your Linux system. System log files, using the syslogd and klogd facilities, can be configured to track as much or as little of your system activity as you choose. Utilities such as logwatch provide easy ways to have the potential problem messages forwarded to your administrative e-mail account. Linux logging features are described later in this chapter.

NOTE Remember that monitoring your system does not mean that you simply turn on logging — you must also carefully monitor those logs and react to what they tell you.

■ **Use SELinux.** SELinux is an extraordinarily rich (and complex) facility for managing the access of nearly every aspect of a Linux system. It addresses the if-I-get-root-access-I-own-your-box shortcomings of Linux and UNIX systems for highly secure environments. Red Hat systems offer a useful, limited set of SELinux policies that are turned on by default in Fedora. Other Linux distributions are working on and including SELinux implementations as well. Figure 6-1 shows an example of the SELinux Administration tool included with Fedora 8 (select Applications ➪ System Tools ➪ SELinux Management), while Figure 6-2 shows the SELinux Troubleshooter (select Applications ➪ System Tools ➪ SELinux Troubleshooter).

FIGURE 6-1

SELinux utilities are included with Fedora.

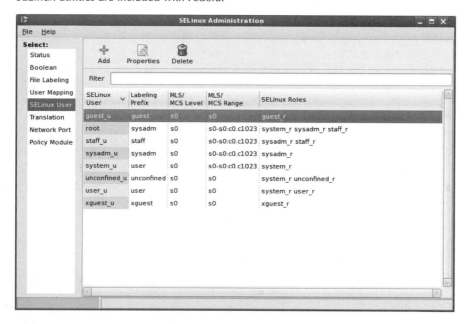

FIGURE 6-2

The SELinux Troubleshooter will identify areas of concern.

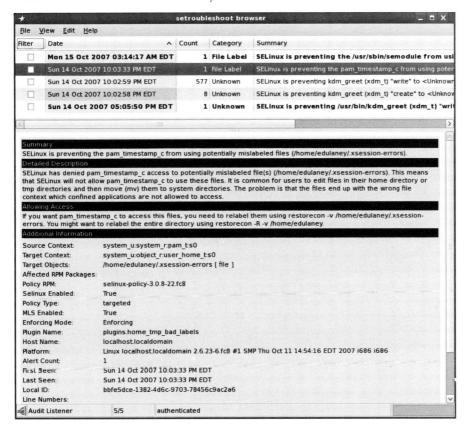

Finding Distribution-Specific Security Resources

Most major Linux distributions have resources devoted to helping you secure Linux and keep up with security information that is specific to that version of Linux. Here are a few online resources that focus on security for several Linux distributions:

- **Red Hat Enterprise Linux and Fedora security** — Check the Red Hat Security site (www.redhat.com/security) for RHEL security issues (that typically relate to Fedora systems as well). From here you can look for and read about available updates. You can also get information on security training and consulting from Red Hat, Inc. For Fedora security issues, see the Fedora Wiki (http://fedoraproject.org/wiki/Security/Features).

Refer to the Red Hat Enterprise Linux 4 Security Guide for an in-depth look at Linux security for Red Hat systems. You can access this guide online from the following address:

`www.redhat.com/docs/manuals/enterprise/RHEL-4-Manual/security-guide/`

- **Debian security** — The Debian Security Information page (`www.debian.org/security`) provides a central point for finding security advisories, answers to common Debian security questions, and links to security documents. You can find the Securing Debian online manual here:

`www.debian.org/doc/manuals/securing-debian-howto`

- **Ubuntu security** — Find security guides and tools for Ubuntu on the Ubuntu security page (`https://help.ubuntu.com/community/Security`).

- **Gentoo security** — Included on the Gentoo Linux Security page (`www.gentoo.org/security`) are tools, announcements, and links to security policy and project documents associated with securing Gentoo systems. Find the Gentoo security handbook here:

`www.gentoo.org/doc/en/security`

- **Slackware security** — To keep up with Slackware security issues, refer to the Slackware Security Advisories (`www.slackware.com/security`). You can also join the security mailing list (`www.slackware.com/lists`) for Slackware.

- **SUSE security** — Online security support for SUSE is provided by SUSE's parent company, Novell. Find links to a variety of SUSE security topics from this site:

`www.novell.com/linux/security/securitysupport.html`

For openSUSE, visit this site:

`www.novell.com/products/opensuse/security.html`

Finding General Security Resources

There are many computer security Web resources that now offer information that is particularly useful to Linux system administrators. Here are a few sites you can check out:

- **CERT** (`www.cert.org`) — The CERT Coordination center follows computer security issues. Check its home page for the latest vulnerability issues. The site has articles on security practices (`www.cert.org/nav/articles_reports.html`). It also has recommendations on what you should do if your computer has been compromised (`www.cert.org/tech_tips/win-UNIX-system_compromise.html`).

- **SecurityFocus** (`www.securityfocus.com`) — In addition to offering news and information on general computer security topics, SecurityFocus also offers several Linux-specific resources. In particular, you can subscribe to receive a weekly Linux Security News newsletter.

- **LinuxSecurity** (`www.linuxsecurity.com`) — This site contains many news articles and features related to Linux security. It also tracks security advisories for more than a dozen Linux distributions.

Using Linux Securely

Getting and keeping your Linux systems secure means not only making good decisions about how you initially set up your system but also how you use it going forward. Whether you are using your Linux system as a desktop or server system, good security practices related to passwords, using secure applications, and monitoring log files are always important.

Setting up a secure firewall (as described in Chapter 18) is critical to having a secure Linux system. There are also other security measures you should apply to Linux. This section describes some good practices for using passwords, keeping track of system activity by watching log files, and communicating with other systems using Secure Shell (ssh) applications.

Using Password Protection

Passwords are the most fundamental security tool of any modern operating system and consequently, the most commonly attacked security feature. It is natural to want to choose a password that is easy to remember, but very often this means choosing a password that is also easy to guess. Crackers know that on any system with more than a few users, at least one person is likely to have an easily guessed password.

By using the "brute force" method of attempting to log in to every account on the system and trying the most common passwords on each of these accounts, a persistent cracker has a good shot of finding a way in. Remember that a cracker will automate this attack, so thousands of login attempts are not out of the question. Obviously, choosing good passwords is the first and most important step to having a secure system.

Here are some things to avoid when choosing a password:

- Do not use any variation of your login name or your full name. Even if you use varied case, append or prepend numbers or punctuation, or type it backwards, this will still be an easily guessed password.
- Do not use a dictionary word, even if you add numbers or punctuation to it.
- Do not use proper names of any kind.
- Do not use any contiguous line of letters or numbers on the keyboard (such as "qwerty" or "asdfg").

Choosing Good Passwords

A good way to choose a strong password is to take the first letter from each word of an easily remembered sentence. The password can be made even better by adding numbers, punctuation, and varied case. The sentence you choose should have meaning only to you, and should not be publicly available (choosing a sentence on your personal Web page is a bad idea). Table 6-1 lists examples of strong passwords and the tricks used to remember them.

TABLE 6-1

Ideas for Good Passwords

Password	How to Remember It
Mrci7yo!	My rusty car is 7 years old!
2emBp1ib	2 elephants make BAD pets, 1 is better
ItMc?Gib	Is that MY coat? Give it back

The passwords look like gibberish but are actually rather easy to remember. As you can see, I can place emphasis on words that stand for capital letters in the password. You set your password using the passwd command. Type the passwd command within a command shell, and it will enable you to change your password. First, it prompts you to enter your old password. To protect against someone "shoulder surfing" and learning your password, the password will not be displayed as you type.

Several distributions include random password generators that can be used to conjure up secure passwords. Figure 6-3, for example, shows a password generator in the Users and Groups tool available in Ubuntu.

Assuming you type your old password correctly, the passwd command will prompt you for the new password. When you type in your new password, the passwd command checks the password against cracklib to determine if it is a *good* or *bad* password. Non-root users will be required to try a different password if the one they have chosen is not a good password.

The root user is the only user who is permitted to assign *bad* passwords. Once the password has been accepted by cracklib, the passwd command asks you to enter the new password a second time to make sure there are no typos (which are hard to detect when you can't see what you are typing). When running as root, it is possible to change a user's password by supplying that user's login name as a parameter to the passwd command. For example:

```
# passwd joe
Changing password for user joe.
New UNIX password: ********
Retype new UNIX password: ********
passwd: all authentication tokens updated successfully.
```

FIGURE 6-3

Generating random passwords

Here the passwd command prompts you twice to enter a new password for joe. It does not prompt you for his old password in this case. This allows root to reset a user's password when that user has forgotten it (an event that happens all too often).

Using a Shadow Password File

In early versions of UNIX, all user account and password information was stored in a file that all users could read (although only root could write to it). This was generally not a problem because the password information was encrypted. The password was encrypted using a *trapdoor algorithm*, meaning the unencoded password could be encoded into a scrambled string of characters, but the string could not be translated back to the non-encoded password. In other words, the trapdoor implies that encryption only goes in one direction, so the encrypted password can't be used to go back to the unencoded password.

How does the system check your password in this case? When you log in, the system encodes the password you entered, compares the resulting scrambled string with the scrambled string that is stored in the password file, and grants you access only if the two match. Have you ever asked a system administrator what the password on your account is only to hear, "I don't know" in response? If so, this is why: The administrator really doesn't have the password, only the encrypted version. The unencoded password exists only at the moment you type it.

Breaking Encrypted Passwords

There is a problem with people being able to see encrypted passwords, however. Although it may be difficult (or even impossible) to reverse the encryption of a trapdoor algorithm, it is very easy to encode a large number of password guesses and compare them to the encoded passwords in the password file. This is, in order of magnitude, more efficient than trying actual login attempts for each user name and password. If a cracker can get a copy of your password file, he or she has a much better chance of breaking into your system.

Fortunately, Linux and all modern UNIX systems support a shadow password file by default. The shadow file is a special version of the passwd file that only root can read. It contains the encrypted password information, so passwords can be left out of the passwd file, which any user on the system can read. Linux supports the older, single password file method as well as the newer shadow password file. You should always use the shadow password file (it is used by default).

Checking for the Shadow Password File

The password file is named passwd and can be found in the /etc directory. The shadow password file is named shadow and is also located in /etc. If your /etc/shadow file is missing, it is likely that your Linux system is storing the password information in the /etc/passwd file instead. Verify this by displaying the file with the less command.

```
# less /etc/passwd
```

Something similar to the following should be displayed:

```
root:DkkS6Uke799fQ:0:0:root:/root:/bin/bash
bin:x:1:1:bin:/bin:
daemon:x:2:2:daemon:/sbin:/bin/sh
     .
     .
     .
mary:KpRUp2ozmY5TA:500:100:Mary Smith:/home/mary:/bin/bash
joe:OsXrzvKnQaksI:501:100:Joe Johnson:/home/joe:/bin/bash
jane:ptNoiueYEjwX.:502:100:Jane Anderson:/home/jane:/bin/bash
bob:Ju2vY7AOX6Kzw:503:100:Bob Reynolds:/home/bob:/bin/bash
```

Each line in this listing corresponds to a single user account on the Linux system. Each line is made up of seven fields separated by colon (:) characters. From left to right, the fields are the login name, the encrypted password, the user ID, the group ID, the description, the home directory, and the default shell. Looking at the first line, you see that it is for the root account and has an encrypted password of DkkS6Uke799fQ. You can also see that root has a user ID of zero, a group ID of zero, and a home directory of /root, and root's default shell is /bin/bash.

All of these values are quite normal for a root account, but seeing that encrypted password should set off alarm bells in your head. It confirms that your system is not using the shadow password file. At this point, you should immediately convert your password file so that it uses /etc/shadow to store the password information. You do this by using the pwconv command. Simply log in as root (or use the su command to become root) and enter the pwconv command at a prompt. It will print no messages, but when your shell prompt returns, you should have a /etc/shadow file, and your /etc/passwd file should now look like this:

```
root:x:0:0:root:/root:/bin/bash
bin:x:1:1:bin:/bin:
daemon:x:2:2:daemon:/sbin:
   .
   .
   .
mary:x:500:100:Mary Smith:/home/mary:/bin/bash
joe:x:501:100:Joe Johnson:/home/joe:/bin/bash
jane:x:502:100:Jane Anderson:/home/jane:/bin/bash
bob:x:503:100:Bob Reynolds:/home/bob:/bin/bash
```

Encrypted password data is replaced with an x. Password data has been moved to /etc/shadow.

There is also an Authentication Configuration utility (available with Fedora and RHEL systems) that you can use to manage shadow passwords and other system authentication information. This tool has features that let you work with MD5 passwords, LDAP authentication, or Kerberos 5 authentication as well. Select System ➪ Authentication, and step through the screens to use it.

To work with passwords for groups, you can use the grpconv command to convert passwords in /etc/groups to shadowed group passwords in /etc/gshadow. If you change passwd or group passwords and something breaks (you are unable to log in to the accounts), you can use the pwunconv and grpunconv commands, respectively, to reverse password conversion.

So, now you are using the shadow password file and picking good passwords. You have made a great start toward securing your system. You may also have noticed by now that security is not just a one-time job. It is an ongoing process, as much about policies as programs. Keep reading to learn more.

Using Log Files

If you make use of good firewalling practices as described in Chapter 18, you will be well prepared to mitigate and prevent most cracker attacks. If your firewall should fail to stop an intrusion, you must be able to recognize the attack when it is occurring. Understanding the various (and numerous) log files in which Linux records important events is critical to this goal. The log files for your Linux system can be found in the /var/log directory.

Most Linux systems make use of log-viewing tools, either provided with the desktop environment (such as GNOME) or as a command you can execute from a Terminal window. GNOME-based desktops often include a System Log Viewer window (gnome-system-log command) that you can use to view and search critical system log files from the GUI. To open the System Log Viewer window from the top panel in Fedora, select Applications ➪ System Tools ➪ System Logs. Figure 6-4 shows an example of the System Log Viewer window.

FIGURE 6-4

Display system log files in the System Log Viewer window.

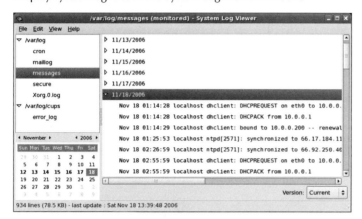

To view a particular log file, click the log name in the left column. Choose a date from the calendar in the lower-left corner to view log messages for a particular date.

Table 6-2 contains a listing of log files displayed in the System Log Viewer window, along with other files in the /var/log directory that may interest you. (Select File ⇨ Open to open a log file that doesn't appear in the left column.) Many of these files are included with most Linux systems and are viewable only by root. Also, some Linux systems may use different file or directory names (for example, /etc/httpd is /etc/apache on some Linux systems).

Because these logs are stored in plain-text files, you can view them using any text editor (such as vi or gedit) or paging command (such as the less command).

TABLE 6-2

Log Files in the /var/log Directory

System Logs Name	Filename	Description
Boot Log	boot.log	Contains messages indicating which systems services have started and shut down successfully and which (if any) have failed to start or stop. The most recent bootup messages are listed near the end of the file.
Cron Log	cron	Contains status messages from the crond, a daemon that periodically runs scheduled jobs, such as backups and log file rotation.
Kernel Startup Log	dmesg	A recording of messages printed by the kernel when the system boots.

TABLE 6-2   *(continued)*

System Logs Name	Filename	Description
FTP Log	xferlog	Contains information about files transferred using the FTP service.
Apache Access Log	httpd/access_log	Logs requests for information from your Apache Web server.
Apache Error Log	httpd/error_log	Logs errors encountered from clients trying to access data on your Apache Web server.
Mail Log	maillog	Contains information about addresses to which and from which e-mail was sent. Useful for detecting spamming.
MySQL Server Log	mysqld.log	Includes information related to activities of the MySQL database server (mysqld).
News Log	spooler	Directory containing logs of messages from the Usenet News server if you are running one.
RPM Packages	rpmpkgs	Contains a listing of RPM packages that are installed on your system. (For systems that are not based on RPM packaging, look for a debian-installer or packages directory to find lists of installed packages.)
Security Log	secure	Records the date, time, and duration of login attempts and sessions.
System Log	messages	A general-purpose log file to which many programs record messages.
Update Agent Log	up2date	Contains messages resulting from actions by the Red Hat Update Agent.
X.Org X11 Log	Xorg.0.log	Includes messages output by the X.Org X server.
[a]	gdm/:0.log	Holds messages related to the login screen (GNOME display manager).
[a]	samba/log.smbd	Shows messages from the Samba SMB file service daemon.
[a]	squid/access.log	Contains messages related to the squid proxy/caching server.
[a]	vsftpd.log	Contains messages relating to transfers made using the vsFTPd daemon (FTP server).
[a]	sendmail	Shows error messages recorded by the sendmail daemon.
[a]	uucp	Shows status messages from the UNIX to UNIX Copy Protocol daemon.

[a] Indicates a log file that is not contained in the System Log Viewer window. Access these files directly from /var/log.

> **NOTE** GNOME 2.18 also includes Seahorse — a front-end to GNU Privacy Guard. Seahorse allows you to digitally sign or authenticate documents and works with OpenPGP and ssh keys. You can find more information at www.gnome.org/projects/seahorse/index.html.

The Role of syslogd

Most of the files in the /var/log directory are maintained by the syslogd service. The syslogd daemon is the system logging daemon. It accepts log messages from a variety of other programs and writes them to the appropriate log files. This is better than having every program write directly to its own log file because it enables you to centrally manage how log files are handled. It is possible to configure syslogd to record varying levels of detail in the log files. It can be told to ignore all but the most critical messages, or it can record every detail.

The syslogd daemon can even accept messages from other computers on your network. This is particularly handy because it enables you to centralize the management and reviewing of the log files from many systems on your network. There is also a major security benefit to this practice.

If a system on your network is broken into, the cracker cannot delete or modify the log files because those files are stored on a separate computer. It is important to remember, however, that those log messages are not, by default, encrypted. Anyone tapping into your local network can eavesdrop on those messages as they pass from one machine to another. Also, although the cracker may not be able to change old log entries, he can affect the system such that any new log messages should not be trusted.

It is not uncommon to run a dedicated loghost, a computer that serves no other purpose than to record log messages from other computers on the network. Because this system runs no other services, it is unlikely that it will be broken into. This makes it nearly impossible for a cracker to erase his or her tracks, but it does not mean that all of the log entries are accurate after a cracker has broken into a machine on your network.

Redirecting Logs to a Loghost with syslogd

To redirect your computer's log files to another computer's syslogd, you must make some changes to your local syslogd's configuration file, /etc/syslog.conf. Become root using the su - command and then load the /etc/syslog.conf file in a text editor (such as vi). You should see something similar to this:

```
# Log all kernel messages to the console.
# Logging much else clutters up the screen.
#kern.*                          /dev/console
# Log anything (except mail) of level info or higher.
# Don't log private authentication messages!
*.info;mail.none;news.none;authpriv.none;cron.none  /var/log/messages
# The authpriv file has restricted access.
authpriv.*                       /var/log/secure
# Log all the mail messages in one place.
mail.*                           /var/log/maillog
# Log cron stuff
cron.*                           /var/log/cron
# Everybody gets emergency messages
*.emerg                          *
# Save news errors of level crit and higher in a special file.
uucp,news.crit                   /var/log/spooler
# Save boot messages also to boot.log
```

```
local7.*                                /var/log/boot.log
#
# INN
#
news.=crit                              /var/log/news/news.crit
news.=err                               /var/log/news/news.err
news.notice                             /var/log/news/news.notice
```

The lines beginning with a # character are comments. Other lines contain two columns of information. The left field is a semicolon-separated list (spaces won't work) of message types and message priorities. The right field is the log file to which those messages should be written.

To send the messages to another computer (the loghost) instead of a file, start by replacing the log filename with the @ character followed by the name of the loghost. For example, to redirect the output normally sent to the messages, secure, and maillog log files, make these changes to the preceding file:

```
# Log anything (except mail) of level info or higher.
# Don't log private authentication messages!
*.info;mail.none;news.none;authpriv.none;cron.none  @loghost
# The authpriv file has restricted access.
authpriv.*                              @loghost
# Log all the mail messages in one place.
mail.*                                  @loghost
```

The messages will now be sent to the syslogd running on the computer named loghost. The name loghost was not an arbitrary choice. It is customary to create such a hostname and make it an alias to the actual system acting as the loghost. That way, if you ever need to switch the loghost duties to a different machine, you need to change only the loghost alias; you do not need to re-edit the syslog.conf file on every computer.

On the loghost side, that machine must run syslogd with the -r option, so it will listen on the network for log messages from other machines. In Fedora systems, that means adding a -r option to the SYSLOGD_OPTIONS variable in the /etc/sysconfig/syslog file and restarting the syslog service (service syslog restart). The loghost must also have UDP port 514 accessible to be used by syslogd (check the /etc/services file), so you might need to add a firewall rule to allow that.

Understanding the messages Log File

Because of the many programs and services that record information to the messages log file, it is important that you understand the format of this file. You can get a good early warning of problems developing on your system by examining this file. Each line in the file is a single message recorded by some program or service. Here is a snippet of an actual messages log file:

```
Feb 25 11:04:32 toys network: Bringing up loopback interface:  succeeded
Feb 25 11:04:35 toys network: Bringing up interface eth0:  succeeded
Feb 25 13:01:14 toys vsftpd(pam_unix)[10565]: authentication failure;
      logname= uid=0 euid=0 tty= ruser= rhost=10.0.0.5  user=chris
Feb 25 14:44:24 toys su(pam_unix)[11439]: session opened for
      user root by chris(uid=500)
```

This is really very simple when you know what to look for. Each message is divided into five main parts. From left to right, they are:

- The date and time that the message was logged
- The name of the computer from which the message came
- The program or service name to which the message pertains
- The process number (enclosed in square brackets) of the program sending the message
- The actual text message

Take another look at the preceding file snippet. In the first two lines, you can see that the network was restarted. The next line shows that the user named chris tried and failed to get to the FTP server on this system from a computer at address 10.0.0.5 (he typed the wrong password and authentication failed). The last line shows chris using the su command to become root user.

By occasionally reviewing the messages and secure files, it's possible to catch a cracking attempt before it is successful. If you see an excessive number of connection attempts for a particular service, especially if they are coming from systems on the Internet, you may be under attack.

Using Secure Shell Tools

The Secure Shell (ssh) tools are a set of client and server applications that allow you to do basic communications (remote login, remote copy, remote execution, and so on) between remote computers and your Linux system. Because communication is encrypted between the server (typically the sshd daemon process) and clients (such as ssh, scp, and sftp), these tools are inherently more secure than similar, older UNIX tools such as rsh, rcp, and rlogin.

Most Linux systems include Secure Shell clients, while many include the sshd server as well. If you are using the Fedora or Red Hat Enterprise Linux distributions, for example, the following client and server software packages include the ssh software: openssh, openssh-clients, and openssh-server packages.

Starting the ssh Service

Linux systems that come with the ssh service already installed often are configured for it to start automatically. In Fedora and RHEL systems, the sshd daemon is started from the /etc/init.d/sshd startup script. To make sure the service is set up to start automatically in Fedora, RHEL, and other RPM-based Linux systems, type the following (as root user):

```
# chkconfig --list sshd
sshd       0:off    1:off    2:on    3:on    4:on    5:on    6:off
```

This shows that the `sshd` service is set to run in system states 2, 3, 4, and 5 (normal bootup states) and set to be off in all other states. You can turn on the ssh service, if it is off, for your default run state by typing the following as root user:

```
# chkconfig sshd on
```

This line turns on the ssh service when you enter run level 2, 3, 4, or 5. To start the service immediately, type the following:

```
# service sshd start
```

Other Linux distributions may simply start the sshd daemon from an entry in the `/etc/rc.d` directory from a file named something like `rc.sshd`. In any case, you can find out if the sshd daemon is currently running on your system by typing the following:

```
$ ps ax | grep sshd
1996 ?      Ss  0:00 /usr/sbin/sshd
```

The preceding example shows that the sshd daemon is running. If that is the case, and your firewall allows Secure Shell service (with TCP port 22 open), you should be able to use ssh client commands to access your system. (Any further configuration you want to do to restrict what the sshd daemon will allow is typically done in the `/etc/ssh/sshd_config` file.)

Using the ssh, sftp, and scp Commands

Three commands you can use with the ssh service are `ssh`, `sftp`, and `scp`. Remote users use the `ssh` command to log in to your system securely or to remotely execute a command on your system. The `scp` command lets remote users copy files to and from a system. The `sftp` command provides a safe way to access FTP sites through the ssh service (for sites that offer ssh access to their FTP content).

Like the normal remote shell services, Secure Shell looks in the `/etc/hosts.equiv` file and in a user's `.rhost` file to determine whether it should allow a connection. It also looks in the ssh-specific files `/etc/shosts.equiv` and `.shosts`. Using the `shosts.equiv` and the `.shosts` files is preferable because it avoids granting access to the unencrypted remote shell services. The `/etc/shosts.equiv` and `.shosts` files are functionally equivalent to the traditional `hosts.equiv` and `.rhosts` files, so the same instructions and rules apply.

Now you are ready to test the ssh service. From another computer on which ssh has been installed (or even from the same computer if another is not available), type the `ssh` command followed by a space and the name of the system you are connecting to. For example, to connect to the system `ratbert.glaci.com`, type:

```
# ssh ratbert.glaci.com
```

If this is the first time ever you have logged in to that system using the ssh command, the system will ask you to confirm that you really want to connect. Type **yes** and press Enter when it asks this:

```
The authenticity of host 'ratbert.glaci.com (199.170.177.18)' can't be
established.
RSA key fingerprint is xx:xx:xx:xx:xx:xx:xx:xx:xx:xx:xx:xx:xx:xx:xx:xx.
Are you sure you want to continue connecting (yes/no)?
```

If you don't specify a user name when you start the ssh connection, the SSH daemon assumes you want to use the user name you are logged in as from the client. If you want to log in as a different user name (such as chris, for example), you could type the following:

```
$ ssh chris@ratbert.glaci.com
```

The scp command is similar to the rcp command for copying files to and from Linux systems. Here is an example of using the scp command to copy a file called memo from the home directory of the user named jake to the /tmp directory on a computer called maple:

```
$ scp /home/jake/memo maple:/tmp
jake@maple's password: ********
memo          100%|****************|  153   0:00
```

Enter the password for your username (if a password is requested). If the password is accepted, the remote system indicates that the file has been copied successfully.

Similarly, the sftp command starts an interactive FTP session with an FTP server that supports ssh connections. Many security-conscious people prefer sftp to other ftp clients because it provides a secure connection between you and the remote host. Here's an example:

```
$ sftp ftp.handsonhistory.com
Connecting to ftp.handsonhistory.com
jake@ftp.handsonhistory.com's password: ********
sftp>
```

At this point you can begin an interactive FTP session. You can use get and put commands on files as you would using any FTP client, but with the comfort of knowing that you are working on a secure connection.

> **TIP** The sftp command, as with ssh and scp, requires that the ssh service be running on the server. If you can't connect to an FTP server using sftp, the ssh service may not be available.

Using ssh, scp, and sftp Without Passwords

For machines that you use a great deal (particularly machines behind a firewall on your LAN), it is often helpful to set them up so that you do not have to use a password to log in. The following procedure shows you how to do that.

These steps take you through setting up password-less authentication from one machine to another. In this example, the local user is named chester on a computer named host1. The remote user is also chester on a computer named host2.

1. Log in to the local computer (in this example, I log in as chester to host1).

NOTE Run Step 2 only once as local user on your local workstation. Do not run it again unless you lose your ssh keys. When configuring subsequent remote servers, skip right to Step 3.

2. Type the following to generate the ssh key:

```
$ ssh-keygen -t dsa
Generating public/private dsa key pair.
Enter file in which to save the key
(/home/chester/.ssh/id_dsa): <Enter>
Enter passphrase (empty for no passphrase): <Enter>
Enter same passphrase again: <Enter>
Your identification has been saved in /home/chester/.ssh/id_dsa.
Your public key has been saved in /home/chester/.ssh/id_dsa.pub.
The key fingerprint is:
3b:c0:2f:63:a5:65:70:b7:4b:f0:2a:c4:18:24:47:69 chester@host1
```

As shown in the example, press Enter to accept the filename where the key is stored. Then press Enter twice to accept a blank passphrase. (If you enter a passphrase, you will be prompted for that passphrase and won't be able to log in without it.)

3. You must secure the permissions of your authentication keys by closing permissions to your home directory, .ssh directory, and authentication files as follows:

```
$ chmod go-w $HOME
$ chmod 700 $HOME/.ssh
$ chmod go-rwx $HOME/.ssh/*
```

4. Type the following to copy the key to the remote server (replace chester with the remote username and host2 with the remote hostname):

```
$ cd ~/.ssh
$ scp id_dsa.pub chester@host2:/tmp
chester@host2's password: *******
```

5. Type the following to add the ssh key to the remote user's authorization keys (the code should be on one line, not wrapped):

```
$ ssh chester@host2 'cat /tmp/id_dsa.pub >>
    /home/chester/.ssh/authorized_keys2'
```

> **NOTE** In the previous two steps you are asked for passwords. This is okay.

For the sshd daemon to accept the `authorized_keys2` file you created, your home directories and that file itself must have secure permissions. To secure that file and those directories, type the following:

```
$ ssh chester@host2 chmod go-w $HOME $HOME/.ssh
$ ssh chester@host2 chmod 600 $HOME/.ssh/authorized_keys2
```

6. Type the following to remove the key from the temporary directory:

```
$ ssh chester@host2 rm /tmp/id_dsa.pub
```

> **NOTE** You should not be asked for a password or passphrase in the previous step.

It is important to note that once you have this working, it will work regardless of how many times the IP address changes on your local computer. The IP address has nothing to do with this form of authentication.

Securing Linux Servers

Opening up your Linux system as a server on a public network creates a whole new set of challenges when it comes to security. Instead of just turning away nearly all incoming requests, your computer will be expected to respond to requests for supported services (such as Web, FTP, or mail service) by supplying information or possibly running scripts that take in data.

Entire books have been filled with information on how to go about securing your servers. Many businesses that rely on Internet servers assign full-time administrators to watch over the security of their servers. So, think of this section as an overview of some of the kinds of attacks to look out for and some tools available to secure your Linux server.

Controlling Access to Services with TCP Wrappers

Completely disabling an unused service is fine, but what about the services that you really need? How can you selectively grant and deny access to these services? For Linux systems that incorporate TCP wrapper support, the `/etc/hosts.allow` and `/etc/hosts.deny` files determine when a particular connection should be granted or refused for services such as rlogin, rsh, telnet, finger, and talk.

Most Linux systems that implement TCP wrappers do so for a set of services that are monitored by a single listening process called the Internet super server. For Fedora and RHEL systems, that server is the xinetd daemon, while in other systems (such as Debian) the inetd daemon is used. When a service that relies on TCP wrappers is requested from the server process, the `hosts.allow` and `hosts.deny` files are scanned and checked for an entry that matches the IP address of the connecting machine. These checks are made when connection attempts occur:

- If the address is listed in the `hosts.allow` file, the connection is allowed and `hosts.deny` is not checked.
- If the address is in `hosts.deny`, the connection is denied.
- If the address is in neither file, the connection is allowed.

Keep in mind that the order in which hosts are evaluated is important. For example, you cannot deny access to a host in the `hosts.deny` file that has already been given access in the `hosts.allow` file.

It is not necessary (or even possible) to list every single address that may try to connect to your computer. The `hosts.allow` and `hosts.deny` files enable you to specify entire subnets and groups of addresses. You can even use the keyword `ALL` to specify all possible addresses. You can also restrict specific entries in these files so they apply only to specific network services. Look at an example of a typical pair of `hosts.allow` and `hosts.deny` files. Here's the `/etc/hosts.allow` file:

```
#
# hosts.allow  This file describes the names of the hosts are
#              allowed to use the local INET services, as decided
#              by the '/usr/sbin/tcpd' server.
#
cups-lpd: 199.170.177.
in.telnetd: 199.170.177., .linuxtoys.net
vsftpd: ALL
```

Here's the `/etc/hosts.deny` file:

```
#
# hosts.deny This file describes names of the hosts which are
#            *not* allowed to use the local INET services, as
#            decided by the '/usr/sbin/tcpd' server.
#
ALL: ALL
```

The preceding example is a rather restrictive configuration. It allows connections to the cups-lpd and telnet services from certain hosts, but then denies all other connections. It also allows connections to the FTP service (vsftp) to all hosts. Let's examine the files in detail.

As usual, lines beginning with a # character are comments and are ignored by xinetd or inetd when it parses the file. Each noncomment line consists of a comma-separated list of daemons followed by a colon (`:`) character and then a comma-separated list of client addresses to check. In this context, a client is any computer that attempts to access a network service on your system.

A client entry can be a numeric IP address (such as 199.170.177.25) or a hostname (such as jukebox.linuxtoys.net), but it is more often a wildcard variation that specifies an entire range of addresses. A client entry can take four different forms. The online manual page for the hosts.allow file describes them as follows:

- A string that begins with a dot (.) character. A hostname is matched if the last components of its name match the specified pattern. For example, the pattern .tue.nl matches the hostname wzv.win.tue.nl.

- A string that ends with a dot (.) character. A host address is matched if its first numeric fields match the given string. For example, the pattern 131.155. matches the address of (almost) every host on the Eindhoven University network (131.155.*x.x*).

- A string that begins with an at (@) sign is treated as an NIS netgroup name. A hostname is matched if it is a host member of the specified netgroup. Netgroup matches are not supported for daemon process names or for client user names.

- An expression of the form *n.n.n.n/m.m.m.m* is interpreted as a *net/mask* pair. A host address is matched if *net* is equal to the bitwise and of the address and the mask. For example, the net/mask pattern 131.155.72.0/255.255.254.0 matches every address in the range 131.155.72.0 through 131.155.73.255.

The example host.allow contains the first two types of client specification. The entry 199.170.177. will match any IP address that begins with that string, such as 199.170.177.25. The client entry .linuxtoys.net will match hostnames such as jukebox.linuxtoys.net and picframe.linuxtoys.net.

Let's examine what happens when a host named jukebox.linuxtoys.net (with IP address 199.170.179.18) connects to your Linux system using the Telnet protocol. In this case, the Linux system is Fedora, which uses the xinetd daemon to listen for service requests associated with TCP wrappers:

1. xinetd receives the connection request.

2. xinetd begins comparing the address and name of jukebox.linuxtoys.net to the rules listed in /etc/hosts.allow. It starts at the top of the file and works its way down the file until it finds a match. Both the daemon (the program handling the network service on your Fedora box) and the connecting client's IP address or name must match the information in the hosts.allow file. In this case, the second rule that is encountered matches the request:

   ```
   in.telnetd: 199.170.177., .linuxtoys.net
   ```

3. The jukebox host is not in the 199.170.177 subnet, but it is in the linuxtoys.net domain. xinetd stops searching the file as soon as it finds this match.

How about if jukebox connects to your box using the CUPS-lpd protocol? In this case, it matches none of the rules in hosts.allow; the only line that refers to the lpd daemon does not refer to the 199.170.179 subnet or to the linuxtoys.net domain. xinetd continues on to the hosts.deny file. The entry ALL: ALL matches anything, so tcpd denies the connection.

The ALL wildcard was also used in the hosts.allow file. In this case, you are telling xinetd to permit absolutely any host to connect to the FTP service on the Linux box. This is appropriate for running an anonymous FTP server that anyone on the Internet can access. If you are not running an anonymous FTP site, you probably should not use the ALL flag.

A good rule of thumb is to make your hosts.allow and hosts.deny files as restrictive as possible and then explicitly enable only those services that you really need. Also, grant access only to those systems that really need access. Using the ALL flag to grant universal access to a particular service may be easier than typing a long list of subnets or domains, but better a few minutes spent on proper security measures than many hours recovering from a break-in.

> **TIP** For Linux systems that use the xinetd service, you can further restrict access to services using various options within the /etc/xinetd.conf file, even to the point of limiting access to certain services to specific times of the day. Read the manual page for xinetd (by typing **man xinetd** at a command prompt) to learn more about these options.

Understanding Attack Techniques

Attacks on computing systems take on different forms, depending on the goal and resources of the attacker. Some attackers want to be disruptive, while others want to infiltrate your machines and utilize the resources for their own nefarious purposes. Still others are targeting your data for financial gain or blackmail. Here are three major categories of attacks:

- **Denial of Service (DOS)** — The easiest attacks to perpetrate are Denial of Service attacks. The primary purpose of these attacks is to disrupt the activities of a remote site by overloading it with irrelevant data. DOS attacks can be as simple as sending thousands of page requests per second at a Web site. These types of attacks are easy to perpetrate and easy to protect against. Once you have a handle on where the attack is coming from, a simple phone call to the perpetrator's ISP will get the problem solved.

- **Distributed Denial of Service (DDOS)** — More advanced DOS attacks are called distributed Denial of Service attacks. DDOS attacks are much harder to perpetrate and nearly impossible to stop. In this form of attack, an attacker takes control of hundreds or even thousands of weakly secured Internet connected computers. The attacker then directs them in unison to send a stream of irrelevant data to a single Internet host. The result is that the power of one attacker is magnified thousands of times. Instead of an attack coming from one direction, as is the case in a normal DOS, it comes from thousands of directions at once. The best defense against a DDOS attack is to contact your ISP to see if it can filter traffic at its border routers.

Many people use the excuse "I have nothing on my machine anyone would want" to avoid having to consider security. The problem with this argument is that attackers have a lot of reasons to use your machine. The attacker can turn your machine into an agent for later use in a DDOS attack. More than once, authorities have shown up at the door of a dumbfounded computer user asking questions about threats originating from their computer. By ignoring security, the owners have opened themselves up to a great deal of liability.

- **Intrusion attacks** — To remotely use the resources of a target machine, attackers must first look for an opening to exploit. In the absence of inside information such as passwords or encryption keys, they must scan the target machine to see what services are offered. Perhaps one of the services is weakly secured and the attacker can use some known exploit to finagle his or her way in.

  A tool called `nmap` is generally considered the best way to scan a host for services (note that `nmap` is a tool that can be used for good and evil). Once the attacker has a list of the available services running on his target, he or she needs to find a way to trick one of those services into letting him or her have privileged access to the system. Usually, this is done with a program called an *exploit*.

While DOS attacks are disruptive, intrusion attacks are the most damaging. The reasons are varied, but the result is always the same. An uninvited guest is now taking up residence on your machine and is using it in a way you have no control over.

Protecting Against Denial of Service Attacks

As explained earlier, a Denial of Service attack attempts to crash your computer or at least degrade its performance to an unusable level. There are a variety of Denial of Service exploits. Most try to overload some system resource, such as your available disk space or your Internet connection. Some common attacks and defenses are discussed in the following sections.

Mailbombing

Mailbombing is the practice of sending so much e-mail to a particular user or system that the computer's hard drive becomes full. There are several ways to protect yourself from mailbombing. You can use the Procmail e-mail–filtering tool or, if you are using sendmail as your mail transport agent, configure your sendmail daemon.

Blocking Mail with Procmail

The Procmail e-mail–filtering tool, installed by default with Fedora, RHEL, and many other Linux systems, is tightly integrated with the sendmail e-mail daemon; thus, it can be used to selectively block or filter out specific types of e-mail. You can learn more about Procmail at the Procmail Web site: `www.procmail.org`.

To enable Procmail for your user account, create a `.procmailrc` file in your home directory. The file should be mode 0600 (readable by you but nobody else). Type the following, replacing *evilmailer* with the actual e-mail address that is mailbombing you:

```
# Delete mail from evilmailer
:0
* ^From.*evilmailer
/dev/null
```

The Procmail recipe looks for the `From` line at the start of each e-mail to see if it includes the string `evilmailer`. If it does, the message is sent to `/dev/null` (effectively throwing it away).

Blocking Mail with sendmail

The Procmail e-mail tool works quite well when only one user is being mailbombed. If, however, the mailbombing affects many users, you should probably configure your sendmail daemon to block all e-mail from the mailbomber. Do this by adding the mailbomber's e-mail address or system name to the `access` file located in the `/etc/mail` directory.

Each line of the `access` file contains an e-mail address, hostname, domain, or IP address followed by a tab and then a keyword specifying what action to take when that entity sends you a message. Valid keywords are `OK`, `RELAY`, `REJECT`, `DISCARD`, and `ERROR`. Using the `REJECT` keyword will cause a sender's e-mail to be bounced back with an error message. The keyword `DISCARD` will cause the message to be silently dropped without sending an error back. You can even return a custom error message by using the `ERROR` keyword.

Thus, an example `/etc/mail/access` file may look similar to this:

```
# Check the /usr/share/doc/sendmail/README.cf file for a description
# of the format of this file. (search for access_db in that file)
# The /usr/share/doc/sendmail/README.cf is part of the sendmail-doc
# package.
#
# by default we allow relaying from localhost...
localhost.localdomain          RELAY
localhost                      RELAY
127.0.0.1                      RELAY
#
# Senders we want to Block
#
evilmailer@yahoo.com    REJECT
stimpy.glaci.com        REJECT
cyberpromo.com          DISCARD
199.170.176.99          ERROR:"550 Die Spammer Scum!"
199.170.177             ERROR:"550 Email Refused"
```

As with most Linux configuration files, lines that begin with a pound (#) sign are comments. The list of blocked spammers is at the end of this example file. Note that the address to block can be a complete e-mail address, a full hostname, a domain only, an IP address, or a subnet.

To block a particular e-mail address or host from mailbombing you, log in to your system as root, edit the /etc/mail/access file, and add a line to DISCARD mail from the offending sender.

After saving the file and exiting the editor, you must convert the access file into a hash-indexed database called access.db. The database is updated automatically the next time sendmail starts. On Fedora and other Red Hat systems, you can convert the database immediately, as follows:

```
# cd /etc/mail
# make
```

Sendmail should now discard e-mail from the addresses you added.

Spam Relaying

Your e-mail services can also be abused by having your system used as a spam relay. *Spam* refers to the unsolicited junk e-mail that has become a common occurrence on the Internet. *Relay* refers to the mail server feature that causes it to send mail it receives to another server. (Normally, only users with valid e-mail accounts on the server are allowed to use a mail server to relay messages on their behalf. A mail server configured as an open relay will allow anyone to forward e-mail messages through it and is, therefore, considered to be a very bad practice.)

Spammers often deliver their annoying messages from a normal dial-up Internet account. They need some kind of high-capacity e-mail server to accept and buffer the payload of messages. They deliver the spam to the server all in one huge batch and then log off, letting the server do the work of delivering the messages to the many victims.

Naturally, no self-respecting Internet service provider will cooperate with this action, so spammers resort to hijacking servers at another ISP to do the dirty work. Having your mailserver hijacked to act as a spam relay can have a devastating effect on your system and your reputation. Fortunately, open mail relaying is deactivated by default on Fedora and Red Hat Enterprise Linux installations. Open mail relaying is one security issue that you will not have to worry about.

You can allow specific hosts or domains to relay mail through your system by adding those senders to your /etc/mail/access file with keyword RELAY. By default, relaying is allowed from the local host only.

> **TIP** One package you might consider using to filter out spam on your mail server is SpamAssassin. SpamAssassin examines the text of incoming mail messages and attempts to filter out messages that are determined to be spam. SpamAssassin is described in Chapter 25.

Smurf Amplification Attack

Smurfing refers to a particular type of Denial of Service attack aimed at flooding your Internet connection. It can be a difficult attack to defend against because it is not easy to trace the attack to the attacker. Here is how smurfing works.

The attack makes use of the ICMP protocol, a service intended for checking the speed and availability of network connections. Using the ping command, you can send a network packet from your computer to another computer on the Internet. The remote computer will recognize the packet as an ICMP request and echo a reply packet to your computer. Your computer can then print a message revealing that the remote system is up and telling you how long it took to reply to the ping.

A smurfing attack uses a malformed ICMP request to bury your computer in network traffic. The attacker does this by bouncing a ping request off an unwitting third party in such a way that the reply is duplicated dozens or even hundreds of times. An organization with a fast Internet connection and a large number of computers is used as the relay. The destination address of the ping is set to an entire subnet instead of a single host. The return address is forged to be your machine's address instead of the actual sender. When the ICMP packet arrives at the unwitting relay's network, every host on that subnet replies to the ping! Furthermore, they reply to your computer instead of to the actual sender. If the relay's network has hundreds of computers, your Internet connection can be quickly flooded.

The best fix is to contact the organization being used as a relay and inform it of the abuse. Usually, they need only to reconfigure their Internet router to stop any future attacks. If the organization is uncooperative, you can minimize the effect of the attack by blocking the ICMP protocol on your router. This will at least keep the traffic off your internal network. If you can convince your ISP to block ICMP packets aimed at your network, it will help even more. (Note that there is some debate about whether or not blocking ICMP packets is a good idea because ICMP services can be useful for various administrative purposes.)

Protecting Against Distributed DOS Attacks

DDOS attacks are much harder to initiate and extremely difficult to stop. A DDOS attack begins with the penetration of hundreds or even thousands of weakly secured machines. These machines can then be directed to attack a single host based on the whims of the attacker.

With the advent of DSL and the cable modem, millions of people are enjoying Internet access with virtually no speed restrictions. In their rush to get online, many of those people neglect even the most basic security. Because the vast majority of these people run Microsoft operating systems, they tend to get hit with worms and viruses rather quickly. After the machine has been infiltrated, quite often the worm or virus installs a program on the victim's machine that instructs it to quietly *call home* and announce that it is now ready to do *the master's bidding*.

At the whim of the master, the infected machines can now be used to focus a concentrated stream of garbage data at a selected host. In concert with thousands of other infected machines, a *script kiddie* now has the power to take down nearly any site on the Internet.

Detecting a DDOS is similar to detecting a DOS attack. One or more of the following signs are likely to be present:

- Sustained saturated data link
- No reduction in link saturation during off-peak hours
- Hundreds or even thousands of simultaneous network connections
- Extremely slow system performance

To determine if your data link is saturated, the act of pinging an outside host can tell much of the story. Much higher than usual latency is a dead giveaway. Normal ping latency (that is, the time it takes for a ping response to come back from a remote host) looks like the following:

```
# ping www.example.com
PING www.example.com (192.0.34.166) from 10.0.0.11: 56(84) bytes of data
64 bytes from 192.0.34.166: icmp_seq=1 ttl=49 time=40.1 ms
64 bytes from 192.0.34.166: icmp_seq=2 ttl=49 time=42.5 ms
64 bytes from 192.0.34.166: icmp_seq=3 ttl=49 time=39.5 ms
64 bytes from 192.0.34.166: icmp_seq=4 ttl=49 time=38.4 ms
64 bytes from 192.0.34.166: icmp_seq=5 ttl=49 time=39.0 ms
--- www.example.com ping statistics ---
5 packets transmitted, 5 received, 0% loss, time 4035ms
rtt min/avg/max/mdev = 38.472/39.971/42.584/1.432 ms
```

In the preceding example, the average time for a ping packet to make the roundtrip was about 39 thousandths of a second.

A ping to a nearly saturated link looks like the following:

```
# ping www.example.com
PING www.example.com (192.0.34.166): from 10.0.0.11: 56(84)bytes of data
64 bytes from 192.0.34.166: icmp_seq=1 ttl=62 time=1252 ms
64 bytes from 192.0.34.166: icmp_seq=2 ttl=62 time=1218 ms
64 bytes from 192.0.34.166: icmp_seq=3 ttl=62 time=1290 ms
64 bytes from 192.0.34.166: icmp_seq=4 ttl=62 time=1288 ms
64 bytes from 192.0.34.166: icmp_seq=5 ttl=62 time=1241 ms
--- www.example.com ping statistics ---
5 packets transmitted, 5 received, 0% loss, time 5032ms
rtt min/avg/max/mdev = 1218.059/1258.384/1290.861/28.000 ms
```

In this example, a ping packet took, on average, 1.3 seconds to make the roundtrip. From the first example to the second example, latency increased by a factor of 31! A data link that goes from working normally to slowing down by a factor of 31 is a clear sign that link utilization should be investigated.

For a more accurate measure of data throughput, you can use a tool such as ttcp. To test your connection with ttcp you must have installed the ttcp package on machines inside *and* outside of your network. (The ttcp package is available with Fedora and other Linux systems.) If you are not sure whether the package is installed, simply type **ttcp** at a command prompt. You should see something like the following:

```
# ttcp
Usage: ttcp -t [-options] host [ < in ]
       ttcp -r [-options > out]
Common options:
       -l ##    length of bufs read from or written to network (default 8192)
       -u       use UDP instead of TCP
       -p ##    port number to send to or listen at (default 5001)
```

```
       -s        -t: source a pattern to network
                 -r: sink (discard) all data from network
       -A        align the start of buffers to this modulus (default 16384)
       -O        start buffers at this offset from the modulus (default 0)
       -v        verbose: print more statistics
       -d        set SO_DEBUG socket option
       -b ##     set socket buffer size (if supported)
       -f X      format for rate: k,K = kilo{bit,byte}; m,M = mega; g,G = giga
Options specific to -t:
       -n##      number of source bufs written to network (default 2048)
       -D        don't buffer TCP writes (sets TCP_NODELAY socket option)
  -w ## number of microseconds to wait between each write
Options specific to -r:
       -B        for -s, only output full blocks as specified by -l (for TAR)
       -T        "touch": access each byte as it's read
  -I if Specify the network interface (e.g. eth0) to use
```

The first step is to start up a receiver process on the server machine:

```
# ttcp -rs
ttcp-r: buflen=8192, nbuf=2048, align=16384/0, port=5001  tcp
ttcp-r: socket
```

The -r flag denotes that the server machine will be the receiver. The -s flag, in conjunction with the r flag, tells ttcp that you want to ignore any received data.

The next step is to have someone outside of your data link, with a network link close to the same speed as yours, set up a ttcp sending process:

```
# ttcp  ts server.example.com
ttcp-t: buflen=8192, nbuf=2048, align=16384/0, port=5001  tcp
     -> server.example.com
ttcp-t: socket
ttcp-t: connect
```

Let the process run for a few minutes and then press Ctrl+C on the transmitting side to stop the testing. The receiving side then takes a moment to calculate and present the results:

```
# ttcp -rs
ttcp-r: buflen=8192, nbuf=2048, align=16384/0, port=5001  tcp
ttcp-r: socket
ttcp-r: accept from 64.223.17.21
ttcp-r: 2102496 bytes in 70.02 real seconds = 29.32 KB/sec +++
ttcp-r: 1226 I/O calls, msec/call = 58.49, calls/sec = 17.51
ttcp-r: 0.0user 0.0sys 1:10real 0% 0i+0d 0maxrss 0+2pf 0+0csw
```

In this example, the average bandwidth between the two hosts was 29.32 kilobytes per second. On a link suffering from a DDOS, this number would be a mere fraction of the actual bandwidth the data link is rated for.

If the data link is indeed saturated, the next step is to determine where the connections are coming from. A very effective way of doing this is with the netstat command, which is included as part of the base Fedora installation. Type the following to see connection information:

```
# netstat -tupn
```

Table 6-3 describes each of the netstat parameters used here.

TABLE 6-3

netstat Parameters

Parameter	Description
-t, --tcp	Show TCP socket connections.
-u, --udp	Show UDP socket connections.
-p, --program	Show the PID and name of the program to which each socket belongs.
-n, --numeric	Show the numerical address instead of trying to determine the symbolic host, port, or usernames.

The following is an example of what the output might look like:

```
Active Internet connections (w/o servers)
Proto  Recv-Q Send-Q Local Address   Foreign Address      State       PID/Program name
tcp    0      0 65.213.7.96:22       13.29.132.19:12545   ESTABLISHED 32376/sshd
tcp    0    224 65.213.7.96:22       13.29.210.13:29250   ESTABLISHED 13858/sshd
tcp    0      0 65.213.7.96:6667     13.29.194.190:33452  ESTABLISHED 1870/ircd
tcp    0      0 65.213.7.96:6667     216.39.144.152:42709 ESTABLISHED 1870/ircd
tcp    0      0 65.213.7.96:42352    67.113.1.99:53       TIME_WAIT   -
tcp    0      0 65.213.7.96:42354    83.152.6.9:113       TIME_WAIT   -
tcp    0      0 65.213.7.96:42351    83.152.6.9:113       TIME_WAIT   -
tcp    0      0 127.0.0.1:42355      127.0.0.1:783        TIME_WAIT   -
tcp    0      0 127.0.0.1:783        127.0.0.1:42353      TIME_WAIT   -
tcp    0      0 65.213.7.96:42348    19.15.11.1:25        TIME_WAIT   -
```

The output is organized into columns defined as follows:

- **Proto** — Protocol used by the socket.
- **Recv-Q** — The number of bytes not yet copied by the user program attached to this socket.
- **Send-Q** — The number of bytes not acknowledged by the host.
- **Local Address** — Address and port number of the local end of the socket.
- **Foreign Address** — Address and port number of the remote end of the socket.
- **State** — Current state of the socket. Table 6-4 provides a list of socket states.
- **PID/Program name** — Process ID and program name of the process that owns the socket.

TABLE 6-4		

Socket States

State	Description
ESTABLISHED	Socket has an established connection.
SYN_SENT	Socket actively trying to establish a connection.
SYN_RECV	Connection request received from the network.
FIN_WAIT1	Socket closed and shutting down.
FIN_WAIT2	Socket is waiting for remote end to shut down.
TIME_WAIT	Socket is waiting after closing to handle packets still in the network.
CLOSED	Socket is not being used.
CLOSE_WAIT	The remote end has shut down, waiting for the socket to close.
LAST_ACK	The remote end has shut down, and the socket is closed, waiting for acknowledgement.
LISTEN	Socket is waiting for an incoming connection.
CLOSING	Both sides of the connection are shut down, but not all of your data has been sent.
UNKNOWN	The state of the socket is unknown.

During a DOS attack, the foreign address is usually the same for each connection. In this case, it is a simple matter of typing the foreign IP address into the search form at www.arin.net/whois/ so you can alert your ISP.

During a DDOS attack, the foreign address will likely be different for each connection. In this case, it is impossible to track down all of the offenders because there will likely be thousands of them. The best way to defend yourself is to contact your ISP and see if it can filter the traffic at its border routers.

Protecting Against Intrusion Attacks

Crackers have a wide variety of tools and techniques to assist them in breaking into your computer. Intrusion attacks focus on exploiting weaknesses in your security, so the crackers can take more control of your system (and potentially do more damage) than they could from the outside.

Fortunately, there are many tools and techniques for combating intrusion attacks. This section discusses the most common break-in methods and the tools available to protect your system. Although the examples shown are specific to Fedora and other Red Hat Linux systems, the tools and techniques are generally applicable to any Linux or UNIX-like operating system.

Evaluating Access to Network Services

Linux systems and their UNIX kin provide many network services, and with them many avenues for cracker attacks. You should know these services and how to limit access to them.

What do I mean by a network service? Basically, I am referring to any task that the computer performs that requires it to send and receive information over the network using some predefined set of rules. Routing e-mail is a network service. So is serving Web pages. Your Linux box has the potential to provide thousands of services. Many of them are listed in the /etc/services file. Look at a snippet of that file:

```
# /etc/services:
# service-name  port/protocol  [aliases ...]    [# comment]
chargen         19/tcp            ttytst source
chargen         19/udp            ttytst source
ftp-data        20/tcp
ftp-data        20/udp
# 21 is registered to ftp, but also used by fsp
ftp             21/tcp
ftp             21/udp         fsp fspd
ssh             22/tcp                          # SSH Remote Login Protocol
ssh             22/udp                          # SSH Remote Login Protocol
telnet          23/tcp
telnet          23/udp
# 24 - private mail system
smtp            25/tcp         mail
```

After the comment lines, you will notice three columns of information. The left column contains the name of each service. The middle column defines the port number and protocol type used for that service. The rightmost field contains an optional alias or list of aliases for the service.

As an example, examine the last entry in the file snippet. It describes the SMTP (Simple Mail Transfer Protocol) service, which is the service used for delivering e-mail over the Internet. The middle column contains the text 25/tcp, which tells you that the SMTP protocol uses port 25 and uses the Transmission Control Protocol (TCP) as its protocol type.

What exactly is a *port number*? It is a unique number that has been set aside for a particular network service. It allows network connections to be properly routed to the software that handles that service. For example, when an e-mail message is delivered from some other computer to your Linux box, the remote system must first establish a network connection with your system. Your computer receives the connection request, examines it, sees it labeled for port 25, and thus knows that the connection should be handed to the program that handles e-mail (which happens to be sendmail).

I mentioned that SMTP uses TCP. Some services use UDP, the User Datagram Protocol. All you really need to know about TCP and UDP (for the purposes of this security discussion) is that they provide different ways of packaging the information sent over a network connection. A TCP connection provides error detection and retransmission of lost data. UDP doesn't check to ensure that the data arrived complete and intact; it is meant as a fast way to send noncritical information.

Disabling Network Services

Although there are hundreds of services (with official port numbers listed in /etc/services) that potentially could be available and subject to attack on your Linux system, in reality only a few dozen services are installed and only a handful of those are on by default. In Fedora and RHEL systems, most network services are started by either the xinetd process or by a start-up script in the /etc/init.d directory. Other Linux systems use the inetd process instead of xinetd.

xinetd and inetd are daemons that listen on a great number of network port numbers. When a connection is made to a particular port number, xinetd or inetd automatically starts the appropriate program for that service and hands the connection to it.

For xinetd, the configuration file /etc/xinetd.conf is used to provide default settings for the xinetd server. The directory /etc/xinetd.d contains files that tell xinetd what ports to listen on and what programs to start (the inetd daemon, alternatively, uses only the /etc/inetd.conf file). Each file in /etc/xinetd.d contains configuration information for a single service, and the file is usually named after the service it configures. For example, to enable the rsync service, edit the rsync file in the /etc/xinetd.d directory and look for a section similar to the following:

```
service rsync
{
    disable = yes
    socket_type        = stream
    wait               = no
    user               = root
    server             = /usr/bin/rsync
    server_args        = --daemon
    log_on_failure     += USERID
}
```

Note that the first line of this example identifies the service as rsync. This exactly matches the service name listed in the /etc/services file, causing the service to listen on port 873 for TCP and UDP. You can see that the service is off by default (disable = yes). To enable the rsync services, change the line to read disable = no instead. Thus, the disable line from the preceding example would look like this:

```
disable = no
```

> **TIP** The rsync service is a nice one to turn on if your machine is an FTP server. It allows people to use an rsync client (which includes a checksum-search algorithm) to download files from your server. With that feature, users can restart a disrupted download without having to start from the beginning.

Because most services are disabled by default, your computer is only as insecure as you make it. You can double-check that insecure services, such as rlogin and rsh (which are included in the rsh-server package in Fedora and RHEL systems), are also disabled by making sure that disabled = yes is set in the /etc/xinetd.d/rlogin and rsh files.

TIP You can make the remote login service active but disable the use of the /etc/host
.equiv and .rhosts files, requiring rlogin to always prompt for a password. Rather
than disabling the service, locate the server line in the rsh file (server = /usr/sbin/in.rshd)
and add a space followed by -L at the end.

You now need to send a signal to the xinetd process to tell it to reload its configuration file. The
quickest way to do that in Fedora and RHEL systems is to reload the xinetd service. As the root
user, type the following from a shell:

```
# service xinetd reload
Reloading configuration:            [ OK ]
```

You can also tell the xinetd process directly to reread the configuration file by sending it a SIGHUP
signal. That works if you are using the inetd daemon instead (on systems such as Debian or
Slackware) to reread the /etc/inetd.conf file. For example, type this (as root user) to have the
inetd daemon reread the configuration file:

```
# killall -s SIGHUP inetd
```

That's it — you have enabled the rsync service. Provided that you have properly configured
your FTP server, clients should now be able to download files from your computer via the
rsync protocol.

Securing Servers with SELinux

Red Hat, Inc. did a clever thing when it took its first swipe at implementing SELinux in Red Hat
systems. Instead of creating policies to control every aspect of your Linux system, it created a
"targeted" policy type that focused on securing those services that are most vulnerable to attacks.
The company then set about securing those services in such a way that, if they were compromised,
a cracker couldn't compromise the rest of the system as well.

Once you have opened a port in your firewall so others can request a service, then started that
service to handle requests, SELinux can be used to set up walls around that service. As a result, its
daemon process, configuration files, and data can't access resources they are not specifically
allowed to access. The rest of your computer, then, is safer.

As Red Hat continues to work out the kinks in SELinux, there has been a tendency for users to see
SELinux failures and just disable the entire SELinux service. However, a better course is to find out
if SELinux is really stopping you from doing something that is unsafe. If it turns out to be a bug
with SELinux, file a bug report and help make the service better.

If you are enabling FTP, Web (HTTPD), DNS, NFS, NIS, or Samba services on your Fedora or
RHEL system, you should consider leaving SELinux enabled and working with the settings from
the Security Level Configuration window to configure those services. For information on SELinux
that is specific to Fedora, refer to this site:

```
http://fedoraproject.org/wiki/SELinux
```

Protecting Web Servers
with Certificates and Encryption

Previous sections told you how to lock the doors to your Linux system to deny access to crackers. The best dead bolt lock, however, is useless if you are mugged in your own driveway and have your keys stolen. Likewise, the best computer security can be for naught if you are sending passwords and other critical data unprotected across the Internet.

A savvy cracker can use a tool called a *protocol analyzer* or a *network sniffer* to peek at the data flowing across a network and pick out passwords, credit card data, and other juicy bits of information. The cracker does this by breaking into a poorly protected system on the same network and running software, or by gaining physical access to the same network and plugging in his or her own equipment.

You can combat this sort of theft by using encryption. The two main types of encryption in use today are symmetric cryptography and public-key cryptography.

Symmetric Cryptography

Symmetric cryptography, also called *private-key* cryptography, uses a single key to both encrypt and decrypt a message. This method is generally inappropriate for securing data that will be used by a third party because of the complexity of secure key exchange. Symmetric cryptography is generally useful for encrypting data for one's own purposes.

A classic use of symmetric cryptography is for a personal password vault. Anyone who has been using the Internet for any amount of time has accumulated a quantity of usernames and passwords for accessing various sites and resources. A personal password vault lets you store this access information in an encrypted form. The end result is that you have to remember only one password to unlock all of your access information.

Exporting Encryption Technology

Before describing how to use the various encryption tools, I need to warn you about an unusual policy of the United States government. For many years, the United States government treated encryption technology like munitions. As a result, anyone wanting to export encryption technology had to get an export license from the Commerce Department. This applied not only to encryption software developed within the United States, but also to software obtained from other countries and then re-exported to another country (or even to the same country you got it from).

Thus, if you installed encryption technology on your Linux system and then transported it out of the country, you were violating federal law! Furthermore, if you e-mailed encryption software to a friend in another country or let him or her download it from your server, you violated the law.

In January 2000, U.S. export laws relating to encryption software were relaxed considerably. However, often the U.S. Commerce Department's Bureau of Export Administration requires a review of encryption products before they can be exported. U.S. companies are also still not allowed to export encryption technology to countries classified as supporting terrorism.

Until recently, the United States government was standardized on a symmetric encryption algorithm called DES (Data Encryption Standard) to secure important information. Because there is no direct way to crack DES-encrypted data, to decrypt DES-encrypted data without a password, you would have to use an unimaginable amount of computing power to try to guess the password. This is also known as the *brute force* method of decryption.

As personal computing power has increased nearly exponentially, the DES algorithm has had to be retired. In its place, after a very long and interesting search, the United States government has accepted the Rijndael algorithm as what it calls the AES (Advanced Encryption Standard). Although the AES algorithm is also subject to brute force attacks, it requires significantly more computing power to crack than the DES algorithm does.

For more information on AES, including a command-line implementation of the algorithm, you can visit `http://aescrypt.sourceforge.net/`.

Asymmetric Cryptography

Public-key cryptography does not suffer from key distribution problems, and that is why it is the preferred encryption method for secure Internet communication. This method uses two keys, one to encrypt the message and another to decrypt the message. The key used to encrypt the message is called the public key because it is made available for all to see. The key used to decrypt the message is the private key and is kept hidden.

Imagine that you want to send me a secure message using public-key encryption. Here is what we need:

1. I must have a public and private key pair. Depending on the circumstances, I may generate the keys myself (using special software) or obtain the keys from a key authority.

2. You want to send me a message, so you first look up my public key (or more accurately, the software you are using looks it up).

3. You encrypt the message with the public key. At this point, the message can be decrypted only with the private key (the public key cannot be used to decrypt the message).

4. I receive the message and use my private key to decrypt it.

Secure Sockets Layer

A classic implementation of public-key cryptography is with Secure Sockets Layer (SSL) communication. This is the technology that enables you to securely submit your credit card information to an online merchant. The elements of an SSL-encrypted session are as follows:

- SSL-enabled Web browser (Mozilla, Internet Explorer, Opera, Konquerer, and so on)
- SSL-enabled Web server (Apache)
- SSL certificate

To initiate an SSL session, a Web browser first makes contact with a Web server on port 443, also known as the HTTPS (Hypertext Transport Protocol Secure) port. After a socket connection has been established between the two machines, the following occurs:

1. The server sends its SSL certificate to the browser.
2. The browser verifies the identity of the server through the SSL certificate.
3. The browser generates a symmetric encryption key.
4. The browser uses the SSL certificate to encrypt the symmetric encryption key.
5. The browser sends the encrypted key to the server.
6. The server decrypts the symmetric key with its private key counterpart of the public SSL certificate.

The browser and server can now encrypt and decrypt traffic based on a common knowledge of the symmetric key. Secure data interchange can now occur.

Creating SSL Certificates

To create your own SSL certificate for secure HTTP data interchange, you must first have an SSL-capable Web server. The Apache Web server (httpd package), which comes with Fedora and other Linux systems, is SSL-capable. The following procedure for creating SSL certificates is done on a Fedora system that includes Apache from the httpd-2.2.3-5 package. This procedure may be different for Apache on other Linux systems.

Once you have a server ready to go, you should familiarize yourself with the important server-side components of an SSL certificate:

```
# ls -l /etc/httpd/conf
-rw-r--r--  1 root     root      36010 Jul 14 15:45 httpd.conf
lrwxrwxrwx  1 root     root         37 Aug 12 23:45 Makefile ->
                                          ../../../usr/share/ssl/certs/Makefile
drwx------  2 root     root       4096 Aug 12 23:45 ssl.crl
drwx------  2 root     root       4096 Aug 12 23:45 ssl.crt
drwx------  2 root     root       4096 Jul 14 15:45 ssl.csr
drwx------  2 root     root       4096 Aug 12 23:45 ssl.key
drwx------  2 root     root       4096 Jul 14 15:45 ssl.prm
# ls -l /etc/httpd/conf.d/ssl.conf
-rw-r--r--  1 root     root      11140 Jul 14 15:45 ssl.conf
```

The /etc/httpd/conf and /etc/httpd/conf.d directories contain all of the components necessary to create your SSL certificate. Each component is defined as follows:

- **httpd.conf** — Web server configuration file
- **Makefile** — Certificate building script
- **ssl.crl** — Certificate revocation list directory
- **ssl.crt** — SSL certificate directory

- **ssl.csr** — Certificate service request directory
- **ssl.key** — SSL certificate private key directory
- **ssl.prm** — SSL certificate parameters
- **ssl.conf** — Primary Web server SSL configuration file

Now that you're familiar with the basic components, take a look at the tools used to create SSL certificates:

```
# cd /etc/httpd/conf
# make
This makefile allows you to create:
  o public/private key pairs
  o SSL certificate signing requests (CSRs)
  o self-signed SSL test certificates
To create a key pair, run "make SOMETHING.key".
To create a CSR, run "make SOMETHING.csr".
To create a test certificate, run "make SOMETHING.crt".
To create a key and a test certificate in one file, run "make SOMETHING.pem".
To create a key for use with Apache, run "make genkey".
To create a CSR for use with Apache, run "make certreq".
To create a test certificate for use with Apache, run "make testcert".
Examples:
  make server.key
  make server.csr
  make server.crt
  make stunnel.pem
  make genkey
  make certreq
  make testcert
```

The make command utilizes the makefile to create SSL certificates. Without any arguments, the make command simply prints the information listed in the preceding example. The following defines each argument you can give to make:

- make server.key — Creates generic public/private key pairs.
- make server.csr — Generates a generic SSL certificate service request.
- make server.crt — Generates a generic SSL test certificate.
- make stunnel.pem — Generates a generic SSL test certificate, but puts the private key in the same file as the SSL test certificate.
- make genkey — Same as make server.key except it places the key in the ssl.key directory.
- make certreq — Same as make server.csr except it places the certificate service request in the ssl.csr directory.
- make testcert — Same as make server.crt except it places the test certificate in the ssl.crt directory.

Using Third-Party Certificate Signers

In the real world, I know who you are because I recognize your face, your voice, and your mannerisms. On the Internet, I cannot see these things and must rely on a trusted third party to vouch for your identity. To ensure that a certificate is immutable, it has to be signed by a trusted third party when the certificate is issued and validated every time an end user taking advantage of your secure site loads it. The following is a list of the trusted third-party certificate signers:

- **GlobalSign** — `https://www.globalsign.net/`
- **GeoTrust** — `https://www.geotrust.com/`
- **VeriSign** — `https://www.verisign.com/`
- **RapidSSL** — `www.freessl.com/`
- **Thawte** — `www.thawte.com/`
- **EnTrust** — `www.entrust.com/`
- **ipsCA** — `www.ipsca.com/`
- **COMODO Group** — `www.comodogroup.com/`

> **NOTE** Because of the fluid nature of the certificate business, some of these companies may not be in business when you read this, while others may have come into existence. To get a more current list of certificate authorities, from your Mozilla Firefox browser select Edit ⇨ Preferences. From the Preferences window that appears, select Advanced ⇨ Manage Certificates. From the Certificate Manager window that appears, refer to the Authorities tab to see Certificate Authorities from which you have received certificates.

Each of these certificate authorities has gotten a chunk of cryptographic code embedded into nearly every Web browser in the world. This chunk of cryptographic code allows a Web browser to determine whether or not an SSL certificate is authentic. Without this validation, it would be easy for crackers to generate their own certificates and dupe people into thinking they are giving sensitive information to a reputable source.

Certificates that are not validated are called *self-signed certificates*. If you come across a site that has not had its identity authenticated by a trusted third party, your Web browser will display a message similar to the one shown in Figure 6-5.

FIGURE 6-5

A pop-up window alerts you when a site is not authenticated.

This does not necessarily mean that you are encountering anything illegal, immoral, or fattening. Many sites opt to go with *self-signed* certificates, not because they are trying to pull a fast one on you, but because there may not be any reason to validate the true owner of the certificate, and they do not want to pay the cost of getting a certificate validated. Some reasons for using a *self-signed* certificate include:

- **The Web site accepts no input.** In this case, you as the end user, have nothing to worry about. There is no one trying to steal your information, because you aren't giving out any information. Most of the time this is done simply to secure the Web transmission from the server to you. The data in and of itself may not be sensitive, but, being a good netizen, the site has enabled you to secure the transmission to keep third parties from sniffing the traffic.

- **The Web site caters to a small clientele.** If you run a Web site that has a very limited set of customers, such as an Application Service Provider, you can simply inform your users that you have no certificate signer. They can browse the certificate information and validate it with you over the phone or in person.

- **Testing.** It makes no sense to pay for an SSL certificate if you are only testing a new Web site or Web-based application. Use a *self-signed* certificate until you are ready to go live.

Creating a Certificate Service Request

To create a third-party validated SSL certificate from a Fedora Linux system, you must first start with a Certificate Service Request (CSR). To create a CSR, do the following on your Web server:

```
# cd /etc/httpd/conf
# make certreq
umask 77 ; \
/usr/bin/openssl genrsa -des3 1024 > /etc/httpd/conf/ssl.key/server.key
     .
     .
     .
```

You will now be asked to enter a password to secure your private key. This password should be at least eight characters long, and should not be a dictionary word or contain numbers or punctuation. The characters you type will not appear on the screen, to prevent someone from shoulder surfing your password.

```
Enter pass phrase:
```

Enter the password again to verify.

```
Verifying - Enter pass phrase:
```

The certificate generation process now begins.

At this point, it is time to start adding some identifying information to the certificate that the third-party source will later validate. Before you can do this, you must unlock the private key you just created. Do so by typing the password you typed for your passphrase. Then enter information as you are prompted. An example of a session for adding information for your certificate is shown here:

```
Enter pass phrase for /etc/httpd/conf/ssl.key/server.key:
You are about to be asked to enter information that will be incorporated
into your certificate request.
What you are about to enter is what is called
a Distinguished Name or a DN.
There are quite a few fields but you can leave some blank
For some fields there will be a default value,
If you enter '.', the field will be left blank.
-----
Country Name (2 letter code) [GB]: US
State or Province Name (full name) [Berkshire]: Connecticut
Locality Name (eg, city) [Newbury]: Mystic
Organization Name (eg, company) [My Company Ltd]: Acme Marina, Inc.
Organizational Unit Name (eg, section) []: InfoTech
Common Name (eg, your name or your server's hostname) []: www.acmemarina.com
Email Address []: webmaster@acmemarina.com
```

To complete the process, you will be asked if you want to add any extra attributes to your certificate. Unless you have a reason to provide more information, you should simply press Enter at each of the following prompts to leave them blank.

```
Please enter the following 'extra' attributes
to be sent with your certificate request
A challenge password []:
An optional company name []:
```

Getting Your CSR Signed

Once your CSR has been created, you need to send it to a signing authority for validation. The first step in this process is to select a signing authority. Each signing authority has different deals, prices, and products. Check out each of the signing authorities listed in the "Using Third-Party Certificate Signers" section earlier in this chapter to determine which works best for you. The following are areas where signing authorities differ:

- Credibility and stability
- Pricing
- Browser recognition
- Warranties
- Support
- Certificate strength

After you have selected your certificate signer, you have to go through some validation steps. Each signer has a different method of validating identity and certificate information. Some require that you fax articles of incorporation, while others require a company officer be made available to talk to a validation operator. At some point in the process, you will be asked to copy and paste the contents of the CSR you created into the signer's Web form.

```
# cd /etc/httpd/conf/ssl.csr
# cat server.csr
-----BEGIN CERTIFICATE REQUEST-----
MIIB6jCCAVMCAQAwgakxCzAJBgNVBAYTAlVTMRQwEgYDVQQIEwtDb25uZWNOaWN1
dDEPMAOGA1UEBxMGTXlzdGljMRowGAYDVQQKExFBY211IE1hcmluYSwgSW5jLjER
MA8GA1UECxMISW5mb1RlY2gxGzAZBgNVBAMTEnd3dy5hY211bWFyaW5hLmNvbTEn
MCUGCSqGSIb3DQEJARYYd2VibWFzdGVyQGFjbWVtYXJpbmEuY29tMIGfMAOGCSqG
SIb3DQEBAQUAA4GNADCBiQKBgQDcYH4pjMxKMldyXRmcoz8uBVOvwlNZHyRWw8ZG
u2eCbvgi6w4wXuHwaDuxbuDBmw//Y9DMI2MXg4wDq4xmPi35EsO1Ofw4ytZJn1yW
aU6cJVQro46OnXyaqXZOPiRCxUSnGRU+OnsqKGjf7LPpXv29S3QvMIBTYWzCkNnc
gWBwwwIDAQABoAAwDQYJKoZIhvcNAQEEBQADgYEANv6eJOaJZGzopNR5h2YkR9Wg
18oBl3mgoPH60Sccw3pWsoW4qbOWq7on8dS/++QOCZWZI1gefgaSQMInKZ1II7Fs
YIwYBgpoPTMC4bpOZZtURCyQWrKIDXQBXw7BlU/3A25nvkRY7vgNL9Nq+7681EJ8
W9AJ3PX4vb2+ynttcBI=
-----END CERTIFICATE REQUEST-----
```

You can use your mouse to copy and paste the CSR into the signer's Web form.

After you have completed the information validation, paid for the signing, and answered all of the questions, you have completed most of the process. Within 48 to 72 hours you should receive an e-mail with your shiny new SSL certificate in it. The certificate will look similar to the following:

```
-----BEGIN CERTIFICATE-----
MIIEFjCCA3+gAwIBAgIQMI262Zd6njZgN97tJAVFODANBgkqhkiG9w0BAQQFADCB
ujEfMB0GA1UEChMWVmVyaVNpZ24gVHJ1c3QgTmV0d29yazEXMBUGA1UECxMOVmVy
aVNpZ24sIEluY4xMzAxBgNVBAsTK1Z1cmlTaWduIEludGVybmF0aW9uYWwgU2Vy
dmVyIENBICOgZ2xhc3MgMzFJMEcGA1OrY2g0Dd3d3LnZlcmlzaWduLmNvbS9DUFMg
SW5jb3JwLmJ51FJlZi4gTElBQklMSVRZIExURC4oYyk5NyBWZXJpU2lnbjAeFwOw
MzAxMTUwMDAwMDBaFwOwNDAxMTUyMzU5NTlaMIGuMQswCQYDVQQGEwJVUzETMBEG
A1UECBMKV2FzaG1uZ3RvHiThErE371UEBxQLRmVkZXJhbCBXYXkxGzAZBgNVBAoU
EklETSBTZXJ2aWM1cywgSW5jLjEMMAoGA1UECxQDd3d3MTMwMQYDVQQLFCpUZXJt
cyBvZiB1c2UgYXQgd3d3LnZlcmlzaWduLmNvbS9ycGEgKGMpMDAxFDASBgNVBAMU
C21kbXNlcnYuY29tMIGfMAOGCSqGSIb3DQEBAQUAA4GNADCBiQKBgQDaHSk+uzOf
7jjDFEnqT8UBalL3yFILXFjhj3XpMXLGWzLmkDmdJjXsa4x7AhEpr1ubuVNhJVIO
FnLDopsx4pyr4n+P8FyS4M5grbcQzy2YnkM2jyqVF/7yOW2pDl30t4eacYYaz4Qg
q9pTxhUzjEG4twvKCAFWfuhEoGu1CMV2qQ1DAQABo4IBJTCCASEwCQYDVROTBAIw
ADBEBgNVHSAEPTA7MDkGC2CGSAGG+EUBBxcDMCOwKAYIKwYBBQUHAgEWHHHh0dHBz
Oi8vd3d3LnZlcmlzaWduLmNvbS9ycGEwCwYDVRRPBAQDAgWgMCgGA1UdJQQhMB8G
CWCGSAGG+EIEMOOcOwIYBQUHAwEGCCsGAQUFBwmCMDQGCCsGAQUFBwEBBCgwJjAk
BggrBgEFBQcwAYYYaHROcDovL29jc2AudmVyaXNpZ24uY29tMEYGA1UdHwQ/MDOw
O6A5oDeGNWh0dHA6Ly9jcmwudmVyaXNpZ24uY29tLONsYXNzMOludGVybmF0aW9u
YWxTZXJ2ZXIuY3JsMBkGCmCGSAgG+E+f4Nfc3zYJODA5NzMwMMTEyMA0GCSqGSIb3
DQEBBAUAA4GBAJ/PsVttmlDkQai5nLeudLceb1F4isXP17B68wXLkIeRu4Novu13
81LZXnaR+acHeStR01b3rQPjgv2y1mwjkPmC1WjoeYfdxH7+Mbg/6fomnK9auWAT
WFOiFW/+a8OWRYQJLMA2VQOVhX4znjpGcVNY9AQSHm1UiESJy7vtd1iX
-----END CERTIFICATE-----
```

Copy and paste this certificate into an empty file called `server.crt`, which must reside in the `/etc/httpd/conf/ssl.crt` directory, and restart your Web server:

```
# service httpd restart
```

Assuming your Web site was previously working fine, you can now view it in a secure fashion by placing an `s` after the `http` in the Web address. So if you previously viewed your Web site at `www.acmemarina.com`, you can now view it in a secure fashion by going to `https://www.acmemarina.com`.

Creating Self-Signed Certificates

Generating and running a self-signed SSL certificate is much easier than having a signed certificate. To generate a self-signed SSL certificate on a Fedora system, do the following:

1. Remove the key and certificate that currently exist:

```
# cd /etc/httpd/conf
# rm ssl.key/server.key ssl.crt/server.crt
```

2. Create your own server key:

```
# make genkey
```

3. Create the self-signed certificate by typing the following:

```
# make testcert
umask 77 ; \
/usr/bin/openssl req -new -key
/etc/httpd/conf/ssl.key/server.key
    -x509 -days 365 -out
/etc/httpd/conf/ssl.key/server.crt
    .
    .
    .
```

At this point, it is time to start adding some identifying information to the certificate. Before you can do this, you must unlock the private key you just created. Do so by typing the password you typed earlier. Then follow this sample procedure:

```
You are about to be asked to enter information that will be
  incorporated into your certificate request.
What you are about to enter is what is called
a Distinguished Name or a DN.
There are quite a few fields but you can leave some blank
For some fields there will be a default value,
If you enter '.', the field will be left blank.
-----
```

```
Country Name (2 letter code) [GB]: US
State or Province Name (full name) [Berkshire]: Ohio
Locality Name (eg, city) [Newbury]: Cincinnati
Organization Name (eg, company) [My Company Ltd]: Industrial Press, Inc.
Organizational Unit Name (eg, section) []: IT
Common Name (eg, your name or your server's hostname)
[]: www.industrialpressinc.com
Email Address []: webmaster@industrialpressinc.com
```

The generation process in this example places all files in the proper place. All you need to do is restart your Web server and add `https` instead of `http` in front of your URL. Don't forget that you'll get a certificate validation message from your Web browser, which you can safely ignore.

Restarting Your Web Server

By now you've probably noticed that your Web server requires you to enter your certificate password every time it is started. This is to prevent someone from breaking into your server and stealing your private key. Should this happen, you are safe in the knowledge that the private key is a jumbled mess. The cracker will not be able to make use of it. Without such protection, a cracker could get your private key and easily masquerade as you, appearing to be legitimate in all cases.

If you just cannot stand having to enter a password every time your Web server starts, and are willing to accept the increased risk, you can remove the password encryption on your private key. Simply do the following:

```
# cd /etc/httpd/conf/ssl.key
# /usr/bin/openssl rsa -in server.key -out  server.key
```

Troubleshooting Your Certificates

The following tips should help if you are having problems with your SSL certificate:

- Only one SSL certificate per IP address is allowed. If you want to add more than one SSL-enabled Web site to your server, you must bind another IP address to the network interface.

- Make sure the permission mask on the `/etc/httpd/conf/ssl.*` directories and their contents is 700 (`rwx------`).

- Make sure you aren't blocking port 443 on your Web server. All `https` requests come in on port 443. If you are blocking it, you will not be able to get secure pages.

- The certificate lasts for one year only. When that year is up, you have to renew your certificate with your certificate authority. Each certificate authority has a different procedure for doing this; check the authority's Web site for more details.

- Make sure you have the mod_ssl package installed. If it is not installed, you will not be able to serve any SSL-enabled traffic.

Using Linux Live CD Security Tools

If you suspect your computers or networks have been exploited, a wide range of security tools is available for Linux that you can use to scan for viruses, do forensics, or monitor activities of intruders. The best way to learn about and use many of these tools is by using dedicated, bootable Linux distributions built specifically for security.

Advantages of Security Live CDs

One great advantage of using a live CD or DVD to check the security of a system is that it separates the tools you use to check a system from the system itself. In other words, because the tools for finding problems on an installed system may themselves be compromised, a live CD of trusted software can be a good way to ensure that you are testing a potentially infected system with clean tools.

If, despite your best efforts (good passwords, firewalls, checking log files, and so on), you believe an intruder may have gained control of your system, you can use a live CD to check it out. Security live CDs such as System Rescue CD, INSERT, and BackTrack (all included on this book's CD or DVD) are great tools for checking and fixing your system.

CROSS-REF   See Chapter 19 for more information on bootable security and rescue CDs.

Using INSERT to Check for rootkits

If an intruder gains access to your Linux system to try to take over control of that system (and use it for more than just a hit-and-run), he or she might install what is called a *rootkit*. A rootkit is a set of software that the intruder will use to:

- Carry out his or her intent (such as hosting false Web content from your server)
- Hide his or her activities from your view

Rootkits can employ different methods for hiding what they do. Often a rootkit will replace common system commands with its own version of those commands. So, for example, you could replace ls and ps to not list the content added to your machine or not show certain processes running on your system, respectively.

The chkrootkit command is a good tool for checking for well-known rootkits, as well as for generally checking system files to see if they have been infected. This tool will check for infections in disk-checking tools (such as du, find, and ls), process table tools (ps and pstree), login-related commands (login, rlogin, and slogin), and many other tools. Here's how to run chkrootkit from INSERT:

1. Insert the CD that comes with this book into the CD drive and reboot.
2. From the boot prompt, type **insert** and press Enter. INSERT should boot to a desktop.

3. To be able to check the Linux system installed on your hard disk, you need to mount the partition representing your installed Linux system. Using the mount.app applet (displayed in the lower-right corner of the screen), click the arrows on that applet to click through the available storage media. If Linux was installed on the first partition of the first hard disk, select hda1. Then click the mount button to mount that partition.

4. Open a Terminal window by right-clicking the desktop and selecting Terminal Session ⇨ Aterm - super user. A Terminal window opens.

5. Run the chkrootkit command and save the output to a file. For example, run the following command to check the file system mounted on /mnt/hda1 and send the output to a file name chkroot-output.txt:

```
# chkrootkit -r /mnt/hda1 > /tmp/chkroot-output.txt
```

6. When the command completes, page through the output. For example:

```
# less /tmp/chkroot-output.txt
ROOTDIR is '/mnt/hda1/'
Checking 'amd' ... not found
Checking 'basename' ... not infected
   .
   .
   .
```

7. Press the spacebar to page through the output. The output should reveal the following:

   ▪ If a rootkit has been planted on your system, some commands will likely come up as infected.

   ▪ If any files or directories implanted by commonly known rootkits are detected, those will be noted. The command checks for more than 60 known rootkits.

   ▪ If any suspicious-looking files appear, they will be listed so you can check them (although they might not represent the presence of a rootkit).

If the search turns up a rootkit, chances are that someone else has control of your machine. Often the best course of action is to reinstall the system. You may be able to replace just the commands that have been infected, but it you do, you first want to make sure that multiple backdoors have not already been placed on your system.

Summary

Securing your Linux system is something you need to do from the very beginning and continue as you use your Linux system. By implementing good security practices (such as practices described in the security checklist at the beginning of this chapter), you stand a better chance of keeping out intruders over the long haul.

Going forward, you can help keep your Linux system secure by using encrypted network applications (such as ssh), monitoring log files, and adhering to good password techniques. If your Linux system is being used as a server, you need to take particular care in narrowing the access to the server and protecting data. To that end, you can use such tools as TCP wrappers (to limit who can use your server) and certificates (to ensure that both ends of communications with your Web server are authenticated).

Part III

Choosing
and Installing
a Linux Distribution

Chapter 7

Installing Linux

If someone hasn't already installed and configured a Linux system for you, this chapter is going to help you get started so you can try out the Linux features described in the rest of the book. With recent improvements to Linux live CDs and installers, getting your hands on a working Linux system is quicker and more solid than ever before.

If you are a first-time Linux user, I recommend that you:

IN THIS CHAPTER

Choosing a Linux distribution

Getting a Linux distribution

Understanding installation issues

- **Try a bootable Linux** — This book's CD and DVD include several bootable Linux systems. The advantage of a bootable Linux is that you can try out Linux without touching the contents of your computer's hard drive. In particular, KNOPPIX is a full-featured Linux system that can give you a good feel for how Linux works. Using the DVD or CD, you can try out several different live CDs, as described in Appendix A. Some of these live CDs also include features for installing Linux to your hard disk. Although live CDs tend to run slower than installed systems and don't keep your changes once you reboot, they are good tools for starting out with Linux.

- **Install a desktop Linux system** — Choose one of the Linux distributions and install it on your computer's hard disk. Permanently installing Linux to your hard disk gives you more flexibility for adding and removing software, accessing and saving data to hard disk, and more permanently customizing your system. Installing Linux as a desktop system lets you try out some useful applications and get the feel for Linux before dealing with more complex server issues.

This chapter provides you with an overview of how to choose a Linux distribution, and then describes issues and topics that are common to installing most Linux distributions. Appendix A describes which Linux distributions are included on this book's DVD and CD and how to run them live or use them to install Linux permanently. Each of the other chapters in this part of the book is dedicated to understanding and installing a particular Linux distribution.

After you've installed Linux, you'll want to understand how to get and manage software for your Linux system. These are important topics that are covered throughout the book, but this chapter describes the major packaging formats and tools to get you going.

Choosing a Linux Distribution

Dozens of popular Linux distributions are available today. Some are generalized distributions that you can use as a desktop, server, or workstation system; others are specialized for business or computer enthusiasts. One intention of this book is to help you choose which one (or ones) will suit you best.

Using the DVD that comes with this book, you can boot directly to KNOPPIX (or several other live CDs to try out Linux) or run an installer (to install Fedora, Ubuntu, Gentoo, or Slackware on your computer's hard disk). Because the Fedora distribution included with the book is the complete distribution, you can install a full range of desktop interfaces and applications, programming tools, and server features. So after you've tried out KNOPPIX and are ready to install Linux on your hard disk, I recommend you try Fedora.

Using the CD that comes with this book, you can boot directly to Damn Small Linux (or several other smaller bootable Linux distros), Debian, or Gentoo (to do a network install of those distributions to your hard disk). Debian and Damn Small Linux are two distributions that can be set up to work well on computers that are older and less powerful, or have a CD drive but no DVD drive. This book also provides descriptions for setting up Debian as a mail and Web server (see Chapters 24 and 25).

Linux at Work

Because I know a lot of people who use Linux, both informally and at work, I want to share my general impressions of how different Linux distributions are being used in the United States. Most consultants I know who set up small office servers used to use Red Hat Linux, but now have mostly moved to Fedora, CentOS (built from Red Hat Enterprise Linux software), Ubuntu, or Debian GNU/Linux. Mandriva Linux (formerly Mandrakelinux) has been popular with people wanting a friendly Linux desktop, but Fedora is also well-liked. The more technically inclined like to play with Gentoo (highly tunable) or Slackware (Linux in a more basic form).

The agreement between Novell and Microsoft at the end of 2006 prompted some open source proponents to abandon SUSE. Whether this will result in a migration from SUSE in the enterprise space, however, has yet to play out. However, right now, Red Hat Enterprise Linux offers the best choice in the enterprise realm for those who object to the alliance.

For people transitioning to Linux with Macintosh hardware, Yellow Dog Linux lets you install on a PowerPC and learn skills that are useful to expand later to Red Hat systems. (Yellow Dog was originally based on Red Hat Linux.) As for the bootable Linuxes, everyone I know thinks they are great fun to try out and a good way to learn about Linux. For a bootable Linux containing desktop software that fits on a full CD (or DVD), KNOPPIX is a good choice, as is Ubuntu; for a bootable mini–CD size Linux, Damn Small Linux works well. However, you can also try out these live CDs from the media that come with this book: INSERT, Puppy Linux, SLAX Popcorn, System Rescue CD, or BackTrack.

This book exposes you to several different Linux distributions. It gives you the advantage of being able to see the strengths and weaknesses of each distribution by actually putting your hands on it. You can also try to connect in to the growing Linux user communities because strong community support results in a more solid software distribution and help when you need it (from such things as forums and online chats).

Other Distributions

There seems to be a new Linux distribution every five minutes, and I really have to stop writing this book at some point. To keep the descriptions of Linux distributions to a reasonable size (and actually have the space to describe how to use Linux), several interesting Linux distributions aren't explored in this book.

Notable Linux distributions not included in this book are TurboLinux, Xandros, and CentOS. TurboLinux (`www.turbolinux.com`) is a popular distribution in Asia-Pacific countries. Xandros (`www.xandros.com`), designed to operate well in Microsoft Windows environments, is a well-regarded desktop Linux system. CentOS has become very popular among consultants who used to use Red Hat Linux. CentOS is a rebuild of the Red Hat Enterprise Linux source code. So, people use it for servers that require longer update cycles that you would get with Fedora. However, because CentOS and Red Hat Enterprise Linux are built from technology developed for Fedora, you can learn a lot about how to use those two distributions by using Fedora. The following sections explain how to look beyond the confines of this book for those and other Linux distributions.

Getting Your Own Linux Distribution

By packaging a handful of Linux distributions with this book, I hoped to save you the trouble of getting Linux yourself. If you have a DVD drive, perhaps you can use this opportunity to at least try KNOPPIX, so you'll better understand what's being discussed. If you have a CD drive only, at least boot directly to Damn Small Linux from the CD that comes with this book.

If for some reason you can't use the software on the CD or DVD, you may want to get your own Linux distributions to use with the descriptions in this book. Reasons you might want to get your own Linux distributions include:

- **No DVD drive** — You need a bootable DVD drive on your computer to use the Linux distributions on the DVD that comes with this book.

- **Later distributions** — You may want a more recent version of a particular distribution than comes with this book.

- **Complete distributions** — Because there's limited space on the CD and DVD and because some distributions require subscriptions or other fees, you may want to obtain your own, more complete distribution with which to work.

Today, there is no shortage of ways to get Linux.

Finding Another Linux Distribution

You can go to the Web site of each distribution (such as `http://fedoraproject.org` or `http://slackware.com/getslack`) to get Linux software. Those sites often let you download a complete copy of their distributions and give you the opportunity to purchase a boxed set.

However, one way to get a more complete view of available Linux distributions is to go to a Web site dedicated to spreading information about Linux distributions. Use these sites to connect to forums and download documentation about many Linux distributions. Here are some examples:

- **DistroWatch** (`www.distrowatch.com`) — The first place I go to find Linux distributions is DistroWatch.com. Go to the Major Distributions link to read about the top Linux distributions (most of which are included with this book). Links will take you to download sites, forums, home pages, and other sites related to each distribution.

- **Linux Help** (`www.linuxhelp.net`) — Select the ISO images link from this site's home page, and you can find download links to ISO images for many of the most popular Linux distributions.

If you don't want to download and burn the CDs yourself, there are plenty of links on those sites from places willing to sell you Linux CDs or DVDs. Distribution prices are often only a little bit higher than the cost of the media and shipping. If you really like a particular Linux distribution, it's a good idea to purchase it directly from the organization that makes it. That can ensure the health of the distribution into the future.

Books such as *Fedora and Red Hat Enterprise Linux Bible* from Wiley Publishing can also be a good way to get a Linux distribution. Finding up-to-date documentation can be difficult when you have nothing but a CD to start out with. Standard Linux documentation (such as HOWTOs and man pages) is often out of date with the software. So, I would particularly recommend a book and distribution (such as this one or *Fedora and Red Hat Enterprise Linux Bible*) for first-time Linux users.

Understanding What You Need

By far, the most common way of getting Linux is on CDs, with DVD being an alternative that's increasing in popularity. Another way is to start with a floppy or CD that includes an installation boot image and get the parts of Linux you need live from the network as you install Linux.

The images that are burned onto the CDs are typically stored on the Internet in what are called *software repositories*. You can download the images and burn them to CDs yourself. Alternatively, the software packages are usually also included separately in directories. Those separate software directories enable you to start an install process with a minimal boot disc that can grab packages over the network during the installation process. (Some of the installations I recommend with this book are done that way.)

When you follow links to Linux software repositories, here's what you look for:

- **Download directory** — You often have to step down a few directories from the download link that gets you to a repository. Look for subdirectories that describe the distribution, architecture, release, and medium format. For example, mirrors for the Fedora 8 Linux distribution might be named `fedora/linux/8/i386/iso`. Other Linux distributions, such as Gentoo and Debian, have tools that will search out online repositories for you, so you don't have to find a mirror directory on your own.

- **ISO images** — The software images you are going to burn to CD are typically stored in ISO format. Some repositories include a README file to tell you what images you need (others just assume you know). To install a distribution, you want the set of ISOs containing the Linux distribution's binary files.

> **NOTE** Although an ISO image appears as one file, it's actually like a snapshot of a file system. You can mount that image to see all the files the image contains by using the `loop` feature of the `mount` command. For example, with an image called `abc.iso` in the current directory, create an empty directory (`mkdir myiso`) and, as root, run the mount command: `mount -o loop abc.iso myiso`. Change to the `myiso` directory and you can view the files and directories the ISO image contains. When you are done viewing the contents, leave the directory and unmount the ISO image (`cd .. ; umount myiso`).

- **MD5SUM** — To verify that you got the right CDs completely intact, after you download them look for a file named MD5SUM or ending in `.md5` in the ISO directory. The file contains one or more MD5 (128-bit) checksums, representing the ISO files you want to check. Other distributions publish SHA1 checksums, which does 160-bit checksums. You can use that file to verify the content of each CD (as described later).

Downloading the Distribution

You can download each ISO image by simply clicking the link and downloading it to a directory in your computer when prompted. You can do this on a Windows or Linux system.

If you know the location of the image you want, with a running Linux system, the `wget` command is a better way to download than just clicking a link in your browser. The advantage of using `wget` is that you can restart a download that stops in the middle for some reason. A `wget` command to download a KNOPPIX CD image (starting from the directory you want to download to) might look like this:

```
$ wget -c kernel.org/pub/dist/knoppix/KNOPPIX_V5.1.1CD-2007-01-04-EN.iso
```

257

If the download stops before it is completed, run the command again. The `-c` option tells `wget` to begin where the download left off, so that if you are 690MB into a 696MB download when it stopped, it just adds in the last 6MB.

A more "good citizen" approach to downloading your ISO images is to use a facility called BitTorrent (`http://bittorrent.com`). BitTorrent enables you to download a file to your computer by grabbing bits of that file from multiple computers on the network that are downloading the file at the same time. For the privilege, you also use your upload capacity to share the same file with others as you are downloading.

During times of heavy demand with a new Linux distribution, BitTorrent can be the best way to go. Recent news articles have portrayed BitTorrent as a tool for illegal activities, such as downloading copyrighted materials (movies, music, and so on). Because most Linux distributions contain only software covered under various open source licenses, there is no legal problem with using BitTorrent to distribute Linux distributions. Check out `www.linuxtracker.org` for a list of Linux distributions that can be downloaded with BitTorrent.

If you are on a dial-up modem, you should strongly consider purchasing Linux CDs (or getting them from a friend) if you don't find what you want on the CD or DVD with this book. You might be able to download an entire 700MB CD in a couple hours on a fast DSL or cable modem connection. On a dial-up line, you might be talking a whole day or more per CD. For a large, multi-CD distribution, available disk space can also become a problem (although, with today's large hard disks, it's not as much of a problem as it used to be).

Burning the Distribution to CD

With the CD images copied to your computer, you can proceed to verify their contents and burn them to CD. All you really need is a CD burner on your computer.

With Linux running, you can use the `md5sum` or `sha1sum` command to verify each CD.

> **NOTE** If you are using Windows to validate the contents of the Linux CD, you can get the MD5Summer utility (`www.md5summer.org`) to verify each CD image.

Assuming you downloaded the MD5 file associated with each CD image, and have it in the same directory as your CD images, run the `md5sum` command to verify the image. For example, to verify the KNOPPIX CD shown previously in the `wget` example, you can type the following:

```
$ md5sum KNOPPIX_V5.1.1CD-2007-01-04-EN.iso
653acc801d4059598bd388de8171a20d  KNOPPIX_V5.1.1CD-2007-01-04-EN.iso
```

The MD5SUM file I downloaded previously from the download directory was called `KNOPPIX_V5.1.1CD-2007-01-04-EN.iso.md5`. It contained this content:

```
653acc801d4059598bd388de8171a20d  *KNOPPIX_V5.1.1CD-2007-01-04-EN.iso
```

As you can see, the checksum (first string of characters shown) that is output from the ISO image matches the checksum in the MD5 file, so you know that the image you downloaded matches the image from the server. If the project uses shalsum to verify its ISO images, you can test your downloaded images with the shalsum command, as follows:

```
$ shalsum FC-6-i386-DVD.iso
6722f95b97e5118fa26bafa5b9f622cc7d49530c FC-6-i386-DVD.iso
```

Once you have verified the shalsum or md5sum of the CD or DVD, as long as you got the image from a reliable site, you should be ready to burn the CD or DVD.

With your Linux distribution in hand, use commands such as cdrecord or k3b to burn your CD or DVD images to disk. Instructions for installing the distributions from the CD or DVD can be found in individual chapters devoted to each distribution (Chapters 8–19). Before you proceed, however, some information is useful for nearly every Linux system you are installing.

Exploring Common Installation Topics

Before you begin installing your Linux distribution of choice, there is some general Linux information you should understand. Reading over this information might help you avoid problems or keep you from getting stuck when you install Linux.

Knowing Your Computer Hardware

Every Linux will not run on every computer. When installing Linux, most people use a Pentium-class PC. There are Linux systems that are compiled to run on other hardware, such as Mac PowerPCs or AMD 64-bit computers. However, the distributions provided with this book run only on 32-bit Pentium-class PCs. Note that because new Mac computers are built from standard Intel components, it's possible to install Linux on those computers as well (see the "Installing Linux on Intel Macs" sidebar).

Installing Linux on Intel Macs

Because of the popularity of MacBook and Mac mini computers, which are based on Intel architecture, several Linux projects have produced procedures for installing their systems to dual-boot with Mac OS X. Most of these procedures involve using the Apple BootCamp software (www.apple .com/macosx/bootcamp).

To install the Fedora Linux that comes with this book, refer to the Fedora on Mactel page (http://fedoraproject.org/wiki/FedoraOnMactel). For Ubuntu, refer to the Ubuntu MacBook page (https://help.ubuntu.com/community/MacBook).

Minimum hardware requirements from the Fedora Project are pretty good guidelines for most Linux systems:

- **Processor** — The latest version of Fedora recommends that you have at least a Pentium-class processor. For a text-only installation, a 200 MHz Pentium is the minimum, while a 400 MHz Pentium II is the minimum for a GUI installation.

> **NOTE** If you have a 486 machine (at least 100 MHz), consider trying Damn Small Linux or Slackware. The problem is that many machines that old have only floppy disks, so you can't use the CD or DVD that comes with this book. In that case, you can try ZipSlack (www.slackware.com/zipslack), which is a Slackware version that comes on about 30+ floppy disk images or a 100MB zip disk and can run on a 486 with at least 100MB of disk space.

- **RAM** — You should have at least 64MB of RAM to install most Linux distributions and run it in text mode. Slackware might run on 8MB of RAM, but 16MB is considered the minimum. If you are running in graphical mode, you will probably need at least 192MB. The recommended RAM for graphical mode in Fedora is 256MB. A GNOME environment generally requires a bit less memory to run than a KDE environment. If you are using a more streamlined graphical system (that runs X with a small window manager, such as Blackbox), you might get by with as little as 32MB. In that case, you might try Damn Small Linux or Slackware.

- **DVD or CD drive** — You need to be able to boot up the installation process from a DVD or CD. If you can't boot from a DVD or CD, there are ways to start the installation from a hard disk or using a PXE install. Some distributions, such as Slackware or SUSE, let you use floppy disks to boot installation. Once the install is booted, the software can sometimes be retrieved from different locations (over the network or from hard disk, for example).

- **Network card** — If you are doing an install of one of the distributions for which we provide a scaled-down boot disk, you might need to have an Ethernet card installed to get the software you need over the network. A dial-up connection won't work for network installs. You don't have to be connected to the Internet necessarily to do a network install. Some people will download the necessary software packages to a computer on their LAN, and then use that as an install server.

- **Disk space** — You should have at least 3GB of disk space for the average GNOME or KDE desktop, although installations can range (depending on which packages you choose to install) from 600MB (for a minimal server with no GUI install) to 7GB (to install all packages).

If you're not sure about your computer hardware, there are a few ways to check what you have. If you are running Windows, the System Properties window can show you the processor you have, as well as the amount of RAM that's installed. As an alternative, you can boot KNOPPIX and let it detect and report to you the hardware you have. (See Chapter 5 for instructions on running the lspci and dmseg commands in Linux to view information about your computer hardware.)

Upgrading or Installing from Scratch

If you already have a version of the Linux you are installing on your computer, many Linux distributions offer an upgrade option. This lets you upgrade all packages, for example, from version 1 of the distribution to version 2. Here are a few general rules before performing an upgrade:

- **Back up data** — There is a possibility that after you finish your upgrade, the operating system won't boot. It's always a good idea to back up any critical data and configuration files (in /etc) before doing any major changes to your operating system.

- **Remove extra packages** — If there are software packages you don't need, remove them before you do an upgrade. Upgrade processes typically upgrade only those packages that are on your system. Upgrades generally do more checking and comparing than clean installs do, so any package you can remove saves time during the upgrade process.

- **Check configuration files** — A Linux upgrade procedure often leaves copies of old configuration files. You should check that the new configuration files still work for you.

TIP Installing Linux from scratch goes faster than an upgrade. It also results in a cleaner Linux system. So if you have the choice of backing up your data, or just erasing it if you don't need it, a fresh install is usually best.

Some Linux distributions, most notably Gentoo, have taken the approach of ongoing updates. Instead of taking a new release every few months, you simply continuously grab updated packages as they become available and install them on your system.

Dual Booting with Windows or Just Linux?

It is possible to have multiple, bootable operating systems on the same computer (using multiple partitions on a hard disk and/or multiple hard disks). Setting up to boot more than one operating system, however, requires some thought. It also assumes some risks.

CAUTION While tools for resizing Windows partitions and setting up multi-boot systems have improved in recent years, there is still considerable risk of losing data on Windows/Linux dual-boot systems. Different operating systems often have different views of partition tables and master boot records that can cause your machine to become unbootable (at least temporarily) or lose data permanently. Always back up your data before you try to resize a Windows (NTFS or FAT) file system to make space for Linux. If you have a choice, install Linux on a machine of its own or at least on a separate hard disk.

If the computer you are using already has a Windows system on it, it's quite possible that that the entire hard disk is devoted to Windows. While you can run a bootable Linux, such as KNOPPIX or Damn Small Linux, without touching the hard disk, to do a more permanent installation you'll want to find disk space outside of the Windows installation. There are a few ways to do this:

- **Add a hard disk** — Instead of messing with your Windows partition, you can simply add a hard disk and devote it to Linux.

- **Resize your Windows partition** — If you have available space on your Windows partition, you can shrink that partition so there is available free space on the disk to devote to Linux. Commercial tools such as Partition Magic from Symantec (`www.symantec.com`) or Acronis Disk Director (`www.acronis.com`) are available to resize your disk partitions and set up a workable boot manager. Some Linux distributions (particularly bootable Linuxes used as rescue CDs) include a tool called QTParted that is an open source clone of Partition Magic (which includes software from the Linux-NTFS project for resizing Windows NTFS partitions).

> **NOTE** An alternative to QTParted is GParted, which is included on the media for this book.

Before you try to resize your Windows partition, you might need to defragment it. To defragment your disk on some Windows systems, so that all of your used space is put in order on the disk, open My Computer, right-click your hard disk icon (typically C:), select Properties, click Tools, and select Defragment Now.

Defragmenting your disk can be a fairly long process. The result of defragmentation is that all the data on your disk are contiguous, creating a lot of contiguous free space at the end of the partition. There are cases where you will have to do the following special tasks to make this true:

- If the Windows swap file is not moved during defragmentation, you must remove it. Then, after you defragment your disk again and resize it, you will need to restore the swap file. To remove the swap file, open the Control Panel, open the System icon, and then click the Performance tab and select Virtual Memory. To disable the swap file, click Disable Virtual Memory.

- If your DOS partition has hidden files that are on the space you are trying to free up, you need to find them. In some cases, you won't be able to delete them. In other cases, such as swap files created by a program, you can safely delete those files. This is a bit tricky because some files should not be deleted, such as DOS system files. You can use the `attrib -s -h` command from the root directory to deal with hidden files.

Once your disk is defragmented, you can use one of the commercial tools described earlier (Partition Magic or Acronis Disk Director) to repartition your hard disk to make space for Linux. An open source alternative to those tools is QTParted.

Boot KNOPPIX or any of several other bootable Linux distributions (particularly rescue CDs) and run QTParted by selecting System Tools ➪ QTParted from the desktop main menu. From the QTParted window, select the hard disk you want to resize. Then choose Options ➪ Configuration to open a window where you can select the ntfsresize tool to resize your NTFS partition.

After you have cleared enough disk space to install Linux (see the disk space requirements in the chapter covering the Linux distribution you're installing), you can choose your Linux distribution and install it. As you set up your boot loader during installation, you will be able to identify the Windows, Linux, and any other bootable partitions so that you can select which one to boot when your start your computer.

Using Installation Boot Options

Sometimes a Linux installation will fail because the computer has some non-functioning or non-supported hardware. Sometimes you can get around those issues by passing options to the install process when it boots up. Those options can do such things as disable selected hardware (`nousb`, `noscsi`, `noide`, and so on) or not probe hardware when you need to select your own driver (`noprobe`).

Although some of these options are distribution-specific, others are simply options that can be passed to an installer environment that works from a Linux kernel. Chapter 11 includes a list of many boot options that can be used with KNOPPIX and other Linux systems.

Partitioning Hard Drives

The hard disk (or disks) on your computer provides the permanent storage area for your data files, applications programs, and the operating system itself. Partitioning is the act of dividing a disk into logical areas that can be worked with separately. In Windows, you typically have one partition that consumes the whole hard disk. However, with Linux there are several reasons you may want to have multiple partitions:

- **Multiple operating systems** — If you install Linux on a PC that already has a Windows operating system, you may want to keep both operating systems on the computer. For all practical purposes, each operating system must exist on a completely separate partition. When your computer boots, you can choose which system to run.

- **Multiple partitions within an operating system** — To protect from having your entire operating system run out of disk space, people often assign separate partitions to different areas of the Linux file system. For example, if /home and /var were assigned to separate partitions, then a gluttonous user who fills up the /home partition wouldn't prevent logging daemons from continuing to write to log files in the /var/log directory.

  Multiple partitions also make it easier to do certain kinds of backups (such as an image backup). For example, an image backup of /home would be much faster (and probably more useful) than an image backup of the root file system (/).

- **Different file system types** — Different kinds of file systems have different structures. File systems of different types must be on their own partitions. In most Linux systems, you need at least one file system type for / (typically ext3 or reiserfs) and one for your swap area. File systems on CD-ROM use the iso9660 file system type.

> **TIP** When you create partitions for Linux, you will usually assign the file system type as Linux native (using the ext2 or ext3 type on some Linux systems, and reiserfs on others). Reasons to use other types include needing a file system that allows particularly long filenames, large file sizes, or many inodes (each file consumes an inode).
>
> For example, if you set up a news server, it can use many inodes to store news articles. Another reason for using a different file system type is to copy an image backup tape from another operating system to your local disk (such as one from an OS/2 or Minix operating system).

COMING FROM WINDOWS If you have used only Windows operating systems before, you probably had your whole hard disk assigned to C: and never thought about partitions. With many Linux systems, you have the opportunity to view and change the default partitioning based on how you want to use the system.

During installation, systems such as SUSE and Fedora let you partition your hard disk using graphical partitioning tools (YaST and Disk Druid, respectively). The following sections describe how to use Disk Druid (during installation) or fdisk. See the section "Tips for Creating Partitions" for some ideas for creating disk partitions.

Partitioning with Disk Druid During Installation

During installation, Fedora gives you the opportunity to change how your hard disk is partitioned using a tool called Disk Druid (in fact, the name "Disk Druid" seems to be going away, but the partitioning tool remains the same). The Disk Druid screen is divided into two sections. The top shows general information about each hard disk. The bottom shows details of each partition. Figure 7-1 shows an example of the Disk Druid window.

FIGURE 7-1

Partition your disk during Fedora installation from the disk setup window.

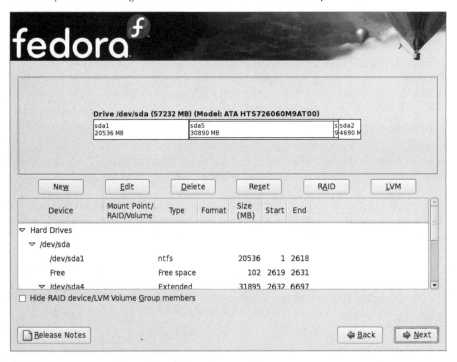

For each of the hard disk partitions, you can see the following:

- **Device** — The device name is the name representing the hard disk partition in the /dev directory. Each disk partition device begins with two letters: sd for IDE or SCSI disks, ed for ESDI disks, or xd for XT disks. After that is a single letter representing the number of the disk (disk 1 is a, disk 2 is b, disk 3 is c, and so on). So, for example, to refer to the entire first hard disk, use the device name /dev/sda. To refer to a particular partition on that disk, add the partition number (1, 2, 3, and so on). For example, /dev/sda1 represents the first partition on the first IDE hard drive on the computer.

- **Mount Point/Raid/Volume** — The directory where the partition is connected into the Linux file system (if it is). You must assign the root partition (/) to a native Linux partition before you can proceed. If you are using RAID or LVM, the name of the RAID device or LVM volume appears here.

- **Type** — The type of file system that is installed on the disk partition. In many cases, the file system will be Linux (ext3), Win VFAT (vfat), or Linux swap. However, you can also use the previous Linux file system (ext2), physical volume (LVM), or software RAID. The NTFS partition shown in Figure 7-1 for device /dev/sda1 implies that Windows is installed on this computer and this can, therefore, be used as a dual-boot computer with Windows and Linux.

- **Format** — Indicates whether the installation process should format the hard disk partition. Partitions marked with a check are erased! So, on a multi-boot system, be sure your Windows partitions and other partitions containing data you don't want to lose are not checked!

- **Size (MB)** — The amount of disk space allocated for the partition (in megabytes). If you selected to let the partition grow to fill the existing space, this number may be much larger than the requested amount.

- **Start/End** — Represents the partition's starting and ending cylinders on the hard disk.

In the top section, you can see each of the hard disks connected to your computer. The drive name is shown first. That's followed by the model name of the disk. The total amount of disk space, the amount used, and the amount free are shown in megabytes.

Reasons for Partitioning

There are different opinions about dividing up a hard disk. Here are some issues:

- **Do you want to install another operating system?** If you want Windows on your computer along with Linux, you will need at least one Windows (Win95 FAT16, VFAT, or NTFS type), one Linux (Linux ext3), and one Linux swap partition.

- **Is it a multiuser system?** If you are using the system yourself, you probably don't need many partitions. One reason for partitioning an operating system is to keep the entire system from running out of disk space at once. That also serves to put boundaries on what an individual can use up in his or her home directory (although disk quotas are good for that as well).

- **Do you have multiple hard disks?** You need at least one partition per hard disk. If your system has two hard disks, you may assign one to / and one to /home (if you have lots of users) or /var (if the computer is a server sharing lots of data).

Deleting, Adding, and Editing Partitions

Before you can add a partition, there needs to be some free space available on your hard disk. If all space on your hard disk is currently assigned to one partition (as it often is in DOS or Windows), you must delete or resize that partition before you can claim space on another partition. The section "Dual Booting with Windows or Just Linux?" discusses how to add a partition without losing information in your existing single-partition system.

CAUTION   Make sure that any data that you want to keep is backed up before you delete the partition. When you delete a partition, all its data is gone.

Disk Druid is less flexible but more intuitive than the fdisk utility. Disk Druid lets you delete, add, and edit partitions.

TIP   If you create multiple partitions, make sure that there is enough room in the right places to complete the installation. For example, most of the Linux software is installed in the /usr directory (and subdirectories), whereas most user data files are eventually added to the /home or /var directory.

To delete a partition in Disk Druid, do the following:

1. Select a partition from the list of Current Disk Partitions on the main Disk Druid window (click it or use the arrow keys).
2. Click Delete.
3. When asked to confirm the deletion, click Delete.
4. If you made a mistake, click Reset to return to the partitioning as it was when you started Disk Druid.

To add a partition in Disk Druid, follow these steps from the main Disk Druid window:

1. Select New. A window appears, enabling you to create a new partition.
2. Type the name of the Mount Point (the directory where this partition will connect to the Linux file system). You need at least a root (/) partition and a swap partition.
3. Select the type of file system to be used on the partition. You can select from Linux native (ext2 or preferably ext3), software RAID, Linux swap (swap), physical volume (LVM), or Windows FAT (vfat).

TIP   To create a file system type different from those shown, leave the space you want to use free for now. After installation is complete, use fdisk to create a partition of the type you want.

4. Type the number of megabytes to be used for the partition (in the Size field). If you want this partition to grow to fill the rest of the hard disk, you can put any number in this field (1 will do fine).

5. If you have more than one hard disk, select the disk on which you want to put the partition from the Allowable Drives box.

6. Type the size of the partition (in megabytes) into the Size (MB) box.

7. Select one of the following Additional Size Options:

   ▪ **Fixed size** — Click here to use only the number of megabytes you entered into the Size text box when you create the partition.

   ▪ **Fill all space up to (MB)** — If you want to use all remaining space up to a certain number of megabytes, click here and fill in the number. (You may want to do this if you are creating a VFAT partition up to the 2048MB limit that Disk Druid can create.)

   ▪ **Fill to maximum allowable size** — If you want this partition to grow to fill the rest of the disk, click here.

8. Optionally, select Force to Be a Primary Partition if you want to be sure to be able to boot the partition or Check for Bad Blocks if you want to have the partition checked for errors.

9. Select OK if everything is correct. (The changes don't take effect until several steps later when you are asked to begin installing the packages.)

To edit a partition in Disk Druid from the main Disk Druid window, follow these steps:

1. Click the partition you want to edit.

2. Click the Edit button. A window appears, ready to let you edit the partition definition.

3. Change any of the attributes (as described in the add partition procedure). For a new install, you may need to add the mount point (/) for your primary Linux partition.

4. Select OK. (The changes don't take effect until several steps later, when you are asked to begin installing the packages.)

Partitioning with fdisk

The fdisk utility is available with most every Linux system for creating and working with disk partitions in Linux. It does the same job as graphical partitioning tools such as Disk Druid, although it's no longer offered as an option during Fedora installation.

TIP During Fedora and other Linux installations that have virtual terminals running, you can switch to a shell (press Ctrl+Alt+F2) and use fdisk manually to partition your hard disk.

The following procedures are performed from the command line as root user.

CAUTION Remember that any partition commands can easily erase your disk or make it inaccessible. Back up critical data before using any tool to change partitions! Then be very careful about the changes you do make. Keeping an emergency boot disk handy is a good idea, too.

The fdisk command is one that is available on many different operating systems (although it looks and behaves differently on each). In Linux, fdisk is a menu-based command. To use fdisk to list all your partitions, type the following (as root user):

```
# fdisk -l
Disk /dev/sda: 40.0 GB, 40020664320 bytes
255 heads, 63 sectors/track, 4865 cylinders
Units = cylinders of 16065 * 512 = 8225280 bytes
    Device Boot    Start      End     Blocks   Id  System
/dev/sda1    *        1       13     104391   83  Linux
/dev/sda2            14     4833   38716650   83  Linux
/dev/sda3          4834     4865     257040   82  Linux swap
```

To see how each partition is being used on your current system, type the following:

```
# df -h
Filesystem           Size  Used Avail Use% Mounted on
/dev/sda2             37G  5.4G   30G  16% /
/dev/sda1             99M  8.6M   86M  10% /boot
none                  61M     0   61M   0% /dev/shm
```

From the output of df, you can see that the root of your Linux system (/) is on the /dev/sda2 partition and that the /dev/sda1 partition is used for /boot.

> **CAUTION** Before using fdisk to change your partitions, I strongly recommend running the df -h command to see how your partitions are currently being defined. This will help reduce the risk of changing or deleting the wrong partition.

To use fdisk to change your partitions, you need to identify the hard disk you are partitioning. For example, the first IDE hard disk is identified as /dev/sda. So, to partition your first IDE hard drive, you can begin (as root user) by typing:

```
# fdisk /dev/sda
```

For different hard drive types or numbers, /dev/sda is replaced by the name of the device you want to work with. Table 7-1 shows some of your choices.

TABLE 7-1

Disk Device Names

Device	Description
/dev/sda	For the first IDE or SCSI hard disk; sdb, sdc, and so on for other disks
/dev/rd/c0d0	For a RAID device
/dev/ida/c0d0	Also for a RAID device

After you have started fdisk, type **m** to see the options. Here is what you can do with fdisk:

- **Delete a partition** — Type **d** and a partition number, and then press Enter. For example, /dev/sda2 would be partition number 2. (The deletion won't take effect until you write the change — you can back out up to that point.)

- **Create a partition** — If you have free space, you can add a new partition. Type **n; l** for a logical partition (5 or over) or **p** for a primary partition (1–4); and a partition number from the available range. Then choose the first cylinder number from those available. (The output from fdisk -l shown earlier will show you cylinders being used under the Start and End columns.)

  Next, enter the cylinder number the partition will end with (or type the specific number of megabytes or kilobytes you want: for example, +50M or +1024K). You just created an ext3 Linux partition. Again, this change isn't permanent until you write the changes.

- **Change the partition type** — Type **T** to choose the type of file system. Enter the partition number of the partition you want to change. Type the number representing the file system type you want to use in hexadecimal code. (Type **L** at this point to see a list of file system types and codes.) For a Linux file system, use the number 83; for a Linux swap partition, use 82; and for a windows FAT32 file system, use the letter *b*.

- **Display the partition table** — Throughout this process, feel free to type **p** to display (print on the screen) the partition table as it now stands.

- **Quit or save** — Before you write your changes, display the partition table again and make sure that it is what you want it to be. If you don't like a change you make to your partitions, type **Q** to exit without saving. Nothing changes on your partition table.

  If your changes are correct, write them to the partition table by typing **W**. You are warned about how dangerous it is to change partitions, and you must confirm the change.

An alternative to the menu-driven fdisk command is sfdisk, which is a command line–oriented partitioning tool. With sfdisk, you type the full command line to list or change partitions, instead of being taken through a set of prompts (as with fdisk). See the sfdisk man page for details. Linux experts often prefer sfdisk because it can be used in combination with other commands to take and output partitioning information.

Tips for Creating Partitions

Changing your disk partitions to handle multiple operating systems can be very tricky, in part because each operating system has its own ideas about how partitioning information should be handled, as well as different tools for doing it. Here are some tips to help you get it right:

- If you are creating a dual-boot system, particularly for Windows XP, try to install the Windows operating system first. Otherwise, the Windows installation may make the Linux partitions inaccessible. Choosing a VFAT instead of NTFS file system for Windows will also make sharing files between your Windows and Linux systems easier and more reliable.

- The `fdisk` man page recommends that you use partitioning tools that come with an operating system to create partitions for that operating system. For example, the DOS fdisk knows how to create partitions that DOS will like, and the Linux fdisk will happily make your Linux partitions. Once your hard disk is set up for dual boot, however, you should probably not go back to Windows-only partitioning tools. Use Linux fdisk or a product made for multi-boot systems (such as Partition Magic).

- You can have up to 63 partitions on an IDE hard disk. A SCSI hard disk can have up to 15 partitions. You won't need nearly that many partitions.

If you are using Linux as a desktop system, you probably don't need a lot of different partitions. There are, however, some very good reasons for having multiple partitions for Linux systems that are shared by a lot of users or are public Web servers or file servers. Multiple partitions within Fedora Linux, for example, offer the following advantages:

- **Protection from attacks** — Denial of Service attacks sometimes take actions that try to fill up your hard disk. If public areas, such as `/var`, are on separate partitions, a successful attack can fill up a partition without shutting down the whole computer. Because `/var` is the default location for Web and FTP servers, and expected to hold a lot of data, entire hard disks often are assigned to the `/var` file system alone.

- **Protection from corrupted file systems** — If you have only one file system (`/`), its corruption can cause the whole Linux system to be damaged. Corruption of a smaller partition can be easier to fix and often allows the computer to stay in service while the correction is made.

Table 7-2 lists some directories that you may want to consider making into separate file system partitions.

Although people who use Linux systems casually rarely see a need for lots of partitions, those who maintain and occasionally have to recover large systems are thankful when the system they need to fix has several partitions. Multiple partitions can localize deliberate damage (such as denial-of-service attacks), problems from errant users, and accidental file system corruption.

TABLE 7-2

Assigning Partitions to Particular Directories

Directory	Explanation
`/boot`	Sometimes the BIOS in older PCs can access only the first 1,024 cylinders of your hard disk. To make sure that the information in your `/boot` directory is accessible to the BIOS, create a separate disk partition (of about 100MB) for `/boot` and make sure that it exists below cylinder 1,024. The rest of your Linux system can exist outside of that 1,024-cylinder boundary if you like. Even with several boot images, there is rarely a reason for `/boot` to be larger than 100MB. (For newer hard disks, you can select the Linear Mode check box during installation. Then the boot partition can be anywhere on the disk.)

TABLE 7-2	(continued)
Directory	**Explanation**
/usr	This directory structure contains most of the applications and utilities available to Linux users. Having /usr on a separate partition lets you mount that file system as read-only after the operating system has been installed. This prevents attackers from replacing or removing important system applications with their own versions that may cause security problems. A separate /usr partition is also useful if you have diskless workstations on your local network. Using NFS, you can share /usr over the network with those workstations.
/var	Your FTP (/var/ftp) and Web server (/var/www) directories are, by default in many Linux systems, stored under /var. Having a separate /var partition can prevent an attack on those facilities from corrupting or filling up your entire hard disk.
/home	Because your user account directories are located in this directory, having a separate /home account can prevent a reckless user from filling up the entire hard disk.
/tmp	Protecting /tmp from the rest of the hard disk by placing it on a separate partition can ensure that applications that need to write to temporary files in /tmp are able to complete their processing, even if the rest of the disk fills up.

Using LILO or GRUB Boot Loaders

A boot loader lets you choose when and how to boot the bootable operating systems installed on your computer's hard disks. Most Linux systems give you the opportunity to use GRUB or LILO boot loaders. The following sections describe both GRUB and LILO boot loaders.

Booting Your Computer with GRUB

With multiple operating systems installed and several partitions set up, how does your computer know which operating system to start? To select and manage which partition is booted and how it is booted, you need a boot loader. The boot loader that is installed by default with Fedora and other Linux systems is the GRand Unified Boot loader (GRUB).

GRUB is a GNU bootloader (www.gnu.org/software/grub) that replaced LILO as the default boot loader in many Linux systems, including Fedora and Ubuntu. GRUB offers the following features:

- Support for multiple executable formats.

- Support for multi-boot operating systems (such as Fedora, FreeBSD, NetBSD, OpenBSD, and other Linux systems).

- Support for non–multi-boot operating systems (such as Windows 95, Windows 98, Windows NT, Windows ME, Windows XP, and OS/2) via a chain-loading function. Chain-loading is the act of loading another boot loader (presumably one that is specific to the proprietary operating system) from GRUB to start the selected operating system.

- Support for multiple file system types.

- Support for automatic decompression of boot images.

- Support for downloading boot images from a network.

For more information on how GRUB works, type **man grub** or **info grub**. The info command contains more details about GRUB.

Booting with GRUB

When you install Linux, you are typically given the option to configure the information needed to boot your computer (with one or more operating systems) into the default boot loader. With GRUB configured, when you boot your computer, the first thing you see after the BIOS loads is the GRUB boot screen (it says GRUB at the top and lists bootable partitions below it). Do one of the following:

- **Default** — If you do nothing, the default operating system will boot automatically after a few seconds. (The timeout is set by the timeout value, in seconds, in the grub.conf file.)

- **Select an operating system** — Use the up and down arrow keys to select any of the titles, representing operating systems you can boot, that are shown on the screen. Then press Enter to boot that operating system.

- **Edit the boot process** — If you want to change any of the options used during the boot process, use the arrow keys to highlight the operating system you want and type **e** to select it. Follow the next procedure to change your boot options temporarily.

If you want to change your boot options so that they take effect every time you boot your computer, see the section on permanently changing boot options. Changing those options involves editing the /boot/grub/grub.conf file.

Temporarily Changing Boot Options

From the GRUB boot screen, you can select to change or add boot options for the current boot session. First, select the operating system you want (using the arrow keys) and type **e** (as described earlier). You will see a graphical screen that looks like the one shown in Figure 7-2.

There are three lines in the example of the GRUB editing screen that identify the boot process for the operating system you chose. The first line (beginning with root) shows that the entry for the GRUB boot loader is on the seventh partition of the first hard disk (hd0,6). GRUB represents the hard disk as hd, regardless of whether it is a SCSI, IDE, or other type of disk. You just count the drive number and partition number, starting from zero (0).

The second line of the example (beginning with kernel) identifies the boot image (/boot/vmlinuz-2.6.20-1.3104.fc7) and several options. The options identify the partition as initially being loaded ro (read-only) and the location of the root file system on a partition with the label root=LABEL=/123. The third line (starting with initrd) identifies the location of the initial RAM disk, which contains the minimum files and directories needed during the boot process.

From the GRUB boot screen, you can select to change boot options.

```
GNU GRUB    version 0.97   (639K lower / 259840K upper memory)


 root (hd0,6)
 kernel /boot/vmlinuz-2.6.20-1.3194.fc7 ro root=LABEL=/123 rhgb quiet
 initrd /boot/initrd-2.6.20-1.3194.fc7.img




    Use the   and   keys to select which entry is highlighted.
    Press 'b' to boot, 'e' to edit the selected command in the
    boot sequence, 'c' for a command-line, 'o' to open a new line
    after ('O' for before) the selected line, 'd' to remove the
    selected line, or escape to go back to the main menu.
```

If you are going to change any of the lines related to the boot process, you would probably change only the second line to add or remove boot options. Here is how you do that:

1. Position the cursor on the kernel line and type **e**.

2. Either add or remove options after the name of the boot image. You can use a minimal set of bash shell command-line editing features to edit the line. You can even use command completion (type part of a filename and press Tab to complete it). Here are a few options you may want to add or delete:

   ■ **Boot to a shell** — If you forgot your root password or if your boot process hangs, you can boot directly to a shell by adding init=/bin/sh to the boot line. (The file system is mounted read-only, so you can copy files out. You need to remount the file system with read/write permission to be able to change files.)

   ■ **Select a run level** — If you want to boot to a particular run level, you can add the word linux, followed by the number of the run level you want. For example, to have Fedora Linux boot to run level 3 (multiuser plus networking mode), add linux 3 to the end of the boot line. You can also boot to single-user mode (1), multiuser mode (2), or X GUI mode (5). Level 3 is a good choice if your GUI is temporarily broken.

3. Press Enter to return to the editing screen.

4. Type **b** to boot the computer with the new options. The next time you boot your computer, the new options will not be saved. To add options so they are saved permanently, see the next section.

Permanently Changing Boot Options

You can change the options that take effect each time you boot your computer by changing the GRUB configuration file. In Fedora and other Linux systems, GRUB configuration centers on the /boot/grub/grub.conf file.

The /boot/grub/grub.conf file is created when you install Linux. Here's an example of that file for Fedora:

```
# grub.conf generated by anaconda
#
# Note that you do not have to rerun grub after making
# changes to this file
# NOTICE: You have a /boot partition.  This means that
#         all kernel and initrd paths are relative to /boot/, eg.
#         root (hd0,6)
#         kernel /vmlinuz-version ro root=/dev/sda7
#         initrd /initrd-version.img
#boot=/dev/sda
default=0
timeout=10
splashimage=(hd0,6)/grub/splash.xpm.gz
title Fedora (2.6.20-1.3104.fc7)
     root (hd0,6)
     kernel /vmlinuz-2.6.20-1.3104.fc7 ro root=LABEL=/123 rhgb quiet
     initrd /initrd-2.6.20-1.3104.fc7.img
title Windows XP
     rootnoverify (hd0,0)
     chainloader +1
```

The default=0 line indicates that the first partition in this list (in this case Fedora) will be the one that is booted by default. The line timeout=10 causes GRUB to pause for 10 seconds before booting the default partition. (That's how much time you have to press **e** if you want to edit the boot line, or to press arrow keys to select a different operating system to boot.)

The splashimage line looks in the seventh partition on the first disk (hd0,6) for the boot partition (in this case /dev/sda7, which is the /boot partition). GRUB loads splash.xpm.gz as the image on the splash screen (/boot/grub/splash.xpm.gz). The splash screen appears as the background of the boot screen.

NOTE GRUB indicates disk partitions using the following notation: (hd0,0). The first number represents the disk, and the second is the partition on that disk. So, (hd0,1) is the second partition (1) on the first disk (0).

The two bootable partitions in this example are Fedora and Windows XP. The title lines for each of those partitions are followed by the name that appears on the boot screen to represent each partition.

For the Fedora Linux system, the root line indicates the location of the boot partition as the second partition on the first disk. So, to find the bootable kernel (vmlinuz-2.20-1.3104.fc7) and the initrd initial RAM disk boot image that is loaded (initrd-2.6.20-1.3104.fc7.img), GRUB looks in the root of hd0,6 (which is represented by /dev/sda7 and is eventually mounted as /boot). Other options on the kernel line set the partition as read-only initially (ro) and set the root file system to LABEL=/123.

For the Windows XP partition, the `rootnoverify` line indicates that GRUB should not try to mount the partition. In this case, Windows XP is on the first partition of the first hard disk (`hd0,0`) or `/dev/sda1`. Instead of mounting the partition and passing options to the new operating system, the `chainloader +1` indicates to hand control the booting of the operating system to another boot loader. The +1 indicates that the first sector of the partition is used as the boot loader.

> **NOTE** Microsoft operating systems require that you use the `chainloader` to boot them from GRUB because GRUB doesn't offer native support for Windows operating systems.

If you make any changes to the `/boot/grub/grub.conf` file, you *do not* need to load those changes. GRUB automatically picks up those changes when you reboot your computer. If you are accustomed to using the LILO boot loader, this may confuse you at first, as LILO requires you to rerun the `lilo` command for the changes to take effect.

Adding a New GRUB Boot Image

You may have different boot images for kernels that include different features. Here is the procedure for modifying the `grub.conf` file:

1. Copy the new image from the directory in which it was created (such as `/usr/src/kernels/linux-2.6.20-1/arch/i386/boot`) to the `/boot` directory. Name the file something that reflects its contents, such as `bz-2.6.20-1`. For example:

```
# cp /usr/src/linux-2.6.20-1/arch/i386/boot/bzImage/boot/bz-2.6.20-1
```

2. Add several lines to the `/boot/grub/grub.conf` file so that the image can be started at boot time if it is selected. For example:

```
title Fedora (My own IPV6 build)
    root (hd0,1)
    kernel /bz-2.6.20-1 ro root=/dev/sda7
    initrd /initrd-2.6.20-1.img
```

3. Reboot your computer.
4. When the GRUB boot screen appears, move your cursor to the title representing the new kernel and press Enter.

The advantage to this approach, as opposed to copying the new boot image over the old one, is that if the kernel fails to boot, you can always go back and restart the old kernel. When you feel confident that the new kernel is working properly, you can use it to replace the old kernel or perhaps just make the new kernel the default boot definition.

Booting Your Computer with LILO

LILO stands for LInux LOader. Like other boot loaders, LILO is a program that can stand outside the operating systems installed on the computer so you can choose which system to boot. It also lets you give special options that modify how the operating system is booted. On Slackware and some other Linux systems, LILO is used instead of GRUB as the default boot loader.

If LILO is being used on your computer, it is installed in either the master boot record or the first sector of the root partition. The master boot record is read directly by the computer's BIOS. In general, if LILO is the only loader on your computer, install it in the master boot record. If there is another boot loader already in the master boot record, put LILO in the root partition.

> **NOTE** If you are new to Linux and not familiar with boot loaders, it is highly recommended that you learn and use GRUB instead of LILO. Support for LILO — and inclusion in distributions — has been reduced recently in favor of GRUB.

Using LILO

When your computer boots with the Fedora version of LILO installed in the master boot record, a graphical Fedora screen appears, displaying the bootable partitions on the computer. Use the up and down arrow keys on your keyboard to select the one you want and press Enter. Otherwise, the default partition that you set at installation will boot after a few seconds.

If you want to add any special options when you boot, press Ctrl+X. You will see a text-based boot prompt that appears as follows:

```
boot:
```

LILO pauses for a few seconds and then automatically boots the first image from the default bootable partition. To see the bootable partitions again, quickly press Tab. You may see something similar to the following:

```
LILO boot:
linux linux-up dos
boot:
```

This example shows that three bootable partitions are on your computer, called linux, linux-up, and dos. The first two names refer to two different boot images that can boot the Linux partition. The third refers to a bootable DOS partition (presumably containing a Windows operating system). The first bootable partition is loaded if you don't type anything after a few seconds. Or you can use the name of the other partition to have that boot instead.

If you have multiple boot images, press Shift, and LILO asks you which image you want to boot. Available boot images and other options are defined in the /etc/lilo.conf file.

Setting Up the /etc/lilo.conf File

The /etc/lilo.conf file is where LILO gets the information it needs to find and start bootable partitions and images. By adding options to the /etc/lilo.conf file, you can change the behavior of the boot process. The following is an example of some of the contents of the /etc/lilo.conf file:

```
prompt
timeout=50
default=linux
boot=/dev/hda
```

```
map=/boot/map
install=/boot/boot.b
message=/boot/message
linear
image=/boot/vmlinuz-18-1.2798.fc6
        label=linux
        initrd=/boot/initrd-2.6.18-1.2798.fc6.img
        read-only
        root=/dev/hda6
        append="root=LABEL=/"
other=/dev/hda1
        optional
        label=dos
```

With `prompt` on, the boot prompt appears when the system is booted without requiring you to press any keys. The timeout value, in this case 50 tenths of a second (5 seconds), defines how long to wait for keyboard input before booting the default boot image. The boot line indicates that the bootable partition is on the hard disk represented by /dev/hda (the first IDE hard disk).

NOTE Depending upon the distribution, "hda" may be "sda". If you are using LILO, the odds are good that you are using an older Linux implementation and thus hda is shown in the example and used in this discussion.

The `map` line indicates the location of the map file (/boot/map, by default). The map file contains the name and locations of bootable kernel images. The `install` line indicates that the /boot/boot.b file is used as the new boot sector. The `message` line tells LILO to display the contents of the /boot/message file when booting (which contains the graphical Fedora boot screen). The linear line causes linear sector addresses to be generated (instead of sector/head/cylinder addresses).

In the sample file, there are two bootable partitions. The first (`image=/boot/vmlinuz-2.6.18-1 .2798.fc6`) shows an image labeled `linux`. The root file system (/) for that image is on partition /dev/hda6. Read-only indicates that the file system is first mounted read-only, although it is probably mounted as read/write after a file system check. The `initrd` line indicates the location of the initial RAM disk image used to start the system.

The second bootable partition, which is indicated by the word "other" in this example, is on the /dev/hda1 partition. Because it is a Windows XP system, it is labeled a DOS file system. The table line indicates the device that contains the partition.

Other bootable images are listed in this file, and you can add another boot image yourself (like one you create from reconfiguring your kernel as discussed in the next section) by installing the new image and changing `lilo.conf`.

After you change `lilo.conf`, you then must run the `lilo` command for the changes to take effect. You may have different boot images for kernels that include different features. Here is the procedure for modifying the `lilo.conf` file:

   1. Copy the new image from the directory in which it was created (such as /usr/src/ kernels/2.6.18-1.2798.fc6/arch/i386/boot) to the /boot directory. Name the file something that reflects its contents, such as zImage-2.6.18-1.2798.fc6.

2. Add several lines to the /etc/lilo.conf file so that the image can be started at boot time if it is selected. For example:

```
image=/boot/zImage-2.6.18-1.2798.fc6
label=new
```

3. Type the **lilo -t** command (as root user) to test that the changes were okay.

4. Type the **lilo** command (with no options) for the changes to be installed.

To boot from this new image, either select new from the graphical boot screen or type **new** and press Enter at the LILO boot prompt. If 5 seconds is too quick, increase the timeout value (such as 100 for 10 seconds).

Options that you can use in the /etc/lilo.conf file are divided into global options, per-image options, and kernel options. A lot of documentation is available for LILO. For more details on any of the options described here or for other options, you can see the lilo.conf manual page (type **man lilo.conf**) or any of the documents in /usr/share/doc/lilo*/doc.

A few examples follow of global options that you can add to /etc/lilo.conf. Global options apply to LILO as a whole, instead of just to a particular boot image.

You can use the default=*label* option, where *label* is replaced by an image's label name, to indicate that a particular image be used as the default boot image. If that option is excluded, the first image listed in the /etc/lilo.conf file is used as the default. For example, to start the image labeled new by default, add the following line to lilo.conf:

```
default=new
```

Change the delay from 5 seconds to something greater if you want LILO to wait longer before starting the default image. This gives you more time to boot a different image. To change the value from 5 seconds (50) to 15 seconds (150), add the following line:

```
delay=150
```

You can change the message that appears before the LILO prompt by adding that message to a file and changing the message line. For example, you could create a /boot/boot.message file and add the following words to that file: Choose linux, new, or dos. To have that message appear before the boot prompt, add the following line to /etc/lilo.conf:

```
message=/boot/boot.message
```

All per-image options begin with either an image= line (indicating a Linux kernel) or other= (indicating some other kind of operating system, such as Windows XP). The per-image options apply to particular boot images rather than to all images (as global options do). Along with the image or other line is a label= line, which gives a name to that image. The name is what you select at boot time to boot that image. Here are some of the options that you can add to each of those image definitions:

- lock — This enables automatic recording of boot command lines as the defaults for different boot options.

- alias=*name* — You can replace *name* with any name. That name becomes an alias for the image name defined in the label option.

- password=*password* — You can password-protect all images by adding a password option line and replacing *password* with your own password. The password would have to be entered to boot any of the images.

- restricted — This option is used with the password option. It indicates that a password should be used only if command-line options are given when trying to boot the image.

For Linux kernel images, there are specific options that you can use. These options let you deal with hardware issues that can't be autodetected, or provide information such as how the root file system is mounted. Here are some of the kernel image-specific options:

- append — Add a string of letters and numbers to this option that need to be passed to the kernel. In particular, these can be parameters that need to be passed to better define the hard disk when some aspect of that disk can't be autodetected. For example: append="hd=64,32,202".

- ramdisk — Add the size of the RAM disk that you want to use in order to override the size of the RAM disk built into the kernel.

- read-only — Mount the root file system read-only. It is typically remounted read-write after the disk is checked.

- read-write — Mount the root file system read/write.

Changing Your Boot Loader

If you don't want to use the GRUB boot loader, or if you tried out LILO and want to switch back to GRUB, it's not hard to change to a different boot loader on Linux distributions that support both boot loaders. To switch your boot loader from GRUB to LILO, do the following:

1. Configure the /etc/lilo.conf file as described in the "Booting Your Computer with LILO" section.

2. As root user from a Terminal window, type the following:

```
# lilo
```

The new Master Boot Record is written, including the entries in /etc/lilo.conf.

3. Reboot your computer. You should see the LILO boot screen.

To change your boot loader from LILO to GRUB, do the following:

1. Configure the `/boot/grub/grub.conf` file as described in the "Booting Your Computer with GRUB" section.

2. You need to know the device on which you want to install GRUB. For example, to install GRUB on the master boot record of the first disk, type the following as root user from a Terminal window:

```
# grub-install /dev/hda
```

The new Master Boot Record is written to boot with the GRUB boot loader.

3. Reboot your computer. You should see the GRUB boot screen.

If for some reason you don't see the GRUB boot screen when you reboot, you can use a rescue CD to reboot your computer and fix the problem. When the rescue CD boots up, mount the file system containing the `/boot/grub/grub.conf` file. Then use the `chroot` command to change to the root of that file system. Correct the `grub.conf` file and run `grub-install` again.

Configuring Networking

If you are connecting your computer to an Ethernet LAN that has a DHCP server available, you probably don't need to do anything to start up automatically on your LAN and even be connected to the Internet. However, if there is no DHCP server on your LAN and you have to configure your TCP/IP connection manually, here is the information you will probably be prompted for during Linux installation:

- **IP address** — If you set your own IP address, this is the four-part, dot-separated number that represents your computer to the network. It would take more than a few sentences to explain how IP addresses are formed and how you choose them (see Chapter 5 for a more complete description). An example of a private IP address is 192.168.0.1.

- **Netmask** — The netmask is used to determine what part of an IP address represents the network and what part represents a particular host computer. An example of a netmask for a Class C network is 255.255.255.0. If you apply this netmask to an IP address of 192.168.0.1, for example, the network address would be 192.168.0 and the host address 1. Because 0 and 255 can't be assigned to a particular host, that leaves valid host numbers between 1 and 254 available for this local network.

- **Activate on boot** — Some Linux install procedures ask you to indicate if you want the network to start at boot time (you probably do if you have a LAN).

- **Set the host name** — This is the name identifying your computer within your domain. For example, if your computer were named "baskets" in the `handsonhistory.com` domain, your full host name may be `baskets.handsonhistory.com`. You can either set the domain name yourself (manually) or have it assigned automatically, if that information is being assigned by a DHCP server (automatically via DHCP).

- **Gateway** — This is the IP number of the computer that acts as a gateway to networks outside your LAN. This typically represents a host computer or router that routes packets between your LAN and the Internet.

- **Primary DNS** — This is the IP address of the host that translates computer names you request into IP addresses. It is referred to as a Domain Name System (DNS) server. You may also have Secondary and Tertiary name servers in case the first one can't be reached. (Most ISPs will give you two DNS server addresses.)

Configuring Other Administrative Features

Depending on which Linux install you are using, there are other types of information you will be asked to enter. These might involve the following:

- **Firewall** — Most Linux distributions these days use iptables to configure firewalls. Older Linux systems use ipchains. When you configure a default firewall, you typically choose which ports will be open to outside connections on your system (although there are many other things a firewall can be configured to do as well). The iptables firewall facility is described in Chapter 18.

- **Languages** — While Linux itself doesn't include support for lots of different languages, some Linux distributions (such as Fedora) and desktop environments (such as KDE) offer support for many different languages. Nearly all Linux distributions will let you configure language-specific keyboards.

- **Root password and additional user** — Every Linux system that uses passwords will have you add at least the root user's password when you install Linux. Some distributions will require that you add at least one additional non-root user as well.

Besides the features just mentioned, every distribution needs to have some initial configuration done before you have a fully functional Linux system. See Chapter 4 for information on basic administrative tasks for Linux.

Installing from the *Linux Bible* CD or DVD

With the knowledge you've gained in this chapter, you're ready to select a Linux distribution to install. Read the descriptions of Linux distributions in the other chapters in Part II of this book. Each chapter includes an "On the DVD" or "On the CD" icon box that tells you if the distribution described there is on the CD or DVD or, if it isn't, where you can get it.

If you need more information about the CD or DVD, Appendix A describes the contents of those discs. It also tells you which Linux distributions can be run live or used to install Linux permanently to your hard disk from those two discs.

Summary

While every Linux distribution includes a different installation method, there are many common activities you need to do, regardless of which Linux system you install. For every Linux system, you need to deal with issues of disk partitioning, network configuration, and boot loaders.

Linux Bible 2008 Edition includes a DVD and a CD with several different Linux systems you can install. If you prefer, you can instead download and burn your own CDs or DVDs to install Linux. If you go the route of burning your own CDs, this chapter helps you find Linux distributions you can download and describes tools you can use to verify their contents.

Chapter 8

Running Fedora and Red Hat Enterprise Linux

In September 2003, the world's leading Linux distribution, Red Hat Linux, disappeared.

Red Hat, Inc., the company that created Red Hat Linux, divided its development efforts in two directions: the Fedora Project, which produces the Fedora operating system (originally called Fedora Core), and Red Hat Enterprise Linux. The split came from trying to better serve two diverse groups with one operating system. Fedora focused on encouraging the open source development community interested in helping develop and test software that would one day go into Red Hat products. Red Hat Enterprise Linux focused on the needs of paying customers who needed enterprise computing solutions.

ON the DVD-ROM Fedora 8 is included on the DVD that comes with this book. You can install the entire Fedora 8 prime DVD, from this DVD, using descriptions in Appendix A and the "Installing Fedora" section later in this chapter. If you don't have a DVD drive, you can obtain the same software on CDs by downloading them from the Internet (`http://fedoraproject.org/wiki/Distribution/Download`) **and burning them to CD, as described in Appendix A.**

Fedora and Red Hat Enterprise Linux both come from a base of code that stems from the Red Hat Linux legacy. The two distributions have different goals and audiences and may drift farther apart over time. For the time being, however, Fedora includes features being developed for future Red Hat Enterprise Linux releases.

Fedora is intended to include the latest Linux technology and to be a proving ground for features slated to go into Red Hat Enterprise Linux products. It is a freely distributed operating system for the Linux community.

Although it is sponsored and directed by Red Hat, Inc., the Fedora Project encourages community involvement. The latest Fedora includes many more features than Red Hat Enterprise Linux, but those features have less guarantee of stability and no guarantee of support. However, important decisions about the direction of Fedora are still very much under the control of Red Hat, Inc. Likewise, Red Hat owns Fedora trademarks and makes legal decisions for Fedora based on its own legal counsel.

NOTE   Fedora follows the legacy of Red Hat Linux. The final version of Red Hat Linux was version 9. Fedora Core 1 and Red Hat Enterprise Linux 3 followed Red Hat Linux 9. At the time of this writing, Fedora 8 (the "Core" having been dropped) and Red Hat Enterprise Linux 5 are the latest versions of those two operating systems.

Red Hat Enterprise Linux (RHEL), which is actually represented by multiple products for desktop, server, and workstation computer systems, is licensed commercially. Red Hat puts all its documentation, training, and support efforts behind RHEL, which it sells to customers in the form of subscriptions. The intent is to have RHEL be a rock-solid Linux system that can be deployed across entire enterprises.

Despite the confusion it unleashed by dumping its flagship Red Hat Linux line and fears by some that Red Hat might become another Microsoft, Red Hat is still the dominant player when it comes to commercial Linux products. Many people have been happy to upgrade their critical Linux systems to Red Hat Enterprise Linux products.

In fact, when Microsoft announced its patent agreement with Novell, Red Hat was reported to have turned down a similar offer of cooperation with Microsoft, calling such an arrangement an "innovation tax." So, Red Hat, which was once viewed by some in the free software community as a threat to the free software movement, is now being viewed more often as a great defender of free and open source software rights.

To its credit, Red Hat has managed to become a profitable venture while making some remarkable contributions to the open source effort. Releasing its installer (Anaconda) and software packaging tools (RPM Package Management) under the GNU Public License (GPL) has enabled other Linux distributions to use and enhance those features. Within Red Hat Linux and now Fedora, Red Hat, Inc. has worked hard to include only software that could be freely distributed (removing most software with patent and copyright issues).

Despite continued emphasis from Red Hat, Inc. that Fedora comes with no guarantees, Fedora is an excellent Linux distribution. I know of universities that have deployed hundreds of Fedora desktop systems in their computer labs and small companies that run their businesses exclusively with Fedora. Even if you prefer to bet your business on Red Hat Enterprise Linux, Fedora is a great way to evaluate and use technology that is in all Linux distributions from Red Hat. Features in the current Fedora 8 are those that are being prepared for the next release of RHEL. Both Fedora and RHEL are discussed in this chapter, so you can determine which distribution is right for you.

Digging into Features

There are many opinions on why Red Hat Linux and other distributions from Red Hat, Inc. have been so popular. The following sections describe some features of Red Hat Linux distributions commonly believed to have led to its success and that now add to the popularity of Fedora and Red Hat Enterprise Linux distributions.

Red Hat Installer (Anaconda)

When many Linux distributions still had you struggling from the command line to get the distribution installed, Red Hat created its own installer called Anaconda. Anaconda includes both graphical and text-based procedures for installing Linux, and is one of the oldest graphical installers continuously shipping. When you're done installing Fedora or Red Hat Enterprise Linux, you have the following:

- A set of software packages installed that suits how you want to use your computer (as a desktop, workstation, server, or some custom configuration)

- Standard information, such as date, time, time zone, and language set

- A configured mouse, keyboard, video card, and monitor

- An appropriately partitioned hard disk

- A configured network card and firewall, to immediately connect to a LAN

- A configured boot loader, to define how Linux starts up

In addition to being easy to use, Anaconda is loaded with features to make it easy to manage the installation of multiple RHEL or Fedora systems. For example, these power features are built into the Anaconda installer:

- **Network installs** — After booting the install process, the actual Fedora or RHEL distribution can be on a network server that is accessible via a Web server (http), FTP server (ftp), or UNIX file server (NFS).

- **Kickstart installs** — It's not so bad to sit there and click through the answers to run the installation of one Fedora system, but if you're doing dozens or hundreds of installs (especially on similar computers), automating that task can be a major time-saver. Anaconda supports kickstart installs, for which you use a preconfigured kickstart file to answer the questions that come up during a Fedora or RHEL installation. If you answer all the questions in the file, you can launch the installation and have it run from start to finish without you in attendance.

- **Upgrades** — With an existing Fedora system installed, Anaconda enables you to easily upgrade to a newer Fedora system. A lot of nice features for saving backups of configuration files and logging the upgrade activities are built into that process. During an upgrade, Anaconda takes into consideration any dependency issues, so the upgraded software packages will have all the libraries and commands that the features in those packages need.

Recent major enhancements to Anaconda have come with recent releases of Fedora. In particular, Anaconda now incorporates the yum facility for gathering, downloading, and installing packages. During initial installation, you can add multiple yum-enabled Fedora software repositories to install software from those repositories.

You'll find a detailed description of installing Fedora using the Anaconda installer at the end of this chapter.

RPM Package Management

All Red Hat and Fedora distributions use the RPM Package Management (RPM) software packaging format to store and maintain software. Fedora and RHEL contain a set of tools for installing, upgrading, maintaining, and querying software packages in RPM format. Essentially, the RPM software packages that are installed are maintained in a database, so you can list the contents of packages, view descriptions, and even check for tampering of the files in those packages.

Using RPM, add-on software can also be easily included in and maintained for Fedora systems. So users who once had to know how to deal with tarballs and makefiles to compile their own software can now simply install an RPM package to get the features they want. With other Linux distributions (such as SUSE and Mandrake) also using RPM packaging, your RPM tool skills can help you manage software on those distributions as well.

Because of the popularity of Red Hat Linux systems, lots of software repositories and third-party software management tools have been created to further automate and simplify handling software in Red Hat systems. Tools such as yum (`www.linux.duke.edu/projects/yum`) and apt4rpm (`http://apt4rpm.sourceforge.net`) are available for updating selected software.

As noted earlier, the yum facility forms the foundation for installing RPM packages in Fedora and RHEL. For several reasons, yum is usually preferred over the `rpm` command. First, it can be used to install from network repositories. Second, it can find and install dependent packages needed by the packages you request. And last, it is preferred because there are related tools for searching and managing repositories. Yum can also be used to install software from local media and, unlike RPM, resolve dependencies automatically.

Kudzu Hardware Detection

Early Linux systems required that someone installing Linux know a lot about their hardware and the Linux drivers needed for that hardware to work. The kudzu feature was created by Red Hat to detect and configure a lot of computer hardware automatically. This feature is a great boost to those who don't want to worry about finding and selecting the drivers needed for their computer hardware.

Kudzu runs during your initial Red Hat installation to detect your system's hardware. It also runs each time you start your Fedora or RHEL system so that if you add or remove hardware and restart the system, it can try to determine what the hardware is and offer you the opportunity to configure it or remove the driver, as appropriate.

NOTE The highly touted hardware detection done by the KNOPPIX bootable Linux distribution is based on the kudzu libraries from Red Hat, Inc. While the kudzu hardware detection is quite good in Fedora and RHEL, if you don't need hardware detection from kudzu, you can save significant time in rebooting if you disable kudzu.

Red Hat Desktop Look-and-Feel

To add a level of consistency to the desktops on its Linux systems, Red Hat created a look-and-feel that is pretty much the same for both GNOME and KDE. In particular, consistent themes (backgrounds, icons, logos, and other elements) are set up by default for KDE and GNOME desktops. With the release of Fedora 8, the Online Desktop is now included — the goal of which is to provide a desktop suitable for running applications directly from the Web and storing information online. This allows the desktop to be the window to applications such as Facebook, Gmail, and other online applications. Figure 8-1 shows an example of the Online Desktop.

FIGURE 8-1

Fedora includes the Online Desktop.

By default, the Online Desktop opens the Firefox Web browser when started. It also includes the Sidebar on the left side of the screen — a panel of the applications you often run online.

System Configuration Tools

Red Hat created a set of simplified, graphical tools for configuring and administering many basic administrative features in Red Hat systems. Using these tools, you can add printers, configure your network, add users, set up your sound card, tune up your video card, and more.

Red Hat's graphical configuration tools (described in Chapter 4) can be launched from the System or Applications menu or from the command line. Several releases ago, the beginnings of these configuration tools' command names changed from `redhat-config` to `system-config`. For example, the tool to configure your network in Fedora is now called `system-config-network` (instead of `redhat-config-network`).

Going Forward with Fedora

With the original Red Hat Linux, you could have the exact same Linux system for free (to run in your home or small business) that was being used in large-scale enterprise deployments. For just a few dollars, you could add official Red Hat support for that system, which included official security patches and upgrade paths for the future.

Today, with the different free (Fedora) and subscription-based (RHEL) Linuxes from Red Hat, some of the same basic advantages hold true — if you are a bit more adventurous. Because Red Hat Linux is such a successful operating system, many who have developed skills in using and deploying Red Hat Linux have rallied to support Fedora in areas where Red Hat, Inc. has bowed out. The following sections explore some of those support efforts.

Growing Community Support for Fedora

Despite some confusion about the future and direction of the Fedora Project, new initiatives and Web sites have popped up to support Fedora. Two of the best new official assets of the Fedora Project are FedoraProject.org (which is transitioning to become the official Fedora Project site) and FedoraForum.org (which has been recognized as the official end-user forum of choice).

FedoraProject.org is the site for official information about schedules, goals, and initiatives that make up the Fedora Project. If you want to become involved in Fedora-related projects, such as Ambassadors, Marketing, Live CD, or Documentation, FedoraProject.org is the focal point for pursuing those initiatives.

FedoraForum.org features news, galleries, and (as you might guess) forums for sharing questions and information about Fedora. As of this writing, there were about one million posts to these forums and the forum for installation help has more than 100,000 posts itself.

The Unofficial Fedora FAQ (www.fedorafaq.org) has become an excellent resource for getting answers to the most constant, nagging questions about Fedora. This FAQ is a good place to start for learning how to get all those things you need (MP3 players, instant messaging, video players, access to your Windows XP NTFS file system, and so on).

On the whole, the total amount of software available and greater stability among software repositories (I discuss them next) has meant that it's possible to get a much better total experience with Fedora than was possible even with Red Hat Linux.

Forums and Mailing Lists

Since Fedora came into existence, many individuals and organizations have rallied to support Fedora going forward. If you want to get into the flow of the Fedora community, I recommend starting with the Fedora Project's own mailing lists. You can choose the Fedora mailing list that interests you from the Red Hat Mailing Lists page (http://redhat.com/mailman/listinfo). Start with the Fedora-list or Fedora-announce-list mailing list.

Many other Fedora resources are also available on the Web, and Appendix B includes a list of many of them.

Fedora Comes of Age

Most people who follow Linux would agree that Fedora has become a strong, viable Linux system in its own right, and not just a test release for Red Hat Enterprise Linux. The project has continued to grow and flourish, and Fedora 8 is but the latest incarnation in a great line. Figure 8-2 shows a standard desktop.

While still laying the foundation for Red Hat Enterprise Linux, Fedora has also added some fun and powerful features to distinguish itself from other Linux systems. Here are some examples:

- **Anaconda** — As noted earlier, the Anaconda installer used with Fedora and RHEL has received a major overhaul in the past two versions of Fedora. For some time, Anaconda has been able to install Fedora from local media (CD/DVD) or network media (using HTTP, NFS, or FTP), but it used to be able to install packages only from the Fedora repository.

  Anaconda is also being used as the heart of the Fedora LiveCD Project (formerly Kadischi). You can run a typical Anaconda install that results in a live CD or DVD ISO image that can be used to run Fedora live from that medium.

- **Xen virtualization** — The ability to run multiple operating systems instances on one computer is just the beginning of the promise that virtualization brings to Linux. In today's server computing model, often an entire server is devoted to running a particular application that may be tied to a particular operating system. As a result, the entire computer may be underutilized if it is not a high-demand application.

FIGURE 8-2

Fedora includes the GNOME or KDE desktop, and many games.

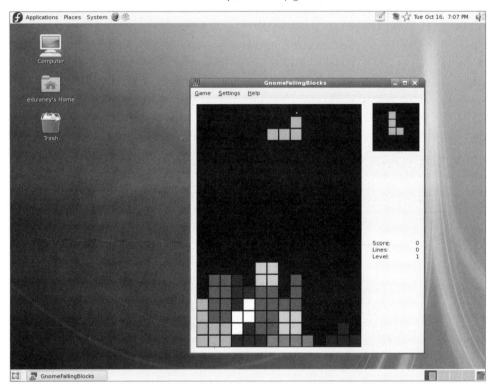

With virtualization, you have the opportunity to run multiple instances, including an entire operating system, an application, and a data combination. Those instances (called *guests*) can be Linux, Windows, or any other operating system that runs on the computer hardware. Guests operate separately from each other, and so remain secure from each other. As demand slows or increases for a guest, it can be moved to different hardware to make the best use of available hardware.

Red Hat, Inc. has thrown some strong development support into the Xen virtualization software (`www.xensource.com`) that is included in Fedora 8. Tools for starting, stopping, and otherwise managing multiple guest operating systems are all included in the Xen version that comes with Fedora 8.

- **AIGLX desktop eye candy** — The Accelerated Indirect GLX (AIGLX) project is a cooperative effort between the Fedora community and the X.Org X Window server project. With a video card that supports DRI and GLX (see `http://fedoraproject.org/wiki/RenderingProject/aiglx` for information on supported cards), you can see some eye-popping desktop effects.

If Fedora is such a great product, you may wonder why someone would want to pay for Red Hat Enterprise Linux. The major reason for using RHEL over Fedora is the promise of support behind your critical systems. You may also need a longer period of promised support for critical fixes and security patches than is available with Fedora.

Many people I know, especially those who like to have the latest cool bits available, use Fedora for their personal desktop and server systems. They don't mind upgrading every six months or so and can accept a certain level of instability. If you have a similar aesthetic, Fedora could be an excellent Linux distribution for you.

Installing Fedora

The Linux operating system Fedora, sponsored by Red Hat, is included on this book's DVD. The rest of this chapter leads you through its installation.

Before you install Fedora on your computer, ensure that your computer hardware supports it. You should also choose a method of installing Fedora. Those topics are discussed in the following sections.

Choosing Computer Hardware

Choosing your computer hardware may not really be a choice. You may just have an old PC lying around on which you want to try Fedora. Or you may have a killer workstation with some extra disk space and want to try Fedora out on a separate partition or whole disk. To install the PC version of Fedora (the version on the accompanying DVD) successfully, the computer must have the following:

- **Processor** — The Pentium-class PC needs to be at least 200 MHz for text mode and 400 MHz Pentium II for GUI.

- **RAM** — You need at least 64MB of RAM to install Fedora. If you are running in graphical mode, you need at least 192MB. The recommended RAM for graphical mode is 256MB.

- **DVD or CD drive** — You need to be able to boot up the installation process from a DVD or CD (the latter requires that you get Fedora installation CDs as described at `http://fedoraproject.org/wiki/Distribution/Download`). If you can't boot from a DVD or CD, there are ways to start the installation from a hard disk or using a PXE install, as the following section, "Choosing an Installation Method," explains.

- **Hard disk** — With no preset install types in Fedora 8, essentially every installation is a custom installation. Therefore, depending on which packages you choose to install, the disk space you need can range from about 600MB (for a minimal server with no GUI installed) to 7GB (to install all packages).

  I recommend at least 2GB to 3GB if you are installing a desktop system. (The Fedora Project recommends at least five percent of additional free space, plus any disk space you require for user data.)

- **Keyboard and monitor** — You need a keyboard and monitor at least during installation. (You can operate Fedora quite well over a LAN using either a shell interface from a network login or an X terminal.)

Although not included with this book, Fedora versions are available for the AMD64 architecture. Red Hat Enterprise Linux versions (which you have to purchase from Red Hat, Inc.) are available for other hardware, such as Intel Itanium, IBM PowerPC, and IBM mainframe. The Fedora distribution that comes with this book and the installation procedures presented here are specific to x86 architecture PCs.

Most of the software described in this book will work the same in any of those hardware environments. (Check out Fedoraproject.org for sites that offer Fedora for different computer hardware architectures.)

To begin installing Fedora, you also need to have installed media, such as the *Linux Bible 2008 Edition* DVD that comes with this book (or a set of installation CDs that you obtain yourself). Also you must either be dedicating your entire hard disk (or an added hard disk) to Linux, have a pre-configured Linux partition, or have sufficient free space on your hard disk outside any existing Windows partition.

NOTE If you are not dedicating your whole hard disk to Fedora and you don't understand partitioning, refer to Chapter 7, which describes how to set up partitioning to allow multiple computer operating systems to coexist on the same hard drive. Always be sure to back up everything before installing a new operating system or making a significant change.

Choosing an Installation Method

You can also install Fedora from any of several different types of media. You can still start the install process by booting the installation DVD. After booting the install process, however, you can type **linux askmethod** at the boot prompt, which offers you the choice of installing Fedora from the following locations:

- **Local DVD or CD-ROM** — This is the most common method of installing Fedora and the one you get by pressing Enter from the Fedora installation boot prompt. Use this section for both DVD and CD installs. (You may need to change the BIOS if the DVD or CD doesn't boot.) All packages needed to complete the installation are on the DVD that comes with this book.

- **HTTP** — Lets you install from a Web page address (http://).

- **FTP** — Lets you install from an FTP site (ftp://).

- **NFS image** — Allows you to install from any shared directory on another computer on your network using the Network File System (NFS) facility.

- **Hard drive** — If you can place a copy of the Fedora distribution on your hard drive, you can install it from there. (The distribution should be on a hard drive partition to which you are *not* installing.)

NOTE Unlike some earlier Fedora and Red Hat Linux versions, the current version of Fedora doesn't support floppy disk boot images because the Linux 2.6 kernel is too large to fit on a floppy disk. So if you don't have a bootable CD or DVD drive, you will need to start the install process from some other medium such as a USB key, PXE server, or hard drive.

Installing on Multiple Computers

If you're installing Fedora on many computers with similar configurations, you can save yourself some time by using the Kickstart installation, which enables you to create a set of answers to the questions Fedora asks you during installation. More information about Kickstart can be found at http://fedoraproject.org/wiki/AnacondaKickstart.

Installation Guides

Fedora 8 installation guides are available in several different languages. To download a tarball of an installation guide or simply read it online, refer to this site:

> http://docs.fedoraproject.org/install-guide/

Choosing to Install or Upgrade

Are you doing a new install or an upgrade? If you are upgrading a Fedora system to the latest version, the installation process will try to leave your data files and configuration files intact as much as possible. This type of installation takes longer than a new install. A new install simply erases all data on the Linux partitions (or whole hard disk) that you choose.

If you are upgrading an existing Fedora system to this release, you should consider first removing any unwanted packages from your old Fedora system. The fewer packages to be checked during an upgrade, the faster the upgrade installation (and the less space used).

NOTE You can upgrade to Fedora 8 from previous Fedora systems. The further you are from the current release, however, the greater the chance of something going wrong. You cannot upgrade to Fedora from a Red Hat Enterprise Linux system or vice versa.

To upgrade, you must have at least a Linux 2.0 kernel installed. With an upgrade, all of your configuration files, modified by the installer, are saved as filename.rpmsave (for example, the hosts file is saved as hosts.rpmsave). The locations of those files, as well as other upgrade information, are written to /tmp/upgrade.log. The upgrade installs the new kernel, any changed software packages, and any packages that the installed packages depend on being there. Your data files and configuration information should remain intact. By clicking the Customize box, you can choose which packages to upgrade.

COMING FROM WINDOWS If you are installing a dual-boot system that includes a Windows operating system, install the Windows system first and the Fedora system afterward. Some Windows systems blow away the Master Boot Record (MBR), making the Fedora partition inaccessible.

If, when installing Windows or Fedora, you find that the other operating system is no longer available on your boot screen, don't panic and don't immediately reinstall. You can usually recover from the problem by booting with the Fedora emergency boot disk and then using either the grub-install or lilo command to reinsert the proper MBR. If you are uncomfortable working in emergency mode, seek out an expert to help you.

Red Hat provides a description of how to configure a dual-boot system at www.redhat.com/docs/manuals/linux/RHL-9-Manual/install-guide/ch-x86-dualboot.html.

Beginning the Installation

Once you have selected the right type of installation for your needs, you can begin the installation procedure. Throughout most of the procedure, you can click Back to make changes to earlier screens. However, once you are warned that packages are about to be written to hard disk, there's no turning back. Most items that you configure can be changed after Fedora is installed.

> **COMING FROM WINDOWS** It is quite possible that your entire hard disk is devoted to a Windows 95, 98, 2000, ME, NT, XP, or Vista operating system, and you may want to keep much of that information after Fedora is installed. While there are installation choices that let you retain existing partitions, they don't let you take space from existing DOS partitions without destroying them. If you like, you can try resizing your Windows partition using the qtparted utility. You can run qtparted by booting the KNOPPIX distribution that comes on the DVD included with this book. Just be aware that, if used improperly, qtparted (or any disk partitioning tool) can damage or erase important data from your hard disk.

Ready to install? (Have you backed up any data you want to keep safe?) Okay, then here's what to do:

1. **Insert the DVD into the DVD drive.** If you are not able to boot from the DVD, obtain an installation CD set, as described earlier in this chapter, and continue with this procedure by inserting the first CD into the drive.

2. **Reboot your computer.** If you see the Fedora installation screen, continue to the next step.

> **TIP** If you don't see the installation screen, your DVD or CD-ROM drive may not be bootable. You may be able to make the drive bootable, however. Here's how: Restart the computer. Immediately, you should see a message telling you how to go into setup, such as by pressing the F1, F2, or Del key. Enter setup and look for an option such as Boot Options or Boot From. If the value is A: First, Then C:, change it to CD-ROM First, Then C: or something similar. Save the changes and try to install again.

3. **Boot the install procedure.** At the boot prompt, type **linux** and press Enter to start the install in graphical mode. If your computer won't let you install in graphical mode (16-bit color, 800 × 600 resolution, framebuffer), refer to the "Choosing Different Install Modes" sidebar. The boot screen is menu-driven. So if you want to change any of the boot options for a menu selection, highlight that selection and press the Tab key. You can then remove or add options before pressing Enter to continue. For example, to install from a different medium (such as over the network), add the askmethod boot option. See the sidebar "Choosing Different Install Modes" for more boot options.

4. **Media check.** If you're asked to check your installation media, press Enter. If the DVD is damaged, this step saves you the trouble of getting deep into the install and then failing. Once the DVD is checked, select Skip to continue.

5. **Continue.** When the welcome screen appears, click Release Notes to see information about this version of Fedora. Click Next when you're ready to continue.

6. **Choose an installation language.** Move the arrow keys to the language you want and then select Next. (Later, you will be able to add additional languages.)

7. **Choose a keyboard.** Some layouts enable dead keys (on by default). Dead keys enable you to use characters with special markings (such as circumflexes and umlauts).

8. **Choose install type.** Select either Install Fedora for a new install or Upgrade an Existing Installation to upgrade an existing version of Fedora.

9. **Choose your partitioning strategy.** You have the following choices related to how your disk is partitioned for a Fedora installation:

   ▤ **Remove all partitions on selected drives and create default layout** — This erases the entire contents of the hard disks you select.

   ▤ **Remove Linux partitions on selected drives and create default layout** — This erases all Linux partitions, but leaves Windows partitions intact.

   ▤ **Use free space on selected drives and create default layout** — This works only if you have enough free space on your hard disk that is not currently assigned to any partition.

   ▤ **Create custom layout** — Select this if you want to create your own custom partitioning.

NOTE Instead of installing to a local hard disk, you can identify an ISCSI initiator as the storage device by selecting the Advanced Storage Configuration button and entering the IP address and ISCSI Initiator Name of the SCSI device. Once that is identified, you can use that device for installing Fedora.

If you have multiple hard disks, you can select which of those disks should be used for your Fedora installation. If you want to configure an ISCSI device to use for the install, select Advanced Storage Configuration. Check the Review and Modify Partitioning Layout check box to see how Linux is choosing to partition your hard disk. Click Next to continue.

10. **Review and modify partitioning layout.** If you choose to review or customize your partitioning, you will see a partitioning tool with your current partitioning layout displayed. You can change any of the partitions you choose, provided you have at least one root (/) partition that can hold the entire installation and one swap partition. A small /boot partition (about 100MB) is also recommended.

The swap partition is often set to twice the size of the amount of RAM on your computer (for example, for 128MB RAM you can use 256MB of swap). Linux uses swap space when active processes have filled up your system's RAM. At that point, an inactive process is moved to swap space. You get a performance hit when the inactive process is moved to swap and another hit when that process restarts (moves back to RAM). For example, you might notice a delay on a busy system when you reopen a window that has been minimized for a long time.

Choosing Different Install Modes

Although most computers enable you to install Fedora in the default mode (graphical), there may be times when your video card does not support that mode. Also, although the install process detects most computer hardware, there may be times when your hard disk, Ethernet card, or other critical piece of hardware cannot be detected and will require you to enter special information at boot time.

The following is a list of commands that you can type at the installation boot prompt to change installation modes to start the Fedora install process. You typically try these modes only if the default mode fails (that is, if the screen is garbled or installation fails at some point). For a list of other supported modes, refer to the /usr/share/doc/anaconda*/command-line.txt file or press F2 to see short descriptions of some of these types.

Command	Description
text	Runs installation in a text-based mode. Do this if the installation doesn't seem to recognize your graphics card.
lowres	Runs installation in 640 × 480 screen resolution for graphics cards that can't support the higher resolution.
nofb	Turns off the framebuffer.
noprobe	Installation won't probe to determine your hardware; you must load any special drivers that might be needed to install it. Normally, installation auto-probes to determine what hardware you have on your computer.
mediacheck	Check your DVD or CDs before installing. Because media checking is done next in the normal installation process, do this only to test the media on a computer you are not installing on.
rescue	Boots from CD, mounts your hard disk, and lets you access useful utilities to correct problems that are preventing your Linux system from operating properly. (Not really an installation mode.)
expert	Bypasses probing so you can choose your mouse, video memory, and other values that would otherwise be chosen for you. Use if you believe that the installation process is not properly auto-probing your hardware.
askmethod	Has the installation process ask where to install from (local CD, NFS image, FTP, HTTP, or hard disk).
updates	To install from an update disk.

You can add other options to the linux boot command to identify particular hardware that is not being detected properly. For example, to specify the number of cylinders, heads, and sectors for your hard disk (if you believe the boot process is not detecting these values properly), you can pass the information to the kernel as follows: linux hd=720,32,64. In this example, the kernel is told that the hard disk has 720 cylinders, 32 heads, and 64 sectors. You can find this information in the documentation that comes with your hard disk (or stamped on the hard disk itself on a sticker near the serial number).

There are also other boot options you can add to the installation prompt to instruct the installation boot prompt how to start the installation. Many of these options are described in Chapter 11.

The reason you need to have enough swap space is that when RAM and swap fill up, no other processes can start until something closes. Bottom line: Add RAM to get better performance; add swap space if processes are failing to start. The Fedora Project suggests a minimum of 32MB and a maximum of 2GB of swap space.

Click the Next button (and select OK to accept any changes) to continue.

11. **Configure the boot loader.** If you selected a custom install, you get the opportunity to configure the boot loader. All bootable partitions and default boot loader options are displayed. By default, the install process uses the GRUB boot loader, installs the boot loader in the master boot record of the computer, and chooses Fedora as your default operating system to boot.

> **NOTE** If you keep the GRUB boot loader (described in Chapter 7), you have the option of adding a GRUB password. The password protects your system from having potentially dangerous options sent to the kernel by someone without that password. This does not have to be the same password you use to log in later.

The names shown for each bootable partition will appear on the boot loader screen when the system starts. Change a partition name by clicking it and selecting Edit. To change the location of the boot loader, click Configure Advanced Boot Loader Options, and continue to the next step. If you do not want to install a boot loader (because you don't want to change the current boot loader), click Change Boot Loader and select Do Not Install a Boot Loader. If the defaults are okay, skip the next step.

12. **Configure the advanced boot loader.** If you selected to configure advanced boot loader options, you can now choose where to store the boot loader. Select one of the following:

   ▪ **Master Boot Record (MBR)** — This is the preferred place for GRUB. It causes GRUB to control the boot process for all operating systems installed on the hard disk.

   ▪ **First Sector of Boot Partition** — If another boot loader is being used on your computer, you can have GRUB installed on your Linux partition (first sector). This lets you have the other boot loader refer to your GRUB boot loader to boot Fedora.

If you have multiple, bootable partitions, the Change Drive Order button is a useful feature. Select this button if you want to change the order in which hard drives are booted. If you have a combination of SCSI and IDE drives, this enables you to indicate that the master boot record should go on a SCSI drive.

You can choose to add kernel parameters (which may be needed if your computer can't detect certain hardware). If a piece of hardware is improperly detected and is preventing your computer from booting, you can add a kernel parameter to disable it (for example, add `nousb`, `noscsi`, `nopcmcia`, or `noagp`). You can select to use linear mode (which was once required to boot from a partition on a disk that is above cylinder 1024, but is now rarely needed).

13. **Configure networking.** This applies only to a local area network. If you will use only dial-up networking, skip this section by clicking Next. If your computer is not yet connected to a LAN, you also should skip this section.

    Network address information is assigned to your computer in two basic ways: statically (you type it) or dynamically (a DHCP server provides that information from the network at boot time). One Network Device appears for each network card you have installed on your computer. The first Ethernet interface is eth0, the second is eth1, and so on. Repeat the setup for each card by selecting the card and clicking Edit.

CROSS-REF Chapter 5 discusses IP addresses, netmasks, and other information you need to set up your LAN.

With the Edit Interface eth0 dialog box displayed, add the following for both IPv4 and IPv6 support:

- **Enable IPv4 support** — This is the most common TCP/IP protocol version in use today. It should be enabled in most cases.

- **Dynamic IP configuration (DHCP)** — For IPv4 support, if your IP address is assigned automatically from a DHCP server, a check mark should appear here. With DHCP checked, you don't have to set IPv4 addresses on this page. Remove the check mark to set your own IP address.

- **Enable IPv6 support** — This is the upcoming TCP/IP standard, which features much longer addresses and some built-in security features. You can enable this without conflicting with IPv4 support.

- **Automatic Neighbor Discovery** — This makes it possible for different machines to exchange messages to implement autoconfiguration. Using this feature, computers can find information on routing and other nearby hosts (neighbors).

- **Dynamic IP configuration (DHCPv6)** — For IPv6 support, if your IP address is assigned automatically from a DHCPv6 server, a check mark should appear here. Remove the check mark to set your own IPv6 address.

- **IPv4 and IPv6 Manual Configuration** — If you are not using DHCP to get IP addresses for your Fedora system, you can enter an IPv4 or IPv6 address here. In most cases, an IPv4 address is all that you need. If you set your own IP address, this is the four-part, dot-separated number that represents your computer to the network. An example of a private IP address is 192.168.0.1. (See Chapter 5 for a more complete description of how IP addresses are formed and how you choose them.)

    In the second part of each IP address, you enter the netmask. The netmask is used to determine which part of an IP address represents the network and which part represents a particular host computer. An example of a netmask for a Class C network is 255.255.255.0.

Click OK. Then add the following information on the main screen:

- **Activate on boot** — Indicate whether you want the network to start at boot time (you probably do if you have a LAN).

- **Set the hostname** — The name identifying your computer within your domain. For example, if your computer were named "baskets" in the `handsonhistory.com` domain, your full hostname may be `baskets.handsonhistory.com`. You can either set the domain name yourself (manually) or have it assigned automatically, if that information is being assigned by a DHCP server (automatically via DHCP).

- **Gateway** — The IP number of the computer that acts as a gateway to networks outside your LAN. This typically represents a host computer or router that routes packets between your LAN and the Internet.

- **Primary DNS** — The IP address of the host that translates requested computer names into IP addresses. It is referred to as a Domain Name System (DNS) server. If the first name server can't be reached, you may also have a Secondary name server. (Most ISPs will give you two DNS server addresses.)

Click Next to continue.

14. **Choose a time zone.** Select the time zone. Either click a spot on the map or choose from the drop-down box. Before you click your exact location on the map, click on the area of the map that includes your continent. Then select the specific city. You can click "System clock uses UTC" to have your computer use Coordinated Universal Time (also known as Greenwich Mean Time). With multiple operating systems installed, you might want to clear this box because some operating systems expect the BIOS to be set to local time.

15. **Set root password.** The root password provides complete control of your Fedora system. Without it, and before you add other users, you will have no access to your own system. Enter the password, and then type it again in the Confirm box. (Remember the root user's password and keep it confidential! Don't lose it!) Click Next to continue.

NOTE If you are enabling Security Enhanced Linux (SELinux) on your computer, the security structure of your computer changes. The root user may no longer have complete control of the computer. Instead, there may be policies set that prevent any one user from having complete control.

16. **Install Classes.** For a new install, the installer automatically selects a set of basic software to install. In addition to that set, you can choose one or more of the following groups of software, referred to as *tasks*. For each of these installation tasks, you have the opportunity to install a set of preset packages or customize that set.

- **Office and Productivity** — Installs software appropriate for a home or office personal computer or laptop computer. This includes the GNOME desktop (no KDE) and various desktop-related tools (word processors, Internet tools, and so on). Server tools, software development tools, and many system administration tools are not installed.

■ **Software Development** — Similar to an Office and Productivity installation but adds tools for system administration and software development. (Server software is not installed.)

■ **Web Server** — Installs the software packages that you would typically need for a Linux Web server (in particular, Apache Web server and print server). It does not include many other server types by default (FTP, DHCP, mail, DNS, FTP, SQL, or news servers). The default server install also includes a GUI (GNOME only).

Unlike previous versions of Fedora, this version does not offer an Everything install type or a Minimal install type. Select the install classes you want, and then you can choose Customize Now (see Step 19) to see the packages to be installed (based on install categories and package groups). Unselecting the major categories can get you a pretty good minimal install, if you like to build from a bare-bones install.

17. **Add software repositories**. A new feature in Fedora 8 lets you select software repositories outside of Fedora from which you can select packages to install during the initial Fedora installation. To use this feature, you need an active Internet connection. Select the "Add additional software repositories" button to establish an Internet connection and to see the Add Repository pop-up.

For example, to use the RPM.livna.org repository to install many multimedia applications and video drivers, you could enter `livna` as the repository name and `http://rpm.livna .org/fedora/8/i386` as the repository URL. Then select the Add repository button to be able to add packages from that repository to your installation.

18. **Customize Now**. Select the Customize Now button after selecting the task (or tasks) you want to install. This lets you see which categories from each task and which packages within those categories are selected to be installed. It also lets you add or remove package selections. Note that packages from multiple repositories can appear in the same category.

You are presented with categories of software on the left side of the screen and package groups on the right side.

19. **Choose optional packages.** Select a category to see which groups it contains. Select a group and click Optional packages to see which optional packages are available in that group and which are selected to be installed. Categories include:

■ **Desktop Environments** — The GNOME desktop environment is selected by default. KDE and XFCE are the other available desktop environments. (GNOME and KDE are described in Chapter 3.)

■ **Applications** — This category includes packages of office applications, games, sound and video players, Internet tools, and other applications.

■ **Development** — General and specialized software development tools are included in packages in this category.

- **Servers** — Packages in this category are for Web, mail, FTP, database, and a variety of other network server types.

- **Base System** — Contains basic system administration tools, many common utilities, and support for basic system features (such as X Window System, Java, and Legacy software support).

- **Languages** — Packages containing support for multiple languages are contained in this category.

After you have chosen the packages you want to install, select Next to continue. The installer will take some time to check for dependencies among the packages you selected.

20. **Decide to install.** You can still back out now, and the disk will not have changed. Click Next to proceed. (To quit without changes, eject the DVD and restart the computer.) The file systems are created and the packages are installed. This typically takes from 20 to 60 minutes to complete, although it can take much longer on older computers.

    If you are using the DVD, you do not need to change media. If you are installing from the five-CD set, you are prompted to insert additional installation CDs as they are needed.

21. **Finish installing.** When you see the Congratulations screen, you are done. Note the links to Fedora information, eject the CD, and click Exit.

22. **Your computer restarts.** If you installed GRUB, you will see a graphical boot screen that displays the bootable partitions. Press the up or down arrow key to choose the partition you want to boot, and press Enter. If Linux is the default partition, you can simply wait a few moments and it boots automatically.

The first time your system boots after installation, the Fedora Setup Agent runs to do some initial configuration of your system. The next section explains how Fedora Setup Agent works.

Running the Fedora Setup Agent

The first time you boot Fedora after it is installed, the Fedora Setup Agent runs to configure some initial settings for your computer.

> **NOTE** The Fedora Setup Agent runs automatically only if you have configured Fedora to boot to a graphical login prompt. To start it from a text login, log in as root and switch to init state 5 temporarily (type **init 5**). Log in to the graphical prompt. From a Terminal window, as root user, type

```
# rm /etc/sysconfig/firstboot
# /usr/sbin/firstboot
```

The Welcome screen displays. From it, step through screens to read (and agree to) the license, configure a firewall, configure SELinux, set the date and time, create a regular user, and configure your sound card. Click the Finish button and you are ready to log in to Fedora.

Summary

Since leaving its well-known Red Hat Linux name behind, Red Hat, Inc. focused its development efforts on the free Fedora Project and commercial Red Hat Enterprise Linux. In the past few releases, Fedora has emerged as an exceptional distribution in its own right, with new features such as Xen virtualization, AIGLX video hardware acceleration, and powerful extensions to its Anaconda installer.

Fedora and Red Hat Enterprise Linux distributions distinguish themselves from other Linux distributions with their simplified installer (Anaconda), graphical configuration tools, and RPM Package Management tools. Fedora is freely available, whereas Red Hat Enterprise Linux is available on a paid subscription basis.

Fedora is included on the DVD that comes with this book. You can install the complete Fedora distribution by following the detailed instructions included in this chapter.

Chapter 9

Running Debian GNU/Linux

IN THIS CHAPTER

Inside Debian

Installing Debian

Managing your Debian system

Debian GNU/Linux is a creation of the Debian Project. Founded in 1993 by Ian Murdock, the Debian Project is an association of individuals who have made a common cause to create a free, coherent, and complete operating system.

ON the CD-ROM A single Debian GNU/Linux network install CD image is contained on the CD that comes with this book. You can install Debian directly from that CD as described in this chapter. This installation is suitable for setting up a Web server (LAMP server) and a mail server (see Chapters 24 and 25, respectively).

NOTE Ian Murdock is now associated with Sun, and continues to be an outspoken visionary on Debian, Linux, and operating systems in general. He regularly contributes to a blog that is worth reading, which you can find at http://ianmurdock.com/.

The principles of the Debian Project are defined in the Debian Social Contract. This contract is a commitment to the free software community that basically states:

- All software within the Debian system will remain free, as defined in the Debian Free Software Guidelines (DFSG).

- The Debian Project will contribute to the free software community by licensing any software developed for the Debian system in accordance with the DFSG, developing the best system it can, and by sharing improvements and fixes with the original developers of any programs incorporated into Debian GNU/Linux.

- Problems will not be hidden from users, and any bug reports filed against Debian components will be made promptly available to the public through the Debian Bug Tracking System (BTS).

- The Debian Project will focus on the needs of its users and on the principles of free software.

- Provisions will be made for the support of programs that do not meet the standards in the DFSG because some users may depend on these programs to make effective use of the system. The bug tracking and support systems will always include mechanisms for handling these programs when they are provided with the Debian system.

Debian's commitment to free software distribution and openness has earned it a huge following in the technical community. More than any other Linux system, Debian has been used as the basis for other Linux distributions, including KNOPPIX, Ubuntu, Damn Small Linux, and many others.

The success of Debian has come despite the lack of large corporate sponsors, formal enterprise initiatives, or official certification and training programs. Debian enthusiasts will tell you that it is the most stable and reliable Linux system. It is thoroughly tested, and new versions aren't released until the Debian leadership believes that software is extraordinarily stable.

Inside Debian GNU/Linux

As with most modern operating systems, software programs in Debian GNU/Linux are bundled into packages for easy distribution and management. The package format and management tools used in Debian GNU/Linux were created by the Debian Project and are arguably the most sophisticated of their type. Additionally, careful adherence to packaging policies and quality-control measures ensure compatibility and help make upgrades go smoothly. Debian is one of the operating system distributions in which all components (except the kernel) can be upgraded without rebooting the system.

Debian Packages

Debian packages come in two forms: binary and source. Binary packages contain files that can be extracted directly onto the system by the package management tools. Source packages contain source code and build instructions that the Debian build tools use to create binary packages.

In addition to programs and their associated data files, Debian packages contain control data that enable the package management tools to support advanced features:

- A main `control` file contains version and package interrelationship data. The version can be compared to an installed version of the same package to determine whether an upgrade is needed. The interrelationship data tell the package management tools which packages must or cannot be installed at the same time as the package.

> **NOTE**   Package interrelationship fields include Depends, Conflicts, Replaces, Provides, Recommends, Suggests, and Enhances. For a complete list of control file fields, see
> `http://debian.org/doc/debian-policy/ch-controlfields.html`.

- Optional preinst, postinst, prerm, and postrm files can instruct the package management tools to perform functions before or after package installation or removal. For example, most packages containing daemons (such as Apache HTTPD) include a postinst script that starts the daemon automatically after installation.

- A conffiles file can designate specific files in the package as configuration files, which are not automatically overwritten during upgrades. By default, all files under the /etc/ directory are configuration files.

Two special package types, meta and virtual, also exist. Meta packages are standard binary packages that do not contain any files, but depend on a number of other packages. Installation of a meta package results in the automatic installation of all packages that they depend on. These can be used as a convenient method for installing a set of related packages.

Virtual packages do not actually exist as files but can be referenced in the package interrelationship fields. They are most commonly used in cases where more than one package fulfills a specific requirement. Packages with this requirement can reference the virtual package in their Depends field, and packages that satisfy this dependency reference it in their Provides field.

Because most programs providing a virtual package are mutually exclusive, they also include the virtual package in their Conflicts field to prevent the installation of conflicting packages. An example of this is the mail-transport-agent virtual package, which is required by most system programs in order to send mail.

NOTE An easy way to browse the list of available packages is through the Debian Web site at www.debian.org/distrib/packages. The current release comes with more than 18,200 packages.

Debian Package Management Tools

Perhaps the most interesting and well-known part of the Debian package management system is APT, the Advanced Package Tool. APT, through the apt-get utility, maintains a database of packages available in the repositories that it is configured to check and can handle automatically downloading new or upgraded packages. A program named aptitude has been added to simplify package management, and it acts as an interface for the command line operations of apt-get.

When installing or upgrading packages, APT downloads the necessary files to a local cache directory and then instructs the dpkg tool to take the appropriate actions. Among other things, this allows the user to select programs for addition or removal without having to manually instruct the system to handle any package dependencies.

Most basic package management functions are performed by dpkg, although not always at the direct request of the user. This tool handles medium-level package installation and removal, and also manages the package status database. That database contains information about every package known to dpkg, including the package meta information and two other important fields: the package state and selection state.

 More information about how to determine the state of a package can be found in the "Querying the Package Database" section of this chapter.

As its name suggests, the package state indicates the present state of the package, which is one of the following:

- **not-installed** — The package is known but is not installed on the system.
- **half-installed** — An attempt was made to install the package, but an error prevented it from finishing.
- **unpacked** — The files have been extracted from the package, but any post-extract configuration steps have not yet been performed.
- **half-configured** — The post-extract configuration was started, but an error prevented it from finishing.
- **installed** — The package is fully installed and configured.
- **config-files** — The package was removed, but the configuration files still exist on the system.

NOTE If you have manually removed a configuration file and want to get it back by reinstalling the package, you can do so by passing the `--force-confmiss` option to dpkg. Doing so will not overwrite the other configuration files for that package. If you want to start over with all of the original configuration files, you can also pass the `--force-confnew` option.

The package selection state indicates what state you want the package to be in. Changes to package status through dpkg happen immediately when using the `--install`, `--remove`, and `--purge` options on a package, but other uses and tools will instead set this flag and then process any pending changes in a batch. The package selection state is one of the following:

- `install` — The package should be installed.
- `deinstall` — The package files should be removed, with the exception of configuration files.
- `purge` — All package files and configuration files should be removed.
- `hold` — dpkg should not do anything with the package unless explicitly told to do so with the `--force-hold` argument.

Some packages are designed to enable you to select configuration options as they are being installed. This configuration is managed through the debconf utility. Debconf supports a number of different interfaces, including a command prompt and a menu-based interface. A database of configuration options is also maintained by debconf, allowing it to automatically answer repeated questions, such as those you might encounter while upgrading or reinstalling a package.

Examples of how to use these utilities are included in the section "Managing Your Debian System" later in this chapter.

Debian Releases

In Debian terms, a distribution is a collection of specific package versions. From time to time, a distribution is declared ready for release and becomes a release. In practice, these two terms are often used interchangeably when referring to Debian distributions that have reached the "stable" milestone.

Debian distributions are given code names (recent ones include potato, woody, and sarge, named for characters in the movie *Toy Story*) to identify their archive directory on the Debian servers. While a particular distribution release is active, it will be referenced by one of three release tags, each one pointing to one of the three active releases. The tags — unstable, testing, and stable — identify the state of the release within the release cycle. At the time of this writing, the current stable release is Etch, and the testing release is Lenny. The unstable release is special in that it is always named Sid (after the kid who broke all the toys).

New packages, and new versions of packages, are uploaded to the Debian archive and are imported into the unstable distribution. This distribution always contains the newest version of every package, which means that changes have not yet been thoroughly tested to verify that installing them will not cause unexpected behavior.

Once a package has been assigned to the unstable area for a few days, and testing shows that it has not had any significant bugs filed against it, it is imported into the testing distribution. The testing distribution remains open to changes (just as the unstable area was) until it is frozen in preparation for release as the next stable distribution. When testing is in the frozen state, only changes necessary to fix significant bugs are imported.

After all release-critical bugs have been fixed in the frozen testing distribution, the release manager declares the release ready, and it replaces the stable distribution. The previous stable version becomes obsolete (but remains on the Debian archive for a reasonable period of time), a new testing distribution is created from the changes that went into packages in the unstable area while testing was frozen, and the process begins again.

Getting Help with Debian

The Debian project has a mature set of resources to support those who use, administer, and develop software for Debian systems. A place to begin learning more about Debian is the Debian Support page (www.debian.org/support). Here are some of the resources you can connect to from that page:

- **Documentation** (www.debian.org/doc) — From this page, you can find links to both Debian-specific and general Linux documentation. For specific Debian information, refer to the Release Notes, Installation Guide, Debian GNU/Linux FAQ, and various user, administrator, and programming manuals. General Linux information includes manuals, HOWTOs, and FAQs.

- **Mailing lists** (`www.debian.org/MailingLists`) — Ways of accessing (and behaving on) a Debian mailing list are described on this page. A complete listing of the more than 200 Debian mailing lists is available from `http://lists.debian.org/completeindex.html`.

- **Bug tracking** (`www.debian.org/Bugs`) — If you are interested in following the bug tracking system for Debian, links from the support page can take you to the Bug Tracking System site. If you are having problems with any Debian software, you can search that site for bug reports and file a bug report, if your bug was not yet reported.

- **Help** (`www.debianhelp.org`) — This site offers connections to a range of information about Debian. In particular, you can find Debian forums from this site, containing literally thousands of posts. The Debian User Forums site (`http://forums.debian.net`) is another place you can go to post questions about Debian.

If you are interested in becoming a Debian developer, start at the Debian Developers' Corner (`www.debian.org/devel`). That site acts as a guide to ways in which you can enter the Debian development community. There are Debian developers all over the world. The largest concentrations of Debian developers are in Europe and the United States, as you can see from the Debian Developer Location map (`www.debian.org/devel/developers.loc`).

Installing Debian GNU/Linux

The Debian CD image included with this book contains the most commonly used packages in the Debian system. Additional packages can be downloaded and installed from the Internet after the base system has been installed and an Internet connection established. For information about how to obtain additional Debian packages on CD or DVD, see `www.debian.org/distrib/`.

Hardware Requirements and Installation Planning

To run Debian, you need at least a 486 processor and 32MB of RAM. For a server or a graphical workstation (running the X Window System), you should plan on having at least 128MB of memory and a Pentium-class processor.

A minimal set of packages requires 250MB of disk space, and a normal installation of desktop applications can require a few gigabytes. Additional space will be needed to store any data files that you want to keep on the system.

Most ISA and PCI network cards are supported under Linux, although ISA models are not usually detected automatically by the installer. Inexpensive cards based on RealTek 8139 chipsets can be found at most PC dealers and will work fine for low-demand applications. Intel PRO/100 and PRO/1000 adapters are supported in Linux and will work well in high-demand applications, as will cards based on the "tulip" chipsets and most 3Com network cards.

Many newer systems include software-based modems that are not supported by the manufacturer under Linux. If you require a dial-up connection for Internet access, see Chapter 5 and check out `http://tldp.org/HOWTO/Modem-HOWTO-2.html` before you start the installation process.

Many other devices, such as sound and video capture cards, can also be used under Linux. For more information about hardware compatibility, see the Hardware Compatibility HOWTO at `http://tldp.org/HOWTO/Hardware-HOWTO/`.

Workstations

In most cases, workstation users will want to run the X Window System (X11). The ability to run X11 depends on compatibility with the video chipset on your video card or mainboard. Debian 4.0 includes version 7.1 of X.org, which includes better autodetection than the XFree86 X11 system previously used.

Servers

A Linux server installation generally consists of only the minimum set of packages required to provide the service for which it was designed. In particular, this means that servers do not usually have a graphical interface installed.

Server hardware is generally more expensive than workstation hardware, although you can still run smaller servers on less-expensive desktop hardware. If you are planning to store important data on your server, you will want to look into a RAID array for storage. A number of inexpensive ATA RAID controllers work well under Linux.

NOTE More information about ATA RAID compatibility is available at the following sites:

```
http://linuxmafia.com/faq/Hardware/sata.html
http://ibiblio.org/pub/Linux/docs/HOWTO/other-formats/html_single/
   Hardware-HOWTO.html#IDERAID
```

Higher-end servers will, of course, require more expensive hardware. In applications such as mail servers where you will have a lot of disk activity, plan on splitting the disk-intensive tasks across multiple arrays. When it comes to CPU and RAM, more of both is good, but most applications benefit more from extra RAM than they do from multiple CPUs.

Running the Installer

To install Debian from the Debian network install CD, you need an Internet connection. After you have installed the base system and done some system configuration, most of the software you choose to install is downloaded from an online Debian repository.

CAUTION Before you begin installing Debian to your hard disk, be sure to back up any data that is important to you. A simple mistake during partitioning can result in your losing some or all of your data. Refer to Chapter 7 for information on disk partitioning. It can help you decide how to divide up your hard disk or even resize existing disk partitions to make room for the new Debian installation.

1. Boot the CD that comes with this book and type **debian** from the boot prompt to start the Debian installer.

NOTE **Some systems may require special parameters in order to boot. Other options are also available, such as the option to install to a particular hardware configuration. Press F4 at the** `boot:` **prompt for more information.**

2. After the installer has finished booting, you are presented with the series of menus that make up the installation process. Use the arrow keys to navigate through the menus and select your language, region, and keyboard mapping.

3. Configure the network connection. This step is skipped automatically if no network card is detected in your system.

    If a network card is detected in your system, the installer will attempt to automatically detect the network using the DHCP protocol. This involves the computer sending out requests on the network for configuration details from a DHCP server. Most networks and broadband routers support this service.

    If the DHCP configuration fails, you are presented with four options:

    ■ **retry** — Select this option if you suspect that there was a temporary problem that prevented your computer from communicating with the DHCP server.

    ■ **retry with hostname** — Select this option if your network provider requires you to enter a DHCP hostname. This used to be common on cable modem networks, but is rarely seen anymore.

    ■ **manual configuration** — Select this option if you have static IP address information that must be entered for your Internet connection.

CROSS-REF **See Chapter 5 for information about IP addresses, network masks, and other material related to setting up a network card connection.**

    ■ **do not configure at this time** — Select this option if you do not have an Internet connection, are using a dial-up connection, or have a broadband connection that requires the use of PPPoE. In the latter two cases, you'll want to establish the connection at the point that it is noted during stage 2 of the installation.

4. Provide a hostname (a single-word name that you give to your system, such as `debian`, `littlebeigebox`, or `yoda`) and a domain name. If you do not have your own domain name, you can make one up, such as `myhouse.local`.

5. You will next be asked to configure your disk partitions for Debian. If you haven't already done so, read Chapter 7 for more information about partitioning.

   If you already have partitions on your drive and have room for more, you are given the option to use this space for your Debian system. Another option is to erase the entire disk and use the whole thing for Debian. Either of these two options takes you through the guided partitioning, which is covered in this section.

   A third option, manually editing the partition, enables you to be more exacting about your partition setup, but you should not try this without help or at least without reading Chapter 7.

   The guided partitioning section presents three partitioning schemes. Each of the options includes a suitable amount of swap space but has different benefits based on your situation. You must select one from the list before you proceed. See the "Selecting a Partition Scheme" sidebar for more information.

NOTE When installing to small disk drives (those under a few gigabytes in size), you should use ext2 file systems instead of ext3. The journaling feature in ext3 requires that a portion of the disk be set aside for the journal, but the feature is of limited usefulness on small file systems. You can change file system types by going into the partition properties. To do this, highlight the partition using the arrow keys and press Enter.

CAUTION The next step will modify the contents of your hard disk. Check your partition settings carefully before proceeding.

6. With your partition configuration chosen, select Finish Partitioning and Write Changes to Disk. This is your last chance to cancel changes that could cause damage to any other operating systems you may have on the disk, so check the screen carefully before proceeding!

7. Select your time zone from a list.

8. The base system includes an empty password for the root (superuser) account, which means that you want to set one here. Select a password that you will remember but that others will not be able to guess easily.

9. Add a non-administrative account that you can use for your day-to-day tasks on the server. Enter your name, your desired username (this should not contain any spaces or punctuation other than dashes, must not start with a number, and is generally all in lowercase), and a password for this account. If you have more users to add, you can do so later, as described in Chapter 4.

   The installer writes the partitions to disk and creates the necessary file systems. After they have been prepared and mounted, the Debian base system is extracted from the CD and installed to the target partitions.

Selecting a Partition Scheme

The guided partitioning feature allows you to select one of three templates to use to create your partitions. Use these guidelines to select the template that is correct for you.

- **All files in one partition** — Makes a single Linux partition for files. This is the easiest option to manage because you don't have to worry about balancing the sizes of your partitions. This can also be dangerous because users have the capability to fill up the entire disk, which can cause problems for the operating system. Do not use this option unless you are prepared to monitor disk space carefully.

- **Desktop machine** — Gives the operating system its own space and gives home directories their own space. This option is a good trade-off between the convenience of a single partition and the increased safety of the multiuser scheme. However, the /tmp/ directory is still part of the operating system partition, meaning that it is still fairly easy for people who habitually use that directory to fill up the operating system partition.

- **Multiuser system** — Creates separate partitions for the root file system, /usr/, /var/, /tmp/, and /home/. You can choose this option when you are using this system as a server. It may also be a good choice for systems that will be used by more than just you, your relatives, and your close friends. The trade-off is that you may run out of room on a given partition even though the others have plenty of space, which means that you will need to plan carefully.

In some situations, you may need to adjust the partition sizes selected by the multiuser partitioning scheme to put more room where you are likely to need it:

- If you are planning to compile a lot of large software packages, you'll need to have plenty of space in the /usr/ partition.

- Active servers (especially Web and mail servers) may need extra room in /var/ for log files. Mail servers also use this space for the mail queue, and the default mail system also stores incoming mail here (you may also want to consider making /var/mail/ a separate partition in these cases).

- Web browsers such as Mozilla use /tmp/ for storing files while they are downloaded. This file system must be big enough to hold any large files that you want to download through there, plus any other files that may be there at the same time.

Note that with the multiuser partitioning scheme, the /home/ partition generally ends up receiving most of the space on larger disks. This usually makes it a good place to "borrow" space from when you want to make other partitions larger. However, because partman (the partitioning tool used by the Debian installer) has already mapped out the partitions, you actually need to delete /home/ and then re-add it after you increase the size of the other partition. If there are other partitions between /home/ and the one that you are increasing in size, you also need to delete them, and then add them back in an appropriate order.

10. If a network connection was not configured during stage 1, you will be given the chance to configure a dial-up PPP connection to an Internet service provider. This is performed using the pppconfig program, which is explained in further detail in the "Dial-Up PPP Connections" section later in this chapter. Keep in mind that the system will try to dial-up once this step has completed.

    If you're using a broadband connection that requires PPPoE, press Alt+F2, log in as root, and run the `pppoeconf` program.

    You can still finish the system installation if you are unable to connect to the Internet at this time. However, you may later need to manually edit your APT sources mirror list (as described in the "Package Management Using APT" section in this chapter) before all of the packages that you want are available for easy installation.

NOTE   Because the Debian CD image included with this book is the network install image, the CD itself will provide software for installing only a minimal Debian system. You will need a network connection or other Debian software CDs to install, for example, a full desktop system or the LAMP and mail servers described in Chapters 24 and 25.

11. Select Yes to enable a network mirror as the source for additional or updated software packages. Then select a country and a mirror server from the list. You are prompted for any HTTP proxy configuration, which may be necessary on some corporate or school networks. If you aren't sure, check with your support desk. If it does not apply, just leave it empty. APT retrieves a list of packages from the site that you selected.

12. The installer attempts to retrieve a list of security updates from the Debian security archive. This step will fail if you do not have an Internet connection, but you can still finish the rest of the installation.

13. You are asked to participate in a package usage survey. The survey is optional.

14. You are presented with a list of predefined software collections that you can select for installation. Use the arrow keys and space bar to choose to install any of these collections now. (Any software you don't install now you can add after installation is complete using task selection, as described later in this chapter.) Press Enter to continue.

15. APT downloads and installs the packages you have selected.

16. The final step is to install GRUB, the boot loader. The default setting is to install to the master boot record (MBR), which is generally the best option. If the installer finds other bootable partitions, it will tell you what it has found and, if you agree, it will add them to the boot loader. Select Yes and press Enter to continue.

Installation of the Debian GNU/Linux system is now complete. Depending on which software categories you selected, you may have a fully functioning desktop system, plus a variety of network server packages (Web server, FTP server, and so on). Reboot to begin using your new Debian system. Figure 9-1 shows an example of a Debian system with the default GNOME desktop.

A default Debian desktop includes browsers, music players, and other popular apps.

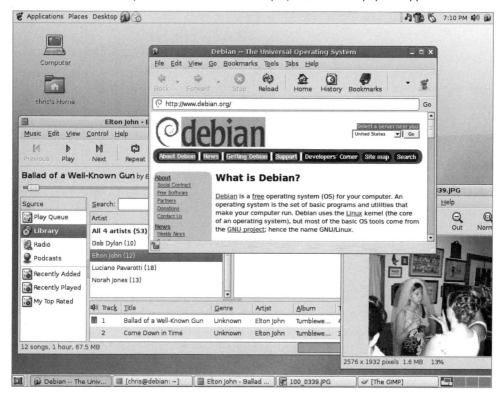

Managing Your Debian System

Some of the basic tasks that you may encounter while running Debian GNU/Linux include package installation, configuration, and removal, as well as handling some special situations that you may come across.

All these steps require that you be logged in as the superuser (root). If you have just finished installing the system, you can log in as root from the login prompt.

Configuring Network Connections

Debian includes a set of tools for managing most types of network interfaces, including Ethernet, PPP, wireless, and even ATM. You may find that you need to add or change network settings after the system has been installed.

IP Networks: Ethernet and Wireless

On Debian systems, standard network connections are configured in the `/etc/network/`
`interfaces` file. If you have a network card configured to obtain an IP address automatically,
the file will look like this:

```
# This file describes the network interfaces available on
# your system and how to activate them. For more information,
# see interfaces(5).

# The loopback network interface
auto lo
iface lo inet loopback

# The primary network interface
auto eth0
iface eth0 inet dhcp
```

> **CAUTION** Do not modify the `loopback` **entry unless you are absolutely certain that you know**
> **what you are doing.**

In some cases, such as when the system will be acting as a server, you want to configure your network interface with a fixed IP address. To do so, edit `/etc/network/interfaces` and replace
the `iface eth0 inet dhcp` line. Use the following block as a template, replacing the parameters with the correct settings for your network:

```
iface eth0 inet static
    address 192.168.1.220
    netmask 255.255.255.0
    gateway 192.168.1.1
```

> **NOTE** **You can obtain IP network settings from your ISP or network administrator.**

Wireless interfaces can also be configured using the interfaces file but require that the wireless-
tools package be installed. Use dpkg or apt-get to install the wireless-tools package. Then add the
necessary parameters to the entry for your wireless network interface. This example shows the settings for a wireless network with an access point (managed mode) set to the ESSID Home, and
operating on channel 11:

```
iface eth0 inet dhcp
    wireless_essid Home
    wireless_mode Managed
    wireless_channel 11
```

> **NOTE** **If your wireless network is using encryption, you will need to specify a** `wireless_key`
> **parameter. You can find a complete list of wireless options in the** `iwconfig` **man page**
> **and** `/usr/share/doc/wireless-tools/README.Debian.`

Dial-Up PPP Connections

Dial-up connections can be managed using the pppconfig utility. Simply run `pppconfig`, and you are provided with a menu from which you can create, modify, and delete dial-up connections. If you have not created a connection yet, you will want to select that option from the menu. Otherwise, you can edit your existing connections.

The pppconfig utility will ask a number of questions during the connection creation process. Start by selecting "Create a connection," and then enter the following information as prompted:

1. **Provider name** — Enter any name you like to identify this connection. For the dial-up entry to your primary ISP, you can simply leave the name `provider` as the Provider name.

2. **DNS server configuration method** — Here you can configure the connection to static DNS servers if needed. This is probably not necessary unless your service provider included the DNS server in the information that it provided about the connection. If you aren't certain, select Dynamic DNS and change it later if needed.

3. **Authentication method** — This is the method that your computer will use to identify itself to the dial-up server. PAP is the most commonly used protocol, and some systems also support CHAP. The CHAP option should be used if the dial-up servers use text prompts to ask for the username and password. If in doubt, select PAP.

4. **User name and password** — Enter the username and password that will be recognized by the dial-up server.

5. **Speed** — This is the speed that your computer and your modem will communicate with one another. In most cases, this should be set to 115200.

6. **Dialing method** — If your telephone system requires pulse dialing, you can configure that here.

7. **Phone number** — Enter the number that you need to dial in order to reach the dial-up server, including any area codes and other codes that may be needed. For instance, if you have to dial 9 in order to reach an outside line, use 9,*<number to dial>*. The comma tells your modem to pause before continuing the dialing process. You may also enter the appropriate numbers for disabling features such as call waiting through your telephone service.

8. **Modem configuration method** — Here, you can have pppconfig attempt to automatically find the port that your modem is on. If a modem is not found, you will then be given the chance to enter the path to the modem device. More information about what to enter here can be found in the sidebar "Identifying and Configuring Your Modem" later in this chapter.

Save your settings by selecting Finished from the menu, and then exit the pppconfig utility.

Dial a connection by using the `pon` command, by replacing *peer* with the name you assigned to your connection, or by leaving it out if your connection is named `provider`:

```
# pon peer
```

You can disconnect using the `poff` command and can view logs (for diagnosing problems or determining status) using the `plog` command. The user that was created during the base system configuration will automatically have access to run these commands. Any other users who need to run them will need to be added to the dialout group through the use of the gpasswd utility:

```
# gpasswd -a <username> dialout
```

Identifying and Configuring Your Modem

If your modem is not automatically on COM1, 2, 3, or 4, you may need to perform some additional configuration steps before it can be used for PPP connections. Plug-and-play and PCI modems are often found on higher ports such as ttyS4 ("COM5"). This information can often be found in the output from the dmesg utility. If you reached this point from stage 2 of the install, you can get to a prompt by pressing Alt+F2 and logging in as root.

```
# dmesg | grep tty
ttyS00 at 0x03f8 (irq = 4) is a 16550A
ttyS04 at port 0xa800 (irq = 5) is a 16550A
```

In this case, `ttyS00` is the on-board serial port (most PC motherboards have at least one of these) and `ttyS04` is probably the modem. If you have several serial ports showing up, you can create devices for all of them (as shown following) and try them until you find your modem.

The system includes only `ttyS0` through `ttyS3` by default, so this device will need to be created using the `MAKEDEV` command. When running `MAKEDEV`, you will need to leave out any leading zeros in the device number. In this example, `ttyS04` becomes `ttyS4`:

```
# (cd /dev && sh MAKEDEV ttyS4)
```

If you reached this point while performing stage 2 of the install, you can get back to the install menu by pressing Alt+F1.

See Chapter 5 for more information on using modems to get on the Internet.

PPPoE Connections

Some DSL and cable modem providers require that you use PPPoE (PPP over Ethernet) to connect to their systems. PPPoE connections are managed using the pppoeconf program. As long as your computer is connected to the broadband connection, it should be able to detect most of the settings automatically.

Package Management Using APT

For most users, APT will be the primary tool for installing, removing, and upgrading packages. This section shows how to use the apt-get and apt-cache utilities. From the console, you can also use the aptitude utility, which acts as an interface to apt-get.

Managing the List of Package Repositories

The configuration file /etc/apt/sources.list contains a list of Debian package repositories that APT will use. Like most configuration files on a Linux system, this file is a plain-text file that can be viewed using any text editor or pager. To view its contents, run the following:

```
# pager /etc/apt/sources.list
deb cdrom:[Debian GNU/Linux _Sarge_ NetInst]/ stable main
deb http://ftp.us.debian.org/debian/ stable main
deb-src http://ftp.us.debian.org/debian/ stable main
deb http://security.debian.org/ stable/updates main
```

NOTE Depending on which pager is configured as your default, you may need to press the q key in order to return to a prompt.

Your output will differ from this example's, of course, but the kind of information remains the same. The first part of each line indicates whether the repository is to be used for binary packages (indicated by the deb prefix) or source packages (deb-src). The rest of the line defines the method (in this case, cdrom or http), the location, the distribution (stable), and the sections (main). If you want to use software from the contrib and non-free sections, you can use a text editor to add them after main.

NOTE Run man sources.list on any Debian system for more information.

If you aren't going to have your Debian CD available all the time, you may want to remove the cdrom: entry from the file. Use a text editor (as root user) to edit the file:

```
# editor /etc/apt/sources.list
```

Make any changes you need to the file, exit the editor, and then update the package database as described in the following section.

NOTE Astute readers may notice that the pager and editor commands used in this section are not common UNIX commands. Both are pointers to programs and are managed using Debian's alternatives system, which is discussed later in this chapter.

Updating the APT Package Database

Because the lists of packages available in the Debian package repositories may change from time to time, you need to instruct APT to download these lists and update its database occasionally. To perform this process, run the following command:

```
# apt-get update
```

You generally want to run this command before installing new packages so that you do not download an older version. Run it before checking for upgrades as well.

Finding and Installing Packages

When looking for new packages to install, you may not always know what package you want. The package database maintained by APT includes package descriptions and other fields that can be searched using the apt-cache utility:

```
# apt-cache search tetris
bsdgames--a collection of classic textual unix games
pytris--two-player networked console tetris clone
stax--collection of puzzle games similar to Tetris Attack.
```

TIP Specifying multiple keywords in a search prevents apt-cache from listing packages that do not contain all of the keywords you specify. This enables you to do very specific searches such as word processor.

You can also use this utility to find out more information about a specific package in the repositories:

```
# apt-cache show pytris
Package: pytris
Priority: optional
Section: games
Installed-Size: 101
Maintainer: Radovan Garabik
Architecture: i386
Version: 0.96
Depends: python (>=2.1), libc6 (>= 2.2.4-4)
Filename: pool/main/p/pytris/pytris_0.96_i386.deb
Size: 16304
MD5sum: 70eb8ad6f5a8a901a95eb37f7336fc57
Description: two-player networked console tetris clone
 two-player networked console based tetris clone, written
 in python, similar to xtet42.
```

NOTE To view information about a specific package that is already installed on your system, use dpkg, as discussed later in this chapter.

Once you know the name of the package you want to install, use the install method to download it and any packages on which it depends. For example, the ssh package is very useful for remotely accessing systems and is probably one of the first programs that you will want to install:

```
# apt-get install ssh
```

On this command, APT retrieves and installs the ssh package. If additional packages are required, a list of those packages is displayed by APT. If you choose to continue, APT will download and install those packages along with the package you requested.

> **NOTE**   When installing packages that support automatic configuration through debconf, you're prompted to answer the appropriate configuration questions. While the Debian package developers have gone to great lengths to ensure that the default options for these questions will work in most situations, it's best to read the questions thoroughly to be sure that the defaults work for you.

Removing Packages

APT can also be used to remove packages from your system. Unlike dpkg, which removes only the package you tell it to remove, `apt-get` also removes any packages that depend on the package you are removing. This is best used in conjunction with the `-s` option to simulate what would happen if the removal were actually performed:

```
# apt-get -s remove python2.3
Reading Package Lists... Done
Building Dependency Tree... Done
The following packages will be REMOVED:
  bittornado python python2.3 python2.3-dev
0 upgraded, 0 newly installed, 4 to remove and 0 not upgraded.
Remv pytris (0.96 Debian:testing)
Remv python (2.3.4 1 Debian:testing)
Remv python2.3-dev (2.3.4-5 Debian:testing)
Remv python2.3 (2.3.4-5 Debian:testing)
```

In this example, several other packages depend on the python2.3 package and also need to be removed. To proceed with removing python2.3 and all packages that depend on it, run the command again without the `-s` flag.

Upgrading Your System

As new versions of packages become available, you can instruct APT to download and install them, automatically replacing the older versions. This is as simple as updating your package list, followed by a simple command:

```
# apt-get upgrade
```

APT will begin by downloading the necessary packages, and will then move on to installing and configuring them. If necessary, you can abort the upgrade during the download process by pressing Control+C. APT may also be able to recover if you have to abort during the installation or configuration steps, but it is still best to let the process run without interruption once it has begun installing packages.

> **NOTE**   When upgrading to a newer distribution, use `dist-upgrade` instead of `upgrade`. This changes the rules that APT uses when deciding which actions to take, making it expect major changes in dependencies and handle them appropriately.

Package Management Using dpkg

As mentioned earlier, the dpkg utility is the core package management tool in Debian. Most other package management tools within the system, including APT, use dpkg to perform the midlevel work, and dpkg in turn uses dpkg-deb and dpkg-query to handle a number of the low-level functions. In most cases, you will want to use APT or aptitude for package management, and use dpkg in only a few situations.

Far too many commands associated with dpkg exist to list in this chapter, but the most common ones are explained in the following sections. In most cases, there are both short and long commands to perform the same function. Use whichever is easier for you to remember.

Installing and Removing Packages

Packages can be installed with dpkg using the `-i` or `--install` flags and the path to the `.deb` file containing the package. The path must be accessible as a file system path (HTTP, FTP, and other methods are not supported), and more than one package can be specified:

```
# dpkg --install /home/wayne/lsof_4.71-1_i386.deb
```

Package removal through dpkg is also straightforward and is done with the `-r` or `--remove` command. When configuration files are to be removed, the `-P` or `--purge` command can be used instead. Both commands can also be used to specify multiple packages to remove:

```
# dpkg --remove lsof
```

or

```
# dpkg --purge lsof
```

Querying the Package Database

You will often need to obtain more information about packages that are already installed on your system. Because these operations do not modify the package database, they can be done as a non-root user.

To list all packages known to dpkg, use the `-l` or `--list` command:

```
$ dpkg --list
```

You can restrict the list by specifying a glob pattern:

```
$ dpkg --list "*lsof*"
```

> **NOTE** The quotes are used to prevent the shell from replacing the wildcard with a list of matching files in the current directory. For more information about wildcards, see Chapter 2 or type **man 7 glob** to see a list of wildcards.

To view detailed information about a specific package, use the -s or --status command:

```
$ dpkg --status lsof
Package: lsof
Status: install ok installed
Priority: standard
Section: utils
...
```

The origin package for a file can be determined using the -S or --search command:

```
$ dpkg --search /bin/ls
coreutils: /bin/ls
```

The list of files in an installed package can be viewed using the -L or --listfiles command:

```
$ dpkg --listfiles lsof
/.
/usr
/usr/sbin
/usr/bin
/usr/bin/lsof
...
```

Examining a Package File

Package files can be examined before installing them using either the --info (-I) or the --contents (-c) command. These options can be used on packages in a local directory, as opposed to using them to examine packages on a remote server.

The following --info option shows the lsof package name, version information, and sizes of different parts of the package. Beyond that (although shortened here for space considerations) you would be able to see a list of packages lsof depends on and descriptive information about the package.

```
$ dpkg --info lsof_4.71-1_i386.deb
 new debian package, version 2.0.
 size 319058 bytes: control archive= 1534 bytes.
     557 bytes,    16 lines      control
    2246 bytes,    32 lines      md5sums
 Package: lsof
 Version: 4.71-1
 ...
```

The following --contents option lets you see the full contents of the package you choose as if you were listing the contents with an ls -l command. You can see the name and path to each file, its permission settings, and file/group ownership:

```
$ dpkg --contents lsof_4.71-1_i386.deb
drwxr-xr-x root/root          0 2004-04-03 07:34:41 ./
drwxr-xr-x root/root          0 2004-04-03 07:34:36 ./usr/
drwxr-xr-x root/root          0 2004-04-03 07:34:39 ./usr/bin/
...
```

Installing Package Sets (Tasks) with Tasksel

Some package sets are too large to be managed practically through meta packages, so tasks have been created as an alternative. Tasks are installed and removed using the tasksel utility. When run without any arguments, tasksel presents a menu from which you can select tasks to install or remove.

> **CAUTION** Do not install any tasks if you plan to use this system in conjunction with the server examples in Chapters 24 and 25.

Additional options are available from the command line:

- To see a list of known tasks, run `tasksel --list-tasks`.
- To list the packages that are installed by a task, run `tasksel --task-packages <task name>`.

> **CAUTION** When a task is removed, all programs associated with that task, whether installed manually or as part of that task, are removed!

An example of a popular task to install is the `desktop` task. The `desktop` task installs three complete desktop environments based on the X Window System: GNOME, KDE, and XFCE environments. Note that this task will take a long time to download and install and requires several gigabytes of disk space to complete. To start the `desktop` task, run the following:

```
# tasksel install desktop
```

Alternatives, Diversions, and Stat Overrides

In cases where there is more than one installed program that provides a specific function, package maintainers have the option of utilizing Debian's alternatives system. The alternatives system manages which program is executed when you run a specific command. For instance, the ed, nano, and nvi packages each provide a text editor. An alternative maintained in the system guarantees that a text editor is accessible through the generic `editor` command, regardless of which combination of these packages is installed.

The system administrator can designate which program is referenced in the alternatives database through the use of the `update-alternatives` command:

```
# update-alternatives --config editor
```

```
These are alternatives that provide 'editor'.
  Selection    Alternative
-----------------------------------------------
       1         /bin/ed
*+     2         /bin/nano
       3         /usr/bin/nvi

Press enter to keep the default[*],
or type selection number: 2
```

You can also use the `--all` command with `update-alternatives` to configure every entry in the alternatives database, one at a time. You can find more details by typing the following: **man update-alternatives**.

NOTE By default, all alternatives are in automatic mode, meaning that the system automatically selects a suitable program from the available candidates. Installing a new candidate program generally results in the automatic updating of the appropriate alternatives. Manually configuring an alternative disables automatic mode, preventing the system from changing these settings without prior knowledge of the system administrator.

The Debian package management tools also provide a mechanism for renaming specific files in a package and for overriding the ownership and permission settings on files. Unlike when these changes are made manually using `mv`, `chmod`, or `chown`, changes made through the Debian tools remain in place across package upgrades and re-installations.

For example, if you want to replace `/usr/bin/users` without modifying the coreutils package, you can divert it to `/usr/bin/users.distrib`:

```
# dpkg-divert --local --rename --add /usr/bin/users
Adding `local diversion of /usr/bin/users to /usr/bin/users.distrib'
```

Removing the diversion returns the original filename:

```
# dpkg-divert --remove /usr/bin/users
Removing `local diversion of /usr/bin/users to /usr/bin/users.distrib'
```

Stat overrides are useful when you want to disable access to a program, or when you want to make it set-UID. For instance, to disable access to the `wall` program, type the following:

```
# dpkg-statoverride --update --add root root 0000 /usr/bin/wall
```

This sets the owner and group of `/usr/bin/wall` to root and root and disables all permissions on the file.

NOTE You can find more information about file permissions in the section "Understanding File Permissions" in Chapter 2.

Unlike `dpkg-divert`, `dpkg-statoverride` does not keep track of the original file permissions. As a result, removing an override does not restore the old permissions. After removing the override, you need to either set the permissions manually or reinstall the package that contained the file:

```
# dpkg-statoverride --remove /usr/bin/wall
# apt-get --reinstall install bsdutils
Reading Package Lists... Done
Building Dependency Tree... Done
0 upgraded, 0 newly installed, 1 reinstalled, 0 to remove and 0 not upgraded.
Need to get 0B/62.5kB of archives.
After unpacking 0B of additional disk space will be used.
Do you want to continue? [Y/n]Y
(Reading database ... 16542 files and directories currently installed.)
Preparing to replace bsdutils 1:2.12-10 (using .../bsdutils_1%3a2.12-
10_i386.deb) ...
Unpacking replacement bsdutils ...
Setting up bsdutils (2.12-10) ...
```

Managing Package Configuration with debconf

All packages that include support for configuration management through debconf are configured as they are being installed. If you want to change a configuration option later, you can do so using the dpkg-reconfigure command. For instance, you can change the configuration options for ssh using the following command:

```
# dpkg-reconfigure ssh
```

Every configuration parameter is assigned a priority by the package maintainer. This allows debconf to select the default values for settings below a specific priority. By default, you will be prompted to answer questions of only medium, high, or critical priority; low-priority questions are answered automatically. You can change this by reconfiguring the debconf package:

```
# dpkg-reconfigure debconf
```

NOTE Advanced users maintaining multiple systems may want to create a database of configuration settings that can be distributed to every computer (or to sets of computers) to reduce the number of repeated steps. This process is documented in the debconf and debconf.conf man pages.

Summary

The reliability of Debian GNU/Linux, combined with the large number of high-quality packages available for it, make Debian a great choice for both workstations and servers. The carefully executed releases and the capability to upgrade most software without rebooting serve to further increase its suitability as a server operating system.

APT is a primary tool for installing, removing, and upgrading packages. This chapter explores how to use the apt-get and apt-cache utilities for package management. The chapter also covers the installation of package sets (tasks) using the tasksel utility and managing package configuration with the dpkg-reconfigure utility.

Chapter 10

Running SUSE and openSUSE Linux

For the past few years, SUSE has been the most popular Linux distribution in Europe. Since the U.S. networking company Novell, Inc. purchased SUSE in November 2003, SUSE has been positioning itself to challenge Red Hat to become the dominant Linux distribution for large enterprise computing environments worldwide.

Like Fedora and Red Hat Enterprise Linux, SUSE is an excellent first Linux for people who prefer to work from a graphical desktop rather than from the command line. Likewise, Novell's Linux product line is geared toward enterprise computing, so the skills you gain using SUSE on your home Linux system will be useful in a business environment as well.

SUSE has a slick graphical installer that leads you through installation and intuitive administrative tools, consolidated under a facility called YaST. SUSE and its parent company, Novell, offer a range of Linux products and support plans that scale from free versions of openSUSE with community support, to supported SUSE distributions for the home and enterprise desktop (SUSE and SUSE Linux Enterprise Desktop), all the way up to SUSE's Linux Enterprise Server product.

In 2005, Novell refocused its development efforts to do as Red Hat does with its Red Hat Enterprise Linux product and Fedora project: Novell formed the openSUSE project, which, like the Fedora project, produces a free community-driven Linux system that feeds into Novell's for-profit Linux systems. Unlike Fedora and RHEL, however, openSUSE and SUSE Linux Enterprise are, so far, following the same release numbers. They are differentiated by the fact that openSUSE offers no official Novell support and SUSE may contain some non–open source software.

ON the DVD-ROM The DVD that comes with this book contains the openSUSE 10.3 KDE install CD.

IN THIS CHAPTER

Understanding SUSE

What's in SUSE

Getting support for SUSE

Installing openSUSE

This chapter describes the features and approach to Linux that sets SUSE apart from other Linux distributions. It also explains how to install the openSUSE Linux 10.3 distribution that is included with this book.

The current versions of openSUSE and SUSE Linux (10.3) feature the YaST installer, and the current versions of KDE 3.5.7 desktop environment, GNOME 2.20.0, Firefox 2.0.0.7, GIMP 2.2.17, Apache 2.2.6, MySQL 5.0.45, and OpenOffice.org 2.3.0. All SUSE Linux packages for the current release are listed at `www.novell.com/products/linuxpackages/suselinux/index_all.html` and `www.novell.com/products/linuxpackages/desktop10/i386/index_all.html`.

At the time of this writing, openSUSE 10.3 has just been released. OpenSUSE and SUSE 10.2 feature KDE 3.5.5, GNOME 2.16, Firefox 2.0, and Apache 2.2.3.

> **NOTE** With the split between SUSE and openSUSE, Linux product names from Novell have changed significantly in the past year. Most significantly, what was previously called SUSE Professional Linux is now called SUSE Linux Enterprise

Understanding SUSE and openSUSE

If you are looking for a Linux system with the stability and support on which you can bet your business, SUSE offers impressive, stable Linux products backed by a company (Novell, Inc.) that has been selling enterprise solutions for a long time. SUSE's product offerings range from personal desktop systems to enterprise-quality servers.

Running with the Enemy: The SUSE/Microsoft Deal

In November 2006, Novell announced that it had struck a deal with Microsoft to further collaboration and interoperability with Microsoft products. This deal includes indemnification against patent-related lawsuits, and has raised a fair amount of concern and controversy in the open source community. In reality, Novell hasn't admitted and doesn't see any evidence of the use of Microsoft's intellectual property (IP) in Linux, but indemnification against patent liabilities has become an important part of the Linux scene ever since SCO launched its series of questionable IP lawsuits against Linux. Red Hat and Oracle already offer indemnification against this sort of thing, so this is an even broader level of protection.

Paranoia aside, this deal is important if for no other reason than that it is a statement by Microsoft that Linux is important to their customers and a viable enterprise operating system. As always, the long-term effects of this deal remain to be seen, but it should be a good thing for all concerned. Many members of the open source community are concerned that Microsoft will sneak its IP into the GNU/Linux code base, setting the stage for future lawsuits against non-partners (primarily Novell, although Linux companies Xandros and Linspire have signed similar deals).

SUSE began as a German version of Slackware in 1992, on 40 floppy disks, and was first officially released on CD (SUSE Linux 1.0) in 1994. Founded by Hubert Mantel, Burchard Steinbild, Roland Dyroff, and Thomas Fehr, SUSE set out as a separate distribution from Slackware to enhance the software in the areas of installation and administration.

Although SUSE had success and respect with its Linux distribution, it was not profitable, and Novell's $210 million offer for SUSE was seen as a good thing both for SUSE and for Linux in general. SUSE was running short on cash, and Novell was looking for a way to regain its stature as a growth company in the enterprise and network-computing arena.

In the 1980s and early 1990s, Novell was the world's number-one computer networking company. Before the Internet took hold, Novell's NetWare servers and IPX/SPX protocols were the most popular ways to connect PCs on LANs. International training, support, and sales teams brought Novell products to businesses and organizations around the world.

Despite Novell's huge lead in the network computing market, file and printer sharing features in Microsoft Windows and late entry into the TCP/IP (Internet) arena caused Novell to lose its market dominance in the 1990s. Although its NetWare products contained excellent features for directory services and managing network resources, Novell didn't have end-to-end computing solutions. NetWare relied on Windows for client computers and lacked high-end server products.

Novell's association with the UNIX operating system in the early 1990s makes an interesting footnote in the history of Linux. Novell purchased UNIX System V source code from AT&T and set out to make its resulting UNIXWare product (a UNIX desktop product for x86 processors) a competitor to Microsoft's growing dominance on the desktop. The effort was half-hearted, and in the mid-1990s Novell gave the UNIX trademark to the Open Group and sold the UNIX source code to SCO (although Novell apparently didn't transfer full rights to that code).

Novell's purchase of SUSE marks its second major attempt to fill in its product line with a UNIX-like desktop and server product. From the early returns, it appears that Novell is doing a better job with Linux than it did with UNIX.

What's in SUSE

Unlike distributions geared toward more technical users, such as Gentoo and Slackware, you can configure and launch most major features of SUSE Linux by selecting menus on the desktop. New Linux users should find SUSE to be very comfortable for daily use and basic administration.

Like Red Hat Enterprise Linux, SUSE is made to have a more cohesive look-and-feel than most Linux distributions that are geared toward Linux enthusiasts. In other words, you aren't required to put together a lot of SUSE by hand just to get it working. Although SUSE is ultimately aimed more toward enterprise computing, it also works well as a home desktop system.

Let's explore what openSUSE and SUSE Linux offer you.

Installation and Configuration with YaST

A set of modules that can be used to configure your SUSE system is gathered together under the YaST facility. Because many of the features needed in a Linux installer are also needed to configure a running system (network, security, software, and other setup features), YaST does double duty as an installer and an administrative tool.

YaST (which stands for Yet Another Setup Tool) was originally proprietary code that was not available as open source. However, to gain wider acceptance for YaST among major computing clients as a framework for managing a range of computing services, Novell released YaST under the GNU Public License in March 2004.

YaST makes obvious what you need to do to install Linux. Hardware detection is done before your eyes. You can set up your disk partitions graphically (no need to remember options to the fdisk command). Setting up the GRUB boot loader is done for you, with the option to modify it yourself.

One of the nice features of YaST installation is that you can scan the configuration process without stepping through every feature. If you scan through the mouse, keyboard, installation mode, partitioning, and other information and they look okay, you can click Accept and just keep going. Or you can change any of those settings you choose. (The "Installing openSUSE" section later in this chapter details the installation process with YaST.)

Because YaST offers both graphical (QT) and text-based (ncurses) interfaces, you can use YaST as a configuration tool from the desktop or the shell. To start YaST from the desktop, click the SUSE button on the desktop panel and select System ⇨ YaST. Figure 10-1 shows what the graphical version of the YaST utility looks like.

Launching the YaST utility actually involves running the /sbin/yast2 command. When you run /sbin/yast2, YaST starts in graphical mode by default. (An alternative is to run kdesu /sbin/yast from a Terminal window, which starts YaST in text mode.) Figure 10-2 shows what YaST looks like when started in text mode from a Terminal window.

YaST offers you some intuitive tools for configuring your system and comes preconfigured so you start with a nice set of defaults. YaST also does a good job detecting your hardware, finding partitions, and the like, so a new user can often just accept the settings YaST chooses. Here are some examples of what YaST does for you:

- **Detects hardware** — You don't have to check through /etc configuration files or run lsmod, lspci, or hwinfo to see the drivers for your hardware or how your hardware has been configured in SUSE. From the Hardware section, you can select icons representing your CD drives, graphics cards, printers, joysticks, scanners, sound cards, and mice. Click the Hardware information icon to see your full list of detected hardware.

- **Manages system configuration** — Like Red Hat Enterprise Linux, SUSE stores much of the information it uses to configure services at boot time in files in the /etc/sysconfig directory. The information in those files is in the form $VARIABLE="VALUE"$.

FIGURE 10-1

Configure common Linux features using the YaST utility.

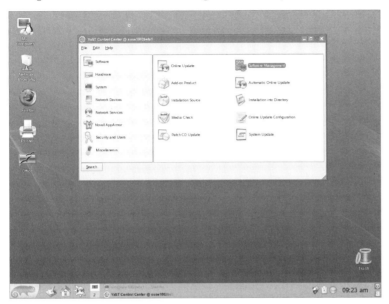

FIGURE 10-2

Use the arrow and Tab keys to navigate YaST in text mode.

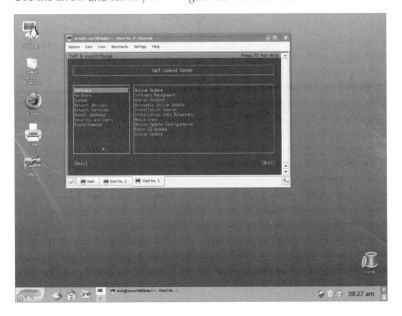

Under the YaST System icon, you can select the sysconfig Editor, which lets you select each file and then view and possibly change each variable so that you don't have to guess what variables are available for each configuration. For more advanced system administrators, this is a great way to fine-tune the startup services for your system.

SUSE also includes a System Configuration Profile Management (SCPM) applet, which lets you store and manage a collection of system settings so it can be used again later.

- **Configures network devices** — YaST detects your dial-up modem, Ethernet card, DSL modem, or ISDN hardware, and gives you the opportunity to configure each piece of hardware. SUSE also does a much better job than most distributions at getting Winmodems working in Linux, which is particularly useful for using dial-up features on laptops that have cheap, built-in modems.

- **Defines network services** — With a connection to your LAN or WAN, YaST provides some helpful graphical tools for configuring some services that can be unintuitive to configure from the command line.

- **Changes security settings** — Security settings in Linux are often among the most unintuitive features to configure, while at the same time being among the most important. Although features such as iptables work great for most Linux gurus for setting up a firewall, people who are accustomed to graphical interfaces may find them challenging.

  From the YaST Security and Users selection, the Firewall icon enables you to step through your network interfaces and add access to those services you want by name (such as Web Server, Mail Server, and Other Services) or by port number. It even enables you to do initial setup of more complex firewall features, such as packet forwarding, IP Masquerading, and logging.

To make your way around the graphical YaST interface, you need only to click the mouse and use the Tab key to move between fields. For the text-based YaST interface, you can use the Tab and arrow keys to move among the selections and the Enter key to select the currently highlighted item.

RPM Package Management

Like Red Hat Enterprise Linux and Fedora, SUSE packages its software using the RPM package management file format and related tools. RPM contains a lot of features for adding, removing, and managing software in SUSE. Although software packages in the Red Hat and SUSE distributions are different, the tools you use for managing packages in those two distributions are the same.

You use the rpm utility to work with RPM software packages. Here's a list of some of its features:

- **Installing local or remote packages** — You can use the rpm command to add a software package to SUSE, and rpm doesn't care if the package is in the local directory, CD, or remote computer (provided you have network access to that computer). A remote package can be available on a Web server (http://) or FTP server (ftp://). Here's an example of using an rpm command to install a software package from an FTP server:

```
# rpm -iv ftp://ftp.linuxtoys.net/pub/suse/10.2/abc.i586.rpm
```

In this example, the -i option says to install the package, and the -v option says to give verbose output as the package is installed. The fictitious package (abc.i586.rpm) is installed from an FTP repository. If there are dependency or access issues, rpm informs you and fails. Otherwise, the package is installed. (The -U option is often used instead of the -i option to install RPMs because -U succeeds even if the package is already installed. The -U says to upgrade the package.)

■ **Querying the RPM database** — One of the best features of the RPM facility is that you can find out a lot of information about the software packages that are installed. The query option (-q) lets you list package names, descriptions, and contents in various ways. Here are a few examples:

```
# rpm -qa xmms
# rpm -ql xmms | less
# rpm -qi xmms | less
```

The first example (-qa) searches for the xmms package and reports the current version of the package that is installed. In the second, -ql lists all files in the xmms package and then pipes that output to the less command to page through it. And finally, -qi displays a description and other information about the xmms package.

■ **Verifying installed packages** — Use rpm to verify the contents of an RPM package. The -V option enables you to check whether any of the files in a package have been tampered with. Here is an example:

```
# rpm -V aaa_base
..5....T c /etc/inittab
S.5....T   /etc/profile.d/alias.ash
```

-V checks whether any of the contents of the aaa_base package (which contains some basic system configuration files) have been modified. The output shows that the inittab and alias.ash files have been modified from the originals. The 5 indicates that the md5sum of the files differ, while the T indicates that the timestamp on the file differs. On the alias.ash file, the S shows that the size of the file is different.

The rpm command has many other options as well. To find out more about them, type **man rpm** or **rpm --help** from any shell.

Automated Software Updates

As of version 7.1, SUSE Linux includes an automatic update agent. The YaST Online Update (YOU) utility is built right into the YaST facility and offers an easy way to get updates, security patches, and bug fixes for SUSE or openSUSE by downloading and installing them from software repositories over the network. You can also execute YOU from the command line, using the `kdesu you` command.

From within YaST, select Online Update. YaST uses software installation sources that have been defined in YaST's Installation Source module to enable you to begin retrieving software updates with a single click. It presents you with a list of patches from which you can choose. Security patches are in red, all recommended patches are selected, and optional patches are shown (unselected). It's easy to see all available patches and read their descriptions to determine if you want them.

After you have selected the updates you want and clicked OK, you can watch the progress as each patch and updated package is downloaded and installed. Having security-related patches and other fixes separated and having the ability to read all about each software update and patch right on the YaST window before you start downloading are features that make YaST Online Update a powerful and easy-to-use software update mechanism.

Managing Software with zypper

Although the `rpm` command is good for managing single applications, SUSE needed a tool that could work well with online repositories and deal with issues of dependent packages and updates. The recently added zypper utility is just such a tool.

The zypper utility is similar to the yum utility that is used with Fedora and other Red Hat systems. With zypper, not only can you install packages, but you can also search, download, and query packages from online SUSE repositories. The zypper utility is also designed to support several different software backends, including Novell Rug (Red Carpet updater), ZENworks software manager, and yum repositories.

Getting Support for SUSE and openSUSE

SUSE has an excellent support database and full-time support staff. You can search many of the articles on the site for free and check out the FAQs. Paid support options are available as well.

The openSUSE.org Wiki (`http://en.opensuse.org`) is the place to search for answers about openSUSE. To try the free search engine at the site, just enter your term in the Search box. Check the news and events box for the latest news about openSUSE. For a more interactive experience, select the Communicate link to gain access to mailing lists, online forums, IRC chats, and other tools for connecting you to the openSUSE community. You can also follow links to PlanetSUSE (`http://planetsuse.org`), where you can read blogs from members of the openSUSE community. If you are really stuck, try the openSUSE Support Database (`http://opensuse.org/SDB:SDB`).

With the split of openSUSE and SUSE Linux Enterprise, many of SUSE's online resources have been divided as well. For example, many general SUSE resources are directed to Novell.com. If you are interested in the commercial SUSE Linux Enterprise products, you should start at the Novell SUSE Enterprise Linux site (`www.novell.com/linux`). From there you can view demos, compare products, and check out costs.

> **NOTE** At the time of this writing, SUSE is offering a free 60-day evaluation for SUSE Linux Enterprise Server if you want to download it. That evaluation includes installation support and upgrade protection. Check the Novell (`www.novell.com`) and SUSE (`www.opensuse.org`) Web sites to see if any evaluation specials are currently available.

Installing openSUSE

The installation procedure described here is for openSUSE Linux 10.3. This edition is available free of charge. Functionally, it is almost exactly the same as the SUSE Linux 10.3 boxed set version that Novell sells. The primary differences between the two are product support (only with SUSE Linux) and inclusion of some non–open source software (also only with SUSE Linux). So, essentially, these instructions should work equally well for both SUSE and openSUSE 10.3.

The DVD that comes with this book includes the openSUSE 10.3 KDE install CD, remastered to coexist with other Linux distributions on the DVD. If you like SUSE and want a commercial version, select the How to Buy link at the SUSE Linux site (`www.novell.com/products/suselinux`). You can purchase a boxed set of SUSE Linux, which includes installation support, some non–open source software (such as multimedia plug-ins and Java support) and hardcopy documentation. Or you can choose one of the other editions, such as the SUSE Linux Enterprise Server edition, that also include support and documentation.

> **NOTE** The installation description in this chapter covers installs on Intel x86 PCs. If you have AMD 64-bit or Intel Extended Memory 64 Technology systems, you need to purchase the SUSE Linux boxed set, which includes installation media for both of those types of hardware, or download the version of openSUSE for the x86_64 platform. If you are using an Itanium-based system, an ia64 version of openSUSE is also available.

Before You Begin

To install openSUSE, you need at least 96MB of main memory, although more is always better, and future releases may require greater amounts of memory for installation and usability. For a desktop install, however, I recommend at least 256MB of main memory.

The default installation of openSUSE 10.3 from the KDE install CD included on the DVD with this book requires at least 2.5GB of disk space. The default installation from an official openSUSE 10.3 DVD requires 3.25GB of disk space. You can get by with less by deselecting packages during installation. Installation should work on any Pentium-class x86 PC. The openSUSE installation DVD contains a total of 4.1GB of data.

The description here explains how to install by booting the installation DVD that comes with this book and installing the software from that medium.

Starting Installation

Here are the steps for installing openSUSE Linux on your hard disk from the openSUSE CD image included on the DVD that comes with this book:

NOTE With previous versions you chose your desktop during the installation. At the time of this writing, openSUSE 10.3 CDs are available for installation in two forms — KDE or GNOME. We have included the KDE CD on the DVD that comes with this book. If you want to download the GNOME version or the full openSUSE 10.3 install DVD, follow the Download link from the openSUSE.org site. From that same site, you can download the Non-Open Source Software CD, which contains software that is not open source but can otherwise be distributed without cost.

1. **Insert the installation DVD in your drive.** Reboot the computer. The installation boot screen appears.

2. **Installation type.** Type **suse** and then press Enter.

3. **Swap space.** Select whether you want to create a swap partition or a swap file. A swap partition is the default, and the one recommended. With a single hard disk, the swap partition will default to sda1. The system will reboot and open YaST. (If your hard disk already has a swap partition, the installer will skip this step.)

4. **License.** Read the Novell Software License Agreement. If you agree, select Yes and click Next. (If you select No, it ends the install process.) You are prompted to select an install mode. The system is probed to make sure minimum hardware requirements are met.

NOTE Sometimes installation can fail because the computer hardware doesn't support certain features, such as power management (ACPI or APM) or DMA on hard drives or removable media. For those cases, you can try starting installation by selecting ACPI Disabled (which turns off ACPI) or Safe Settings (which turns off ACPI and APM as well as turning off DMA for any IDE CD, DVD, or hard drives).

5. **Installation mode.** Here you can choose whether to run a new installation or upgrade from an older version. Choosing to upgrade an existing openSUSE Linux installation will take more time than a clean (new) installation. You also select the Include Add-On Products From Separate Media option if you have downloaded and burned a copy of the Add-On CD for openSUSE 10.3.

CAUTION For either an upgrade or a new installation, you should back up all your data before you start.

6. **Network setup.** You are prompted to set up your network connection, so you can get files from remote repositories if they are needed. When prompted, choose the type of network connection to use (DHCP or static addressing).

7. **Online repositories**. A list of online repositories for SUSE appears. The main OSS repository and no–open source repository are both available for download.

8. **Clock and time zone.** Select the geographic region and time zone in which you're located. If the time is wrong, click Change, type your new date and/or time, and click Apply. Note that other operating systems may not expect the Hardware Clock (in the BIOS) to be set to UTC (Coordinated Universal Time). If you dual-boot, you may want to consider setting this to Local time so it does not conflict with other operating systems. Linux will work with either mode. Select Next to continue. You are asked to choose a Desktop.

Installation Settings

The installation settings that appear allow you to select either the Overview or Expert tab. Review the settings on these tabs. The following steps describe the options on the Expert tab, which provides more detailed information than the Overview tab:

9. **System.** Select System to probe your computer hardware. You get details about the type and model of each hardware item on your computer. You can save this information to your hard disk (if there is an available partition) or to a floppy disk. Click Details to see further information about any selected item. You might find this information useful if, for some reason, the hardware is not properly configured after the install is complete. It will give you information you need to search the Web or ask a question in a Linux forum about your hardware problem.

10. **Keyboard layout.** Make sure the language/country associated with the keyboard you are using are properly identified.

11. **Partitioning.** Partitioning is very important, especially if you want to protect any data currently on your hard disk. Select Partitioning. openSUSE recommends a partitioning scheme. (If your disk is already partitioned, openSUSE tries to use that scheme.) You can simply accept that scheme (choose Accept Proposal As-Is and click Next) or elect to create a custom partition setup.

    The Expert partitioning selection enables you to use a partitioning interface that is very similar to Disk Druid. See the description of partitioning in Chapter 7 for information on partitioning your hard disk. If you ever plan to move your partitions around with a tool such as Partition Magic, you should assign your Linux partition to the ext3 file system type. (If you are an expert and want to use the fdisk command, press Ctrl+Alt+F2 to get to a shell, run fdisk, and then press Ctrl+Alt+F7 to return to the graphical installer.)

12. **Software.** Select Software to see a list of packages available to install on your hard disk. The openSUSE install CD offers various groups of software, including graphical software, word processing and document production software, applications for software development, and much more.

Choose a group to see the specific packages in each group. Figure 10-3 shows the pre-selected packages associated with the openSUSE Base System group. Check marks indicate which packages will be installed. If you want to customize the standard installation, it's a good idea to look through this list to see what you are getting. If you change any of the selections, click the Check button to make sure that all packages which other packages depend on are being installed.

FIGURE 10-3

Install additional software using the YaST software module.

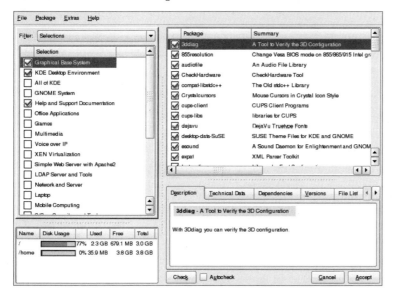

The YaST software packages module used for adding, removing, and finding out about software packages during installation is the same one used on a running openSUSE system. In either case, you can find out a lot of information about packages that interest you. With a package selected, click tabs in the box at the bottom-right corner of the screen to see its description, technical data (its size, packager, and so on), dependencies, and version numbers.

13. **Booting.** Select Booting to see the information that is added to your boot loader (GRUB, by default, but you can use the LILO boot loader as well). The boot loader includes the information needed to boot Linux: the location of the boot loader, the default operating system to boot, and other information.

14. **Time zone.** Select Time Zone to change your system's default idea of the time zone in which you are located.

15. **Language.** Select the default language to use. (You can add support for other languages later, if you like.)

16. **Default runlevel.** Normally you'd use the default (5) to boot to a full multiuser, networked desktop system with a graphical login screen. The other common default is 3, which provides a text-based login screen but is otherwise the same. (If you choose 3, you can start the GUI after login by typing the `startx` command.)

17. **Start the install.** If the Installation settings all look okay, click Accept to begin the install process. Remember that this is your last chance to back out! When the confirmation dialog box appears, click Back to return to the installer so that you can modify or abort the install process, or select Install to start the installation.

    If you click Yes, openSUSE formats your hard disk and installs the selected packages. After installation finishes, openSUSE prompts for some final configuration information to complete the installation process.

Configuration Settings

After the basic software installation completes, the YaST installer prompts you for some additional information:

18. **Root password.** Enter the root password (twice). Enter up to eight characters. DES is the default encryption type used to protect your password. (You can select Expert Options to choose MD5 or Blowfish instead.) Refer to Chapter 6 for suggestions on choosing a good password.

19. **Host name and domain name.** Enter the name that you want to use for this host on your network. Enter the name of the Internet domain that this machine is a member of.

20. **Network configuration.** YaST probes to find any network cards, DSL connections, ISDN adapters, or modems connected to your computer, and proposes a default configuration. Select any of the items that appear on the screen, as appropriate, to examine and, optionally, reconfigure it. For example, select Network Interfaces to view any installed network cards. You can configure any card found to use DHCP (if available) or your own network settings to connect to the LAN and/or the Internet. (See Chapter 5 for information on configuring Internet connections.)

    The automatic network configuration enables a firewall and disables remote access to your machine via SSH. You can change either of these by clicking their default settings so that, for example, you can allow ssh requests through your firewall, so you can log in and transfer files to and from the machine using OpenSSH tools (ssh, sftp, and so on).

    After you are done, click Next. openSUSE sets up and lets you test your network connections.

21. **Online update.** YaST tests network connectivity through the network interface that you defined in the previous step, and downloads the latest release notes as a test. This step also enables you to upload configuration information about your system to Novell and identify any new updates that are available. To skip this step, you can select the Configure Later radio button and click Next. If you leave the Configure Now radio button selected, you can click Next to upload information about your system and retrieve information about any available updates. This does not actually install any updates, but only registers

the network locations where updates are available so that you can subsequently use them to update your system. You can skip this step by selecting the Configure later radio button. Click Next to proceed.

22. **User authentication method.** Typically, you will use your home computer in standalone mode, as it relates to user accounts. However, in a business setting, you may use NIS, LDAP, or Samba to get user account lists that allow access to your computer and other computers on your LAN. If the latter is the case, select Network Client and choose either NIS (a common facility used by UNIX systems to share configuration files) or LDAP (a standard directory service, used to share address books and other kinds of information on a network), depending on what your company supports. Choosing Samba lets you use Windows SMB file- and print-sharing features for authentication. Then click Next.

23. **New local user.** You will want to add at least one user account, as prompted, for your computer. Right now, you have only the root user account set up for use on a standalone machine. Using that account for e-mail, Web browsing, or other common tasks is considered bad security practice. So you should add at least one user account for non-administrative use of your computer. Add your full name; a short, one-word login name; and a password to protect that account.

If you want to have this user automatically logged in on the system whenever you restart, leave the Automatic Login check box selected. Otherwise, de-select it to see a standard login prompt whenever you boot your system. You can also check the Receive System Mail check box to ensure that the user account you have just created automatically receives a copy of any mail sent to the root user on your system, which is often sent by administrative applications. To proceed, click Next.

When you are done, YaST writes the system configuration information to your computer. It then displays the Release Notes for your current version of openSUSE. Click Next to continue.

24. **Hardware configuration.** The openSUSE Installer displays a screen listing all of the hardware that was detected in your system. You can use this screen to configure other hardware devices to use with your system, or to verify the configuration of your existing hardware. You can select the headers on this screen to configure your graphics card, printer, sound card, or TV card.

> **NOTE** If you reconfigure your graphics hardware, you should test your display as prompted. If the settings you choose don't work, select Ctrl+Alt+Backspace to exit and try to configure it again.

When you are done testing or updating your system hardware, or if you just want to use openSUSE's default hardware configuration settings, click Next. The settings are written to hard disk. An Installation Completed screen appears.

25. **Finish.** On this screen, you can optionally click Clone system for Autoyast to save a record of your system's configuration if you are planning to install other SUSE 10.3 systems. Click Finish when you are ready to proceed. The system starts the graphical user interface that you selected during installation and is ready for you to log in.

Starting with openSUSE

If you created a user account during the preceding installation and left Automatic Login selected when you created that account, openSUSE should automatically log you in as that user and present you with the KDE desktop. (If you are presented with a graphical login screen instead, log in as that user now.) Here are a few things to help you get started using openSUSE:

- **Desktop applications** — The default openSUSE install is configured as a desktop system that includes a set of easily accessible desktop applications. On the desktop, try the Office icon to open OpenOffice.org to work with documents, spreadsheets, presentations, drawings, Web pages, or a variety of other content types. From the openSUSE icon on the panel, select from among dozens of applications to try them out.

- **My Computer** — A My Computer icon on the desktop enables you to see removable media and mounted partitions, and also gives you access to your Desktop, Documents, and public_html folders in a Konqueror window.

- **Reconfigure your computer** — Get to the YaST administration tool by selecting Applications ➪ System ➪ Administrator Settings from the openSUSE menu. You can reconfigure your system hardware and software from the YaST Control Center that appears.

If you want to configure your desktop (change backgrounds, screen savers, or themes), use the KDE control center as you would with any modern KDE desktop. You can launch the control center from the openSUSE menu (select My Favorites ➪ Configure Desktop).

Summary

SUSE is generally considered to be the next best choice for enterprise-quality Linux systems, after Red Hat Enterprise Linux. Its graphical installation and administrative tools (implemented in a facility called YaST) set it apart from other Linux distributions geared more toward technical users.

Since SUSE was acquired by Novell in 2003, SUSE Linux has become part of a larger, enterprise-ready product line. Boxed sets of SUSE Linux are available. Support offerings are available at many different levels. With Novell's worldwide sales and training organization, SUSE Linux has the backing it needs to compete to become the world's most popular commercial Linux system. The release of SUSE to the open source community as the openSUSE project ensures that the latest and greatest features are available or are in the SUSE development pipeline.

Because so much work has gone into the YaST installer and administrative interface, even an inexperienced user can be up and running on a newly installed SUSE or openSUSE system within an hour. It's then easy to begin using a variety of desktop and personal productivity applications from the SUSE desktop.

Chapter 11

Running KNOPPIX

A computer's operating system usually resides on the hard disk — but it doesn't have to. When a computer boots up, it typically checks first if there is a CD, floppy disk, or DVD in a drive and tries to boot from there (depending on BIOS settings). So, with up to 700MB (CD) or 8.4GB (dual-layer DVD) of space on those media, why not use them to boot whole operating systems?

Well, that's exactly what bootable Linux distributions (also called *live CDs*) such as KNOPPIX do. In the case of KNOPPIX, one CD holds up to 2GB of compressed software for you to run that uncompresses on-the-fly. Start it up and you can try out all the features of a well-stocked Linux system, without touching the contents of your hard disk.

N the DVD-ROM KNOPPIX is included on the DVD that comes with this book. In fact, it is the default option. Insert the DVD into your PC's DVD drive, and when you see the boot screen, press Enter. KNOPPIX should just start up, and you can begin using it as described in this chapter.

If you have never used Linux before, KNOPPIX gives you the chance to do so in a very safe way. If you are experienced with Linux, KNOPPIX can be used as a tool to take Linux with you everywhere, troubleshoot a computer, or check whether a computer will run Linux. In any case, you can use this chapter to take a little tour of some great Linux features that you can try out with KNOPPIX.

KNOPPIX Features

KNOPPIX has so many features it's hard to find a place to start. The latest official version of KNOPPIX at the time of this writing (KNOPPIX 5.1.1), features X.Org7.1, OpenOffice.org 2.1.0, KDE 3.5.5, GIMP 2.2.11, Linux kernel 2.6.19, as well as many multimedia applications. More information can be found on the KNOPPIX homepage (www.knoppix.com).

One of the most useful features of the most recent versions of KNOPPIX is the ease with which you can create your own, personalized KNOPPIX disk. The available options are so vast that there is not enough room to cover them in this book. For more information on how to create your own version of KNOPPIX, see www.knopper.net.

COMING FROM WINDOWS KNOPPIX includes support for NTFS file systems, so you can use KNOPPIX on a computer with Windows XP installed and access your files from your hard disk. This is a good way to try out your documents, music, movies, or other content from Windows using Linux applications (before you switch permanently). NTFS transparent write access, which was newly supported in KNOPPIX 5.0, is said to make writing to NTFS partitions safer than it was in previous versions.

Understanding KNOPPIX

If you are impatient to get started, you don't have to read any further. In most cases, you can just insert your DVD into your PC, reboot the computer, and start using KNOPPIX. If you have the time, however, read on a bit more.

KNOPPIX is a bootable Linux that includes a nice selection of open source software. Originally, there was a CD version of KNOPPIX (about 700MB image). Now, there is also a DVD version (about 4GB image). It is the KNOPPIX CD image that is included on the DVD that comes with this book.

KNOPPIX is considered to be the best bootable Linux available. In fact, KNOPPIX is used as the basis for many specialized Linux live CDs, including Gnoppix (featuring GNOME instead of KDE), KNOPPIX STD (security), KnoppMyth (MythTV media player), and KnoppiXMAME (console game player), to name a few. To try out the latest features, however, you should start with the most recent version of KNOPPIX, as described in the rest of this chapter.

KNOPPIX News

With release 5.0.1 in June 2006, KNOPPIX became more like a complete operating system. Extensions were added to make it easier to install KNOPPIX to hard disk. The ability to update certain critical packages was added in the Live Update feature. Packaging, in general, is now more focused on staying closer to the Debian packages on which KNOPPIX is based. Release 5.1.1 continued this and added more hardware detection and configuration capabilities.

Looking Inside KNOPPIX

After automatically detecting and configuring your computer hardware, KNOPPIX boots right up to a full-featured desktop system complete with hundreds of ready-to-use desktop applications (no login required). It includes some powerful server and power user features. In fact, there are so many features, I won't even try to mention them all here, but take a look at the following list of some of KNOPPIX's major components:

- **KDE** — A full-featured KDE desktop (which runs on the X Window System) that includes tools for configuring the desktop and a bunch of applications tailored for the KDE environment. (See Chapter 3 for descriptions of KDE.)

NOTE If you prefer the GNOME desktop environment, there are several customized versions of KNOPPIX that include GNOME. Most notable is the Gnoppix (http://en .wikipedia.org/wiki/Gnoppix) distribution, which uses GNOME as its default desktop.

- **OpenOffice.org** — The OpenOffice.org suite of office productivity tools so that you can create documents, graphics, presentations, spreadsheets, and most anything you expect to be able to do with office applications. With KNOPPIX, you can give a presentation created in OpenOffice.org software anywhere that you have access to a PC. (See Chapter 21 for descriptions of OpenOffice.org productivity applications.)

- **Internet tools** — Web browsers (Firefox, Konqueror, and Lynx), e-mail clients (Thunderbird, Kmail, Thunderbird, and mutt), a chat client (XChat IRC), a newsreader (KNode), an instant messaging client (Gaim), and many more applications for using the Internet. (See Chapter 22 for descriptions of popular Web browsers and mail clients.)

- **Multimedia software** — Applications for playing music (xmms), editing music (Audacity), watching TV (xawtv), playing movies (Kaffeine), working with graphics (GIMP and ImageMagick), using Webcams (gqcam), and displaying images (KView and Kuickshow). (Chapter 20 covers music and video players.)

- **Games** — A few dozen diverting board games, card games, strategy games, and puzzles to play. Try Potato Guy to keep the young ones busy, and Kasteroids for the older kids. (Chapter 23 talks about KDE games and other games that you can run with KNOPPIX.)

- **Administrative tools** — A nice set of system and network administration tools that enables you to do some pretty advanced setup, monitoring, and debugging of your computer and network. (The Knoppix-STD distribution is configured specifically as a rescue CD to do almost anything you can imagine to check and fix your computer and network.)

- **Servers** — A few of the powerful server projects available for Linux, many of which don't require a lot of disk space: a Web server (Apache), file server (NFS), Window file/print server (Samba), proxy server (Squid), DNS server (bind9), login server (sshd), and DHCP server (dhcpd).

COMING FROM WINDOWS Using KNOPPIX (or any of the other bootable server Linux systems described in Chapter 19) as a server opens some amazing possibilities for serving the data from a Windows or other operating system to a network, while completely bypassing that operating system on the computer's hard disk.

- **Programming tools** — A good set of tools for developing software across a variety of programming environments.

KNOPPIX is based on Debian Linux, so a Debian user will be particularly comfortable with the selection and organization of features. KNOPPIX software packages are also done in deb package format, so you can use apt, dpkg, and related tools to list and otherwise manage the packages. A graphical tool for working with software packages that comes with KNOPPIX is KPackage.

CROSS-REF   Refer to Chapter 9 for information on using apt and dpkg tools for managing software in Debian. Even if you don't install any new software, those tools provide an excellent way to search, list, or even upgrade software packages that are running in KNOPPIX.

What's Cool About KNOPPIX

The features just described are ones that come with many different Linux distributions. What makes them special with KNOPPIX is that you can often be up and using those features within a few minutes — without having to repartition your disk, install software, or do any configuration. For just trying out Linux or using it for some special, quick task such as playing or displaying music, documents, or spreadsheets from a computer's hard disk, KNOPPIX is quite awesome.

Some features, however, are specific to KNOPPIX (as compared to a Linux system you would run from a hard disk). Many of those special features are there to help you through issues that relate to the fact that you are not working in a permanent setup. In particular, KNOPPIX includes the following:

- **Extraordinary hardware detection** — The capability to properly detect and configure hardware is one of the best features. During the bootup procedure, KNOPPIX finds most common PC hardware components and loads the proper modules so it can use them. Its hwsetup tool relies on the Red Hat libkudzu facility to identify hardware, load appropriate modules, and create necessary device files.

   For hardware that can't be detected, there are many boot options you can add to properly identify (or skip over) selected hardware devices. Some of them deal with particularly sticky issues related to video cards and running on laptop computers. (See Tables 11-1 through 11-3.)

- **Automatic desktop startup** — Instead of just dropping you to a command line, KNOP-PIX does its best to start up a complete KDE desktop environment. Along the way, it adds some nice features, such as desktop icons that give you access to your computer's hard disk partitions.

- **Configuration tools** — Some hardware either can't be perfectly detected or requires some extra setup. You can access KNOPPIX-specific configuration tools for configuring your printer, TV card, sound card, network connections, and other features by clicking the desktop icon that looks like a squished penguin.

- **Save setup** — You don't have to lose the configuration you have done for KNOPPIX every time you reboot. Click the configuration menu to save your configuration — including your personal desktop configuration, files on the desktop, network settings, and graphics setup (X) — to floppy disk, hard disk, or USB memory stick.

- **Persistent desktop** — You can use the configuration icon to create a persistent KNOPPIX home directory on your hard disk or other medium so that you can store and reuse your desktop setup information and any data you save from session to session. (See the "Creating a Persistent Home Directory" section later in this chapter for details on setting up a persistent desktop.)

■ **Add swap** — If you are using KNOPPIX from a computer with Linux installed, it automatically uses a swap partition that is set up there. On DOS and Windows systems, KNOPPIX enables you to create an extra swap area if you have space on an available DOS partition. (The mkdosswapfile command is used for this purpose.)

■ **Work with Windows files** — KNOPPIX includes drivers for using Microsoft Windows NTFS file systems. The drivers enable you to read and write files from your hard disk if you are booting KNOPPIX from a PC with Windows installed. (Writing to NTFS partitions from KNOPPIX is still considered experimental, so consider using an NTFS partition in read-only mode if the partition contains critical data.)

For example, say that you have your entire music collection, images downloaded from your digital camera, and personal Web pages on your hard disk on a computer that was set up to be booted by Microsoft Windows XP. You boot KNOPPIX instead (notice that Microsoft Windows is not running at all). Suddenly your hard disk is just a place that holds a lot of files. You can now use applications that come with KNOPPIX to open the files on your hard disk to play the music, view or manipulate images, and display or change Web pages.

A testament to how well KNOPPIX is respected is how many other bootable Linux distributions are based on it. The KNOPPIX project even provides a KNOPPIX-customize package that lets anyone make his or her own customized KNOPPIX. There are specialized KNOPPIX derivatives that can be used to rescue a broken computer, play a range of multimedia content, or run a specific application.

CROSS-REF See Chapter 18 for information on using a bootable Linux as a firewall/router and Chapter 19 for descriptions of many other bootable Linux distributions.

Examining Challenges with KNOPPIX

For most people, KNOPPIX is a special-use Linux system. It's a great way to try Linux or to access a computer that isn't set up the way you like. However, there are a few challenges with using KNOPPIX that you should keep in mind:

■ **Reboot clears out KNOPPIX** — Unless you save your data to some other media (which you can do, as I describe later in this chapter), the entire KNOPPIX system goes away when you reboot. That means files on the desktop, installed software, system configuration, and anything else you do during your KNOPPIX session will be gone unless you explicitly save that information to a hard disk or some removable medium (floppy, CD, and so on).

■ **Memory limitations** — KNOPPIX is made to be able to run without touching your hard disk, so when you save files to KNOPPIX, they are (by default) stored in your computer's memory (RAM). As a result, precious memory is devoted to holding files that might otherwise be used for running demanding applications.

■ **Performance hits** — Even with today's faster CD and DVD drives, it's still slower getting data from CDs and DVDs than it is getting them from a local hard disk. Almost every component needed to run KNOPPIX (commands, libraries, and so on) is grabbed from the CD or DVD and decompressed on-the-fly. So it can take a bit longer to run commands with KNOPPIX than it would to run them from hard disk. Watch the blinking light on your CD or DVD drive to see how often KNOPPIX goes there to get data.

■ **Uses your CD/DVD drive** — Because KNOPPIX relies so heavily on data from the CD or DVD, you can't remove it while you are using the system. So, if you have only one drive for removable media, you can't use it to access a music CD, install from another software disk, or burn data while you are using KNOPPIX.

> **NOTE** If you have more than 1GB of RAM on your computer, you can use the `toram` boot option to KNOPPIX. This will not only allow you to remove the KNOPPIX disk, because everything is running from RAM, but will also cause KNOPPIX to run faster than a Linux system installed on a hard disk.

I must admit that the challenges described here are more of an explanation of how KNOPPIX works than they are problems with KNOPPIX itself. The idea that you can run a full-blown desktop and server operating system from a single CD (with nearly 2GB of available applications) is an awesome concept for someone who still remembers DOS and character terminals.

Seeing Where KNOPPIX Comes From

KNOPPIX was created by Klaus Knopper in Germany. Knopper follows in the great tradition of naming a distribution using a part of the creator's own name with "ix" or "ux" stuck on the end.

While a groundswell of interest and support has appeared for KNOPPIX in the past few years, Knopper himself admits that KNOPPIX started out more as a collection of tools he needed than as a full Linux distribution. Knopper works to provide only software that can be distributed freely, for both noncommercial and commercial use. He doesn't even include some free software (such as browser plug-ins) that might restrict free redistribution, although he doesn't object to including non–open source software that can still be freely distributed.

There is no big company behind KNOPPIX, and development efforts continue to be headed up by Knopper himself. There are, however, many people who contribute bug reports and enhancement requests (see `www.knoppix.net/wiki/bugs`), and there are other developers who have helped create software specifically for KNOPPIX (in particular, Fabian Franz who, among other things, has contributed significant work to KNOPPIX installer-related features).

The only official KNOPPIX Web site is Knopper's own personal site: `www.knopper.net/knoppix/index-en.html`. If you are looking for a way to get information and become involved with others who use and develop the system, the Knoppix.net site offers a very active forum and links to information about other KNOPPIX resources. It's a great place not only to get your questions answered, but also to find a wealth of links to FAQs, HOWTOs, and related projects. There is also an IRC channel (#knoppix on `irc.freenode.net`) and a wiki used primarily to gather documentation (`www.knoppix.net/wiki/Main_Page`).

Exploring Uses for KNOPPIX

Because there is so much you can do with KNOPPIX, it's hard to choose just a few uses to high-light. Consider the following possibilities:

- **Your own portable operating system** — You don't have to carry around a laptop or whole PC to make sure you have the software you need. Instead, you can use any PC that is available (with the exception of some unsupported hardware) and boot your whole computing environment with a single CD. By customizing your own KNOPPIX, you can add your own data and pick and choose applications as well.

- **A tool for managing data on any PC** — You can bypass the operating system and other software on any computer and use the applications on your KNOPPIX disk to manage the data on that computer.

Of course, these concepts are not exclusive to KNOPPIX because you could conceptually do the same thing with any boot floppy since the days of DOS (as well as any other bootable Linux). The difference is that KNOPPIX does those things so well. It lets you take over a computer, not just with a tiny rescue disk capable of running a few obtuse commands, but with a full-scale desktop, server, and administrative toolkit operating system. With that in mind, here are some ways people are using KNOPPIX:

- **Showing off Linux** — A demo can lack some punch when you have to spend an hour installing before you can make your point. With KNOPPIX, it can take about 5 minutes from the time you tell your friend about Linux to the time you have a complete desktop system running on his PC. And in the process, you don't have to worry about harming anything on his computer because you don't even need to touch his hard disk.

- **Testing a computer for Linux** — Instead of getting halfway through an install to see if your PC is capable of running Linux, you can boot KNOPPIX. If it works, you can check to see what drivers were loaded to deal with your hardware (type **lsmod** from a shell) and then go ahead and install any Linux you like to the hard disk.

- **Rescuing a computer or network** — Many tools for tracking down and fixing problems on both Linux and Windows systems are included in KNOPPIX. There is also a Knoppix-STD edition that includes dozens more tools for rescuing broken systems and tracing net-work problems (see www.knoppix-std.org).

- **Taking over a broken server** — If a Web server, file server, or firewall has been cracked or otherwise broken, you might be able to use KNOPPIX to safely serve the data from a KNOPPIX boot disk while you fix the problem.

- **Doing anything you want** — For those of us who have gotten used to using Linux, it's a pain to go somewhere and have to do work or make a presentation on a computer that doesn't have the tools you need. By bringing the whole operating system, all your software tools and sometimes even your data (with a customized CD, separate floppy disk, pen drive, or downloaded files), your computing environment can be the same wherever you go.

Now that you have some idea of what to do with KNOPPIX, let's get started.

Starting KNOPPIX

In most cases, it's very easy to start KNOPPIX. With KNOPPIX in hand, all you really need is a PC that meets the minimum specifications.

Getting a Computer

If you are ready to start KNOPPIX, I recommend the following:

- **A PC** — You need a PC that meets the minimal processor and memory requirements described a bit later. There are no hard disk space requirements because you don't need to touch the hard disk. To get better performance on low-RAM systems, however, you might want to create a swap partition, or swap file, on hard disk to enable you to run more processes (as described later).

- **Permission to reboot** — KNOPPIX is going to take over operation of the PC, so you need to be sure that it's okay to reboot it. Make sure that nobody else is currently using the computer or relying on it to be accessible over a network. (It is possible to run KNOPPIX on a running Windows or Linux system, using virtualization tools such as Qemu or VMWare. To run KNOPPIX, however, you will need a computer that has a lot of available RAM. Otherwise, you will get poor performance.)

- **Internet connection (optional)** — It isn't necessary, but if your computer has an Ethernet card and a connection to the Internet, you can immediately start using KNOPPIX to browse the Web and otherwise take advantage of its communications tools. KNOPPIX will try to detect a DHCP server (to get an IP address and other information) and automatically configure itself to use the Internet or other network that is available. If you need a dial-up connection instead, KNOPPIX includes Kppp for configuring a dial-up modem.

The system requirements for running KNOPPIX are much lower than you need for most of the latest Linux systems. According to Klaus Knopper, you need:

- **CPU** — Intel-compatible i486 or better.

- **RAM** — 20MB (for text mode), 82MB (for graphics mode with KDE), or 128MB (to also run most office applications).

- **Bootable drive (DVD drive to use the DVD or CD to use a CD)** — KNOPPIX is able to boot from drives that are IDE/ATAPI, FireWire, USB, or SCSI (provided that your computer can boot from those devices). Otherwise, you can create a boot floppy to start the process of booting KNOPPIX (described later). If you have a DVD drive, you can boot KNOPPIX directly from the DVD that comes with this book.

- **Graphics card** — Must be SVGA-compatible.

- **Mouse** — Supports any standard serial mouse, PS/2 mouse, or IMPS/2-compatible USB mouse.

Booting KNOPPIX

If you have a PC in front of you that meets the requirements, you can get started by following these steps:

1. Insert your KNOPPIX DVD or CD into the appropriate drive.

2. Reboot the computer. After a few moments, you will see the boot screen.

> **NOTE** Although the boot screens look different for the *Linux Bible 2008 Edition* DVD and a regular KNOPPIX CD, you can proceed with the boot process the same way.

3. Press Enter. If all goes well, you should see the KNOPPIX desktop, and you can proceed to the section "Using KNOPPIX." If KNOPPIX doesn't boot up properly or if you want to tune it further before it boots, continue on to the next section. In particular, you might want to use some of the boot options shown in Table 11-1.

Correcting Boot Problems

By understanding a bit about the boot process you will, in most cases, be able to overcome any problems you might have installing KNOPPIX. Here are some things you should know:

- **Check boot order** — Your computer's BIOS has a particular order in which it looks for bootable operating systems. A typical order would be floppy, CD or DVD, and hard disk. If your computer skips over the KNOPPIX boot disk and boots right from hard disk, make sure that the boot order in the BIOS is set to boot from CD or DVD. To change the BIOS, restart the computer and as it first boots the hardware, enter Setup (quickly) as instructed (usually by pressing F1, F2, or DEL). Look for a selection to change the boot order so that your CD or DVD boots before the hard disk.

- **Add boot options** — Instead of just letting the boot process autodetect and configure everything about your hardware, you can add options to the boot prompt that will override what KNOPPIX autoconfiguration might do. Press F2 from the boot prompt to see additional boot options.

Some boot options are available with which you can try to overcome different issues at boot time. KNOPPIX refers to these options as *cheat codes*. For a more complete list, refer to the file `knoppix-cheatcodes.txt`, which you'll find in the `KNOPPIX` directory when you mount the CD or the DVD that comes with this book on any operating system.

> **NOTE** Many boot options can be used with different Linux systems. So if you are having trouble installing or booting a different Linux distribution, you can try any of these options to see if they work. Instead of the word "knoppix," you will probably use a different word to launch the install or boot process for other distributions (such as "linux" for Fedora systems or "morphix" for Morphix Live-CD, depending on the distribution).

When KNOPPIX first begins the boot process, you see the boot screen, with the `boot:` prompt at the bottom. The following tables provide boot prompt options that can help you get KNOPPIX running the way you like. Table 11-1 shows options to use when you want specific features turned on that may not be turned on by default when you boot.

TABLE 11-1

Boot Options to Select Features

Option	Feature
knoppix lang=??	Choose a specific language/keyboard. Replace ?? with one of the following: cn, de, da, es, fr, it, nl, pl, ru, sk, tr, tw, uk, or us.
knoppix desktop=??	Instead of using the KDE desktop (kde), replace ?? with one of the following window managers: fluxbox, icewm, larswm, twm, wmaker, or xfce.
knoppix blind	Start BrailleTerminal (running without X).
knoppix brltty=type,port,table	Add parameters to use for the Braille device.
knoppix wheelmouse	For a wheel mouse, enable IMPS/2 protocol.
knoppix nowheelmouse	For a regular PS/2 mouse, force PS/2 protocol.
knoppix keyboard=us xkeyboard=us	Assign different keyboard drivers to use with text (shell) and graphical (X) interfaces.
knoppix dma	Turn on DMA acceleration for all IDE drives.
knoppix gmt	Use time that is based on Greenwich Mean Time (GMT). You can use utc instead of gmt to get the same result.
knoppix tz=country/city	Specify a particular time zone, based on country and city.
knoppix noeject	Don't eject the CD after KNOPPIX has stopped.
knoppix noprompt	Don't prompt to remove the CD after KNOPPIX stops.

If there is hardware being improperly detected or configured, you can have KNOPPIX skip over that hardware. Table 11-2 contains options for skipping or turning off various hardware features.

TABLE 11-2

Boot Options to Turn Off Hardware

Option	Result
knoppix atapicd	No SCSI emulation for IDE CD-ROMs.
knoppix noagp	No detection of an AGP graphics card.
knoppix noapic	Disable the Advanced Programmable Interrupt Controller (APIC). (This can overcome some problems on SMP computers.)

TABLE 11-2 *(continued)*	
Option	**Result**
knoppix acpi=off	Disable the Advanced Configuration and Power Interface (ACPI).
knoppix noapm	No Advanced Power Management (APM) support. (With a working acpi, apm will be off by default. Only one can be active at a time.)
knoppix noaudio	No sound support.
knoppix nodhcp	Don't try to start your network connection automatically via DHCP.
knoppix fstab	Don't read the fstab file to find file systems to mount or check.
knoppix firewire	No detection of Firewire devices.
knoppix nopcmcia	No detection of PCMCIA card slots.
knoppix noscsi	No detection of SCSI devices.
knoppix noswap	No detection of swap partitions.
knoppix nousb	No detection of USB devices.
knoppix nousb2	Disable extensions for USB 2.0.
knoppix pnpbios=off	Don't initialize plug-and-play (PnP) in the BIOS.
knoppix failsafe	Do almost no hardware detection.

Table 11-3 lists options that may help if you are having trouble with your video card. Several of these options are particularly useful if you are having trouble with X on a laptop.

TABLE 11-3	

Boot Options to Fix Video Problems

Option	**Result**
knoppix screen=??	Pick X screen resolution. Replace *??* with 640 × 480, 800 × 600, 1024 × 768, 1280 × 1024, or any other resolution supported by your video card.
knoppix xvrefresh=60	Set vertical refresh rate to 60 Hz for X (or other value as specified by monitor's manual).
knoppix xhrefresh=80	Set horizontal refresh rate to 80 Hz for X (or other value as specified by monitor's manual).
knoppix xserver=??	Replace *??* with XFree86 or XF86_SVGA.
knoppix xmodule=??	Select the specific driver to use for your video card. Replace *??* with one of the following: ati, fbdev, i810, mga, nv, radeon, savage, s3radeon, svga, or i810.
knoppix 2	Run level 2, text mode only.

continued

TABLE 11-3	(continued)
Option	**Result**
knoppix vga=normal	No-framebuffer mode, but X.
knoppix fb1280x1024	Use fixed framebuffer graphics (1).
knoppix fb1024x768	Use fixed framebuffer graphics (2).
knoppix fb800x600	Use fixed framebuffer graphics (3).

Customizing KNOPPIX

Several boot options exist that tell KNOPPIX to look for a customized home directory or configuration information on hard disk or floppy. See the section "Keeping Your KNOPPIX Configuration" later in this chapter for information on how to both save a customized KNOPPIX configuration and tell KNOPPIX where to look for that customized information at boot time. (Unless they were created from KNOPPIX, most other Linux distributions will not use these boot options.)

Table 11-4 lists options you can use to identify the location of your customized data or tell KNOPPIX to run in ways that will make it perform better. Some of these options are described in detail in sections that follow.

TABLE 11-4

Boot Options to Find Data or Boot Faster

Option	Result
knoppix myconf=/dev/????	Tells KNOPPIX to run the knoppix.sh script from a particular partition. For example, replace ???? with hda1 (first partition on the first IDE drive) or sda1 (first partition on the USB flash drive or SCSI drive).
knoppix myconf=scan	Search available drives for the knoppix.sh script.
knoppix home=/mnt/????/filename.img	Identify the location of an image file that should be mounted and used as the /home directory during your KNOPPIX session. For example, using the file /mnt/hda1/knoppix.img gets an image file (knoppix.img) from the top-level directory of the first partition of the first IDE drive.
knoppix home-scan	Search available drives for a home directory image.
knoppix mem=???M	Make the specified amount of memory available to KNOPPIX (for example, 128M).
knoppix toram	Copy the contents of the CD to RAM and run it from there. (For a live CD, you should have at least 1GB of RAM available to use toram.)

TABLE 11-4 (continued)	
Option	**Result**
knoppix tohd=/dev/????	Copy the contents of the CD to a hard disk partition and run it from there. Replace *????* with the device name, such as hda1 or sda1. The partition must be ext2 or VFAT to use this feature.
knoppix fromhd	Look for KNOPPIX to run on the hard disk, instead of the CD.
knoppix fromhd=/dev/????	Look for KNOPPIX to run from a particular partition on the hard disk, instead of the CD. Replace *????* with the device name, such as hda1 or sda1.
knoppix bootfrom=/dev/????	If the KNOPPIX image is on an NTFS or ReiserFS file system, use this option to boot the image from there.
knoppix bootfrom=/dev/????/KNX.iso	Select a particular image name to boot from, when the image exists on an NTFS or ReiserFS file system on the selected hard disk. The kernel versions on the CD and hard disk image must match.

Special Features and Workarounds

The following list suggests some workarounds for booting and running KNOPPIX that you may find helpful. Other boot options are described in the knoppix-cheatcodes.txt file that comes on the KNOPPIX CD (open the KNOPPIX folder from the KNOPPIX icon on the desktop to find the file). Things you can do with boot options include changing the splash screen when KNOPPIX boots, running in expert mode so you can load your own drivers, testing your computer's RAM, and trying to overcome special problems with laptop computers.

■ **Testing the CD** — If you suspect that you have a bad KNOPPIX CD, I recommend running this from the boot prompt:

```
knoppix testcd
```

If you are still not able to boot KNOPPIX at this point, it might be that your hardware is either not supported or is broken in some way. To further pursue the problem, check out an appropriate forum at www.knoppix.net.

■ **Running KNOPPIX from RAM** — To improve performance, KNOPPIX offers a way to run the entire KNOPPIX distribution from RAM (provided you have enough available) or install it on your hard disk and run it from there. Provided that you have more than 1GB of RAM, you can run KNOPPIX entirely from RAM (so you can remove the KNOPPIX DVD or CD and use that drive while you run KNOPPIX) by typing the following from the boot prompt:

```
knoppix toram
```

■ **Installing KNOPPIX to hard disk** — You can run KNOPPIX entirely from hard disk if your hard disk is either a FAT or EXT2 file system type and contains at least 800MB of space. To do this, you must know the name of the hard disk partition you are installing on. For example, to use the first partition on the first IDE drive, you would use /dev/hda1. In that case, to copy KNOPPIX to that disk partition, you would type this at the boot prompt:

```
knoppix tohd=/dev/hda1
```

You can watch as KNOPPIX is copied to your hard disk partition and then boots automatically from there. The next time you want to boot KNOPPIX, you can boot it from hard disk again by inserting the KNOPPIX medium and typing the following:

```
knoppix fromhd=/dev/hda1
```

With KNOPPIX running from your hard disk, you can safely eject your CD or DVD and use the drive for other things (type **eject /dev/cdrom**). Refer to the knoppix-cheatcodes.txt file for information on other things you can do from the KNOPPIX boot prompt.

Using KNOPPIX

KDE is the default desktop environment that comes with KNOPPIX. You can change that at the boot prompt to use one of several window managers instead, or get a Gnoppix disk instead to use the GNOME environments.

The KNOPPIX version of KDE matches pretty closely the descriptions in Chapter 3, although a few items related to the KNOPPIX KDE desktop are worth noting:

■ **Desktop icons** — To get information about KNOPPIX, click the KNOPPIX icon (choose a language, and then find links to FAQs, Knopper.Net, and general KNOPPIX information) or the LinuxTag icon (to read the licenses). There is also the requisite Trash icon.

■ **Disk icons** — Any CD, DVD, floppy, or other removable medium drive is displayed as an icon on the desktop. Of course, this includes the drive holding the KNOPPIX disk, which you can get to directly to do such things as find boot images or KNOPPIX documentation.

Hard disk partitions are also represented by icons on your KNOPPIX desktop. Click one of those icons and you can access (read-only) the files on that hard disk partition. This is a great feature for getting the information you need without, by default, enabling you to change or otherwise damage the data on the computer. To make a disk writable, right-click on the disk icon and select Actions ➪ Change read/write mode. If you are not able to write to the disk, refer to the section on making disks writable later in this chapter.

■ **KDE Panel** — KNOPPIX loads the KDE Panel with applets and launchers for a few useful applications. Click the K button to display the menu containing most KDE applications for you to select. The Web Browser icon launches the Konqueror browser, which is the KDE file manager as well.

- **KNOPPIX configuration** — Click the squished penguin icon in the KDE Panel to see a menu of configuration tools specific to KNOPPIX. This is where you can tune up your TV card, configure printers, get your network connection going, and even start a few servers. I describe some of these subjects — in particular, how to save data and configuration information across sessions with this otherwise ethereal operating system — later in this chapter.

- **Launching games, players, and other stuff** — From the KDE menu, you can launch applications as you would from any desktop operating system.

Running KNOPPIX, at this point, is just like running any other Linux system with a KDE desktop, with one major exception. By default, you can't save any data permanently. There are a few ways around this issue, especially if you expect to use KNOPPIX on a regular basis. Refer to the sections on creating persistent desktops and opening disks for writing later in this chapter.

Getting on the Network

If you have an Ethernet card and a connection to a network that has a DHCP server, your KNOPPIX system should just start up and offer immediate access to that network (and possibly the Internet if it offers such a connection). If not, KNOPPIX offers several tools for configuring your network connection, including:

- **Dial-up modem** — From the squished penguin, select Network/Internet ➪ /dev/modem connection setup. The menus that appear help you create a dial-up connection to the Internet, or other TCP/IP network, using a serial modem, USB modem, IRDA cell phone/PDA, or Bluetooth cell phone/PDA.

- **ADSL router** — From the squished penguin, select Network/Internet ➪ ADSL/PPPOE configuration. It will help you connect your broadband ADSL router to connect to the Internet.

- **GPRS connection** — From the squished penguin, select Network/Internet ➪ GPRS/UMTS connection to set up a connection via your cell phone provider.

- **Network card** — From the squished penguin, select Network/Internet ➪ Network card configuration to configure your Ethernet card (assuming you don't just want to use DHCP to get your network address).

- **ISDN** — From the squished penguin, select Network/Internet ➪ ISDN to use ISDN to connect to the network.

- **Wireless card** — From the squished penguin, select Network/Internet ➪ Wavelan to use a wireless Ethernet card to connect to the network. You can instead select ndiswrapper configuration if there is no Linux driver for your card but you have a Windows driver you can try.

In addition to the interfaces available here, you can use the wvdialconf command to create your dial-out connection as described in Chapter 5.

Installing Software in KNOPPIX

Despite the fact that KNOPPIX includes a wide range of software applications, there may be some software package you want to use with it that isn't included. For installing software while you are running KNOPPIX from the DVD, you can use Synaptic.

To start Synaptic, click the squished penguin on the KNOPPIX panel and select Utilities ➪ Manage Software in KNOPPIX. The Synaptic window opens, displaying lists of installed packages. Here's what you do to install a package:

1. **Reload the package list.** To see which packages are available for you to install, select the Reload button. Synaptic searches online repositories configured for KNOPPIX for available packages and loads them into the Synaptic window. New package categories and packages appear.

2. **Select a package.** Choose a category on the left and any package you want from that category on the right. A description of the package appears in the lower pane. Figure 11-1 shows an example of Synaptic with the bzflag package selected.

FIGURE 11-1

Choose packages to install in KNOPPIX using Synaptic Package Manager.

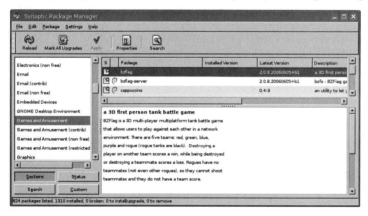

3. **Mark a package for installation.** With the package that you want to install highlighted, select Package ➪ Mark for Installation. If any changes to existing packages or additional packages are needed, a pop-up window alerts you. Click Mark to continue.

4. **Apply changes.** After you have selected all the new packages you want, select Apply. If the changes noted in a pop-up window are okay, select Apply again. Synaptic begins downloading and installing the selected packages.

Remember that the software is being installed in the version of KNOPPIX that is running in RAM. So, the software will disappear the next time you reboot, unless you do something to preserve your data (such as creating a persistent desktop before you install the software you want to keep).

Saving Files in KNOPPIX

When you reboot your computer with KNOPPIX, you lose not only KNOPPIX itself but any data and configuration information you may have created along the way. That's because, by default, KNOPPIX runs from your system's RAM and a nonwritable CD or DVD. Using tools and procedures that come with KNOPPIX, there are ways in which you can keep that information going forward.

KNOPPIX happily gives you a login name (knoppix) and a home directory (/home/knoppix), each time you boot from KNOPPIX. You can save files to that directory, as well as change your desktop and system configuration information (which is stored in that directory and in /etc files). The problem is that those directories are in RAM, so they disappear when you reboot.

The following sections give you some ideas about how to save what you do in your KNOPPIX session to use in future sessions.

Writing to Hard Disk

Although hard disk partitions are mounted read-only by default, you can make them read/write if you like. Then you can store any data you want to save on those partitions. (You can simply drag and drop files to those partitions when they are displayed in a Konqueror window, or save files there from an application.)

CAUTION   Up to this point, there's not much risk of damaging any data on your hard disk. Once you make your disks writable, you have the potential for deleting or changing that data. Keep that in mind if the computer doesn't belong to you or if you are not used to using Linux. Regardless of which user you are logged in as, KNOPPIX does not prevent you from changing any file in a writable hard disk partition.

Mounting Linux Partitions for Writing

KNOPPIX usually identifies all hard disk partitions and adds entries for each one in your /etc/fstab file. If you click the icon representing that partition, the partition is automatically mounted and a folder opens to the root of that directory.

The name of each partition (hda1, hda2, and so forth for IDE partitions; sda1, sda2, and so on for SCSI disk partitions, including USB flash drives) is shown on the desktop icon representing each partition. Hover the mouse pointer over the icon to see information about the partition's mount point and device name. With that information, you can make any of those partitions writable by following these steps:

1. Right-click the icon representing the hard disk partition you want to write to on the KNOPPIX desktop. A menu opens, displaying functions available for that partition.

2. Choose the Change read/write mode option. You are asked if you really want that partition to be writable. Select Yes.

At this point, you can open the folder to the partition (hda2 in our example) or open a shell and write to that directory (/mnt/hda2 and any subdirectories). To make that change permanent (in the KNOPPIX sense), you need to change /etc/fstab to add rw to the entry for the partition so it is mounted read/write by default. Again, with the example of /dev/hda2, an entry in /etc/fstab to mount that partition read/write could look as follows:

```
/dev/hda2 /mnt/hda2 ext3 noauto,users,exec,rw 0 0
```

With that change, simply typing **sudo mount /dev/hda2** mounts the directory with read/write permissions. You can save that change permanently, as described in the section "Keeping Your KNOPPIX Configuration" later in this chapter.

Mounting Windows Partitions for Writing

Provided your partitions are properly detected, mounting Windows partitions is no different than mounting Linux partitions. For Windows file system types FAT and VFAT, there should be no problem mounting and writing to those file systems. For NTFS file systems, there are a few things you should consider before writing to them.

Earlier versions of KNOPPIX allowed you to download a feature called Captive NTFS. With Captive NTFS, you could use native Windows drivers to access NTFS partitions from KNOPPIX. This was considered to be reliable enough that you could write to NTFS partitions without much fear of corruption.

The current version of KNOPPIX uses drivers from the Linux-NTFS Project (www.linux-ntfs.org/) to provide support for accessing NTFS file systems from Linux. The advantage of using Linux-NTFS is that NTFS partitions can be mounted and used just like any other Linux file system. In other words, you don't need Windows drivers. The downside is that writing to NTFS partitions using Linux-NTFS is considered unreliable and could cause corruption to your NTFS partition. So, I recommend you not try to write to an NTFS file system from KNOPPIX if it contains critical data, but feel free to read from NTFS during a KNOPPIX session.

Creating a Persistent Home Directory

If you are going to use the computer more than once with KNOPPIX (or if you just want more storage space for files than your computer has available in RAM), you can assign your KNOPPIX home directory (/home/knoppix) to use some of the available space on your hard drive. That can be done in either of two ways:

- Assign an entire partition to be used for your home directory.
- Assign a part of that partition for your home directory, in the form of an image file.

You can also put your persistent home directory on rewritable, removable media, such as a memory stick. Once you create that area to use as your home directory, you can tell KNOPPIX to use it every time you restart KNOPPIX. Here's what you do:

1. Click the squished penguin in the panel, and then select Configure ➪ Create a Persistent KNOPPIX disk image. A window appears, asking if you are ready to create a persistent home directory.

2. Click Yes to continue. You are asked which partition you want to use for your persistent home directory.

3. Select the partition you want to use to store your persistent desktop and click OK. You are asked if you want to save the home directory in an encrypted format.

4. Select No, to not have the directory selected as encrypted (if you choose Yes, you'll have to specify a long password that you will need to access the persistent home directory at boot time). You are asked to enter the size of your home directory.

5. Type the number of megabytes to assign to your home directory and click OK. Be sure that that much space is available on the partition. (When the partition is mounted later, you can type **df -h** to see how much space is available on it.) The partition or image file should be created now.

When I ran this procedure to create a 100MB image on the hda5 partition, it created the file /mnt/hda5/knoppix.img, which had 97MB of available space. To see how to use that directory, see the section "Restarting KNOPPIX" later in this chapter.

Keeping Your KNOPPIX Configuration

After you have gone through all the work to configure your desktop, printer, network, disks, and other preferences for your KNOPPIX setup, it's a shame to lose all that on your next reboot. Well, KNOPPIX offers a way that you can save your configuration information and reuse it for your next session. That saved information can be stored on a floppy disk or any other medium that is accessible (such as your hard disk) the next time you reboot KNOPPIX. Here's how:

1. From the squished penguin icon on the panel, click Configure ➪ Save KNOPPIX configuration.

2. Choose the configuration files to save. You can choose to save your personal configuration (from /home/knoppix.kde and .mozilla directories), files on the desktop, your network configuration, X configuration, and other system configuration files (from /etc).

3. Choose to save your configuration files to your floppy disk or to any available disk partition that is writable. Choosing floppy can make the configuration portable, whereas using the hard disk makes the configuration easily reusable on the same machine.

4. If you are saving to floppy, insert the floppy and click OK. The data is saved to floppy disk.

The results from this action are that the knoppix.sh and configs.tbz files are created on floppy disk. The configs.tbz file contains all the saved configuration files from your /home and /etc directories. The knoppix.sh file is a script that tells KNOPPIX how to install those files when KNOPPIX boots up. The next time you start KNOPPIX, you can use the configuration files, as described in the next section.

NOTE Those who create their own customized KNOPPIX boot disks can simply add their knoppix.sh and config.tbz files to the top-level directory of the CD, so KNOPPIX will just boot to their personalized configuration without worrying about an extra floppy or other medium.

Restarting KNOPPIX

You can start KNOPPIX anytime by just inserting your KNOPPIX CD or DVD and restarting your computer. However, if you want to take advantage of the persistent desktop you set up or the saved configuration information, you need to add some options to the KNOPPIX boot prompt. Here's how:

1. Insert your KNOPPIX CD or DVD into the computer and reboot. You should see the KNOPPIX boot prompt.

2. Press F3 (before KNOPPIX boots) to see if any additional boot options are required.

3. If you have a configuration floppy boot disk (or other removable media created in an earlier procedure), insert that disk now.

4. At the boot prompt, type one of the following command lines, which are different ways to load your configuration files:

```
boot: knoppix floppyconfig
boot: knoppix myconfig=/dev/hda1
boot: knoppix myconfig=/dev/sda1
boot: knoppix myconfig=scan
```

These KNOPPIX boot commands, respectively, get configuration information from the floppy disk, look for that information on the first IDE drive partition (/dev/hda1), look for it on the first SCSI drive partition (/dev/sda1), or scan all available drives to find the information. To boot to a persistent desktop (assuming you set one up earlier), you can instead type:

```
boot: knoppix home=/dev/hda1/knoppix.img
boot: knoppix home=/dev/sda1/knoppix.img
boot: knoppix home=scan
```

The previous boot commands, respectively, assign the KNOPPIX home directory (/home/knoppix) to the /dev/hda1/knoppix.img file, to the /dev/sda1/knoppix .img file, or to the image file found by scanning all available directories for that file. You can also combine one from each of the two preceding command sets to both read your configuration files and assign a persistent desktop, as follows:

```
boot: knoppix floppyconfig home=/dev/hda1/knoppix.img
```

Now you are ready to continue your KNOPPIX session where you left off last time, with the same configuration and data files available.

Summary

KNOPPIX offers what many feel is the best bootable Linux today. It gives you a fully configured Linux desktop system available virtually anywhere you can find a bootable PC.

Besides its desktop features, KNOPPIX contains software needed to use many server, programming, and troubleshooting features of Linux as well. Despite the fact that KNOPPIX runs as a bootable system in RAM, by default, there are ways to configure it to save data and configuration information across multiple boot sessions.

The fact that KNOPPIX can be used to come up to a consistent state every time you boot it is another advantage to using KNOPPIX. If you believe that your saved customizations have become corrupted, you can always reboot KNOPPIX without them to start with a clean KNOPPIX system again.

KNOPPIX is particularly valuable as a tool for accessing a damaged computer so that you can troubleshoot it. With a KNOPPIX disk booted on a computer that was installed to use Microsoft Windows or other operating system, you can use KNOPPIX to access and work with data on that computer's hard disk.

Chapter 12

Running
Yellow Dog Linux

Yellow Dog Linux is one of the premier Linux distributions for the PowerPC (PPC) platform. Offered by Terra Soft Solutions (www .terrasoftsolutions.com), Yellow Dog Linux provides unparalleled concentration on the needs of the PowerPC users.

Because most Linux distributions focus on the Intel/AMD (x86) platform, it's sometimes startling to realize that there's a major Linux distribution, with a passionate community of its own, providing a strong presence in the world of PowerPCs. Distributions such as Ubuntu provide PowerPC versions of their releases and have dedicated PowerPC developers. Yellow Dog, however, is solely dedicated to PowerPC and similar processors. To go after PowerPC enthusiasts, Terra Soft Solutions tailors its Yellow Dog Linux to include the multimedia and ease-of-use features that Apple users expect.

This chapter aims at introducing you to Yellow Dog Linux and how it is moving forward to cater to those who love Apple's PowerPC hardware but are drawn to Linux.

Yellow Dog Linux is not included on the CD or DVD that come with this book. You can purchase Yellow Dog Linux from Terra Soft Solutions (www.terrasoftsolutions.com/store) or download the four-CD installation set from a Yellow Dog Linux mirror site (for a list of mirror sites, see www.terrasoftsolutions.com/resources/ftp_mirrors.shtml). See Appendix A for information on burning CDs.

IN THIS CHAPTER

Digging into Yellow Dog Linux

Installing Yellow Dog Linux

Running Mac-on-Linux

Understanding Yellow Dog Linux

Terra Soft Solutions has focused its efforts on making Yellow Dog Linux work for a wide range of Apple products, which has resulted in less chance of hardware incompatibilities. This is one of the distribution's strengths.

Another heartening note is that Terra Soft Solutions is an Apple Authorized OEM Value Added Reseller with permission from Apple to install Linux on Apple hardware, retaining any hardware warranties provided by Apple.

> **NOTE** The latest Apple hardware uses x86 chips in the form of Intel's Cure Duo processors. Yellow Dog Linux will not work on these systems because that's not Terra Soft's mission. See the section "Going Forward with Yellow Dog" for more information.

Mac OS X, in the form of Aqua, is considered one of the most advanced graphical user interfaces on the market today. With a sophisticated interface available on the Apple platform, a user might question putting Linux on Apple hardware, but there are many valid reasons to install Linux on the PowerPC architecture, including:

- **Cost of applications** — Commercial applications usually have a higher price of ownership than their open source counterparts for similar functionality. For instance, the latest word processor on the Mac OS X platform can cost hundreds of dollars, whereas the open source alternatives are generally free. The free software available for Linux far exceeds that available for the Mac OS X platform.

> **NOTE** While some of the more popular open source programs are available for Mac OS X, they may require a port of the software, as opposed to a recompile. Porting applications is a more complicated process and usually requires expertise in operating system programming. Porting is outside the sphere of this book.

- **Extended hardware life** — Linux is well known for its low operation requirements. You can use Yellow Dog Linux on machines that aren't necessarily supported by the latest Mac OS X version and still run the latest Linux applications.

- **Uniformity** — Linux is widely deployed, especially for back-office functions. By using Yellow Dog Linux (often referred to as YDL), you can mix PowerPC hardware with Intel hardware in the same production environment, with application and operating system uniformity, thus reducing costs associated with the support of two different operating systems. Because Linux is open source and widely available, you also reduce your dependence on one entity for your operating systems.

- **Security** — Yellow Dog Linux has the support of thousands of programmers who constantly develop patches and updates for software, as opposed to depending on a commercial entity to release patches (or doing them yourself).

- **Ease of administration/use** — Linux (and particularly Fedora, on which Yellow Dog Linux is based) is so widely deployed, with more installations occurring every day, that it's understood and managed by a large user/administrator group. It's often easier for system administrators and users to complete tasks on a familiar system with a standard interface.

- **Mac-on-Linux** — Mac-on-Linux software enables you to run Mac OS X (10.1 through 10.3.3), Mac OS 7.5.2 through 9.2.2, or another instance of Linux within your active Yellow Dog Linux session on a PowerPC system, so you get the best of both worlds.

A few different versions of Yellow Dog Linux are available, covering a wide spectrum of current and legacy PowerPC hardware:

- **Yellow Dog Linux 5.0.2** — This version provides support for Power Architecture Cell processors, cell-based systems such as Sony PlayStation 3, Mercury Computer systems, and IBM and Apple systems that use G5, IBM 970, G4, and G3 PowerPC processors.

- **Yellow Dog Linux 4.1** — An updated and enhanced release of Yellow Dog Linux that provides full support for all of the specialized hardware found in the latest PowerPC Mac Minis and G5 systems, as well as continued support for G3 and G4 systems.

- **Yellow Dog Linux 3.0.1** — The last version of Yellow Dog Linux (October 1, 2004) to support the beige G3 hardware (66 MHz) and previous Old World ROM Macs. This version also supports most of the same hardware that Yellow Dog Linux 4.0 supports.

- **Y-HPC** — A variation of Yellow Dog based on the 64-bit Fedora Core 5.0 version of Linux. This version is for high-performance computing and focuses on offering high-performance support for Xserve G5s or cluster nodes.

Going Forward with Yellow Dog

Despite the fact that Apple has moved its product line from the PowerPC to the x86 (standard PC) architecture, Terra Soft Solutions continues developing Yellow Dog Linux for the Power Architecture. While Terra Soft remains a top-tier value-added partner of Apple's, it has also begun selling pre-installed Linux systems on hardware from other manufacturers.

Simply put, Yellow Dog's mission is to support the latest Power Architecture systems (such as Sony Playstation 3, and cell-based and high-end PowerPC systems from vendors such as IBM and Mercury Computer), and to continue to deliver PowerPC-focused Linux for the 10 or 20 million people like myself who have PowerPC-based Macs but want to take advantage of the power of Linux on those systems.

For high-end server systems, Terra Soft Solutions offers its Y-HPC operating system on IBM 970 BladeCenter 42U rack servers and Mercury Computer XR9 64-bit extended ATX 1U and 4U rack servers. Along with Y-HPC on these machines comes the Y-Imager cluster management software suite, so you can centrally manage multiple Power-based Y-HPC servers.

On the workstation end, Terra Soft is the Linux vendor of choice for the Sony PlayStation 3. After having worked closely with Sony to ensure complete support and interoperability, Terra Soft delivered Yellow Dog Linux 5.0 for the PS3 at the end of November 2006. Similarly, Terra Soft has also partnered with Genesi USA (`www.genesippc.com`) to sell the Open Desktop Workstation with Yellow Dog Linux pre-installed. The Open Desktop Workstation has a micro-ATX form factor, both Gigabit and 10/100 Ethernet ports, an AGP slot, three low-profile PCI slots, and multiple FireWire and USB ports.

The bottom line here is that you can expect Yellow Dog Linux to continue its support for Power Architecture on both server and desktop systems. So, Apple users who love their PowerPCs can find a way to continue using that hardware by moving over to a Yellow Dog Linux system. Also, because of the Power Architecture's support for multimedia hardware and Yellow Dog's inclusion of software for playing a variety of audio and video content, the combination adds a bit of sparkle to the standard Linux desktop systems that are around today.

Digging into Yellow Dog

Yellow Dog Linux offers a Fedora, RPM-based distribution that is highly compatible with most available open source software. By basing the Yellow Dog distribution on a widely deployed and used x86 distribution such as Red Hat's Fedora, Terra Soft Solutions has been able to quickly deploy a very uniform, user-friendly experience for its user base. This section takes a look at some of the highlights of the Yellow Dog distribution.

 This chapter focuses on Yellow Dog 5.0.2, which was released in June 2007 and is the latest version of Yellow Dog Linux that is freely available at the time of this writing.

Yellow Dog Linux 5.0.2 offers four full CDs of software with some of the following applications:

- 2.6.22 Linux Kernel
- X Window System server (X.Org 1.0.1)
- KDE 3.5.5 desktop (unified with GNOME to provide easy access to programs from either desktop environment)
- GNOME 2.14.1 desktop (again, unified with KDE to provide easy access to programs from either desktop environment)
- OpenOffice 2.0.2 (suite of productivity tools including a spreadsheet program, drawing program, presentation software, and a full-featured, Microsoft Word–compatible word processor)
- More than 1,300 other application packages from programming tools to Web browsers

The wide range of applications included on the Yellow Dog CDs is enough to keep even the most computer-savvy person happy, but many more choices are available on the Internet, so you should be able to find an application that fits your needs.

Fedora is the community-supported version of what was previously the ubiquitous Red Hat Linux distribution. As a derivative of Fedora, Yellow Dog Linux can offer the advantages of Fedora features on a Mac platform, including:

- **Red Hat Package Manager (RPM) software** — Starting with software packages from the Fedora Project helps Yellow Dog Linux avoid compatibility problems suffered by some Linux distributions. Users can also rely on well-known RPM packaging tools for adding, removing, and managing software.

- **Anaconda installer** — Yellow Dog takes advantage of the well-tested Anaconda installer for easy installation.

- **Kudzu hardware detection** — By starting with the Fedora kudzu facility for detecting and configuring hardware, Yellow Dog has a stable foundation for probing equipment that has been extended to work with Mac hardware.

CROSS-REF Refer to Chapter 8 for more information on the Fedora Project and some of the specifics regarding its implementation.

Installing Yellow Dog Linux

Before you can install Yellow Dog Linux, you need to get a copy of it from some of the many resources available. The first and most recommended avenue is to purchase it from the vendor. You benefit because you acquire the distribution from the source as well as support from the company that creates Yellow Dog Linux so it can continue development for the PowerPC platform.

NOTE Yellow Dog Linux always makes the previous version of its distribution freely available and downloadable from its Web site. At the time that this book was written, version 5.0.2 was commercially available, meaning that YDL 4.1 is available as downloadable CD images. See www.terrasoftsolutions.com/resources/downloads.shtml for information about downloading the latest version that is available.

To purchase Yellow Dog Linux from Terra Soft Solutions, visit the Terra Soft Solutions Web store at http://terrasoftsolutions.com/store/. When purchasing from Terra Soft Solutions, you receive the following in a box set:

- Install and source DVDs

- *Getting Started with Yellow Dog Linux,* a book that covers all the information a beginning Linux user would need to know to get a fully operational Yellow Dog Linux system running

- Optional 60 days of installation support (you can purchase the box set with or without support, depending on your needs and skill level with Linux)

- Other goodies (sticker, flexible flier depending on package purchased)

- The knowledge that you are supporting the company that created the product, allowing further development

Alternatives to purchasing the Yellow Dog Linux box set include:

- **Purchasing a subscription to YDL.net** — This is Terra Soft Solutions' online resource for Yellow Dog Linux users. You can get e-mail accounts and Web space as well as prerelease access to the latest version of Yellow Dog Linux before it is available for general release. The costs vary depending on which version you choose. More information is available at www.ydl.net.

■ **Downloading and creating your own ISO** — You can download the distribution from one of the many Linux mirrors as identified at `http://yellowdoglinux.com/resources/ftp_mirrors.shtml` and burn your own ISO.

■ **Purchasing online** — If you have a slow Internet connection and want to try Yellow Dog, you can purchase burned CDs or DVDs (depending on the release of Yellow Dog that you want to run) from various Linux stores on the Internet. Use your favorite search engine to locate one near you.

Hardware Support

Hardware support with the Linux operating system was a major issue in the past, but as Linux's popularity has grown, many device makers have provided access to their hardware drivers or in some cases have created hardware drivers for Linux. While this is still an issue with hardware that is brand new in the x86 community, the effects are lessened with the PowerPC platform because all hardware is generally created to Apple's exacting standards. Terra Soft Solutions' focus on Apple hardware and generally fewer variations in hardware add up to support being much faster for the PowerPC platform.

One of the great things about Yellow Dog Linux is that as you dig into it, you discover that some of the hardware compatibility issues faced by the x86 Linux crowd (such as with Winmodems, the plethora of hardware configuration options, and so forth) are minimized or eliminated. With Terra Soft Solutions, a fully authorized Apple Value Added Reseller, you are assured that the hardware you are using will be supported. There are some notable hardware support differences with the release of YDL 5.0 and 4.1, and the fully capable 3.0.1 version covers any older hardware that is not supported in the 5.*x* product.

In addition to being able to install Yellow Dog Linux on your own Apple hardware, you can purchase Apple hardware from Terra Soft Solutions with Yellow Dog Linux preinstalled.

Terra Soft Solutions has developed official lists of hardware configurations that have been specifically tested with Yellow Dog Linux (`http://yellowdoglinux.com/support/hardware/breakdown/index.php`). The Yellow Dog list includes:

■ Power Mac G3 (Yosemite Blue and White 300–450 MHz G3)

■ Power Mac G4 (Power Mac G4 PCI 350–400 MHz G4 and above)

■ Power Mac G5 (1.6 GHz G5 and above)

■ Mac Mini

■ iMac (Rev A,B 233 MHz G3), eMac G4, and iMac G5

■ PowerBook (Lombard 333–400 MHz G3, Pismo 400–500 MHz FW G3, Titanium 400 MHz–1 GHz G4, Powerbook 12″ 867 MHz–1.33 GHz, and Powerbook 15–17″ 1.0–1.5 GHz G4)

- iBook (300–366 MHz G3 — 800 MHz 1.2 GHz G4)
- HPC (Xserver Cluster Node 1.33 MHz G4, Single/Dual 1.33 GHz G4, Cluster Node 2.0 GHz G5, and Single/Dual 2.0 GHz G5)

In general, Yellow Dog 5.0.2 should run on any PPC-based Mac system released before January 2006, with the exception of Old World ROM or beige G3 and earlier hardware such as 8500s, 7200s, and Performa PowerPCs. YDL 3.0.1 supports this older hardware and much of the hardware currently supported by Yellow Dog Linux 4.1 (certainly anything that was manufactured by Apple before September 2003, which is when 3.0.1 was released). The hardware supported and tested for Yellow Dog Linux 3.0.1 includes:

- Power Mac 4400–9600
- Power Mac beige G3 models and blue-and-white G3 models
- Most hardware supported by Yellow Dog Linux 4.0 and 4.0.1

If you have older PPC hardware that isn't officially supported, you should still be able to use Yellow Dog Linux 4.1, but you'll be running in an unsupported configuration, so *caveat emptor*. Terra Soft Solutions dropped support for many older hardware configurations so that it could focus on the most likely configurations. Also, trying to support outdated computer architectures, which on the Old World ROM systems were particularly troublesome, doesn't offer much return for a commercial Linux venture.

Planning Your Installation

Installing Linux on PowerPC and cell-based systems is slightly more complex than installation on x86 systems because of differences in the bootloader and associated requirements for specific partitions on certain systems. Specifically, repartitioning existing systems on which some version of the Mac OS is already installed can be very difficult because of the types of file systems used on modern Macintosh computers. This section does not discuss repartitioning.

CAUTION Before you start installation, back up any data you want to retain on external media (CD, hard drive, and so on). If you are installing Yellow Dog on a separate disk, this is a precautionary measure in case your system overwrites data that is important to you (or you accidentally select the wrong disk). In all other cases, the standard mechanisms (described in this section) for partitioning a disk require that you format your disk, erasing all of your existing data. If you want to repartition an existing disk without losing data, I suggest using software such as ProSoft's Drive Genius, which is as good as its name suggests.

After backing up your important data, the next step is to determine whether you are going to multi-boot Mac OS with Yellow Dog Linux or install Yellow Dog Linux as a standalone product. If you choose to multi-boot, you must decide whether you will use two hard drives or partition (that is, logically divide) a single hard drive to house both Linux and Mac OS.

> **CAUTION** If you choose to multi-boot, the Yellow Dog installer gives you the option to resize an existing volume to make room for Yellow Dog. *You should always do backups* before attempting something like this. See the Yellow Dog documentation for more information.

Installing Mac OS X and Yellow Dog Linux on One Hard Drive

If you choose to use one hard drive to house both Mac OS and Yellow Dog Linux, you need to load Mac OS (X or 9) first and then create a partition for Yellow Dog Linux as the first partition. In Mac OS X do the following:

1. Boot off the Mac OS X CD by holding down the C key with the Mac OS X CD-ROM inserted.

2. From the Install menu, select Open Disk Utility.

3. Select your hard drive and then click the partition tab on the right side.

4. Choose how many partitions you want. (Two partitions is a good selection if you are installing Mac OS X and Yellow Dog Linux, or if you want to install Mac OS 9 or earlier and Mac OS X, you can choose the number of partitions needed.)

5. Choose the first gray partition that is untitled (it should be the top one).

6. In the Format menu, select Free Space for your Yellow Dog Linux partition. Note that you can change the size of the partition if you don't want to use the defaults by entering the size you want or by using the slider. You can also name the partition if you like.

> **NOTE** Be sure to create a partition large enough for your Linux installation. The default sizes for some types of installations (discussed later in this chapter) are Personal Desktop (2GB), Workstation (2.5GB), Server (1GB), and Everything (6GB).

These are size estimations, and you will need more room for any other applications you want as well as for personal files, and so on.

7. Choose the second gray partition and leave it as the default (Mac OS Extended) for your Mac OS X partition. You can name this as well if you like and adjust the size according to your needs.

8. Click the Partition button and then quit the partition tool.

Resume your installation of Mac OS X as normal.

Installing Mac OS 9 or Earlier and Yellow Dog Linux on One Hard Drive

If you want to install Mac OS 9 or earlier in addition to Yellow Dog Linux on one hard drive, you can perform the following for a dual-booted machine:

1. Boot off the Mac OS CD by holding down the C key with the Mac OS CD-ROM inserted.

2. Double-click the Utilities or Disk Tools folder. Double-click the Drive Setup application.

3. Select your hard drive in the List of Drives in the Drive Setup window.

4. Click the Initialize button, and then click the Custom Setup button.

5. Choose how many partitions you want in the Custom Setup pop-up window (3 partitions is a good selection for both Mac OS and Yellow Dog Linux, or 4 partitions for Mac OS, Mac OS X, and Yellow Dog Linux). You can use the slider bar to change the size of the partitions here.

6. Choose the top partition and select Unallocated in the menu that by default displays Mac OS Extended. The second partition should be Mac OS Standard for Mac OS, and if you are loading Mac OS X as well, the third partition should be Mac OS Extended (available only if you chose 3 partitions). Make sure to label the partitions appropriately.

7. Select OK and then Initialize.

Resume your installation of Mac OS as normal.

Installing Mac OS 9 or Earlier, Mac OS X, and Yellow Dog Linux on Multiple Hard Drives

Because of the way the system boots, you should have the drive to which you plan to install Yellow Dog Linux as the first hard drive in the IDE chain, set as Master. Mac OS or Mac OS X should be placed as the second drive in the chain and have the jumper set to Slave.

Then install the other versions of Mac OS (9 or earlier, or X) onto the other hard drives. You need only to select a drive other than the first one during the installation procedure. You must install Yellow Dog Linux as the last operating system on the first drive.

Yellow Dog Linux 3.0.1 Special Considerations

All the planning noted previously applies to Yellow Dog Linux 3.0.1, but there is one special consideration to take into account. The newest releases of Yellow Dog Linux support only New World ROM systems, which are the blue-and-white G3 and above systems.

 **There are two versions of the G3, one that has a beige case and another that has the blue-and-white case.**

If you are installing Yellow Dog on a New World ROM system, go right to the next section, "Beginning the Installation."

If you are using an Old World ROM system, which are beige G3 systems and earlier hardware, refer to the Yellow Dog Linux Web site (www.yellowdoglinux.com) for more information.

Beginning the Installation

After you have determined how you will boot your system (multi-boot or single Yellow Dog Linux boot) and have loaded Mac OS X or Mac OS 9 or earlier as appropriate, you can begin installing Yellow Dog Linux. This procedure focuses on the newest release of Yellow Dog Linux, but special notes on aspects of the 3.0.1 install are included where appropriate.

1. Insert Yellow Dog Linux CD 1 into your CD-ROM drive, reboot your system, and press C to boot off the CD-ROM.

2. If you downloaded Yellow Dog or have a burned CD-R, you may want to check your media by appending `mediacheck` to the end of any of the install types (see Step 3 for install types). For example:

```
install-safe mediacheck
```

This goes through all your media to determine if it is suitable for loading the operating system. This can save you a lot of time by determining that all of your CDs are good before you invest your time in the installation procedure.

> **NOTE** Although it doesn't show up in the Yellow Dog 3.0.1 text menu, you can still type `mediacheck` after `install` or `install-text` to check your CD-ROMs.

3. After some cursory probing messages, you are prompted with a menu asking how you want to boot the CD-ROM. If you are using a New World ROM G3 or G4 system (blue-and-white G3 and above machine), type **install** at the prompt to use the graphical user interface method of installation. If you are using a G5 machine, type **install-g5** at the prompt to install using the graphical user interface.

If you can't get either of these methods to work, type **install-safe** for G3 or G4 machines or **install-g5-safe** for G5 machines to use a generic video mode for installation. If neither of these methods works, you can type **install text** for G3 or G4 machines or **install-g5 text** for G5 machines to install with the text installation method.

> **NOTE** Yellow Dog Linux 3.0.1 has only `install` and `install-text` options available. Choose `install` first, and if that doesn't work, choose `install-text` after rebooting.

4. The system will have been probed prior to this point to determine the hardware configuration. After the text messages, you are presented with a welcome screen. (You can choose to review the release notes by clicking the Release Notes button at the bottom-left side.) When you're ready to move on, click the Next button on the bottom-right side.

5. Select the language with which you are most comfortable. All future information presented by the installer will be in the language you select.

6. Choose the keyboard type that matches your current configuration.

7. Choose the type of installation you want. The options are:

   ■ **Personal Desktop** — Most home users will want this installation because it contains the most appropriate software set for home or office users (including laptops). Games, word processors, Internet tools, and other useful packages are included.

   ■ **Workstation** — Similar to the personal desktop type but includes tools for system administration and software development.

   ■ **Server** — Installs software needed for providing external services, including file and print, Web, and mail services. This is an advanced installation type and should be used only if you need it because you could misconfigure your system and create a security vulnerability. You can choose to install a graphical user interface as well, so if you don't want the extra overhead of a GUI, you can go without one on this type.

- **Custom** — Provides the most flexibility because you can configure the partitions and software packages you want (everything!). This is your choice if you want to have more control over the installation. If you want to experience a large set of applications, you can choose this instead of installing applications one by one. You can also choose a more specific set of packages if this is to be a server used for external services, providing a higher level of security.

For this chapter, the Custom installation type is used.

8. Decide how you want to partition your hard drive. You have two choices:

- **Option 1: Automatically partition** — If you choose this method, click Next and you are presented with three options:

  - **Remove all Linux partitions on this system** — Deletes all previous Linux partitions and replaces only previously identified Linux partitions.

  - **Remove all partitions on this system** — Use this only on New World ROM systems or on a single-drive Yellow Dog installation. If you use this option on a multi-boot system, it removes *all* previous installations, including any Mac OS or MAC OS X installation. If you use this on an Old World ROM system, regardless of the installation type, it destroys the installation and requires a reformat and reload of Mac OS.

> **CAUTION** Be extremely careful using the Remove All Partitions option. Avoid using it at all if possible because you can accidentally destroy your Mac OS installation!

  - **Keep all partitions and use existing free space** — The one you want to use in most cases because it won't alter your Mac OS or Mac OS X installations and uses only the identified free space (as created previously). This is the option you should select if you are using Automatically partition. You can also select the Review (and modify if needed) the partitions created option, which will enable you to double-check the partitions that the installer creates for you and change them if need be.

- **Option 2: Manually Partition with Disk Druid** — This is the more advanced option that allows you to create your partitions to your preference. Here is the sequence for creating new Linux partitions:

  a. Choose the drive on which you want to install Yellow Dog Linux.

  b. Choose New to create a new partition. You must create three partitions. First, choose Filesystem Type ➪ Apple BootStrap. No mount point is needed. It should be 1MB and fixed size. This partition is for booting and should be the very first partition. Second, choose Filesystem Type ➪ Swap. No mount point required. It should be a minimum of 256MB (256MB is generally enough, although some say this should be set to twice the size of your physical RAM. More won't degrade system performance, however, and it doesn't hurt to be safe) and fixed size. This partition is the swap space that Linux uses for processes when the RAM is full. Third, create your root partition by selecting / as the mount point. This is where the file system is mounted. The root partition is absolutely critical because your other file systems will mount from this. You generally want to have your root partition consume the rest of the hard drive unless you are creating more partitions. Additional partitions are optional.

TIP   On most multi-boot systems, you will want to select Automatically partition. Then select the "Keep all partitions and use existing free space" option and the "Review (and modify if needed) the partitions created" check box to make sure that you are using the correct portion of your hard drive.

9. Identify your network settings, including DHCP. You use your network configuration for LAN (local area network) connections, such as when you are using a router between your cable or DSL connection and the local, internal network. Because you need to know these settings ahead of time, be sure to check them out before you start.

CROSS-REF   Refer to Chapter 5 for descriptions of IP addresses, netmasks, and other information you need to set up your LAN.

NOTE   If you are not prompted for network configuration information at this point, the installer could not identify your network card. This is extremely rare, but it can happen with older Macs. If this occurs, contact Yellow Dog support for help in resolving this problem.

Select eth0 (your first network interface card) and click Edit. You have the following options:

- **Configure using DHCP** — Enables you to automatically obtain a DHCP address from your LAN if there is a DHCP server (such as Linksys or D-Link routers). If you select this option, you do not need to fill out anything else in this section.

- **Activate on boot** — Enables you to turn on your network connection during boot. Under most circumstances, you will want to select this option if you are using a LAN.

- **IP Address** — A four-octet number that uniquely identifies your computer address. Your system will have a unique IP on your LAN or WAN (wide area network) connection.

- **Netmask** — Identifies the host and network portions of the IP address. A class A network is 255.0.0.0, a class B is 255.255.0.0, and a class C is 255.255.255.0 by default (if no subnet masking is in place).

Click OK and, if you aren't using DHCP, set your hostname by selecting Hostname ⇨ Manually. This can be any name you want to represent your computer. If this is a server, follow your company's naming convention. If you prefer to have DHCP set your hostname, select the Automatically via DHCP radio button.

The last options are grayed out if you selected DHCP. If you chose to manually configure your network options, enter the following:

- **Gateway IP address** — The IP address of the machine that is the gateway or router between your network and the outside networks. For instance, 192.168.1.1 might be your gateway if you have a Linksys or D-Link router between your computer and your cable or DSL connection.

- **Primary, secondary, and tertiary DNS** — The server that your system uses for address name translation (converting a hostname into an IP address). Your ISP usually gives you this information.

10. Configure the firewall. A firewall acts as a conduit between your computer and other computers that request access to the services it is providing. If you are connected to the Internet or other networks, enable your firewall. Even if you are not connected to an untrusted network, you should enable the firewall in case you connect at a later date. Two choices are available in this section:

- **No firewall** — Don't choose this option because it does not check against requests for services. Even if your system is not currently providing services, it's best to not select this option (things can change as the system grows).

- **Enable firewall** — The preferred selection. It provides a modicum of security against malicious entities that may want to attack your systems. Only the default services are allowed at this level, and you can configure access for more services as needed. Some of the defaults are:

  - *Remote login (SSH)* — An encrypted protocol that replaces the vulnerable telnet protocol. With SSH you can log in to the system with an interactive shell, as well as securely transfer files interactively (SFTP) or noninteractively (SCP). For more information on this, type **man ssh** at the command line after installation.

NOTE When SSH is unchecked, you can still use these utilities on outgoing connections. This controls only incoming requests from outside your computer. If you need to access your system remotely, you can choose this, but it is best to leave it unchecked for security reasons. The same applies to the other options presented.

  - *Web Server (HTTP, HTTPS)* — Allows your system to serve regular (HTTP) Web pages or encrypted (HTTPS) Web pages. Unless you need to run a Web server, I recommend you not check this.

  - *File Transfer (FTP)* — Allows users to interactively log in to your system and transfer files. This protocol is unencrypted and not needed by most users. If you must allow file transfers, SFTP (provided with SSH) is the preferred method because the password and username are sent encrypted.

  - *Mail Server (SMTP)* — Allows your system to accept mail requests or mail relay requests. You can still send and receive mail if you do not check this; it just allows your machine to act as a mail server. If you install and improperly configure SMTP, your system can become a spam relay, so only more experienced users should check this.

NOTE These settings can be reconfigured later using iptables. See the man page for iptables for more information.

On this screen, you also specify whether you want SELinux (Security-Enhanced Linux) policies activated on your system. These access control policies provide a much richer and more powerful environment for defining the access that users and applications can have to various system resources.

11. If you need additional language support, select it here. Your default language (chosen during install language selection) should already be selected. Click Next to continue.

12. Select the time zone in which you reside or the time zone you want to use for your server. If your hardware uses UTC (Coordinated Universal Time) or GMT (Greenwich Mean Time), select the check box at the bottom. Click Next to continue.

13. Set your root password. This password provides the keys to the kingdom; with the root account, a user can do *anything*, including destroy the entire file system. You must set a strong password (not any personally identifiable information such as identification number, phone number, pet's name, family member's birthday, and so on). Enter your password twice (to ensure you've entered it correctly), and then press Enter.

> **CAUTION** The importance of a good root or any other account password should not be minimized. This is crucially important to the security of your system. See Chapter 6 and the Guide to Better Password Practices (`http://securityfocus.com/infocus/1537`) for more information on choosing good passwords.

14. Select the different packages you want to install on the system. Choose Everything (for all software packages) or Minimal (only the basics to run the system). Selecting the package groups enables you to see the individual packages included in each group (you can select or deselect from that list for more granularity). Note that KDE is chosen by default; if you prefer to use GNOME or want to use both, check GNOME. When you're finished, click Next.

15. You've reached the About to Install phase. You're warned that the system will begin writing to the disk. You can back out of anything at this point with no damage to the system, so if you made a mistake or are not sure about installing, you can simply reboot.

If you are ready to commit your configuration to the system, click Next. Your system begins writing the software to the hard drive. This can take from 10 minutes to an hour or more depending on the speed of your system and the amount of software you decided to load. You are shown a list of the CDs that your system needs to load the software. Be sure to have those CDs ready to load into the system. After each CD is completed, you are prompted to insert another CD until the installation is complete.

16. After the installation finishes, the Congratulations! screen appears. Click Reboot when you are ready.

17. The system reboots and goes through system initialization. Afterward, a welcome screen appears.

18. The initial setup begins here. Click Next to move forward.

19. The license agreement appears in a text box. Read it and then click No if you do not agree to the terms, and the process stops. Click Yes if you agree to the terms.

20. Set the date and time for the system. If you want to use Network Time Protocol (NTP) to synchronize your system date and time with a remote network system for maximum assurance of the correct date and time, check the Enable Network Time Protocol box, and then select one of the two NTP servers provided.

21. Set the display resolution and color depth to your preference. (You can change this in the system after installation.)

22. Create your non-root daily user account. Enter a username (the name you use to log in with) and the full name of the user (for administrative purposes), and then enter the password twice. If you need to use a network login, you can configure that here as well (your system administrator can provide this information if needed).

CAUTION Do not log in with the root account for normal day-to-day activities. That can be very dangerous in that you could accidentally damage the system with an errant command, but it also means that you might surf the Web using root or install software with root without thinking twice about it, possibly introducing malicious software. Use the non-root account for all non-administrative purposes and regular interaction with the system.

23. Configure your sound card. If everything seems to be configured properly, try to play a test sound. A pop-up window asks if you heard the sound. Answer appropriately. If you have multiple sound devices (such as a USB audio device), you may need to select multiple device tabs and test each associated device. When you are done, click Next when you're ready to move on.

24. If you have any additional CDs from which to install software, insert them into the CD-ROM, and select them here (the CD you insert will show on the list). Click Next to continue.

25. At this point you are done installing and configuring your system, and you are booted up into the graphical user interface with a prompt for the username and password.

Rebooting Your Linux Mac

If you've followed the instructions in this chapter to create a system that can boot either Mac OS X or Yellow Dog Linux, you will see a new step in your system's boot process. When you reboot your system, you will see a small text menu in the upper right corner of the screen that enables you to specify the system that you want to boot. Your choices are:

- l — Boot Yellow Dog Linux
- x — Boot Mac OS X
- c — Boot from the CD-ROM drive

If you do not specify one of these three options, your system will automatically boot into Yellow Dog Linux in 10 seconds.

Updating Yellow Dog Linux

Yellow Dog Updated, Modified (yum) is included with Yellow Dog and ships with Fedora, Mandriva, and other Linux distributions as well. It's a utility that enables you to update your system packages to the latest available version. Because new security vulnerabilities are released on all operating systems frequently, updating your system packages regularly is essential.

Updating your packages also gives you the newest features available for the applications you are using. Table 12-1 shows some of the most widely used options available with yum (replace *package* with the name of your package).

TABLE 12-1

Using Yum to Work with Software Packages

Option	Description
yum list	Shows all the packages available to be installed (but not installed).
yum list installed	Shows installed packages.
yum list updates	Shows all installed packages that have updates (patches) available.
yum install *package*	Installs the package you identify in *package*.
yum update *package*	Updates the package you identify in *package*. The great thing about this is it installs all package dependencies, which used to be a major headache when administering patches.
yum update	Updates all packages on the system. (Same as preceding option but does not specify package name.)
yum remove *package*	Removes the package identified in *package*.
yum info *package*	Provides detailed information on the package identified in *package*.

Using this information, assume that you want to run the GNU Image Manipulation Program (aka GIMP, a very popular graphics editing program), and you haven't installed it previously. If you want to get more information on it, run:

```
yum info gimp
```

If you decide you want to install it, run:

```
yum install gimp
```

If an update becomes available a week later and you want to patch it, run:

```
yum update gimp
```

If it has been a month and you decide you no longer need gimp, you can remove it with the following:

```
yum remove gimp
```

Yum makes updating packages very easy and should be used regularly to keep your system updated with the latest patches (you can even run it from a cron job for true automation).

Running Mac Applications with Mac-on-Linux

Mac-on-Linux is a very interesting project that enables Mac users to have the best of both Linux and Mac. With this software, you can run Linux as the primary operating system and still access your Mac OS or Mac OS X operating system (or even another Linux operating system) via a window within your operating Linux session.

Mac-on-Linux presents a virtual machine that provides a real environment to the Mac OS or Mac OS X installation. Because there is no emulation, Mac-on-Linux is very fast and capable, but will only run on PowerPC Macintosh systems. Mac-on-Linux is very stable and works with minimal configuration. For more information on what Mac-on-Linux provides and instructions for its use, visit `http://maconlinux.org/`.

Support Options

If you run into problems using or installing Yellow Dog Linux, you can obtain support in many ways. The Linux community is very supportive, proffering numerous Web pages available to assist the newcomer. If you encounter problems with hardware, try one of the following options:

- **Yellow Dog Community Board** — Another free support option that is run by Yellow Dog Linux enthusiasts. It is available at `http://yellowdog-board.com/`.

- **Yellow Dog Mailing Lists** — If your questions don't get answered through the preceding sites, you can subscribe to some of the numerous Yellow Dog mailing lists where you can ask your questions. Directions for use are at `http://lists.terrasoftsolutions.com/mailman/listinfo`.

- **Yellow Dog Linux User Channel** — If you are comfortable with IRC (Internet Relay Chat), you can use `irc.freenode.net` and join #yellowdog for community-driven interactive support.

- **Yellow Dog Official Support** — If you can't find the information you need from the previous sources or `http://terrasoftsolutions.com/support/installation/`, you can purchase support from Terra Soft Solutions through `http://terrasoftsolutions.com/tss_contact.shtml`. If you purchased Yellow Dog Linux through Terra Soft Solutions with 60 days of support, you can contact the company through `http://terrasoftsolutions.com/support/`.

If you need software support after your installation, use some of the other more generic support options available from the Linux community. These options include using a search engine to search for the problem and visiting community-driven Web sites such as the following:

- **The Linux Documentation Project** (`http://tldp.org/`) — The premier Web site for how-to guides for using the Linux operating system.

- **Linux Journal Help Desk** (http://linuxjournal.com/xstatic/community) — Offers guidance on using Linux.

- **Just Linux** (http://justlinux.com/) — Offers some basic guidelines on Linux use.

You can use your favorite search engine to find more of the many, many helpful Linux Web sites out there.

The Linux community is generally very supportive of new users, and you can find help from local Linux User Groups (LUGs) or via many places on the Internet.

Summary

Yellow Dog Linux is a very stable, fully functioning version of Fedora available on the PowerPC platform. It has the capability to extend the life of your PowerPC Mac hardware and to run Mac OS 9 or earlier or even Mac OS X on your running Linux installation using Mac-on-Linux. Linux is not the sole domain of the x86 community. Yellow Dog Linux enables PowerPC users to use Linux through multi-booting or using the innovative Mac-on-Linux software, while still enjoying their Mac OS or Mac OS X environment.

Apple's move from the PowerPC to the x86 architecture has made Linux an even more attractive proposition for existing PowerPC systems. Although Mac OS X itself is based on a free version of Linux (FreeBSD), running Linux on your PPC Mac software is the easiest way to guarantee that you'll always be able to run the latest and greatest open source software on your PowerPC Macintosh hardware. Terra Soft Solutions has also begun delivering Linux on newer Power Architecture systems (most notably Sony PlayStation 3). Terra Soft also provides Linux for various high-performance, rack-mounted computers and continues to support Linux for Macintosh systems and other PPC workstations with a focus on strong multimedia support and high-quality graphics.

Chapter 13

Running Gentoo Linux

IN THIS CHAPTER

Understanding Gentoo

What's in Gentoo

Installing Gentoo

S everal years ago, Gentoo (www.gentoo.org) was the rising star of Linux distributions among Linux enthusiasts. Of all the popular Linux distributions, this is the first one I'd recommend to a technically oriented friend who wanted to learn Linux, and the last one I'd recommend to my wife ("Just show me what button to click for my e-mail"). That's because to install and maintain Gentoo effectively, you have to care (to an almost unnatural extent) about what is going on with your computer.

Gentoo is named after the gentoo penguin, believed to be the fastest underwater swimmers of all penguin species. So Gentoo Linux gives a nod both to the Linux mascot (a penguin named Tux) and the distribution's own goals to provide tools to create a fast and efficient operating system. (To pronounce Gentoo, use the G sound as you would in the word *gentle*.)

This chapter describes why you might want to use Gentoo, what the Gentoo community is like, and how to get and install Gentoo Linux.

ON the CD-ROM The Gentoo live/install CD is included on the DVD that comes with this book. You can use this Gentoo CD as described in Appendix A. The Gentoo live/install CD image lets you run, and then install, a solid, basic desktop system. You will need an Internet connection or some medium containing the needed Gentoo packages (CD, DVD, or hard disk) to get additional packages for your Gentoo installation.

Understanding Gentoo

Performance and efficiency were the critical goals that led to the creation of the Gentoo Linux distribution. A dedication to the spirit of open source software (and to those drawn to it) has been vital to Gentoo's rapid and incredible growth.

In the few years it has been in existence, Gentoo has grown from having one maintainer — its creator, Daniel Robbins — to having more than 250 active developers. Although Robbins has moved on to other endeavors, Gentoo still boasts one of the strongest user communities among all Linux distributions. Gentoo users seem willing to contribute so freely because they feel that they get back what they give to Gentoo.

The Portage software distribution management system is the key technology that separates Gentoo from other Linux distributions. Based on the BSD Ports system, Portage can be used to build almost the entire Gentoo distribution from source codes, and manage and upgrade that software as well.

Gentoo's Open Source Spirit

Although Gentoo could some day produce a commercial Linux distribution, the Gentoo project is committed to the goals of open source software, while still allowing those who use the software to make money. Ways that those goals are reflected in Gentoo — and not in some other distributions — include:

- **Passing bug fixes upstream** — Software bugs in open source projects are often shaken out when actual Linux distributions are put together. When a distribution finds a bug, it is considered good practice to pass the fix to that bug upstream, to the project maintaining the original software.

  Not passing bug fixes upstream could potentially give a commercial Linux distribution an advantage over other distributions that don't have the fix. There have been many cases where fixes in some distributions have not made it to the upstream projects. Gentoo, on the other hand, has a reputation for sharing bug fixes with the open source community.

- **Transparent development process** — Not only is the open source software made available to everyone, but the tools for building that software are also freely distributed. Gentoo users can see exactly what their software contains, along with all the decisions made to build that software. It is also a fairly simple procedure for users in the process of building their own Gentoo software to change any of those build decisions.

- **Choices for creating Gentoo** — You can build your own Gentoo Linux from the source code pages or start from prebuilt binary packages provided by the Gentoo project. Freedom, in the Gentoo philosophy, means letting users create the kind of Linux system they want. So, if users don't want to make decisions about how their packages are built, they can simply take ready-made packages from the Gentoo project.

- **Not-for-profit organization** — When the Linux distribution is dedicated to the community and not beholden to stockholders, open source enthusiasts often feel better about freely contributing to improving that distribution. Gentoo is a not-for-profit organization.

This open source spirit has also helped Gentoo gain a community that is extraordinarily active and helpful to one another.

The Gentoo Community

The open source spirit of Gentoo pervades its community. The size and activity of that community is best reflected in its forums (http://forums.gentoo.org), in which there are literally hundreds (and sometimes thousands) of new posts per day. If there's something about Gentoo you can't find using Google, try searching the Gentoo forums.

To get a sense of the activity levels on the forums, check out the board statistics (http://forums.gentoo.org/statistics.php). You can see how many posts, topics, and users there are in the forums per day. You can also see, and visit, the most active topics in the forums.

Many Gentoo enthusiasts seem to live on the forums. Although most of the posts stick closely to Linux, nobody seems to blink an eye when someone posts questions about the existence of God or what to do when a guy's wife has left him. At times, the forums have the distinct feel of a coffee house.

It never hurts to start with the Frequently Asked Questions (FAQ) forums. However, I think most will want to start with the Installing Gentoo forum (because it's quite possible to get hung up on installation when you first try installing it). If you are interested in live communications about Gentoo, try the Gentoo IRC #gentoo channel at irc.freenote.net (you can use xchat in most Linux systems to access IRC channels). Another good starting forum is the Documentation, Tips, & Tricks forum, where you can find cool little tricks to tweak your system.

Building, Tuning, and Tweaking Linux

Gentoo is sometimes referred to as the build-from-source Linux system. Most other Linux distributions give you a set of prebuilt packages to install and never expect you to build the whole system yourself. While you can get Gentoo with packages prebuilt for you, the distribution was made for you to be able to build the Linux kernel and all packages right on the machine where you will install it.

When you install from prebuilt binary software packages, which is expected with Gentoo and most other Linux distributions, many decisions have already been made for you about what each package includes and what it is tuned for. For a first-time user, the Gentoo project has made a first installation easy by including an installer that you can launch right from the desktop of the Gentoo live CD (which is included on the DVD that comes with this book).

By building a Gentoo distribution from source code, however, you can create a distribution that specifically takes into account the following about your situation:

- **What processor you are running** — Most distributions choose a particular architecture (such as x86, PowerPC, or Sparc) and a generic selection of settings for using the processor. With Gentoo, however, you can choose the exact type of processor you're using and compile all software to take advantage of features from that processor (while not including features specific to other processors).

- **What hardware you might have** — Most distributions install tons of modules to support hardware that you might some day add (it loads them as you need them into the kernel). It also builds a kernel for you that includes support for features that it believes you do need (for example, some distributions include ext3 file system support, expecting that to be your basic file system type, but may not have reiserfs file system support built into the kernel). With Gentoo, you can choose exactly which features are in the kernel to support only the hardware you know you have. Likewise, you can get and install drivers for hardware not connected to your computer if you expect to install that hardware later.

- **What services you want** — Some Linux distributions suffer performance problems because they have processes taking up memory for services that you don't necessarily want (such as daemons for Web, file, print, and other server types). With Gentoo, you can be selective down to the most minute detail about the services that are installed and running on Gentoo (including the order in which they are started).

- **What software is available** — Linux distributions such as Red Hat Enterprise Linux offer a preset selection of software packages that are well-tested and integrated into a set of CDs or DVDs. Gentoo has a massive repository of software packages from which you can choose the exact packages you need. Each package carries its own set of dependencies with it as well, so you don't have to add every library or utility to your system to support software you might want some day. With an Internet connection and Gentoo's emerge tool, you can always add software you need, when you need it.

- **What features are available** — Because in Gentoo you are making decisions about what software you use at compile time, you can select to turn on or off optional features within each software component. For example, if you are building Mozilla mail, you can choose whether the package you build will include support for LDAP address books. In theory, removing support for unneeded features makes the software you end up with run faster and use less memory. However, if you need the support at a later date, you will need to recompile the application (and possibly others that depend on it).

The features just described help characterize the type of person who is attracted to Gentoo. Gentoo enthusiasts like to configure, tune, tweak, and update their Linux systems continuously, and Gentoo users generally end up with systems that run faster, take up less disk space, and run in less memory than would be the case with any other Linux that you get off a shelf.

Where Gentoo Is Used

As you may have guessed by now, Gentoo is most popular with Linux enthusiasts as their personal Linux systems. Among Gentoo users, you find those who like to tinker with desktops and run servers where performance is critical (such as game servers). Because Gentoo can be so easily configured and tuned, users can make very efficient Linux desktop and server systems that include only the software needed for the particular job.

Given its slant toward personal use, there is a lot of interest in Gentoo forums for configuring desktops, configuring multimedia applications, and getting popular games running. There are also significant discussions on securing Gentoo because most of its security tools don't come with friendly, graphical interfaces and require a lot of manual setup.

Despite the fact that you can use Gentoo to create an extraordinarily efficient, finely tuned Linux desktop or server, the distribution is not yet widely accepted in business or educational institutions. There are probably several reasons for that:

- **Stability** — To stay on the bleeding edge of the latest Linux software, Gentoo sacrifices the level of stability demanded by most businesses.

> **NOTE** People I know who use Gentoo on their personal computers tend to use Debian or Fedora for small Web, file, or print servers when they do consulting work, and Red Hat Enterprise Linux or SUSE Linux Enterprise for larger enterprise installations.

- **Support** — No official support packages are offered with Gentoo, so if something goes wrong, no official help is available (although the forums can be quite helpful).
- **Training** — If you are setting up many machines, the people who use those machines will need training. Unlike Red Hat or SUSE Linux, you can't get official training from Gentoo's developers.

So far, the factors just mentioned have kept Gentoo from making any significant inroads into enterprise computing. However, as a learning tool and a personal Linux distribution, Gentoo is hard to beat.

What's in Gentoo

No two Gentoo systems are alike because you can select and build only the pieces of Linux you want to use. In late 2007, there were more than 10,000 software packages available for the project, and the list was growing.

Unlike distributions such as Red Hat Enterprise Linux and SUSE Linux, Gentoo tends to not force its own look-and-feel on the projects it includes. Each software package ported to a Gentoo system gives the user a view of the included open source software packages as they were intended from the individual projects. For example, a KDE desktop will look like a KDE desktop as it was delivered from the KDE project itself; there are no "Gentoo-ized" menus and icons or graphical administration tools to alter it.

Gentoo's focus on tools for managing and building source code has helped make Gentoo extraordinarily portable. Besides the common Intel x86 (PC) version of Gentoo, there are packaged versions of Gentoo ports for HP Alpha, AMD64, HPPA, iA64, PowerPC, PowerPC64, and Sparc 64 computer architectures. Available, but unsupported architectures include ARM, MIPS, and s390. Optimized Linux kernels are also available with Gentoo for different specific processors within each architecture. Still, some of the ports are works in progress, so for the time being you will probably get the best experience using an x86 platform to run Gentoo.

To explore Gentoo, it's more appropriate to start with the tools for getting what you want than it is to talk about what you end up with. If you build Gentoo tuned to your hardware and include just the software that you need, your system isn't going to look like any other Gentoo system.

Managing Software with Portage

At the heart of Gentoo is the Portage software management system. Based on the FreeBSD Ports system, Portage enables you to find, download, configure, build, and install the exact software you choose.

Using the Portage system can give you some excellent insights into how Linux is created. As Daniel Robbins said, " . . . we are documenting how to build a Linux system at the same time we are moving Gentoo Linux development forward."

Those developing software are encouraged not only to contribute their software to the Gentoo project but also to contribute the scripts they use to build that software. Portage tools and build scripts open up Linux technology beginning at the source-code level.

Key components of the Portage package management system include the `emerge` command and the package build scripts (contained in the `/usr/portage` directory). You can use these tools to build the entire Gentoo distribution from scratch, or rely on some prebuilt binaries to save some compile time. In most cases, you won't have to modify any configuration files to get a solid Gentoo installation.

For examples of how to use the `emerge` command with Gentoo, refer to the section "Getting Software with emerge" later in this chapter.

Finding Software Packages

Part of the Gentoo installation process includes installing the Portage directory tree in the `/usr/portage` directory. You can step around that directory to see the packages that are available. As I mentioned earlier, several thousand are available.

Most software packages fall into the following major categories:

- **app** — Applications software packages, such as editors, antivirus software, administrative tools, accessibility tools, CD writing applications, and many other packages.
- **dev** — A wide variety of development tools.
- **games** — Dozens of board, arcade, first-person-shooter, puzzle, and strategy games, and games servers.
- **media** — A variety of audio, video, and other multimedia tools.
- **net** — Communications, server, firewall, and other network tools.
- **sys** — System configuration tools.
- **www** — Web communications servers and related software packages.
- **x11** — Miscellaneous tools for the X Window System graphical interface, along with related themes and window managers.

Simply step through the `/usr/portage` directory structure to see the software packages you can install, information about how each is built, and patches that are available.

New Gentoo Features

Because the emphasis of Gentoo is on providing the infrastructure to make the kind of Linux you want, many of the features recently added to Gentoo resulted in support for new computer architectures and in the tools for installing Gentoo systems. Gentoo provided two major releases in 2006, and one in 2007.

The Gentoo 2006.0 release in February 2006 featured a new live CD that combined a complete GNOME desktop environment with a Gentoo installer. The installer can be used to install the live CD's desktop system permanently to hard disk. In terms of support for multiple hardware architectures, the PPC64 team produced optimized stages for G5 and Power5 processors.

The Gentoo 2006.1 release in August 2006 brought improved support for Alpha, SPARC, PPC, and HPPA architectures. On the x86 and AMD64 platforms, networkless installs were added to provide a much easier and more streamlined installation experience for users. Other advancements to the Gentoo Catalyst installer included improvements to features that enabled you to run a Gentoo install that resulted in your own, custom live CD image.

The Gentoo 2007.0 release in May 2007 included a rewriter version of the Gentoo Linux Installer as well as updated applications. Another release is scheduled, but at the time of this writing it is not available. If released in late 2007, it is expected to be called Gentoo 2007.1, continuing the current Gentoo numbering scheme.

Installing Gentoo

A traditional Gentoo installation is more like building your own Linux than it is like typical Linux installs. However, improvements to the Gentoo installer, including the ability to install directly from the Gentoo live CD, makes installing Gentoo a much easier proposition for the first-time Gentoo user.

Two different Gentoo installation procedures are included in this chapter:

- **Live CD Install** — Using the Gentoo live CD included on the DVD that comes with this book, you can boot to a live Gentoo system. Then, by opening an icon on the desktop, you can begin the process of installing Gentoo on your hard disk with a basic, preset desktop system. If you are new to Gentoo, you should use this install type.
- **Minimal CD Install** — If you prefer a more tuned and selective Gentoo install, boot the CD that comes with this book to run a minimal Gentoo install procedure.

Getting Gentoo

The Gentoo Linux distribution is available in several different forms. The live CD install is the easiest to do and is the one that is included with this book. However, there are more customizable install types you might want to look into as well.

If you are new to Gentoo, I recommend you try the live CD install procedure described below. If you are more experienced with Linux or you want to learn more about the detailed features that go into an installation, use the Minimal/Universal install described later.

Live CD Install

The Gentoo live CD, included on this book's DVD, can be used to install a basic desktop system. This CD is for x86 computer architectures. If you are installing for a different architecture, you can find other live/install CDs from the "Where to Get Gentoo Linux" page (`www.gentoo.org/main/en/where.xml`). Then follow the procedures in the section "Starting Gentoo Installation from a Live CD" later in this chapter.

Minimal/Universal Install CD

To provide the full feel of installing Gentoo, you could begin with as little as a minimal disk image. From a minimal install disk, you can download and compile most of the software you need (including the kernel itself). To do this procedure, you need a broadband Internet connection (no dial-up). For architectures other than i686 and AMD64, there are also Universal and Package Gentoo CDs that you can use without having a live Internet connection.

For the minimal install, begin with the following CD image: `install-x86-minimal-2007.0.iso`. This bootable minimal install CD image (up to 130MB) includes just enough software to begin the install procedure. This CD image is included on the CD that comes with this book, so you can boot it directly from the CD. You can also find this image in any Gentoo mirror site (in the `releases/x86/2007.0/installcd` directory).

If you have computers that have non-x86 or AMD64 architectures, I recommend that you get the universal CD for your particular architecture instead, as well as the Packages CD before you begin installing.

- **install-*-universal-2007.0.iso** — This bootable install CD image contains enough software to enable you to have a working Gentoo system without going on the Internet. Look for the Universal Install CD link on the "Where to Get Gentoo Linux" page for your architecture (`www.gentoo.org/main/en/where.xml`).

- **packages-*-2007.0.iso** — This non-bootable CD image contains many popular packages you might want with Gentoo. The contents include popular, precompiled packages that you can add after the basic Gentoo system is installed. While this CD saves you download and compile time, it does not let you do the optimization for your particular machine on the packages it includes. Look for the Package CD link on the "Where to Get Gentoo Linux" page for your architecture.

Those two CDs enable you to do a complete Gentoo install without requiring that you access the Internet. You can download the disk images from Gentoo mirror sites (refer to `www.gentoo.org/main/en/mirrors.xml` for the locations of these sites).

For a more detailed description of the Gentoo install process, refer to the *Gentoo Linux x86 Quick Install Guide* and the larger, more general *Gentoo 2007.0 Handbook*. Look for these documents from links on the Gentoo Documentation Resources page (`www.gentoo.org/doc/en/index.xml`). Select Installation Related Resources for guides directly related to installation.

Starting Gentoo Installation from a Live CD

Here are the minimum computer requirements for a Gentoo installation using the live CD procedure described in this section:

- 1.5GB of hard disk space
- 256MB of RAM
- A 686 processor (or better) is recommended
- 256MB of swap space

Boot the Gentoo live CD from the DVD that comes with the book as follows:

1. **Insert the DVD.** Insert the DVD that comes with this book. Then, restart the computer and select to boot the Gentoo live CD image contained on that DVD. Log in as root with no password when you see the login prompt. You can get a list of available kernels by pressing F1 from the boot screen, shown in Figure 13-1.

FIGURE 13-1

The Gentoo boot screen

2. **Start the graphical installer.** From icons on the desktop, you have a choice of starting a graphical or text-based install. Then select either a standard or networkless install. If possible, I recommend starting the graphical (GTK) install.

3. **Click Forward.** Go forward from the Welcome screen.

4. **Configure networking.** Configure a connection on this page and click Forward. The page also includes a Misc tab from which you can start the Secure Shell daemon (sshd) and view loaded modules. You will see a partitioning screen.

5. **Partition your hard disk.** Choose which drive to install Gentoo on. Then choose either of the following:

   ▪ **Choose the unallocated space** — Select the gray part of the disk bar and add the partitions you want.

   ▪ **Choose the recommended layout** — Gentoo will recommend a partitioning layout for your disk.

   Create at least a 1GB swap partition and probably at least a 3GB or 4GB root (/) partition. A 100MB /boot partition is also recommended. If you have extra space, assign it to the root partition. You can delete partitions if you need more space, but first make sure to back up any data you need.

6. **Share your NFS connection.** You can connect to another machine if it contains a /usr/portage directory. The Stage screen appears after you click Forward.

7. **Select the type of install.** Choose Stage 3, GRP Install, and Dynamic if you want to do a quick install from the Live CD (no network connection is required for this). As an alternative, you can use other stage files. Click Forward to proceed to the Portage tree screen.

8. **Select the portage tree.** Click Forward to use the portage tree from the live CD. Otherwise, you need to choose the location of the Portage tree you want. You will see the make.conf screen.

9. **Change make.conf settings.** If you like, you can change the USE flags, CFLAGS, and other settings to use for your installation. Select Forward to see the kernel screen.

10. **Select a kernel.** Select livecd-kernel to use it as the kernel for the installed Gentoo system. To go to the bootloader screen, click Forward.

11. **Make your bootloader selection.** Select Grub as your bootloader. In most cases, you will want to install it in the master boot record (MBR) on the hard disk you want to boot from. (For multi-boot situations, you may want to install the boot loader to a different partition and update your master boot record later to point to all of your bootable partitions.) Click Forward to see the time zone screen.

12. **Select your time zone.** Choose your time zone from the map or list shown on the screen. Then click Forward to go to the Networking screen.

13. **Configure networking.** Choose your network interface (usually eth0) from the Interface box. Then either select DHCP or select Static (and add your IP address and other information by hand) and a hostname. If you need to connect to the Internet via a proxy server, you can enter the location of the proxy server on this screen as well. Click the Save button to save the interface settings. Click Forward to see the Daemons page.

14. **Select Logger and Cron.** Use the default Cron and System Logger daemons, unless you have some reason to do otherwise. Click Forward to go to the Extras Packages screen.

15. **Choose software packages.** Choose the packages you want on your system. Choose GRP packages to use prebuilt binaries. This will speed up the install process. Click Forward to see the Services screen.

16. **Choose services.** Turn on the services that will start up at boot time. Click Forward to go to the Other Settings screen.

17. **Select settings.** Choose settings associated with the display manager, keymaps, and other features that interest you. You also have the choice of setting the BIOS clock to UTC time. Click Forward to continue to the Users screen.

18. **Assign a root password.** Type in your root password and repeat. Select Add User to add an account for a regular user. Click Forward to see the Review screen.

19. **Check options.** Carefully review the install options you have selected. Click Save to save the settings for a future install. This is your last chance to exit before erasing your disk and installing packages! Select Install to reformat your hard disk and install Gentoo. The installation process will take a long time to complete. In fact, it could take a very long time!

20. **Finish installing.** Close the installer after you see the Install Complete! message.

21. **Exit and reboot.** Select to log out, and then choose to reboot the computer. After the system shuts down, remove the live CD and reboot the newly installed Gentoo system.

At this point, you can use the `emerge` command to add additional software packages to your installed Gentoo system. See the "Getting Software with emerge" section later in this chapter.

Starting Gentoo Installation from a Minimal CD

Here are the minimum computer requirements for a Gentoo installation using the minimal install procedure described in this chapter:

- 1.5GB of hard disk space
- 256MB of RAM
- A 686 processor (or better)
- 256MB of swap space

If you have a slow processor, consider getting precompiled packages because the full compilation process can take a long time.

Use the CD that comes with this book, as described in Appendix A. With this CD in hand, here's how to install Gentoo on your computer:

1. **Insert the CD.** Insert the CD into your computer's CD or DVD drive.

2. **Reboot.** Reboot your computer.

3. **Boot the CD.** From the boot prompt, press Enter. (If you are not able to boot the install medium, press F1 or F2 to see other install options that might help you get going.) Type **gentoo** at the boot: prompt to start the Gentoo live CD, or press the designated Gentoo function key to see other options for running Gentoo.

   Gentoo should detect your computer hardware, start the install process, and display a boot prompt.

4. **Set the date.** Type the `date` command to make sure the date and time are set correctly. If they need to be changed, use the `date` command (with options) to change them. For example, to set the date to 8:15 a.m., June 15, 2008, type:

   ```
   # date 061508152008
   ```

5. **Load modules.** If some piece of hardware was not autodetected, you may have to load the module you need to access that hardware. Use the `modprobe` command with the name of the module you want to load. For example, to load the module for an Orinoco wireless LAN card, you can type:

   ```
   # modprobe orinoco
   ```

 Do a Web search for "Linux" and the name of the hardware not being detected to find out what module to load.

6. **Configure the network.** Type **ifconfig eth0** to see if the Internet connection to your first Ethernet card is up and running. Then try to ping a computer on the Internet to make sure you can get out (for example, `ping www.gentoo.org`). If you are not able to pick up a DHCP server to automatically connect to the Internet, you can set up your Internet connection manually, by typing:

   ```
   # net-setup eth0
   ```

   Refer to the network configuration information in the installation procedure in Chapter 8 to help you answer questions about setting up your Internet connection manually.

7. **Partition the hard disk.** Partition your hard disk to prepare it to receive your Gentoo installation. You can use the `fdisk` utility to do this. Gentoo recommends a 64MB boot volume (ext2 file system), a swap partition that's double the size of your RAM, and a large root (/) partition (ReiserFS file system). Start `fdisk` by following the command with the name of your first hard disk (such as `/dev/hda` or `/dev/sda` for your first IDE or SCSI hard disk, respectively). Then type **h** to display a list of commands. (See Chapter 7 for information on using `fdisk` to partition your hard disk.)

   ```
   # fdisk /dev/hda
   ```

CAUTION   Repartitioning your disk destroys existing data on your hard disk. Back up any data you value before starting this procedure. Be sure not to delete or change any partitions that have data on them that you want to keep.

8. **Make file systems.** To create the appropriate file systems on your disk partitions, use the mk2fs and mkswap commands. For example, with an IDE hard drive that has the first partition as the boot partition (/dev/hda1), the second as swap (/dev/hda2), and the third as the root (/) partition (/dev/hda3), you can type the following:

```
# mke2fs /dev/hda1
# mkswap /dev/hda2
# mkreiserfs /dev/hda3
```

9. **Turn on swap.** Use the swapon command to turn on your swap partition. For our example (with hda2 being the swap partition), type:

```
# swapon /dev/hda2
```

10. **Mount the root (/) partition.** You need to mount the root (/) partition temporarily to begin installing Gentoo to it. In this example (with the root file system on /dev/hda3), type:

```
# mount /dev/hda3 /mnt/gentoo
```

11. **Mount the /boot partition.** Mount the boot partition so you can install boot files to that partition:

```
# mkdir /mnt/gentoo/boot
# mount /dev/hda1 /mnt/gentoo/boot
```

12. **Get the stage1 tarball.** Assuming that you have the minimal Gentoo installation CD, you need to download the stage1 tarball. Find a mirror site near you (as described earlier). Then make a directory on your hard disk to copy it to and download the tarball using a tool such as wget. Here is an example:

```
# mkdir /mnt/gentoo/tmp2
# cd /mnt/gentoo/tmp2
# wget -c http://gentoo.osuosl.org/releases/x86/2007.0/
  stages/stage1-x86-2007.0.tar.bz2
```

If you are using the universal CD, the stage1 tarball is available there. Instead of downloading it, jump to the next step and extract the tarball from /mnt/cdrom/stages/stage1*.tar.bz2.

NOTE The wget command, which appears on multiple lines here, should all be typed on one line. (There's no space between the slash at the end of the first line and the word "stages" at the beginning of the next.) If the download should stop in the middle, you can restart it by running the same command again in the same directory.

13. **Extract the stage 1 tarball.** Use the following commands:

```
# cd /mnt/gentoo
# tar -xvjpf /mnt/gentoo/tmp2/stage1-*.tar.bz2
```

You can remove the stage1 tarball once you have untarred it.

14. **Select the mirror site.** Use the `mirrorselect` command to search for a Gentoo mirror site from which you can efficiently download the files you need to do the install. Run the following command to select an efficient mirror and add it to your `make.conf` file (it will take a while to test the download speed from more than 150 servers):

```
# mirrorselect -s4 -o |grep GENTOO_MIRRORS >> /mnt/gentoo/etc/make.conf
```

> **NOTE** If, when you run `emerge` commands later in this procedure, you see messages that files are not found from any of the download sites, you might need to add other mirror sites to the `make.conf` file.

15. **Mount the file system.** Mount the `/proc` file system as follows:

```
# mount -t proc proc /mnt/gentoo/proc
```

16. **Change the root directory.** Use the `chroot` command to change `/mnt/gentoo` to be your root directory, but first copy the `resolve.conf` file so it can be used from there:

```
# cp /etc/resolv.conf /mnt/gentoo/etc/resolv.conf
# chroot /mnt/gentoo /bin/bash
```

17. **Update the Portage tree.** Type the following command to have the latest package information installed to your `/usr/portage` directory:

```
# emerge --sync
```

18. **Update the environment.** Read in environment variables as follows:

```
# env-update; source /etc/profile
```

19. **Modify the** `make.conf` **file.** Use the nano text editor to change the `make.conf` file that is used to build your Gentoo system, because that is the text editor available at this point. Use the `-w` option of `nano` so that configuration lines aren't wrapped around. (For more `nano` options, type **nano --help**.)

```
# nano -w /etc/make.conf
```

If you don't know what to change, refer to the `/etc/make.conf.example` file for information on the settings you may want to change before continuing. If you don't know what processor your computer has, type **cat /proc/cpuinfo**.

20. **Bootstrap Gentoo.** Run `bootstrap.sh` to bootstrap Gentoo as follows:

```
# cd /usr/portage/ ; scripts/bootstrap.sh
```

21. **Install Gentoo.** Before running the next command, understand that it could take a *very* long time to complete. With an old computer and slow Internet connection, it could take anywhere from hours to days to complete. If you are okay with that, run the following `emerge` command to install Gentoo:

```
# emerge -e system
```

 As noted earlier, it takes a long time for `emerge -e system` **command to complete. If it fails before it is finished, check that the settings in your** `make.conf` **file are correct.**

22. **Set the time zone.** Use the following command:

```
# ln -sf /usr/share/zoneinfo/path /etc/localtime
```

You need to replace `path` with the path to the file that represents the time zone your computer is in. For example, the entire path for Central time in the United States is `/usr/share/zoneinfo/US/Central`. (If your date and time are set incorrectly, you can run the `hwclock -s` command to set the system date and time from the BIOS.)

23. **Create a file system table.** Add the file systems you want to mount automatically at boot time to your `/etc/fstab` file. Here's an example:

```
# nano -w /etc/fstab
```

Here's what `/etc/fstab` might look like (given the partitions created earlier in this example procedure):

```
# <fs>                  <mountpoint> <type>   <opts>          <dump/pass>
/dev/hda1               /boot        ext2     noauto,noatime  1 2
/dev/hda2               none         swap     sw              0 0
/dev/hda3               /            reiserfs noatime         0 1
/dev/cdroms/cdrom0      /mnt/cdrom   auto     noauto,user     0 0
none                    /proc        proc     defaults        0 0
none                    /dev/shm     tmpfs    defaults        0 0
```

24. **Build a kernel.** Either install a prebuilt kernel or build one yourself. To build one, you need a kernel sources package (gentoo-sources is recommended). Type the `emerge` command as follows to get the gentoo-sources package:

```
# emerge gentoo-sources
```

Next, use the following command to get the genkernel package and configure a kernel using `menuconfig`:

```
# emerge genkernel
# genkernel --menuconfig all
```

After you have made any changes you want to your kernel configuration, select Exit, and then choose Yes to save it. At this point, genkernel makes your new kernel. This takes a while.

After genkernel is complete, note the names of the kernel and boot loader. (Type **ls /boot** to see the names.)

25. Add coldplug. Type the following to enable coldplug (so hardware outside of that which is detected during initialization is detected and configured automatically):

```
# emerge coldplug
# rc-update add coldplug boot
```

26. Configure system services. Install your system services — system logger, cron service, hotplug, and reiserfs service — and set the domain name. Then turn on each of those services, as follows:

```
# emerge syslog-ng
# rc-update add syslog-ng default
# emerge vixie-cron
# rc-update add vixie-cron default
# emerge hotplug
# rc-update add hotplug default
# emerge reiserfsprogs
```

27. Add special driver support. There may be particular kernel modules required by your computer at this point. For example, if you have a special Ethernet adapter or a special type of video card, use the emerge command to install kernel modules now. You may not need any of them. Here are a few examples:

```
# emerge nvidia-kernel
# emerge nforce-audio
# emerge e1000
# emerge ati-drivers
```

These emerge command lines are used only if you have special hardware associated with the kernel drivers. Respectively, those commands load drivers for accelerated NVidia video cards, audio for Nvidia NForce motherboards, fIntel e1000 Gigabit Ethernet cards, and ATI Radeon+/FireGL graphics acceleration video cards.

28. Add user and machine information. Add a password for the root user, a regular user account name of your choosing (chris in this example), a machine name, and a domain name. If you like, you can also edit the /etc/hosts and /etc/rc.conf files to add IP addresses and a hostname or change the basic system startup script.

```
# passwd
# useradd chris -m -G users,wheel,audio -s /bin/bash
```

```
# passwd chris
# echo mymachine > /etc/hostname
# echo mydomain.com > /etc/dnsdomainname
# nano -w /etc/hosts
# nano -w /etc/rc.conf
```

29. **Set up networking.** Edit the net file, and then run rc-update to add the eth0 interface as the default. (Uncomment the line iface eth0="dhcp" to have the network use DHCP to start up automatically.)

```
# nano -w /etc/conf.d/net
# rc-update add net.eth0 default
```

30. **Add kernel modules.** Add any extra kernel modules that you need to add at boot time. You usually need to do this only if some piece of hardware isn't detected and the module needed to use it isn't automatically loaded. Edit either the kernel-2.4 or kernel-2.6 file, depending on which kernel you are using.

```
# nano -w /etc/modules.autoload.d/kernel-`uname -r`
```

You can type **uname -a** to see what your current kernel version is.

31. **Configure the boot loader.** You need to install a boot loader (grub in this example) and configure it. The example makes the following assumptions about your setup. You need to replace any of the following information with the settings for your particular setup:

- Gentoo is installed on your first IDE hard disk (/dev/hda).
- You have a separate /boot partition on /dev/hda1.
- Your initrd file in the /boot directory is initramfs-genkernel-x86-2.6.18-gentoo-r2.
- Your kernel file in the /boot directory is kernel-genkernel-x86-2.6.18-gentoo-r2.

If any of that information is different for your setup, you need to adapt the following step appropriately. To configure grub, install it with emerge, run the grub command, and then create the grub.conf file as follows:

```
# emerge grub
# grub
grub> root (hd0,0)
grub> setup (hd0)
grub> quit
```

When you create the grub.conf file, you need to do the following:

```
# cd /boot/grub
# cp grup.conf.sample grub.conf
# nano -w /boot/grub/grub.conf
```

```
default 0
timeout 15
splashimage=(hd0,0)/grub/splash.xpm.gz
title=Gentoo Linux
  root (hd0,0)
  kernel /kernel-genkernel-x86-2.6.18-gentoo-r2 root=/dev/hda0
  initrd /initrd-genkernel-x86-2.6.18-gentoo-r2
```

32. **Reboot.** Exit from your chroot partition by running `umount` to unmount all partitions and then rebooting as follows:

```
# exit; cd /
# umount /mnt/gentoo/proc /mnt/gentoo
# reboot
```

Remove the installation disk and allow the computer to boot from hard disk. After a few moments, you should see the GRUB boot screen. Select Gentoo Linux (press Enter).

NOTE From here on, you will be booting from the hard disk and working directly from the operating system you installed. If you see error messages, such as missing kernel drivers, I recommend that you go to `http://forums.gentoo.com` and search for the driver that's causing problems. Chances are that someone else has had the same problem and can offer you a solution.

33. **Install a desktop.** For most of us, it's not much fun just working from the command line. The following command installs a basic set of desktop packages, including the X Window System (xfree), KDE desktop (kde), Mozilla browser (mozilla), and Openoffice.org office suite (openoffice-bin). (This takes a long time to install over the network.)

```
# emerge xorg-x11
```

At this point you can add a simple window manager, such as enlightenment. You could add the entire KDE desktop (`emerge kde`) or GNOME desktop, but I warn you that it will take a very, very long time to complete over the network. The Gentoo Quick Install Guide shows an example GNOME install (`emerge -vp gnome`) as taking nearly nine hours to complete and a complete KDE install (`emerge -vp kde-meta`) taking more than 19 hours to complete.

Here is an example of installing the enlightenment window manager:

```
# emerge enlightenment
```

After that, you should choose some desktop applications to install. For example, here's how to install the Firefox Web browser and Abiword word processor:

```
# emerge mozilla-firefox abiword
```

34. Configure the X server. Now that your desktop software is installed, you need to configure the X Window System to work properly with your video card and monitor. Type the following to configure your video card and monitor:

```
# Xorg -configure
```

The previous command creates a sample configuration file: `/root/xorg.conf.new`. Type the following command to test that configuration file:

```
# X -config /root/xorg.conf.new
```

If you see a gray screen with your mouse cursor represented by an X and able to move, the configuration file is basically working. To exit from X, press Ctrl+Backspace. Copy the file to its permanent location:

```
# cp /root/xorg.conf.new /etc/X11/xorg.conf
```

Now, you should be able to start your desktop interface:

```
# startx
```

If no window manager is found, or if you get a window manager you don't want such as twm, create a `$HOME/.xinitrc` file and indicate the file manager to use. For example, to use fluxbox as your window manager, add the following line to your `.xinitrc` file:

```
XSESSION=enlightenment
```

You can run `startx` again to start your desktop with the new window manager.

At this point you should have a working desktop. If you need help getting it working, refer to the Gentoo X Server Configuration HOWTO (`www.gentoo.org/doc/en/xorg-config.xml`). For documentation on configuring other parts of your Gentoo system, I recommend that you check out `www.gentoo.org/doc/en/index.xml`.

Getting Software with emerge

Following are some examples of some common uses of the `emerge` command that you can use with Gentoo. To use some of the examples, you need to either have a connection to the Internet or have downloaded all package updates to your local computer.

When the `emerge` command is run to install software or to get updated software packages, it looks on a Gentoo mirror site if it can't find the packages it needs locally. The first example lets you search (`-s`) the `/usr/portage` directory tree for packages that interest you. For example, to search for the package named bzflag, type the following:

```
# emerge -s bzflag
```

To build and install a package you choose, simply type **emerge** with the package name:

```
# emerge bzflag
```

To update your Portage directory tree so that it contains the latest information to install software packages, type the following:

```
# emerge sync
```

To get your Gentoo system up-to-date, use the `-uD world` option. The following command checks all the software packages you have installed on your computer, and then goes to a Gentoo mirror site to download and install the latest versions of each of those packages:

```
# emerge -uD world
```

To view the many other options available with `emerge`, type **man emerge** or run `emerge` with the help option:

```
# emerge -h | less
```

You can use `emerge` to install packages contained on your local computer or have the packages downloaded automatically from Gentoo software mirror sites. During the build process, `emerge` handles getting all the dependencies that the software you choose requires.

Summary

In just a few years, Gentoo distinguished itself as a premier distribution for Linux enthusiasts who are interested in complete control of the components and settings of their Linux systems.

The jewel of the Gentoo system is the Portage package management system. Using the Portage `emerge` command, you can install any of thousands of Gentoo software packages. Those packages can be downloaded and built from scratch, using settings you choose, to tune them for how you use your Linux system.

An improved Gentoo installer that is bootable from the Gentoo live CD has made it much easier to get started using Gentoo. Using the more detailed minimal installation, also contained in this chapter, you have more opportunities to tune and tweak your operating system exactly as you want it to be.

Chapter 14

Running Slackware Linux

A sk old-time Linux users about the first Linux distribution they used and many will tell you it was Slackware. Slackware is the oldest Linux distribution still actively developed today. Although it does not have a fancy graphical installer or specialized GUI tools, Slackware still has a loyal following and is a good way to get a basic Linux system that is both secure and stable.

This chapter explores the Slackware distribution, discusses its strengths and weaknesses, and introduces those who use it. It also explains how to install Slackware.

[the DVD-ROM] The first CD of the Slackware 12.0 three-CD set is included on the DVD that comes with this book. The SLAX live CD (which is based on Slackware) is also included and can be booted directly. You can buy the complete Slackware 12.0 from the Slackware Store (`http://store .slackware.com`) or find out where to download the DVD or other CD images from the Slackware site (`www.slackware.com/getslack`).

Getting into Slackware

Although full graphical installs and GUI administration tools can make installing and configuring Linux easy, those tools carry with them some overhead. They also hide some of the details of how Linux is being configured.

Ask Slackware devotees the value of Slackware and they might recite their mantra, the "4S Rule": Stable, Solid, Simple, and Sensible. By keeping things basic, Slackware offers the following advantages:

- **Better comprehension** — Because you use commands and configuration files with Slackware, you learn more about how Linux works on the inside. Most graphical installers and GUI tools hide the actual configuration that is going on and often limit the features you can use. If something goes wrong, it can be hard to debug a problem with most graphical interfaces. The Slackware installer is menu-based, very flexible, and quite intuitive.

- **Less bloat** — In general, graphical interfaces consume far more resources than their command-line counterparts. GUIs require more room on the distribution medium, plus more hard disk space and more RAM. GUIs also may not run well, or at all, on certain underpowered or unsupported video cards. Slackware relies primarily on basic Linux commands, text-based configuration files, and some simple menu-driven administration tools.

- **Better for low-end computers** — Slackware is the first distribution I recommend to run on low-end machines. A special ZipSlack distribution (`www.slackware.com/zipslack`) can be installed from a 100MB Zip drive or floppy disks. ZipSlack can install on a 386 PC with as little as 4MB of RAM. Even with the latest Slackware distribution, if you want a GUI, the installation procedure for Slackware lets you choose small, efficient window managers, Web browsers, mail clients, and other graphical tools.

- **Stable and secure** — While other Linux distributions deliver the latest kernel, glibc, and other critical components of Linux as their default, Slackware opts for more stable, well-tested versions. In Slackware 12.0, the default kernel is 2.6.21.5 while later kernels are available in `/extra` and `/testing` directories. As security issues come up, new packages are made available and announcements are posted (`www.slackware.com/security`).

- **Packages as projects intended** — Slackware doesn't mold the software it includes into one look-and-feel. The Apache Web server, KDE desktop, or Samba file/printer sharing projects work pretty much as they are delivered from those projects. So, again, the knowledge you gain from using those projects will transfer fairly easily to those same projects on other Linux systems.

Instead of providing a unified look-and-feel, Slackware gives you the maximum amount of control. It allows the desktop environment or window manager you choose to dictate the desktop presentation. You can change your desktop as you like, using the menus or preference windows that come with those environments. A full KDE desktop environment is included with Slackware. Or you can opt for a lighter, more efficient window manager, such as XFCE4, fvwm2, or twm.

NOTE The GNOME desktop environment was dropped from Slackware 10.2 and remains out of the distribution. Patrick Volkerding, Slackware's creator/maintainer, cited demands of keeping up with GNOME development changes and some GNOME features that don't match Slackware objectives (such as including PAM and replacing some system packages, such as X11). Volkerding suggests `http://gware.sf.net` if you want to add GNOME to your own installation of Slackware.

For system administration, Slackware offers some tools based on the ncurses text-mode windowing library. Ncurses allows an application to provide a screen-oriented interface on a character terminal, so you can use forms, menus, and sometimes even a mouse to configure some basic Linux features from any shell (no X-based GUI required).

Recently added Slackware package management tools (such as the `slackpkg` command) have made the tasks of adding, removing, and upgrading packages much easier. For information on `slackpkg` see `http://slackpkg.sourceforge.net`. There are also tools for creating your own Slackware packages (such as the `slacktrack` command). In the true Slackware tradition, Slackware packages are quite simple: basically a tarball of files with an install script.

Anything you can do with other Linux distributions, you can do with Slackware. It might just take a bit more manual work to get there.

NOTE Slackware comes with a good set of libraries that will take care of the dependency needs of most Linux applications. However, for video, audio, and some other types of applications, you may find yourself hunting around for libraries.

Characterizing the Slackware Community

Like many other successful Linux distributions, Slackware was started by a strong-minded individual who created the kind of Linux system that suited him. Slackware users are generally people who pretty much agree with him.

The Slackware Creator

Patrick Volkerding started Slackware in 1993 as a Linux distribution to use for himself and his friends. He was kind enough to answer some questions I had about Slackware, and I want to share his answers with you here.

Patrick originally used a Linux distribution called SLS Linux (named after Soft Landing Linux, the company that made it).

Q: Why didn't you just contribute to SLS instead of starting your own distribution?

A: I tried. By April of 1993 I had collected a huge list of bugs in SLS, along with the fixes for most of them. Plenty of people tried to get these to Peter MacDonald (SLS's author/maintainer) but the bugs in SLS (many of which were quite obvious) never seemed to get fixed.

Of course, I'd started work on my patched version of SLS with no plan to try to launch a lasting distribution. I figured I'd get it online and SLS would fix the issues, and that might just be that. SLS was a great distribution and isn't given enough credit for all the ideas that started there. Unfortunately it was while Peter was busy working on inventing kernel modules that SLS sat online for a few months full of bugs and not getting any updates.

Patrick decided to take the leap to separate Slackware from SLS after MacDonald suggested that Slackware was infringing on his copyrights (despite the only license on the SLS code saying, "Distribute freely; do not restrict").

Q: So, what did you do?

A: I promised Peter that I would write a new installer for Slackware instead of using a modified SLS one, and that the new installer would be the next change made to Slackware online.

Q: Did the great success of Slackware from the get-go surprise you?

A: Absolutely. I knew it worked better than the other distributions that were out at the time, but I didn't expect the kind of mass exodus from SLS that occurred.

Q: What kind of person is attracted to Slackware over other Linux distros?

A: It seems to attract the kind of users who want to configure software the old-fashioned way (using a text editor), and who don't want a lot of unnecessary things running in the background. I try to compile software with as few of my own changes as possible, which also makes it pretty easy to update things from source if you decide to go that route.

In the early days of Linux I think most of the users were like this, and as time has moved on and various distributions have focused on different markets, the profile of the average Linux user has changed quite a lot. Most of today's commercial Linux distributions seem to target a user who wants to administer his machine with a point-and-click interface much like Windows. Slackware and other lower-level distributions serve a different niche — users who don't mind a learning curve if it means the operating system will stay out of their way.

Today, Patrick is still the Project lead and maintains complete control over Slackware's features and release schedule. In this arrangement, Patrick can choose the features to include, and he doesn't add features that don't suit him (even popular ones).

Q: How would you characterize the Slackware development process?

A: Most of what I do is research — trying to figure out where Linux is going so I can make (I hope) sane choices about what to implement. There's not really a core development team (which really streamlines the development process by sidestepping the usual time-wasting squabbles that usually happen in any official development hierarchy). But I get a ton of help from people who e-mail me with problems or suggestions that lead to an upgrade or fix somewhere in the system.

The best way to keep up with Slackware development issues is to read the Change Logs (available from the Slackware home page). Slackware aficionados expect releases on an "it's ready when it's ready" schedule, as the Slackware FAQ notes: "As things are built for the upcoming release, they'll be uploaded into the -current tree. If the -current does not exist, it probably means we have just released a new version of Slackware."

Slackware Users

From a purely subjective perspective, my friends who use Slackware tend to be technically oriented, but not the extreme overclockers and tweakers who might be drawn to Gentoo, for example. They like Slackware because it works so simply and so well that they believe it gives them more time to slack.

Slackware users often think of themselves as loners, despite the fact that they all hang out together at LAN parties and Internet cafes. They like the more purist, less commercial approach of Slackware. For their personal desktop, gaming box, or small-office server, they see no need for the graphical tools that you get with Red Hat Enterprise Linux or SUSE Linux systems. They are comfortable with commands and man pages.

I've often heard users refer to Slackware as being easier to use than other Linux distributions. To someone coming from a UNIX or BSD background, this is probably true. You don't have to wait for graphical tools to pop up and almost everything is covered on a man page.

NOTE Man pages are the traditional means of documenting commands, file formats, devices, system calls, and most any other component of a UNIX or Linux system. Man pages date back to the very first UNIX systems. You can read man pages using the `man` command, followed by a component name, from any shell. To learn about how the man page system itself works, type **man man**.

Slackware Internet Sites

The Slackware home page (`www.slackware.com`) is a good place to start looking for information about Slackware. There are two main mailing lists plus an IRC channel available through the Web site, as well as links to download sites, some documentation, and the Slackware Store (`store.slackware.com`).

There's a Slackware Linux Essentials online book (`www.slackbook.org/`) and four FAQs (`www.slackware.com/faq/`) available from the Slackware site. There's no "news" to speak of at the Slackware site, so the best way to keep up on what's happening with the project is to read the change logs (`www.slackware.com/changelog/`).

For information on the Slackware version described in this chapter (Slackware 12.0), refer to the release announcement (`www.slackware.com/announce/12.0.php`). Refer to the package changes list (`www.slackware.com/announce/12.0.php`) for details on working with this release.

Outside of the official Slackware site, a lot of new sites have been popping up recently that provide information about Slackware. A good place to bring questions about Slackware is `http://linuxquestions.org` (follow the links: Forums ➪ Linux Distributions ➪ Slackware). The Linux Packages site (`www.linuxpackages.net`) offers some active Forums on different aspects of Slackware.

Challenges of Using Slackware

There is no commercial organization behind Slackware and no official support, so, if something goes wrong with your Slackware system, you are on your own to solve the problem. The Slackware project, however, does maintain a list of third-party organizations that provide technical support at `www.slackware.com/support/`.

Although functionally Slackware can be used in most any computing environment, in places where you feel the need to have a company behind the computer systems you install (such as a large enterprise), you would do better to look toward a Red Hat or SUSE system.

The lack of official package management tools used to pose another challenge to Slackware users. While Slackware's packaging tools are a great improvement over just installing from tarballs, those tools have not yet reached the level of sophistication you get with those available with RPM-based (Red Hat, SUSE, Mandriva, and so on) or Deb-based (Debian, Ubuntu, KNOPPIX, and so on) distributions.

When a software package made to add to Slackware requires a library that is not in the standard Slackware distribution, the developers often build the needed library into the package. If the software fails, however, indicating a missing library, you can try a couple of things:

- Look in the software package's README file for descriptions of the libraries it needs.
- Use the ldd command to determine the libraries a command needs (for example, typing ldd /bin/cat shows the libraries needed by the cat command).
- Search the Web for the terms "Slackware" and the name of the missing library.

COMING FROM WINDOWS As someone comfortable with UNIX and Linux, I find the text-based tools that come with Slackware helpful and fairly simple to use. If you are coming from a Windows environment, however, you may find the lack of GUI-based tools and cohesive end-to-end procedures for setting up features a bit disconcerting.

Because Slackware is not backed up by a big support organization, it has not made much headway into the corporate enterprise arena. The fact that most commercial applications are created specifically for Red Hat Enterprise Linux or, to a lesser extent, SUSE distributions, and won't just run out-of-the-box on Slackware, makes Slackware an even harder sell for corporate environments.

Using Slackware as a Development Platform

Slackware has long been a preferred platform for developing open source software. It contains a large set of libraries and includes nearly every tool you could want for developing applications. There are special spin-off projects for Slackware developers as well, such as the Slackware for ARM processor project for developing embedded Linux applications (www.armedslack.org).

Because Slackware is a clean, basic Linux system, applications that run in Slackware will run on most other Linux systems as well. In other words, you won't be encouraged to add a lot of special Slackware hooks that would prevent software from being portable across a wide range of Linux, UNIX, and BSD systems.

Slackware can easily provide an efficient development workstation environment for technical people because the distribution doesn't get in the way of its powerful features. It's easy to configure a simple window manager and not incur the overhead of background processes that try to "help" you when you insert a CD or need software updates. Slackware simply gives you an efficient desktop that lets you do what you need to do, keeps you as close to the silicon as possible, and otherwise stays out of your way.

If you become interested in building and submitting packages for Slackware, there are some good descriptions of how to do so at the Linux Packages site (www.linuxpackages.net). Look for links to building and submitting packages on the site's home page in the Information box.

Installing Slackware

Slackware is freely available from several different sources. It installs and runs well on low-end computers. Some Linux or UNIX expertise would be useful, especially if something goes wrong.

Getting Slackware

Slackware 12.0 comes on a single DVD (about 3.7GB) or six CDs: three installation CDs and three source code CDs. The first Slackware CD can be used for a good, basic install. That CD is included on the DVD that comes with this book. I recommend installing from that CD for a computer that has limited disk space and an older processor.

The full Slackware distribution set is also available from a few dozen mirror sites on the Web (see www.slackware.com/getslack). Because of disk space issues and to maximize bandwidth, the Slackware project recommends you get the DVD or CD images (ISOs) using BitTorrent. For a list of available torrents, see www.slackware.com/getslack/torrents.php.

 For many years, Slackware was available on one install CD, but adding KDE to the distribution made additional CDs necessary.

To help support the project, you can purchase the boxed set of Slackware from http://store.slackware.com. At the store, you also can get a subscription to Slackware so that the Slackware Store sends you a new version each time one is released (every six to eight months). The store will just ship it when it's available and charge your credit card. People who like Slackware often pay the subscription fee just to show their support.

New Features in Slackware 12.0

With Slackware 12.0, the distribution consists of three installation CDs (plus three source code CDs) and/or a DVD version that holds everything. While still offering a stable foundation (the 2.6.21.5 kernel is used by default), Slackware includes bleeding-edge components for the desktop (KDE 3.5.7 or XFCE 4.4.1) and applications (the latest Firefox browser and Thunderbird e-mail client).

Here are a couple of applications that were added to Slackware recently that might interest you:

- **X11 7.2.0** — The X.Org Foundation's modular X Window System. This offers improvements with performance and hardware support.
- **SeaMonkey 1.1.2** — Contains a combination Web browser, e-mail client, IRC chat client, newsgroup client, and HTML client. In Slackware, SeaMonkey replaces the Mozilla suite as the all-in-one Internet suite.

Along with these applications, Slackware has added recent popular updates to many of its existing applications and facilities (Firefox, Thunderbird, XFCE, and many others). To work with software packages in Slackware 12.0, the distribution now includes the Slackware Package Browser. This Web application enables you to search a Slackware packages database, making it much easier than it was in the past to find the Slackware software you want.

Hardware Requirements

While some older versions of Slackware will run on a 386, the Slackware site recommends 486 as a minimum processor. Without a graphical interface (X Window System), the minimum amount of RAM required is 16MB. With the GUI, at least 128MB of RAM is recommended. If you intend to use the KDE desktop environments, you can't have too much RAM (KDE in Slackware runs effectively with 256MB RAM or more, depending on your applications).

The ZipSlack distribution is a small Slackware distribution that you can install from a Zip drive or floppy disks. ZipSlack can install on a hard disk with as little as 100MB space. You can find ZipSlack on any Slackware mirror site.

If you are installing Slackware 12.0, 500MB is the minimum amount of disk space you should have available on your Linux partition. The recommended amount of hard disk space is at least 3.5GB for a full desktop install.

Slackware supports all IDE and SCSI controllers supported by the Linux kernel itself.

Starting Installation

Although the Slackware installer has evolved over the years, its basic look-and-feel hasn't changed much. There are some things you still need to do manually, such as setting up RAID or doing partitioning.

The following steps describe how to install Slackware from the first installation CD. For the purposes of this book, this procedure demonstrates a minimal installation from the first Slackware CD. If you want to install Linux on low-end hardware (slow CPU and minimal RAM), this procedure is a great way to end up with a workable, minimal desktop system.

If you want to do a more complete installation of Slackware, you should obtain the Slackware 12.0 DVD or three-CD installation set. For more detailed information (or if something goes wrong during the installation that isn't covered here), refer to the Slackware-HOWTO, which is on the first Slackware CD.

1. Obtain a Slackware installation disc. (As mentioned earlier, you can boot the CD image from the DVD that comes with this book as described in Appendix A, or download it from a Slackware mirror site and burn it to CD.)

2. Insert the DVD that comes with this book into the drive and reboot your computer.

3. From the boot prompt, type **slack** and press Enter to start the default boot process. If you are using a Slackware CD instead of this book's DVD, simply press Enter.

If the Slackware installation boots properly, you are prompted to enter a keyboard map.

> **NOTE** If your Slackware medium won't boot, refer to the BOOTING.TXT file on the Slackware CD for information on things you can try to get around the problem. (If you can't access the CD at all, you can get this file from any Slackware mirror site.)

4. If you are using a U.S. keyboard map, press Enter; to use a keyboard map for a different language/country, type **1**, press Enter, and then select the language/country you want. The Slackware login prompt appears.

5. Type **root** and press Enter. A shell prompt appears.

6. Partition your hard disk. Chapter 7 explains how to partition your hard disk. Slackware doesn't have a graphical partitioning tool, such as Disk Druid, so you have to use the fdisk or cfdisk command to partition your hard disk (again, refer to Chapter 7 or see the Slackware-HOWTO for details).

To install Slackware, you should have at least one swap partition (up to twice the size of your RAM, with a maximum of about 500MB) and one Linux partition (such as ext3). You should have at least 500MB of hard disk space, with a recommended 3GB of disk space available for a full install of Slackware 12.0.

7. Enter setup mode. Type the following command to enter setup mode:

`# setup`

The Slackware Linux Setup screen appears, with the following options:

```
HELP       Read the Slackware Setup Help file
KEYMAP     Remap your keyboard if you're not using a US one
ADDSWAP    Set up your swap partition(s)
TARGET     Set up your target partitions
SOURCE     Select source media
SELECT     Select categories of software to install
INSTALL    Install selected software
CONFIGURE  Reconfigure your Linux system
EXIT       Exit Slackware Linux Setup
```

Type the first letter in the option name (or use the arrow keys) to highlight the option you want, and then press Enter. The following steps describe options you need to configure Slackware.

8. Select ADDSWAP. The Swap Space Detected menu appears, listing the swap partitions you have available. Select the one you want (there will usually be just one) and select Yes to install it as your swap partition. (If you don't have a swap partition, exit the setup screen and run fdisk to create one.)

The swap partition will be checked for bad blocks, formatted, and activated. Select OK to continue. The Select Linux Installation Partition menu appears.

9. Select a root partition. From the Linux partition that is displayed, highlight the one that you want to use as your root (/) partition and choose Select. The / partition is where Linux and all your data will go by default. (Other partitions can be added later.)

   Choose to do a quick format (Format) or a slow format that includes bad block checking (Check). Or you can select No to not format the partition.

NOTE Typically you would overwrite your / partition, although you might keep data from another partition. I often maintain a separate data partition that I will attach to the file system in a location such as /mnt/data. With that technique, I can keep my data and still install a whole new operating system.

   Choose the file system type for the root file system. These days, most people select either the ext3 or reiserfs file system as their Linux root partition. Both of those file system types do journaling, so they can recover quickly if the system is shut down improperly (such as when someone kicks out the power cord).

   Choose the Inode Density. Select 4096 (the default, which is fine in most cases), 2048, or 1024 bytes. (A smaller number allows more inodes on the file system, which is useful only if you have many small files, as you might on a news server.)

10. Select other partitions. If you created other Linux partitions, you can assign file system types and format them as well. Identify where in the file system the other partitions are connected. (Again, check Chapter 7 for information on where you might want to attach a partition to you Linux file system.)

11. Choose your source media. Select 1, in most circumstances, so that Slackware is installed from the CD. You can also install Slackware from a partition on your hard drive, from an NFS shared file system, or from a premounted directory.

   You can have Setup scan for your Slackware CD or tell it a particular device to use (if you have multiple drives and you want to tell it which to use).

12. Select the different package series that you want to install and press OK. General package series include:

   ▪ Base Linux system (the core of the operating system and basic utilities)

   ▪ Various applications that do not need X (non-graphical commands)

   ▪ Program Development (C, C++, Lisp, Perl, and so on)

   ▪ GNU Emacs (a text editor)

   ▪ FAQ lists, HOWTO documentation

   ▪ Linux kernel source

   ▪ Qt and the K Desktop Environment for X

   ▪ International support for KDE

- System libraries (needed by X, KDE, and others)
- Networking (TCP/IP, UUCP, mail, news, and so on)
- TeX typesetting
- Tcl/Tk scripting languages
- X Window System
- X Applications
- Games

If you are installing from the single CD image, deselect KDE and KDEI because they come on the second CD. Later in the installation process, you have an opportunity to select a simple window manager such as XFCE, Blackbox, Fluxbox, or fvwm2.

> **NOTE** While it's safest just to install everything with the three install CDs so that you're sure to have everything you want and won't miss a dependent package, Slackware CD I had no dependency problems simply deselecting the KDE package group.

13. Choose how you are prompted to select packages. After you have selected the package series you want to install, you can choose to further refine the installation of those packages or simply go with the defaults by selecting one of the following:

- **Full** — Installs everything without prompting or interaction. You can use this option if you have only the first CD or the DVD.
- **Expert** — Enables you to choose individual packages interactively.
- **Menu** — Enables you to choose groups of packages interactively.
- **Newbie** — Shows you a lot about what is being installed on your Slackware system and lets you choose whether to install optional packages. You just have to sit there for a long time and keep pressing Enter.

When prompted, either choose to continue (if you have another Slackware CD you want to install) or Quit (to just install from the first CD). You are asked to install a kernel.

14. Choose a Linux kernel. In most cases where you have an IDE controller, you can use the kernel from the installation boot disk or choose the Slackware CD as the location for getting the kernel your installed Slackware system will ultimately use. Remove Slackware CD 2 and reinsert the Slackware CD 1 and press Enter. In most cases, you should choose the default `bare.i` kernel. If you have a SCSI controller, choose one of the kernels with a `.s` at the end. If your computer has very little RAM, try the `lowmem.i` kernel.

15. Make a boot disk. If you have a floppy drive, make a boot disk. It will enable you to reboot your computer if your hard disk ever becomes unbootable. If you don't have a floppy drive, you can use the Slackware install CD as a boot disk in an emergency.

16. Configure a modem. Select No Modem if you don't plan to use a modem with your computer. If you have an external, serial modem, choose the COM port it is connected to (represented by `/dev/tty?`, with COM1 associated with `ttyS0`). For PCI modems (slots directly in the motherboard), device names usually begin at `/dev/ttyS4`.

17. Enable the hotplug subsystem. Select Yes to enable the hotplug subsystem at boot time. This lets Slackware try to activate devices that are plugged into the computer while it is running (such as Cardbus and USB devices). By enabling the system at boot time, it can also detect other hardware, including PCI cards.

18. Install the LILO boot loader. Choose Simple to have the setup process try to automatically install the LILO boot loader, or choose Expert if you want to configure the boot loader to do something special. If you want to add kernel parameters and set framebuffer console features, you can use either mode, but certain tasks require Expert mode:

- Adding other bootable Linux partitions

- Adding a bootable Windows partition

- Installing an existing lilo.conf file, instead of creating a new one

You can have graphics appear on the boot screen by enabling the frame buffer console. Choose the resolution and number of colors (such as 1024 × 768 × 256) to use with the frame buffer console.

When prompted, add any parameters you want fed to the kernel when you boot. In particular, you might add kernel parameters if you want to turn off autoprobing on certain devices (for example, nousb) or turn off power management features (noacpi). Chapter 11 describes some kernel parameters that might be useful to you.

LILO is usually placed in the root of the Linux partition or in the master boot record for the entire hard disk. It's safest to put LILO in the superblock (Root) of the Linux partition or on a formatted floppy disk. For the former, you need to indicate that the Linux partition is bootable (using the fdisk command when you return to a shell prompt). It can be unsafe to put LILO in the master boot record. However, for a system on which only one operating system is installed (in this case, Slackware), the master boot record is a common place to put LILO.

19. Configure the mouse. Select the type of mouse connected to your system. You are also given the opportunity to configure gpm, which lets you use your mouse to select, cut, and paste text in virtual consoles (text windows).

20. Configure the network. Select Yes to configure your network (that is, your LAN connection from your Ethernet card). Refer to Chapter 7 for information on configuring your network connection.

21. Select startup services. For server software that you installed, you need to tell Slackware whether to start that service at boot time. In general, you should turn on only services you want to have on (you can always turn any others on later). Among the services that will be on by default (assuming you installed the packages) are the sshd service, to enable remote login using SSH; system logging (rc.syslog), to log system activity; and Sendmail, to receive e-mail. To share your printer, you may want to enable CUPS; to be a Web server, you should turn on Apache (rc.httpd).

22. Configure console fonts. You can try some custom screen fonts. If you find one you particularly like, you can choose to use it instead of the default.

23. Set the hardware clock. The clock on your computer can be set to local time or to UTC time (or Greenwich Mean Time). Most often, you will set it to local time, especially if you dual-boot between operating systems (see `http://tldp.org/HOWTO/Clock-2.html` for information on how Linux keeps track of time).

24. Choose a time zone. Select your current time zone from the list.

25. Select a default window manager. Choices include the KDE and XFCE desktop environments or any of a number of smaller simple window managers, such as Blackbox, Fluxbox, fvwm2 (selections look like Windows systems), and TWM (too lightweight for most people). If you installed only from the first Slackware CD, KDE is not among your choices because it is installed from the second installation CD.

26. Set root password. Select a root password when you are prompted to do so.

    At this point you can return to the Slackware Linux Setup menu.

27. Select EXIT to leave the setup screen. The install CD should eject.

28. Press Ctrl+Alt+Delete to reboot your computer.

Starting with Slackware

The LILO Boot menu appears when you first boot Slackware. It should contain at least a listing for your Linux partition and possibly for a Windows partition (if there is one on your computer).

Press Enter at the boot prompt to start Slackware. Log in as the root user when you see the login prompt. You are going to be at a Linux command line prompt; if you don't know what that is, refer to Chapter 2.

Here are a few things you might want to do to get started with Slackware:

- **Get mail** — Type **mail** at the command-line prompt. You should have a couple of mail messages there for the root user, including one from Patrick Volkerding. Type the number of that message and page through it (using the Enter key) to read some additional setup steps that may interest you. (Type **q** to exit the message and **x** to exit mail).

- **Add another user** — Because you shouldn't use the root user account for your daily use of Linux, you should add a regular user account and give it a password. Here's what you run to add a user named robby:

```
# useradd -m robby
# passwd robby
Changing password for robby
New password: ********
Re-enter new password: ********
```

Be sure to use the `-m` option to `useradd` (to automatically create the new user's directory) or you will have to create a home directory for that user manually.

- **Start the desktop** — If you installed X and either a window manager or whole desktop environment (KDE or XFCE), you can start it by typing:

```
# startx
```

If X and your chosen desktop don't start properly (the screen may be unreadable or X may simply crash), press Ctrl+Alt+Backspace to exit X and return to the shell. Instructions for solving X problems, choosing different window managers, and configuring X are included in Chapter 3's "Configuring Your Own Desktop" section.

- **Configure sound** — When you first boot Slackware, the ALSA sound system should be set up to work, but the volume is muted. To configure ALSA and check that your sound card is ready to go, as root user run the `alsaconf` command. It searches for installed sound cards, and when it finds one, it adds any modules needed to use the card, raises the volume, and tests the card.

Once your sound card is configured, use the `alsamixer` command to adjust volume levels for your sound card.

- **Add modules** — If any of your computer hardware was not properly detected and configured, you can add the modules you need after Slackware is running.

NOTE   If some of your computer hardware is not being detected properly, and you don't know what module is required for it to work, try booting KNOPPIX (from the DVD included with this book). If the hardware works in KNOPPIX, run the `lsmod` command to see what modules are loaded. From that list, you should be able to add the necessary modules as just described.

- **Configure a printer** — Because Slackware now includes the CUPS facility for printing (replacing LPRng), you can configure your printers using any Web browser. The best way to begin adding and configuring a printer is to type the following into a location box on any Web browser on your Slackware system:

```
http://localhost:631:/admin
```

Enter the root username and your root password when prompted. Then select the Add printer button to begin adding your printer to your CUPS printing server on your Slackware system.

- **Configure networking** — If you didn't configure your Ethernet cards at installation time, you can do it now. Type the following command:

```
# netconfig
```

The menu system enables you to configure your network interface using the same screens as at installation.

- **Install additional software packages** — The `slackpkg` command is the preferred tool for downloading and installing software for Slackware. You can download the slackpkg package from `http://slackpkg.sourceforge.net`. Once you have the slackpkg package, install it by typing **installpkg slackpkg***. With slackpkg installed, edit the `/etc/slackpkg/mirrors` file and uncomment a single repository that you will use to get software packages.

  You are now ready to start using slackpkg. First, type **slackpkg update** to get available updates for your Slackware system. Then you can install the packages you want by typing **slackpkg install** *packagename*, where *packagename* is the name of the package you want to install.

NOTE One place to find Slackware packages is `LinuxPackages.net`. Likewise, you can install software packages from any open source project (such as `sourceforge.net`) that are either identified as being created for Slackware or simply tar.gz packages that you can build from scratch.

If you are used to other Linux systems, you should familiarize yourself with a few things you might find different in Slackware. For example, system startup scripts are contained in `/etc/rc.d`, rather than a whole series of links to various `/etc/rc?.d` directories.

Summary

Slackware is the oldest active Linux distribution. It is run by Patrick Volkerding, as it has been for more than a decade, and keeps as its goals stability and security. Slackware has a loyal following, but the project is not geared for wide deployment in enterprise computing situations. Slackware is a great distribution to learn Linux on because it keeps its configuration simple and near to the command line and configuration files.

Look for Slackware to continue to be among the most efficient Linux distributions. There are currently no plans to add a graphical installer, although the project recently began encouraging the use of slackpkg for installing packages. You can expect Slackware to remain trim and true to its roots, making it one of the best Linux distributions to run on older computer hardware.

Chapter 15

Running Linspire and Freespire

T he brief history of Linspire is colorful and has been portrayed as a "David and Goliath" story, at least in some of the news media. In this case, Linspire is David and a PC desktop market share is Goliath. While Goliath seems to have gotten his way, to some extent, David is still breathing.

Linspire is a commercial, desktop-oriented Linux system that has made a play for the retail market. Linspire, Inc. has marketed itself as a direct competitor to Microsoft Windows by offering boxed sets of Linspire, as well as preinstalled versions on inexpensive PCs.

Freespire is a community project backed by Linspire, Inc., which provides a more traditional Linux distribution freely available on the Internet. Selected versions of Freespire will become the basis of future Linspire releases.

This chapter describes what Linspire and Freespire are, their major features, how to install them, and where to find more information.

IN THIS CHAPTER

Understanding Freespire, Linspire, and Lindows

Linspire support and software

Installing Linspire

Overview of Linspire

Linspire began as Lindows, founded by Michael Robertson in 2001, after his tenure with MP3.com. His goal was to bring Linux to the desktop once and for all.

The general concept was to develop an operating system that would be inexpensive, easy to install and use, and a competitive alternative to Microsoft Windows on the desktop PC. To accomplish that, Lindows needed to be simple enough for a nontechnical user (even someone who has never really used a PC before) to install, configure, and use. While this is, indeed, a laudable goal, most of this product's press has come as the result of its tension with Microsoft Corporation.

The main point of public contention with Microsoft was the name *Lindows*. In several legal proceedings, Microsoft claimed that the Lindows name infringed on the term Windows, which Microsoft claimed as a trademark. Lindows and many others contended that the term *windows* was generic before Microsoft began using the term.

Microsoft's attempts to get U.S. courts to protect the Windows trademark were not initially successful, but in countries including Finland, Sweden, Belgium, the Netherlands, and Luxembourg, Microsoft was able to get injunctions against Lindows. Because of those rulings, and related threats of massive fines being imposed, Lindows stated that it could not remedy the situation without changing its name.

The rulings supported Microsoft's contentions that Lindows infringed on the Microsoft Windows trademark, and that Lindows could not allow citizens of those countries to access the Lindows Web site or access products with the Lindows name. Because keeping any country's residents off of a particular Web site would have proved very difficult, Lindows had to make some drastic changes, most notably the alteration of its name.

Microsoft was still pursuing an injunction or summary judgment and would soon see its Windows trademark challenged in court. To avoid a costly court battle, Microsoft offered a reported $20 million and some other items, including some technology licensing, to settle the case. Linspire accepted, and that was the end of the dispute.

Early in 2006, Linspire, Inc. announced the launch of the Freespire project. Rather than being a corporate product, Freespire is to be developed in the tried-and-true Linux style via an open community of developers and users communicating over the Internet. As well as expanding Linspire's user base beyond the core constituency of consumers and Windows converts to more experienced (or at least more adventurous) users, Freespire serves as a test bed for future versions of Linspire.

An ISO image of the Freespire 2.0 CD is included on the DVD that comes with this book. You can also follow the instructions in Appendix A to copy and burn the Freespire ISO to a CD-ROM for use as a live CD or in the installation process described in this chapter. The Web page `http://wiki .freespire.org/index.php/Download_Freespire` describes alternative ways of acquiring copies.

Linspire is a commercial product and is not included on the media that comes with this book You can purchase Linspire directly from `www.linspire.com`, or you can download its live CD from `http://media.linspire.com/cnr_linspirelive/`. You will need to run a bittorrent client to download the CD. (In Fedora, you can install bittorrent as root user by typing **yum install bittorrent-gui**.)

The installation procedure for Linspire and Freespire is mostly the same and is described later in this chapter.

Which Version Is Right for You?

Both Linspire and Freespire were built on the solid base of Debian/Ubuntu Linux, the KDE desktop, and the OpenOffice.org office suite. With recent releases, the distributions have moved to embracing Ubuntu 7.04 (itself a Debian derivative) as their foundation, or base. Unlike many other Linux distributions, both come with a set of licensed commercial codecs for multimedia formats such as MP3, drivers, and other proprietary software. Although vendors provide such things for all varieties of Linux, bringing them together and integrating them while observing all the legal niceties is a big headache, so most distributions tend to leave it all up to the individual user to work out. This is a big annoyance for the typical PC user who has come to expect playing video clips or adding new hardware to "just work." Even experienced Linux users find it a chore. It is a serious hindrance to the adoption of desktop Linux. Linspire and Freespire take care of the hassle for you.

All versions of Freespire and Linspire can also access the Click-N-Run (CNR) warehouse. CNR is an easy-to-use software delivery mechanism that makes over 20,000 applications available. Linspire and Freespire are somewhat different in both content and aim, and each contains a couple of variants. Here is a brief overview of the various versions:

■ **Linspire 6.0** — This is the commercial product sold and supported by Linspire, Inc. and its partners. The digital version is available for $49.95. Linspire is also available preinstalled on PCs from a number of vendors. See `www.linspire.com/featured_partner/featured_partner.php` for a list.

Linspire is a good choice for new Linux users. It contains multimedia tutorials that show step-by-step how to perform common tasks such as connecting to a wireless network. Tech support is also available via e-mail and in user-to-user forums. In addition to the well-known open source desktop software you would expect to see in a KDE desktop (OpenOffice.org office suite, Konqueror Web browser, GAIM instant messaging, and so on), Linspire has some added, proprietary features, including the capability to play MP3 music and other multimedia formats.

> **NOTE**   Most commercial DVD titles are in an encrypted format that is not normally possible to play legally under Linux, but Linspire users can purchase a licensed DVD player from the CNR warehouse for $49.95.

■ **Linspire Five-0 CNR Edition** — This version includes the core Linspire Five-0 operating system and a year's subscription to the gold level of the CNR service. As with the basic level of service, gold level lets you easily install and remove thousands of software packages. It also enables you to organize your downloads in groups or "aisles," which is handy when you want to duplicate a favorite set of programs on multiple computers. Aisles can also be shared with other CNR users. Gold-level users also get priority support and discounts on Linspire merchandise and third-party software. For example, they pay only $9.95 for the licensed DVD player.

- **Freespire 2.0.3** — Available as a download from the Internet, Freespire is designed and developed with the assistance of the user community. While the range of software included is similar to that in Linspire, there is more emphasis on tools for software developers and Linux veterans. Because of the ongoing development, it may at times be less stable and rougher around the edges than Linspire. It is a good choice for the kind of user who is comfortable with Linux or doesn't require extensive handholding. It can also be a cheap way to take Linspire for a test drive before committing to the price of a boxed set.

- **Freespire OSS Edition** — I mentioned earlier that Freespire and Linspire include some proprietary software such as codecs and drivers. To cater to the user who would like an operating system made up of free software only, there is a special build of Freespire called the Open Source Software edition in which everything non-free is omitted. People trying Linux for non-ideological reasons are likely to find the other varieties of Linspire and Freespire more appealing.

 That's free software in the sense of "without restrictions." All varieties of Freespire are free in the sense of costing nothing.

Figure 15-1 shows the Freespire desktop.

FIGURE 15-1

The Freespire desktop

Installing Software with Click-N-Run

One of the biggest complaints from Linux neophytes is the difficulty they encounter installing additional software. It has become very clear that in order to make serious inroads onto the desktop PCs of Joe and Jane Q. Public, Linux needs to keep improving ease of use.

Continuing with the "it's so easy" theme, Linspire has developed one of the most trouble-free software installation processes in use on a desktop Linux system: Click-N-Run (CNR). This process connects users with tons of applications and requires almost no effort at all to install.

Click-N-Run has been described, accurately, as apt-get taken to new, graphical heights. Apt-get is a tool used to manage software packages. The beginnings of apt-get are most closely associated with Debian and .DEB packages, yet apt-get has been adapted to handle RPMs and is widely available for platforms other than Debian.

Apt-get is complemented by detailed man pages, although it is a command-line application. A graphical front end called Synaptic is available, but it is not as easy to use as CNR. The CNR process enables you to select the desired application, click a little green button, and wait while the package downloads and installs. You need only an existing Linspire installation and to click the green globe with a running man in the middle to get started. Here are some of the CNR tool's features:

 The following description is based on the Freespire version of CNR. Some of the tabs and buttons are labeled slightly differently in the Linspire version.

- **Sign in/Sign out** — Use this button to configure your logon information for CNR. To use the CNR Warehouse, you need a valid user account.

- **Configure** — This option enables you to specify where CNR will look for files when you are installing new applications. If you do not have your own repository, leave this setting alone.

  The capability to select your source location is relevant only if you choose to install packages not in the CNR Warehouse, such as an application your network administrator has made available for installation by users on the local network. For most users, this is not a real selling point because the real return for buying Linspire comes from accessing applications in the CNR Warehouse.

- **Install/Update Selected** — After you've selected a software package to install from your source location (local files, CD-based, on the network, or from the CNR Warehouse), you can initiate the installation process. Items in the warehouse can be installed by clicking the green globe icon next to the product name in lieu of using CNR's Install button.

  Most software in the warehouse is freeware. Some commercial applications are available, but, of course, you have to purchase them before you can install them. You can also select an application and then use the Update feature to check for newer versions of the software. Gold-level users are automatically notified when updates are available.

- **Run It!** — After you have installed an application you can use this option to run the program immediately. You can also run the program from the launch menu or a desktop shortcut.

- **Pause** — You can pause your download of online installation files. This makes working with large installation files over slower or shared network connections easier.

- **Add to Desktop** — Creates a desktop shortcut to any of your applications in addition to the launch menu icons.

- **Uninstall Selected** — When you run the uninstall option on a selected application, all of the program files, icons, and folders for that application are automatically removed.

CNR is a great tool for getting software from the warehouse, and Click-N-Run Express is a CNR version that can be used to install applications from any location. It enables you to designate local or remote repositories and then install the products.

If you configure the download option, CNR Express stores a local copy of the installed applications for later use, enabling you to install, remove, and reinstall when you want without having to download the installation package all over again. When your installation is complete, the application waits for you to use it by browsing to the application title in your K menu.

COMING FROM WINDOWS One of the truly handy, proprietary applications available in the CNR Warehouse is Win4Lin, which can be used to get many Win32 applications up and running on your Linspire system.

Other Installation Options

While the Click-N-Run application is the quickest means of managing software on your Linspire installation, it may not meet every user's needs. With this in mind, here are a couple of other options for managing software on your Linspire installation:

- .DEB packages can be used to manually install software. Open a Terminal window and run the command `'dpkg - i filename.deb'`.

TIP For more information on using the dpkg installation utility, check out the related Debian FAQ at http://debian.org/doc/FAQ/ch-pkgtools.en.html.

- RPM packages can be used if you make use of an installation package converter such as Alien (www.kitenet.net/programs/alien/). This method should be employed only if you have no other convenient options. Package conversion is not a sure thing, and unexpected consequences can arise from using converted packages.

- As mentioned, apt-get can be used to install .DEB packages over the network.

NOTE See Chapter 9 for a thorough description of Debian's apt-get utility and related software management tools.

- Software not available in .DEB or RPM format can often be installed from installer scripts (.sh) or by compiling source code from a tarball. A tarball is an archive of files created with a special utility (named tar) and usually compressed using another utility, gzip. Source code distributions are often packaged as gzipped tarballs. Compiling from source enables you to do things the "old way" if needed and to exercise granular control of unpackaged software. This functionality helps keep Linspire a flexible platform for running a variety of software.

Linspire and Freespire Support

The level of support available from Linspire is not particularly expansive, especially when compared to other Linux project communities. It is, however, very easy to find information on the support site, and make contact with users willing to help you out should you have any questions or need help with using Linspire or most of the Click-N-Run applications (although most application support is unofficial).

Many of the online Linspire support options are available by clicking the Help Center icon (it looks like a life jacket) in the panel. The menu that appears not only connects you to official Linspire online support and community forums, but it also lets you view HowTo tutorials and run demos of Linspire software.

Freespire has no paid support options or the Audio Assistant included with Linspire. Members of the Freespire community support each other via the Internet. You can also access the Freespire support options via the Help Center icon. (In Freespire, the Help Center icon is on the Launch menu, not the panel.)

Forums and Information

If you should encounter any problems or simply want to ask some questions about Linspire, you can start by checking out the Linspire support pages. By taking your Web browser to `http://support.linspire.com/support.jsp` or `http://support.freespire.org/support.jsp`, you can access user forums, FAQs, and (if you have a product logon) personalized support.

While the FAQs and personalized support are very useful at times, you will get the most mileage out of the user forums. Most of the forums allow posts by registered users only, but there are guest areas as well. These forums are frequented by other users and product developers and are a great resource for getting future product information and providing feedback on how Linspire works for you.

Freespire has its own set of forums at `http://forum.freespire.org/`.

Audio Assistant

What good would new software be without a product tour peppered with a touch of product evangelism? Linspire offers both with the Audio Assistant. This animated tour of the Linspire OS runs after your initial installation. The Assistant walks you through using Click-N-Run, configuring your desktop, and a lot more.

NOTE You can check out the online version of the Audio Assistant at `http://media.linspire.com/howto/kiosk.swf`.

Should you install Linspire and bypass the Audio Assistant tutorial, have no fear. You can re-launch the tutorials by clicking the life jacket icon in the lower-left corner of your desktop (in the toolbar).

Installing Linspire or Freespire

If you plan ahead, a Linspire or Freespire installation is one of the most straightforward operating system software installations. This includes Apple and Microsoft as well as other Linux distributions. Because of its experimental nature, Freespire installation may be a little rough around the edges at times, but it is still easy for even non-gurus to perform. In the following section, I guide you through the installation of Freespire 2.0, which is included on the DVD, but the same instructions apply to Linspire 6.0.

There are very few configuration options and no disk partitioning options other than either selecting an installation partition or wiping the entire hard disk. For maximum joy, make sure you have no data on the computer/partition/drive where Freespire will be installed. The target location for the installation will be wiped out.

Also, make sure that you check the supported hardware list (`www.linspire.com/linspire_hardware_compatibility.php`) before you begin your installation to make sure there are no surprises there.

Hardware Requirements

While Freespire is top-notch when it comes to ease of use, it won't be very easy if your hardware doesn't work with the software. Freespire system requirements follow the product's "keep it simple" theme, and there is no discussion of RAID controllers or other such arcane items. As with any version of Linux, the minimum requirements are pretty sparse, but you need to make sure your PC meets them:

- **800 MHz or faster processor** — Any processor that crosses this performance threshold will work.

- **128MB of RAM** — This will get you by, but Freespire recommends you splurge and install 256MB or more of RAM for optimum performance.

- **Hard disk** — Freespire recommends a hard disk with 4GB of free space.

- **Video** — You need a color monitor capable of supporting a screen resolution of 1024 × 768. Some of the games and screen savers included with various packages or available from the CNR Warehouse require some kind of 3D graphics accelerator hardware.

- **Sound** — You need a Freespire-compatible soundcard with speakers and/or headphones. Check your soundcard at `www.linspire.com/linspire_hardware_compatibility.php` before beginning your installation.

- **Modem** — Your 56K, cable, or DSL modem also needs to be Freespire-compatible. Before beginning your installation, check your equipment at `www.linspire.com/linspire_hardware_compatibility.php`.

- **Network card** — Any Ethernet card is acceptable. Although Freespire does not specifically recommend it, you would be wise to check the hardware compatibility list to ensure your Ethernet adapter is supported.

- **Keyboard and mouse**

Like most flavors of Linux, the range of hardware supported is quite wide. If you find that your hardware is not on the supported devices list, check the hardware vendor's Web site for Debian drivers for your device. It is entirely possible that you can install the driver manually (if Freespire cannot configure it).

NOTE To debug hardware problems, select the Advanced option from the menu and then select Diagnostics when booting from the Freespire CD or DVD. Running diagnostics shows you any errors relating to the configuration or detection of your hardware. If you have already installed Freespire, Diagnostics is available as the second option on the initial boot menu.

Installing Linspire or Freespire

Want to take Freespire for a test run? An ISO image of the Freespire 2.0 CD is included on the DVD that comes with this book. Refer to Appendix A for information on copying and burning that CD image to a CD. The resulting CD can be used to install Freespire to hard disk or run Freespire live, directly from this CD.

Before installing Freespire on your hard drive, boot from the CD and at the initial menu, use the arrow keys to select "RUN Freespire directly from the CD without installing (FreespireLive!)." Then press Enter. Freespire will now start up in live mode with full functionality. After you have experimented with it to your satisfaction, you can either begin the installation process or remove the CD or DVD and reboot to restore your system to its prior state.

The Freespire installer is simple and effective. You select the appropriate option from the boot screen of the installation CD, and from that point on you pretty much follow the prompts. The entire installation usually takes 15 to 20 minutes to complete, depending on the speed of your computer and your CD drive. The following steps walk you through the installation and the initial startup process:

1. Start the computer and boot the install CD. You'll see several options, as shown in Figure 15-2. The first is to install. Select option 1 and press Enter, or simply wait and the installation proceeds after a few moments.

2. After a welcome screen that gives you the choice of canceling or continuing with the install, you are asked about your keyboard layout, and then you proceed to the Install Methods screen (see Figure 15-3). Here you can select a basic or advanced installation. A basic installation is useful when you have only one hard disk and partition. An advanced installation enables you to select the hard disk and/or partition to which you want to install. Make your selection, and click Next.

CAUTION Both basic and advanced installations wipe out all data on the target drive/partition. Back up anything you think you might want to keep before proceeding. If you select the advanced method, it is recommended that your data partition be at least 4GB or more.

3. The screen to select your computer name, username, and password appears (see Figure 15-4). You need to name the PC and provide the details for a user account, including a password if you opt to provide one. For a home configuration replacing a Windows installation, for example, leaving the password blank might be acceptable. In any working environment or if the PC is not going to be shielded from the Internet, providing a strong password is essential. When you have made your selection, click Next.

FIGURE 15-2

The Freespire boot screen

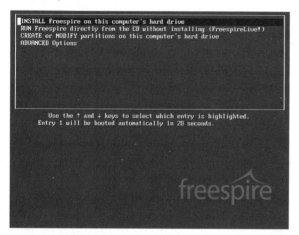

FIGURE 15-3

Select an installation method

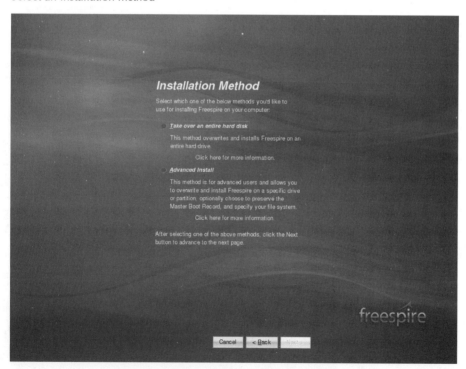

FIGURE 15-4

Select a computer name, username, and password.

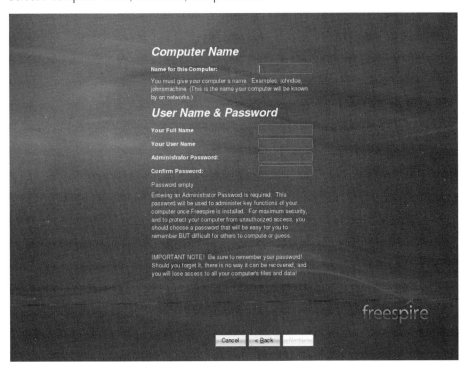

TIP   Most distributions, including Linspire, follow the UNIX tradition of having a superuser or *root* account to handle privileged tasks such as installing and removing software and other stuff normal users should not be able to do. Freespire is different; the root account is locked down and the user account created in this screen is designated as an admin account, with the power to temporarily assume superuser powers via the sudo command. (See the manual page for sudo to understand how this works.) After installation, you can create other accounts with or without sudo powers or even restore the root account to its customary position.

4. You are asked to confirm your computer name, account information, and the installation method you selected. If you are happy with your selections, click Next.

5. A Warning window asks you to make absolutely certain that you want to proceed. You are again warned that all data on the target drive/partition will be lost. You are given the options "Yes, I am sure" and "Let me make changes." Select "Yes, I am sure" and you go to the next step. Select "Let me make changes" and you return to the installation type screen.

TIP   At any point up to and including Step 5, you can use the Back button to review and/or change your previous configuration decisions.

6. The next screen indicates the progress of the installation process. Scrolling messages fill the space, and in a few minutes you see the message:

```
Freespire setup complete
press OK to restart your computer.
```

Click OK.

7. A final message appears, instructing you to remove your CD and press any key. Your CD tray opens. Grab the CD and press any key. Your installation is complete.

8. When Freespire starts up, you can specify which startup path you would like to take. The startup options are called *boot options*, and there are four boot options in your startup screen (called the Linux Loader or LILO): Freespire, Redetect, Diagnostics, and Advanced Menu.

   ▪ Freespire, the default option, boots into the Freespire operating system; you can select it or just wait for Freespire to load. Unless you have installed hardware since the last time you started Freespire or you are having some serious startup issues, always select the default option to launch Freespire.

   ▪ Redetect identifies installed hardware, which is useful if you've added new items since your last installation. This is roughly equivalent to the plug-and-play functionality most Windows users enjoy.

   ▪ Diagnostics is an option used when you are experiencing some kind of system issues, such as failed or improperly configured hardware. A series of applications runs, and the results of the detection and diagnosis are displayed. This screen can be very intimidating and difficult to interpret if you are not familiar with the Linux startup process.

   ▪ The Advanced Menu lets you boot up without any hardware detection, which could be useful if the detection process causes a peripheral to hang.

   Select Freespire (or Linspire as the case may be), and the operating system finishes loading.

The Settings window (see Figure 15-5) provides a button for setting the system time and a settings dialog that enables you to set or change the admin account password. Set the desktop (display) resolution that you prefer and that your hardware supports, and invoke the Freespire User Manager, with which you can create new users, assign them capabilities, and delete them as needed. You also get one opportunity to rename your PC. You set the computer name and administrator password during startup, so there is not likely to be a reason to change them here, but you can if you like.

With Freespire installed, with the exception of the few special Freespire applications (mostly associated with playing multimedia content and getting help), Freespire behaves like most KDE desktop systems, so you can learn how to get around the Freespire desktop using descriptions from Chapter 3.

FIGURE 15-5

The Settings window

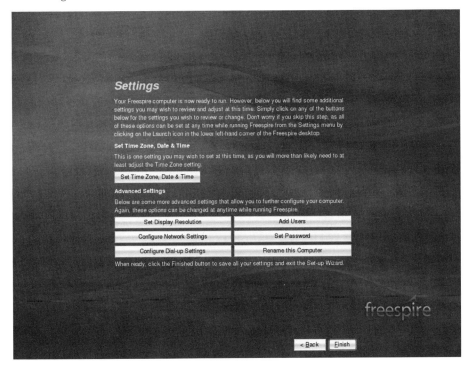

Securing Linspire and Freespire

When you install Linspire, or if you run Linspire or Freespire with the live CD option, you are given the choice of creating a user account. If you skip this step, you will be running the system as the root or superuser account. Every application you run will also have the privileges of the root account.

As you learned in Chapter 4, the root account has complete power over the entire Linux system. It should be used sparingly, only for the tasks that truly need it. Running common applications such as a Web browser or instant-messaging client as root will raise the hackles of any Linux security expert, because you are essentially giving anyone who can exploit those applications the keys to your entire system. Linspire probably allowed this to cater to the type of users coming from non-Linux systems who run everything as Administrator. But then again, those were the type of users whose PCs were usually infested with viruses and spyware. Don't let the same thing happen to your Linux system; create a user account and use root only when absolutely necessary. The Freespire installer is good in this regard, because it forces you to create a user account.

For the times when you do have to do work as root, it can be a pain to log out and log back in or to open a separate terminal window, so Linspire and Freespire include the `sudo` command. This allows you to run a single command as root and then immediately revert to your account's normal level of privilege. The default setup is that users in the `admins` group have the ability to use `sudo`. The accounts that you create during the installation process are automatically added to `admins`, and you can add or remove other user accounts to it later. Here, too, you can take steps to increase the default level of security. The problem is that the configuration file for sudo, `/etc/sudoers`, contains a line like this:

```
%admins ALL=(ALL) NOPASSWD: ALL
```

This means that any user in the `admins` group can run `sudo` without having to type in his password, which is quite convenient but allows any malicious hacker who can exploit an `admins` account full access to the system. The fix is to use your favorite editor to open up `/etc/sudoers` and change the preceding line of code to:

```
%admins ALL=(ALL) ALL
```

Now the first time a user runs `sudo`, he will be asked for his password. He won't be asked for it again for a period of 15 minutes, which ought to be enough time to complete whatever task needed to be done as *root*. This value can also be configured if you want to change the timeout value. See the `sudo` man page and `http://wiki.freespire.org/index.php/Making_Admin_Accounts_More_Secure` for more details.

This is by no means the last word on securing your Linspire or Freespire system, but taking these simple steps will go a long way in keeping your system safe.

Summary

Linspire may not excite the battle-hardened Linux-using community, but it serves as a positive example of a user-oriented desktop Linux system. Linspire is by far the most accessible version of Linux for new users. With a computer that has supported hardware, literally anyone can install Linspire and get up and running with new applications, Web surfing, and e-mail in a couple of hours.

Freespire offers more room for experimentation while remaining within the comfort level of the average user. The ability for users to have a say in its future direction and to choose what mix of proprietary and free software to include in an installation makes it attractive for all kinds of custom uses.

The Click-N-Run (CNR) application takes ease of installation to a new level, making Linspire and Freespire hopeful proof of the concept that a desktop version of Linux can succeed in the home and office. The installation walkthrough at the end of the chapter demonstrates that there are some tradeoffs for this ease of use.

While Linspire and Freespire do support a wide range of both Windows and Linux applications, it is still difficult to run some of the more popular commercial Windows games and applications on them without having to go well beyond the graphical tools offered with these distributions. Presumably, because Linspire, Inc. has paid to include software for playing MP3 and a variety of video formats, Linspire and Freespire can play many more types of multimedia content than other Linux systems can play out of the box.

Chapter 16

Running Mandriva

Before becoming Mandriva Linux, Mandrakelinux was created as a fork of Red Hat Linux (in 1998). It initially had such tight ties to Red Hat Linux that the Mandrakelinux installer even stated that you were installing Red Hat.

After those early days, Mandrakelinux became a solid distribution in its own right, with the main focus on an easy-to-use desktop distribution. It is often mentioned along with Linspire when people talk about the easiest distributions for someone new to Linux to install and use.

From the beginning of 2005 to the present, Mandrakelinux has gone from the brink of bankruptcy to its current incarnation as *Mandriva,* after MandrakeSoft (the parent company of Mandrakelinux) merged with Conectiva Linux in February 2005. Conectiva Linux is a South American–based Linux company with goals similar to those of Mandrakelinux.

N the DVD-ROM The Mandriva live CD, called Mandriva One, is included on the DVD that comes with this book. This is a desktop-oriented live CD that can also be used as an installer, to install the contents of that live CD to your hard drive.

Mandriva Features

Unlike Linux distributions that are community-driven, Mandriva is a company that sells Linux products. Community-like activities are available through the Mandriva Club (http://club.mandriva.com), which provides more of a customer support–type function than a Linux development center.

IN THIS CHAPTER

Exploring Mandriva

The Mandriva community

Installing Mandriva

In addition to the merger with Conectiva, Mandriva also acquired the desktop-oriented Lycoris Linux distribution in June 2005. Therefore, the product offerings have changed significantly in the past few years. (Expect changes to continue for a while as the dust settles.) Actual Mandriva products are divided into Enterprise and Individual offerings. Mandriva gears the support and services it offers to those two categories.

On the Enterprise side, products focus on corporate desktops and servers, as well as some specialty firewall and clustering products. To support those products, Mandriva offers a variety of consulting, support, and training options. For the Individual line, Linux products range from beginner desktop products to products aimed at home and small office servers. For a short period of time after the acquisition, Mandriva offered a Lycoris desktop product. However, that offering has since been dropped and Lycoris technology has been integrated into other Mandriva products.

At the time of this writing, the most current version of Mandriva Linux is Mandriva 2008. Version numbers for business-oriented products follow a different scheme, with the latest business server product called Mandriva Linux Corporate Server 4.0.

Here is a brief overview of the versions of Mandriva that you can download for free:

- **Mandriva One** — A live CD version of Mandriva Linux that contains a well-stocked set of desktop applications. In addition to offering the full OpenOffice productivity suite, Mandriva One includes tools for graphics (GIMP and F-Spot), Internet (Firefox, Evolution, and GAIM), and multimedia (Totem movie player, Sound Juicer, and TVtime television viewer). Mandriva One is included on the DVD that comes with this book.

- **Mandriva Linux Free** — This four-CD set of free software is aimed at power users. There are both i586 and x86-64 versions of Mandriva Linux Free that are freely available for download.

- **Mandriva Spring** — Designed for individual use, with the entry-level desktop user in mind. The package includes basic productivity software such as OpenOffice, Kdeprintfax, and planning/finance software. Also included are the requisite networking tools for e-mail, FTP, and Web browsing. Several multimedia components are also installed, enabling audio and video playback, image editing, and scanning documents as well as CD recording.

COMING FROM WINDOWS Mandriva Linux 2007 Spring is the product that Mandriva recommends for beginners who are looking to switch to Linux from Windows. By adding commercial software for watching DVD movies (LinDVD), Windows gaming (Transgaming's Cedega), and 3D desktop effects (drak3D), Mandriva makes transitioning from Windows to Linux a fairly easy proposition.

The following is a list of Mandriva product offerings for business:

- **Corporate Desktop** — Available in x86 and x86-64 versions for corporate desktops. It offers five-year product maintenance with unlimited Web support that features Web response within two business days. Many features you would expect in an open source, corporate desktop system are included: OpenOffice productivity suite, Evolution e-mail/groupware, Totem media player, and Kopete instant messaging. Value-added software includes CrossOver Office for running Windows applications, and (optionally) VMware virtualization software.

- **Mandriva Linux Clustering** — Includes software for deploying clustering systems for a variety of modeling, simulation, and other applications that require high-performance clustering. This is available on x86 and x86-64 versions.

- **Mandriva Pulse** — A solution for monitoring and managing Linux and Windows networks. It is an open source product that simplifies remote management.

- **Mandriva Corporate Server** — Along with popular server software (Apache, MySQL, Samba, and so on), business-oriented Mandriva products come with more extensive product support. Both the Corporate and Premium Corporate Server products come with 24/7 Web support, with a Web response time of two business days. Both offer unlimited phone support as well, with the premium package offering quicker response time and other extended options. One, three, and five-year maintenance contracts are available.

If you just want to try out Mandriva, Mandriva One can be booted directly from the DVD that comes with this book. Open the Live Install icon on the desktop to install the contents of the Mandriva One CD to your hard drive. A four-CD Mandriva Linux Free edition is also available for free download (see www.mandriva.com/en/download).

As noted earlier, the Mandriva Club (www.mandrivaclub.com) helps Mandriva end users get the most out their Mandriva systems. Different levels of membership are available, from Standard Membership ($66 per year) to Platinum Membership ($1,320 per year). Membership gives you access to a special Mandriva Club edition of Mandriva and other offerings that include commercial software, along with their open source offerings.

Exploring Mandriva

The Linux distribution that has now evolved into Mandriva has long hung its hat on the concept of "ease of use," the idea being that its distributions should be readily accessible to a large pool of users. Mandrakelinux was heralded early on for its exceptional use of a graphical installer and configuration tools. Its support for hardware, video acceleration, and audio playback also tends to be top-notch.

When coupled with the fact that the Mandrakelinux installer frequently detected and configured hardware that left other distributions' installation routines mystified, you can see why Mandrakelinux has been, and will probably continue, under the name Mandriva, to be a popular distribution.

Mandriva Linux 2008 comes with a number of attractive features, including the following:

- The largely automated installation process has new features such as the capability to resize NTFS partitions.

- Hardware detection and configuration have been improved over previous Mandrakelinux releases. In particular, the security, printing, and user configuration tools have been completely overhauled to provide additional functionality and ease of use.

- Updated versions of the RPM Package Manager and the Internet update software have improved the ease of installing new software as well as system patches.

- Security maintenance is comprehensive. Mandriva Linux 2008 includes easy-to-use configuration tools for setting general system security and setting up a firewall. It also supports a range of security protocols such as SSH, SSL, LDAP, and NIS.

- The user interface is consistent across desktop environments.

In addition, there are a few "Drak" tools that make a particularly big impact on the usability and consistency of Mandriva. These utilities are DrakX installer, RPMDrake software management window, and Mandriva Linux Control Center.

Mandriva Installer (DrakX)

DrakX is a highly acclaimed and user-friendly installer that has been one of Mandriva's key differentiators against other Linux builds. Included since version Mandrakelinux 7.0, this installer was one of the first attempts at automated installers that most novice Linux users could successfully use.

Although the installer is almost "newbie"-proof, it's still possible to invoke advanced installation options enabling detailed control of the install at any point during the installation process. As with most versions of Linux, you can install from a boot CD, another drive, or a network. Here are the key features of the DrakX installer included in the current version of Mandriva:

- Convenient installation configuration options using predefined packages, rather than requiring you to choose individual packages from the wide selection that is available. You can select individual packages if you do not want to use one of the predefined package options. Workstation and Server Package groups are available for various roles and needs, for example.

- The ability to format hard disks, configure RAID, and resize partitions of many types, including NTFS, FAT32, EXT3, ReiserFS, and XFS.

- Support for a wide range of network file systems.

- Improved upgrade support.

- Automated installation tools.

- Rescue mode for failed/problematic installation.

In addition to the straightforward boot CD, the DrakX installer supports a number of other installation methods, including:

- **Network installs** — If needed, you can start the DrakX installation process and connect to a variety of network servers to access the installation files. This includes NFS, HTTP, SBM, SSH, Web Proxy, and FTP servers.

- **Kickstart installs** — In environments such as customer support call centers, school computer labs, and large offices, you might find yourself needing to install and configure large numbers of computers in a short period of time. Kickstart installations use an answer file to automate most of the installation process. Mandriva's installation routine enables you to create floppies to use when performing kickstart installations. Mandriva enables you to make semi-interactive or completely automated setup floppies.

- **Upgrades** — The DrakX installer supports an upgrade path to bring older installs up to snuff with the newest release.

You can try out the DrakX installer in the walk-through included in this chapter.

RPM Package Management with RPMDrake

Adding software to and removing software from your Linux installation should not be a time-consuming chore. RPMDrake provides an intuitive graphical interface for managing installed software. You can easily see what is installed and add or remove packages as needed. To open RPMDrake, select Applications ➪ System ➪ Install, Remove & Update Software. Figure 16-1 shows an example of the RPMDrake window.

FIGURE 16-1

Add, remove, and update Mandriva software from the RPMDrake Software Management window.

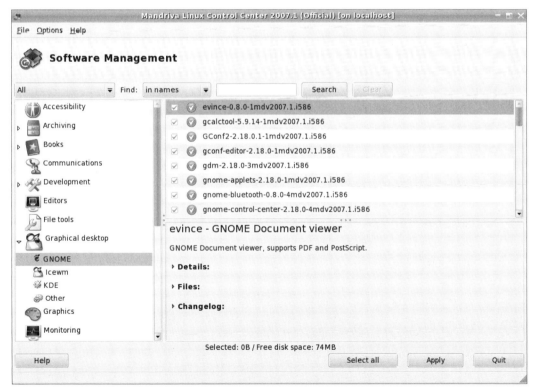

You should know the following when using RPMDrake:

- You can configure your list of sources by invoking the Define Sources feature. This enables you to specify the location of installable packages, which could be local network locations, CD-ROM media, or HTTP/FTP archives of installation packages. You can refresh the List of Mirrors option to make sure you're ready to get access to the latest security and system updates.

- Using the Mandriva Update button is probably the easiest way to maintain your system because it automatically downloads and installs updates for your system when you initiate the updates.

- You need the root password when installing packages. RPMDrake prompts you for it as needed.

- RPMDrake offers improved upgrade support. You can use it to scan for software updates, download them, and offer them in the list of installable programs for the user to select.

RPMDrake supports a search feature that enables you to use a variety of criteria to search for desired software within configured sources. You can search by package name, or you can search based on a description. Either way, once you find the package you want, simply select the target package and use the Install/Remove button to get going.

But what if you just want to remove software? This is a very straightforward process as well. Locate the package you want to remove under the Installed Applications tab. Select it, and click the Install/Remove button. The package, along with any that depend on it, is removed from the system. (You may also choose not to remove the dependent packages.)

Mandriva Linux Control Center

The Mandriva Linux Control Center (MLCC), also called DrakConf, provides an intuitive and accessible means of configuring various system resources. You can use this tool to add new hardware, configure installed applications, add or remove applications (by invoking RPMDrake), and change the configuration of your existing hardware.

To open the MLCC, select Applications ➪ System ➪ Configure Your Computer. Figure 16-2 shows an example of the Mandriva Linux Control Center.

You can also use the control center to adjust your default system security levels, change your display options, schedule events, manage user accounts, and even change the system time/date setting. The MLCC uses a number of installation and configuration wizards to help you get rolling. For example, a wizard for Apache Web server setup enables you to get your HTTP server online in just a few minutes. Some of the key improvements and features of MLCC in Mandriva Linux are:

- Secure, remote system configuration from any network
- Automatic detection of hot swappable devices without restarting the system
- Large icons that are easy to see and appropriately related to the functions they invoke

FIGURE 16-2

The Mandriva Linux Control Center is a simplified tool for system administration.

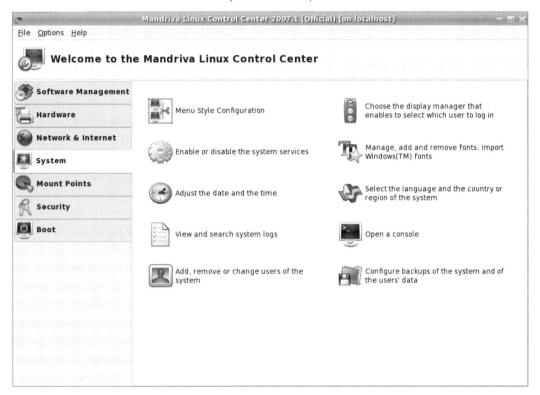

The Mandriva Community

Like many distributions of Linux, Mandriva Linux has developed a split personality of sorts. Mandriva distributes value-added versions of Mandriva Linux complete with numerous utilities, applications, and support. The core Mandriva development effort produces an unsupported, but just as useful, version of the core Mandriva build. With this "free" copy, called Mandriva Linux Free, you get the OS and the basic utilities and applications but no access to the Mandriva Club or commercial add-on software (DVD players, multimedia plug-ins, and so on). Mandriva One represents a live CD, reduced set of the Mandriva Linux Free software.

Mandriva Club allows folks with a paid membership to access early builds; the full suite of downloadable one-click applications; and forums, support, and downloads of current releases using its club-member–only bit torrent system. It also gives you access to commercial software (such as Flash plug-ins and NVIDIA drivers) that cannot be freely distributed. For someone trying to make

Linux a desktop system for use by folks coming from Apple and Microsoft GUI operating systems, these added features are extremely useful.

RPM Repository on Mandriva Club

The Mandriva Club Web site (`http://club.mandriva.com`) has a massive collection of software that is tested for use with Mandriva and is directly accessible to members. (A nonmember can view the available packages, but will not be able to access the files without providing a valid Mandriva Club membership.) A search tool and various precompiled lists by category, creation date, product name, maintaining organization/user, and distributor are features of this site.

To find mirror sites that host packages for Mandriva, refer to the Mandriva Club Mirror Finder (see `http://club.mandriva.com` and select Downloads ➪ Mirror Finder). In addition to finding software in the main Mandriva distribution, you can search Club software repositories that include commercial software, JPackage software, club contributions, and software that is still in testing.

Mandriva Forums

If you have any interest in tracking product development and maybe getting a little help if you need it, you'll want to keep on top of Mandriva news, forums, and Linux User Groups (LUGs).

User forums are a priceless tool for finding solutions to problems, getting involved in software-related projects, or just connecting with other Mandriva users. The Mandriva users' forum (`http://mandrivausers.org/`) is a great one with especially in-depth information on installation and configuration.

The Mandriva Club forums (`http://forums.mandriva.com`) are also popular. You get temporary free access to Mandriva Club when you purchase any retail Mandriva product, or you can separately enroll in the club and make use of its services. If you find you like Mandriva and will be using it long-term, it's probably a good idea to join the Mandriva Club because you'll have access to official support and your funds will help the development of the product.

Another critical resource for information on all things Linux is your local Linux user group (LUG). Each LUG is different, but you are apt to find a number of like-minded users with whom to interact in a variety of situations. If you have no idea how to find the nearest LUG, you can try using your favorite search engine to look for the words "Linux Users Group," along with the name of the nearest big town or city.

Installing Mandriva Limited Edition

To check out Mandriva for the first time, you have several options. Mandriva One is a live CD that can also be used as a basic installer. The other free option is to download the four-CD set of Mandriva Linux Free. If you like the distribution, I encourage you to purchase a Mandriva Linux 2008 product and/or join the Mandriva Club Edition.

To review your options, refer to the Mandriva Linux Download page at www.mandriva.com/en/download.

If you are content to try out the live CD and install the contents of the CD to your hard disk, you can follow the instructions in this section. An image of the Mandriva One live CD is included on the DVD that comes with this book and can be booted directly from the DVD.

NOTE The DVD that comes with this book includes the English GNOME version of Mandriva One. If you prefer the KDE version or any of several different language versions, refer to the Mandriva One Download page (www.mandriva.com/en/download/mandrivaone). Appendix A explains how to burn the installation CDs from the CD images, if you decide to download Mandriva CDs yourself.

The Right Hardware for Mandriva

As with software packages, look before you leap. It is important to make sure your hardware is up to the task before you install Mandriva. Fear not, users of less-than-stellar hardware; the hardware requirements are far from onerous. To use Mandriva you need (or you can use) the following:

- **x586 class processor or above** — The Intel Pentium I–IV, AMD K6/II/III, Duron, or Athlon/XP/MP.

- **RAM** — At least 256MB of memory is recommended (although 512MB will work much better). If you need to run Mandriva on a machine with less RAM, consider starting the installation from Mandriva Free instead of Mandriva One because live CDs generally require more RAM to run effectively.

- **Hard disk** — At least 1GB is recommended for installing Mandriva One.

- **RAID controllers** — There is wide support for SCSI RAID controllers. In addition, 3Ware IDE and Serial ATA controllers are supported.

- **DVD or CD drive** — To run the installation from a CD/DVD source disk, you need the appropriate drive. This drive will need to support bootable CD/DVD media.

- **Input/Output** — Of course, if you want to interact with your Mandriva install, you'll at least need a keyboard and a monitor. A mouse is not needed for the installation, but it is handy and recommended.

NOTE For those who live life on the bleeding edge, there is a version of Mandriva that supports the AMD Athlon64 processor. See the Mandriva Powerpack product (www.mandriva.com/en/linux/2007/powerpack).

As you can see from the system specifications, you can use a wide range of hardware to run your Mandriva installation. Do you have an old PIII with 128MB of RAM, a CD-ROM, and a blank 1GB hard disk? No problem. How about a "gaming war machine" sporting a 3.2 GHz P4, 1GB of RAM, a DVD-R, and an ocean of hard disk space? Bring it on!

The vast assortment of hardware supported includes popular video cards such as NVIDIA FX series and ATI Radeon video adapters. Large numbers of Ethernet and Wi-Fi network adapters, USB 2.0, and other hardware make your chances of installation and configuration success very high.

This installation requires no special hard disk configuration. As mentioned, this install assumes a preexisting Microsoft Windows operating system using the NTFS file system. You will "make room" on the existing partition and install Mandriva there. In addition to using a boot disk (as you will here), you can take advantage of the installation options such as FTP and NFS as outlined briefly in this chapter and in more detail in Chapter 7.

CAUTION Do not make your first installation attempt on a mission-critical system. Resizing an NTFS partition can have unintended effects. Back up any information you cannot live without, especially if you resize existing partitions as the following instructions show.

Installing Mandriva with the DrakX Installer

The first part of starting a Mandriva install from the Mandriva One live CD is to boot up that live CD. Once the live CD is up and running, you start the installation process by opening the Live Install icon from the live CD's desktop.

1. Back up any important data from your computer's hard disk before starting this procedure.

2. Insert the DVD that comes with this book and reboot the computer. You will see the boot screen.

3. Type **mandriva** and press Enter. The Mandriva One live CD starts and you are prompted to select your language.

4. Select your language and click Next. You are asked to enter your country name.

5. Select your country name and click Next. You are asked to accept the warranty.

6. Read the warranty. Select to accept it and click Next. You are asked to choose your keyboard layout.

7. Select your keyboard layout and click Next. You are asked to select your time zone.

8. Choose the time zone you are in, based on your country, state, and city. You are asked to set your time.

9. Choose whether or not to set your computer's hardware clock to local time or UTC time. As an alternative, you can choose to have your time set by an NTP server (you can choose the server as well). Click Next to continue. You are asked if you want to enable 3D desktop effects.

10. Choose to either not use 3D desktop effects or to use Xgl-based desktop effects. (Your video card needs to support hardware acceleration to be able to use 3D desktop effects, which include wobbly window moves and desktops spinning on a cube.) Click Next to continue.

    At this point, Mandriva One continues to boot up to a desktop, such as the one shown in Figure 16-3. In particular, notice the Live Install icon on the left side of the screen.

11. Open the Live Install icon on the desktop. The Mandriva Live Wizard starts. Click Next to continue. You are asked how you want to partition your disk.

FIGURE 16-3

Start a Mandriva One installation from an icon on the Mandriva One desktop.

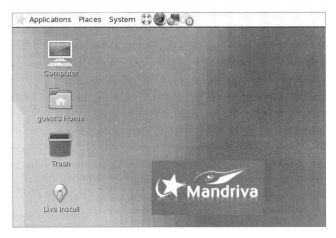

12. The next screen begins the disk partitioning portion of the Mandriva installation. (General guidance regarding the size and types of partitions you'll need is included in Chapter 7.) Select one of the following approaches to configuring your hard disk:

- **Use Existing Partitions** — Use any available Linux partitions to install Mandriva.

- **Erase and Use Entire Disk** — Wipes the existing hard disk in preparation for your install. This is a great option for critical server systems where you want to start with a completely clean system or if there is no data on the disk you need.

- **Custom** — Here's where the real magic happens: You can create custom volumes, resize existing volumes, and in general torture your hard drives as much as you like.

Selecting the Custom option opens a new window that shows all the existing hard drives and configured partitions. If your system has only an existing Windows installation on an NTFS partition, all that will be visible are the blue markers indicating a Windows partition.

Once you click on the partition that you want to use for your Mandriva installation, a new option appears in the left portion of the disk configuration window. By clicking the Resize button, you can change the size (within limitations) of the existing NTFS partition.

Give it a shot if you have the opportunity. Click the Resize button, and a new window appears. It has a slider that's all the way to the right by default. As you slide the indicator to the left, the corresponding value displayed gets smaller. This number reflects the size (in MB) that the NTFS partition will be after you've completed the resizing operation. For example, if you have a 30GB NTFS partition and you want to free up 10GB of space for the creation of a set of native Linux partitions, simply slide the indicator from the maximum value of 30000MB to 20000MB, and you will have freed the required 10000MB.

The amount of space you can create depends on the size of the disk, how much data is stored, and whether the partition has been defragmented. To find out the degree to which you can resize the partition, move the slider all the way to the left. That displays the smallest size you can make the existing Windows partition.

When you've selected the size you want, click the Next button. You are shown a warning to make sure you have backed up any information you depend on before performing the partition resizing. If you're ready to commit, click OK.

It is foolish to tinker with partitions and volumes if you have important information on them and no backup. Resizing is a pretty predictable process, but the process is not perfect, and you can end up with a working Mandriva install and a sizeable, useless Windows partition.

If all went well, you now have an unformatted partition available. Click the empty partition and create the native Linux partitions you need or want. After you've sorted all your partitions in the manner you would like, click Done. A warning message asks if you're sure you want to do this. Click Next and the deed is done.

13. In a normal Mandriva install, you would be given the opportunity to select packages to install at this point. Because this procedure installs from the live CD, however, the operating system on the live CD is simply copied to your hard drive. Once that's done, you are asked to choose a boot loader.

14. Choose either the GRUB or LILO boot loader. Then choose the boot device (typically the device representing the first hard disk that is booted on your computer, such as /dev/hda). See Chapter 7 for descriptions of GRUB and LILO. Click the Advanced button to choose other boot options. Click Next to continue. Your current boot entries are displayed.

15. The entries that Mandriva has set up to put on your boot menu are displayed. You can edit those entries or create some of your own. If you have multiple operating systems on your computer, you can add your own entries so that those systems can be selected from the boot loader. Click Next to continue.

16. You are instructed to restart the computer and remove the live CD. Click Finish and select System ⇨ Shutdown, and then choose Restart.

After the live CD shuts down, the DVD is ejected. Remove the DVD and press Enter to boot your newly installed Mandriva system.

The first time your installed system boots, you have the opportunity to configure settings for that installation. You can configure the following:

■ **Network & Internet Configuration** — Configure your Ethernet, wireless, or other Internet connection.

■ **Root password** — Enter a password for the root user (twice).

- **Add user** — Enter the real name, login name, and password (twice) for a regular user account.

- **Mandriva account** — You can create a Mandriva online account. With this account, you can take advantage of a variety of services available from Mandriva, such as keeping up with security updates and upgrades.

Summary

Although Mandriva may not be as widely known as other Linux distributions, it is arguably one of the most accessible versions for novice desktop users. It is especially useful to those who want their Linux installations to exist alongside Windows installations that may not have free partitions for a dedicated Linux installation.

This chapter explores some of the defining features of Mandriva, including the installer, which incorporates the capability to resize existing Windows partitions nondestructively; an RPM package management (RPMDrake); and system configuration tools.

In addition to enabling you to wedge a Linux installation onto a 100 percent Windows partition, the Mandriva installer reliably detects your hardware and provides you with the option of simplified or very granular package selection. The RPM package management enables you to install, uninstall, and update software from a consistent and user-friendly graphical interface.

If you need to add or troubleshoot hardware, Mandriva provides graphical configuration tools (HardDrake) to make the task easier after the initial installation, and DrakX for detection during the installation. If you join the Mandriva Club, there's a wealth of support and application downloads available.

Chapter 17

Running Ubuntu Linux

U buntu Linux (www.ubuntu.com) has experienced a meteoric rise in popularity since its first release at the end of 2004. Relying on a constantly expanding number of core developers and contributions from its growing legion of advocates and users, Ubuntu has become one of the leading Linux distributions in the world.

"Ubuntu" is an African word that means "humanity to others." The project pursues the meaning of its name by:

- Making the distribution freely available; in fact, the project will even mail you pressed CDs without charge (http://shipit .ubuntu.com).

- Providing support for many languages.

- Offering features to make it usable by people with disabilities.

Ubuntu is based on Debian GNU/Linux but offers more focused goals than Debian. The primary goals of Ubuntu are to provide a tested, easy-to-use Linux distribution with a regular release schedule (every six months), to provide support and updates for those releases for an extended period of time, and to fit this easy-to-use desktop Linux on one installation CD. Ubuntu provides its own repositories of freely available software on the Internet, providing a huge assortment of software organized in the traditional licensing-oriented Debian fashion. These packages can be installed using the familiar apt-get, aptitude, and synaptic software management tools.

This chapter describes some of the major features of Ubuntu. It also describes how to install it on your computer or run the live CD version of Ubuntu.

Overview of Ubuntu

Although Ubuntu is primarily a Debian distribution on the inside, Ubuntu's focus on internationalization and general usability, its regular release schedule, and its simplified installation process are what make it different from Debian.

South African businessman, Internet entrepreneur, and longtime Debian advocate Mark Shuttleworth sponsors Ubuntu Linux through his organization Canonical Limited (www.canonical.com). Some of the best and brightest open source developers are on Canonical's team for producing Ubuntu. The organization's commitment to free distribution and rapid development has attracted a large and active user and development community for Ubuntu.

Ubuntu Releases

Coming into 2008, the Ubuntu project has produced seven releases, which have basically stuck to Ubuntu's promised every-six-month release cycle. Each release carries a version number derived from the year and month in which it was released, and is named after a woodland creature (your woodlands may differ from those in South Africa, home of Ubuntu):

- **Warty Warthog** — Released in October 2004 under Ubuntu version number 4.10.
- **Hoary Hedgehog** — Released in April 2005 under Ubuntu version number 5.04.
- **Breezy Badger** — Released in October 2005 under Ubuntu version number 5.10.
- **Dapper Drake** — Released in June 2006 under Ubuntu version number 6.06.
- **Edgy Eft** — Released in October 2006 under Ubuntu version number 6.10.
- **Feisty Fawn** — Released in April 2007 under Ubuntu version number 7.04.
- **Gutsy Gibbon** — Released in October 2007 under Ubuntu version number 7.10.

> **NOTE** In addition to the regular releases, Ubuntu also releases an LTS version for Long Term Support for those who want reliability above features. The LTS version offers support for three years on desktop versions and five years on server versions.

If you are new to Linux, Ubuntu is designed with you in mind. The standard Ubuntu desktop installer provides a great set of defaults for most installation options. Ubuntu, however, also provides other installers that include many more choices for customization when you install it. If you are transitioning from Debian (or another Debian derivative, such as KNOPPIX), you will find it easy to work with Ubuntu. You install and remove packages and manage services with Ubuntu using the same methods as with Debian.

Beginning with the Dapper Drake release, the Ubuntu project offers each release as three different CDs or a single DVD. The CDs are as follows:

- **Desktop Install CD** — This boots directly to Ubuntu, where you can either experiment with Ubuntu (without changing anything on your existing system) or install Ubuntu to a hard drive. This is the equivalent of the live CD provided by many distributions, except that it also provides an easy way to install Ubuntu Linux permanently if you decide to do so.

- **Server Install CD** — Lets you install various server configurations, ranging from a basic server to a standard LAMP (Linux/Apache/MySQL/Perl) Web server.
- **Alternate Desktop CD** — Enables you to install an Ubuntu desktop system from the command line in a more complex fashion than that provided by the Desktop CD's graphical installer (such as using Logical Volume Management). It also supports OEM firms that want to customize and ship Ubuntu-based systems, and provides a custom server installation mechanism. It does not include the live CD.

Getting started with Ubuntu is easy because the Desktop Install CD boots to a fully functioning desktop system. The Ubuntu Desktop Install CD does a great job at detecting hardware, setting up your video card environment (mouse, keyboard, and video card), and booting right to a GNOME desktop without changing anything on your existing system. It includes an icon on the desktop that enables you to install Ubuntu to your system after walking through six simple configuration screens (discussed later in this chapter).

The following sections describe the desktop and server features in Ubuntu 7.10 (Gutsy Gibbon).

Ubuntu Installer

The Ubuntu installer has helped make Ubuntu a tremendously popular distribution, showing Ubuntu's commitment to usability right out of the gate. The desktop Ubuntu install process does an excellent job of detecting hardware and system configuration information. Ubuntu's Desktop Install CD "test-drive" needs only a few additional bits of information in order to install its whole set of software packages to your hard drive. The other Ubuntu CDs feature a more traditional, text-based installer that should be familiar to users of any Debian-like system and are designed to work on almost any system with VGA graphics and 128MB or so of memory. This chapter focuses on the graphical Ubuntu installer, but the text-based installer on the Server and Alternate Desktop Install CDs is also quite easy to use.

Many ease-of-use features are built into the Ubuntu installer. For example, if you are not sure which type of keyboard you have, you have the option to type a few keys (as prompted by the installer) and have it try to figure out the type of keyboard you have. You also have the option to resize existing partitions on your disk during installation (a very handy feature if you have a hard disk with only one big Windows partition that you don't want to completely delete).

Ubuntu as a Desktop

As promised, Ubuntu 7.10 contains the latest desktop features available at the time it was released. Along with the latest desktop components you would expect (GNOME, OpenOffice.org, and so on), Ubuntu 7.10 also includes improved features for installing applications and customizing the desktop experience. Here are some of the features in Ubuntu 7.10:

- **GNOME Desktop** — GNOME 2.20 provides the desktop environment for this release of Ubuntu. Ubuntu's default desktop theme, Human, is a calm, brown theme in keeping with the standard Ubuntu color scheme.
- **PDF File Generator** — A virtual PDF printer is now created by default that allows you to print to PDF files from applications that do not include native PDF support.

451

- **Updates to Firefox** — An apt-enabled plug-in finder is now included as a wizard, and Extension Manager integration is now included.

- **Tracker Search Tool** — You can now find documents, photos, music, chat logs, and all other types of files quickly.

- **Evolution** — The Evolution e-mail and personal information manager (PIM) continues to improve, making it easy to manage e-mail, calendars, appointments, tasks, and contacts from a single application.

 Evolution provides a default interface that is reminiscent of Microsoft Outlook, making it easy for users new to Linux to make a smooth transition to a Linux mail reader.

- **Totem video player** — As for multimedia support, GNOME continues to improve its Totem video player, which is based on the GStreamer multimedia framework. Playlists are now integrated into the Totem sidebar, and DVD menus and subtitles are supported. Totem includes increased support for multiple playlist formats, including the standard CML Sharable Playlist Format, QuickTime Metalink playlists, and RealAudio playlists.

- **Application installation and management tools** — After Ubuntu is installed, you can use the Add/Remove Programs selection from the System Administration menu to install new applications or to remove existing ones you don't want anymore. You can also use the Synaptic package manager to browse all available packages in the Ubuntu repositories, making it easy to find and install the open source applications that do exactly what you need to do.

Beyond these features, Ubuntu contains a broad range of open source applications suitable for the desktop. Leading the list are the latest versions of OpenOffice.org (popular office productivity suite), the GIMP (image manipulation software), and Firefox (Web browser).

Many of the tools for configuring and setting preferences for the desktop that come with the GNOME project also fit well into the Ubuntu goals of accessibility and ease-of-use. GNOME's Removable Drives and Media Preferences window is set to immediately launch appropriate applications when you insert a CD or DVD, attach an external hard disk, or plug in a camera, printer, or scanner. The Assistive Technology Preferences window enables someone who is visually or physically impaired to use magnifiers and onscreen keyboards.

Figure 17-1 shows examples of some of these GNOME tools and applications.

Ubuntu as a Server

Many features that are not useful for a desktop Linux system but are important to servers have been built into the Ubuntu default server installer, available on the Ubuntu Server Install CD (or the complete Ubuntu Install DVD). As a central computing resource, servers tend to need to grow, and features such as the Ubuntu server installer's ability to create LVM partitions during installation make it easier for you to add disk space to your server on-the-fly in the places it is needed. Unlike the graphical Ubuntu Desktop installer described later in this chapter, the Ubuntu server installer is a non-graphical, terminal-oriented installer that is fast and easy to use regardless of the graphical capabilities of your server.

FIGURE 17-1

Assistive technology and easier device management with Ubuntu

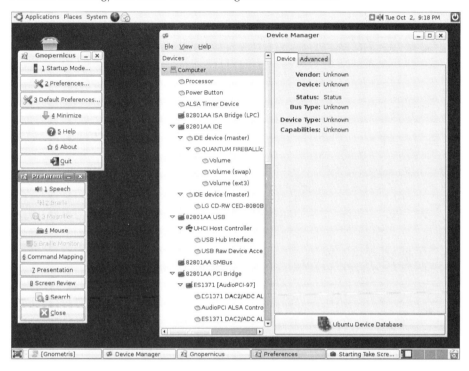

The default server installation supports up to 4GB of RAM on 32-bit PCs, and also provides kernel support for the GFS and OCFS2 cluster file systems. While GFS and OCFS2 are still relatively new file systems, and therefore may not be ready for use on your production systems, they are available for you to try out in Ubuntu.

To use Ubuntu as a thin-client server, Linux Terminal Server Project software is included in the Ubuntu server. You can read about how to use LTSP on the Ubuntu Thin Client HOWTO (https://help.ubuntu.com/community/ThinClientHowto).

The default server install takes up only about 400MB of disk space, although it is a very bare-bones system. In addition to base system packages and core utilities, you get software for managing your network connections and file systems, but not much else. Luckily, however, you do get application management utilities (such as apt-get), so any open source software you want to add to your server is just an apt-get away with an Internet connection.

The most common type of server that many people install is a LAMP server system, which uses Linux to support an Apache Web server and provides the MySQL database. It also supports the Perl programming language, in which many Web applications are written. The Ubuntu Server Install

CD provides a separate installer for this type of server system, highlighting Ubuntu's awareness of (and sensitivity) to the needs of its users, regardless of whether they are sitting in front of their desktop computer system or are cloistered in a machine room somewhere.

Ubuntu Spin-Offs

Because no single CD set of software is going to please everyone, some spin-off projects have already been created from Ubuntu. The following are three partner projects associated with Ubuntu Linux:

- **Kubuntu** (www.kubuntu.org) — This project combines the latest version of the KDE desktop with each desktop Ubuntu release. KDE replaces the GNOME desktop, which is used by default with Ubuntu.

- **Xubuntu** (www.xubuntu.org) — This project blends the power and usability of Ubuntu with the lightweight Xfce desktop system, delivering a full-featured Ubuntu system that is less demanding of system and graphics resources. Xubuntu runs well on older or less-powerful systems, and is ideal for laptops.

- **Edubuntu** (www.edubuntu.org) — This project focuses on producing a version of Ubuntu that is suitable for use in classrooms. Edubuntu combines Ubuntu with software geared toward education (such as KDE Edutainment software) and software used for creating inexpensive computer clusters (such as the Linux Terminal Server Project). As a result, Edubuntu can be used to fill a school's whole computer lab with working, educational workstations at very little cost.

Because of Ubuntu's commitment to help people of different cultures, with support for many different languages and keyboard types, there are Ubuntu communities to support users from all over the world. There's Ubuntu China (www.ubuntu.org.cn), Ubuntu Germany (www.ubuntu-forum.de), Ubuntu Sweden (www.ubuntulinux.se), Ubuntu Indonesia (www.ubuntulinux.or.id), Ubuntu Portugal (www.ubuntu-pt.org), and many other international Ubuntu sites.

Challenges Facing Ubuntu

Despite its rise to stardom, Ubuntu is bound to suffer some growing pains. Some possible challenges Ubuntu faces include:

- **Peaceful coexistence with Debian** — As a Debian-inspired distribution, Ubuntu was originally quite dependent on Debian and continued to use many of the licensing, usability, and stability features that are heavily emphasized in Debian Linux. Some members of the Debian community initially saw Ubuntu as hijacking the hard work of the Debian project. The success of Ubuntu, however, speaks for both itself and the technical excellence and commitment of the Debian community. Ubuntu pushes its fixes and enhancements back to the Debian community, as well as to the developers who support individual open source packages. The two distributions need to continue to work together to improve both distributions and GNU/Linux in general.

- **Fast release cycles** — Ubuntu has set itself a pace of six-month release cycles. In terms of major free Linux distributions, only Fedora has stayed close to a six-month release cycle. Debian has certainly not been known to rush to release new versions — the slowness of Debian releases was one of the initial inspirations for Ubuntu. Some delays have already occurred — for example, the Ubuntu 6.06 release was originally scheduled for April 2006 (6.04), but was intentionally slipped to include significant improvements. The Ubuntu 6.10 release was essentially on time, as have been subsequent releases, but a six-month release schedule is still an aggressive target.

- **Business model** — While the Ubuntu project does offer shirts, hats, teddy bears, and other products you can purchase that carry the Ubuntu logo (`https://shop.canonical.com/`), proceeds from that and donations are clearly not going to be enough to support a long-term development effort. The project has made it clear that it intends to be committed to software that is "100% free of charge" going forward. Canonical, Ltd, and many other vendors around the world, provide paid commercial support for Ubuntu releases, but "paid support" business models for Linux have rarely been successful. Only time (and a growing number of home, small, and medium business and enterprise Ubuntu users) will tell if Ubuntu can manage to succeed without adopting a free/paid community model such as those of Fedora/Red Hat, openSUSE/SUSE, and Freespire/Linspire.

- **Freedom and responsibility** — Endeavors with goals such as freedom and equality as guiding lights can sometimes suffer from a lack of control. As philosophically inspired distributions become more popular, technical discussions can sometimes spin out of control to become almost religious discussions. Ubuntu seems to resist the response that some profit-oriented Linux projects ultimately resort to: "Because we say so," but the line between openness and determinism is a tough one to walk.

  Ubuntu's leadership has done a good job setting up a structure to make hard decisions in a free environment. For example, Ubuntu now has a Community Council (to create teams and projects, as well as leaders for each team) and a Technical Board (to guide the technical direction of Ubuntu). There is also now a Code of Conduct (`www.ubuntu.com/community/conduct`) presented to keep everyone participating in the project on the same path.

Ubuntu has prospered and increased in popularity far beyond the initial excitement inspired by being the new kid on the block. Ubuntu is holding up well under the pressure and continues to grow both in the size of its development and support communities and its popularity.

Installing Ubuntu

Installing Ubuntu to hard disk requires a computer with at least 64MB of RAM for an Ubuntu Server, and 256MB of RAM for an Ubuntu Desktop installation. As for hard disk space, you will need at least 4GB of space to install a desktop system or 500MB of disk space for a minimal server system. For the minimal server, you need to be able to work from the command line (no GUI is installed).

The Ubuntu 7.10 Desktop Install CD image is included on the DVD that comes with this book. To install from that DVD, instead of the procedure described below, do the following: Boot the DVD, type **ubuntu** at the boot prompt, and after the Ubuntu desktop boots, open the Install icon and follow the instructions.

If you are setting up Ubuntu to dual-boot on a desktop computer with a Windows system currently installed, you can resize your Windows partition during the installation process. It is easier, however, to first make sure that the free disk space exists outside of the Windows partition. See Chapter 7 for information on resizing hard disk partitions to make space for a Linux installation. Of course, you should also back up any important data files at this point.

The following procedure describes how to boot and install Ubuntu:

1. Insert the Ubuntu Desktop Install CD and reboot your computer. You should see the Ubuntu CD's boot screen, as shown in Figure 17-2. (If your system doesn't boot from the CD or you don't see the Ubuntu splash screen, make sure your computer is capable of booting from a CD, as described in Chapter 7.)

FIGURE 17-2

The Ubuntu Desktop Install CD boot screen

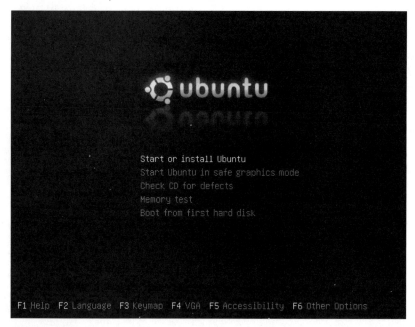

2. The boot screen for the Ubuntu Desktop Install CD provides a number of different options for booting your system, testing the installation CD or your system's memory, and so on. It also provides a number of special menus and screens that you can view to activate capabilities that might help you if you have special requirements during the install. The following is a list of the function keys that you can press and descriptions of each resulting menu or screen:

   ▪ **Help (F1)** — Lists what is available on the boot screens.

   ▪ **Language (F2)** — Enables you to set the language used by Ubuntu and the Ubuntu installer.

   ▪ **Keymap (F3)** — Enables you to specify the type of keyboard used by Ubuntu and the Ubuntu installer.

   ▪ **VGA (F4)** — Enables you to specify the graphics capabilities and screen resolution of the system on which you are booting or installing Ubuntu.

   ▪ **Accessibility (F5)** — Enables you to activate various accessibility-related options in the Ubuntu installer, including a screen magnifier, onscreen keyboard, audio reading of various prompts, and so on.

   ▪ **Other Options (F6)** — Enables you to modify the kernel command line used to boot Ubuntu, which lets you deactivate certain hardware systems (such as power control), turn on more verbose debugging, and so on.

3. To proceed without modifying any of these options, simply press Enter to boot Ubuntu and start a default desktop, as shown in Figure 17-3.

4. Once the Ubuntu desktop displays, you can experiment with Ubuntu Linux on your current system without making any changes to your hard drive, or install Ubuntu to your system. To install Ubuntu on your computer system, double-click the Install icon to begin the installation process.

FIGURE 17-3

The Ubuntu desktop and the icon for the graphical installer

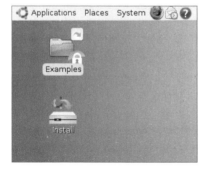

5. Select the language you want to use for Ubuntu. (The default is English.) To accept the selected value and proceed to the next screen, click Forward. You are asked to enter your location.

6. Choose your location. Your location will refine the language used (in other words, U.S. English might be different from Canadian English), and will also be used to set the current time. If the time shown is incorrect for your location, you can click the Set Time button to display a dialog box that enables you to correctly specify the local time. To accept the selected values and proceed to the next screen, click Forward. You are asked to enter your keyboard layout.

7. Select your keyboard type. To accept the selected value and proceed to the next screen, click Forward.

8. Provide information about a user account that you want to create on this system. This account will have administrative privileges, so you should create your own account at this point. Enter your full name (for example, John Smith), a username (for example, jsmith) that you will use to log in as this user, a password (twice) for the new user, and a name for this computer (which can be anything). To accept the selected values and proceed to the next screen, click Forward.

   You are asked to begin partitioning your hard disk.

CAUTION   Changing or removing existing disk partitions can result in data being lost. Consider your options carefully before selecting a partitioning method.

9. Select one of the following choices for partitioning your hard disk. (See Chapter 7 for further information on disk partitioning.)

   - **Erase entire disk** — This erases your entire hard disk, and then repartitions it automatically. Choose this method if you are prepared to remove all the data on your hard disk. Ubuntu installer will repartition using common Linux file system types.

   - **Use the largest continuous free space** — This allows you to install Ubuntu on a system on which another operating system is already installed, as long as you have sufficient, unallocated space available on your system's disk(s). Chapter 7 explains how to repartition an existing system in order to free up space for this option.

   - **Manually edit partition table** — This enables you to manually create your own hard disk partitions. This is the best choice if you want to keep existing partitions from being erased. This is also the best choice if you have special needs, such as creating separate partitions to hold user data (/home) or server data (/var), or using a particular file system type for an area of your hard disk. Manual partitioning is considered to be a more advanced skill.

   If you selected to manually edit the partition table, proceed to the next step. Otherwise, skip ahead to Step 11.

10. During the manual partitioning phase, you can graphically select or resize existing partitions on your disk and specify a variety of information about how you want to use them

on the system where you are installing Ubuntu. You must define at least two partitions. One partition is used as swap space, which is a special partition format that Linux systems use for managing virtual memory. A second partition is used to hold the top-level directory of your Ubuntu Linux installation, known as the root directory and mounted as / on your Ubuntu system.

In the initial partitioning dialog box, you select the free disk space in which you want to create a partition and click New, which displays a dialog box that enables you to graphically size the partition by dragging its borders. In this dialog box, you also specify the type of file system that you want to use on the partition, and whether it is a primary or extended partition. You can have only four primary partitions on a single disk drive — to create more than four partitions on a single disk drive, one of the four primary partitions must be defined as an extended partition, in which other (logical) partitions can then be defined.

11. After dividing your disk into partitions, click Forward to proceed to a second dialog box, in which you define where your primary and logical partitions should be mounted on your Ubuntu system. Mounted partitions are associated with specific directories on an Ubuntu system.

When you are done, click Forward to continue with the installation process.

12. A confirmation screen summarizes the installation options that you have selected. To begin the installation, click Install. You can click Back to return to previous screens and change the values that you selected, or click Cancel to abort the installation process without changing anything on your system. If you select Forward, the Ubuntu installer begins the installation process. When the process is complete, the installer ejects the CD, reminds you to remove it from your system's CD drive, and asks you to press Enter to reboot your system.

13. When installation is complete, the Desktop CD installer displays an Installation Complete dialog box that confirms a successful installation. When you see this dialog box, you can either click Continue Using the live CD to continue experimenting with Ubuntu from the CD, or click Restart Now to reboot your system and begin running Ubuntu directly from your system's hard drive(s).

When you boot your system, Ubuntu displays a splash screen and progress dialog box as it boots, followed by a graphical login screen. Congratulations — you're running Ubuntu Linux!

Ubuntu systems automatically run a graphical application called the Update Manager to notify you when system updates are available and to simplify retrieving and installing those updates. If updates to your system are available, the Update Manager displays a message to this effect and provides an icon at the right of the top panel that you can select to install those updates and keep your system current. You will need to provide your password in order to perform this (or any other) administrative operation. You can also check for updates manually at any time by selecting the System ➪ Administration ➪ Update Manager menu item.

To add other software packages, you can open the Synaptic Package Manager Window (select System ➪ Administration ➪ Synaptic Package Manager) or Add/Remove Applications window (select System ➪ Administration ➪ Add/Remove Programs). Using Synaptic, you can add the software you want individually. Software not available on the CD will be downloaded from the Internet (provided you have an active Internet connection).

Starting with Ubuntu

On the surface, Ubuntu is not very different in appearance from other Linux desktop systems using GNOME. Underneath, the tools for managing your software packages are the same as you would expect with Debian systems. Many of the differences are subtle and do a lot to make using Linux easier for the end user.

Log in using the username and password you entered during installation. Figure 17-4 shows an example of an Ubuntu desktop that uses an alternate Ubuntu desktop background.

FIGURE 17-4

The Ubuntu desktop incorporates GNOME with ease-of-use additions.

Trying Out the Desktop

With the latest GNOME interface, menus are available on the top panel. By default, you won't have as many applications to choose from as you have with the default Fedora install, which should be expected because Ubuntu comes on one rather than multiple CDs. However, the selection of desktop applications that you have with Ubuntu is good.

- The **Applications menu** offers the following categories of software:

  - **Accessories** — From this menu, select some basic desktop utilities that are part of the GNOME project. Choose Archive Manager to launch the File Roller application. File Roller provides a simple GUI interface that is useful for backing up personal files in a variety of archive and compression types. Text Editor starts the gedit graphical text editor (so you don't have to use the unintuitive vi editor to edit plain text documents). To go to a shell, you can launch the Terminal application from this menu. Other accessories include a Calculator, Character Map (for mapping special keyboard characters), and Dictionary.

  - **Games** — Under the Games menu, you have a selection of about 17 GNOME games. Some are similar to ones you would find on a Windows desktop (for example, Mines, AisleRiot Solitaire, and FreeCell Solitaire). There are also Tetris-like games (Gnometris) and board games (Mahjongg). You don't get any of the more demanding open source games (such as Tux Racer) or networked games (such as the BZFlag networked tank battle game), but these can easily be installed using the Synaptic Package Manager.

  - **Graphics** — The Ubuntu desktop install includes the GIMP open source graphic manipulation application. It also includes the F-Spot Photo Manager for managing collections of digital photographs, and the gthumb Image Viewer. To import images from a scanner, Ubuntu includes the XSane image scanning application. No document viewers are included here, such as Evince (which can be used to view PostScript and PDF files), but this, and the more traditional Adobe Acrobat viewer, can be installed using Synaptic.

  - **Internet** — Popular, standard open source Internet clients can be launched from this menu. The Ekiga Softphone application enables you to make voice-over-IP phone calls directly from your Ubuntu system. Evolution (a resource-intensive but full-featured mail client and personal information manager) can be used for reading and managing your e-mail. Firefox is the default Ubuntu Web browser, and Pidgin (formerly known as GAIM) is used for instant messaging. This menu also includes a Terminal Server Client if you need to connect to Microsoft Windows Terminal servers (in the rare event that you still need access to a Microsoft Windows system).

  - **Office** — A full set of OpenOffice.org office productivity applications is included with Ubuntu. Selections include OpenOffice.org Calc (spreadsheet), Draw (drawing and flowcharts), Impress (presentations), Math (formulas and equations), and Writer (word processing). OpenOffice.org Database lets you create and access a database.

  - **Sound & Video** — Ubuntu provides a movie player, the Sound Juicer CD player and ripper, the Rhythmbox Music Player for online audio, the Serpentine CD creator, and the Sound Recorder audio recording application. Like other commercial Linux distributions, Ubuntu doesn't include the software needed to play MP3 music out of the box, but you can easily add these capabilities from the Ubuntu repositories.

The movie player included with Ubuntu (and other GNOME desktops) is the Totem media player. Additional non–open source codecs are needed to enable that video player to play commercial DVD movies. Movie players such as Xine and MPlayer, whose use requires codecs that cannot be freely distributed, are not included with Ubuntu by default, but can be added through the Ubuntu repositories.

- The **Places menu** keeps track of places you want to go, lets you connect to remote servers, and lets you see (and, if you like, connect to) recently opened documents. There is also an option available to search your system for files.

- The **System menu** provides selections for changing desktop preferences and doing system administration tasks.

- The **Administration menu** is where you go to select languages, set up your printer, manage disks, and add users or groups.

Adding More Software

While Ubuntu manages to install around 2GB of applications from a single Ubuntu CD, it's still only 2GB. By contrast, other implementations with multiple CDs in a set can install up to about 7GB of applications. To add more software to Ubuntu, you can use the common Debian packaging tools (apt-get, aptitude, and even dpkg). You can also use the Synaptic Package Manager for adding and removing software packages, which provides a friendly graphical interface, a handy Search function to help you find packages, and many other usability improvements over the command-line tools.

To open the Synaptic Package Manager window, select System ➪ Administration ➪ Synaptic Package Manager. Figure 17-5 shows the Synaptic Package Manager window.

Using Synaptic Package Manager, you can install more software by selecting the Not Installed entry in the next column, and then selecting the package you want to install on the left. With one or more packages selected, select Apply, and the software packages you selected will be downloaded from an Internet repository and installed.

As Ubuntu is delivered, it will check only official Ubuntu software repositories to find and download the software you add to Ubuntu. There are times, however, when you want to add community-built software that is outside the official distribution, in areas referred to as Universe and Multiverse:

- **Universe** — Packages stored in Ubuntu Universe repositories include software that is not yet stable enough to be officially included in the project. Although the software has been built against Ubuntu libraries by the Ubuntu community, and will work well in most cases, it comes without guarantee of support or security fixes.

FIGURE 17-5

Synaptic Package Manager displays and installs Ubuntu software.

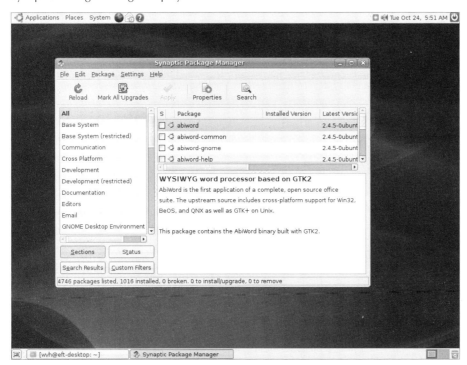

- **Multiverse** — Packages in Multiverse repositories contain software that is not free. This means that the software licensing might not meet Ubuntu requirements, that the software may be encumbered by patent issues, or that only binary versions are available. Users are encouraged to research licensing and other legal issues themselves before using software from these repositories.

Follow these steps to add the Universe and Multiverse repositories to Synaptic Package Manager so that you can use them to get additional Ubuntu software that simply might not be stable enough to be part of the Ubuntu release:

1. From the Synaptic Package Manager main window, select Settings ➪ Repositories. The Software Sources window appears, displaying the software repositories that are active for your system, as shown in Figure 17-6.

2. Select the Community-maintained Open Source software (Universe) or Software restricted by copyright or legal issues (Multiverse) repositories to enable you to explore or install software from them.

FIGURE 17-6

Add repositories to get software from Universe or outside the official distribution.

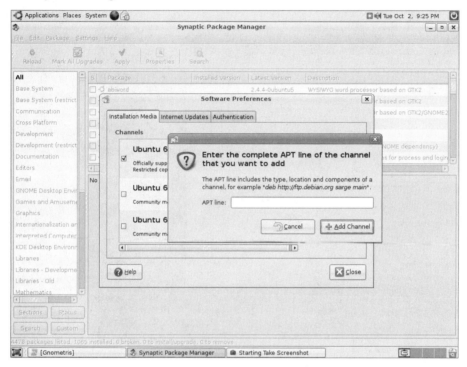

3. Click Close to close this dialog box and return to Synaptic. You will see a confirmation dialog box, alerting you to update Synaptic's package list. Click OK.

4. Select Reload from the Synaptic Package Manager main window. Software from the added repositories now appears in the list of software you can install in your system.

At this point, you can install any of the software that was added to your software list. Keep in mind, however, that because software in the Universe and Multiverse repositories is not supported by Ubuntu, it will not receive official patches or security updates from the Ubuntu development team. In other words, you are on your own (aside from asking for help on the Ubuntu forums or from the open source community in general).

If you want to stray further from the officially supported Ubuntu software, you can add custom repositories to your Ubuntu repository list. Here is where you need to be particularly careful, so be sure to read the caution before proceeding.

CAUTION As with any Linux distribution, any time you use a repository other than the official repositories supported by that distribution, you should carefully scrutinize that repository. Unofficial repositories can break software compatibility, can contain software that you cannot use legally, and might even contain malicious software. Although it is still no guarantee of safety, check Ubuntu forums and mailing lists to find outside repositories that others have found to be reliable before using them yourself. Also, look for repositories that are specific to your version of Ubuntu because software from earlier Ubuntu releases or Debian-specific releases may not work.

To add a custom repository to Ubuntu, do the following from the Synaptic Package Manager window:

1. Select Settings ⇨ Repositories. The Software Sources window appears.

2. Select the Third-Party tab.

3. Click Add. You are asked to add a complete line identifying the repository.

4. Type the line identifying the repository that contains the outside software you want to install. (The following is an example of a line identifying a fictitious repository.)

   ```
   deb http://ubuntu.example.com/ubuntu eft main
   ```

5. Click Add Source to have the line you just created added to your list of Ubuntu software repositories.

6. Click Close in the Software Sources dialog box. You are warned that your repository information changed and that you can now reload your package list.

7. Click Close.

At this point, you can install any packages that appear in your new package list. (Click Not Installed in the left column to see any packages that have not yet been installed from any of the repositories identified in your repository list.)

Getting More Information About Ubuntu

Ubuntu's popularity has led to the creation of many online resources. One of the best places to start learning more about Ubuntu or finding answers to specific questions is the Ubuntu Forums site (www.ubuntuforums.org). To begin participating in that site, I suggest you read the usage guidelines and policies in the Ubuntu Forums FAQ at http://ubuntuforums.org/faq.php.

This FAQ describes conduct rules and suggests the best ways of having your technical support questions answered. As with most forums, browsing through topics of interest or doing keyword searches are good ways to find the information you need.

There are a few resources from the Ubuntu forums that are particularly useful for someone starting out with Ubuntu. I recommend the following:

■ **FAQs, HowTo, Tips, & Tricks**

`http://ubuntuforums.org/forumdisplay.php?f=100`

This forum lists common steps that many people follow after installing Ubuntu, such as adding support for certain video cards or multimedia software.

■ **Absolute Beginner Talk**

`http://ubuntuforums.org/forumdisplay.php?f=73`

Posts in this forum can help you understand what Linux is all about and whether or not Ubuntu will suit your needs. You can ask very basic questions here as well.

■ **Ubuntu Café**

`http://ubuntuforums.org/forumdisplay.php?f=11`

To catch the spirit of the Ubuntu community, you can check out the Ubuntu Café forum and get a taste of what's on people's minds.

The Ubuntu community also has a wiki (`https://wiki.ubuntu.com`) that continues to gain useful content for people using Ubuntu. Currently, the wiki includes areas for Ubuntu documentation, community information, support for different languages, events, and much more. There are also specific areas devoted to each Ubuntu release.

Summary

Ubuntu is certainly the rising star of Linux distributions. Ubuntu started with Debian (one of the most respected but challenging distributions for beginners), simplifying the packaging and installation. It has demonstrated a commitment to frequent, well-designed, and supported releases. Today, Ubuntu is far more than a Debian spin-off, with its own community, advocates, and well-established development and maintenance groups.

Using a single installation CD, a user can install a set of useful desktop software or a streamlined server system. Ubuntu's graphical installer greatly simplifies the installation process by combining a graphical installer with a live distribution that you can run directly from the CD. It is easier than ever to test-drive and install Linux.

Along with the growth in popularity of Ubuntu has come an active community of developers and users. To become involved with Ubuntu, a good place to start is with community forums and the Ubuntu wiki.

Chapter 18

Running a Linux Firewall/Router

T he Internet is a potentially hostile place, so you need to be able to protect your computer from attacks coming in from the Internet. One essential element of security for Internet-facing computers is a firewall. A firewall can protect your computer or private network from outside intruders. Placing a firewall on the route between your local network and the Internet gives you tremendous power and flexibility to manage your network traffic. You can react to every packet coming in or going out of your network based on where it's from, where it's going, and what it is requesting to do.

Linux is often used as a firewall. In fact, several Linux distributions are configured to act exclusively as a firewall (running on media as small as a floppy disk). Because firewall tools can also be used to protect personal desktop systems, several Linux distributions include graphical tools for managing firewalls in an appropriate way for desktops. So, in effect, almost any Linux distribution can be used as a dedicated firewall or can simply be configured to use firewall features to protect itself from unwanted outside access.

In this chapter, you explore the features used in nearly every Linux system today for creating firewalls (using iptables features) and discover how to use graphical firewall tools in Fedora and Mandriva Linux. To comprehend how a lot of firewall features can fit in a very small space, you look at how to use the Coyote Linux Floppy Firewall distribution (which comes with this book).

ON the CD-ROM The CD that comes with this book contains what you need to create a bootable floppy-disk firewall with Coyote Linux. The iptables firewall feature is included with every Linux distribution that comes with this book.

IN THIS CHAPTER

Understanding firewalls

Protecting desktops with firewalls

Managing firewalls with iptables

Making a Coyote Linux bootable firewall floppy

Getting other bootable firewalls

Understanding Firewalls

A *firewall* refers to hardware or software tools that limit access to a computer or network based on a defined security policy. As used in this chapter, firewall refers to a piece of software that examines every network packet coming from the Internet to decide whether it should be allowed in, rejected completely, ignored, or modified. Every recent Linux system has firewall features available because they are built into the Linux kernel in a facility called *iptables*. But firewalls in Linux can be used differently, depending on what you are doing with your Linux system:

- **Desktop system** — A Linux system used only to run applications and browse the Web may simply use its firewall to block all (or nearly all) incoming requests for services. By doing so, the only data that can come into the desktop system is in response to requests initiated by that computer itself. When that desktop itself is behind a corporate firewall, firewall rules can often be relaxed to allow various kinds of file and printer sharing to take place behind that firewall.

- **Server system** — On a Linux server, a firewall can be used to block requests to all incoming ports except those used to provide the specific services offered by that server. It can also be used to block any requests from addresses known to be particularly abusive or to allow more services to computers known to be friendly.

- **Firewall/router system** — Linux is often used as a dedicated firewall, providing a buffer between a private network and a public network (such as the Internet). Using Linux in this scenario, you can make the best use of the full range of firewall features in iptables. Any packet trying to pass through the firewall can be filtered and then allowed to pass, be dropped, or be redirected in some way. The firewall can even hide (masquerade) the identity of private computers coming through the firewall to use the Internet.

Firewalls don't require fancy graphical interfaces (in fact, dedicated firewalls usually don't have X running at all, although they often serve up Web content to others). In fact, a Linux firewall in a home or small-office environment might run on a discarded 486 computer. Its footprint can be so small that it doesn't even need a hard disk — just a bootable floppy or CD that includes (or can access) the needed configuration information.

Firewalls are a prime example of an opportunity to use a special-purpose Linux distribution. (Later in this chapter you see how to build and run your own Coyote Linux firewall distribution, which fits on a floppy disk.) Linux firewall distributions typically:

- Are tuned to include primarily those components needed to be a firewall.

- Contain scripts for easily configuring firewall settings.

- Don't include X, which requires that you use the command line or a Web browser from another machine on the network, allowing the distribution to fit in a much smaller space.

- Include a few other tools for diagnosing network problems or serving the local network in some way.

For the average desktop user, however, graphical tools are available with Linux to set up a basic, secure firewall without the user having to understand the syntax of iptables. Let's examine some of those tools.

Protecting Desktops with Firewalls

If you are using a desktop Linux system, a simplified GUI firewall tool is a good way to begin protecting your computer. At the very least, you can use your firewall to explicitly allow others to use selected services from your computer, while blocking requests for other services.

Tools that come with Mandriva, Fedora, and Red Hat Enterprise Linux (RHEL) offer a few ways to configure a firewall using GUI tools. During installation of Fedora or RHEL, the anaconda installer offers a screen for selecting your level of firewall protection. Mandriva offers a firewall tool with its Control Center.

Starting Your Firewall in Fedora

During the first boot process, after installing Fedora or RHEL systems, the Firewall Configuration screen enables you to put a basic firewall in place. Once Fedora is installed, you can use the Firewall Configuration Window (select System ⇨ Firewall), as shown in Figure 18-1.

FIGURE 18-1

Change settings for your Fedora firewall in the Firewall Configuration Window.

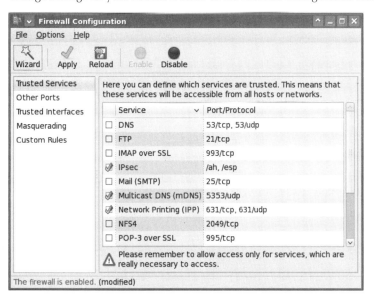

The Fedora Firewall Configuration screen handles almost everything the average desktop user needs in a firewall. Here is what you can do with the settings on that page:

- **Disable the firewall** — Although this option is not generally recommended, some people choose Disable firewall if they are directly connected to a router firewall or feel no threat from their network connection. This allows connection requests through to all ports. Requests to configured services are allowed, while requests for other services are ignored. The firewall just passes these requests through without question.

- **Enable the firewall** — Select the Enable option for the system to set up a basic set of iptables firewall rules for you, without your having to figure out how iptables works. Once your firewall is enabled, you can choose to allow selected services to your Linux system using those listed in the Service column.

- **Select trusted services** — If you are offering access to services from your system, select the check box next to the service you want to allow. You can enable access to the listed server types from your system by selecting the appropriate check boxes.

- **Open other ports** — To allow access to other ports (which represent particular services), click the arrow next to the Other Ports heading. Click Add, and then type either the port name (such as imap) or number (such as 143) and select the protocol (TCP or UDP).

> **NOTE** Open your IMAP and POP3 ports only if your computer is a mail server. If you're just downloading and reading mail from your computer, you can get your mail just fine from an IMAP or POP3 server without opening those ports.

After you have saved your firewall rules, you can examine the /etc/sysconfig/iptables file to see the firewall rules you created from your selections on the Firewall Configuration window. Those rules are loaded into the kernel from the /etc/init.d/iptables script (which is automatically set to run when you start Fedora). See the section "Using Firewalls with iptables" for details on how to work with your firewall manually.

> **NOTE** I like to check a few services just to see the rules that the Firewall Configuration screen creates. Later, if I want to add access to other services on my computer, I can simply copy one of the lines that allow a service and then change the service number or name to the one I want to allow. Service numbers and names are included in the /etc/services file. A common service that a desktop system might want to use and offer is Windows file and printer sharing (using Samba in Linux). To share files with Samba, you might need to open ports 137, 138, and 139 in your firewall. (Open Samba ports to local, trusted networks and never to the Internet.)

Configuring a Firewall in Mandriva

Mandriva offers a way of configuring your firewall after Mandriva is installed:

1. From the top panel, select System ➪ Administration ➪ Configure your computer. You are prompted to enter the root password.

2. Type the root password and click OK. The Mandriva Linux Control Center appears.

3. Select Security ➪ Set up a Personal Firewall. The Firewall service appears in the window.

4. Select particular services you would like to have available from your desktop system and click OK.

   The default settings shown might be appropriate for many desktop systems because they don't allow any incoming service requests. With SSH, FTP, and Echo request on, someone could log in to your system over the network (with appropriate login and password), get files you offer through your own FTP service, and ping your computer to see if it is up and running on the network. Of course, opening your firewall to allow SSH and FTP services assumes you have those two services turned on and configured as you like.

   Other services you can enable from check boxes on this window include Web server, Domain Name System Server, and CUPS server (for printing). If your system is configured as a mail server, you can select Mail Server and, optionally, POP and IMAP servers (to allow mail users to get their e-mail messages).

   If you want to add other ports, click the Advanced button. The Mandriva tool uses a different syntax for adding ports than does Fedora. You need to separate port numbers and protocols with a slash (for example, `123/udp 123/tcp` to open the network time protocol for those two protocols). Open a range of ports for a protocol by separating them with a colon (for example, `137:139/tcp 137:139/udp` to allow Windows file and printer sharing from your computer). Separate multiple entries with spaces instead of commas.

5. Click OK to accept your setting and continue. You are asked if you want to use an Interactive Firewall.

6. With Use Interactive Firewall selected, you will be warned when someone tries to access any of the services you have selected on this page. For example, you can be warned when someone uses a port scanner, presumably in an attempt to find vulnerable ports on your system. You can also be alerted when someone tries to access services you are sharing, such as SSH, FTP, CUPS, or Echo services. Click OK to continue.

7. Select the Ethernet interfaces on which the firewall will be enabled and click OK to continue.

Mandriva uses a facility called Shorewall to set up and manage its iptables rules. So, instead of looking in `/etc/sysconfig/iptables` for the changes you just made, look in the `/etc/shorewall` directory for files such as `rules`, `policy`, and `interfaces`. You can have those rules take effect immediately by restarting the Shorewall service (as root user, from a Terminal window):

```
service shorewall restart
```

When Shorewall restarts, look for any messages displayed. The output can give you information about any problems with the rules you have set up. Periodically check the `/var/log/messages` file to see if anyone has tried to intrude on any of your ports.

To find out more about how Shorewall works to configure your iptables firewalls, refer to the Shorewall Web site (`www.shorewall.net`). You can still use iptables commands to view the current firewall (`iptables -L`) or temporarily flush your firewall (`iptables -F`). However, other changes you might make with iptables will be temporary because the next time you reboot, Shorewall will take over again.

Using Firewalls with iptables

Understanding how iptables works will help you with any firewall you have configured in a Linux system. Previous firewall features — ipchains and ipfwadm — are no longer included in the Linux kernel. Unless you are using a Linux with an older kernel (which only a few floppy firewall distributions still have), iptables is your primary tool for firewall configuration in Linux.

The commands used to configure iptables are not very intuitive. Using the `iptables` command, you add rules (one by one) to your running Linux kernel. When you have a set of rules you like, save those rules to a file using `iptables-save`. Then, when you are ready to use them again, you read them back in using `iptables-restore`.

Although most Linux systems offer some sort of interface to manage and load your iptables firewall automatically, very few offer the full range of features you might want. So you will need to understand iptables to do some configuration by hand if you do more than simply open or close access to ports. Just understanding iptables will help you go from one Linux system to another, regardless of the interface an individual distribution will put on top of it.

Starting with iptables

If you have a running Linux system in front of you, you can immediately get a feel for how your firewall is working in a number of ways. To go beyond just listing the current firewall rules, however, I recommend that you try the procedure I describe in the next section on a Linux system that is set up for you to play with. Booting KNOPPIX is a great way to try that procedure without doing any harm (because everything disappears at your next reboot). Otherwise, just read along.

Setting Some Rules

Studying the following steps will help you understand the syntax of firewall rules and the types of information you can set with them. This procedure is made to run from beginning to end on a computer that you have complete control over. In the process of setting up your firewall rules, you will temporarily cut off all communications to and from the machine, so do not try this on a machine that must stay connected to the network.

This example procedure illustrates a case where you have two Ethernet interfaces on a computer (as is typical with a dedicated firewall). The interface defined as eth0 is connected to the Internet, and the interface defined as eth1 is connected to a private network of computers that the firewall is protecting. Presumably, the private computers are a bunch of desktop computers that need to go through the firewall to browse the Internet.

Iptables lets you set up tables containing rules for how to handle Internet Protocol (IP) packets that enter the computer. The filtering table is the table you use by default (`-t filter`) if none is specified on the iptables command line. Other firewall tables you can configure include NAT (`-t nat`) and mangle (`-t mangle`). Special uses of NAT and mangle tables will be explained later. It's the filter table that's used in this example.

Rules for what to do with packets that enter and leave the firewall are defined within the context of what are called *chains*. Available chains for filter tables are INPUT (packets received by the firewall), FORWARD (packets to be routed through the firewall), and OUTPUT (packets created on the local firewall itself). Filtering is done on those chains based on the rules you set up.

When a packet comes to the firewall, it steps through the rules in the chain until it finds a rule that matches. A match might depend on where a packet came from or where it is going, for example. When a match is made, the chain jumps to the action (also called a *target*) for that rule, which might define that the packet should be accepted or dropped, or have some other action done on it.

> **CAUTION** Setting up a firewall can be serious business. A misconfigured firewall can reject legitimate requests, forward packets to the wrong places, or even make your computer completely inaccessible from the network. Be very cautious if you are trying the following procedure on a computer that you rely on to be safe and accessible from a network.

1. From a Terminal window, become root user:

```
$ su -
Password: ********
#
```

2. Type the following to see what filtering firewall rules are set on your system:

```
# iptables -L
Chain INPUT (policy ACCEPT)
Target     prot opt source                destination

Chain FORWARD (policy ACCEPT)
Target     prot opt source                destination

Chain OUTPUT (policy ACCEPT)
target     prot opt source                destination
```

The example output shows that no filtering rules are currently set for this Linux system, meaning that all packets are accepted (`policy ACCEPT`) by default. If you see a complex set of firewall rules, you might consider using a different machine to try this.

3. These three commands change the default behavior for how packets are filtered for your computer:

```
# iptables -P INPUT DROP
# iptables -P OUTPUT DROP
# iptables -P FORWARD DROP
```

In this example, the default behavior is changed such that all packets that come into your network interfaces (INPUT), go out of your network interfaces (OUTPUT), or request to travel through them (FORWARD) are dropped. At this point, no packets should be able to come in or go out of any network interfaces. You can run iptables -L again to see that all policies have changed from ACCEPT to DROP. (If this concerns you, don't worry. You can run the commands again, changing DROP to ACCEPT, to make your firewall wide open once more. Likewise, a reboot gets you back to your original state.)

4. This step configures how your firewall will accept or reject ICMP packets. ICMP (Internet Control Message Protocol) messages are for reporting error conditions and controlling connections to your server. Your server receives ICMP packets from computers that want to find out the state of your machine, such as if the machine is currently accessible.

    Packets from the Internet that are accepted for ICMP protocol requests in the following example are those for ICMP types 8 and 11. Type 8 service allows your computer to accept echo reply messages, making it possible for people to ping your computer to see if it is available. Type 11 service relates to packets with a time to live (TTL) that was exceeded in transit, and for which you are accepting a Time Exceeded message that is being returned to you. (You need to accept type 11 messages to use the traceroute command to find broken routes to hosts you want to reach.)

```
# iptables -A INPUT -p ICMP -i eth0 -s 0/0 --icmp-type 8 -j ACCEPT
# iptables -A INPUT -p ICMP -i eth0 -s 0/0 --icmp-type 11 -j ACCEPT
```

    These two lines define rules for ICMP packets that come into the computer on the first Ethernet interface (eth0) from any source (-s 0/0). The first line says to ACCEPT type 8 service, and the second says to ACCEPT type 11 service.

5. The following are examples of commands that define the packets that will be allowed to come into and go out of the computer from the local computer or the private LAN that the firewall is protecting:

```
# iptables -A INPUT -p ALL -i lo -s 127.0.0.1 -j ACCEPT
# iptables -A INPUT -p ALL -i lo -s 10.0.0.1 -j ACCEPT
# iptables -A INPUT -p ALL -i lo -s 323.45.67.89 -j ACCEPT
# iptables -A INPUT -p ALL -i eth1 -s 10.0.0.0/24 -j ACCEPT
# iptables -A INPUT -p ALL -i eth1 -d 10.0.0.255 -j ACCEPT
```

    The result of these commands is that any packets sent from the local host (lo) are accepted, whether the source of those packets is the local host itself (-s 127.0.0.1), an interface to the local LAN (-s 10.0.0.1), or the Internet (-s *323.45.67.89*). The IP addresses 10.0.0.1 and 323.45.67.89 are examples of local interfaces to those networks (your addresses will probably be different). The last two lines indicate that the firewall should accept input of packets that are from the private LAN (-s 10.0.0/24) or destined for any address on that LAN (-d 10.0.0.255) network, respectively.

The *323.45.67.89* address is not a real IP address. You will replace it with the IP address assigned from your ISP for your external Internet interface. No valid IP address can include a part higher than 255.

The following commands define acceptable outgoing packets from the firewall computer:

```
# iptables -A OUTPUT -p ALL -s 127.0.0.1 -j ACCEPT
# iptables -A OUTPUT -p ALL -s 10.0.0.1 -j ACCEPT
# iptables -A OUTPUT -p ALL -s 323.45.67.89 -j ACCEPT
# iptables -A OUTPUT -p ALL -s 10.0.0.0/24 -j ACCEPT
# iptables -A OUTPUT -p ALL -d 10.0.0.255 -j ACCEPT
```

As with the input commands, the firewall accepts outgoing packets that come from any of the local firewall interfaces (127.0.0.1, 10.0.0.1, and 323.45.67.89). It also accepts outgoing packets associated with destinations on the private LAN (10.0.0.0/24 and 10.0.0.255).

6. This last set of commands defines what packets that originated from the Internet are allowed into the firewall. For packets attempting to enter your computer from the Internet, you want to be more restrictive, allowing in packets only for services you want to provide. Here are some examples of specific rules you might set to allow requests for services from a server:

```
# iptables -A INPUT -p TCP -i eth0 -s 0/0 --destination-port 21 -j ACCEPT
# iptables -A INPUT -p TCP -i eth0 -s 0/0 --destination-port 22 -j ACCEPT
# iptables -A INPUT -p TCP -i eth0 -s 0/0 --destination-port 80 -j ACCEPT
# iptables -A INPUT -p TCP -i eth0 -s 0/0 --destination-port 113 -j ACCEPT
# iptables -A INPUT -p UDP -i eth0 -s 0/0 --destination-port 53 -j ACCEPT
# iptables -A INPUT -p UDP -i eth0 -s 0/0 --destination-port 2074 -j ACCEPT
# iptables -A INPUT -p UDP -i eth0 -s 0/0 --destination-port 4000 -j ACCEPT
```

The first four lines open up the ports for the TCP services you want to provide to anyone from the Internet: for FTP service (--destination-port 21), secure shell service (22), Web service (80), and IDENTD authentication (113), the last of which might be necessary for protocols such as IRC.

You want to ensure that the services on the ports to which you are allowing access are properly configured before you allow packets to be accepted. In other words, don't open port 80 until you have a Web server configured or port 53 before you have a DNS server configured.

The last three lines define the ports where connection packets are accepted from the Internet for UDP services. This example assumes that DNS service (--destination-port 53) is configured on the computer. It also illustrates lines that accept requests for two other optional ports: Port 2074 is needed by some multimedia applications the users on your LAN might want to use, and port 4000 is used by the ICQ protocol (for online chats).

At this point you can run `iptables -L` again to see your new set of rules. If you have a connection to the computer from your LAN, as I illustrated with some options previously, you can try to ping the computer from the LAN. You can also try configuring different services and accessing them from your network interfaces.

With this part of the procedure completed, your new firewall rules are built into the Linux kernel but do not exist anywhere in a configuration file. Unless you save those rules, they will be gone the next time you reboot your computer. The following section discusses saving your firewall settings so you can use them permanently.

Saving Firewall Settings

If you think you have a good set of rules in your current kernel, you can save those rules using the `iptables-save` command so they can be reloaded later using the `iptables-restore` command. Here's an example of how to use the `iptables-save` command:

```
# iptables-save > /root/iptables
```

In this example, the current firewall rules are stored in the `/root/iptables` file (you can put them anywhere you like for the time being). These rules can be copied to a location where they can be loaded automatically on some Linux systems. For example, in Fedora systems, copy this file to `/etc/sysconfig/iptables`, and the rules are installed when the computer reboots. If they don't load automatically, you can restore them yourself as follows:

```
# iptables-restore < /root/iptables
```

The previously saved rules are now restored to the currently running kernel.

> **NOTE**   Remember that if you are using a bootable Linux, you need to be sure to save the iptables rules file to a location (such as a directory on a USB pen drive or hard disk partition) that will not disappear when you reboot.

Checking Your Firewall

Now that your firewall is configured, you should check it to make sure that it appears to the outside world — in our example, to the Internet on eth0 and your local LAN on eth1 — as you would like it to. A popular tool for checking what services are available on a network interface is nmap.

> **CAUTION**   While nmap is an excellent tool for checking network interfaces on your own computer or private LAN, it should not be used to check for available services on computers that are not yours. Using nmap on someone else's computer is like checking all the doors and windows on a person's house to see if you can get in. It is considered an intrusive act. Use nmap only to make sure your own "doors and windows" are secure.

Following is an example of using nmap to scan a large number of ports on the firewall system you just configured to see what services appear to be available from the two network interfaces on the firewall (eth0 and eth1). To do this effectively, you need to run the `nmap` command from a computer outside your local firewall. That's because you don't want to see what is going on inside your firewall; you want to see the outside world's view of your firewall.

From the firewall computer, you'd first get the IP address of the external Internet interface on eth0 by running `ifconfig eth0`. For this example, that IP address is *323.45.67.89*. (Remember that that is not a real IP address; it's used so you don't use nmap to scan a real computer on the Internet.)

Then, from another Linux machine on the Internet, type the following:

```
# nmap 323.45.67.89
Starting nmap 4.11 ( http:// www.insecure.org/nmap/ ) at 2007-11-16 14:56 CDT
Interesting ports on 323.45.67.89:
(The 1653 ports scanned but not shown below are in state: closed)
PORT     STATE  SERVICE
21/tcp   open ftp
22/tcp   open ssh
53/tcp   open domain
80/tcp   open http
113/tcp  open auth
4000/tcp open remoteanything
MAC Address: 00:0D:61:22:D3:11 (Giga-Byte Technology Co.)
Nmap run completed -- 1 IP address (1 host up) scanned in 72.951 seconds
```

The output shows that 1653 ports scanned on this address were closed (blocked from access) and 6 were open. Services not filtered include TCP ports 21, 22, 53, 80, 113, and 4000 (which you made available when you set up the firewall earlier). The seven services shown as open in the example all have servers running currently and listening on the open ports.

It's possible that you won't have access to a Linux machine on the Internet to test outside access to your computer. If you have another computer on your LAN, try running nmap from that computer. If you have only Windows machines, you can always run a bootable Linux and try nmap from that.

Using iptables to Do SNAT or IP Masquerading

You can use Source Network Address Translation (SNAT) or IP Masquerading (MASQUERADE) to allow computers on your LAN with private IP addresses to access the Internet through your iptables firewall. Choose SNAT if you have a static IP address for your Internet connection, and use MASQUERADE if the IP address is assigned dynamically.

When you create the MASQUERADE or SNAT rule, it is added to the NAT table and the POSTROUTING chain. For MASQUERADE, you must provide the name of the interface (such as eth0, ppp0, or slip0) to identify the route to the Internet or other outside network. For SNAT you must also identify the actual IP address of the interface.

The following examples assume that the connection to the Internet is provided through the first Ethernet card (eth0). Here's an example of a MASQUERADE rule:

```
# iptables -t nat -A POSTROUTING -o eth0 -j MASQUERADE
```

And here's an example of a SNAT rule:

```
# iptables -t nat -A POSTROUTING -o eth0 -j SNAT --to-source 12.12.12.12
```

You can add several source addresses if you have multiple addresses that provide a route to the Internet (for example, `--to-source 12.12.12.1-12.12.12.254`). Although `MASQUERADE` uses some additional overhead, you probably need to use it instead of `SNAT` if you have a dial-up connection to the Internet for which the IP address changes on each connection.

Make sure that IP forwarding is turned on in the kernel because it is off by default on most Linux systems. To turn it on temporarily, use one of the following commands:

```
# echo 1 > /proc/sys/net/ipv4/ip_forward
```

or

```
# sysctl net.ipv4.ip_forward=1
```

To turn on IP forwarding permanently, add the following line to the `/etc/sysctl.conf` file:

```
net.ipv4.ip_forward = 1
```

If you require it, here's how to turn on dynamic IP addressing:

```
# echo 1 > /proc/sys/net/ipv4/ip_dynaddr
```

or

```
# sysctl net.ipv4.ip_dynaddr=1
```

To turn on dynamic IP addressing permanently, add the following line to the `/etc/sysctl.conf` file:

```
net.ipv4.ip_dynaddr = 1
```

Adding Modules with iptables

Some firewall features require that modules be added to the kernel. For example, if a client behind your firewall needs to access an FTP server using passive FTP, special modules are required. With passive FTP, the FTP client sends its IP address and the port number on which it will listen for data to the server. If that client is on a computer that is behind your firewall, for which you are doing NAT, that information must be translated as well or the FTP server will not be able to communicate with the client.

The iptables facility uses modules to track connections, looking inside the FTP data themselves (that is, not in the IP packet header) to get the information it needs to do NAT (remember that computers from the Internet can't talk directly to your private IP addresses). For FTP connection tracking, you need to have the following modules loaded:

```
ip_conntrack
ip_conntrack_ftp
ip_nat_ftp
```

For client computers to use some chat servers from behind the firewall, you need to add connection tracking and NAT as well. In those cases, addresses and port numbers are stored within the IRC protocol packets, so those packets must be translated, too. To allow clients on your LAN to use IRC services, you need to load the following modules:

```
ip_conntrack_irc
ip_nat_irc
```

The default port for IRC connections is 6667. If you don't want to use the default, you can add different port numbers when you load the connection-tracking modules:

```
# modprobe ip_conntrack_irc.o ports=6668,6669
```

Using iptables as a Transparent Proxy

You can use REDIRECT to cause traffic for a specific port on the firewall computer to be directed to a different port. This feature enables you to direct host computers on your local LAN to a proxy service on your firewall computer without those hosts knowing it.

Here's an example of a command line that causes a request for Web service (port 80) to be directed to a proxy service (port 3128):

```
# iptables -t nat -A PREROUTING -p tcp --dport 80 \
        -j REDIRECT --to-ports 3128
```

(This example should actually appear on one line. The backslash indicates continuation on the next line.)

In this example, any packet destined for port 80 (--dport 80) is redirected to port 3128 (--to-ports 3128). Note that the packet is changed before it is routed (-A PREROUTING).

You can use REDIRECT targets only in PREROUTING and OUTPUT chains within a NAT table. You can also give a range of port numbers to spread the redirection across multiple port numbers.

Using iptables for Port Forwarding

What if you have only one public IP address but you want to use a computer other than your firewall computer to provide Web, FTP, DNS, or some other service? You can use the Dynamic Network Address Translation (DNAT) feature to direct traffic for a particular port on your firewall to another computer.

For example, if you want all requests for Web service (port 80) that are directed to the firewall computer (-d 15.15.15.15) to be directed to another computer on your LAN (such as 10.0.0.25), you can use the following iptables command:

```
# iptables -t nat -A PREROUTING -p tcp -d 15.15.15.15 --dport 80 \
        -j DNAT --to-destination 10.0.0.25
```

You can also spread the load for the service you are forwarding by providing a range of IP addresses (for example, --to-destination 10.0.0.1-10.0.0.25). Likewise, you can direct the request to a range of ports as well.

479

Getting iptables Scripts

Rather than type in all your firewall rules by hand, many scripts are available on the Internet (licensed under the GPL) that you can modify to suit your needs. Many of these scripts contain sections in the front where you can add IP addresses, port numbers, and other information that is specific to your firewall setup.

A nice set of scripts that illustrate how to use iptables comes from Oskar Andreasson, the author of the iptables tutorial. The set can be found at `http://iptables-tutorial.frozentux.net/scripts/`. In particular, `rc.firewall.txt` is a good file to step through.

Finding Out More About iptables

So far, you've seen an overview of many of the features in iptables and gotten a basic understanding of what it can do. Creating complex firewalls, especially in situations where there are a lot of people trying to break in, requires a much deeper knowledge of iptables. I suggest that, from here, you refer to the following:

- **iptables Tutorial** (`http://iptables-tutorial.frozentux.net`) — This tutorial by Oskar Andreasson is the standard by which other iptables information is measured.

- **netfilter project** (`www.netfilter.org`) — Get the latest information about iptables development, patches, security issues, mailing lists, and news.

- **LinuxGuruz** (`www.linuxguruz.com/iptables`) — This site provides a nice range of links to iptables FAQs, scripts, chat locations, HOWTOs, tutorials, tools, security sites, and mailing lists.

Making a Coyote Linux Bootable Floppy Firewall

Using just a 1.4MB floppy disk, you can have a firewall that does a good job protecting your LAN against unwanted access from the Internet. With a CD-ROM, you can add literally hundreds of tools for managing your firewall and keeping your network running smoothly.

A handful of bootable Linux firewall distributions are available today. The rest of this chapter steps you through the setup of Coyote Linux (`www.coyotelinux.com`) and then describes a few others that might interest you.

> **NOTE**   Coyote Linux Firewall is described here primarily as a demonstration of how small a useful Linux system can be. If you like, you can even use Coyote Linux from a CD (see `http://rzero.com/coyote/bootcd.html`). However, if the computer you plan to use for your firewall has a CD drive, consider using a more feature-rich and up-to-date firewall distribution such as Devil Linux (`www.devil-linux.com`).

Creating a Coyote Linux Firewall

Using a single, simple script, Coyote Linux lets you create a bootable Linux firewall that fits on a floppy disk. Once you install and boot Coyote Linux, you can manage it from another computer on your LAN. You can use a Web interface or log into it using ssh and manage Coyote Linux from a Linux shell.

Coyote Linux contains an amazing set of features for such a small space. After booting the Coyote Linux boot floppy you create, you have a firewall with which you can:

- Route packets between your LAN and the Internet.

- Provide network interfaces to Ethernet LAN (TCP or PPPoE) or dial-up (PPP) network connections.

- Create firewall rules supported by iptables. (It starts with a few basic rules, but you can add your own rules to include IP Masquerading and NAT, port forwarding, transparent proxies, or many other iptables features.)

- Enable DHCP. Coyote Linux can act as a DHCP server, providing IP addresses and other information to the computers on your LAN.

- Log activities. In addition to creating logs of activities on the firewall, Coyote can be set to pass those log files to another computer on your LAN.

- Monitor network activities. There are a few basic administrative tools in Coyote Linux to check out your network a bit. Those tools include traceroute and nslookup.

- Log in remotely (ssh) and get around the shell. The sshd daemon in Coyote Linux lets you log in from another computer on your LAN. The busybox utility (www.busybox.net/) provides a good set of basic shell tools.

- Open a Web interface to Coyote Linux. From any Web browser on your LAN, you can open the Coyote Linux Web Administrator interface by typing your firewall's IP address and port 8180 (for example, http://192.168.0.1:8180).

The following section shows you how to create a Coyote Linux boot floppy firewall/router. Once you have your Coyote Linux firewall up and running, you can change settings for that firewall from another computer on your LAN using the Web browser or shell (SSH) interface to the computer. If you are familiar with the shell and firewall features (described earlier in the chapter), there are a lot of things such as routing, demand dialing, and using a DHCP service that you can do with this nice little distribution.

NOTE For more information, refer to the Web site of Vortech Consulting, LLC (www.vortech .net), which created the Coyote Linux project. Like many companies that support open source software, it offers commercial products that relate to its open source project. If you want more advanced products and support, you can consider purchasing its corporate and small-office firewall products.

Building the Coyote Linux Floppy

To get just what you want in your Coyote Linux firewall floppy, you need to build it yourself. That entails the following:

- **Creating the floppy** — You'll need a computer with a floppy drive to which you can write raw data. That machine should be running Linux (KNOPPIX should work fine if you don't have a Linux already installed).

- **Running the firewall** — For this, you want a computer that can boot from a floppy disk and have two network interfaces. That computer can have as little power as a discarded 486 machine. In the example, the firewall computer will have a dial-up modem to connect to the Internet and an Ethernet card to connect it to your LAN (although a better and simpler way is to have an Ethernet connection to the Internet that can basically turn on automatically in most cases).

And, of course, you need a floppy disk.

The computer with which you create the floppy disk and the computer on which you run it may be the same computer (but doesn't have to be).

> **CAUTION** You need to know the Linux driver name for your Ethernet cards before you run the procedure to create your firewall floppy. If you don't know what it is, I recommend starting KNOPPIX on your machine and then using the `lsmod` and `lspci` commands to determine the driver names for your Ethernet cards (they should have been autodetected). Use `modinfo` if you are not sure if the driver name is the right one (for example, `modinfo 8139too`).

If possible, it's better to use a broadband or other Ethernet interface to connect to the Internet because dial-up modems can require extra configuration to work, provide slower connections, and make you bring dial-up connections up and down all the time. Because this section is meant to illustrate how to use minimal hardware with an extraordinarily compact Linux, it shows how to use an inexpensive connection type as well.

Figure 18-2 shows an example of the firewall configuration you'll create in the following Coyote Linux procedure.

To create a firewall with Coyote Linux, follow these steps:

1. On a computer that has a CD drive and a floppy drive, copy the Coyote Linux directory from the CD that comes with this book to your computer's hard drive. Then open a Terminal window (or other shell) and change to that directory. (See Appendix A for the location of Coyote Linux on the CD.)

2. Unzip and untar the Coyote Linux file by typing the following:

```
# tar xvfz coyote*tar.gz
```

FIGURE 18-2

A Coyote Linux firewall runs from a floppy disk, managing traffic between your network and the Internet.

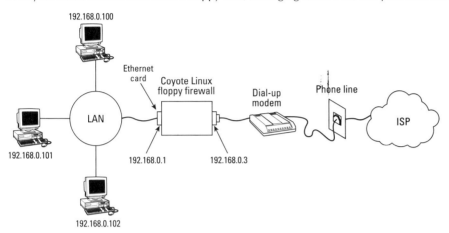

3. Change to the coyote directory that was just created and start the makefloppy.sh batch script to build the Coyote Linux floppy disk, as follows:

```
# cd coyote
# ./makefloppy.sh
Coyote floppy builder script v2.9
Please choose the desired capacity for the created floppy:
1) 1.44Mh (Safest and most reliable but may lack space needed
   for some options)
2) 1.68Mb (Good reliability with extra space) - recommended
3) 1.72Mb (Most space but may not work on all systems or with
   all diskettes)
```

4. Choose the capacity of your floppy disk. I used 3 (1.72MB) and it worked fine. With an older floppy drive, you may have to use a lower capacity, which will include fewer features.

```
Enter selection: 3
Please select the type of Internet connection that your
system uses.
1) Standard Ethernet Connection
2) PPP over Ethernet Connection
3) PPP Dialup Connection
```

5. This example uses a PPP dial-up connection here, so type **3**:

```
Enter Selection: 3
        .
        .
        .
By default, Coyote uses the following settings
for the local network interface:
IP Address: 192.168.0.1
Netmask:    255.255.255.0
Broadcast:  192.168.0.255
Network:    192.168.0.0
```

> **NOTE**   If you have a broadband (DSL, cable modem, or other Ethernet) connection to the Internet, you would typically select 1 here. Select 2 if your ISP said you have a PPPoE connection. Configuring an Ethernet connection is actually simpler than configuring dial-up. Instead of defining the dialer, you typically just select to connect to the Internet via DHCP and enter a hostname (when prompted).

6. You can simply accept the default IP address (and related Netmask, Broadcast, and Network numbers) by typing **N**. If you are creating a new set of addresses for your LAN, this is a common set of IP addresses for you to use (192.168.0.1, 192.168.0.2, and so on). Consider changing the IP address if it conflicts with your current network numbering or if that set of IP addresses is being used on your interface to the Internet.

```
Would you like to change these settings? [Y/N]: N
OPTIONS CONFIGURATION
Demand Dial:
Initiate the link only on demand, i.e. when data
traffic is present.
```

7. Now set up your dial-up features (if you are using dial-up to get to the Internet, as this example does). The first question is whether to allow demand dialing. Type **y** if you want the Internet connection to start up every time someone tries to open a connection to that interface (say, for trying to browse the Web or sending e-mail from the local system or any computer on your LAN using this as a route to the Internet):

```
Do you want to enable the demand dial option [y/n]: y
```

8. Type the number of seconds of idle time (time when no data is sent over the network connection) after which the dial-up connection to the Internet is dropped. The default is 180 (three minutes). I changed it to 600 (10 minutes).

```
Enter number of seconds for idle disconnect [180]: 600
```

9. To connect to the Internet with a particular IP address (assigned from the ISP), type **y** and then add the IP address as requested. In most cases, however, you just have the ISP assign an IP address by typing **n** here.

```
Did your ISP assign you a static IP ADDRESS? [y/n]: n
Setting up for dynamic PPP Address
Set the local PPP interface IP address. Should not be the
same as 192.168.0.1, but on the same subnet.
```

10. You need an initial IP address to start the PPP interface. As noted, you should use an IP address that is on the same network as your LAN.

```
Press enter for [192.168.0.3]: 192.168.0.3
```

11. The next several questions relate to setting up your dial-out connection. The tty device is the serial port where your modem is connected (ttyS0 for COM1, ttyS1 for COM2, and so forth). The port speed refers to how fast your computer can talk to the modem (the default, 115200, is fine). ATZ is the normal script for initializing a modem (check your modem manual if you need something else). Type any name representing your ISP (no spaces). Enter the phone number to dial to get your Internet connection. Finally, enter the username and then the password that was provided to you by the ISP for this Internet account.

```
Enter tty device name for modem (ttyS0, etc)[ttyS0]: ttyS0
Enter ttyS0's port speed (115200, 57600, etc)[115200]: 115200
Enter modem init string (Enter = ATZ): ATZ
Enter name of ISP (no whitespace)[isp]: att
Enter phone number to dial: 5551212
Enter username: jsmith
Enter password: tkNOstf
```

12. Type **n** to not send clear-text passwords during login. You may need to change this to **y** if your ISP requires CHAP or PAP authentication.

```
If you enable this, your password will be sent in clear
text over the line. Say yes here only if despite having
verified everything, you still cannot connect to your ISP.
Login during chat? [y/n]: n
```

13. Because this example firewall will provide IP addresses to the other computers on the LAN, it needs to be enabled as a DHCP server (**y**). Then you list the range of addresses it can assign to those computers. If you plan to have 100 or fewer computers on your LAN, the address range in this example should work fine for you:

```
Do you want to enable the coyote DHCP server? [y/n]: y
Enter DHCP range starting IP [192.168.0.100]: 192.168.0.100
Enter DHCP range ending IP [192.168.0.200]: 192.168.0.200
```

14. A DMZ is a way of further shielding your local network from the outside world if you want to have a Web server protected by the same firewall. In this case, you can add another Ethernet card to the firewall, connect that to the Web server, and then allow incoming requests for Web services to go through to the Web server. This enables you to continue blocking all incoming traffic to the desktop systems on your LAN. For this example, I just chose N.

```
If you don't know what a DMZ is, just answer NO
Would you like to configure a De-Militarized Zone? [Y/N]: N
```

15. Set the domain name with which this firewall is associated, and enter the IP address(es) of the DNS server(s) it will use to resolve addresses (probably provided by your ISP, unless you are running your own DNS server):

```
Enter Domain Name: example.com
Enter DNS Server 1: 123.45.68.799
Enter DNS Server 2 (optional): 123.45.68.800
If you have a syslog server on your LAN you want Coyote to
send its syslog data to, you can specify the address here.
If unsure or you do not have a syslog server, leave this
entry blank.
```

16. You can have Coyote log its activities to another server on your network. This can be very handy because it removes logs from the firewall (so someone can't tamper with them) and enables you to centrally administer logs on your network. Before you can use this feature, you need to configure support for remote logging on your logging computer. To do this, I recommend reading the syslog daemon man page (man syslogd on most Linux systems). Look for the "Support for Remote Logging" section. To disable the feature, as in this example, just press Enter to continue.

```
Syslog server address:
```

17. Coyote Linux supports a nice range of Ethernet cards. You must know the name of the Ethernet driver module for each Ethernet card on your firewall and enter it here. (You should already have this information if you followed the Caution at the beginning of this section.) For ISA cards, which you probably don't have unless it's a much older machine, you need to add IO and IRQ information.

```
Enter the module name for your local network card: 8139too
Enter IO address (Leave blank for PCI cards):
Enter IRQ (Leave blank for PCI cards):
Checking module dependencies...
8139too deps = mii
The default language of the Coyote Web Administrator
is English. Do you like to configure a
different language ? [Y/N]: N
```

18. To configure Coyote Web Administrator for a language other than English, select Y. Then choose from more than a dozen available languages. The Coyote setup script will then build the floppy image:

```
Building package: etc
Building package: local
Building package: modules
Building package: root
Building package: dhcpd
Building package: webadmin
```

19. Insert a blank floppy into the floppy drive and press Enter to build your floppy-disk Coyote Linux distribution:

```
Make sure that you have a floppy in the first floppy drive
in this system and press enter to continue...
Formatting /dev/fd0u1440
Double-sided 80 tracks 18 sec/track. Total capacity 1440 kB
Formatting ... done
Verifying ... done
bin/mkdosfs 2.2 (06 Jul 1999)
Installing boot loader...
Copying files...
cp: omitting directory `floppy/config'
`floppy/dhcpd.tgz' -> `mnt/dhcpd.tgz'
`floppy/etc.tgz' -> `mnt/etc.tgz'
`floppy/linux' -> `mnt/linux'
`floppy/local.tgz' -> `mnt/local.tgz'
`floppy/modules.tgz' -> `mnt/modules.tgz'
`floppy/root.tgz' -> `mnt/root.tgz'
`floppy/syslinux.cfg' -> `mnt/syslinux.cfg'
`floppy/SYSLINUX.DPY' -> `mnt/SYSLINUX.DPY'
`floppy/webadmin.tgz' -> `mnt/webadmin.tgz'
`floppy/config/coyote.cfg' -> `mnt/config/coyote.cfg'
`floppy/config/fireloc.cfg' -> `mnt/config/fireloc.cfg'
`floppy/config/firewall.cfg' -> `mnt/config/firewall.cfg'
`floppy/config/hosts.dns' -> `mnt/config/hosts.dns'
`floppy/config/portfw.cfg' -> `mnt/config/portfw.cfg'
`floppy/config/qosfilt.cfg' -> `mnt/config/qosfilt.cfg'
`floppy/config/reserve.cfg' -> `mnt/config/reserve.cfg'
```

20. After the floppy is created, you are asked if you want to create another floppy disk. Type **y** if you want another floppy disk and insert another floppy disk to create it. Otherwise, just type **n** and you are done:

```
Would you like to create another copy of this disk [y/n]? n
```

Now you're ready to try out your Coyote Linux floppy disk firewall.

Running the Coyote Linux Floppy Firewall

To start up your firewall, simply insert the floppy disk into your firewall computer and reboot. The firewall should come up as you configured it to run. There is no direct shell interface from the firewall's console once it's up and running. In fact, you don't even have to have a monitor on the firewall because you won't see a login prompt anyway. Any administration of the firewall should be done over your LAN.

If you configured it as just described, your firewall is now:

- Offering addresses to the computers on your LAN using DHCP
- Launching a dial-up connection from your firewall to your ISP as soon as anyone from your LAN or the firewall itself tries to access the Internet
- Allowing traffic from your LAN to the Internet
- Offering login (sshd) and Web administration service to you from your LAN

If the firewall is not behaving as you would like it to, go to the next section to further tune it.

Managing the Coyote Linux Floppy Firewall

With the firewall up and running, you almost surely will want to manage it further. There are a couple of ways to access your running firewall so that you can change its configuration with a Web interface or a remote login. Before you can use the remote login, however, you must change the system (root user) password, and that can be done only through the Web interface.

Using a Web Interface

The Coyote Linux Web Administrator can be run from any browser on your LAN to view and change your firewall configuration. It is available from that machine on port 8180. To access the site you configured in the preceding example, type the following in the location box on your browser: **http://192.168.0.1:8180**.

The first thing you want to do is click the System Password button in the main menu and add a password for the root user. Figure 18-3 shows the Internet configuration that was set up to dial out to the Internet in the previous section.

Using a Remote Login

The firewall floppy was configured to run the sshd daemon, enabling you to log in over your LAN (using the ssh command) to access your Coyote Linux firewall from the shell. In the example, you can type:

```
# ssh -l root 192.168.0.1
root@192.168.0.1's password: *******
```

FIGURE 18-3

Administer Coyote Linux from your Web browser.

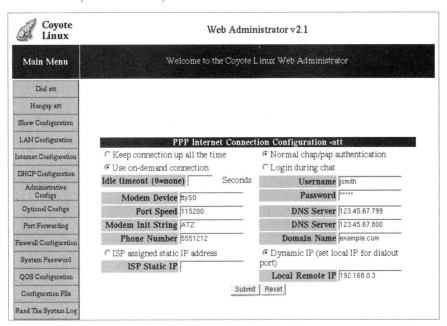

Enter the password (that you added from your Web interface as just described), and you are taken to the following Configuration menu:

```
Coyote Linux Gateway -- Configuration Menu
   1) Edit main configuration file    2) Change system password
   3) Edit rc.local script file       4) Custom firewall rules file
   5) Edit firewall configuration     6) Edit port forward configuration
   c) Show running configuration      f) Reload firewall
   r) Reboot system                   w) Write configuration to disk
   d) Dial PPP connection             h) Hangup PPP connection
   q) Exit Menu                       l) Logout
   --------------------------------------------------------------------
   Selection:
```

Select the letter of the configuration item you want to change. Type **q** when you are done, and you are left at a regular Linux shell prompt. At that point, you can use Coyote Linux as you would any (somewhat limited) Linux system from a shell. (Type **menu** if you want to return to the menu interface.)

As previously noted, the first time you open the browser interface to Coyote Linux, you change the root password. As for basic administrative tasks, you want to read the system log on occasion and back up your configuration changes (which you have made in RAM) so they are copied back to the floppy.

> **NOTE** To use ssh from a Windows machine to get to your firewall, or to get to any other Linux system for that matter, many people use the putty utility. You can get putty from its development home page at http://chiark.greenend.org.uk/~sgtatham/putty/.

Using Other Firewall Distributions

Coyote Linux was chosen for this book to illustrate how small, yet still really useful, a Linux distribution can be. It also uses the iptables facility, which, once you learn how to use it, is useful in all recent Linux distributions.

There are, however, many other bootable firewalls available today. I strongly recommend that you check some of these other distributions if you want more or different features than those offered by Coyote Linux.

- **Devil-Linux** (www.devil-linux.com) is the live CD firewall distribution that is most often recommended by the people I know. Not only is it recommended because of its excellent features, but also because it is being actively developed. A firewall is your first line of defense against Internet intruders, so choosing a firewall distribution to protect your home or small office computing systems that has an up-to-date firewall with the latest security patches is a very valuable asset.

  In addition to offering common Linux firewall features (such as iptables firewall rules and syslogd logging), Devil-Linux supports a wide range of hardware drivers, including many network cards and SCSI devices. You can configure your own firewall settings to be fed to the live CD from a floppy disk or USB drive. You can also configure many supporting services from the firewall, such as remote login (ssh), DHCP (dhcpd), Web service (httpd), Samba file/print sharing (smbd), and many other services.

- **Sentry Firewall CD** (www.sentryfirewall.com) is another very nice bootable CD firewall, but one that has not been actively developed for a while. Sentry Firewall CD takes advantage of the additional space on its CD to provide many extra tools for managing and watching your network. You can create a virtual private network connection using FreeS/WAN, manage SNMP services with net-snmp, and set up a variety of servers (using Apache, sendmail, bind, and others).

  Sentry Firewall supports many different types of IDE and SCSI hardware (so you are not limited to PCI Ethernet cards and modems). It offers both a shell and Web interface for managing your firewall.

- **IP Cop Firewall** (http://ipcop.org) is a stateful firewall distribution based on netfilter. A number of add-ons are available for it and development is constantly underway. As of this writing, the latest version is 1.4.16.

For a list of some additional firewall/router distributions, see the DistroWatch.com site at www.distrowatch.com/dwres.php?resource=firewalls.

Summary

No computer should be connected to the Internet or any public network without either being behind a firewall or being configured as a firewall itself. All of the latest Linux systems have iptables built right into the kernel to offer excellent firewall features (earlier Linux systems included ipchains or ipfwadm).

Desktop Linux systems often offer simplified, graphical tools for configuring a firewall. Every Linux system, however, enables you to use the `iptables` command directly to change the rules in your running Linux system. There are also tools to save and restore your firewall rules.

Coyote Linux illustrates how a Linux distribution with many valuable features can fit on a medium as small as a floppy disk. You stepped through the creation of the firewall floppy, booting it, and configuring the running firewall. For your permanent home or small office firewall, there are live CD–based firewalls you can use, such as Devil-Linux and Sentry Firewall live CDs.

Chapter 19

Running Bootable Linux Distributions

While KNOPPIX is probably the best-known bootable Linux distribution, it's by no means the only one. In the past few years, bootable Linux systems have gone from little more than simple, shell-command rescue floppies to full-blown desktop, server, and security operating systems.

Tools for creating bootable Linux systems have improved quite a lot recently. Because open source software can be pieced together and redistributed, individuals are beginning to create custom bootables that include their own music, presentations, or movies, along with a personal toolkit of software.

This chapter describes some popular and interesting bootable Linux distributions. It also explores ways that you can customize some of these bootable Linux systems to suit your needs.

NOTE If you haven't already done so, I recommend you try the KNOPPIX distribution included with this book and described in Chapter 11. It will help you get a good hands-on view of a bootable Linux system by describing how KNOPPIX works, how to use different boot options to start it, and ways of saving changes across reboots. You can also check out Appendix A for a list of other bootable Linux distributions that come on the CD and DVD included with this book.

Overview of Bootable Linux Distributions

There are now dozens, and probably will soon be hundreds, of bootable Linux distributions (also sometimes called *live CDs*). By stuffing removable media (CDs, DVDs, floppies, and even USB flash drives) with a select mix of open source software, bootable Linuxes enable you to bypass the hard disk completely (if you like) and have a special Linux distribution running on almost any computer within minutes.

A bootable Linux distribution can offer you some amazing opportunities. On a removable medium, you can take with you:

- Your favorite operating system
- As many of your favorite applications as will fit on your medium
- As much of your music, video, documents, and other data as will fit on your medium
- A fully customized set of features and configuration settings

In other words, if you are willing to build your own custom bootable distribution, the concept of bootable Linux distributions can be extended any way you like. Your bootable business card (mini-CD) or CD can carry all the applications you are used to having, so you can use them anywhere from a handy PC. But it can also hold your presentations, documents, mail-server settings, address books, favorite backgrounds and screensavers, personal photos, and any other kinds of data you want as well.

Most bootable Linux systems are based on established Linux distributions that are typically installed to hard disk. For example, KNOPPIX is based on Debian, as is Damn Small Linux (DSL). SLAX is based on Slackware. The System Rescue CD is based on Gentoo. So if, for example, you want to choose a bootable Linux to customize as a personal desktop or server, you might choose one based on a Linux system you are familiar with.

More than the distribution it comes from, however, you will likely choose a particular bootable Linux system because it contains a specialized set of tools (such as a security toolkit) or is built to provide a specific function (such as playing multimedia). For example, tools that are included with the BackTrack Network Security Suite live CD are focused on securing, checking, and recovering computers and networks. BackTrack's menus are organized based on the security tools it provides. Components in MoviX^2 include those geared toward playing movies, music, and images.

Choosing a Bootable Linux

Whether you choose a bootable Linux to do a special job (security, multimedia playback, gaming, and so on) or just to have a portable version of a Linux you are familiar with, several bootable Linux distributions are included with this book that you can try out. For descriptions of those, and other bootable Linux distros, I recommend you visit the following sites:

- **Knoppix Customizations** — The Knoppix Customizations page (`www.knoppix.net/wiki/Knoppix_Customizations`) lists just under 100 distributions based on KNOPPIX.
- **LinuxLinks.com** — This site has a list of mini-distributions, many of which are bootable Linux systems. The page that contains this list is `www.linuxlinks.com/Distributions/Mini_Distributions/`.

■ DistroWatch.com — DistroWatch keeps a list of CD-based Linux distributions and live Linux CDs (`http://distrowatch.com/dwres.php?resource=cd`). Its site also contains information and links to hundreds of distributions.

If you have trouble running any bootable Linux distributions, try adding options to the boot prompt. Because so many of the distributions are based on KNOPPIX, refer to the KNOPPIX boot options (also called *cheat codes*) described in Chapter 11 to help get your Linux distribution to start up the way you would like. View these codes online at `www.knoppix.net/wiki/Cheat_Codes`.

This book comes with several bootable Linux distributions, which you can find out about in Appendix A. You can get more recent versions of distributions that interest you (some are updated quite often) by following links from the sites just mentioned.

CAUTION Most bootable Linux distributions are created by individuals and should still be considered experimental in nature. The quality can vary widely and sometimes the controls are not as stringent as they would be for commercial Linux systems, such as Red Hat Enterprise Linux or SUSE. You can limit your risks by doing such things as mounting all hard disk partitions read-only (as is usually, but not always, done by default), but remember that this software is distributed with no warranty.

Although KNOPPIX, the most popular bootable Linux, has already been covered in this book, the following sections describe interesting bootable Linux distributions, categorized by the type of content they contain.

Security and Rescue Bootables

Rescuing broken systems and diagnosing network problems are among the most popular uses of bootable Linuxes. If you find yourself with a seemingly inaccessible hard disk, bootable rescue CDs or DVDs can literally save damaged or infected computers. Some rescue CDs are touted as complete security toolkits, offering a wide range of tools for monitoring Linux or Windows systems, scanning for viruses, debugging networks, and doing forensics.

Most bootable Linux systems will boot up on your network if a DHCP server is on the line. (If there isn't one, many include the netcardconfig utility to let you set up a wired Ethernet card manually.) So, with your computer booted and connected to a network with a bootable Linux, you could proceed to check, fix, back up, and otherwise control the local computer as well as other computers on your network.

NOTE Some security live CD projects note that the tools their live CDs include were chosen, in part, from the Insecure.org "Top 100 Network Security Tools" list (`http://sectools` `.org`). The list was put together from over 3,200 responses to a survey on the nmap-hackers mailing list.

Here are suggestions of some of the ways you can use most Linux security/rescue CDs:

■ **Assessing vulnerability** — Tools for assessing vulnerabilities of your computer include those to let you scan shared Windows SMB folders (nbtscan), CGI scripts (nikto and screamingCobra), and the computer's ports (nmap), as well as scan for viruses (clamAV). You can also check if someone has used a rootkit to replace critical system files (chkrootkit), or you can use a scanner dispatch (warscan) to test any exploit you like across lots of machines.

- **Running forensics on Windows machines** — If you believe a Windows system has been compromised, there are many tools you can use to find problems and correct them. Boot a security CD, such as KNOPPIX-STD, and you can recover Internet Explorer cookies (galleta), convert Outlook Express dbx files to mbox format (readdbx and readoe), check system integrity (ftimes), and check the Windows recycle bin (rifiuti).

- **Recovering data** — If a Windows or other operating system won't boot or is otherwise impaired, you can get data off that computer. You can copy files over the network (using rsync, scp, or others) or back up to local CD or tape (cpio, tar, or others). You can selectively recover file types from disk images (foremost) or check and recover lost partitions (testdisk).

- **Dealing with intruders** — Tools such as Snort (www.snort.org) enable you to analyze network traffic in real time, as well as log and analyze data as attacks are happening. Honeypots let you watch intruders' moves as the honeypots lead intruders to believe they've compromised your system. Honeypots in security-related Linux CDs include honeyd (http://honeyd.org), thp, and thpot (www.alpinista.org/thp). Kill zombies from DDoS attacks with zz.

- **Using and analyzing encryption techniques** — Many tools enable you to use encryption techniques to protect your data and find when others have tried to compromise it. GNP privacy guard (gpg) is used for verifying the authenticity of computers and people. For setting up virtual private networks, there are stunnel and super-freeSWAN VPNs. You can find images (giffshuffle, stegbreak, and stegdetect) and music (mp3stego) that contain hidden messages created by a technique called *steganography*.

- **Managing a firewall** — Bring a firewall up quickly or assess what's happening on a running firewall. The blockall script can block all inbound TCP traffic, flushall flushes your firewall rules, and fwlogwatch can monitor firewall logs. The firestarter and floppyfw utilities offer quick ways to start up a firewall. Tools for managing iptables firewalls include gtk-iptables and shorewall.

Popular Linux rescue CDs that illustrate very well how many tools you can get on a single CD include System Rescue CD, BackTrack, Knoppix-STD, and the Inside Security Rescue Toolkit (INSERT) rescue CDs.

> **CAUTION**   When you use a rescue CD to change a master boot record, fix partition tables, or clean viruses from a system, you risk doing irreparable damage to your computer system. Remember that GPL software comes with no warranty, so you use that software at your own risk.

BackTrack Network Security Suite

A wide-range of powerful, well-organized security tools are on the Backtrack Network Security Suite (http://remote-exploit.org/index.php/BackTrack) live CD. BackTrack is based on two live Linux distributions used to test if your computer system has been compromised: Whax and Auditor.

BackTrack offers a good combination of GUI and command-line security tools. The BackTrack menus (shown in Figure 19-1) organize all of those tools together. This enables you to look in one place for all similar tools. When you select a command from a menu, the command runs with the help (-h) option so you can see how it works. It's up to you to then type the command and add the options you want.

FIGURE 19-1

BackTrack organizes graphical and command-line security tools.

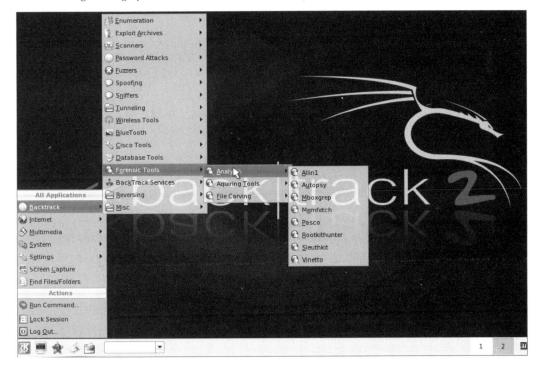

ON the DVD-ROM The BackTrack CD is included on the DVD that comes with this book. Refer to Appendix A for information on running BackTrack.

SystemRescueCd

The SystemRescueCd (www.sysresccd.org) is aimed squarely at recovering crashed systems. Tools included on this distribution include those specifically for repairing and saving your data, such as:

- **Disk partitioning tools** — You can check, add, remove, move, and resize disk partitions with tools such as parted and qtparted.

- **Logical Volume Management tools** — For file systems created with LVM, there are lvm and evms tools. (Logical volume management lets you add space to areas of a file system without changing the physical partitions.)

- **Security tools**—Check whether the data on your system has been compromised with tools such as chkrootkit (to check for software installed by hackers to let them access your system), as well as clamav and clamd (to scan for existing and incoming viruses). Use nmap (scan network computers for open ports) and nc (the Netcat utility for checking connections to remote hosts) for checking network security.

- **Backup tools**—As you might expect, this distribution contains standard Linux tools for archiving data (tar, cpio, dump, rar, and so on) and compressing data (such as bzip2, gzip, and compress). Likewise, it contains standard tools for copying your data over the network (scp, sftp, ftp, and so on).

Because SystemRescueCd doesn't include a graphical interface, it can get a lot of commands into about 100MB of disk space. Some of the tools, however, such as the midnight commander (mc command) file manager, provide a GUI-like interface from a regular Linux shell via the ncurses libraries.

> **ON the CD-ROM** The SystemRescueCd image is included on the CD that comes with this book. Refer to Appendix A for information on running the SystemRescueCd.

KNOPPIX Security Tools Distribution

The Knoppix-STD goes lightweight on the window manager to go heavyweight on the diagnostic tools. The distribution contains hundreds of tools that can be used for repairing and assessing computer and network security (see `http://s-t-d.org/`).

Instead of a full GNOME desktop, Knoppix-STD uses the Fluxbox window manager. It will run on lesser machines, but you'll get a usable GUI on almost any Pentium-class machine with at least 64MB of RAM. With at least 640MB of RAM, you can run the entire distribution from RAM (type **knoppix toram** to boot it to run entirely from RAM). With Knoppix-STD running in RAM, the system operates faster and your CD or DVD drive is available for other purposes.

Go to the project's Tools page (`http://s-t-d.org/tools.html`) to find out about more features in the project. Or go to the download page (`http://s-t-d.org/download.html`) to download and try it yourself.

The Inside Security Rescue Toolkit

INSERT (Inside Security Rescue Toolkit) is another KNOPPIX derivative that includes features from Damn Small Linux as well. INSERT bills itself as a disaster recovery and network analysis system. It contains a more compact set of tools to fit on a bootable business card (about 50MB). Check it out at `www.freshmeat.net/projects/INSERT/`. Chapter 6 shows how to use INSERT to check for rootkits.

> **ON the CD-ROM** INSERT is included on the CD that comes with this book. Refer to Appendix A for information on using INSERT.

The Fluxbox window manager offers some docked system monitors for monitoring CPU, network traffic, memory and swap use, and battery (if you are on a laptop). Another applet displays the Matrix screensaver (double-click it to launch a Terminal window). The mount applet lets you step through the CD, floppy, and hard disk partitions on your computer. Click the key button on that applet (so it turns green), and you can double-click it to mount and open that device or partition.

Right-click the desktop to see a menu that lets you select from a handful of graphical tools for troubleshooting your computer and network, most of which will run from the shell. Figure 19-2 shows the INSERT desktop.

FIGURE 19-2

Use INSERT to troubleshoot computers and networks.

You can find what's in INSERT from the List of Applications page on the Inside Security site (www.inside-security.de/applicationlist.html).

Demonstration Bootables

Individuals and organizations that want to promote their businesses or software projects can create custom live CDs to incorporate their own content or display their wares. And software developers can rest assured that the project they want to show off will work because it can be adapted to an entire operating system. An organization that wants to demonstrate what it's about can boot up to play any content (images, presentations, movies, music, and so on) on any existing open source player.

Here are some examples of bootable CDs that are used for demonstration purposes:

- **Linux distributions** — Several Linux distributions offer official live CDs that let you start using or playing with that distribution before committing to a full install. Two such live CDs are delivered with the Ubuntu (`www.ubuntu.com/download`) and Gentoo Linux (`www.gentoo.org/main/en/where.xml`) projects. Both of these live CDs also offer an icon on the desktop that lets you install the distribution from the live CD (a basic desktop install) directly to hard disk when you are ready.

- **Software projects** — There are open source projects that produce a live CD to let people try out their projects. The GNOME Live Media project (`http://live.gnome.org/GnomeLiveMedia`) offers a live CD that can be used to try the features of GNOME.

- **Any content you choose** — Live CDs are becoming a popular medium to hold and play specific content. GeeXBoX Generator and eMoviX[2] are spin-offs of GeeXboX and MoviX[2] projects for creating live CDs to play any video you include (see the following section). I've created custom versions of Damn Small Linux that boot directly to a slide show of images from my family vacation.

  Because Linux can act as both a client and server, it is a great medium to demo custom Web applications. The book *Practical PHP and MySQL* by Jono Bacon (Prentice Hall, 2006) includes a live CD that contains all the Web applications described in the book. Because a complete LAMP server package is also on the live CD, that live CD is all you need to run the sample projects, display them in a Web browser, and modify them in an HTML editor.

Because open source software can be manipulated as you choose and redistributed, live CDs are becoming an increasingly popular method of demonstrating software projects and content.

Multimedia Bootables

Some bootable Linuxes are tailored specifically to let you play movies, music, and images. Most let you play whatever content you have on your hard disk or can point to from the Internet. Many run in a small enough amount of memory to let you remove the bootable DVD or CD containing Linux and insert your own content (such as a music CD or movie DVD) to play.

MoviX

With MoviX (`http://sourceforge.net/projects/movix/`), you run a multimedia player that disregards the operating systems (Windows, Linux, or otherwise) installed on your system. Because MoviX is small enough to run in your system memory, after it has booted you can remove it and insert the CD or DVD containing the content you want to run. With MoviX, you can play:

- **Videos** — You can play video from many different formats, including DivX/XVID, MPEG 1 and 2, and MPEG 4. So that MoviX can be freely distributed, it does not include the capability to play most DVD movies.

CAUTION The U.S. Digital Millennium Copyright Act (DCMA) prohibits the creation or distribution of software that is made to circumvent encryption that protects copyrighted material. The libdvdcss library, needed to decrypt DVD movies (even if only for playback), has been the subject of much discussion. Although this library is available on the Internet, most Linux systems in the U.S. have chosen not to distribute this library because using it may be illegal under the DCMA. You should research this issue yourself if you plan to add libdvdcss to MoviX or any other Linux distribution that includes MPlayer or xine media players.

- **Music** — You can play audio files in AVI, MP3, Ogg Vorbis, and other formats.
- **Images** — You can run a slide show using the Linux Frame Buffer Image (fbi) viewer that displays images in JPEG, PNG, and a variety of other image formats.

The MoviX player itself doesn't include any video, music, or images for you to play. Instead, it lets you choose the location of your content. Here are the possibilities, depending on what is available on your computer:

- **DVDs** — If you have a DVD drive on your computer, you can play supported content from there. (As previously stated, that doesn't include most commercial movies, by default.)
- **VCDs and SVCD** — These are video formats that can be put on standard CDs.
- **Audio CDs** — You can play standard music CDs (including AVI, MP3, and other formats).
- **Hard disk files** — Any supported content on the local hard disk can also be played from MoviX. As with KNOPPIX, MoviX detects hard disk partitions and then mounts them as you request files from those partitions. The mounts are done read-only, by default, so you can play your content without any risk of deleting or otherwise damaging it.
- **Network** — MoviX boots onto the network if a DHCP server is detected. Although the friendly user interface doesn't appear to support it yet, software in MoviX should enable you to get content from your LAN or the Internet to play back using an NFS (UNIX file sharing) or FTP (standard Internet file sharing facility) file server.

MoviX boots right up to MPlayer, so you can eject the MoviX disk; insert a CD, DVD, or VCD into your drive; and play any supported content. Right-click the desktop to see your choices for selecting content.

If you are comfortable moving around in Linux, you can go to different virtual terminals while you are using MoviX. Press Ctrl+Alt+F2 to view a sound mixer or Ctrl+Alt+F3 to go to a Linux shell. Then press Ctrl+Alt+F4 to get back to the main screen (with MPlayer). Select Switch to MoviX from the menu, and you can choose to run your audio player, slide show, or TV viewer (the latter if you have a television card installed).

If you think MoviX is cool, you'll really like the idea of the eMoviX project. With eMoviX, you put a mini-MoviX distribution on a CD or DVD with your video so that your video content comes with its own bootable player! (See `http://movix.sourceforge.net/Docs/eMoviX` for details.)

 Both eMovix and MoviX are described in my book *Linux Toys II*, in a project devoted mainly to creating your own bootable movies.

GeeXboX

GeeXboX (`www.geexbox.org`) is another bootable multimedia player distribution. From the screen that appears after GeeXboX boots, you can use your cursor to select the location of the content you want. Like MoviX, you can play a variety of audio and video content. It also boots up on your network, so you can get audio and video content from it.

Because GeeXboX is so small (just a few megabytes), you can fit it easily on a mini-CD, bootable business card, or even a pen drive (provided your computer can be booted from those media). There is no graphical interface; you just use the keyboard to select content and simple controls from menus.

Use arrow keys to move among the few GeeXboX selections (Open, Controls, Options, Help, and Quit). Press Enter to make a selection. You can open a file from hard disk, a music playlist, directory of images, or removable media (DVD, VCD/XCD, or audio CD) containing video content. Press M to show or hide menus and use P to pause.

KnoppMyth

I've included KnoppMyth (`http://freshmeat.net/projects/knoppmyth`) because it represents a new and interesting class of bootable Linux distributions. MythTV is a fairly complex set of software used to configure an entertainment center that can include a personal video recorder (complete with downloaded local TV listings and tools for managing recording and playback), music player, weather center, and tools for getting news and other information.

KnoppMyth is a CD distribution based on KNOPPIX that is intended to help simplify getting a MythTV installation up and running. Boot up KnoppMyth, answer a few questions, and MythTV is installed on your hard disk.

KnoppMyth also includes another nice feature: a MythTV front end. With MythTV configured on a computer on your LAN, you can use the KnoppMyth disk to boot up a MythTV front end. That way, you can use your MythTV entertainment center from any TV on your local area network.

Dyne:bolic

The Dyne:bolic GNU/Linux live bootable CD (www.dynebolic.org) provides a full range of multimedia production tools on a single bootable operating system. The distribution is intended for artisans who want to create and work with a variety of digital media: audio, video, digital images, HTML, and so on.

Tools included with Dyne:bolic include MuSE, TerminatorX, GDam, SoundTracker, and PD (for mixing and streaming audio). Video editors include Kino, Cinelerra, and LiVES. For 3D modeling, there is Blender. For image manipulation, Dyne:bolic includes GIMP. Bluefish is included for creating Web pages.

Tiny Desktops

A small CD, shaped in the form of a business card, can fit in your wallet. A USB pen drive can hang from your keychain. There are whole bootable Linux distributions that enable you to boot up a desktop with which you can connect to the Internet, browse the Web, play music, send and receive e-mail, do instant messaging, write documents, and work with spreadsheets. And they can do all that in about 50MB of space on a removable medium.

NOTE   CD business cards are really just regular CDs that have been cut into the shape of a business card. Depending on the one you choose, it can hold from 40MB to 52MB of data. A mini-CD can hold about 180MB of data. You can purchase these CDs in bulk from many locations that sell regular CDs, and you can play them in any CD drive. (However, it's best to use these CDs in trays that have a mini-CD inset because they have been known to fly loose and break CD drives.)

Many bootable Linuxes these days are either based on KNOPPIX or the Bootable Business Card project (http://www.lnx-bbc.com/). I know of several Linux user groups that have tailored their own bootable business card projects from the lnx-bbc.org BBC project to hand out to represent their groups. Many bootable Linux distributions for media with capacity that is larger than that of a business-card-size CD tend to be based on KNOPPIX.

Two examples of tiny desktop Linux distributions are Damn Small Linux and Puppy Linux.

Damn Small Linux

If you want your desktop Linux distribution to fit in your wallet, Damn Small Linux is one of your best choices. Damn Small is one of the first distributions based on KNOPPIX to fit on a bootable business card (about 48MB currently).

ON the CD-ROM   Damn Small Linux is included on the CD that comes with this book. You can use it as described in Appendix A.

With KNOPPIX inside, you have many of the features you get with KNOPPIX: excellent hardware detection and bootup to a desktop with network connectivity (provided you have an Ethernet connection with DHCP). Many features specific to Damn Small, however, are there to let you get a workable desktop system in a small medium (mini-CD) and low RAM. Figure 19-3 shows an example of the DSL desktop.

FIGURE 19-3

Damn Small Linux fits a lot of features in under 50MB.

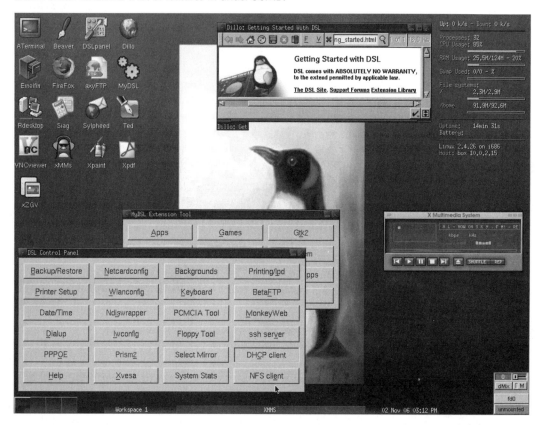

Damn Small's default desktop is pretty simple. The window manager is the powerful, yet efficient, FluxBox window manager (based on BlackBox). Right-click the desktop to see a menu of features you can select. Here are a few things you want to do when you first boot up Damn Small:

- **Enhance your desktop** — Right-click to see the Damn Small menu, and then select Desktop ➪ Full Enhanced Desktop. This adds some icons to your desktop to launch applications, some applets in the lower-right corner to display system information, and a workspace editor. Select Desktop again if you want to change the styles (colors and window borders), or Configuration to change desktop behavior.

- **Get a network connection** — If you don't automatically get on the Internet at boot time, select System ➪ Net Setup from the Damn Small menu. Then you can choose to configure your Ethernet card, DSL connection, dial-up modem, or wireless card.

- **Browse the Web** — Damn Small comes with the Firefox and Dillo Web browsers. Select Apps ➪ Net ➪ Browsers, and then choose either Firefox or Dillo to start browsing. The Dillo browser is small and fast, and can run on any X window manager because it doesn't require GNOME libraries.

- **Configure and read e-mail** — The Sylpheed e-mail client is also very compact and runs fast. Select Apps ➪ Net ➪ Sylpheed to open it. Configure it and you can be up and reading your e-mail within a few minutes.

- **Try out other applications** — Right-click and look through the menu for applications that interest you. To see descriptions of those applications, visit `http://damnsmalllinux .org/applications.html`.

- **Get other applications** — Select the MyDSL icon on the desktop to see a selection of application categories you can choose from. If you are connected to the Internet, you can see lists of applications in each category for downloading and installing.

NOTE You can get other DSL files that will let you download other applications from your desktop as well. Visit `www.damnsmalllinux.org` and select the link to packages to see the myDSL repository.

Damn Small Linux has recently added some excellent customization features. For example, packages you download, desktop settings, and configuration information can be saved across reboots. By creating a list of files and packages you want to save, those files and packages can be saved to a backup file that is stored on your hard disk or any removable medium. The next time you reboot, you can tell Damn Small Linux where to find that backup file and all settings and applications will be inserted into your current Damn Small Linux session.

More information about using Damn Small Linux is available at the project FAQ page, `www.damnsmalllinux.org/faq.html`.

Puppy Linux

The other heavyweight contender for lightweight Linux bootables is Puppy Linux (`www.puppylinux .com/`). The Puppy Linux ISO image is about 71MB. So, for example, you can install and boot Puppy Linux on a 128MB flash drive and still have another 50+ megabytes of space left for data.

Puppy Linux is built for speed, small size, and ease of use. To emphasize the ease-of-use aspects, Puppy Linux tends to lean more toward open and easy than closed and secure. Here are some examples:

- **Backs up data** — Puppy Linux lets you save files and configuration settings to memory the first time you use it. When you are done with your session, you are asked if you want to save that information permanently to a USB flash drive, zip drive, floppy drive, or hard disk partition. If you choose to save your information, it will be backed to a single archive file (named `pup_save.3fs` in ext3 format) on the permanent storage location you selected. You can choose the size of that archive as well. The next time you boot Puppy Linux on that computer, it will find your archive and restore its contents to your Puppy Linux session.

505

- **Loads to RAM** — When you load Puppy Linux it will, by default, run in RAM. So you should get excellent performance, provided your machine has at least 128MB of RAM available. With Puppy Linux in RAM, that also frees up your CD/DVD drive. So you can pop in a CD or DVD and play it without disturbing the running Puppy Linux system.

- **Sets no firewall rules** — Because Puppy Linux uses a Linux 2.6 kernel, the iptables firewall is built in. However, no firewall rules are set by default. So, if you are thinking of expanding Puppy Linux to offer some services (Web server, mail server, and so on), keep in mind that it is intended for a desktop system and not built to securely offer services.

Every major category of desktop applications is represented in Puppy Linux. For word processing, you have abiword. You can play music with GPlayer and video with Gxine. Much of the SeaMonkey Internet Application Suite (derived from code that was previously part of the Mozilla Application Suite) is included for Web browsing, mail, news, and HTML editing. For other Internet client applications, you have GAIM (instant messaging), Gftp (FTP client), and several remote login and remote execution tools (secure shell and telnet).

Other personal productivity tools that come with Puppy Linux include calendar (Ical Calendar), spreadsheet (Gnumeric), contacts (Gabby and SeaMonkey Addressbook), finance manager (Xfinans), and personal information (DidiWiki) applications. Most of these applications are lightweight but serviceable utilities.

Puppy Linux is still a relative newcomer to bootable Linuxes, but it seems to have a good following and fairly active forums and development efforts. Tools for configuring your network and detecting devices seem to work better in KNOPPIX derivatives, such as Damn Small Linux, at the moment. But look for these areas to improve as Puppy Linux develops.

Special-Purpose Bootables

As people begin learning about and playing with customizing bootable Linux distributions, I believe more special-purpose distributions will begin to emerge. The eMoviX[2] distribution (part of the MoviX project) is an example of a distribution geared specifically toward a particular function (in this case, playing video content that you package yourself with the distribution).

Here are examples:

- **Gaming distributions** — The GamesKNOPPIX distribution (http://games-knoppix .unix-ag.uni-kl.de) is currently being developed and will be a collection focusing on games.

CROSS-REF Refer to Chapter 23 for descriptions of many open source games available today.

- **Windows applications distribution** — The SLAX project (www.slax.org), which is based on Slackware, offers some good examples of special-purpose bootable Linuxes. By including WINE, DOSBox, and QEMU software, along with an easy-to-use KDE inter-face, SLAX KillBill offers a special Linux system designed particularly to get Windows applications running in a bootable Linux. Figure 19-4 shows an example of the SLAX KillBill desktop with the Windows WINAMP application running under WINE.

FIGURE 19-4

Try on Windows applications in the bootable SLAX KillBill distro.

ON the CD-ROM While the SLAX KillBill CD image is not included on the media that comes with this book, the SLAX Popcorn Edition is included. SLAX Popcorn edition is a pocket operating system that fits on a 128MB USB flash drive. It includes a basic desktop interface along with some useful Internet applications and desktop productivity tools. Refer to Appendix A for information on using SLAX Popcorn Edition.

Using the features just mentioned, many Windows applications can run natively, without any modification. This distribution offers a great way to try different kinds of Windows compatibility and emulation software to see if you can move your application to Linux.

■ **Firewall distributions** — A firewall is a very good application for a bootable Linux dis-tribution. Using almost any PC and a CD (or even a floppy disk) Linux distribution, you can protect your LAN from intruders and provide a route for multiple computers to the Internet. Popular firewall distributions include Devil-Linux (www.devil-linux.org) and Sentry Firewall CD (www.sentryfirewall.com). Firewall/router distributions are described in Chapter 18.

There are also bootable Linux distributions that are suited for education and for the visually impaired. There are bootable Linux distributions that are suited to be run as a server or to centralize management of clusters. The cool thing is that if there isn't the exact kind of bootable Linux available for you to use, you can start with an existing bootable Linux and customize it yourself.

Customizing a Bootable Linux

A Linux live CD is like a Linux system running from a hard disk, with a few significant differences. It has to be tailored to run from a read-only medium, it usually doesn't (by default) save information across reboots, and it needs to be able to detect and configure hardware each time it starts. Many live CD distributions have created ways of working around these limitations, including allowing you to customize the CD and to save your customizations across reboots.

If you are setting out to create your own customized live CD, or simply save your own custom settings to go with an existing live CD, you can go about it in a few ways:

- **Customizing data** — Live CD distributions, including KNOPPIX and Damn Small Linux, let you save your settings, data files, and even installed applications in a couple of different ways. One approach is to save all your changes to a single archive file to any available writable medium (hard disk, pen drive, and so on), and then restore that archive the next time you boot the CD. Another approach is to create a "persistent desktop," which assigns your home directory and possibly other directories to a writable, mounted file system on your hard disk or other medium. The latter saves your data as you go along.

  Live CDs such as SLAX and Damn Small Linux have their own packaging format that consists of tarballs you can store to be added to the live CD. At boot time, you just point the live CD to the Damn Small MyDSL files or SLAX modules and the archive containing the application is distributed to its proper location in the file system. (See Installing_MyDSL_Extension at `damnsmalllinux.org/wiki` or `www.slax.org/modules.php`.)

- **Remastering** — You can make many more changes to a live CD by remastering it. Remastering is typically done by copying the contents of a live CD to a directory on your hard disk (uncompressing the compressed file system), opening that directory in a chroot environment, adding and deleting software as you please, and then packaging it back up into an ISO image. This approach lets you start with a CD that is basically working, while allowing you to fix problems, update software, and add any data you like so it is included on the CD. See the KNOPPIX Remastering Howto at `www.knoppix.net/wiki/Knoppix_Remastering_Howto`.

- **Fresh install** — Several Linux distributions have projects that take advantage of their basic installers to create a live CD. Fedora Linux's Kadischi project uses its Anaconda installer to produce Fedora live CDs. You basically step through a regular Fedora install and end up with a live CD ISO image. Gentoo can make live CDs from Catalyst, the Gentoo installer.

- **Live CD projects** — There are also several projects that focus on building live CDs from the ground up. The Linux From Scratch project has its own tools and procedures for building live CDs (`www.linuxfromscratch.org/livecd`). Linux live CD/USB scripts (`www.linux-live.org`) enable you to make a live CD from an existing installed Linux system. (The SLAX distribution is made using Linux live CD scripts.)

Here are links to information about how to customize several popular live Linux distributions:

- **KNOPPIX** — There is a very extensive KNOPPIX remastering HowTo available for those who want to create their own custom KNOPPIX distributions. You can find that document here:

`www.knoppix.net/wiki/Knoppix_Remastering_Howto`

  To remaster a KNOPPIX CD, you should have at least 3GB of disk space on a Linux (ext2, ext3, xfs, or other) file system along with at least 1GB of available memory (combining RAM and swap space). It's also a good idea to have an active Internet connection during any remastering because there is almost surely some software you will want to download in the process.

- **Damn Small Linux (DSL)** — This is the Linux distribution I have used the most to customize my own live Linux distributions. DSL does good hardware detection and good selection of working desktop applications. I can start with the 48MB ISO image, and then add lots of software and customized features to fill up a CD. In fact, the CD that comes with the book *Linux Toys II* (Wiley, 2006) is a remastered version of DSL that includes software for building *Linux Toys* projects as well.

  If you simply want to install DSL to a pen drive or other media, DSL offers an automated feature for doing that. Once DSL is on a rewritable pen drive, you can easily add applications (using the MyDSL feature) and customize desktop features in a way that persists across reboots.

- **Puppy Linux** — The project uses its own package management system (called PupGet) that now offers more than 300 packages you can add to Puppy Linux. By adding and deleting these packages, you can create a customized version of Puppy Linux. For information on adding packages and saving your configuration to a custom Puppy Linux distribution, refer to the Puppy Unleashed feature:

`www.puppyos.com/puppy-unleashed.htm`

- **Gentoo** — Tools for building a potentially more finely tuned live CD are available with the Gentoo distribution. While creating a Gentoo live CD is supported through the livecd-ng tool, there is currently no complete document describing a simple way to use this, or other tools, to create a custom Gentoo live CD. Here is a link, however, that can get you started:

`http://gentoo-wiki.com/HOWTO_build_a_LiveCD`

- **FedoraLiveCD** — Originally started as the Kadischi project, this project can help you get a custom Fedora live CD you can take on the road. Check it out here:

```
http://fedoraproject.org/wiki/FedoraLiveCD
```

- **LiveCD Project** — The LiveCD project (`http://livecd.berlios.de`) is an initiative aimed specifically at creating a live CD from a Linux distribution. Because the tools currently work only on Mandrakelinux and PCLinuxOS, this project is probably a good place to start if you want to produce a live CD that is compatible with either of those distributions. There are currently more than a dozen live CD distributions that have been created from the LiveCD project.

Of the projects I've just mentioned, I'd recommend starting with a KNOPPIX or Damn Small Linux distribution for your first attempt at remastering. Because a lot of people are using those, or other distributions based on Debian/KNOPPIX technology, there are mature procedures and forums to help you get over any bumps in the road.

Summary

Dozens of bootable Linux distributions have appeared in the past few years. Those distributions can contain anywhere from 1.4MB of data on a firewall bootable Linux to many gigabytes of data on a bootable DVD. Without needing to touch the computer's hard disk, these distributions can offer full-featured systems that are tailored to be desktop systems, multimedia players, rescue systems, or many other types of systems.

Many bootable Linuxes are based on KNOPPIX (described in Chapter 11), so they feature very fine hardware detection and strong network connectivity. If you want to try out a mini-bootable Linux distribution, try Damn Small Linux or Puppy Linux. For a Linux distribution that fits on a floppy disk, try Coyote Linux (described in Chapter 18).

Nearly all bootable Linux distributions offer ways to access data from the hard disks of the computers on which they are running. While many bootable Linuxes are still experimental in nature, you can have lots of fun playing with them. Also, with the extraordinary improvements in custom features, you can create your own customized bootable Linux distribution to take with you on a floppy, CD, DVD, or USB flash drive (also referred to as pen drives, thumb drives, or other names).

Part IV

Running Applications

Chapter 20

Playing Music and Video

O ne of the most popular and enjoyable activities on a computer is playing audio and video. With improved multimedia players and tools for storing and managing content, Linux has become a great platform for storing, playing, and managing your music and video files.

In this chapter, you learn to use the sound, video, digital imaging, and other multimedia tools available for Linux. You explore the process of configuring audio and selecting video devices. You examine the kinds of media formats available for the Linux platform, how they work, and how to make the most of them by using the right applications.

Linux is an excellent platform for taking advantage of widely used formats such as MPEG, AVI, OGG, QuickTime, and RealMedia. A wide variety of players are available for the various formats, and this chapter discusses several of them to help you determine which might be the right one (or combination) for your interests and/or needs.

NOTE Because many devices holding multimedia content are removable (CDs, DVDs, digital cameras, Webcams, and so on), recent features in Linux to automatically handle removable hardware and media have greatly improved the Linux desktop experience. See the section on managing hardware in Chapter 4 for descriptions of how features such as Udev and HAL are used to manage removable media.

Some Linux distributions are more multimedia-friendly right after the install than others. An example of this is Freespire, which comes pre-loaded and able to support Flash, Java, MP3, Real, QuickTime, and Windows Media files the minute the installation completes. This can save you a great deal of time trying to track down licensing issues and resolve problems. You can find features that are not included with the installation, such as DVD playback support, at the Linspire Click-N-Run service (www.cnr.com). Ubuntu users can also use Click-N-Run to get both free and commercial software.

Playing Digital Media and Obeying the Law

Debate about just what an end user can legally do with digital media is a hot topic right now. What exactly can you do as far as making copies of your CDs, DVDs, and other media? Unfortunately, there is no really good answer. This issue affects just about every computer user, either directly or indirectly.

How you are allowed to use the audio, video, and other media you keep on your computers is increasingly dictated by national and international law. There was a time when you could essentially disregard this issue, but in the era where individual computer users have been successfully sued by corporations and industry groups, a little more caution is required.

Copyright Protection Issues

The biggest factor in the new world of digital media policy is the 1998 Digital Millennium Copyright Act (DMCA). This law ostensibly establishes a framework for implementing several international treaties concerning copyright protection.

The DMCA has been widely criticized because it seems to intrude on the free-speech provisions of the U.S. Constitution. Many people view computer code as a protected form of speech. A conflict arises because the DMCA forbids the development of applications that are designed to intentionally circumvent content security. For example, Dmitry Sklyarov, a Russian cryptographer employed by a Russian software company, ElcomSoft, was arrested by the FBI while attending a conference in Las Vegas because he demonstrated an application that could decrypt Adobe eBooks. A jury found Sklyarov and ElcomSoft not guilty in December 2002, but the point is that companies *will* use the DMCA to litigate against those who publicize methods to decrypt encrypted content.

If nothing else, this event demonstrated that the DMCA has teeth. Unfortunately, these teeth have been used not only to protect legitimate commerce, but to pursue computer scientists at academic institutions researching content protection schemes, encryption, and a range of other technologies. Because the DMCA makes it a crime to manufacture and transport technology used to circumvent copyright protection schemes, many researchers have abandoned valuable research that could yield better (stronger and more useful) protection schemes or reveal critical flaws in existing ones.

While DCMA has provided some clout for content providers to legitimately protect their material, such as persuading search engines to drop information about links to illegally posted and copyrighted information, there are times when that clout has been abused. Some copyright holders, it seems, are more than willing to use the DMCA to curtail three "rights" allowed under pre-DMCA copyright law. Copyright law stipulates:

- Users can make a copy of any copyrighted work for academic purposes, reporting, or critique. This includes a wide range of uses, from students or instructors copying materials for research to someone creating a parody of published materials. But what about a student making a copy of some DVD materials for a multimedia presentation? The student has fair-use access to the material on the DVD, but the DMCA makes it illegal for the student to break the DVD encryption that would allow the student to copy the material.

> **NOTE** The fair-use rule is a privilege that permits someone other than the owner of the copyright to use the copyrighted material in a reasonable and limited manner without the owner's consent.

- Users can sell copyrighted works that they own. You can sell your books, DVDs, audio CDs, and other materials as long as you are not retaining a copy for yourself, or (of course) selling copies of the work without permission from the copyright holder. Some people arguing in favor of file trading with copyrighted materials claim that the DMCA infringes on their ability to "share" content they "own." In fact, under existing copyright law they do not "own" the copyrighted material and certainly do not possess the rights to redistribute the content unless they are reselling it in an allowed manner.

- Copyrights will expire at some time in the future and fall into the public domain. Basically, this point raises the same issue as with the first item: Your DVD movie falls into the public domain (eventually), but to freely copy the content you must again circumvent the protection inherent on the DVD, and by doing so, you run afoul of the DMCA.

It is important to realize the DMCA is very vague about how it defines many of the acts that are illegal. What is a "protection scheme"? Some argue that it could be nearly anything. Many pundits fear that the DMCA can be used to curtail the use of nondigital copyrighted works such as books because the law is so vague in defining its own borders.

While the courts are trying to clarify where the legal line is in any particular situation, the problem is that, often, the company suing to protect its copyrights is a large corporation or group and the defendant is either a new small company or even an individual user. Court battles are expensive, and the broad scope of the DMCA essentially prevents "the little guy" from ever making his case, because he cannot afford to fight.

> **NOTE** In 1998, a law known as the Sonny Bono Copyright Term Extension Act, or CTEA, was passed. This act took the already lengthy copyright protection period (generally 70 years) and extended it by another 20 years, preventing several valuable properties, including film and images of Steamboat Willie (the first Mickey Mouse), from entering the public domain.

From a practical standpoint, what does all this mean to you as a Linux user? Well, it means that if you have to use any trickery to copy MP3s off your CD collection, you could be breaking the law.

Several CD protection schemes used by record companies are designed to prevent digital piracy, but they are very easy to circumvent in many cases. But should you get caught making MP3s off a protected CD, you can be sued and/or arrested (hypothetically speaking). It is quite possible that some of the security on CDs is intentionally weak. It saves development costs and allows the copyright holder to pursue anyone who has ripped the CD because there is no legal means of doing so. But that is just speculation.

Relatively few audio CDs come with protection of any kind, particularly those CDs already owned by the world's audiophiles. If you make fair-use copies of materials you own for your own use, you're not likely to have to worry about anything. If you should decide to transport copyrighted works in a public forum (peer-to-peer networks for example), you are rolling the dice. The RIAA (Recording Industry Association of America) and MPAA (Motion Picture Association of America) have both successfully located and sued users—including children—distributing content illegally online.

> **NOTE**   One attempt to allow sharing, remixing, and reusing legally is the Creative Commons Project. As of this writing, the project is five years old and over 25,000 items are posted. You can find more information at `http://creativecommons.org/`.

Two sites worth exploring are Jamendo (`www.jamendo.com/en/`) and Magnatune (`www.magnatune.com`). Both are libraries offering free access to music. Jamendo focuses on free distribution of music to help musicians grow their audiences. Magnatune helps musicians by licensing their music to those who would like to use it in commercial ventures (such as films, commercials, Web sites and so on), while still allowing the musicians to maintain rights to their music.

Exploring Codecs

If you want to play a video or audio file, you need the appropriate codec installed and ready for use by your media player. A *codec* is a software-based encoder-decoder used to take existing digital audio/video data and decode the content. Often, codecs use compression technology to reduce the size of the data files while retaining the quality of the output.

If you encounter a media file that you know is a working, playable file and you cannot play the file, you might need to identify and install the proper codec. This often involves installing the proper playback application, such as DivX 5.0.5 for Linux, which installs the MPEG4 codec for video and audio playback.

Many codecs are available, so getting the ones you need is usually not an issue. Advances in codec technology have continued to increase the quality of the encoded content, while reducing file size. Fortunately, most widely distributed videos and audio files (from news sites, for example) are created using a few commonly used codecs.

While there are some commonly used encoding standards, there are also a slew of proprietary codecs in use today as well. This is really a battleground of sorts with each vendor/developer trying to produce the superior standard and obtain the spoils of market share that can follow. For the end user, this means you might have to spend time chasing a variety of playback utilities to handle multiple video and audio formats.

Another debate: Can digital media match the quality of analog formats? This hardly seems much of a question anymore because DVD has shown the potential for high-quality digital video, and MPEG codecs have made huge strides in digital audio fidelity. The quality of digital media files is very high and getting better all the time. Some of the key technologies that reflect improvements in how audio and video codecs have improved include:

- **Ogg Vorbis** — This audio codec has been developed as a freely available tool — no patents or licensing needed. Ogg is the "data container" portion of the codec, and Vorbis is the audio compression scheme. There are other compression schemes that can be used with Ogg such as Ogg FLAC, which is used for archiving audio in a lossless format, and Ogg Speex, which is used specifically to handle encoding speech.

- **Real Networks** — Real has developed a set of audio and video codecs that have an amazing ability to serve up streaming content. This protocol is not widely supported by anyone but Real. The Helix project produces a player for Linux that enables playback of Real media encoded files.

- **WMA** — Windows Media Audio is used to create high-quality digital audio. WMA is considered a *lossless* codec, which means the audio doesn't lose quality or data as a result of repeated compression-decompression cycles. Among its other benefits is that it's one of the first widely used codecs to support digital surround sound.

- **WMV** — Windows Media Video is used, not surprisingly, to encode and decode video. This is also a very high-quality encoder and is billed to produce a video that is half the size of an MPEG-4 encoded video at a comparable quality level.

- **DivX** — This video codec has revolutionized digital video. Extremely high-quality video can be stored with amazingly small file sizes when using this codec. DivX (Digital Video Express) is based on the MPEG-4 video standard and can produce 640 × 480 video that is about 15 percent of the size of the source DVD material.

Some of these codecs are integral parts of Digital Rights Management (DRM) scenarios. For example, WMA, WMV, and DivX have elements that support DRM. DRM is basically proprietary copy protection.

The term "DRM" applies to a wide range of technologies that use server-based activation, encryption, and other elements to control who can access content and what they can then do with the content once it has been accessed. While it is very attractive to distributors of audio and video, who are trying to prevent unchecked digital piracy of their content, it can be a real stumbling block for the consumer.

Many DRM solutions require proprietary software and even hardware to work with the protected content. A prime example is the recent production of some DRM-protected audio CDs, particularly in Europe. Some of these disks will not play in older standalone CD players, some will play only on a computer that supports the DRM application on the CD itself, and (especially frustrating) some will not play on a computer at all. In almost all cases, such DRM solutions do not support Linux. Most support only Windows, and a few support Windows and Mac OS X.

Just to make things clear, while the codecs just discussed do not include built-in DRM features, some codecs are specifically designed to integrate with DRM solutions. In other words, all of these codecs can theoretically be used to play encoded content on a Linux system. If the content is protected by a DRM solution, the likelihood that the content is playable on a Linux system is fairly remote. Despite this fact, or perhaps because of it, Linus Torvalds has not excluded the possibility of including support for DRM in Linux. Likewise, several open source projects are working on Linux DRM solutions.

Playing Music

With an understanding of the challenges and advances in digital media under your belt, let's move on to actually putting digital media to use. This section shows you how to set up your Linux installation for audio playback. It examines the process for getting the hardware up and running and then explores available software options for audio playback.

Setting Up Audio Cards

To start your "quadraphonic wall of sound," you need to have a sound card in your PC. A sound card can be an add-in PCI (or even ISA) card, or it can be integrated on your motherboard. Your card will have a ton of uses — from gaming to audio/video playback. Having a multimedia system just isn't the same without sound.

Fortunately, most modern PCs include a sound card, often of the integrated variety. In the rare case that one isn't included (or the slightly more common case where it isn't supported in Linux), you can add a supported sound card starting for only a few dollars. If you're really pinched, check out eBay, where you probably can get a decent SoundBlaster-compatible card (still *the* standard) for next to nothing.

NOTE If you try the procedures in this book but still don't have a working sound card, visit www.alsa-project.org, home of the Advanced Linux Sound Architecture (ALSA). ALSA is the preferred sound software for Linux and is built into the Linux kernel itself (beginning with the 2.6 kernel). The ALSA site offers support, information, and help.

The following list summarizes the basic features that are included in the popular SoundBlaster family of sound cards:

- **Sound recording and playback** — The card can convert analog sound into 8-bit or 16-bit digital numbers. To convert the sound, the board samples the sound in waves from 5 KHz to 48 KHz, or 5,000 to 48,100 times per second. The higher the sampling rate, the better the sound and the larger the output files.

- **Full-duplex support** — Full-duplex means that recording and playback occur at the same time. This is particularly useful for bidirectional Internet communication, such as Voice-Over-IP (VOIP) telephony or simultaneous recording and playback.

- **Input/output ports** — Several different ports on the board enable you to connect other input/output devices. These ports include:

  - **Line-In** — Connects an external CD player, cassette deck, synthesizer, MiniDisc, or other device for recording or playback. If you have a television card, you might also patch that card's line-out to your sound card's line-in.

  - **Microphone** — Connects a microphone for audio recording or communications.

  - **Line-Out (Speaker Out)** — Connects unpowered speakers, headphones, or a stereo amplifier.

■ **Joystick/MIDI** — Connects a joystick for a gaming or MIDI device.

■ **Internal CD Audio** — Connects the sound card to your computer's internal CD-ROM board. (This port isn't externally visible when the board is installed.)

Sound drivers provided in Linux come from many sources. However, as previously mentioned, Advanced Linux Sound Architecture (ALSA) is the sound system that is integrated into the 2.6 kernel. You may find older Open Sound System (OSS) drivers are useful if ALSA does not support your sound card. Commercial support for OSS drivers is available for a small cost from 4Front Technologies (`www.opensound.com`), which is the company that still maintains OSS.

> **CAUTION** Before you install a separate sound driver distribution, check to see if your current distribution already has a recent driver. Using the driver that came with the kernel is always a safe bet if you are not experiencing a specific driver-related issue.

At times, a sound application will ask you to identify the device from which to access sound on your system. With the introduction of the Udev feature in the 2.6 kernel, some of the device names are different from those used with the 2.4 kernel. The following are audio device nodes that may be of interest to you as you use sound in Linux:

■ `/dev/audio`, `/dev/audio1` — Compatible with Sun workstation audio implementations (audio files with the `.au` extension). These devices are not recommended for new sound applications. Under Udev, these devices are symbolic links to `/dev/sound/audio` and `/dev/sound/audio1`, respectively.

■ `/dev/cdrom` — Represents your first CD-ROM drive. `/dev/cdrom` is usually a symbolic link to the device node, such as `/dev/hdc`, that corresponds to your CD-ROM drive. Additional CD-ROM drives are located at `/dev/cdrom1`, `/dev/cdrom2`, and so on.

■ `/dev/dsp`, `/dev/dsp1` — Digital sampling devices, which many audio applications identify to access your sound card. Under Udev, these devices are symbolic links to `/dev/sound/dsp` and `/dev/sound/dsp1`, respectively.

■ `/dev/mixer`, `/dev/mixer1` — Sound-mixing devices. Under Udev, these devices are symbolic links to `/dev/sound/mixer` and `/dev/sound/mixer1`, respectively.

■ `/dev/sequencer` — Provides a low level interface to MIDI, FM, and GUS. Under Udev, these devices are symbolic links to `/dev/sound/sequencer` and `/dev/sound/sequencer1`, respectively.

■ `/dev/midi00` — Provides raw access to MIDI ports. Under Udev, raw access to MIDI ports is handled by symbolic links to device-special files in `/dev/snd` named `midiC[D0-9]`. For example, `/dev/midi00` would be a symbolic link to `/dev/midiCD0`.

For general information about sound in Linux, see the Sound-HOWTO (for tips about sound cards and general sound issues) and the Sound-Playing-HOWTO (for tips on software for playing different types of audio files). You can find Linux HOWTOs at `www.tldp.org`.

Choosing an Audio CD Player

The GNOME CD player (gnome-cd) is the default CD player for many GNOME desktop systems. It has standard play buttons and lets you get track information automatically from a CD database, such as freedb.org. (If your CD isn't listed in the database, you can enter your own track information manually.)

However, a variety of CD players come with Linux distributions or may be downloaded and installed. Here is a cross-section of your other choices for playing CDs with Linux:

- **Rhythmbox** (rhythmbox) — Import and manage your CD collection with Rhythmbox music management and playback software for GNOME. It uses GStreamer on the audio back end and compresses music using Ogg Vorbis audio format. In addition to enabling you to create playlists of your music library, Rhythmbox also has features for playing Internet radio stations. Free music stores were added to Rhythmbox in recent releases, allowing you to play free music from Jamendo (www.jamendo.com/en/) and Magnatune (www.magnatune.com), and possibly purchase CDs or license use of that music for commercial projects.

- **KsCD player** (kscd) — The KsCD player comes with the KDE desktop. To use it, the kdemultimedia package must be installed. From the main menu on the KDE desktop, select Multimedia ⇨ KsCD (or type **kscd** in a Terminal window). Like gnome-cd, this player lets you get title, track, and artist information from the CD database. KsCD, however, also lets you submit information to a CD database (if your CD isn't found there).

- **Grip** (grip) — While Grip is primarily used as a CD ripper, it can also play CDs. Select Multimedia ⇨ Grip (or type **grip** in a Terminal window). It includes tools for gathering data from and submitting data to CD databases. It also includes tools for copying (ripping) CD tracks and converting them to different formats (encoding). Naturally, the grip package must be installed to use this command.

- **Amarok** (amarok) — With Amarok, you get a nice graphical interface where you can manage music by moving elements around with your mouse. Amarok uses SQLite (or other databases) to store your music. It also supports playlists and streaming audio playback from online radio stations.

- **X Multimedia System** (xmms) — The XMMS player plays a variety of audio formats but can also play directly from a CD.

 If you try some of these CD players and your CD-ROM drive is not working, see the sidebar "Troubleshooting Your CD-ROM" for further information.

Playing CDs with gnome-cd

Like most graphical CD players, the gnome-cd player has controls that look similar to those you would see on a physical CD player. If you are using the GNOME desktop, from the main menu select Sound & Video ⇨ CD Player, or from a Terminal window, type:

```
$ gnome-cd &
```

Troubleshooting Your CD-ROM

If you are unable to play CDs on your CD-ROM drive, here are a few things you can check to correct the problem:

- Verify that your sound card is installed and working properly.

- Verify that the CD-ROM drive was detected when you booted Linux. If your CD-ROM drive is an IDE drive, type **dmesg | grep ^hd**. You should see messages about your CD-ROM that resemble this: hdc: CD-ROM CDU701, ATAPI CDROM drive or hdc: ATAPI 14X CD-ROM drive, 128kB Cache.

- If you see no indication of a CD-ROM drive, verify that the power supply and cables to the CD-ROM are connected. To make sure that the hardware is working, you can also boot to Windows (if it is installed and you are running a dual-boot machine) and try to access the CD.

- Try inserting a software CD-ROM. If you are running the GNOME or KDE desktop, a desktop icon should appear indicating that the CD mounted by itself. If no such icon appears, go to a Terminal window, and, as the root user, type **mount /dev/cdrom**. Then change to the /media/cdrom or /dev/media directory and list the contents using the command cd /media/cdrom; ls. This tells you if the CD-ROM is accessible.

- If you get the CD-ROM working but it fails with the message CDROM device: Permission denied when you try to play music as a non–root user, the problem may be that /dev/cdrom (which is typically a link to the actual hardware device) is not readable by anyone but root. Type **ls -l /dev/cdrom** to see what the device is linked to. Then if, for example, the CD device is /dev/hdc, type **chmod 644 /dev/hdc** as the root user to enable all users to read your CD-ROM and to enable the root user to write to it. One warning: If others use your computer, they will be able to read any CD you place in this drive.

If your computer is connected to the Internet, for most CDs you'll see the title and artist information. Even obscure artists are (usually) represented in the free online databases. If the information isn't available, you can enter it yourself.

The interface for adding information about the CD and its tracks is very nice. Click the Open Track Editor button. You can add Artist and Title information about the CD. Then you can select each track to type in the track name. To add the name of the artist and the disk title, click in the appropriate text box, and type in that information. Figure 20-1 shows the CD player and the CDDB Track Editor.

FIGURE 20-1

Play CDs and store artist, title, and track information with gnome-cd.

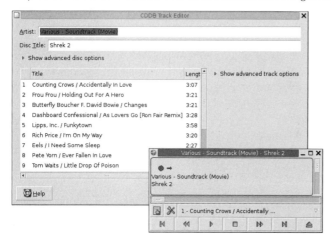

Playing Music with the Rhythmbox Audio Player

Rhythmbox provides the GNOME music player that lets you do everything, at least according to the Rhythmbox documentation. Rhythmbox is built on the GStreamer framework for developing media players, video editors, and streaming media. You can play music files, import music from CDs, and play Internet radio stations, all from one interface. Recent additions let you play podcasts and free music from Magnatune and Jamendo online music services.

The first time you run Rhythmbox, consider setting some Rhythmbox Preferences by selecting Edit Preferences (see Figure 20-2). On the Music tab, you can tell Rhythmbox where you store your music files and how Rhythmbox should organize and store your music (including how folders are named and how songs are titled, and the format in which music is stored).

After you've set up your preferences, you'll see the main music library interface (see Figure 20-3). Rhythmbox makes it easy to organize even large collections of music files.

NOTE If your distribution does not include support for MP3 playback with Rhythmbox, fear not — there is hope! In Fedora, you can use the Codeina feature to download free MP3 decoder support from Fluendo (www.fluendo.com). For Ubuntu and Linspire, check out support in the Click-N-Run service (www.cnr.com).

In addition to playing music files, Rhythmbox can easily rip CDs. Just insert the CD you want to rip, right-click the CD when it appears under the Devices heading in the left column, and select Copy to Library. The CD will be ripped and stored with your Rhythmbox music collection.

FIGURE 20-2

Defining where you store your music

FIGURE 20-3

Viewing a music library with Rhythmbox

Rhythmbox can also play Internet radio stations. The easiest way to do this is to find a streaming radio station (look for Shoutcast PLS files, usually with a `.pls` extension). Save the PLS file, and then double-click the file in the Nautilus file browser. Nautilus comes configured to launch Rhythmbox for playing audio. Figure 20-4 shows Rhythmbox with a variety of Internet radio stations.

FIGURE 20-4

Rhythmbox playing Internet radio

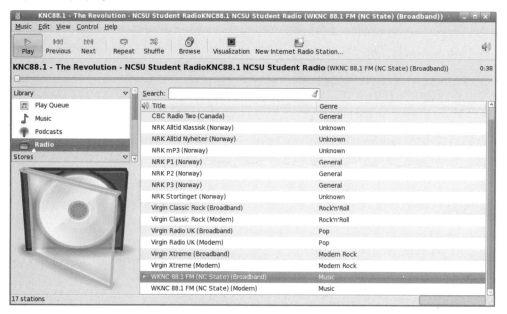

 The site www.di.fm lists a number of free Internet radio channels.

Playing Music with the XMMS Multimedia Player

The XMMS (X Multimedia System) multimedia player provides a graphical interface for playing music files in MP3, Ogg Vorbis, WAV, and other audio formats. XMMS has some nice extras, too, including an equalizer, a playlist editor, and the capability to add more audio plug-ins. One of its greatest attributes is that XMMS is easy to use. If the player looks familiar to you, that's because it is styled after the Windows Winamp program.

NOTE Red Hat removed all software that does MP3 encoding or decoding because of patent concerns related to the MP3 format. Although the XMMS player was designed to play MP3 files, the XMMS plug-in required to actually decode MP3 is not included. To add MP3 support back into your Red Hat or Fedora distribution, you can get and install an MP3 plug-in. One place to get RPM packages that support MP3 decoding is http://rpm.livna.org. They are also available from other sources, including www.xmms.org and www.gurulabs.com/downloads.html. This issue does not necessarily apply to other Red Hat–derived distributions.

Start the XMMS audio player by selecting Sound & Video ➪ Audio Player or by typing **xmms** from a Terminal window. Figure 20-5 shows the XMMS audio player with the associated equalizer (to the left) and the Playlist Editor (to the right).

Play Ogg Vorbis and other audio files from the XMMS playlist.

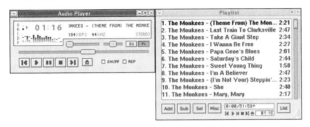

As noted earlier, you can play several audio file formats. Supported formats include:

- MP3 (with added plug-in)
- Ogg Vorbis
- WAV
- AU
- CD audio
- CIN movies

NOTE If XMMS is not able to find a configured sound card, it redirects its output to the Disk Writer plug-in. This causes the files you play to be written to hard disk as WAV files.

You can get many more audio plug-ins from www.xmms.org. The XMMS audio player can be used in the following way:

1. Obtain music files by ripping songs from a CD or copying them from the Web so that they are in an accessible directory, or by inserting a music CD in your CD-ROM drive. (XMMS expects the CD to be accessible from /dev/cdrom.)

2. From the applications menu, select Sound & Video ➪ Audio Player. The X Multimedia System player appears.

3. Click the Eject button. The Load files window appears.

4. If you have inserted a CD, the contents of /mnt/cdrom appear in the Files pane. Select the files you want to add to your Playlist and click the Add Selected Files or the Add All Files in Directory button to add all songs from the current directory. To add audio files from your file system, browse your files and directories and click the same buttons to add the audio files you want. Select Close.

5. Click the Play List button (the tiny button marked PL) on the console. A Playlist Editor window appears.

6. Double-click the music file, and it starts to play.

7. With a file selected and playing, here are a few actions you can take:

   ▪ **Control play** — Buttons for controlling play are what you would expect to see on a standalone CD player. From left to right, the buttons let you go to a previous track, play, pause, stop, go to the next track, and eject the CD. The eject button opens a window, enabling you to load the next file.

   ▪ **Adjust sound** — Use the left slider bar to adjust the volume. Use the right slider bar to change the right-to-left balance.

   ▪ **Display time** — Click in the elapsed time area to toggle between elapsed time and time remaining.

   ▪ **View file information** — Click the button in the upper-left corner of the screen to see the XMMS menu. Then select View File Info. You can often find out a lot of information about the file: title, artist, album, comments, and genre. For an Ogg Vorbis file, you can see specific information about the file itself, such as the format, bit rate, sample rate, frames, file size, and more. You can change or add to the tag information and click Save to keep it.

8. When you are done playing music, click the Stop button to stop the current song. Then click the X in the upper-right corner of the display to close the window.

Special features of the XMMS audio player let you adjust frequencies using a graphic equalizer and gather and play songs using a Playlist Editor. Click the button marked EQ next to the balance bar on the player to open the Equalizer.

Using the Equalizer

The Equalizer lets you use slider bars to set different levels to different frequencies played. Bars on the left adjust lower frequencies, and those on the right adjust higher frequencies. Click the EQ button to open the Equalizer window. Here are tasks you can perform with the Equalizer:

   ■ If you like the settings you have for a particular song, you can save them as a Preset. Set each frequency as you like it and click the Preset button. Then choose Save ➪ Preset. Type a name for the preset and click OK.

   ■ To reload a preset you created earlier, click the Preset button and select Load ➪ Preset. Select the preset you want and click OK.

The small window in the center/top of the Equalizer shows the sound wave formed by your settings. You can adjust the Preamp bar on the left to boost different levels in the set range.

Using the Playlist Editor

The Playlist Editor lets you put together a list of audio files that you want to play. You can add and delete files from this list, save them to a file, and use them again later. Click the PL button in the XMMS window to open the Playlist Editor.

The Playlist Editor enables you to:

■ **Add files to the playlist** — Click the Add button. The Load Files window appears. Select the directory containing your audio files (it's useful to keep them all in one place) from the left column. Then either select a file from the right column and click Add Selected Files or click Add All Files in the Directory. Click OK. The selected file (or files) appears in the playlist. You can also add music files by dragging them from the Nautilus file manager onto the playlist window.

■ **Select files to play** — To select from the files in the playlist, use the previous track and next track buttons in the main XMMS window. The selected file is highlighted. Click the Play button to play that file. Alternatively, you can double-click any file in the playlist to start it playing.

■ **Delete files from the playlist** — To remove files from the playlist, select the file or files you want to remove (use the next track and previous track buttons), right-click the playlist window, and click Remove ➪ Selected. The selected files are removed.

■ **Save the playlist** — To save the current playlist, hold the right mouse button down on the List button and then select Playlist ➪ Save List from the pop-up menu. Browse to the directory you want, and then type the name you want to assign to the playlist and click OK. The filename should end with a .m3u extension, such as monkees_hits.m3u.

■ **Load the playlist** — To reload a saved playlist, click the List button. Select a playlist from the directory in which you saved it and click OK.

There is also a tiny set of buttons on the bottom of the Playlist Editor screen. These are the same buttons as those on the main screen used for selecting different tracks or playing, pausing, stopping, or ejecting the current track.

One of the most fun aspects to XMMS is that you can change the skin, or the look, of the user interface. XMMS skins allow you to see wildly different interfaces, even though the application remains the same. Not only can you control the look of XMMS, you can also use skins to adjust for any issues in the XMMS interface. For example, the current song in the playlist window may not be highlighted enough, especially if you have a high-resolution monitor. You can select a skin that provides better highlighting. You can also choose skins that make XMMS look like Winamp on Windows, or like the Mac OS X interface.

You can select and download XMMS skins from www.xmms.org/skins.php. In addition, XMMS supports Windows Winamp skins (files with a .wsz extension), so you can download those skins and see Scarlett Johansson or Bob Marley for your music player.

Using MIDI Audio Players

MIDI (Musical Instrument Digital Interface) files are created from synthesizers and other electronic music devices. They tend to be smaller than other kinds of audio files because instead of storing the complete sounds, they contain information about the notes played, tempo, and articulation. You can think of a MIDI file as electronic sheet music. The MIDI player reproduces the notes to sound like a huge variety of MIDI instruments.

There are lots of sites on the Internet for downloading MIDI files. Try the Ifni MIDI Music site (www.ifnimidi.com), for example, which contains songs by the Beatles, Led Zeppelin, Nirvana, and others organized by album. Most of the MIDI music is pretty simple, but you can have some fun playing with it.

Linux distributions that include the KDE desktop (such as Fedora) often come with the kmid MIDI player. Kmid provides a GUI interface for midi music, including the capability to display karaoke lyrics in real time. To start kmid in Fedora, select Sound & Video ⇨ KMid (or type **kmid &** from a Terminal window).

Performing Audio File Conversion and Compression

There are many different formats for storing and compressing speech and music files. Because music files can be large, they are usually stored in a compressed format. While MP3 has been the compression format of choice, Ogg Vorbis is quickly becoming a favorite for compressing music in the open source community. Ogg Vorbis has the added benefit of not being encumbered by patents as MP3 is.

Linux tools for converting and compressing audio files include:

- **SoX (Sound eXchange)** — A general-purpose tool for converting audio files among a variety of formats.
- **oggenc** — A tool for specifically converting music files to Ogg Vorbis format.

Converting Audio Files with SoX

If you have a sound file in one format, but you want it to be in another format, Linux offers some conversion tools. The SoX utility can translate to and from any of the audio formats listed in Table 20-1.

 Type **sox -h** to see the supported audio types, as well as supported options and effects.

TABLE 20-1

Sound Formats Supported by the SoX Utility

File Extension or Pseudonym	Description	File Extension or Pseudonym	Description
.8svx	8SVX Amiga musical instrument description format.	.aiff	Apple IIc/IIgs and SGI AIFF files. May require a separate archiver to work with these files.
.au, .snd	Sun Microsystems AU audio files. This was once a popular format. (The .snd extension is ambiguous because it's also been used on the NeXT format and the headerless Mac/PC format.)	.avr	Audio Visual Research format, used on the Mac.
.cdr	CD-R files used to master compact disks.	.cvs	Continuously variable slope delta modulation, which is used for voice mail and other speech compression.
.dat	Text data files, which contain a text representation of sound data.	.gsm	Lossy speech compression (GSM 06.10), used to shrink audio data in voice mail and similar applications.
.hcom	Macintosh HCOM files.	.maud	Amiga format used to produce sound that is 8-bit linear, 16-bit linear, A-law, and u-law in mono or stereo.
.ogg	Ogg Vorbis compressed audio, which is best used for compressing music and streaming audio.	.ossdsp	Pseudo file, used to open the OSS /dev/dsp file and configure it to use the data type passed to SoX. Used to either play or record.
.prc	Psion record.app format, newer than the WVE format. Note that the .prc extension is also used for programs for Palm handheld devices.	.sf	IRCAM sound files, used by the CSound package and the -MixView sample editor.
.sph	Speech audio SPHERE (Speech Header Resources) format from NIST (National Institute of Standards and Technology).	.smp	SampleVision files from Turtle Beach, used to communicate with different MIDI samplers.

continued

TABLE 20-1	(continued)		
File Extension or Pseudonym	**Description**	**File Extension or Pseudonym**	**Description**
.sunau	Pseudo file, used to open a /dev/audio file and set it to use the data type being passed to SoX.	.txw	Yamaha TX-16W from a Yamaha sampling keyboard.
.vms	Used to compress speech audio for voice mail and similar applications.	.voc	Sound Blaster VOC file.
.wav	Microsoft WAV RIFF files. This is the native Microsoft Windows sound format.	.wve	8-bit, a-law, and 8 KHz sound files used with Psion Palmtop computers.
.raw	Raw files (contain no header information, so sample rate, size, and style must be given).	.ub, .sb, .uw, .sw, .ul, .al, .lu, .la, .sl	Raw files with set characteristics. ub is an unsigned byte; sb is a signed byte; uw is an unsigned word; sw is a signed word; and ul is u-law.

If you are not sure about the format of an audio file, you can add the .auto extension to the file-name. This triggers SoX to guess what kind of audio format is contained in the file. The .auto extension can be used only for the input file. If SoX can figure out the content of the input file, it translates the contents to the sound type for the output file you request.

In its most basic form, you can convert one file format (such as a WAV file) to another format (such as an AU file) as follows:

```
$ sox file1.wav file1.au
```

To see what SoX is doing, use the -V option. For example:

```
$ sox -V file1.wav file1.voc
sox: Reading Wave file: Microsoft PCM format, 2 channel, 44100 samp/sec
sox: 176400 byte/sec, 4 block align, 16 bits/samp, 50266944 data bytes
sox: Input file: using sample rate 11025
        size bytes, style unsigned, 1 channel
sox: Input file1.wav: comment "file1.wav"
sox: Output file1.voc: using sample rate 44100
        size shorts, encoding signed (2's complement), 2 channels
sox: Output file: comment "file1.wav"
```

You can apply sound effects during the SoX conversion process. The following example shows how to change the sample rate (using the -r option) from 10,000 KHz to 5,000 KHz:

```
$ sox -r 10000 file1.wav -r 5000 file1.voc
```

To reduce the noise, you can send the file through a low-pass filter. Here's an example:

```
$ sox file1.voc file2.voc lowp 2200
```

For more information on SoX and to get the latest download, go to the SoX — Sound eXchange — home page (www.sourceforge.net/projects/sox/).

Compressing Music Files with oggenc

The oggenc command takes music or other audio data and converts it from uncompressed formats (such as WAV, RAW, or AIFF) to the compressed Ogg Vorbis format. Using Ogg Vorbis, audio files can be significantly reduced in size without a noticeable loss of sound quality. (I used the default settings in oggenc and reduced a 48MB WAV music file to 4MB.)

In its most basic form, you can use oggenc with one or more WAV or AIFF files following it. For example:

```
$ oggenc *.wav
```

This command would result in all files ending with .wav in the current directory to be converted to Ogg Vorbis format. An OGG file is produced for each WAV file, with oggenc substituting .ogg for .wav as the file suffix for the compressed file. Ogg Vorbis files can be played in many different audio players in Linux, including the XMMS player (described earlier).

In addition, a number of handheld music players support Ogg Vorbis formats. These include a number of iRiver, Jens of Sweden, MobiBLU, Neuros, and Samsung models. Verify with your product's manual, however, as models and player firmware change often.

> **TIP** If you want to rip music files from a CD and compress them, you can use the Grip window (described later in this chapter). Grip enables you to select oggenc as the tool to do the file compression.

If you are interested in making a CD jukebox that rips, records, and compresses music CDs using oggenc and other open source software, check out *Linux Toys* by Christopher Negus and Chuck Wolber from Wiley Publishing (2003).

Recording and Ripping Music

A writable CD-ROM drive is a standard device on computers. Where once you had to settle for a floppy disk (1.44MB) or a Zip disk (100MB) to store personal data, a CD-ROM burner lets you store more than 600MB of data in a format that can be exchanged with most computers. On top of that, you can create CD music discs!

Both graphical and command-line tools exist for creating CDs on Linux. The cdrecord command enables you to create audio and data CDs from the command line, writing to CD-recordable (CD-R) and CD-rewritable (CD-RW) drives. This command is discussed in the following section.

Creating an Audio CD with cdrecord

You can use the `cdrecord` command to create either data or music CDs. You can create a data CD by setting up a separate file system and copying the whole image of that file system to CD. Creating an audio CD consists of selecting the audio tracks you want to copy and copying them all at once to the CD.

This section focuses on using `cdrecord` to create audio CDs. `cdrecord` can use audio files in `.au`, `.wav`, and `.cdr` formats, automatically translating them when necessary. If you have audio files in other formats, you can convert them to one of the supported formats by using the `sox` command (described previously in this chapter).

One way to create an audio CD is to use `cdda2wav` to extract (copy) the music tracks to a directory and then use `cdrecord` to write them from the directory to the CD. Here's an example:

> **NOTE** If you prefer a graphical tool for copying and burning CDs and DVDs, refer to Appendix A, which describes how to use the K3b CD/DVD burning facility for burning CD images. That tool can also be used for copying audio CDs.

1. Create a directory to hold the audio files, and change to that directory. (Make sure the directory can hold up to 660MB of data — less if you are burning fewer songs.) For example:

   ```
   # mkdir /tmp/cd
   # cd /tmp/cd
   ```

2. Insert the music CD into your CD-ROM drive. (If a CD player opens on the desktop, close it.)

3. Extract the music tracks you want by using the `cdda2wav` command. For example:

   ```
   # cdda2wav -D /dev/cdrom -B
   ```

   This reads all of the music tracks from the CD-ROM drive. The `-B` option says to output each track to a separate file. By default, the `cdda2wav` command outputs the files to the WAV audio format.

   Instead of extracting all songs, you can choose a single track or a range of tracks to extract. For example, to extract tracks 3 through 5, add the `-t3+5` option. To extract just track 9, add `-t9+9`. To extract track 7 through the end of the CD, add `-t7`.

> **NOTE** If you have a low-quality CD drive or an imperfect CD, `cdda2wav` might not be the best ripping tool. You might try `cdparanoia -B` to extract songs from the CD to hard disk instead.

4. When `cdda2wav` is done, insert a blank CD into your writable CD drive.

5. Use the cdrecord command to write the music tracks to the CD. For example:

```
# cdrecord -v dev=/dev/cdrom -audio *.wav
```

The options to cdrecord tell the command to create an audio CD (-audio) on the writable CD device located at /dev/cdrom. The cdrecord command writes all .wav files from the current directory. The -v option causes verbose output.

6. If you want to change the order of the tracks, you can type their names in the order you want them written (instead of using *.wav). If your CD writer supports higher speeds, you can use the speed option to double (speed=2) or to quadruple (speed=4) the writing speed.

After you have created the music CD, indicate the contents of the CD on its label side. It's now ready to play on any standard music CD player.

Ripping CDs with Grip

For GNOME users, the Grip window provides a more graphical method of copying music from CDs to your hard disk so that you can play the songs directly from your hard disk or burn them back onto a blank CD. Besides just ripping music, you can also compress each song as you extract it from the CD.

You can open Grip from the red hat menu by selecting Sound & Video ⇨ Grip (or by typing **grip** from a Terminal window). Figure 20-6 shows an example of the Grip window.

FIGURE 20-6

Rip and play songs from the Grip window.

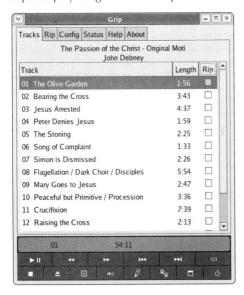

To rip audio tracks from a CD with grip, do the following:

1. With the Grip window open, insert a music CD into your CD drive. If you have an active connection to the Internet and the CD is known to the CD database, the title, artist, and track information appears in the window.

2. Click each track that you want to rip (that is, copy to your hard disk). A check mark appears in that track's Rip column.

3. Click the Config tab at the top of the page, and then select Encode.

4. You can choose the type of encoder used to compress the music by clicking the Encoder box and selecting an encoder (by default, oggenc compresses files in Ogg Vorbis, assuming that Ogg Vorbis was installed on your Linux distribution).

5. Click the Rip tab at the top of the page.

6. Click one of the following:

   ■ **Rip+Encode** — This rips the selected songs and (if you left in the default oggenc compression in Step 4) compresses them in Ogg Vorbis format. You need an Ogg Vorbis player to play the songs after they have been ripped in this format (there are many Ogg Vorbis players for Linux).

   ■ **Rip only** — This rips the selected songs in WAV format. You can use a standard CD player to play these songs. (When I tried this, the same song ripped in WAV was 12 times larger than the Ogg Vorbis file.)

   Songs are copied to the hard disk in the format you selected. By default, the files are copied into a subdirectory of $HOME/ogg (such as /home/jake/ogg). The subdirectory is named for the artist and CD. For example, if the user jake were ripping the song called "High Life" by the artist Mumbo, the directory containing ripped songs would be /home/jake/ogg/mumbo/high_life. Each song file is named for the song (for example, fly_fly_fly.wav).

7. Now you can play any of the files using a player that can play WAV or Ogg files, such as XMMS. Or you can copy the files to a CD using cdrecord. Because the filenames are the song names, they don't appear in the same order as they appear on the CD, so if you want to copy them back to a writable CD in their original order, you may have to type each filename on the cdrecord command line. For example:

```
# cdrecord -v dev=/dev/cdrom -audio fly_fly.wav \
        big_news.wav about_time.wav
```

The Grip window can also be used to play CDs. Use the buttons on the bottom of the display to play or pause, skip ahead or back, stop, and eject the CD. The toggle track display button lets you shrink the size of the display so it takes up less space on the desktop. Click toggle disc editor to see and change title, artist, and track information.

Creating CD Labels with cdlabelgen

The cdlabelgen command can be used to create tray cards and front cards to fit in CD jewel cases. You gather information about the CD, and cdlabelgen produces a PostScript output file that you can send to the printer. The cdlabelgen package also comes with graphics (in /usr/share/cdlabelgen) that you can incorporate into your labels.

Here's an example of a cdlabelgen command line that generates a CD label file in PostScript format (type it all on one line or use backslashes, as shown, to put it on multiple lines):

```
$ cdlabelgen -c "Grunge is Gone" -s "Yep HipHop" \
-i "If You Feed Me%Sockin Years%City Road%Platinum and Copper%Fly Fly \
Fly%Best Man Spins%What A Headache%Stayin Put Feelin%Dreams Do Go \
Blue%Us%Mildest Schemes" -o yep.ps
```

In this example, the title of the CD is indicated by -c "Grunge is Gone" and the artist by the -s "Yep HipHop" option. The tracks are entered after the -i option, with each line separated by a % sign. The output file is sent to the file yep.ps with the -o option. To view and print the results, use the evince command like this:

```
$ evince yep.ps
```

The result of this example is shown in Figure 20-7.

FIGURE 20-7

Generate CD jewel case labels with cdlabelgen and print them with evince.

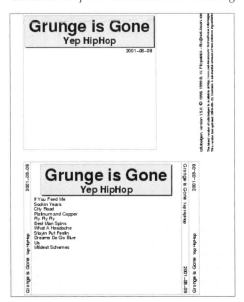

535

You'll want to edit the `cdlabelgen` command line to include the title and song names for the CD label and rerun the program a few times to get the label correct. When you are ready to print the label, click Print All.

Working with TV, Video, and Digital Imaging

Getting TV cards, Webcams, and other video devices to play in Linux is still a bit of an adventure. Most manufacturers of TV cards and Webcams are not losing sleep to produce Linux drivers. As a result, most of the drivers that bring video to your Linux desktop have been reverse-engineered (that is, they were created by software engineers who watched what the video device sent and received, rather than seeing the actual code that runs the device).

The first and probably biggest trick is to get a TV card or Webcam that is supported in Linux. Once you are getting video output from that device (typically available from `/dev/video0`), you can try out a couple of applications to begin using it.

This section explores the tvtime program for watching television and the Ekiga program for video conferencing.

Watching TV with tvtime

The tvtime program (`tvtime` command) enables you to display video output—television channels, in particular—on your desktop. You can change the channels, adjust the volume, and fine-tune your picture. In addition, tvtime sports a slick onscreen display and support for a widescreen display.

The following sections describe how to choose a TV capture card and use tvtime to watch television on your desktop.

Getting a Supported TV Card

Video4Linux (V4l/V4l2) is the video interface available for Linux. It supports a variety of TV capture cards and cameras, and is included in some distributions. If your distribution does not include V4l or V4L2, you can install it on your own, although it is not the easiest task to accomplish. For more information about obtaining and installing V4l and the appropriate driver, visit `http://linux.bytesex.org/v4l2/index.html`.

To see a list of supported TV cards that you can use with tvtime, refer to the `CARDLIST` and `Cards` files of your V4l installation. To view these files, you need to have the kernel-source package installed. You'll find the `Cards` file in `/usr/src/linux*/Documentation/video4linux/bttv/Cards` on your Linux system. The `Cards` file applies to the Video4Linux bttv driver. In addition, look at all files starting with `CARDLIST` in `/usr/src/linux*/Documentation/video4linux/CARDLIST*`.

Video4Linux is designed to autodetect your TV capture card and load the proper modules to activate it. Install the TV-card hardware (with the appropriate connection to your TV reception), boot Linux, and run the `tvtime` command as described in the next section. You should see video displayed in your tvtime window.

If your card doesn't appear to be working, here are a few things you can try:

- Check that your TV card was properly seated in its slot and detected by Linux by typing:

```
$ /sbin/lspci
```

  This shows you a list of all valid PCI cards on your computer. If your card doesn't show up, you probably have a hardware problem.

- It is possible that the card is there but that the right card type is not being detected. Improper detection is most likely if you have a card for which there are several revisions, with each requiring a different driver. If you think your card is not being properly detected, find your card in the `CARDLIST` files. Then add the appropriate line to the `/etc/modprobe.conf` file. For example, to add a Prolink PV-BT878P, revision 9B card, add the following line to the file:

```
options    bttv   card=72
```

- You can also add other options listed in the Insmod-options file for the bttv driver. If you are still having problems getting your card to work, a mailing list is available on which you can ask questions about Video4Linux issues: `http://listman.redhat.com/mailman/listinfo/video4linux-list`. While this list is for Red Hat specifically, the information is germane to most distributions.

One possible reason that you don't see any video when you try to run tvtime or other video applications is that some other person or video application already has the video driver open. Only one application can use the video driver at a time. Another quirk of Video4Linux is that the first person to open the device on your system becomes the owner. So you might need to open the permissions of the driver to allow people other than the first person to use it to access the Video4Linux driver.

Running tvtime

To start up the tvtime viewer, simply select TVtime Televison Viewer from the Sound & Video or Multimedia menu (depending on your Linux distribution), or type the following from a Terminal window on your desktop:

```
$ tvtime &
```

A video screen should appear in a window on the desktop. Click on the window to see a list of stations. Right-click to see the onscreen Setup menu.

Here are a few things you can now do with your tvtime onscreen display:

- **Configure input** — Change the video source, choose the television standard (which defaults to NTSC for the U.S.), and change the resolution of the input.

- **Set up the picture** — Adjust the brightness, contrast, color, and hue.

- **Adjust the video processing** — Control the attempted frame rate, configure the deinterlacer, or add an input filter.

- **Adjust output** — Control the aspect ratio (for 16:9 output, for example), apply a matte, or set the overscan mode.

Video Conferencing with Ekiga

The Ekiga window lets you communicate with other people over a network through video, audio, and typed messages. Because Ekiga supports the H323 protocol (a standard for multimedia communications), you can use it to communicate with people using other popular videoconferencing clients, such as Microsoft NetMeeting, Cu-SeeMe, and Intel VideoPhone.

NOTE Ekiga does not support the NetMeeting shared whiteboard functions, just videoconferencing.

To be able to send video, you need a Webcam that is supported in Linux — you'll find a few dozen models from which to choose. The following sections show you how to set up your Webcam and use Ekiga for videoconferencing.

NOTE Ekiga was previously known as GnomeMeeting. Both names may be in use on any given Linux platform.

Getting a Supported Webcam

As with support for TV capture cards, Webcam support is provided through the Video4Linux interface. To see if your Webcam is supported, check the /usr/src/linux*/Documentation directory. A few parallel-port video cameras are described in the video4linux subdirectory; however, the bulk of the supported cameras are listed in the usb directory.

TIP After doing some research, I purchased a Logitech QuickCam Pro 3000. The driver for this Webcam was made for a Philips USB Webcam, but it also works for Webcams from Logitech, Samsung, Creative Labs, and Askey. The pwc driver needed to use these cameras is available with most popular Linux distributions.

Supported USB cameras should be autodetected, so that when you plug them in, the necessary modules are loaded automatically. Just start up Ekiga (ekiga command), and you should see video from your Webcam on your Linux desktop.

You can check to see that your Webcam is working properly by typing the following:

```
# lsmod
pwc                     43392    1
videodev                 5120    2  [pwc]
usbcore                 59072    1  [audio pwc usb-uhci]
```

The output from lsmod shows that the pwc driver is loaded and associated with the videodev module and usbcore module.

Opening Your Firewall for Ekiga

You need to open a variety of ports in your firewall to use Ekiga. In particular, you need to open TCP port 1720 and TCP port range 30000 to 30010. For UDP ports, you must open ports 5000 through 5007 and ports 5010 through 5013. Examples of exact iptables settings you can use to open these ports are contained in the Ekiga FAQ (www.ekiga.org/faq).

Running Ekiga

To start Ekiga in most distributions, select Applications ➪ Internet ➪ Ekiga Softphone. To start Ekiga from a Terminal window, type **ekiga &**. If it is not installed, you can get the package for your Linux distribution when you install the GNOME desktop. The first time you run Ekiga, the Ekiga Configuration Assistant starts, enabling you to enter the following information:

- **Personal Data** — Your first name, last name, e-mail address, comment, and location. You can also choose whether you want to be listed in the Ekiga ILS directory.
- **Connection Type** — Indicate the speed of your Internet connection (56K modem, ISDN, DSL/Cable, T1/LAN, or Custom).

Once you have entered the data, the Ekiga window opens.

Figure 20-8 shows the Ekiga window with the call log to the right. Select Tools ➪ Calls History to open that log. It shows a history of the calls you make during this session. To open the Address book, select the address book icon from the left side of the Ekiga window. Add ILS servers and friends to that window, and then select the user or server you want to contact and click Contact ➪ Call Contact.

Use the tabs beneath the video window to adjust your audio levels and video appearance. The History tab shows a log of your activities.

FIGURE 20-8

Connect to ILS servers to videoconference with Ekiga.

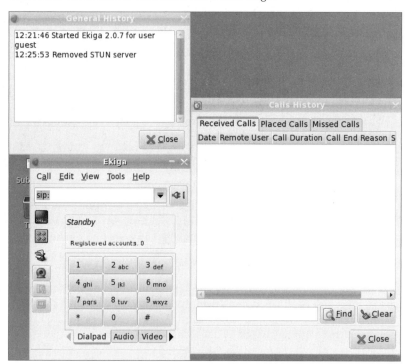

Watching Movies and Video

Although several fairly high-quality video players are available for Linux, it is rare to see the players included in formal distributions because of legal complications. The issues surrounding the playing of encoded DVD movies in Linux might be responsible for keeping players such as the MPlayer (`freshmeat.net/mplayer`), Ogle (`www.dtek.chalmers.se/groups/dvd`), and xine (`http://xinehq.de/`) video players out of common distributions.

By most accounts, however, you can get and use these video players to play a variety of video content for personal use as long as you don't download and use the DeCCS (software for decrypting DVD movies). The following sections provide descriptions of some commonly used video players.

Watching Video with xine

The xine player is an excellent application for playing a variety of video and audio formats. You can get xine from `xine.sourceforge.net` or from software repositories associated with your Linux distribution.

You can start the xine player by typing **xine&** from a Terminal window. Figure 20-9 shows an example of the xine video player window and controls.

FIGURE 20-9

Play video CDs, MP3s, QuickTime, and other video formats with xine.

> **NOTE** When you try to install xine, it tells you if you need any additional packages. If your xine player fails to start, see the "xine Tips" section later in this chapter.

xine supports a bunch of video and audio formats, including:

- MPEG (1, 2, and 4)
- QuickTime (see "xine Tips" if your QuickTime content won't play)
- WMV
- DVDs, CDs, and VCDs
- Motion JPEG
- MPEG audio (MP3)
- AC3 and Dolby Digital audio
- DTS audio
- Ogg Vorbis audio

xine understands different file formats that represent a combination of audio and video, including `.mpg` (MPEG program streams), `.ts` (MPEG transport streams), `.mpv` (raw MPEG audio/video streams), `.avi` (MS AVI format), and `.asf` (Advanced Systems Format). While xine can play video CDs and DVDs, it can't play encrypted DVDs or the Video-on-CD hybrid format (because of legal issues mentioned earlier related to decrypting DVDs).

Using xine

With xine started, right-click in the xine window to see the controls. The quickest way to play video is to click one of the following buttons, and then press the Play button (right arrow or Play, depending on the skin you are using):

- VCD (for a video CD)
- DVD (for a DVD in /dev/dvd)
- CDA (for a music CD in /dev/cdaudio)

Next, you can use the Pause/Resume, Stop, Play, Fast Motion, Slow Motion, and Eject buttons to work with video. You can also use the Previous and Next buttons to step to different tracks. The controls are very similar to what you would expect on a physical CD or DVD player.

To select individual files, or to put together your own list of content to play, use the Playlist feature.

Creating Playlists with xine

Click the Playlist button on the left side of the xine control window. A Playlist Editor appears, showing the files on your current playlist. You can add and delete content and then save the list to call on later.

xine content is identified as media resource locators (MRLs). Each MRL is identified as a file, DVD, or VCD. Files are in the regular file path (/path/file) or preceded by file:/, fifo:/, or stdin:/. DVDs and VCDs are preceded by dvd and vcd, respectively (for example, vcd://01).

Table 20-2 shows what the xine Playlist Editor buttons do.

TABLE 20-2

Using the xine Playlist Editor

Button	Description
CDA, DVD, or VCD	All content from that CD or DVD is added to the playlist.
Add	See the MRL Browser window. From that window, click File to choose a file from your Linux file system, and then click Select to add that file to the Playlist Editor. (MRL stands for Media Resource Locator, which defines the form in which remote and local content are identified.)
Move Up Selected MRL Move Down Selected MRL	Move up and down the playlist.
Play	Play the contents of the playlist.
Delete Selected MRL	Remove the current selection.
Delete All Entries	Clear the whole playlist.
Save	Save the playlist to your home directory ($HOME/.xine/playlist).
Load	Read in your (saved) playlist.

xine Tips

Getting video and audio to work properly can sometimes be a tricky business. Here are a few quick tips if you are having trouble getting xine to work correctly (or at all):

- **xine won't start** — To work best, xine needs an X driver that supports xvid. If there is no xvid support for your video card in X, xine shuts down immediately when it tries to open the default Xv driver. If this happens to you, try starting xine with the X11 video driver (which is slower, but should work) as follows:

```
$ xine -VXSHM
```

- **xine playback is choppy** — If playback of files from your hard disk is choppy, there are a couple of settings you can check: 32-bit IO and DMA, features that, if supported by your hard disk, generally improve hard disk performance. Here's how to check:

CAUTION Improper disk settings can result in destroyed data on your hard disk. Perform this procedure at your own risk. This procedure is for IDE hard drives only (no SCSI)! Also, be sure to have a current backup and no activity on your hard disk if you change DMA or I/O settings as described in this section.

1. Test the speed of hard disk reads. To test the first IDE drive (/dev/hda), type:

```
# hdparm -t /dev/hda
Timing buffered disk reads: 64 MB in
      19.31 seconds = 3.31 MB/sec
```

2. To see your current DMA and I/O settings, as root user type:

```
# hdparm -c -d /dev/hda
/dev/hda:
 I/O support = 0 (default 16-bit)
 using_dma   = 0 (off)
```

3. This result shows that both 32-bit I/O and DMA are off. To turn them on, type:

```
# hdparm -c 1 -d 1 /dev/hda
/dev/hda:
 I/O support = 1 (32-bit)
 using_dma   = 1 (on)
```

4. With both settings on, test the disk again:

```
# hdparm -t /dev/hda
Timing buffered disk reads: 64 MB in
      2.2 seconds = 28.83 MB/sec
```

In this example, buffered disk reads of 64MB went from 19.31 seconds to 2.2 seconds after changing the parameters described. Playback would be much better now.

- **xine won't play particular media** — Messages such as `no input plug-in` mean that either the file format you are trying to play is not supported or it requires an additional plug-in (as is the case with playing DVDs). If the message is that xyx may be a broken file, the file may be a proprietary version of an otherwise supported format. For example, I had a QuickTime video fail that required an SVQ3 codec (which is currently not supported under Linux), although other QuickTime files played fine.

Using Helix Player and RealPlayer 10

A tremendous amount of content is available on the Internet in the RealMedia and RealAudio formats. You can see and hear video clips of popular musicians and comics; view live events such as conferences, news stories, and concerts; and listen to your favorite radio stations when you are out of town.

To play RealMedia and RealAudio content, you need, as you may have guessed, RealPlayer. RealNetworks (`www.real.com`) is a leader in streaming media on the Internet. More than 50 million unique users have registered with RealNetworks and its Web site, downloading more than 175,000 files per day. And that's not even the good news. The good news is that RealPlayer is available to run in Linux.

RealPlayer 10 for Linux is available via the Linux area of `www.download.com` and `www.tucows` `.com` and at `www.real.com/linux/`. This player is not supported by RealNetworks directly. In addition, RealNetworks has opened up the source code to the RealPlayer under the name Helix Player. Fedora 8 (on the DVD included with this book) includes a version of the Helix Player that you can try out.

The instructions for configuring RealPlayer are delivered in HTML format, so you can read them in Mozilla or some other Web browser. If any patches or workarounds are required, you can find them by querying for the word "Linux" in the RealNetworks Knowledge Base. To get there, click Support (from most RealNetworks pages), and then click Knowledge Base.

When you install RealPlayer, you are asked if you want to configure it to be used as a Netscape plug-in (which I recommend so that you can play Real content in Mozilla Firefox). After that, when you open any Real content in your browser, RealPlayer opens to handle it. Alternatively, you can start RealPlayer from a Terminal window on your desktop by typing the following:

```
$ realplay &
```

RealNetworks has gone to a subscription model for its content (you sign up and pay a monthly fee). To see what's available, and to decide if it is worth signing up, I suggest starting at the RealGuide site (`www.realguide.real.com`), which includes a few clips you can try out.

Using a Digital Camera with gtkam and gPhoto2

With the gtkam window, you can download and work with images from digital cameras. The gtkam window is a front end to gPhoto2, which provides support for dozens of digital cameras in Linux. The gtkam window works by attaching a supported digital camera to a serial or USB port on your computer. You can view thumbnails of the digital images from the camera, view full-size images, and download the ones you select from the camera to your hard disk.

> **NOTE** If you have a camera that saves images to a floppy disk, just insert that disk into your disk drive and the contents of the disk should open automatically on your desktop. In addition, if your camera saves images to SD or CF cards, you can purchase a USB card reader and view these files from Linux.

Check the gPhoto2 Web site (`www.gphoto.org/proj/libgphoto2/support.php`) for information on supported cameras as well as other topics related to gPhoto. If you include experimental units and cameras under testing, there are over 900 supported cameras. New cameras are added frequently, so check the support page regularly if you do not see your camera listed.

Downloading Digital Photos with gtkam

The following procedure describes how to download images from your digital camera.

1. Using a cable provided with your digital camera, connect your camera to the USB or COM port on your computer (I had better luck with the USB port).

2. Set your camera to Send and Receive mode.

3. From the main menu on your desktop, choose Graphics ⇨ Digital Camera Tool. The gtkam window appears.

4. Select Camera ⇨ Add Camera. The Select Camera window appears.

5. Click the down arrow next to the Model box, select your camera, and click Detect.

6. Click Apply, and then click OK. Your camera model should be listed in the gtkam window.

7. To begin downloading images from your digital camera, click the camera name that appears in the left column, and then select the folder containing the images from that camera. After the images download (which can take a while), thumbnails appear in the main gtkam window.

8. Select the images that interest you, and click the Save Selected Photos button to save the selected images. The Save Photos window that appears lets you choose a directory to save them to. You can rename the images or just use the names assigned by the camera.

9. Choose images you want to delete, and click the Delete button.

Using Your Camera as a Storage Device

Some digital cameras let you treat them like storage devices to manage pictures. By mounting a digital camera as a USB mass storage device, you can view, copy, delete, and move the pictures on your camera as you would files on a hard disk or CD (just at a lower speed).

Table 20-3 is a partial summary of digital cameras that can be used as USB storage devices. For a current list, visit www.qbik.ch/usb/devices/showdevcat.php?id=10.

> **NOTE**   At the Linux-USB Device Overview site (www.qbik.ch/usb/devices/index.php), you can also find the latest information on devices other than cameras: audio, networking, video, and so on.

TABLE 20-3

Cameras That Can Be Used as USB Storage Devices

Brand	Supported Models
Casio	QV-2400UX, QV-2x00, QV-3x00, QV-4000, and QV-8000
Fuji	FinePix 1300, 1400Zoom, 2300Zoom, 2400Zoom, 2800Zoom, 4200Z, 4500, 4700 Zoom, 4900 Zoom, 6800 Zoom, A101, A201, and S1 Pro
HP	PhotoSmart 315, 318xi, 618, and C912
Konica	KD200Z, KD400Z, and Revio KD300Z
Kyocera	Finecam s3
Leica	Digilux 4.3
Minolta	Dimage 5, Dimage 7, and Dimage X
Nikon	CoolPix 2500, 885, 5000, 775, and 995
Olympus	Brio Zoom D-15, C-100, C-200Z, C-2040, C-220Z, C-2Z, C-3020Z, C-3040Z, C-4040Zoom, C-700, C-700UZ, C-860L, D-510, D-520Z, E-10, and E-20
Pentax	EI2000, Optio 330, and Optio 430
Sony	DSC-F505, DSC-F505V, DSC-F707, DSC-P1, DSC-P20, DSC-P5, DSC-P71, DSC-S30, DSC-S70, DSC-S75, DSC-S85, MVC-CD300, and MVC-FD92
Vivitar	Vivicam 3550
Yashica	Finecam s3

To Linux, the USB mass storage camera appears as a SCSI drive containing a VFAT file system with image files on it. Here's a procedure for using your digital camera as a USB storage device:

1. Use the cable provided with your digital camera to connect your camera to a USB port on your computer, and turn the camera on so it is ready to send and receive data.

2. Boot your computer.

3. Open the /etc/fstab file as root user and see if an entry was created for your digital camera. If you have no other SCSI devices on your computer, the camera is probably detected as a /dev/sda1 device. Here's what the entry might look like:

```
/dev/sda1    /mnt/camera    auto    defaults, user,noauto    0 0
```

If no such entry appears, create the entry. Create the mount point directory (as root user, type **mkdir /mnt/camera**).

4. As root user, type the command to mount the camera: **mount /mnt/camera**.

5. Open the /mnt/camera directory as you would any other directory from the shell or from a file manager. Copy, delete, move, and rename files as you would any files on your hard disk.

6. When you are done, unmount the camera (as root user from a Terminal window):

```
# umount /mnt/camera
```

 If you unplug your camera without unmounting the file system, it can damage the files on your camera.

You can follow this procedure to use other USB mass storage devices (CD drives, keychains, and so on) in Linux. Use different mount directories (such as /mnt/keychain) and check which SCSI device is being assigned to the USB storage device.

To see if your USB storage device can be seen by Linux, check the /var/log/dmesg file or run the usbview command. Either will tell you if the device is being detected properly by Linux.

Summary

Getting up and running with digital media can take some doing, but once it's set up, you can play most audio and video content available today. This chapter takes you through the steps of setting up and troubleshooting your sound card and explains how to find software to play music through that card.

Every desktop Linux distribution comes with one or more ways of playing music from files or CDs. Popular music players include XMMS and Rhythmbox. Tools for ripping and recording CDs include Grip and command-line utilities such as cdda2wav and cdrecord.

The chapter also covers playing live video from TV cards and Webcams in the sections on tvtime and Ekiga, respectively. Finally, the chapter describes how the xine player can be used to play a variety of video formats and explored the gtkam window for downloading images from a digital camera. If your computer has a CD burner, use the descriptions in this chapter to create your own music CDs and CD labels.

Chapter 21

Working with Words and Images

Computers are great for collecting and recording music, playing games, and communicating with far-off lands. While these functions are popular and exciting, one tool has been considered essential since the earliest days of personal computers: document-creating applications. From ultra-simple text-only editors to feature-rich groupware systems, you'll be hard-pressed to find a PC without this basic functionality. Such software is so important that Microsoft makes billions of dollars each year selling productivity tools for the Windows OS.

Linux users are, on most levels, no different from any other PC user. They need to write letters, make presentations, write books, and sort information in spreadsheets. For the Linux user, a copy of Microsoft Office is simply not in the cards yet, but there are many powerful tools from which to choose.

OpenOffice.org is a powerful open-source office suite available as a download and as part of many Linux distributions. Based on Sun Microsystems' StarOffice productivity suite, OpenOffice.org includes a word processor, spreadsheet program, presentation manager, and other personal productivity tools. In most cases, OpenOffice.org can be used as a drop-in replacement for Microsoft Office.

The first document and graphics tools for Linux were mostly built on older, text-based tools. Recently, more sophisticated tools for writing, formatting pages, and integrating graphics have been added. Despite their age, many of the older publishing tools (such as Groff and LaTeX) are still used by people in the technical community.

This chapter examines both text-based and GUI-based document preparation software for Linux, and discusses tools for printing and displaying documents, as well as software for working with images.

 **If you've been using Microsoft Office applications such as Microsoft Word, Excel, and PowerPoint, this chapter shows you how to work with your existing files or create new ones using Linux tools, such as the utilities in the OpenOffice.org suite.**

Using OpenOffice.org

Some have called OpenOffice.org the most significant threat to Microsoft's dominance of the desktop market. If a need to work with documents in Microsoft Word format has kept you from using Linux as your desktop computer, OpenOffice.org is a big step toward removing that obstacle. You can use a program such as WINE that (among other things) allows you to run versions of Microsoft Office directly on your Linux PC, but for the vast majority of users there is no reason to bother doing so. In this section we take a high-level overview of the suite and spend a little time examining one of the more commonly used elements, Writer (the word processor), in some detail.

Many distributions of Linux include the entire OpenOffice.org suite of desktop applications. Some include the StarOffice suite in addition to or in lieu of OpenOffice.org. If neither is present, you can always download and install OpenOffice.org from its Web site, www.openoffice.org. StarOffice is commercial software and can be purchased from www.sun.com.

NOTE At the time of this writing, the latest version of OpenOffice is 2.2.1. Version 2.3 is in development.

OpenOffice.org, which shares its source code with StarOffice, consists of the following office-productivity applications:

- **Writer** — A word-processing application that can work with documents in file formats from Microsoft Word, StarOffice, and several others. Writer also has a full set of features for using templates, working with fonts, navigating your documents, including images and effects, and generating tables of contents.

- **Calc** — A spreadsheet application that lets you incorporate data from Microsoft Excel, StarOffice, Dbase, and several other spreadsheet formats. Some nice features in Calc enable you to create charts, set up database ranges (to easily sort data in an area of a spreadsheet), and use the data pilot tool to arrange data in different points of view.

- **Draw** — A drawing application that enables you to create, edit, and align objects; include textures and colors; and work with layers of objects. It lets you incorporate images, vector graphics, AutoCAD, and a variety of other file formats into your drawings. Then, you can save your drawing in the OpenOffice.org Drawing or StarDraw format.

- **Math** — A calculation program that lets you create mathematical formulas.
- **Impress** — A presentation application that includes a variety of slide effects. You can use Impress to create and save presentations in the Microsoft PowerPoint, StarDraw, and StarImpress formats.

Unlike other applications that were created to work with Microsoft document and data formats, OpenOffice.org (although not perfect) does a very good job of opening and saving those files with fewer problems. Very basic styles and formatting that open in OpenOffice.org often don't look noticeably different from the way they appear in Microsoft Office. In other cases, such things as bullets, alignment, and indentation can appear quite different in Writer than they do in Word. Also, some Word features, such as macros and scripting features, may not work at all in Writer. For the most part, however, the recent versions of the OpenOffice.org suite handle most Microsoft Office files.

In addition, the OpenOffice.org suite supports the ODF, or Open Document Format, a recently standardized file format for office documents. ODF is becoming more and more important with government and scientific organizations that need to be able to access the documents they create for many years in the future. Using the Microsoft Office formats, for example, locks an organization into paying Microsoft's fee in order to access the organization's data. In the future, that fee could become too high for the organization, or worse yet, Microsoft may choose not to support files created by older versions of the software. Even today, for example, OpenOffice.org supports older versions of Microsoft Word than Word does.

Another nice feature of the OpenOffice.org suite is document signing, so that you can provide better security to shared documents.

To open OpenOffice.org applications, select the relevant menu item (such as the OpenOffice.org Writer icon) from the System menu. In most distributions, there's a folder called Office (or something very similar) located on the system menu as well. Figure 21-1 shows a Microsoft Word document open for editing in OpenOffice.org Writer.

The controls in Writer are similar to the ones you find in Word. Toolbars include boxes for changing styles, font types, and font sizes. Buttons let you save and print the file, change the text alignment, and cut, copy, and paste text. In other words, Writer includes almost everything you expect in an advanced word processor. In addition, Writer includes a handy PDF button to output a file directly to the PDF format, which is very useful for exchanging documents or placing data on the Internet.

> **NOTE** Although this book cannot cover all the OpenOffice.org applications, you can try them out directly from KNOPPIX or most other Linux distributions that offer KDE or GNOME desktops.

Work with Microsoft Word documents in OpenOffice.org Writer.

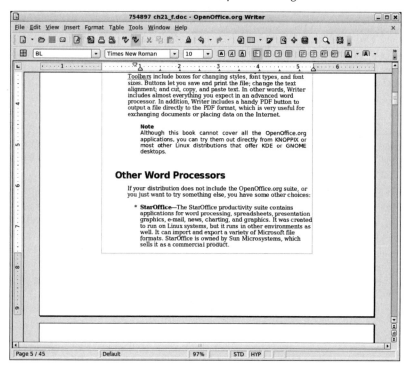

Other Word Processors

If your distribution does not include the OpenOffice.org suite, or you just want to try something else, you have some other choices:

- **StarOffice** — The StarOffice productivity suite contains applications for word processing, spreadsheets, presentation graphics, e-mail, news, charting, and graphics. It was created to run on Linux systems, but it runs in other environments as well. It can import and export a variety of Microsoft file formats. StarOffice is owned by Sun Microsystems, which sells it as a commercial product.

- **AbiWord** — The AbiWord word processor (`abiword` command), is noncommercial software and is the first application produced by the AbiSource project (`www.abisource.com`). In addition to working with files in its own formats (`.abw` and `.zabw`), AbiWord can import files in Microsoft Word and several other formats.

- **KOffice** — The KOffice package contains a set of office productivity applications designed for the KDE desktop (you must have the KDE desktop environment). The noncommercial software includes a word processor (KWord), spreadsheet (KSpread), presentation creator (KPresenter), and diagram-drawing program (KChart). These applications can be run separately or within a KOffice Workspace.

Using StarOffice

The StarOffice suite from Sun Microsystems, Inc. (www.sun.com/staroffice) is a product that runs on Linux, UNIX, and Windows operating systems. Like OpenOffice.org, StarOffice contains many features that make it compatible with Microsoft Office applications. In particular, it includes the capability to import Microsoft Word and Excel files.

StarOffice is probably the most complete integrated office suite for Linux. It includes:

- **Writer** — StarOffice's word-processing application. It can import documents from a variety of formats, with special emphasis on Word documents.

- **Calc** — The StarOffice spreadsheet program. You can import spreadsheets from Microsoft Excel and other popular programs.

- **Impress** — Create presentations with this application.

- **Draw** — A vector-oriented drawing program that includes the capability to create 3D objects and to use texturing.

- **Base** — Manage your data sources. You can access a variety of database interfaces.

Other tools in StarOffice enable you to create business graphics, edit raster images, and edit mathematical formulas.

You can download StarOffice 8 for Linux or purchase a boxed set from the StarOffice Web site at www.sun.com/staroffice. Although StarOffice was once available free for download, the current price to download the software for home users is $69.95 U.S., or $99.95 if you purchase it through retail outlets. (You can also get a volume discount.) There is a trial version available that you can enable (using a license key) if you decide that you like it enough to purchase the product.

One reason to pay for StarOffice when you can get OpenOffice.org software for free is that you get a bunch of extras with StarOffice. The extras include a spell-checker, clip art, many more file converters (although the best ones are for converting Microsoft formats), a database module, and technical support.

NOTE OpenOffice.org is an open source project sponsored by Sun Microsystems. Sun takes the shared source code used to create OpenOffice.org and combines it with other modules to produce the StarOffice suite. This is very similar to Mozilla, an open source Web browser, and Netscape, a commercial product built from the Mozilla sources.

Using AbiWord

The AbiWord word processor is a very nice, free word processor from the AbiSource project (www.abisource.com). If you are starting documents from scratch, AbiWord includes many of the basic functions you need to create good-quality documents.

With AbiWord, you can select the type of document the file contains, and select to read the file in the following formats:

- AbiWord (.abw)
- GZipped AbiWord (.zabw)
- Rich Text Format (.rtf)
- Microsoft Word (.doc)
- UTF8 (.utf8)
- Text (.txt)

In addition, AbiWord can import and export ODF, DocBook, and OpenOffice.org files.

AbiWord doesn't yet import all these file types cleanly. Although the recent version supports Word styles, sometimes tables, graphics, and other features don't translate perfectly. If you want to work with a Word document in AbiWord, open it as AbiWord, correct any font problems, and save the document in AbiWord format. AbiWord has vastly improved in the past few releases, but you may still experience problems if you need to exchange files with others who are using Word. (If you want to keep files in the Word format, you'll find that OpenOffice.org and StarOffice work much better, but not perfectly.)

AbiWord is a great first try as a usable word processor. Recently added features such as styles and bullets continue to make it a more useful word-processing tool. It's not yet competitive with comparable commercial products, but its developers continue to improve it.

If you do not have a lot of formatting needs, or if you do not care about Microsoft file formats, AbiWord provides a realistic alternative to larger application suites such as OpenOffice.org. The AbiWord program is small and executes fast, requiring less system resources such as RAM than OpenOffice.org. The speed and size make it a joy to use.

Using KOffice

The K Desktop Environment, KDE, provides an office suite along with hundreds of other programs. The KOffice package has the basic applications you would expect in an integrated office suite: a word processor (KWord), a spreadsheet program (KSpread), a presentation creator (KPresenter), and a diagram-drawing program (KChart).

Start by opening the KOffice Workspace (usually from a KDE panel menu). In the workspace window that opens, you can select from the different office applications presented in the left column.

Open multiple documents in any of the applications, and then click Documents in the left column to choose which one to display at the moment.

Figure 21-2 shows the KOffice Workspace, displaying a KWord document.

FIGURE 21-2

The KOffice Workspace enables you to work with multiple KDE office applications at once.

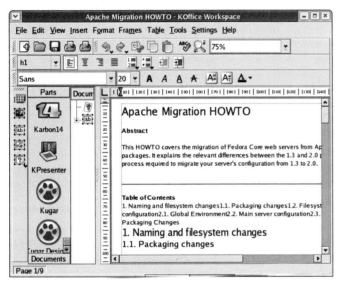

You can work with a variety of document, spreadsheet, and image types. Not many commercial document types are supported yet, so you may need to import documents using other tools before you can read them into KWord. KSpread, however, can open several different spreadsheet styles, including Microsoft Excel and GNUmeric spreadsheets.

Getting Away from Windows

For casual home users, small-office workers, and large corporation personnel alike, moving away from Microsoft Office to another Office suite is an experience that can range from simple to harrowing. In general, it is useful to examine this migration in terms of "home use" versus "work use."

Home users typically have to concern themselves with maintaining access to their own documents. In a personal context, it might be rare for friends and relatives to send Excel spreadsheets, Word documents, and PowerPoint presentations. But over the years you may have accumulated term papers, recipes, letters to the editor, account spreadsheets, and other such documents that you'd like to be able to read and print. In most cases, OpenOffice.org applications will handle files in Microsoft formats just fine.

At work, in addition to the accumulation of documents over time, there is a more pressing issue: Other people will be sending you Microsoft Office documents. So while home users need to concern themselves most with access to historical documents, in the workplace you probably need to accommodate new documents as well as your historical information.

Because you can convert your documents, there are no real challenges to migrating simple documents. However, if your Microsoft Office documents include extensive macro, scripting, or embedded object usage, you may find the conversion is not a very clean one. Make sure you attempt conversions using the following options before moving on to the last resort of using multiple applications or re-creating documents.

Using Microsoft Office to convert documents enables you to save your files in an alternative format. For example, Word 2002 allows you to save your .doc files (the Word versions anyway) to a variety of formats, including:

- **HTML** (.htm/.html) — HTML is a great format for your information if it is basically text and you need only a few formatting options and some embedded images and links. The resulting HTML document will be smaller than the corresponding .doc file.

- **Rich Text Format** (.rtf) — Another wonderful minimalist format (owned by Microsoft but an open standard nonetheless) that preserves some formatting and graphics, but any scripting or macro usage is lost.

- **Plain Text** (.txt) — Works if all you need to save is the text of the file. Everything else is lost.

- **Word 6.0/95** (.doc) — An alternative format that may save some of the elements you want yet make it more accessible to OpenOffice.org. Using this format may not resolve all of the issues you have with converting those hard-to-change documents, but it just might do the trick.

> **NOTE**   The default format for Word 2007 files is .docx — Office Open XML.

Other Microsoft Office applications offer similar functionality. PowerPoint can convert presentations to HTML and general image formats such as JPEG and TIFF. Excel can save tab- and comma-delimited files that are easily importable into a large number of applications.

If you make use of Access to save data, you may want to move data stored in Access's .mdb format into a SQL database. SQL is more scalable, powerful, and virtually platform-independent. Migrating to SQL will preserve your data, but if your .mdb file will not open in OpenOffice.org, you will need to re-create any forms for accessing the data that you would like to continue using.

If you are likely to continue to receive Microsoft Office files and you are concerned about interoperability, here are some options to consider:

- Keep a copy of Microsoft Office installed using WINE and the CodeWeavers CrossOver Office plug-in. For more information about CrossOver Office, visit CodeWeavers' Web site at www.codeweavers.com.

- Ask individuals sending you documentation to use a less vendor-specific format, such as Adobe PDF. Document formatting can be exquisitely preserved and will be viewable by anyone capable of installing a PDF viewer, which supports virtually every operating system in widespread use today. Documents posted on Web sites, for example, should be in PDF and not Microsoft Word format for security reasons.

- For forms that have user-editable fields, scripting, or complex embedded information, use HTML documents instead. Anyone with a compliant Web browser will be able to interact with the document, and Microsoft Office applications universally support saving files into this format.

  If you will want to access your documents a long time from now, say a few years, consider storing your documents in the Open Document Format, or ODF. ODF, being open and not encumbered by patents, will make it easier for you to access your documents in the future. If your organization has any requirements for long-term data storage, use ODF. Remember, Microsoft does not support old versions of Word documents today. Furthermore, Word's latest document format is encumbered by patents, so you may lose the right to access your documents in the future, or need to pay any fee required by the vendor. Use ODF.

CAUTION Before making any wholesale conversion away from Microsoft Office, make sure the files you need to use will work as expected with the new office suite you have selected or that you can construct suitable replacements if needed. Testing things ahead of time enables you to make necessary adjustments without later having to endure the frustration of finding some important document inaccessible or unusable.

Many organizations start their transition away from Microsoft Office by switching to OpenOffice.org on Windows. This way you can have both Office and OpenOffice.org running on the same systems as you gradually work out any conversion issues. Once the issues have been resolved, you can migrate to Linux. In any migration effort, follow good practices such as starting with smaller groups to ensure any glitches or problems are properly handled.

Using Traditional Linux Publishing Tools

With old-school text processors such as Groff and TeX, you can ignore document appearance while writing. Plain-text macros instruct postprocessors how to lay out a document for printing after writing is done. With word processors such as OpenOffice.org Word and StarOffice Writer, you mark up text and see the basic layout of the document as you write.

Some attributes of the traditional Linux document preparation tools make them particularly well suited for certain types of projects. TeX and Groff are a pair of these "classic" tools and have been popular among technical people because:

- You can manipulate files in plain text. Using tools such as sed and grep, you can scan and change one document or hundreds with a single command or script. This makes it easier when company or product names change, for example.

- Scientific notation is supported. With the `geqn` command, you can create complex equations. LaTeX and TeX are suited for technical notation, and some math publications require LaTeX.

- Editing can be faster because traditional Linux documents are created with a text editor. You usually get better performance out of a text editor than a word processor.

Simple page layouts work well with Linux documentation tools. For example, a technical book with a few flow charts and images can be easily produced and maintained using Groff or TeX documentation tools. Letters and memos are also easy to do with these tools. And, of course, Linux man pages are created with text-based tools.

Additionally, Linux likes PostScript. Although people think of PostScript as a printing language, it is really more of a programming language (you could write PostScript code directly). Most Linux document-processing software includes print drivers for PostScript. Some documents on the Web are distributed in PostScript (`.ps`).

The drawback to the traditional Linux document tools is that they are not intuitive. Although there are some easier front ends to LaTeX (see the description of LyX later in this chapter), if you are creating documents in a text editor, you need to learn what macros to type into your documents and which formatting and print commands to use.

NOTE   For many years, the UNIX system documentation distributed by AT&T was created in troff/nroff formats, which predate Groff. The documents used separate macro packages for man pages and guide material. Using a source code control system (SCCS), AT&T ported thousands of pages of documentation to different UNIX systems.

Creating Documents in Groff or LaTeX

You can use any text editor to create documents for both Linux's Groff (troff/nroff) and LaTeX styles of publishing. Most Linux distributions come with several text editors. You always have the option to download others from the Internet. (See the "Choosing a Text Editor" sidebar for more information.)

Here are the general steps for creating documents in Groff or LaTeX:

1. Create a document with any text editor. The document will contain text and markup.

2. Format the document using a formatting command that matches the style of the document that you created (for example, with `groff` or `latex`). During this step, you may need to indicate that the document contains special content, such as equations (`eqn` command), tables (`tbl` command), or line drawings (`pic` command).

3. Send the document to an output device (a printer or a display program).

If you are accustomed to a word processor with a GUI, you may find these publishing tools difficult to learn at first. In general, Groff is useful for creating man pages for Linux. LaTeX is useful if you need to produce mathematical documents, perhaps for publication in a technical journal.

Choosing a Text Editor

Hardcore UNIX or Linux users tend to edit files with either the vi or emacs text editor. These editors have been around a long time and are hard to learn but efficient to use because your fingers never leave the keyboard. The emacs editor has some GUI support, although it runs fine in a Terminal window. There are also GUI versions of vi and emacs that add menu and mouse features to the editors. These are GVim (`gvim` command in the vim-X11 package) and Xemacs (`xemacs` command) editors.

The following table shows some of the other, simpler text editors that can run on your graphical desktop.

Text Editor	Command	Description
gedit	`gedit`	Lightweight text editor that comes with the GNOME desktop environment. It has simple edit functions (cut, copy, paste, and select all), and you can set indentations and word wrap. Special functions, such as a spell-checker and a diff feature, are included. Start by typing **gedit** from a Terminal window. Go to `www.gnome.org/projects/gedit/` for more information.
Advanced Editor	`kwrite`	Includes a menu bar to create, open, and save files, and simple edit functions (cut, copy, paste, undo, and help). Other features enable you to set indents, find and replace text, and select all. This tool comes with the KDE desktop; access it by selecting Accessories ⇨ More Accessories ⇨ Kwrite.
Text Editor	`kedit`	A simple text editor that comes with the KDE desktop. Features let you open files from your file system or from a URL. It also includes a convenient toolbar and a spell-checker. Access it by selecting Accessories ⇨ More Accessories ⇨ Text Editor.
nedit	`nedit`	A rather plain-looking, but very advanced, X-based text editor. It provides all the usual editing functions, syntax-highlighting modes for a plethora of programming languages, and an advanced macro system. Despite its advanced features, it's easy for beginners to use.
joe	`joe`	A text-mode editor that's much simpler than either vi or emacs and has the capability to mimic other text editors, such as vi, emacs, pico, and even the late, lamented WordStar. In addition to standard features such as search and replace, arrow key movements for the cursor, and so on, it offers macros, code-editing features, and the capability to move or format large chunks of text easily.

Text Processing with Groff

The nroff and troff text formatting commands were the first interfaces available for producing typeset-quality documents with the UNIX system. They aren't editors, but commands through which you send your text, with the result being formatted pages. The nroff command produces formatted plain text and includes the capability to do pagination, indents, and text justification, as well as other features. The troff command produces typeset text, including everything nroff can do, plus the capability to produce different fonts and spacing. The troff command also supports kerning, adjusting the spacing between characters in variable-width fonts to look better.

The groff command is the front end for producing nroff/troff documentation. Because Linux man pages are formatted and output in Groff, most of the examples here help you create and print man pages with Groff.

People rarely use primitive nroff/troff markup. Instead, there are common macro packages that simplify creating nroff/troff–formatted documents, which include:

- **man** — These macros are used to create Linux man pages. You can format a man page using the -man option to the groff command.

- **mm** — The mm macros (memorandum macros) were created to produce memos, letters, and technical white papers. This package includes macros for creating tables of contents, lists of figures, references, and other technical-document–style features. You can format an mm document using the -mm option to the groff command.

- **me** — These macros are popular for producing memos and technical papers on Berkeley UNIX systems. You format an me document using the groff command option -me.

Groff macro packages are stored in /usr/share/groff/*/tmac. The man macros are called from the an.tmac file, mm macros are from m.tmac, and me macros are from e.tmac. The naming convention for each macro package is xxx.tmac, where xxx represents the macro package. In each case, you can deduce the name of the macro package by adding an m to the beginning of the file prefix.

 Instead of noting a specific macro package, you can use -mandoc to choose one.

When you run the groff formatting command, you can indicate on the command line which macro packages you are using. You can also indicate that the document should be run through any of the following commands that preprocess text for special formats:

- eqn — Formats macros that produce equations in Groff.
- pic — Formats macros that create simple line drawings in Groff.
- tbl — Formats macros that produce tables within Groff.

The formatted Groff document is output for a particular device type. The device can be a printer, a window, or (for plain text) your shell. Here are the output forms Groff supports:

- **ps** — PostScript output for a PostScript printer or a PostScript previewer

- **lj4** — Output for an HP LaserJet4 printer or other PCL5-compatible printer
- **ascii** — Plain-text output that can be viewed from a Terminal window
- **dvi** — Output in TeX dvi, to output to a variety of devices described later
- **X75** — Output for an X11 75 dots/inch previewer
- **X100** — Output for an X11 100 dots/inch previewer
- **latin1** — Typewriter-like output using the ISO Latin-1 character set

Formatting and Printing Documents with Groff

Try formatting and printing an existing Groff document using any man pages on your system. You'll find some in /usr/share/man/*; they're compressed, so copy them to a temporary directory and unzip them to try out Groff.

The following commands copy the chown man page to the /tmp directory, unzip it, and format it in plain text so you can page through it on your screen:

```
$ cp /usr/share/man/man1/chown.1.gz /tmp
$ gunzip /tmp/chown.1.gz
$ groff -Tascii -man /tmp/chown.1 | less
```

In this example, the chown man page (chown.1.gz) is copied to the /tmp directory, unzipped (using gunzip), and output in plain text (-Tascii) using the man macros (-man). The output is piped to less, to page through it on your screen. Instead of piping to less (| less), you can direct the output to a file (> /tmp/chown.txt). You can also make the command shorter by piping the commands together. For example:

```
$ gunzip < /usr/share/man/man1/chown.1.gz | groff -Tascii -man | less
```

To format a man page for typesetting, you can specify PostScript or HP LaserJet output. Direct the output to a file or to a printer. Here are a couple of examples:

```
$ groff -Tps -man /tmp/chown.1 > /tmp/chown.ps
$ groff -Tlj4 -man -l /tmp/chown.1
```

The first example creates PostScript output (-Tps) and directs it to a file called /tmp/chown.ps. That file can be read by a PostScript previewer (such as Ghostscript) or sent to a printer (lpr /tmp/chown.ps). The next example creates HP LaserJet output (-Tlj4) and directs it to the default printer (-l option).

Creating a Man Page with Groff

Before HOWTOs and info files, man pages were the foundation for information about UNIX and UNIX-like systems. Each command, file format, device, or other component either had its own man page or was grouped on a man page with similar components. To create your own man page requires that you learn a few macros (in particular, man macros). Figure 21-3 shows the source for a fictitious man page for a command called waycool.

FIGURE 21-3

Simple markup is required to create man pages.

```
.\"
.\" waycool.1 - the *roff document processor source for the waycool command
.\"
.TH waycool 1 "May 12, 2002" GNU "Linux Programmer's Manual"
.SH NAME
waycool \- my cool command
.SH SYNTAX
\fBwaycool\fR [ \fB-abcv\fR ] [ \fI file ... \fR ]
.SH VERSION
This man page documents the GNU waycool version X.XX
.SH DESCRIPTION
\fBwaycool\fR is a way cool command.
.SP
This version of \fBwaycool\fR is better than the last one.
.SH OPTIONS
.IP -a
Run all options with it.
.IP -b
Run some options.
.IP -c
affect symbolic links instead of any referenced file
(available only on systems that can change the
ownership of a symlink)
.IP -v
Print the version number with the command.
.SH COMMENTS
If you don't like the command, don't tell me. It will just hurt my feelings.
.SH ENVIRONMENT VARIABLES
These environment variables are used by  \fBwaycool\fR:
.IP "DISPLAY"
This sets the X Display variable.
.IP "WAYCOOL"
This contains the location of the waycool database.
.SH FILES
/usr/local/waycool - Directory containing waycool stuff.
.SH AUTHOR
Chris Craft <chris@handsonhistory.com>
.SH "REPORTING BUGS"
Report bugs to <bug-fileutils@gnu.org>.
.SH COPYRIGHT
Copyright \(co 2001 Free Software Foundation, Inc.
.br
This is free software; see the source for copying conditions.  There is NO
warranty; not even for MERCHANTABILITY or FITNESS FOR A PARTICULAR PURPOSE.
.SH ACKNOWLEDGEMENTS
I'd like to thank all my friends.
```

TIP   Most man pages are stored in subdirectories of /usr/share/man. Before you create a man page, refer to similar man pages to see the markup and the headings they include. man1 has commands; man2 has system calls; man3 has library functions; man4 has special device files (/dev/*); man5 has file formats; man6 has games; man7 has miscellaneous components; and man8 has administrative commands.

A few other kinds of macros are used in the man page. The .IP macros format indented paragraphs for things such as options. The man page also contains some lower-level font requests; for example, \fB says to change the current font to bold, \fI changes the font to italic, and \fR changes it back to regular font. (This markup is better than asking for a particular font type because it just changes to bold, italic, or regular for the current font.) Figure 21-4 shows what the waycool man page looks like after it is formatted with groff (and sent to the printer with the -l option):

```
$ groff -man -Tps -l waycool.1
```

Table 21-1 lists the macros that you can use on your man pages. These macros are described on the man(7) manual page (type **man 7 man** to view that page).

FIGURE 21-4

Man page formatting adds headers and lays out the page of text.

TABLE 21-1

man Macros

Macro	Description
.B	Bold.
.BI	Bold, then italics (alternating).
.BR	Bold, then Roman (alternating).
.DT	Set default tabs.
.HP	Begin a hanging indent.
.I	Italics.
.IB	Italics, then bold (alternating).
.IP	Begin hanging tag. Used for options. Long tags use .TP.

continued

TABLE 21-1	*(continued)*
Macro	**Description**
.IR	Italics, then Roman (alternating).
.LP	Begin paragraph.
.PD	Set distance between paragraphs.
.PP	Begin paragraph.
.RB	Roman, then bold (alternating).
.RE	End relative indent (after .RS).
.RI	Roman, then italics (alternating).
.RS	Begin relative indent (use .RE to end indent).
.SB	Small text, then bold (alternating).
.SM	Small text. Used to show words in all caps.
.SH	Section head.
.SS	Subheading within a .SH heading.
.TH	Title heading. Used once at the beginning of the man page.
.TP	Begin a hanging tag. Begins text on next line, not same line as tag.

Creating a Letter, Memo, or White Paper with Groff

Memorandum macros (which are used with the -mm option of groff) were once popular among UNIX users for producing technical documents, letters, and memos. Although more modern word processors with a variety of WYSIWYG (What You See Is What You Get) templates have made the mm macros outdated, in a pinch they are still a quick way to create a typeset-style document in a text environment.

To format and print (to a PostScript printer) a document with mm macros, use the following:

```
$ groff -mm -Tps -l letter.mm
```

To convert to a PDF instead of to PostScript, use a command like the following:

```
$ groff -mm -Tps letter.mm | ps2pdf - letter.pdf
```

Here's a simple example of how to use mm macros to produce a letter:

```
.WA "Christopher T. Craft"
999 Anyway Way
Anytown, UT 84111 USA
.WE
.IA
John W. Doe
```

```
111 Notown Blvd.
Notown, UT 84111
.IE
.LO RN "Our telephone conversation"
.LO SA "Dear Mr. Doe:"
.LT
In reference to our telephone conversation on the 4th, I am
calling to confirm our upcoming appointment on the 18th. I
look forward to discussing the merger. I believe we have a
win-win situation here.
.FC "Yours Truly,"
.SG
```

Use the following command to format the document and save the output to a file named
`letter.ps`:

```
$ groff -mm -Tps -l letter.mm > letter.ps
```

As before, you can make PDF output instead of PostScript with a command like the following:

```
$ groff -mm -Tps letter.mm | ps2pdf - letter.pdf
```

The output will look like Figure 21-5.

FIGURE 21-5

Create a simple letter using mm macros.

TIP If you get output from the `groff` command that says `letter.mm:15:`
`warning 'let*wa-title!1' not defined`, **you can safely disregard
it. Alternatively, add a set of empty double quotes to the end of the first line. That is, change the first
line of** `letter.mm` **to read**

```
.WA "Christopher T. Craft" ""
```

The mm macros were often used to produce technical memos. The following is an example of a sign-off sheet that might go at the front of a larger technical memo:

```
.TL
Merger Technical Specifications
.AF "ABC Corporation"
.AU "Christopher Craft"
.AT "President"
.AS
This memo details the specifications for the planned merger.
.AE
.MT "Merger Description and Marching Orders"
As a result of our talks with XYZ corporation, we plan to go
forward with the merger. This document contains the following:
.BL
.LI
Schedule and time tables.
.LI
Financial statements.
.LI
Asset allocations.
.LE
.SP
Please add any corrections you have, then sign the approval
line indicated at the bottom of this sheet.
.FC
.SG
.AV "John W. Doe, XYZ Corporation President"
.AV "Sylvia Q. Public, XYZ Corporation CFO"
.NS
Everyone in the corporation.
.NE
```

Figure 21-6 shows the output of this memo.

> **NOTE** For a complete listing of mm macros, see the `groff_mm` man page. More than 100 mm macros exist. Also, dozens of defined strings enable you to set and recall information such as figure names, tables, table of contents information, and text automatically printed with different headings.

Adding Equations, Tables, and Pictures

To interpret special macros for equations, tables, and line drawings, you must run separate commands (`eqn`, `tbl`, and `pic` commands) on the source file before you run the `groff` command. Alternatively, you can add options to the `groff` command line to have the file preprocessed automatically by any of the commands (`-e` for `eqn`, `-t` for `tbl`, and `-p` for `pic`).

FIGURE 21-6

Add headings and approval lines automatically to memos.

Here are some examples of EQN, TBL, and PIC markup included in a Groff document. The first example shows an equation that can be processed by eqn:

```
.EQ
a ~ mark = ~ 30
.EN
.sp
.EQ
a sup 2 ~ + ~ b sup 2~lineup = ~ 1000
.EN
.sp
.EQ
x sup 3 ~ + ~ y sup 3 ~ + ~ z sup 3~lineup = ~ 1400
.EN
```

If this appeared in a memo called memoeqn.mm, the memo would be preprocessed by eqn and then sent to the printer using the following command:

```
$ groff -Tps -l -mm -e memoeqn.mm
```

All data between the .EQ and .EN macros are interpreted as equations. The resulting output from the equation would appear as shown in Figure 21-7.

FIGURE 21-7

Produce equations in documents with the use of the eqn command's .EQ and .EN macros.

$$a = 30$$

$$a^2 + b^2 = 1000$$

$$x^3 + y^3 + z^3 = 1400$$

To create a table in a Groff document, use the .TS and .TE macros of the tbl preprocessor. The following is an example of the markup used to produce a simple table:

```
.TS
center, box, tab(:);
c s s
c | c | c
l | l | l.
Mergers and Acquisitions Team
=
Employee:Title:Location
=_
Jones, James:Marketing Manager:New York Office
Smith, Charles:Sales Manager:Los Angeles Office
Taylor, Sarah:R&D Manager:New York Office
Walters, Mark:Information Systems Manager:Salt Lake City Office
Zur, Mike:Distribution Manager:Portland Office
.TE
```

The .TS macro starts the table, and the next line indicates that the table should be centered on the page (center) and surrounded by a line box and that a colon will be used to separate the data into cells (tab(:)). The third line shows that the heading should be centered in the box (c) and should span across the next two cells (s s). The fourth line says that the heading of each cell should be centered (c | c | c) and the fifth line indicates that the data cells that follow should be left justified (l | l | l).

CAUTION There must be a period at the end of the table definition line. In this example, it is after the l | l | l. line. If the period is not there, tbl tries to interpret the text as part of the table definition, fails, and stops processing the table; the table does not print.

The rest of the information in the table is the data. Note that the tab separators are colon characters (:). End the table with a .TE macro. If the table were in a memo called memotbl.mm, the tbl command could preprocess the memo and then send it to the printer using the following command:

```
$ groff -Tps -l -mm -t memotbl.mm
```

Data between .TS and .TE macros are interpreted as tables. Figure 21-8 displays the output from this example.

FIGURE 21-8

Set how text is justified and put in columns with the use of the tbl command's .TS and .TE macros.

Employee	Title	Location
Jones, James Smith, Charles Taylor, Sarah Walters, Mark Zur, Mike	Marketing Manager Sales Manager R&D Manager Information Systems Manager Distribution Manager	Jones, James Smith, Charles Taylor, Sarah Walters, Mark Zur, Mike

The PIC macros (.PS and .PE) enable you to create simple diagrams and flow charts to use in Groff. PIC is really qualified to create only simple boxes, circles, ellipses, lines, arcs, splines, and some text. The following is some PIC code that could be in a Groff document:

```
.PS
box invis "Start" "Here"; arrow
box "Step 1"; arrow
circle "Step 2"; arrow
ellipse "Step 3"; arrow
box "Step 4"; arrow
box invis "End"
.PE
```

The first line after the .PS indicates an invisible box (invis) that contains the words Start Here, followed by an arrow. That arrow connects to the next box, containing the words Step 1. The next elements (connected by arrows) are a circle (Step 2), an ellipse (Step 3), another box (Step 4), and another invisible box (End). The .PE indicates the end of the PIC drawing.

If these lines appear in a document called memopic.mm, you can preprocess the PIC code and print the file using the following command:

```
$ groff -Tps -l -mm -p memopic.mm
```

Figure 21-9 shows an example of this drawing.

FIGURE 21-9

Create simple flow diagrams with the pic command's .PS and .PE macros.

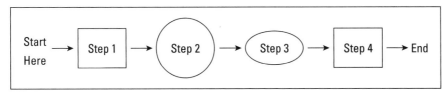

Text Processing with TeX/LaTeX

TeX (pronounced *tech*) is a collection of commands used primarily to produce scientific and mathematical typeset documents. The most common way to use TeX is by calling a macro package. The most popular macro package for TeX is LaTeX, which takes a higher-level approach to formatting TeX documents. TeX and LaTeX tools are contained in the tetex-latex package.

TeX interprets the LaTeX macros from the LaTeX format file (`latex.fmt`). By default, the `latex.fmt` and `plain.fmt` format files are the only ones that are automatically built when the TeX package is installed. Other macro files that you can use with TeX include:

- **amstex** — Mathematical publications, including the American Mathematical Society, use this as their official typesetting system.

- **eplain** — Includes macros for indexing and compiling a table of contents.

- **texinfo** — Macros used by the Free Software Foundation to produce software manuals. Text output from these macros can be used with the `info` command.

You can create a TeX/LaTeX file using any text editor. After the text and macros are created, you can run the `tex` command (or one of several other related utilities) to format the file. The input file is in the form `filename.tex`. The output is generally three different files:

- **filename.dvi** — Device-independent output file that can be translated for use by several different types of output devices (such as PostScript).

- **filename.log** — A log file that contains diagnostic messages.

- **filename.aux** — An auxiliary file used by LaTeX.

The `.dvi` file produced can be formatted for a particular device. For example, you can use the `dvips` command to output the resulting `.dvi` file to your PostScript printer (`dvips filename.dvi`). Or you can use the `xdvi` command to preview the `.dvi` file in X.

Creating and Formatting a LaTeX Document

Because LaTeX is the most common way of using TeX, this section describes how to create and format a LaTeX document. A LaTeX macro (often referred to as a command) appears in a document in one of the two following forms:

- `\string{option}[required]` — A backslash (\) followed by a command. (Replace *string* with the name of the command.) Optional arguments are contained in braces ({ }), and required arguments are in brackets ([ ]).

- `\?{option}[required]` — A backslash (\) followed by a single character (not a letter) command. (Replace *?* with the command character.) Optional arguments are contained in braces ({ }), and required arguments are in brackets ([ ]).

Each command defines some action to be taken. The action can control page layout, the font used, spacing, paragraph layout, or a variety of other actions on the document. The following is the minimum amount of formatting that a LaTeX document can contain:

```
\documentclass{name}
\begin{document}
    TEXT GOES HERE!
\end{document}
```

Replace *name* with the name of the class of document you are creating. The text for the file, along with your formatting commands, goes between the `begin` and `end` document commands.

The best way to get started with LaTeX is to use the LyX editor, which provides a GUI for creating LaTeX documents. It also contains a variety of templates you can use instead of just creating a document from scratch. Figure 21-10 shows an example of the LyX editor.

FIGURE 21-10

Create LaTeX documents graphically with the LyX editor.

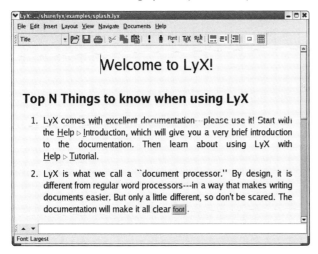

If you want to edit LaTeX in a regular text editor, you must be familiar with the LaTeX commands. For a complete listing of the LaTeX commands, type **info latex** and then read the "Commands within a LaTeX Document" text that appears.

Using the LyX LaTeX Editor

Start the LyX LaTeX editor with the `lyx` command. LyX comes with a lot of supporting documentation. Click Help to select a tutorial, user's guide, or other information.

To start your first document, I recommend that you select one of the templates provided with LyX. Templates are located in /usr/share/lyx/templates. To open a template, click File ⇨ New from Template. A list of available templates appears. You can use the templates to create letters, slides, articles, and so on.

In addition to offering standard editing functions, such as cut, copy, and paste, the Layout menu enables you to perform a variety of markup functions. As for mathematical functions, the Math menu enables you to insert fractions, square root, exponent, sum, and integral functions into your document. When you are done, you can:

- **Print** the file to a PostScript printer or output a PostScript (.ps) file. (Click File ⇨ Print, select the printing method, and then click OK.)

- **Export** the file to LaTeX, DVI, PostScript, or ASCII Text. (Click File ⇨ Export and choose from the list of file formats.)

LyX calls itself a WYSIWYM editor — What You Say Is What You Mean. As a result, what you see on the screen as you edit is not exactly what the printed document will look like. For example, no extra white space appears between lines by pressing Enter multiple times.

Because LyX supports style files, it enables you to create documents that meet several different standards. For example, LyX supports typesetting for the American Mathematics Society (AMS) journals using the article text class. Other text classes supported include:

- **article** — One-sided paper with no chapters.
- **report** — Two-sided report that tends to be longer than an article.
- **book** — Same as report, with additional front and back matter.
- **slides** — For producing transparencies.
- **letter** — Includes special environments for addresses, signatures, and other elements.

Printing LaTeX Files

Whether you create your own LaTeX file, export one from the LyX LaTeX editor, or download one from the Internet, several utilities are available to format, print, or display the output. Here are some of your choices:

- To format a LaTeX file (*filename*.tex), run the following command:

```
$ latex filename.tex
```

- To print a DVI file (*filename*.dvi), send it to your default PostScript printer, and type the following:

```
$ dvips filename.dvi
```

■ To display a DVI file in an X window, type the following:

```
$ xdvi filename.dvi
```

■ To print a DVI file to a PCL printer, such as an HP LaserJet, type the following:

```
$ dvicopy filename.dvi
$ dvilj filename.dvi
```

The `dvilj` command doesn't support virtual fonts directly. The `dvicopy` command converts the fonts so that the PCL printer can handle them.

Converting Documents

Documents can come to you in many different formats. Search just some of the Linux FTP sites on the Internet and you will find files in PostScript, DVI, man, PDF, HTML, and TeX. There are also a variety of graphics formats. Table 21-2 is a list of common document and graphics conversion utilities.

TABLE 21-2

Document and Graphics Conversion Utilities

Utility	Converts	To
dos2unix	DOS text file	UNIX (Linux) text file
fax2ps	TIFF facsimile image files	Compressed PostScript format (The PostScript output is optimized to send to a printer on a low-speed line. This format is less efficient for images with a lot of black or continuous tones, for which tiff2ps might be more effective.)
fax2tiff	Fax data (Group 3 or Group 4)	TIFF format (The output is either low-resolution or medium-resolution TIFF format.)
g32pbm	Group 3 fax file (either digifax or raw)	Portable bitmap
gif2tiff	GIF (87) file	TIFF format
man2html	Man page	HTML format
pal2rgb	TIFF image (palette color)	Full-color RGB image
pbm2g3	Portable bitmap image	Fax file (Group 3)
pdf2dsc	PDF file	PostScript document dsc file (The PostScript file conforms to Adobe Document Structuring Conventions. The output enables PostScript readers such as Ghostview to read the PDF file one page at a time.)

continued

TABLE 21-2	(continued)	
Utility	Converts	To
pdf2ps	PDF file	PostScript file (level 2)
pfb2pfa	Type 1 PostScript font (binary MS-DOS)	ASCII-readable
pk2bm	TeX pkfont font file	Bitmap (ASCII file)
ppm2tiff	PPM image file	TIFF format
ps2ascii	PostScript or PDF file	ASCII text
ps2epsi	PostScript file	Encapsulated PostScript (EPSI) (Some word-processing and graphics programs can read EPSI. Output is often low quality.)
ps2pdf	PostScript file	Portable Document Format (PDF)
ps2pk	Type 1 PostScript font	TeX pkfont
pstotext	PostScript file	ASCII text (pstotext is similar to ps2ascii but handles font encoding and kerning better. It doesn't convert PDFs.)
ras2tiff	Sun raster file	TIFF format
texi2html	Texinfo file	HTML
tiff2bw	RGB or Palette color TIFF image	Grayscale TIFF image
tiff2ps	TIFF image	PostScript
unix2dos	UNIX (Linux) text file	DOS text file

Many graphical applications, such as GIMP, also enable you to save images into several different formats (BMP, JPEG, PNG, TIFF, and so on) through the use of the Save As feature.

Building Structured Documents

Documentation projects often need to produce documents that are output in a variety of formats. For example, the same text that describes how to use a software program may need to be output as a printed manual, an HTML page, and a PostScript file. The standards that have been embraced most recently by the Linux community for creating what are referred to as structured documents are SGML and XML. The specific document type definition (DTD) used to produce Linux documentation is called DocBook.

Understanding SGML and XML

Standard Generalized Markup Language (SGML) was created to provide a standard way of marking text so that it could be output later in a variety of formats. Because SGML markup is done with text tags, you can create SGML documents using any plain-text editor. Documents consist of the text of your document and tags that identify each type of information in the text.

Unlike markup languages such as Groff and TeX, SGML markup is not intended to enforce a particular look when you are creating the document. So, for example, instead of marking a piece of text as being bold or italic, you would identify it as an address, a paragraph, or a name. Later, a style sheet would be applied to the document to assign a look and presentation to the tagged text. HTML is an example of SGML markup.

Because SGML consists of many tags, other projects have cropped up to simplify producing documents based on SGML and to better focus the ways in which SGML is used. In particular, the Extensible Markup Language (XML) was created to offer a manageable subset of SGML that would be specifically tailored to work well with Web-based publishing.

So far in this description of SGML and XML, I've discussed only the frameworks that are used to produce structured documents. Specific documentation projects need to create and, to some extent, enforce specific markup definitions for the type of documents they need to produce. These definitions are referred to as Document Type Definitions (DTDs). For documentation of Linux itself and other open source projects, DocBook has become the DTD of choice.

Understanding DocBook

DocBook is a DTD that is well suited for producing computer software documents in a variety of formats. It was originally created by the OASIS Consortium (`www.oasis-open.org`) and is now supported by many different commercial and open source tools.

DocBook's focus is on marking content, instead of indicating a particular look (that is, font type, size, position, and so on). It includes markup that lets you automate the process of creating indexes, figure lists, and tables of contents, to name a few.

DocBook is important to the Linux and open source community because many open source projects use it to produce documentation. For example, the following is a list of organizations that use DocBook to create the documents that describe their software:

- The Linux Documentation Project (TLDP)

  `www.tldp.org/LDP/LDP-Author-Guide`

- GNOME Documentation Project

  `http://developer.gnome.org/projects/gdp/handbook/gdp-handbook`

- KDE Documentation Project

  `www.kde.org/documentation`

- FreeBSD Documentation Project

  `www.freebsd.org/docproj/`

If you want to contribute to any of these documentation projects, refer to the Web sites for each organization. In all cases, they publish writers' guides or style guides that describe the DocBook tags that they support.

Creating DocBook Documents

You can create the documents in any text editor, using tags that are similar in appearance to HTML tags (with beginning and end tags appearing between less-than and greater-than signs). Certain word-processing programs also allow you to create DocBook markup.

The following steps show an example of a simple DocBook XML document produced with a plain-text editor and output into HTML using tools that are available in many Linux systems.

NOTE The DocBook DTD is available in both SGML and XML forms. Of the two, the XML form is actively maintained.

1. Create a directory in your home directory to work in and go to that directory. For example, you can type the following from a Terminal window:

```
$ mkdir $HOME/doctest
$ cd $HOME/doctest
```

2. Open a text editor to hold your DocBook document. For example, you can type:

```
$ gedit cardoc.xml
```

(A text editor such as jedit, which you can get at www.jedit.org, can also be useful for dealing with the long tag names used in DocBook.)

3. Enter the tags and text that you want to appear in your document. Most DocBook documents are either <book> type (large, multichapter documents) or <article> type (single-chapter documents). To try out a DocBook document, type the following:

```
<?xml version="1.0" ?>
<article>
  <title>Choosing a new car</title>
  <artheader>
    <abstract>
      In this article, you will learn how to price,
      negotiate for, and purchase an automobile.
    </abstract>
  </artheader>
  <section>
    <title>Getting Started</title>
    <para>
      The first thing you will learn is how to figure out
      what you can afford.
    </para>
  </section>
  <section>
```

```
      <title>The Next Step</title>
      <para>
       After you know what you can afford, you can begin
       your search.
      </para>
    </section>
</article>
```

You should notice a few things about this document. The entire document is wrapped in article tags (`<article> </article>`). The article title is in title tags (`<title> </title>`). The section tags (`<section> </section>`) indicate sections of text that each have a title and paragraph. These sections can later be treated separately in the Table of Contents.

4. Save the file and exit from the text editor.

5. You can try translating the document you just created into several different formats. For example, to create HTML output, you can type the following:

```
$ db2html cardoc.xml
```

The result is a new directory called `cardoc`. The result from `db2html` in the `cardoc` directory is the creation of a stylesheet-images directory, a `t1.html` file, and an `x8.html` file. (You will also see a lot of scary-looking error messages when you run the `db2html` program. For now, you can ignore them. Ideally, the `cardoc.xml` document should have a reference to the DocBook DTD.)

To view the HTML file just created, I typed the following:

```
$ epiphany $HOME/doctest/cardoc/t1.html
```

Figure 21-11 shows an example of the output created from the `db2html` command. The screen on the left shows the first page. Click the Next link at the top of the page. The second page that you see is shown on the right. During conversion to HTML, the `db2html` command adds Next/Previous buttons to each page. It also puts the title of each section in a Table of Contents on the first page and in the browser's title bar.

From this point, you can continue to add content and different types of tags. If you are writing documents for a particular project (such as the Linux projects mentioned earlier), you should get information on the particular tags and other style issues they require.

Converting DocBook Documents

The previous example shows how to create a simple DocBook document and convert it to HTML output. The following utilities convert DocBook to other formats:

- **docbook2dvi** — Device-independent file format
- **docbook2html** — HTML format

- **docbook2man** — Man page format
- **docbook2pdf** — Portable Document Format (PDF)
- **docbook2ps** — PostScript format
- **docbook2rtf** — Rich Text Format (RTF)
- **docbook2** — TeX Text format
- **docbook2texi** — GNU TeXinfo format
- **docbook2txt** — Bare text format

FIGURE 21-11

The DocBook file is output in HTML with the db2html command.

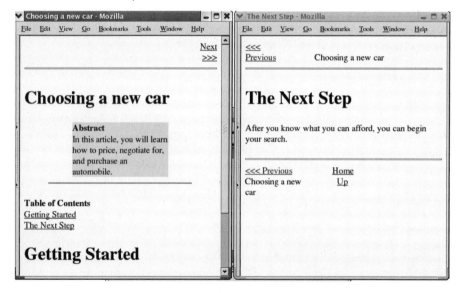

Printing Documents in Linux

Printing in most Linux systems these days is provided by the Common UNIX Printing System (CUPS) service. As a non-administrative user, you don't have a lot of control over how the printers are configured. You can, however, check which printers are available to print to, check the status of print queues (documents waiting to print), and remove any of your own queued print jobs.

CROSS-REF   Refer to Chapter 26 for information on configuring a printer using the CUPS service.

Printing to the Default Printer

When your system administrator (or you) configured printers for your computer, one of those printers was defined as the default printer. If you are not sure which printer is your default in a Fedora or other Red Hat Linux distribution, type **system-config-printer** and look for the printer with the check by it. For other Linux distributions, check the CUPS Web-based interface to see how your printers are configured.

Most graphical word processors, such as StarOffice Writer and OpenOffice.org Writer, enable you to choose a printer from those available. Some of the less sophisticated Linux utilities that run from the command line, however, use only the default printer. For example, `dvips` (to print a PostScript file) and `groff -l` (to print a troff/nroff file) automatically send the output to the default printer.

As a regular user, you can override the default printer using the `PRINTER` environment variable. If the default printer on your computer is `lp0`, for example, and you want to print regularly to `lp1`, change your default printer by setting the `PRINTER` variable as follows:

```
$ export PRINTER=lp1
```

To have this in effect all the time, you can add this line to one of your shell configuration files (such as `$HOME/.bashrc`, if you use the bash shell).

CROSS-REF **Refer to Chapter 2 for more information on using the shell.**

Printing from the Shell

The `lpr` command is used to print files from the shell. You can use `lpr` to print whether the LPRng or CUPS print service is being used. If you have a file already formatted, use `lpr` to print it. For example, if you have a PostScript output file (`file.ps`) and you want to print it to your PostScript printer, use the following command line:

```
$ lpr file.ps
```

If you want to specify a particular printer (other than the default), add the `-Pprinter` option. For example, to print to the lp0 printer, type the following:

```
$ lpr -Plp0 file.ps
```

If you want to print more than one copy of a document, use the `-#num` option, where *num* is replaced by the number of copies you want. For example, to print five copies of a file, use:

```
$ lpr -#5 file.ps
```

The `lpr` command can also accept standard output for printing. For example, you can print the output of a `groff` command by piping that output to `lpr` as follows:

```
$ groff -Tps -man /tmp/chown.1 | lpr -Plp0
```

 The `enscript` command (in the enscript package) is another useful tool for printing plain-text files. It converts the files to PostScript and sends them to a printer or to a specified file.

Checking the Print Queues

To check the status of print jobs that have been queued, you can use the `lpq` command. By itself, `lpq` prints a listing of jobs that are in the queue for the default printer. For example:

```
$ lpq
hp is ready and printing
Rank      Owner      Job   Files           Total Size
active    root       3     hosts           1024 bytes
1st       root       7     (stdin)         625 bytes
2nd       root       8     memo1.ps        12273 bytes
3rd       chuck      9     bikes.ps        10880 bytes
```

The output from `lpq` shows the printer status and the files waiting to be printed. `Rank` lists the order in which they are in the queue. `Owner` is the user who queued the job. `Job` shows the job number. The `Files` column shows the name of the file or standard output (if the file was piped or directed to `lpr`). `Total Size` shows how large each file is in bytes.

You can add options to `lpq` to print different kinds of information. By adding `-Pprinter`, you can see the queue for any available printer. You can also add the job number (to see the status of a particular print job) or a username (to see all queued jobs for a user).

Removing Print Jobs

If you have ever printed a large document by mistake, you understand the value of being able to remove a print job from the queue. Likewise, if a printer is going to be down for a while and every-one has already printed their jobs to another printer, it's sometimes nice to be able to clear all the print jobs when the printer comes back online.

Remove print jobs using `lprm`. For example, to remove all jobs for the user named bill (assuming you are either bill or the root user), type the following:

```
$ lprm bill
```

The root user can remove all print jobs from the queue. To do this, you add a dash (-) to the `lprm` command line, as follows:

```
$ lprm -
```

You may need to enter the root password or be logged in as root to run this command. You can also remove queued print jobs for a particular printer (`-Pprinter`) or for a particular job number by just adding the job number to the `lprm` command line.

Checking Printer Status

Sometimes nothing comes out of a printer, and you have no idea why. `lpc` is a printer status command that might give you a clue about what's going on with your printer. It is intended for administrators, so it may not be in your default PATH. To start the `lpc` command, type the following:

```
# /usr/sbin/lpc
```

When the command returns the `lpc>` prompt, type the word **status**:

```
lpc> status
hp:
            printer is on device 'lpd' speed -1
            queuing is enabled
            printing is enabled
            no entries
            daemon present
lpc>
```

This example shows the status of printer hp: queuing and printing are enabled, the printer shows no problems, and no print jobs are waiting. To quit the `lpc` command, type **exit** at the `lpc>` prompt.

Displaying Documents with ghostscript and Acrobat

Document publishing can be very paper-intensive if you send a Groff or LaTeX document to the printer each time you want to make a change to the document's content or formatting. To save paper and time spent running around, use a print preview program to display your document on the screen as it will appear on the printed page. The following sections describe the `ghostscript` command for displaying PostScript files and the Adobe Acrobat Reader for displaying Portable Document Format (PDF) files.

Using the ghostscript and gv Commands

To display PostScript or PDF documents in Linux, you can use the `ghostscript` command. It is a fairly crude interface, intended to let you step through documents and interpret them one line at a time.

You can display any PS or PDF file you happen to have on your computer. For example, if the samba package is installed, you can type the following to display a PDF file (otherwise, you can find your own PDF file to try it):

```
$ ghostscript -sDEVICE=x11 /usr/share/doc/samba-*/docs/Samba-HOWTO-
Collection.pdf
>>showpage, press <return> to continue<<
```

At the prompt, press Enter (or Return) to go through the file one page at a time. When you have reached the end of the document, you can type the name of another PostScript or PDF file and page through that file. When you are done, type **quit**.

You may also see warning or error messages if `ghostscript` detects problems in the PostScript or PDF file. In most cases, if you can see the document's contents, you can ignore the messages.

The `ggv` command (GNOME ghostview) is another, more friendly way of viewing PostScript files. To use `ggv` to open a file called `rbash.ps`, type the following:

```
$ ggv /usr/share/doc/bash-doc-*/bashref.ps
```

When the ghostview window opens, you can see the document. Left-click on the page and move the mouse up and down to scroll the document. Use the Page Up and Page Down keys to page through the document. You can click a page number in the left column to jump to a particular page or click the Print All button to print the entire document.

Using Adobe Acrobat Reader

The Portable Document Format (PDF) provides a way of storing documents as they would appear in print. With Adobe Acrobat Reader, you can view PDF files in a very friendly way. Adobe Acrobat makes it easy to move around within a PDF file. A PDF file may include hyperlinks, a table of contents, graphics, and a variety of type fonts.

You can get Adobe Acrobat Reader for Linux from the Adobe Web site (`www.adobe.com/products/acrobat/readstep2.html`). Select Linux as the platform from that site. A recent version of the Adobe Acrobat Reader is available in RPM format for Fedora from Guru Labs (`www.gurulabs.com/downloads.html`).

After you install Adobe Acrobat Reader, type the following command to start the program:

```
$ acroread
```

Choose File ➪ Open, and then select the name of a PDF file you want to display. Figure 21-12 shows an example of a PDF file viewed in Adobe Acrobat.

Adobe Acrobat has a lot of nice features. For example, you can display a list of bookmarks alongside the document and click a bookmark to take you to a particular page. You can also display thumbnails of the pages to quickly scroll through and select a page.

Using the menu bar or buttons, you can page through the PDF document, zoom in and out, go to the beginning or end of the document, and display different views of the document (as well as display bookmarks and page thumbnails). To print a copy, choose File ➪ Print.

Other document-viewing programs include Evince, a GNOME viewer, and KghostView, a KDE version of the gv, or GhostView, program.

FIGURE 21-12

Display PDF files in the Adobe Acrobat Reader.

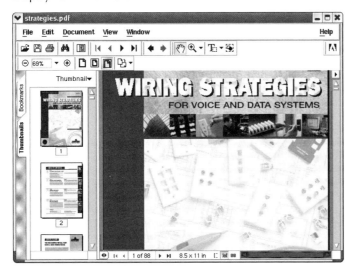

Working with Graphics

Tools for creating and manipulating graphics are becoming both more plentiful and more powerful in Linux systems as a whole. Leading the list is the GNU Image Manipulation Program (GIMP). GIMP lets you compose and author images as well as retouch photographs. Other tools for creating graphics include ksnapshot (a program for taking screen captures) and kpaint (for working with bitmap images).

Manipulating Images with GIMP

GIMP is a free software program for manipulating photographs and graphical images. To create images with GIMP, you can either import a drawing, photograph, or 3D image, or you can create one from scratch. You can start GIMP from the system menu by selecting Graphics ⇨ The GIMP or by typing **gimp&** from a Terminal window.

Figure 21-13 shows an example of GIMP.

In many ways, GIMP is similar to Adobe Photoshop. Some people feel that GIMP's scripting features are comparable to or even better than Actions in Adobe Photoshop. One capability that GIMP lacks, however, is support for CMYK (cyan-magenta-yellow-black) separations. If CMYK is not critical for your graphics needs, you will probably find GIMP to be just as powerful and flexible as Photoshop in many ways.

FIGURE 21-13

GIMP is a powerful tool for graphics manipulation.

TIP   See www.blackfiveservices.co.uk/separate.shtml **for a CMYK plug-in for GIMP. This plug-in provides only rudimentary support for CMYK, according to its documentation. Even so, that may be enough for your needs.**

One of the easiest ways to become familiar with GIMP is to crop, or trim, an image file already on your computer. To crop a file, follow these steps:

1. Start GIMP and open an image file.

2. Right-click on the image. From the contextual menu that appears, select Tools ⇨ Transform Tools ⇨ Crop and Resize. The crop cursor appears (two overlapping L shapes), as does the Crop and Resize Information window.

3. Position the crop cursor at the upper-left corner of the area of the image that you want to crop. Click and drag the cursor to the lower-right corner of the area to be cropped. A selection rectangle appears around the selected area as you do so.

4. Release the mouse button. Four selection handles appear in the corners of the border around the selected area. Click and drag the handles to resize the border.

5. When the border is in the right place, click the Crop button in the Information window. The image is cropped to the border.

 If you make a mistake, select Edit ⇔ Undo from the GIMP menu, or press the Ctrl+Z key combination.

Acquiring Screen Captures

If you want to show examples of the work via screenshot, use the Screen Capture program.

To open Screen Capture, select Graphics ⇨ Ksnapshot from most Linux KDE menus, or type **ksnapshot**. Figure 21-14 shows an example of the Screen Capture program. (You can also take screen captures from GIMP, described previously.)

Grab a picture of your desktop or selected window with Screen Capture.

When Screen Capture first opens, it takes a snapshot of the full desktop. To take a new snapshot, choose the Capture Mode (Full Screen, Window Under Cursor, or Region) and click the New Snapshot button. Use the Save As button to save the snapshot to a file in X bitmap, MS Windows icons, PNG, portable pixmap, JPEG, X pixmap, Encapsulated PostScript, or Windows BMP format. Click the Print button to send the snapshot to your printer.

Modifying Images with KPaint

Using the KPaint window, a utility that comes with KDE, you can work with and convert images in several formats. Figure 21-15 shows an example of KPaint.

Start KPaint from either the desktop (from most KDE desktops, select Graphics ⇨ Paint Program) or from a Terminal window (/usr/bin/kpaint&). Start with either a blank canvas or by opening an image in one of the supported formats (File ⇨ Open, browse for a file, and then click OK). Look in the /usr/share/backgrounds directory for graphics to try.

FIGURE 21-15

Edit bitmap images with KPaint.

The painting tools let you draw ovals, boxes, lines, and other shapes. You can save the file to several different formats, including MS Windows PCX format, Encapsulated PostScript image, MS Windows icons, JPEG, PNG, PNM, TIFF, X bitmap, and X Window pixmap.

Using Scanners Driven by SANE

Software for using a scanner with Linux is being driven by an effort called Scanner Access Now Easy (SANE). This effort hopes to standardize how device drivers for equipment such as scanners, digital still cameras, and digital video cameras are created, as well as help simplify the interfaces for applications that use those devices. SANE is now included with a variety of Linux distributions.

Someone wanting to use Linux as a publishing platform is generally interested in two issues about scanners: which scanners are supported and which applications are available to use the scanners. In general, more SCSI scanners are supported than parallel scanners.

Because of the ongoing development effort, new scanners are being supported all the time. You can find a current list of supported scanners at `www.sane-project.org/sane-supported-`

`devices.html`, with USB scanners listed at `www.buzzard.me.uk/jonathan/scanners-usb.html`. As for applications, some of the more widely used tools available today include:

- **xsane** — An X-based graphical front end for SANE scanners, xsane can work as a GIMP plug-in or as a separate application (from most KDE desktops, select Graphics ➪ Scanning). It supports 8-bit output in JPG, TIFF, PNG, PostScript, and PNM formats. There is experimental 16-bit support for PNM (ASCII), PNG, and raw formats.

- **scanimage** — Use this command-line interface to obtain scanned images. The command acquires the scanned image, and then directs the data to standard output (so you can send it to a file or pipe it to another program). It supports the same formats as xsane.

In addition to these applications, the OpenOffice.org suite supports SANE.

Because of the architecture of SANE scanner drivers, it is possible to separate scanner drivers from scanner applications. This makes it possible to share scanners across a network.

Summary

In recent times, modern GUI-based publishing tools have augmented the text-based publishing tools that have always been available with Linux. Powerful open source publishing tools such as OpenOffice.org are becoming competitive with commercial office suites. Traditional publishing tools such as Groff (which implements traditional troff/nroff text processing) and LaTeX (a TeX macro interface particularly suited for scientific and mathematical publishing) are still available with many Linux distributions.

Chapter 22

E-Mailing and
Web Browsing

Web browsers and e-mail clients available with Linux have seen incredible improvements over the past few years. Their features rival those you can get on the most popular Windows clients. Security issues with Outlook mail clients and Internet Explorer browsers have many people taking a fresh look at Linux and open source software for accessing the Internet.

This chapter describes some of the best Web, e-mail, chat, and related tools for accessing the Internet that you can get with the Linux distributions described in this book. If you have never worked with the Internet from Linux, or haven't for a few years, you might be blown away by what's available today.

Using E-Mail

Any Linux desktop system worth the name "desktop system" will have at least one or two applications for sending, receiving, and managing your e-mail. Many users believe that superior tools for managing spam and generally better security mechanisms make Linux a great desktop platform for managing your e-mail.

Choosing an E-Mail Client

Choices of e-mail clients range from those that look like clones of popular Windows e-mail programs to those that run in plain text from the shell, and interfaces vary widely with the e-mail clients that are available with Linux. Here are some different ways in which e-mail clients are integrated into Linux:

- **Standalone** — These days, most e-mail clients are standalone applications in their own right. The primary standalone e-mail application is Mozilla Thunderbird 2 (`www.mozilla.com/en-US/thunderbird/`), although you can find 50 or more choices on Linux, such as Sylpheed (`sylpheed.sraoss.jp/en/`).

- **With a Web browser** — Many popular Web browsers include an integrated e-mail client. By configuring the e-mail client that comes with your browser, you are ready to launch a new e-mail message by clicking on a mailto link from a browser window. You can also easily open the e-mail client from your Web browser's toolbar.

  Feature-rich Mozilla Mail (`www.mozilla.org`) is probably the most popular e-mail client for Linux to come with a Web browser. Netscape Communicator (`www.netscape.com`) is another Web browser that has its own mail client (although it has been dropped from many Linux distributions because of licensing issues). Most users, however, use the separated clients Thunderbird for e-mail and Firefox for Web browsing. These applications were split out of the unified Mozilla suite (now called SeaMonkey).

  The Opera Web browser (`www.opera.com`) also includes an integrated e-mail client. It is perhaps the most elegant of the e-mail clients that comes with a Web browser. Opera is available for personal use without cost.

- **With groupware** — Some e-mail clients have been bundled with other personal productivity applications to form integrated groupware applications. The most popular of these in Linux is Evolution, which is bundled as the default e-mail client with several different Linux distributions. Besides e-mail, Evolution includes a calendar, task list, and contacts directory. (A company named Ximian originally produced Evolution. Novell, Inc. purchased Ximian, and then later renamed and rebranded Ximian Evolution as Novell Evolution.)

- **From the shell** — Many old-school UNIX and Linux power users prefer to use an e-mail client that runs without a graphical desktop. Although not always intuitive to use, text-based e-mail readers run much faster than their graphical counterparts. The `mail` command dates back to the earliest UNIX systems (where there was no GUI). The mutt e-mail client is popular among power users because of its capability to manage large mailboxes and attachments efficiently.

Features inside each e-mail client can help you distinguish between them. While most e-mail clients let you get, compose, send, and manage e-mail messages, here are a few extra features you might look for:

- **Filters and spam catchers** — Thunderbird, Evolution, and other mail clients offer message filters and junk mail detectors. You use filters to set up rules to sort incoming mail into different folders, delete certain messages, or otherwise respond to incoming mail. Some e-mail clients also have features that try to automatically detect when junk mail has arrived. If you get a lot of e-mail, these can be invaluable tools for managing your e-mail. (Select the Tools menu from your e-mail client, and then look for a Filters or Junk Mail selection.)

- **Security features** — E-mail clients such as Thunderbird (`www.mozilla.com/en-US/thunderbird/`) enable you to use message encryption, digital signatures, and other security features to keep your e-mail private.

- **Sorting, searching, marking, and displaying** — Again, if you are managing lots of e-mail messages at once (some people manage thousands of messages), the capability to refer back to the one you want can be critical. Some clients let you sort by date, sender, priority, subject, and other items. You might be able to search message contents for text or choose how to display the messages (such as without showing attachments or with source code shown).

- **Mail composition tools** — Some mail composers let you include HTML in your messages, which enables you to add images, links, tables, colors, font changes, and other visual enhancements to your messages. One warning: Some mailing lists don't like you to send messages in HTML because some people still use plain-text readers that aren't HTML-aware.

- **Multiple accounts** — Many e-mail clients enable you to configure multiple e-mail accounts to be served by your e-mail reader. Early plain-text e-mail clients pointed to only one mailbox at a time.

- **Performance** — Some lightweight graphical e-mail clients give you much better perform-ance than others. In particular, the Sylpheed e-mail client (which comes with Damn Small Linux) was created to use a minimal amount of memory and processing power, yet still provide a graphical interface. E-mail clients that run from the keyboard, in particular the mutt e-mail client, will run much faster than, say, most full-blown graphical e-mail clients such as Evolution.

COMING FROM WINDOWS For most home and small business users, Evolution and the standalone Thunderbird are often available from a Linux desktop and will give you much the same experience you would expect from Microsoft Windows mail clients, such as Outlook Express. If you are using the KDE desktop, you can use the KDE groupware client Kontact, which includes Kmail (the e-mail client), along with a contact manager, calendar, to-do list application, and more.

Even though the Linux distribution you are using may have only one or two of the e-mail clients described in this section, you can always add a client that interests you.

Getting Here from Windows

To understand how to transition your e-mail client from Windows to Linux, you need to know a bit about your current e-mail setup. Whether you are using Outlook, Outlook Express, or any other e-mail client running in Windows, here are some things you should know:

- **Server type** — Is your e-mail server a POP3 or IMAP server? If it is an IMAP server, all your messages are being stored on the server. Transitioning to a different e-mail server might simply mean pointing the new e-mail client at your server and continuing to use e-mail as you always have. If it is a POP3 server, your messages have probably been downloaded to your local client. To keep your old messages, you need to somehow bring your current mail folders over to your new client, which is a potentially tricky undertaking.

- **Address book** — You need to export your current address book to a format that can be read by your new e-mail client, and import it to your new e-mail client.

To transition to Linux, you may want to add a cross-platform e-mail client such as Thunderbird to your Windows system so that you can get at your resources (addresses, stored mail messages, and so on) during the transition to your new mail client. When you eventually move off Windows altogether, Thunderbird for Linux will work almost exactly as it does in Windows.

If your current e-mail server is a Microsoft Exchange server (2000 or 2003), you need to get a Ximian Connector for Microsoft Exchange license to allow Evolution to access information from that server. The connector now comes from Novell, which purchased Ximian, and is available under an open source license.

Getting Started with E-Mail

Most Linux systems include an e-mail client that you can select on a panel or by left-clicking on the desktop to bring up a menu. Look for an envelope icon on a panel or a submenu labeled something like Internet. If you want a graphical e-mail reader, you can start by looking for one of these clients: Evolution, Mozilla Mail, Thunderbird, or KMail.

After you have launched your chosen e-mail client, you need some information to use it. When you first start most graphical e-mail clients, a configuration screen of some sort asks you to set up an account. Here's how to begin setting up a mail account for the e-mail clients described in this chapter:

- **Evolution** — The Evolution Setup Assistant starts the first time each user opens Evolution. After that, select Tools ➪ Settings from the main Evolution window. Then choose Mail Accounts and double-click the mail account you want to modify.

- **Mozilla Mail** — An account wizard starts the first time you open Mozilla Mail. After that, you can set up or modify accounts from the Mozilla Mail window by clicking Edit ➪ Mail & Newsgroups Account Settings.

- **Thunderbird** — This is the next-generation mail client from the people that bring you Firefox and Mozilla (mozilla.org). Now at version 1.5, and with more advanced security features, you might consider Thunderbird. Not only is it faster than Mozilla Mail and Evolution, Thunderbird is an ideal complement to Mozilla Firefox Web browser. Firefox and Thunderbird run on a number of operating systems, including Linux, Solaris, Microsoft Windows, and Mac OS X.

- **KMail** — From the KMail window, select Settings ➪ Configure KMail. From the Configure KMail window that appears, select the Network icon. From there, you can click Sending or Receiving tabs to configure your outgoing and incoming e-mail settings.

Initial configuration for text-based e-mail clients is described later in this chapter.

Information you will need to configure your e-mail accounts is much the same for the different graphical e-mail clients covered in this chapter:

- **Name** — Enter your name as you want it to appear on outgoing messages.

- **Email Address** — Enter the e-mail address from which you are sending. You may also be offered the opportunity to supply a different reply-to address, if you want replies to go to an address other than the one you sent from.

- **Mail server type** — Most mail servers are POP3 or IMAP servers. (Configuring those types of servers is discussed in Chapter 25.)

- **Server names** — Enter the names of the servers you will use to send outgoing e-mail and receive incoming e-mail. The names can be fully qualified domain names (such as mail.linuxtoys.net) or IP addresses. In many cases, the incoming and outgoing mail servers are the same.

- **Username** — Enter the name by which the mail server knows you. For example, if your e-mail address is chris@linuxtoys.net, your username to the mail.linuxtoys.net server might simply be chris. However, it's possible that your username on the mail server might be different, so you should find that out from the administrator of your mail server.

- **Account title** — Enter the name that you want to call this mail account so you can refer to it later in your list of mail and news group accounts.

- **Authentication type** — Indicate the type of authentication to use when you get your mail (sometimes authentication is needed to send your mail as well). Password authentication is normal. Usually you can have your e-mail client remember your password if you want. Typically, you are prompted for the password the first time you connect to get your mail.

That is most of the basic information you need to start getting and sending e-mail. However, you may want to further tune how your e-mail client interacts when it gets and sends e-mail.

Tuning Up E-Mail

With your basic settings done, you should be ready to start sending and receiving your e-mail. Before you do, however, you should consider some of the other settings that can affect how you use mail:

- **Automatically check messages** — You can set your e-mail client to automatically check and download your messages from the mail server every few minutes.

- **Leave messages on server** — If you turn this feature on for a POP server, your e-mail messages remain on the server after you have downloaded them to your e-mail client. People sometimes turn this feature on if they want to check their mail messages while they are on the road yet want to download their messages from their permanent desktop computer later.

- **Certificates** — Your e-mail client may provide a way of using certificates to sign your outgoing messages. For example, Evolution and Mozilla Mail both have Security tabs for your mail settings that let you enter information about your certificates and indicate that your e-mail be signed. You can also choose to use the certificates for encryption.

Step through your mail account settings because they are slightly different for each e-mail client.

Reading E-Mail with Thunderbird

The Thunderbird e-mail client program is a full-featured mail and newsgroup reader that usually comes with most Linux systems.

NOTE In the past, you may have run the integrated Mozilla suite of applications, now called Mozilla SeaMonkey. The more recent versions of Linux, however, have replaced SeaMonkey with separate e-mail and Web-browsing applications, Thunderbird and Firefox, respectively. If you are used to the older Mozilla suite, you should consider upgrading to Thunderbird.

Thunderbird includes features for:

- Sending, receiving, reading, and managing e-mail
- Managing multiple mail and newsgroup accounts
- Composing HTML e-mail messages
- Controlling junk e-mail
- Message encryption and signing

COMING FROM WINDOWS Thunderbird runs on Windows as well as Linux, so you can convert your organization to Thunderbird now, and then later migrate to Linux.

On most Linux systems, either Thunderbird or Evolution will be the primary e-mail client for your Linux distribution. You can launch the e-mail application from the desktop from a menu such as Internet. For example, in Fedora, you run an e-mail client from the Applications ⇨ Internet menu. Fedora defaults to Evolution as the primary e-mail client, so Evolution is listed simply as Email on the Applications ⇨ Internet menu. Thunderbird is listed as Thunderbird Email.

When you launch Thunderbird for the first time, the application will offer to import your e-mail folders from another application, which is really, really handy, especially if you use a POP3 e-mail server, as described previously.

The first time you launch Thunderbird, you will see a window like that in Figure 22-1.

In Figure 22-1, Thunderbird detected no other compatible e-mail applications to import data from. On your system, you may see a dialog to import e-mail.

Next, Thunderbird presents the New Account Setup dialog, which leads you through setting up an e-mail account (you can create more than one). Figure 22-2 shows this window. In most cases, you'll want to begin by setting up an e-mail account, as shown here.

Figure 22-3 shows the information you need to enter for your identity, including your e-mail address.

Figure 22-4 shows the server information you need to enter. In most cases, the incoming and outgoing servers will be the same system.

Running Thunderbird for the first time

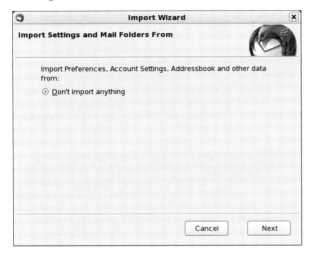

The Thunderbird New Account Setup wizard

FIGURE 22-3

Enter your name and e-mail address.

FIGURE 22-4

Enter the name of the incoming and outgoing e-mail servers.

Figure 22-5 shows the window where you enter your username on the e-mail server.

Enter your username on the e-mail server.

Next, the window shown in Figure 22-6 allows you to enter a name for this e-mail account. You can use the default value (your e-mail address) or enter anything you'd like.

After you enter all this data, the confirmation screen shown in Figure 22-7 appears.

If you want, check the Download messages now box to download all the messages from the e-mail server. Thunderbird downloads messages again every 10 minutes, or you can click the Get Msgs button at any time in the main Thunderbird window.

When you are all done, Thunderbird displays the mail user interface, shown in Figure 22-8.

TIP With the Junk Mail feature, Thunderbird automatically tags any message it believes to be junk mail with a blue recycle-bin icon. Using the Junk toolbar, you train the Junk Mail feature by telling it when a message is or isn't junk mail. After you have identified which messages are junk mail, you can automatically move incoming junk mail to the Junk folder.

FIGURE 22-6

You can choose any name for the e-mail account.

FIGURE 22-7

Before creating your e-mail account, you can confirm all the settings.

FIGURE 22-8

Handle multiple mail accounts in Thunderbird.

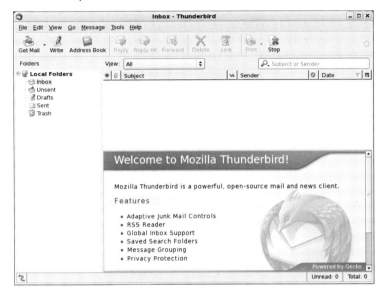

Connecting to the Mail Server

After you have set up your mail accounts in Thunderbird, you can explicitly ask to download any available mail messages from the server (for POP accounts). To do that, click the Get Msgs button.

You are prompted for the password for your account on the mail server. Using that password, Thunderbird downloads all your messages from the mail server. It downloads messages again every 10 minutes, or you can click the Get Msgs button at any time.

If you want to change how often mail is downloaded, or other features of your account, choose Edit ⇨ Account Settings. Under the e-mail account you added are categories to change the setup and behavior of the account. (Click Server Settings to change how often, if at all, new messages are automatically downloaded from the mail server.)

Managing Incoming Mail

There are various ways to store and manage e-mail messages in Thunderbird. Here's a quick rundown of how to manage incoming mail:

- **Mail folders** — Mail messages are stored in folders in the left column. There should be a separate heading for each mail account you have. For each mail account, incoming messages are stored (by default) in your Inbox folder. You can create additional folders to better keep track of your mail (right-click on Inbox, and select New Folder to add a folder). Other folders contain drafts of messages set aside for a time (Drafts), templates for creating messages (Templates), messages you have sent (Sent), and messages that you have discarded (Trash). You can also specify that Thunderbird use a global Inbox where messages from all accounts get placed in the same Inbox folder.

■ **Sort messages** — Messages are sorted by date for the folder you select, in the upper-right corner of the display. Click the headings over the messages to sort by subject, sender, or priority.

■ **Read messages** — When you select a message, it appears in the lower-right corner of the display. Click the e-mail address from the sender, and a menu enables you to add that address to your address book, compose mail to that address, copy mail to that address, or create a filter from that message.

■ **Filter mail** — When Thunderbird grabs your e-mail from the mail server, it drops it into the Inbox associated with your mail account by default. Thunderbird provides some nice features for checking each message for information you choose, and then acting on that message to move it to another folder, label it, or change its priority. See the section "Filtering Mail and Catching Spam" later in this chapter for details.

■ **Search messages** — You can use the search feature to retrieve messages that are in one of your mail folders. With the folder you want to search being the current folder, type a word to search on into the Subject or Sender Contains box. Messages with sender names or subject lines that don't contain that string will disappear from the list of messages. To do more detailed searches, choose Edit ➪ Find ➪ Search Messages.

Composing and Sending E-Mail

To compose e-mail messages, you can either start from scratch or respond to an existing e-mail message. The following are some quick descriptions of how to create outgoing mail:

■ **New messages** — To create a new message, choose Message ➪ New Message (or click Write on the toolbar).

■ **Reply to messages** — To reply to a mail message, click the message on the right side of your screen and then choose Message ➪ Reply (to reply only to the author of the message) or Message ➪ Reply to All (to reply to everyone listed as a recipient of the message).

■ **Forward messages** — To forward a mail message, click the message on the right side of your screen and then choose Message ➪ Forward. You can also forward a message and have it appear in the text (Message ➪ Forward As ➪ Inline) or as an attachment (Message ➪ Forward As ➪ Attachment).

In each case, a Compose window appears, in which you compose your e-mail message. As you compose your message in the Compose window, you can use the following:

■ **Address book** — Add e-mail addresses from your personal address book (or from one of several different directory servers) by selecting Tools ➪ Address Book. Click the Contacts button to select recipients for your missive.

■ **Attachments** — Add attachments such as a word processing file, image, or executable program by choosing File ➪ Attach ➪ File and then selecting a file from your file system to attach. (You can also choose File ➪ Attach ➪ Web Page to choose the URL of a Web page that you want to attach.)

■ **Certificates** — Add certificates or view security information about your mail message by selecting View ➪ Message Security Info.

When you are finished composing the message, click Send to send the message. If you prefer, queue the message to be sent later by choosing File ➪ Send Later. (Send Later is useful if you have a dial-up connection to the network and you are not currently online.)

> **TIP** If you want to quit and finish the e-mail message later, choose File ➪ Save As ➪ Draft, and then click the X in the upper-right corner to close the window. When you are ready to resume work on the message, open the Draft folder in the Thunderbird window and double-click the message.

Filtering E-Mail and Catching Spam

Thunderbird can do more with incoming messages than just place them in your Inbox. You can set up filters to check each message first and then have Thunderbird take an action you define when a message matches the rule you set up.

For example, your filter can contain a rule that checks the subject, sender, text body, date, priority, status, recipients, or age in days of the message for a particular word, name, or date, as appropriate. If there is a match, you can have Thunderbird put that message in a particular folder, label it with a selected phrase, change its priority, or set its junk mail status. You can add as many rules as you like. For example, you can:

■ Have all messages sent from a particular address sorted into a separate mail folder. For example, I do this so that important mail doesn't get lost when there's a lot of activity on the mailing lists to which I subscribe.

■ Mark incoming messages from important clients as having highest priority.

■ Have messages from particular people or places that are being mistakenly marked as spam change their junk status to Not Junk.

To set up filter rules in Thunderbird, click Tools ➪ Message Filters. The Message Filters pop-up appears. If you have multiple mail accounts, select the account you want to filter. Then click New. From the Filter Rules pop-up window, choose the following:

■ **For incoming messages that** — There are different ways to check parts of a message. For example, you can check whether the Sender is in the address book. You can check what the Priority is: low, medium, or high. You can create multiple rules for a filter (click More to add another rule), and then choose if you want to match all or any of the rules to continue to the action.

■ **Perform these actions** — The information in this section describes what to do with a message that matches the rules you've set. You can have the message moved to any existing folder, or label the message. With labels, the message appears in a different color depending on the label: important (red), work (orange), personal (green), to do (blue), or later (purple). You can also change the message priority.

Figure 22-9 shows a rule I created to highlight mail from my friend Tweeks in red (Important) when it comes in.

FIGURE 22-9

Create filter rules to sort or highlight your e-mail messages.

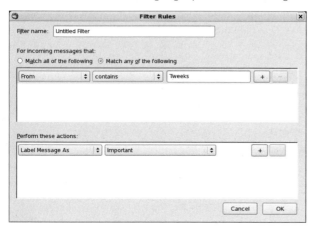

A nice feature of Thunderbird's filtering rules is that you can apply the rules after the fact as well. If you decide you want to move all messages in your Inbox from a particular person to a different folder, for example, you can open the Message Filters window, create a rule to move the selected messages, select Inbox, and click Run Now.

For junk mail, with a mail message selected, click the Junk button in the toolbar. The message is marked as junk. Your selection helps teach Thunderbird what you think is junk mail. Click Tools ➪ Run Junk Mail Controls on Folder, and Thunderbird looks for other messages that look like junk mail. (You can take the junk marker off of any message you think is not junk.) Then select Tools ➪ Delete Mail Marked as Junk in Folder, and the junk mail is deleted. To open a window to configure how you handle junk mail, select Tools ➪ Junk Mail Controls.

Managing E-Mail in Evolution

If you are using Fedora or Debian, Evolution is the e-mail client that you can start right from the desktop (look for the envelope icon on the panel). After you launch Evolution for the first time and run the Startup Assistant, the Evolution window appears, showing the different types of operations you can perform. Figure 22-10 shows an example of the Evolution window.

FIGURE 22-10

Evolution can be used to manage your mail, appointments, and tasks.

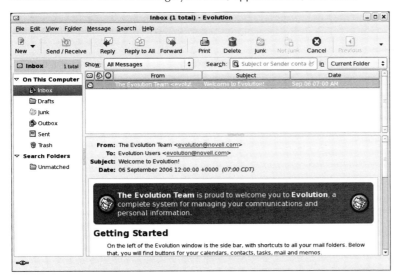

Evolution is a groupware application, combining several types of applications that help groups of people communicate and work together. The features of Evolution include:

- **E-mail** — A complete set of features for getting, reading, managing, composing, and sending e-mail on one or more e-mail accounts.

- **Contacts** — Create contact information such as names, addresses, and telephone numbers for friends and associates. A Categories feature helps you remember who gets birthday and anniversary gifts.

- **Calendar** — Create and manage appointments on your personal calendar. You can e-mail appointment information to others and do keyword searches of your calendar.

- **Tasks** — Organize ongoing tasks into folders.

COMING FROM WINDOWS Evolution provides a default interface that looks a lot like that of Microsoft Outlook, making it easy for new users to make a smooth transition to a Linux system.

New features recently added to Evolution include improved junk mail handling and Search Folders (for managing multiple physical folders as one folder).

Receiving, Composing, and Sending E-Mail

Evolution offers a full set of features for sending, receiving, and managing your e-mail. Here's a quick rundown of these tasks:

- **Read e-mail** — Click Inbox in the left column. Your messages appear to the right. Message headers are in the upper right; the current message is displayed in the lower pane. Double-click a message header to display it in a separate window

- **Delete e-mail** — After you have read a message, select it and press the Delete key. Click View ⇨ Hide Deleted Messages to toggle whether you can see deleted messages. Click Folder ⇨ Expunge to permanently remove all messages marked for deletion in the current folder.

- **Send and receive** — Click the Send/Receive button to send any e-mail queued to be sent and receive any e-mail waiting for you at your mail server. (You may not need to do this if Evolution is configured to download your messages every few minutes. Check Edit ⇨ Preferences, and then double-click on your mail account. The Receiving Options tab indicates if automatic mail checking is being done.)

- **Compose e-mail** — Click New ⇨ Mail Message. A Compose a Message window appears. Type your recipient's e-mail address, enter a subject line, and fill in the body of the message. Click Send when you are finished. Buttons on the Compose window enable you to add attachments, cut and paste text, choose a format (HTML or plain text), and sign the message (if you have set up appropriate keys).

- **Use address books** — Click the View ⇨ Window ⇨ Contacts menu choice to see a list of names, addresses, and other contact information for the people in your address book. When you compose a message, click the To or CC button to select addresses from the book to add as recipients for your message.

- **Create folders** — If you like to keep old messages, you may want to save them outside your Inbox (so it won't get too junked up). To create a folder in which to keep them, right-click on the Inbox and select New Folder. You can choose to store the new folder as a subfolder to any existing folder. Type a folder name and click OK.

- **Move messages** — With new folders created, you can easily move messages from your Inbox to another folder. The easiest way is to simply drag-and-drop each message (or a set of selected messages) from the message pane to the new folder.

- **Search messages** — Type a keyword in the search box over your e-mail message pane and select whether to search your message subject lines, sender, recipient, or message body. Click Find Now to search for the keyword. After viewing the messages, click Clear to have the other messages reappear.

Managing E-Mail with Search Folders

Managing large amounts of e-mail can become difficult when the messages you want to refer to span several folders, dates, or senders. With Search Folders (also called virtual folders or vFolders), you can identify criteria to group messages from all your mail folders so you can deal with them in one Search Folder.

Here's a procedure for creating a Search Folder:

1. With Evolution open to read mail (click Inbox to get there), select File ⇨ New ⇨ Folder. A Create New Folder pop-up appears.

2. Select Search Folders, type a folder name (such as FromJohn), and select OK. A New Search Folder pop-up appears.

3. Click Add and select criteria for including a message in your Search Folder. You can search to see if the sender, recipient, subject, message body, or other part of the message contains or doesn't contain the string you type in the next box. Click Add again if you want to add more criteria.

4. If you want to search only specific folders, click Add in the Search Folder Sources box and select the folder you want to search. You can repeat the Add to choose more than one folder. Otherwise, you can select to search all local folders, all active remote folders, or all local and active remote folders. Then click OK.

5. Make sure the folder bar is visible (View ⇨ Layout ⇨ Show Side Bar). The folder you just created is listed under the Search Folders heading. Click that folder to see the messages you gathered with this action.

At this point, you can work with the messages you gathered in the Search Folder. Although it appears that there are multiple versions of each message across your mail folders, there is really only one copy of each. So deleting or moving the message from a Search Folder actually causes it to be deleted or moved from the original folder in which the real message resides.

TIP You can also create a Search Folder by performing a search, a sort of query by example. Select Search ⇨ Create Search Folder from the Search menu and enter your search criteria.

Filtering E-Mail Messages

You can take action on an e-mail message before it even lands in your Inbox. Click Message ⇨ Create Rule, and then select the type of filter to create. Evolution shows a Filters window to enable you to add filters to deal with incoming or outgoing messages. Click Add to create criteria and set actions.

For example, you can have all messages from a particular sender, subject, date, status, or size sorted to a selected folder. Or you can have messages matching your criteria deleted or assigned a color, or play a sound clip.

Evolution also supports many common features, such as printing, saving, and viewing e-mail messages in various ways. The help system that comes with Evolution (click the Help button) includes a good manual, FAQ, and service for reporting bugs.

Reading E-Mail with Mozilla Mail

The Mozilla Mail client program is a full-featured mail and newsgroup reader that comes with the Mozilla suite on many Linux systems. In general, the Mozilla suite is considered an older application, replaced by Thunderbird and Firefox, the e-mail and Web browser clients, respectively. Thunderbird and Firefox were split from the large Mozilla suite and each now runs as a separate application. If you are used to the older Mozilla suite, now called SeaMonkey, you should consider upgrading to Thunderbird.

In most respects, Mozilla Mail works like Thunderbird, described previously. The only difference is that Mozilla Mail, because it's an older application, won't have all the features of the latest Thunderbird. This is a big change. In the last year or so, Thunderbird has all but replaced Mozilla Mail.

You can download the Mozilla SeaMonkey suite from `www.mozilla.org/projects/seamonkey/`.

Working with Text-Based E-Mail Readers

The first text-based mail clients could be configured quite simply. Mail clients such as mutt, mail, or pine were often run with the user logged in to the computer that was acting as the mail server. So instead of downloading the messages, using POP3 or IMAP, the mail client would simply open the mailbox (often under the user's name in `/var/spool/mail`) and begin working with mail.

There are many text-based mail programs for reading, sending, and working with your mail. Many of these programs have been around for a long time, so they are full of features and have been well debugged. As a group, however, they are not very intuitive.

> **TIP**   Most of these programs use the value of your `$MAIL` environment variable as your local mailbox. Usually, that location is `/var/spool/mail/user`, where `user` is your user-name. If you use Thunderbird but want to try out one of the text-based e-mail clients, you can set your `$MAIL` so that it points to your Thunderbird mailbox. This will enable you to use either Thunderbird or a text-based mail program. Add the following line to one of your startup files:
>
> ```
> export MAIL=$HOME/.thunderbird/*.default/*/Mail/accountname/Inbox
> ```
>
> Replace *accountname* in the command with the name of an e-mail account you set up. If you usually use Thunderbird for mail, set this variable temporarily to try out some of these mail programs.

Mail readers described in the following sections are text-based and use the entire Terminal window (or other shell display). Although some features are different, menu bars show available options right on the screen.

Mutt Mail Reader

The `mutt` command is a text-based, full-screen mail user agent for reading and sending e-mail. The interface is quick and efficient. Type **mutt** to start the program. Move arrow keys up and down to select from your listed messages. Press Enter to see a mail message, and type **i** to return to the Main menu.

The menu bar indicates how to mark messages for deletion, undelete them, save messages to a directory, and reply to a message. Type **m** to compose a new message, and it opens your default editor (vi, for example) to create the message. Type **y** to send the message. If you want to read mail without having your fingers leave your keyboard, mutt is a nice choice. (It even handles attachments!)

Pine Mail Reader

The pine mail reader is another full-screen mail reader, but it offers many more features than does mutt. With pine, you can manage multiple mail folders and newsgroup messages as well as mail messages. As text-based applications go, pine is quite easy to use. It was developed by a group at the University of Washington for use by students on campus, but has become widely used in UNIX and Linux environments.

Start this mail program by typing **pine**. After a brief startup message that invites you to count yourself as a pine user, you should see the following menu, from which you can select items by typing the associated letter or using up and down arrows and pressing Enter:

```
?  HELP             - Get help using Pine
C  COMPOSE MESSAGE  - Compose and send a message
I  MESSAGE INDEX    - View messages in current folder
L  FOLDER LIST      - Select a folder to view
A  ADDRESS BOOK     - Update address book
S  SETUP            - Configure Pine Options
Q  QUIT             - Leave the Pine program
```

To read your e-mail, select either I or L. Commands are listed along the bottom of the screen and change to suit the content you are viewing. Use the left (←) and right (→) arrow keys to step backward and forward among the pine screens.

Mail Reader

The mail command was the first mail reader for UNIX. It is text-based, but not screen-oriented. Type **mail**, and you will see the messages in your mailbox. You get a prompt after message headings are displayed — you are expected to know what to do next. (You can use the Enter key to step through messages.) Type **?** to see which commands are available.

While in mail, type **h** to see mail headings again. Simply type a message number to see the message. Type **d#** (replacing # with a message number) to delete a message. To create a new message, type **m**. To respond to a message, type **r#** (replacing # with the message number).

Choosing a Web Browser

Many Web browsers available in Linux are based on the Mozilla Web browser engine, called Gecko. Web browsers that might come with your Linux distribution include:

- **Mozilla Navigator** — Based on the former industry-leading Netscape Navigator browser, Mozilla Navigator was once the most popular open source Web browser. It has been all but replaced by Firefox.

- **Konqueror** — Comes as the default browser with many KDE desktop environments. Konqueror is a file manager as well as a Web browser and helps bring together many features of the KDE desktop.

- **Firefox** — Being touted as Mozilla's next-generation browser, Firefox is designed to be fast, efficient, and safe for Web browsing.

- **Opera** — A commercial application that runs on many small devices such as mobile phones or the Nokia Linux–based Internet Tablet, this browser is available for free on Mac OS X, Microsoft Windows, and Linux.

- **links, lynx, and w3m** — If you are in a text-based environment (operating from the shell), these are among several text-based Web browsers you can try out.

> **NOTE** Some streamlined Linux versions, such as Damn Small Linux, include a very lightweight Web browser called dillo (www.dillo.org). Although its small size (only about 350KB binary) comes with some limitations (such as limited font and internationalization support), dillo is a good choice for displaying basic HTML on handheld devices and mini Linux distributions. Another small-footprint browser is minimo (www.mozilla.org/projects/minimo/), short for mini-Mozilla.

The following sections describe Mozilla, Firefox, and some text-based Web browsers that are available with many Linux systems.

Exploring the Mozilla Suite

During the early 1990s, Netscape Navigator was the most popular Web browser. When it became apparent that Netscape was losing its lead to Microsoft Internet Explorer, its source code was released to the world as open source code.

Mozilla.org (www.mozilla.org) was formed to coordinate the development of a new browser from that code. The result was the Mozilla browser that is now available with many computing platforms, including many Linux distributions. The availability on multiple platforms is great, especially if you must switch between Linux and Windows — for example, using Windows at work and Linux at home. Mozilla looks and acts the same on many platforms.

As mentioned earlier, the original Mozilla is actually a suite of Internet communications tools. In addition to viewing Web pages, you can also manage e-mail, newsgroups, IRC, and address books, and even create your own Web pages with Mozilla Composer.

Recently, the Mozilla Project's development has been diverted away from the Mozilla browser (and associated composer, mail, and chat components) to focus on development of the Firefox Web browser and Thunderbird e-mail client. Most Linux distributions have made the move to Firefox as their featured browser (including Fedora), replacing Mozilla. In most respects, however, the Mozilla Web browser acts the same as an older version of Firefox. The development effort has clearly been with Firefox for the last few years.

> **NOTE** Slackware kept Mozilla so that the project could offer the Mozilla Composer. The Slackware project noted that Mozilla Composer is a WYSIWYG HTML editor that is still used by many open source enthusiasts as an alternative to Microsoft FrontPage for ease-of-use Web page development.

In addition to the Navigator Web browser, the Mozilla suite also includes the following features:

- **Mail and Newsgroups** — A full-featured program for sending, receiving, and managing e-mail, as well as for using newsgroups. (The mozilla-mail RPM must be installed.) Mozilla Mail has mostly been replaced by the Thunderbird application, covered previously.

- **IRC Chat** — An Internet Relay Chat (IRC) window, called ChatZilla, for participating in online, typed conversations. (The mozilla-chat package must be installed.)

- **Composer** — A Web page (HTML) composer application.

- **Address Book** — A feature to manage names, addresses, telephone numbers, and other contact information. This is also part of Thunderbird.

Using Firefox

Most Linux distributions ship Firefox as the default browser, instead of the older Mozilla suite. In many desktop Linux distributions, you start the Firefox Web browser from an Applications menu. For example, in Debian, select Applications ➪ Internet ➪ Firefox Web Browser. If you don't see it on a menu, you can start Firefox by simply typing **firefox** from a Terminal window. Figure 22-11 shows the Mozilla page for Firefox (`www.mozilla.com/en-US/firefox/`) as displayed by the browser.

FIGURE 22-11

Firefox is the leading open source Web browser based on Netscape source code.

Firefox has all the basic features you need in a Web browser plus a few special features. The following sections describe how to get the most out of your Firefox Web browser.

Setting Up Firefox

There are many things you can do to configure Firefox to run like a champ. The following sections describe some ways to customize your browsing experience in Firefox.

Setting Firefox Preferences

You can set your Firefox preferences in the Preferences window (see Figure 22-12). To open Firefox preferences, select Edit ➪ Preferences.

FIGURE 22-12

Change settings for navigating the Web from Firefox's Preferences window.

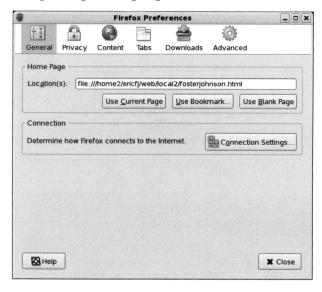

> **TIP**   If you are upgrading from the Mozilla suite, you will notice that the Preferences window looks completely different. Don't despair, however; the browser preferences have not changed much. Firefox just sports a simpler window layout.

The following are some Firefox preferences that you might want to change:

- **General** — Select the location to use as your home page, and choose which buttons you see on the toolbar. Click the Connections Settings button to set further options.

■ **Proxies** — If you have direct access to the Internet, you don't need to change any proxy settings. However, if you need to access the Internet via a proxy server, you can identify the location of that server (or servers) here. To access the Web via proxy servers, you must explicitly identify the proxy server to use for each type of content you request (HTTP, SSL, FTP, Gopher, or SOCKS). Set this from the Connections window on the General tab.

■ **HTTP Networking** — If you are using a proxy server, that proxy server may require that you make HTTP requests using either HTTP/1.0 or HTTP/1.1 standards (1.1 is the default). You can set which version of HTTP requests you should use. Set this from the Connections window on the General tab.

■ **Tabs** — Use these selections to control how Firefox uses tabs, one of the most useful features of this browser.

■ **Downloads** — Choose what you see during downloads from the Internet (a download manager, a progress dialog box, or nothing).

■ **Content** — Set Content preferences to control how Firefox should render Web content. This includes whether to block pop-up windows. These options include:

▓ **Java and JavaScript** — You can control whether these languages are enabled.

▓ **Warn on installation** — Specify this to warn you when a site tries to install a Firefox extension or theme. This is an important security feature.

■ **Privacy** — Choose how long to store a history of addresses of the sites you have typed in your location bar. (These addresses appear in the History tab on the Firefox sidebar.) Set Privacy preferences to control how Firefox caches data and allows Web sites to find out information about you. These preferences include:

▓ **Cache** — By default, the most recent 1MB of Web pages you visit are stored in RAM, and the most recent 50MB of pages you visit are stored on your hard disk. If a page is not out-of-date, caching makes it possible to return to a page quickly, without the browser's needing to reload from the original Web server. Cache preferences let you change how much information is cached, and where the hard-disk cache is located. Other preferences let you clear all memory and disk cache immediately.

▓ **Passwords** — Control whether Firefox saves the passwords you type onto Web forms. Most of us log into a number of Web services every time we browse the Web, so this setting can save you a lot of hassle in remembering passwords. But, this does open up a security issue, in that Firefox will now store these passwords on your hard disk.

▓ **Cookies** — The Web content you choose can try to open, move, resize, raise, and lower windows. It can request to change your images, status bar text, or bits of information stored in what are called *cookies*. These preferences let you restrict what the content you request can do.

- **Advanced** — Set Advanced preferences to fine-tune your Web browsing experience. That includes setting accessibility options, and whether Firefox should automatically download updates. Here are some preferences that might interest you:

  - **Languages** — For Web pages that can appear in multiple languages, this sets the order in which you would prefer languages to be displayed. For example, you might choose English/United States, English, French, and German. Then Firefox tries to display a Web page you open in each of those languages successively, until one is matched. You can set other advanced features on this tab.

  - **Software Installation** — Choose to allow or disallow requested Web content attempts to install software, such as updates, on your computer.

Adding Plug-ins

Although the main type of content provided by Web pages is HTML, many other content types can be displayed, played, or presented by a Web browser. Most additional data encountered by the browser is handled by plug-ins.

> **TIP** Applications that help Firefox display content, such as a Flash plug-in, used to be called Helper Apps. If you are migrating from the Mozilla suite, these helper applications are now called extensions or plug-ins (both names are used).

Plug-ins are self-contained programs that allow data to play within the Mozilla window.

At the time you open a Web page and data of a specific type is encountered, the browser evaluates the data based on the following criteria, and then launches the appropriate plug-in.

- **Suffixes** — If the browser is reading a file that has a particular extension (such as .exe for an application or .gz for a compressed zip file), it can use that suffix to determine the file's contents. When a file's extension matches a suffix configured for a particular plug-in, the plug-in is used to play or display the data.

- **MIME type** — Because data may come to the browser in a stream or have no suffix, the browser can use the Multipurpose Internet Mail Extensions (MIME) type attached to the data to determine which plug-in to use.

Here are some of the most popular extensions to Firefox that are available from Mozilla.org:

- **Downloading tool (FlashGot)** — If you like to download groups of files from your Web browser, FlashGot can be a very useful tool. With FlashGot installed, you can select to download an individual file, files identified by highlighting links on a Web page, or all files linked from the current Web page. There is also a Build Gallery feature that lets you identify a range of filenames to download at once.

  When FlashGot is installed, you can access it from Firefox by selecting Tools ➪ FlashGot and then choosing a feature from the menu. In Fedora, FlashGot passes requests to kGet to complete the download. You can get other download tools to use instead of kGet.

- **Selectively block ads (Adblock)** — Using Adblock, you can selectively prevent ads from being displayed on the Web pages you visit. With Adblock installed, an Adblock button appears on the lower-right corner of Firefox. Click that button to see a window containing items on the current page you want to block. Right-click on an image and select Adblock Image to choose to block that image. Use an asterisk to block all content from a particular site (for example, `www.example.com/*`). Open the Adblock preferences window from Firefox (Tools ⇨ Adblock ⇨ Preferences) to see, edit, or remove blocked sites.

- **Watch your weather (ForecastFox)** — With ForecastFox, the latest weather for any region you select can be just a click away in Firefox. After you install ForecastFox and restart Firefox, a pop-up window lets you configure ForecastFox options. Select at least Find Code to choose the area in which you want to keep up on weather. Save your options, and a weather icon appears in the lower-right corner of Firefox. Move your mouse over that icon to see a quick view of the current weather. Double-click the icon to have a more detailed weather report displayed from `www.weather.com`.

- **Check Internet speed (Bandwidth Tester)** — The Bandwidth Tester can give you a sense of how fast you are able to download data over your Internet connection. The tester downloads five files, based on the type of connection you indicate, and tells you the speed at which that data was downloaded.

Follow the installation instructions that come with the plug-in you downloaded. If the plug-in comes in an RPM file, install it as you would any other software package if you are using an RPM-based Linux distribution (`rpm -Uvh package` command). If the plug-in doesn't come with instructions, just copy the plug-in file (the `.so` file) to the system plug-in directory (such as `/usr/lib/firefox*/plugins`) or your personal plug-ins directory (probably `$HOME/.mozilla/firefox/plugins`), if you are not otherwise instructed. When you restart Firefox, the plug-ins are automatically picked up from those locations.

After you have installed an extension, you need to restart Firefox for it to take effect. In some cases, a change to an extension's option will also require you to restart Firefox.

If you want to uninstall an extension, change an extension's options, or get more extensions, select Tools ⇨ Extensions from Firefox. The window that appears shows you a list of installed extensions and lets you change them. Select Get More Extensions to go directly to Mozilla's Firefox Extensions page.

Changing Firefox Themes

Several themes are available for changing the look and feel of your Firefox window. From the Mozilla update site (`http://addons.mozilla.org`), select Firefox themes. When you download a theme for Firefox, it knows that it is a Firefox theme and, on the download window, it gives you the option to install the theme by clicking the Use Theme button.

To change a theme later or get more themes, select Tools ⇨ Themes. After you have installed a new theme and selected it as your current theme, you need to restart Firefox for the new theme to take effect.

Mozilla Plug-ins

Many plug-ins are available for use in most Linux versions of Mozilla. To see a list of plug-ins associated with the browser, enter **about:plugins** in the address box where you normally type URLs.

Go to `https://addons.mozilla.org/firefox/plugins/` to download the most popular plug-ins, and look at `plugindoc.mozdev.org/linux.html` for links to less-popular plug-ins. Some of the most popular plug-ins are:

- **Adobe Acrobat Plug-in** (`www.adobe.com/support/downloads`) — Displays files in Adobe Systems' Portable Document Format (PDF).

- **DjVuLibre Plug-in** (`djvu.sourceforge.net`) — Displays images in DjVu image compression technology. This plug-in is from AT&T.

- **RealOne Player** (`www.real.com/linux`) — Plays Real Audio and Video content. Real Networks and its open source Helix project have recently made RealVideo 10 codecs available to the Linux community.

- **Adobe Flash Player** (`www.adobe.com`) — Displays multimedia vector graphics and animation. This plug-in is from Adobe, Inc. Flash Player is available for Mozilla, but the Shockwave plug-in is not yet available for Linux.

- **CrossOver Plugin** (`www.codeweavers.com`) — Linux plug-ins are not yet available for some of the more interesting and popular plug-ins. QuickTime movies, Shockwave Director multimedia content, and various Microsoft movie, file, and data formats simply will not play natively in Firefox. Using software built on WINE for Linux on x86-based processors, CodeWeavers created the CrossOver Plugin. Although no longer offered as a separate product (you must buy the entire Crossover Office product for $39.95 US), the CrossOver Plugin lets you play some content that you could not otherwise use in Linux. (Download a demo from `www.codeweavers.com/site/products/download_trial` and choose CrossOver Linux.)

  After you install the CrossOver Plugin, you see a nice Plugin Setup window that lets you selectively install plug-ins for QuickTime 6.5, Windows Media Player, Shockwave 8.5, Flash, iTunes, and Lotus Notes, as well as Microsoft Word, Excel, and PowerPoint viewers. (Support for later versions of these content formats may be available by the time you read this.) You can also install other multimedia plug-ins, as well as a variety of fonts to use with those plug-ins.

Securing Firefox

Security has been one of the strongest reasons for people to switch to Firefox. By prohibiting the most unsafe types of content from playing in Firefox, and by warning you of potentially dangerous or annoying content before displaying it, Firefox has become the Web browser of choice for many security-conscious people. Here are some ways that Firefox helps make your Web browsing more secure:

- **ActiveX** — Because of major security flaws found in ActiveX, Firefox will simply not play ActiveX content. If you absolutely must be able to play ActiveX content, a plug-in is in development to provide controlled support for ActiveX. Follow the progress of this project at the Mozilla ActiveX Project home page (`www.iol.ie/~locka/mozilla/mozilla.htm`).

- **Pop-ups** — When pop-up windows are encountered as you browse with Firefox, a message (by default) tells you that "Firefox prevented this site from opening a popup window." By clicking on that message, you have an opportunity to allow all pop-ups from that site, just allow the requested pop-up, or edit your pop-up settings.

- **Privacy preferences** — From the Privacy window in Firefox (select Edit ➪ Preferences, and then click the Privacy button), you can clear stored private information from your browser in a single click. This is a particularly good feature if you have just used a computer that is not yours to browse the Web. You can select to individually clear your History, information saved in forms you might have filled in, any passwords saved by the browser, history of what you have downloaded, cookies, and cached files. As an alternative, you can click Clear All and clear all that information from Firefox in one click.

- **Certificates** — In Firefox, you can install and manage certificates that can be used for validating a Web site and safely performing encryption of communications to that site. Using the Preferences window (select Edit ➪ Preferences and then click the Advanced button), you can manage certificates under the Certificates heading. Select Manage Certificates to display a window that lets you import new certificates or view certificates that are already installed. Firefox will check that certificates you encounter are valid (and warn you if they are not).

Along with all the excellent security features built into Firefox, it's important that you incorporate good security practices in your Web browsing. Here are some general tips for safe Web browsing:

- Download and install software only from sites that are secure and known to you to be safe.

- For any online transactions, make sure you are communicating with a secure site (look for the `https` protocol in the location box and the closed lock icon in the lower-right corner of the screen).

- Be careful about being redirected to another Web site when doing a financial transaction. An IP address in the site's address or misspellings on a screen where you enter credit card information are warning signs that you have been directed to an untrustworthy site.

Because new exploits are being discovered all the time, it's important that you keep your Web browser up-to-date. That means that, at the least, you need to get updates of Firefox from the Linux distribution you are using or directly from Mozilla.org. To keep up on the latest security news and information about Firefox and other Mozilla products, refer to the Mozilla Security Center (`www.mozilla.org/security/`).

Tips for Using Firefox

There are so many nice features in Firefox, it's hard to cover all of them. Just to point you toward a few more fun and useful features, here are some tips for using Firefox:

- **Add smart keywords** — Many Web sites include their own search boxes to allow you to look for information on their sites. With Firefox, you can assign a smart keyword to any search box on the Web, and then use that keyword from the location bar in the Firefox browser to search that site.

  For example, go to the Linux Documentation Project site (`http://tldp.org`). Right-click in the Search/Resources search box. Select Add a Keyword for this Search from the menu that appears. Add a name (Linux Documentation) and a keyword (tldp), and select Add to add the keyword to your Bookmarks.

  After you have added the keyword, you can use it by simply entering the keyword and one or more search terms to the Firefox location box (on the navigation toolbar). For example, I entered `tldp Lego Mindstorms` and came up with a list of HOWTOs for using Lego Mindstorms in Linux.

- **Check config** — Firefox has hundreds of configuration preferences available to set as you please. You can see those options by typing **about:config** into the location box. For true/false options, you can simply click on the preference name to toggle it between the two values. For other preferences, click the preference to enter a value into a pop-up box. While many of these values can be changed through the Preferences menu (Edit ⇨ Preferences), some technical people prefer to look at settings in a list like the one shown on the about:config page.

- **Multiple home pages** — Instead of just having one home page, you can have a whole set of home pages. When you start Firefox, a separate tab will open in the Firefox window for each address you identify in your home page list. To do this, create multiple tabs (File ⇨ New Tab) and enter the address for each page you want in your list of home pages. Then select Edit ⇨ Preferences ⇨ General and click the Use Current Pages button. The next time you open Firefox, it will start with the selected tabs open to the home pages you chose. (Clicking the Home icon will open new tabs for all the home pages.) You can also manually enter multiple URLs into the text box. Separate each URL with a pipe character (|).

Using Firefox Controls

If you have used a Web browser before, the Firefox controls are probably as you might expect: location box, forward and back buttons, file and edit menus, and so on. There are a few controls with Firefox, however, that you might not be used to seeing:

- **Display Sidebar** — Select View ⇨ Sidebar to toggle the bookmarks or history sidebars on and off. The sidebar is a left column on your Firefox screen for allowing quick access to Bookmarks and History. Use the Bookmarks tab to add your own bookmarks and the History tab to return to pages on your history list.

- **Send Web Content** — You can send an e-mail containing either the current Web page (File ⇨ Send Page) or the URL of the current Web page (File ⇨ Send Link) to selected recipients. Firefox will load your default e-mail client such as Thunderbird or Evolution to send the e-mail message.

- **Search the Internet** — You can search the Internet for a keyword phrase in many different ways. Choose Tools ⇨ Web Search to start a search. Selecting this menu choice moves the mouse cursor to the search box, where you can enter search terms. Press the Enter key to search.

- **View Web Page Info** — You can view information about the location of a Web page, the location of each of its components, the dates the page was modified, and other information by clicking the right mouse button over a Web page and then choosing View Page Info. In the Page Info window, click the Links tab to see links on that page to other content on the Web. Click the Security tab to see information about verification and encryption used on the page.

Improving Firefox Browsing

Not every Web site you visit with Firefox is going to play well. Some sites don't follow standards — they use unreadable fonts, choose colors that make it hard to see, or demand that you use a particular type of browser to view their content. To improve your browsing experience, there are several things you can add to Firefox.

NOTE If you encounter a problem with Firefox that you can't overcome, I recommend that you refer to the Mozilla Bugzilla database (www.mozilla.org/bugs/). This site is an excellent place to search for bugs others have found (many times you can get workarounds to your problems) or enter a bug report yourself.

Adding a Preferences Toolbar

Did you ever run into a Web page that required you to use a particular type or version of a browser or had fonts or colors that made a page unreadable? The Firefox preferences toolbar called PrefBar3 enables you to try to spoof Web sites into thinking you are running a different browser. It also lets you choose settings that might improve colors, fonts, and other attributes on difficult-to-read pages.

You can install the neat little toolbar from the Mozdev.org site (http://prefbar.mozdev.org). Click the Install link, and after it is installed, restart Firefox.

The default set of buttons lets you do the following:

- **Colors** — Change between default colors and those set on the Web page.
- **Images** — Toggle between having images loaded or not loaded on pages you display.
- **JavaScript** — Allow or disallow JavaScript content to play in Firefox.
- **Flash** — Allow or refuse all embedded Flash content on the current page.
- **Clear Cache** — Delete all cached content from memory and disk.

- **Save Page** — Save the current page and, optionally, its supporting images and other content, to your hard disk.

- **Real UA** — Choose to have your browser identified as itself (current version of Firefox) or any of the following: Mozilla 1.0 (in Windows 98), Netscape Navigator 4.7 (in Macintosh), Netscape 6.2 (in Linux), Internet Explorer 5.0 (in Macintosh), Internet Explorer 6.0 (in Windows XP), or Lynx (a text-based Web browser).

The user agent (UA) setting is very useful when you're dealing with Web sites that require Internet Explorer (IE) (and usually IE on Windows, not Mac OS). The IE 6.0 WinXP setting is good enough to allow Firefox to log on to the Microsoft Exchange webmail service, which is usually set up to require IE. If you want to run Linux in a mostly Windows organization, install the Preferences toolbar.

Click the Customize button to add other buttons to the toolbar. You can add buttons to clear your History or Location bar entries. You can even add a Popups button to prevent a page from opening a pop-up window from Firefox.

Many of the preferences take effect immediately. Others may require you to restart Firefox.

Adding Java Support

If you want to display some Java content, but you see only a broken puzzle piece and a failure message that says you need a plug-in to view application/x-java-whatever content, you can install the software you need from the Sun Microsystems Web site (www.sun.com). Look for the Java Runtime Environment package from java.sun.com/download. It should say something like Java Platform, Standard Edition. Be sure to select the edition that runs on Linux.

Doing Cool Things with Firefox

Some neat bells and whistles are built into Firefox that can make your browsing more pleasant. The following sections explore a few of those features.

Blocking Pop-ups

You can block annoying pop-up windows using the Firefox Preferences window. Here's how:

1. Click Edit ➪ Preferences. The Preferences window appears.

2. Click Popup Windows under the Content category.

As the Preferences window notes, by blocking all pop-ups you might keep some Web sites from working properly. Click the Allowed Sites button to allow pop-ups on certain sites that you choose.

Using Tabbed Browsing

If you switch back and forth among several Web pages, you can use the tabbed browsing feature to hold multiple pages in your browser window at once. You can open a new tab for browsing by simply selecting File ➪ New Tab or by pressing Ctrl+T. You can open any link into a new tab by right-clicking over the link and then selecting Open Link in New Tab.

You can also tailor how tabbed browsing works from a Web page or from the Location box. Here's how:

1. Click Edit ➪ Preferences. The Preferences window appears.

2. Click the Tabs tab.

3. Click the tab-related options you desire.

A tab for each tabbed page appears at the top of the Firefox pane. To close a tab, create a new tab, bookmark a group of tabs, or reload tabs, right-click one of the tabs and choose the function you want from the drop-down menu.

One of the easiest ways to open a link in a tab is to right-click over a link on an HTML page. Select the Open Link in New Tab choice.

Using the DOM Inspector

If you are debugging a Web page that you are creating, the Document Object Model (DOM) Inspector can be useful for checking out the structure of your page and dynamically updating the DOM you are traversing. To open the DOM Inspector, from the Firefox window click Tools ➪ DOM Inspector.

In the DOM Inspector window, type the URL to the Web page you want to check out. The nodes representing the head, body, tables, fonts, and so on appear in the left column. Values for each node appear in the right column. Click a node name, and the selected area is highlighted on the page below, with the node value appearing to the right. You can also use the DOM Inspector to inspect a window.

Resizing the Web Page

There is a nice keyboard shortcut that lets you quickly resize the text on most Web pages in Firefox. Hold the Ctrl key and press the plus (+) or minus (–) key. In most cases, the text on the Web page gets larger or smaller, respectively. That page with the insanely small type font is suddenly readable.

There are many more things you can do with Firefox than I have covered in this chapter. If you have questions about Firefox features or you just want to dig up some more cool stuff about Firefox, I recommend checking out the MozillaZine forum for Firefox support:

```
http://forums.mozillazine.org/viewforum.php?f=38
```

This page has a sticky link to Miscellaneous Firefox Tips and a good FAQ post.

Using Text-Based Web Browsers

If you become a Linux administrator or power user, over time you will inevitably find yourself working on a computer from a remote login or where there is no desktop GUI available. At some point while you are in that state, you will want to check an HTML file or a Web page. To solve the problem, many Linux distributions include several text-based Web browsers.

With text-based Web browsers, any HTML file available from the Web, your local file system, or a computer where you're remotely logged in can be accessed from your shell. There's no need to fire up your GUI or read pages of HTML markup if you just want to take a peek at the contents of a Web page. In addition to enabling you to call up Web pages, move around with those pages, and follow links to other pages, some of browsers even display graphics right in a Terminal window!

Which browser you use is a matter of which you are more comfortable with. Browsers that are available include:

- **links** — You can open a file or a URL, and then traverse links from the pages you open. Use search forward (/string) and back (?string) features to find text strings in pages. Use up and down arrows to go forward and back among links. Press Enter to go to the current link. Use the right and left arrow keys to go forward and back among pages you have visited. Press Esc to see a menu bar of features from which to select.

- **lynx** — The lynx browser has a good set of help files (press the ? key). Step through pages using the spacebar. Although lynx can display pages containing frames, it cannot display them in the intended positioning. Use the arrow keys to display the selected link (right arrow), go back to the previous document (left arrow), select the previous link (up arrow), and select the next link (down arrow).

- **w3m** — This browser can display HTML pages containing text, links, frames, and tables. It even tries to display images (although it is a bit shaky). Both English and Japanese help files are available (press H with w3m running). You can also use w3m to page through an HTML document in plain text (for example, cat index.html | w3m -T text/html). Use the Page Up and Page Down keys to page through a document. Press Enter on a link to go to that link. Press B to go back to the previous link. Search forward and back for text using the / (slash) and ? (question mark) keys, respectively.

The w3m seems the most sophisticated of these browsers. It features a nice default font selection and seems to handle frames neatly; its use of colors also makes it easy to use. The links browser lets you use the mouse to cut and paste text.

You can start any of these text-based Web browsers by entering a filename, or if you have an active connection to the network, you can use a Web address as an option to the command name. For example, to read the w3m documentation (which is in HTML format) with a w3m browser, type the following from a Terminal window or other shell interface:

```
$ w3m /usr/share/doc/w3m*/MANUAL.html
```

An HTML version of the W3M Manual is displayed. Or you can give w3m a URL to a Web page, such as the following:

```
$ w3m www.handsonhistory.com
```

After a page is open, you can begin viewing the page and moving around to links included in it. Start by using the arrow keys to move around and select links. Use the Page Up and Page Down keys to page through text.

Summary

A lot of high-quality applications are available to fulfill your needs for a Web browser and e-mail client in Linux. Most Web browsers are based on the Mozilla gecko engine (which came originally from Netscape Navigator). Firefox has become the main Linux Web browser. The combination of security, ease-of-use features, and extensions has made Firefox an extremely popular Web browser for both Linux and Windows users.

Graphical and text-based e-mail clients include Evolution, Mozilla Mail, and KMail. Thunderbird has become the next-generation e-mail client to replace Mozilla Mail.

Chapter 23

Gaming with Linux

There are literally hundreds of games that run in Linux. Freely distributed games include popular card games, board games, strategy games, and first-person shooter (FPS) games. The list of commercial games that will run in Linux has also grown steadily in recent years.

These days, many native Linux games are also network-enabled. You can battle tanks (BZFlag), create civilizations (freeciv), or play standard board games (gnuchess) against others on the Internet. In most cases, both the clients (playing the games) and the game servers (managing dozens or hundreds of players) will all run natively in Linux.

This chapter provides an overview of the state of Linux gaming today. It describes games that were created specifically to run in Linux, and explains how to find commercial games that run in Linux (either with a Linux version or running a Windows version along with Windows compatibility software, such as Cedega).

IN THIS CHAPTER

Gaming in Linux

Playing open source games

Running commercial Linux games

Playing Windows games in Linux

Overview of Linux Gaming

Linux is a wonderful platform for both running and, perhaps more especially, developing computer games. Casual gamers have no shortage of fun games to try. Hardcore gamers face a few more challenges with Linux. Here are some of the opportunities and challenges as you approach Linux gaming:

- **Plenty to play** — If you just like to be diverted by playing some solitaire or shooting some asteroids, start with the Games menu on your desktop. Both GNOME and KDE desktops come with many more games than you will get on default desktop Windows systems. I provide a list of popular desktop games later in this chapter. If your Linux system doesn't have them, you can certainly get them.

623

- **3D acceleration** — If you are a more serious gamer, you will almost certainly want a video card that provides hardware acceleration. Open source drivers for some video cards are available from the DRI project. Video cards from NVIDIA and ATI often have binary-only drivers available. Fun open source games such as PenguinPlanet Racer, BZFlag, and others that recommend hardware acceleration, will run much better if you get one of these supported cards and drivers.

- **Commercial games** — The latest commercial computer games are not all ported to run in Linux. Boxed commercial games for Linux include Unreal Tournament 2003 and 2004, as well as about 50 first-rate commercial games that have been ported to run in Linux. Using Cedega software from Transgaming.com, you can get hundreds more commercial games to run. To see if the game you want is running in Cedega, visit the Transgaming.Org Games Database (`http://transgaming.org/gamesdb`). Commercial Linux games are described in more depth later in this chapter.

- **Gaming servers** — Many commercial computer games that don't have Linux clients available do have Linux game servers associated with them. So Linux is a great operating system for hosting a LAN party or setting up an Internet gaming server.

- **Linux gaming development** — Some of the most advanced tools and application programming interfaces (APIs) for developing computer games run on Linux systems. If you are interested in developing your own games to run in Linux, check out the OpenGL (`http://opengl.org`) and Simple Directmedia Layer (`www.libsdl.org`) projects. Blender (`www.blender.org`) is an open source project for doing animations, 3D models, post-production, and rendering that is being used today in commercial games and movie animations.

 An offshoot of the Blender project is GameBlender (`www.gameblender.org`). Game Blender is working to develop and share technology needed to use Blender for gaming.

While the development tools available for developing open source games are awesome, a primary goal of this book is to get you up and using Linux as quickly as possible. To that end, I want to tell you first how to get hold of games that already run well in Linux and then how to get games working in Linux that are intended for other platforms (particularly Windows and some classic gaming consoles).

Basic Linux Gaming Information

There isn't much you need to know to run basic X Window–based games that come with Linux. The following sections describe basic information about Linux gaming.

Where to Get Information about Linux Gaming

Many Web sites provide information about the latest games available for Linux, as well as links to download sites. If you're looking for information about Linux gaming, start with your distribution's home page (`www.redhat.com`, for example) or the home page of your desktop environment (`www.kde.org` or `www.gnome.com`, for example), or simply search for "Linux Games" or your favorite game title and "Linux" in any search engine. Here are several sites to get you started:

- **TransGaming Technologies** (`www.transgaming.com`) — This company's mission is to bring games from other platforms to Linux. It is the provider of Cedega, formerly known as WineX, a powerful tool that enables you to play hundreds of PC games on your Linux system.

- **The Linux Game Tome** (`http://happypenguin.org`) — Features a database of descriptions and reviews of tons of games that run in Linux. You can do keyword searches for games listed at this site. There are also links to sites where you can get the games and to other gaming sites.

- **Linuxgames.com** (`http://linuxgames.com`) — This site can give you some very good insight into the state of Linux gaming. There are links to HOWTOs and Frequently Asked Questions (FAQs), as well as forums for discussing Linux games. There are also links to Web sites that have information about specific games.

- **id Software** (`www.idsoftware.com`) — Go to the id Software site for information on Linux demo versions for Quake and Return to Castle Wolfenstein.

- **Linuxgamepublishing.com** (`www.linuxgamepublishing.com`) — Linuxgamepublishing.com aims to be a one-stop shopping portal for native Linux games, as well as for ports of games from other platforms. At the time of this writing, it offers about a dozen games. To purchase games from this site, you must create a user account.

- **Loki Entertainment Software** (`www.lokigames.com`) — Loki provided ports of best-selling games to Linux but went out of business in 2001. Its products included Linux versions of Civilization: Call to Power, Myth II: Soulblighter, SimCity 3000, Railroad Tycoon II, and Quake III Arena. The Loki Demo Launcher is still available to see demo versions of these games, and some boxed sets are available for very little money. The Loki site also offers a list of commercial resellers for its games, which may or may not still carry those games.

- **Tux Games** (`www.tuxgames.com`) — The Tux Games Web site is dedicated to the sale of Linux games. In addition to offering Linux gaming news and products, the site lists its top-selling games and includes notices of games that are soon to be released.

- **Wikipedia** (`http://en.wikipedia.org`) — In the past few years, Wikipedia has become a wonderful resource for information on both commercial and open source games available for Linux. From the Wikipedia Linux games list (`http://en.wikipedia.org/wiki/Linux_games`) you can find links to free Linux games, Commercial Linux Games, and Professionally Developed Linux Games.

- **Linux Gamers' FAQ** (`http://icculus.org/lgfaq`) — Contains a wealth of information about free and commercial Linux games. It lists gaming companies that have ported their games to Linux, tells where to get Linux games, and answers queries related to common Linux gaming problems. For a list of Linux games without additional information, see `http://icculus.org/lgfaq/gamelist.php`.

While the sites just mentioned provide excellent information on Linux gaming, not all games have been packaged specifically for every version of Linux. Even though you can always nudge a game into working on your particular Linux distribution, it's probably easiest to start with games that are ready to run. The following list provides information about where to find out about games packaged for different Linux distributions:

- **Fedora** — Much of the recent increase in Fedora games has come from the Fedora Games SIG (Special Interest Group). You can check out that SIG's activities for information on other games of interest that have not made it into Fedora at `http://fedoraproject .org/wiki/SIGs/Games`.

- **Debian** — Debian games resources are listed at the DebianLinux.Net wiki. Visit the games section at `http://debianlinux.net/games.html`.

- **Ubuntu** — The Games Community Ubuntu Documentation page offers some good information about available games and gaming initiatives related to Ubuntu (`http://help .ubuntu.com/community/Games`).

- **Gentoo** — Visit the Gentoo Games project at `http://www.gentoo.org/proj/en/ desktop/games/index.xml` to select games that are of interest to you that run in Gentoo.

- **Slackware** — While GNOME and KDE games run fine in Slackware, not a lot of gaming resources are particular to Slackware. However, because Slackware contains a solid set of libraries and development tools, many open source games will compile and run in Slackware if you are willing to get the source code for the game you want and build it yourself.

Choosing a Video Card for Gaming

Because 3D games place extraordinary demands on your video hardware, choosing a good video card and configuring it properly are key to ensuring a good gaming experience. For advanced gaming, you need to go beyond what a basic 64-bit card can do for you.

Binary-Only Video Card Drivers

Most serious Linux gamers have either an NVIDIA or ATI card, so that's the short answer to starting out with serious Linux gaming. Although open source drivers are available for most NVIDIA and ATI cards, those drivers do not support 3D hardware acceleration. While that's fine for most desktop applications, for gaming you want to get the binary-only drivers for those cards from the following locations:

- **NVIDIA** — To get NVIDIA drivers that run in Linux, go to the Unix Drivers Portal Page (`www.nvidia.com/object/unix.html`).

- **ATI** — To find Linux drivers for ATI video cards, visit the ATI support Knowledge Base page, which describes Linux drivers, at `http://support.ati.com/` and click on the Knowledgebase tab.

When you go to get a binary-only video driver, be sure that you know not only the video card model you are using, but also the name and version of your X server. (XFree86 used to be the most popular server, but many of the biggest Linux distributions now use X.Org.) Resulting video driver modules may be specific to the Linux kernel you are running. So, know that if you upgrade your kernel, you might need to reinstall your video driver as well.

NOTE The rpm.livna.org site has greatly simplified the process of installing ATI and NVIDIA drivers for Fedora Core and other Red Hat systems. Refer to the Livna Switcher page (`http://rpm.livna.org/`) to learn how to install RPM packages containing the ATI or NVIDIA drivers you need.

CAUTION If you load a binary-only driver, it does what is referred to as "tainting the kernel." As a result, you won't be able to get support if you run into problems (at least from `kernel.org`) because, lacking the source code, it is hard to debug driver-related problems. Also, binary-only drivers are known to cause obscure problems because they get out of sync with kernel code changes. Similarly, binary-only drivers aren't updated as frequently as the kernel. While many people, including myself, use binary-only drivers in special cases, they do have shortcomings that you should be aware of.

Open Source Video Drivers

If you want to use open source drivers for 3D accelerated gaming, whether you are running the games using Cedega or natively in Linux, look for cards that have drivers that support OpenGL. The DRI project is one initiative that is creating OpenGL driver implementations. Information about the DRI project can be found on their site (`http://dri.freedesktop.org/wiki/`).

- **ATI Technologies** — You don't have to use binary-only drivers to get 3D acceleration for some ATI video cards with open source drivers. Chip sets from ATI Technologies that support DRI include the Mach64 (Rage Pro), Radeon 7X00 (R100), Radeon 2 / 8500 (R200), and Rage 128 (Standard, Pro, Mobility). Cards based on these chip sets include All-in-Wonder 128, Rage Fury, Rage Magnum, Xpert 99, Xpert 128, and Xpert 2000.

- **3dfx** — If you can find a used unit on eBay (3dfx is no longer in business), there are several 3dfx cards that support DRI. In particular, the Voodoo (3, 4, and 5) and Banshee chip sets have drivers that support DRI. Voodoo 5 cards support 16 and 24 bpp. Scan Line Interleaving (SLI), where two or more 3D processors work in parallel (to result in higher frame rates) is not supported for 3dfx cards.

- **3Dlabs** — Graphics cards containing the MX/Gamma chip set from 3Dlabs have drivers available that support DRI in Linux.

- **Intel** — Supported video chip sets from Intel include the i810 (e, e2, and -dc100), i815, and i815e.

- **Matrox** — The Matrox chip sets that have drivers that support DRI include the G200, G400, G450, and G550. Cards that use these chips include the Millennium G450, Millennium G400, Millennium G200, and Mystique G200.

To find out whether DRI is working on your current video card, type the following:

```
$ glxinfo | grep rendering
direct rendering: Yes
```

This example shows that direct rendering is enabled. If it were not supported, the output would say No instead of Yes. While DRI can be important, many games implement OpenGL rendering, which is a feature supported by both NVIDIA and ATI video cards. To enable rendering for cards that support it, add the following line to your /etc/X11/xorg.conf file:

```
Load    "render"
```

Running Open Source Linux Games

A handful of games are delivered with most desktop-oriented Linux distributions. The GNOME and KDE environments, which are available with most desktop Linux distributions (described in Chapter 3), each has a set of games associated with it.

GNOME Games

More than a dozen basic games are delivered with the GNOME desktop. If you are just looking for a game to pass a bit of time, one of the GNOME games will probably work fine for you.

COMING FROM WINDOWS GNOME games consist of some old card games and a bunch of games that look suspiciously like those you would find on Windows systems. If you are afraid of losing your favorite desktop diversion (such as Solitaire, FreeCell, and Minesweeper) when you leave Windows, have no fear. You can find many of them under GNOME games.

Default installations of Ubuntu, Fedora, and other Linux systems include the gnome-games package. Table 23-1 lists the games included in the gnome-games package. See the GNOME Games site (http://live.gnome.org/GnomeGames/) for further details.

TABLE 23-1

GNOME Games

Game	Description
AisleRiot Solitaire	You can select from among 28 different solitaire card games.
Ataxx	Board game where you flip over circles to consume enemy pieces.
Blackjack	Card game where you try to get closer to 21 (without going over) than the dealer.
Five or More	Clone of the color lines game (glines).
Four-In-A-Row	Drop balls to beat the game at making four in a row.

TABLE 23-1	(continued)
Game	**Description**
FreeCell Solitaire	A popular solitaire card game.
GnomeFallingBlocks / Gnometris	GNOME Tetris-like game.
Iagno	Disk flipping game, similar to reversi.
Klotski	Move pieces around to allow one piece to escape.
Mahjongg	Classic Asian tile game.
Mines	Minesweeper clone. Click on safe spaces and avoid the bombs.
Nibbles	Steer a worm around the screen while avoiding walls.
Robots	Later version of Gnobots, which includes movable junk heaps.
Same GNOME	Eliminate clusters of balls for a high score.
Sodoku	A Japanese logic puzzle where you fill in numbers instead of words.
Tali	Yahtzee clone. Roll dice to fill in categories.
Tetravex	A clone of Tetravex from the GNOME project. Move blocks so that numbers on each side align.

KDE Games

A bunch of games are available for the KDE desktop environment. (In Fedora, Ubuntu, and other versions of Linux that include KDE, these games come in the kdegames package.) Table 23-2 contains a list of KDE games. There may be a different set of games included with your Linux distribution.

TABLE 23-2	
Games for the KDE Desktop	
Game	**Description**
Arcade Games	
KAsteroids	Destroy asteroids in the classic arcade game.
KBounce	Add walls to block in bouncing balls.
KFoul Eggs	Squish eggs in this Tetris-like game.
Klickety	Click color groups to erase blocks in this adaptation of Clickomania.
Kolf	Play a round of virtual golf.
KSirtet	Tetris clone. Try to fill in lines of blocks as they drop down.

continued

TABLE 23-2   (continued)

Game	Description
KSmileTris	Tetris with smiley faces.
KSnakeRace	Race your snake around a maze.
KSpaceDuel	Fire at another spaceship as you spin around a planet.

Board Games

Game	Description
Atlantik	Play this Monopoly-like game against other players on the network.
KBackgammon	Online version of Backgammon.
KBlackBox	Find hidden balls by shooting rays.
Kenolaba	Move game pieces to push opponents' pieces off the board.
KMahjongg	Classic oriental tile game.
KReversi	Flip game pieces to outmaneuver the opponent.
Shisen-Sho	Tile game similar to Mahjongg.
Kwin4	Drop colored pieces to get four pieces in a row.

Card Games

Game	Description
KPoker	Video poker clone. Play five-card draw, choosing which cards to hold and which to throw.
Lieutenant Skat	Play the card game Skat.
Patience	Choose from nine different solitaire card games.

Tactics and Strategy

Game	Description
KAtomic	Move pieces to create different chemical compounds.
KGoldrunner	Strategy puzzle game.
KJumping Cube	Click squares to increase numbers and take over adjacent squares.
KMines	Minesweeper clone. Click safe spaces and avoid the bombs.
Kolor Lines	Move marbles to form five-in-a-row and score points.
Konquest	Expand your interstellar empire in this multiplayer game.
Potato Guy	Build your own potato head face.
SameGame	Erase game pieces to score points.

The games on the KDE menu range from amusing to quite challenging. If you are used to playing games in Windows, KMines and Patience will seem like old favorites. KAsteroids and KPoker are good for the mindless game category. For a mental challenge (it's harder than it looks), try KSokoban.

Games in Fedora

As with many other Linux distributions, Fedora offers an extensive set of games. Table 23-3 lists some of the games that are included in Fedora 8.

TABLE 23-3

Games from Fedora

Game	Description
Beneath a Steel Sky (beneath-a-steel-sky)	A popular commercial science fiction adventure game from the early 1990s, set in a repulsive, futuristic city.
BSD Games (bsd-games)	Text-based card games and adventure games dating back to early UNIX systems of the 1970s and run from the shell.
BZFlag (bzflag)	3D multiplayer tank battle game.
Celestia (celestia)	OpenGL real-time visual space simulation. (Available under the Other menu.)
Flight Gear (FlightGear)	Flight simulator game.
FooBilliard (foobilliard)	OpenGL billiard game.
Freeciv (freeciv)	The Freeciv multiplayer strategy game.
Freedoom (freedoom)	Data files for Doom game engines. (Use with prboom package, which provides an open source port of the Doom engine.)
Freedroid (freedroid)	Clone of the C64 game Paradroid.
Freedroid RPG (freedroidrpg)	Freedroid theme for role playing game with Tux as hero.
GL-117 (gl-117)	Action flight simulator.
Chess (gnuchess)	The GNU chess program. Used with the xboard package to provide a graphical chess game.
Lacewing (lacewing)	Asteroid game sporting different types of ships.
Lincity (lincity-ng)	Build simulated cities.
LMarbles (lmarbles)	Atomix clone where you create figures out of marbles.
Maelstrom (Maelstrom)	A space combat game.
Nexuiz (nexuiz)	Death match–oriented first person shooter (multiplayer).
Overgod	Another Asteroid-like game.
Powermanga (powermanga)	Arcade 2D shoot-'em-up game.
PPRacer (ppracer)	3D racing game featuring Tux.

continued

TABLE 23-3	(continued)
Game	**Description**
Rogue (rogue)	Graphical version of a classic adventure game.
Scorched Earth (scorched3d)	Game based loosely on the classic DOS game Scorched Earth.
Sirius (sirius)	Othello for GNOME.
Starfighter (starfighter)	Project: Starfighter, a space arcade game. (Available by typing the `/usr/games/starfighter` command.)
SuperTux (supertux)	Jump-and-run game similar to Mario Bros.
TORCS (torcs)	The Open Racing Car Simulator.
The Ur-Quan Masters (uqm)	The Ur-Quan Masters, a port of the classic game Star Control II.
Vega Strike (vegastrike)	Spaceflight simulator (3D OpenGL).
Virus Killer (viruskiller)	Frantic shooting game where viruses invade your computer.
Worminator (worminator)	Multi-level shoot-'em-up game.
Chess (xboard)	An X Window System graphical chessboard.
X Pilot (xpilot-ng)	Multiplayer space arcade game. (The xpilot-ng-server is also available.)
xplanet (xplanet)	Render a planetary image into an X window. (Available by typing the `xplanet` command.)

The following sections describe two of the more interesting games that come with Fedora or that can be downloaded from `http://fedoraproject.org/wiki/Games`: Freeciv and PlanetPenguin Racer (ppracer).

Freeciv

Freeciv is a free clone of the popular Civilization game series from Atari. With Freeciv, you create a civilization that challenges competing civilizations for world dominance.

NOTE   **A commercial port of Civilization for Linux (Civilization: Call to Power) was created a few years ago by Loki Games (described later in this chapter).**

The commonly distributed version of Freeciv contains both client software (to play the game) and server software (to connect players). You can connect to your server and try the game yourself or (with a network connection) play against up to 14 other players on the Internet. To install Freeciv, check out the download page on the `www.freeciv.org` Web site. Choose your language, start downloading, install, and have fun.

You can start Freeciv from a Terminal window by typing:

```
$ civclient &
```

Figure 23-1 shows the window that appears when you start Freeciv.

FIGURE 23-1

Play Freeciv to build civilizations and compete against others.

NOTE If Freeciv won't start, you may be logged in as root. You must be logged in as a regular user to run the c i v command.

You can play a few games by yourself, if you like, to get to know the game before you play against others on the network. Follow these steps to start your first practice Freeciv game:

1. Select Start New Game. (In addition to starting the client, this action also starts civserver, which will allow others to connect to your game, if you like.) You are asked to choose the number of players, skill level, and other game options.

2. Select 2 to play against the computer or another number if you want others to join in; then click Start. A What Nation Will You Be? window appears on the client, as shown in Figure 23-2.

3. Choose a nation, name a leader, select your gender, choose the style of the city, and then click OK. At this point, you should be ready to begin playing Freeciv.

FIGURE 23-2

Choose a nation to begin Freeciv.

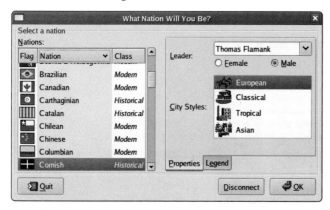

Beginning with Freeciv

Check out the Freeciv window before you start playing the game:

- Click the Help button for topical information on many different subjects that will be useful to you as you play. (You can find more help at the Freeciv site.)

- The world (by default) is 80 × 50 squares, with 11 × 8 squares visible at a time.

- The active square contains an icon of the active unit (flashing alternatively with the square's terrain).

- Some squares contain special resources. Press and hold the middle mouse button for information on what special resources a square contains. (With a two-button mouse, hold down the Ctrl key and click the right mouse button.) Try this a few times to get a feel for the land around you. This action also identifies any units on the terrain, as well as statistics for the unit.

- To see the world outside your 11 × 8 viewing area, click the scroll bars outside the map. At first, the part of the world you haven't explored yet will be black. As units are added, areas closer to those units will be visible. (Press C to return to the active part of your map.)

- An overview map is in the upper-left corner of the Freeciv window. As the world becomes more civilized, this provides a good way to get an overview of what is going on. Right-click a spot on the overview map to have your viewport centered there.

- The menu bar contains buttons you can use to play the game. The Game menu enables you to change settings and options, view player data, view messages, and clear your log. The Kingdom menu enables you to change tax rates, find cities, and start revolutions. The View menu enables you to place a grid on the map or center the view. The Orders menu enables you to choose the items you build and the actions you take. The Reports menu enables you to display reports related to cities, military, trade, and science, as well as other special reports.

■ A summary of the economy of your civilization appears under the overview map. Information includes number of people, current year, and money in the treasury.

■ Ten icons below the overview information represent how money is divided among luxuries (an entertainer), science (a researcher), and taxes (a tax collector). Essentially, these icons represent how much of your resources are placed into improving each of those attributes of your community.

■ When you have made all your moves for a turn, click Turn Done. Next to that, a light bulb indicates the progress of your research (increasing at each turn). A sun icon starts clear, but becomes brighter from pollution to warn of possible global warming. A government symbol indicates that you begin with a despotic government. The last icon tells you how much time is left in a turn.

■ The Unit box shows information about your current unit. You begin with two Settlers units (covered-wagon icons) and one Explorer (a man icon) unit. Click on a Settler, Explorer, city, or other unit to use it or learn about it.

Building Your Civilization

Start building your civilization. The Freeciv manual makes these suggestions:

■ To change the distribution of money, choose Government ➪ Tax Rates. Move the slider bars to redistribute the percentage of assets assigned to luxury, science, and taxes. Try increasing science and reducing taxes to start off.

■ Change the current unit to be a Settler as follows: Click the stack of units on the map and click one of the Settlers from the menu that appears.

■ Begin building a city by clicking Orders ➪ Build City. When prompted, type a name for the city and click OK. The window that appears shows information about the city. It starts with one happy citizen, represented by a single icon (more citizens will appear as the game progresses).

■ The Food, Prod, and Trade lines reflect the raw productivity statistics for the city. The first number shows how much is being produced; the second (in parentheses) shows the surplus above what is needed to support the units. The Gold, Luxury, and Science lines indicate the city's trade output. Granary numbers show how much food is stored and the size of the food store. The pollution level begins at zero.

■ Close the city window by clicking Close.

Exploring Your World

To begin exploring, move the Settlers and the Explorer:

1. Using the numeric keypad, press the 9 key three times to begin exploring. You can move the Explorer up to three times per turn. You begin to see more of the world.

2. When the next unit (a Settler) begins blinking, move it one square in another direction. When you have made all the moves you want to make (or all that the game allows), the Turn Done button is highlighted. Click Turn Done to start your next turn. Information for the city is updated. (The city changes and grows, simply through the passage of time reflected in the turns.)

3. Click the City to see the city window. Notice that information about the city has been updated. In particular, you should see food storage increase. Close the city window.

4. Continue exploring and build a road. With the Explorer flashing, use the numeric keypad to move it another three sections. When the Settler begins blinking, press R to build a road. A small R appears on the square to remind you that the Settler is busy building a road. Click Turn Done.

Using More Controls and Actions

Now that you have some understanding of the controls and actions, the game can go in a lot of different directions. Here are a few things that might happen next and things you can do:

- After you take a turn, the computer gets a chance to play. As it plays, its actions are reported to you. You can make decisions on what to do about those actions. Choose Game ➪ Message Options. The Message Options window appears, containing a listing of different kinds of messages that can come from the server and how they will be presented to you.

- As you explore, you will run into other explorers and eventually other civilizations. Continue exploring by selecting different directions on your numeric keypad.

- Continue to move the Settler one square at a time after it has finished creating the road. The Settler will blink again when it is available. Click Turn Done to continue.

- At this point, you should see a message that your city has finished building Warriors. When buildings and units are complete, you should usually check out what has happened. Click the message associated with the city, and then click Popup City. The city window appears, showing you that it has additional population. The food storage may appear empty, but the new citizens are working to increase the food and trade. You may see an additional warrior unit.

- A science advisory may also appear to let you choose your city's research goals. Click Change and select Writing as your new research goal. You can then select a different long-term goal as well. Click Close when you are done.

- If your new Warrior is now blinking, press the S key to assign sentry mode to the Warrior.

- Select Reports from time to time to keep track of statistics about your Cities, Units, Economy, Science, and other attributes of your world.

Those moves provided familiarity with some of the actions of Freeciv. To learn some basic strategies for playing the game, choose Help ⇨ Help Playing.

PlanetPenguin Racer (TuxRacer)

With PlanetPenguin Racer, you guide Tux the penguin (the Linux mascot) down a snow-covered hill as fast as you can. Planet Penguin Racer (`ppracer` command) is an open source (GPL) version of TuxRacer, which was once freeware, but was later made into a commercial game by Sunspire Studios.

To advance in PlanetPenguin Racer, you need to complete courses in the allotted time while overcoming whatever obstacle is presented (gathering herring or negotiating flags). You move up to try different courses and achieve higher-level cups. Figure 23-3 shows a screenshot of PlanetPenguin Racer.

FIGURE 23-3

Race Tux the penguin down a mountain.

Commercial Linux Games

When Loki Software, Inc. closed its doors a few years ago, the landscape of commercial gaming in Linux changed. Loki produced Linux ports of popular games, including Myth II and Civilization: Call to Power, to name a couple, and many hoped it would help Linux become the premier gaming platform. Since then, no other company has stepped up to port that wide a range of best-selling games to Linux. Today, commercial games that run natively are led by several popular games from id Software (described in the next section) and a few gaming companies that have ported individual titles to Linux.

Some Loki games are still available for purchase on the Web. They sell for a fraction of their original price, but you are on your own if they don't work because Loki Software is no longer there to support them. The Loki Games Demo is still around, if you want to get a feel for a particular Loki game before it disappears completely. (I describe how to find demo and packaged Loki Games later in this chapter.)

Although the state of Linux gaming has improved somewhat in the last few years, Linux is still emerging as a gaming platform. Linux has some of the technology needed to support advanced games, but the technology and developer support have not yet really come together. Most serious gamers still maintain a Windows partition to support their gaming habits.

According to top game developers, there are significant hurdles — both technological and economic — that hinder development of games for Linux. In particular, the relatively small size of the Linux gaming market means that incentives to overcome some technical issues are not particularly strong. However, these limitations are not overwhelming. As you'll see later in this chapter, even the hardcore game nut can successfully use Linux.

Getting Started with Commercial Games in Linux

How you get started with Linux gaming depends on how serious you are about it. If all you want to do is play a few games to pass the time, I've already described plenty of diverting X Window games that come with Linux. If you want to play more powerful commercial games, you can choose from the following:

- **Games for Microsoft Windows (Cedega 6.0)** — Many of the most popular commercial games created to run on Microsoft operating systems will run in Linux using Cedega. To get RPM versions of Cedega, you must sign up for a Cedega subscription at www.transgaming.com. Make sure to check in with www.linuxgames.com to see if there is a relevant HOWTO for working with the particular game you have in mind. Many games are covered there, including Half-Life and Unreal Tournament. To see if your favorite Windows game will run in Linux and Cedega, refer to the TransGaming.Org Games Database at http://transgaming.org/gamesdb.

- **Games for Linux (id Software and others)** — Certain popular games have Linux versions available. Most notably, id Software offers its Doom and Return to Castle Wolfenstein in Linux versions. Other popular games that run natively in Linux include Unreal Tournament 2004 and 2005 from Atari (www.unrealtournament.com). Commercial games that run in Linux without WINE, Cedega, or some sort of Windows emulation typically come in a boxed version for Windows with some sort of Linux installer included.

Linux games that were ported directly to Linux from the now defunct company Loki Software, Inc. are still available. While you cannot purchase the titles directly from Loki, you can go online to one of Loki's resellers at www.lokigames.com/orders/resellers.php3. For example, Amazon.com (one of the listed resellers) shows 16 titles, including Quake III, Myth II: Soulblighter, and Heretic II for Linux.

Playing Commercial Linux Games

To get your commercial games running in Linux, you should start from a site such as The Linux Game Tome (www.happypenguin.org) or Linux Gamers' FAQ (http://icculus.org/lgfaq), which provide information on commercial games that run in Linux and help in getting them to run. In most cases, you need to:

- Purchase a legal copy of the game.
- Go to a Web site that describes how to install, get patches for, and work around any issues related to playing the game in Linux.

Here are examples of a few commercial games that run well in Linux:

- **Duke 3D Atomic Edition for Linux (3D Realms)** — Duke Nukem returns to earth to face aliens and clean up Los Angeles in this third chapter in the Duke Nukem series. Visit 3D Realms for official information about Duke 3D Atomic Edition (www.3drealms .com/duke3d). See the Icculus.org site (http://icculus.org/duke3d/) for tips on getting it running.

- **Unreal Tournament 2003 (Epic Games)** — Multiplayer death match set in the future, where warriors face each other with awesome weapons and stuff. Includes a Linux installer. Go to Epic Games (www.epicgames.com) or the Unreal Tournament site (www.unrealtournament.com) for the official information. Visit the Icculus.org site for tips on installing in Linux (www.icculus.org/lgfaq#ut2k3_install).

- **Unreal Tournament 2004 (Epic Games)** — Adds new maps, characters, vehicles, weapons, and modes of play to the 2003 edition.

The following sections describe Linux games from id Software, information about running Windows games using Cedega in Linux, and games from the now-defunct Loki Games still available from other sources today.

id Software Games

Among the most popular games running natively in Linux are Quake II, Quake III Arena, and Return to Castle Wolfenstein from id Software, Inc. You can purchase Linux versions of these games or download demos of each game before you buy.

 **NOTE** If you have trouble getting any id Software games running in Linux, refer to the Linux FAQs available from id Software at http://zerowing.idsoftware.com/linux.

Quake III Arena

Quake III Arena is a first-person, shooter-type game where you can choose from lots of weapons (lightning guns, shotguns, grenade launchers, and so on) and pass through scenes with highly detailed 3D surfaces. You can play alone or against your friends. There are multiplayer death-match and capture-the-flag competitions. Standalone play allows you to advance through a tournament structure of skilled AI opponents. This version of the game has a selectable difficulty level, from fairly easy to beat to downright impossible.

A demo version of Quake III Arena for Linux is available from the id Software Web site (click the demo link at www.idsoftware.com/games/quake/quake3-gold/ and then look for the Linux demo). Because the demo is in the form of a large shell script, to save it you can right-click the link and select Save Link As from your Web browser. Figure 23-4 shows a screenshot from Quake III Arena.

FIGURE 23-4

Quake III Arena is a popular first-person shooter game that runs in Linux.

Return to Castle Wolfenstein

You battle with the Allies to destroy the Third Reich in Return to Castle Wolfenstein, which mixes World War II action with creatures conjured up by Nazi scientists. It's based on the Quake III Arena engine and offers single-player mode as well as team-based multiplayer mode.

If you purchase Return to Castle Wolfenstein for Linux, you actually get the Windows version with an extra Linux installer. If you already have the Windows version, you can download the Linux installer and follow some instructions to get it going. I downloaded the installer called `wolf-linux-1.31.x86.run` from `www.idsoftware.com/games/wolfenstein/rtcw/index.php?game_section=updates`. The `INSTALL` file (in `/usr/local/games/wolfenstein`) describes which files you need to copy from the Windows CD.

To get a demo of Return to Castle Wolfenstein, go to `www.idsoftware.com/games/wolfenstein/rtcw/index.php?game_section=overview`. Both single-player and multiplayer demos are available.

 You need an NVIDIA card to run Return to Castle Wolfenstein.

Figure 23-5 is a screenshot from Return to Castle Wolfenstein running in Linux.

FIGURE 23-5

Return to Castle Wolfenstein combines strange creatures and World War II battles.

Playing TransGaming and Cedega Games

TransGaming Technologies brings to Linux some of the most popular games that currently run on the Windows platforms. Working with WINE developers, TransGaming is developing Cedega, which enables you to run many different games on Linux that were originally developed for Windows. Although TransGaming is producing a few games that are packaged separately and tuned for Linux, in most cases it sells you a subscription service to Cedega instead of the games. That subscription service lets you stay up-to-date on the continuing development of Cedega so you can run more and more Windows games.

COMING FROM WINDOWS To get Windows games to run in Linux, Cedega particularly needs to develop Microsoft DirectX features that are required by many of today's games. There are also issues related to CD keys and hooks into the Windows operating system that must be overcome (such as requiring Microsoft Active Desktop). A Cedega subscription has value, in part, because it lets you vote on which games you'd like to see TransGaming work on next.

A full list of games supported by TransGaming, as well as indications of how popular they are and how well they work, is available from the TransGaming site (`www.transgaming.org/gamesdb/`). Browse games by category or alphabetically. An asterisk marks games that are officially supported by TransGaming. On each game description page is a link to a related Wiki Node, when one exists, that gives you details about how well the game works under Cedega and tips for getting it to work better.

NOTE Depending on your distribution, you may need to get the vanilla kernel from kernel.org and boot that on your system before running games with Cedega. TransGaming has added several new features to the Cedega GUI (formerly called Point2Play). The Cedega GUI provides a graphical window for installing, configuring, and testing Cedega on your computer. This application also lets you install and organize your games so you can launch them graphically. Figure 23-6 shows an example of the TransGaming Cedega window.

FIGURE 23-6

Use the Cedega window to launch Windows games in Linux.

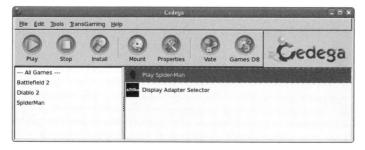

Features in the new Cedega GUI window include a new look-and-feel and tools for individually configuring how each game runs under Cedega. (If a game won't run from the GUI, try launching it from a Terminal window.)

To get binary copies (ones that are already compiled to run) of Cedega, you need to subscribe to TransGaming. For details on how to become a "TransGamer," click the Sign Up Today link on the TransGaming home page (`www.transgaming.com`). Benefits currently include:

- Downloads of the latest version of Cedega
- Access to Cedega support forums
- Ability to vote on which games you want TransGaming to support next
- Subscription to the Cedega newsletter

Cedega used to be known as WineX. The source code for WineX may become available in the near future if you want to build your own WineX/Cedega package. To check availability, try the SourceForge.net project site for WineX (`sourceforge.net/projects/winex`).

Loki Software Game Demos

To encourage people to get to know its games, Loki Software, Inc. offered a demo program that let you choose from among more than a dozen of its games to download and try. You can still find some of its games for sale. For example, a recent search for Loki at Amazon.com turned up 16 different Loki games (including the ones described here), many selling for $9.99.

CAUTION If you try to download any of the demos described in the following sections, make sure you have enough disk space available. It is common for one of these demos to require several hundred megabytes of disk space.

The Loki Demo Launcher page (`www.lokigames.com/products/demos.php3`) still offers links to FTP sites from which you can download the Demo Launcher. The file that you want to save is `loki_demos-full-1.0e-x86.run`. Save it to a directory (such as `/tmp/loki`) and do the following:

1. Change to the directory to which you downloaded the demo. For example:

`# cd /tmp/loki`

NOTE You may not need to be root user to install these games. However, the paths where the Demo Launcher tries to write by default are accessible only to the root user.

2. As root user, run the following command (the program may have a different name if it has been updated):

`# sh loki_demos-full-1.0e.x86.run`

3. If you have not used the Demo Launcher before, a screen appears asking you to identify the paths used to place the Install Tool. If the default locations shown are okay with you, click Begin Install.

4. Assuming that there was no problem writing to the install directories, you should see an Install Complete message. Click Exit.

5. The Uninstall Tool window displays. If the paths for holding the Uninstall Tool are okay, click Begin Install. The Install Complete message appears. Click Exit.

6. The next window enables you to set the locations for installing the Demo Pack. If the paths are okay, click Begin Install.

7. A box shows the different demo games available. As you move the cursor over each game, the disk space needed for the game is displayed. Click the games you want to install and then click Continue.

8. A window displays the progress of each download. You may need to click an Update button to complete the update and then click Finish to finish it.

9. The demo should now be ready to start. Either click Play or type **loki_demos** from a Terminal window to start the program.

10. Select to start the game, and you're ready to go.

The following sections describe a few games that may still be available. Again, these games may not be available for long.

Civilization: Call to Power

You can build online civilizations with Civilization: Call to Power (CCP). Like earlier versions and public spinoffs (such as the Freeciv described earlier in this chapter), Civilization: Call to Power for Linux lets you explore the world, build cities, and manage your empire. The last version offered by Loki Games includes multiplayer network competition and extensions that let you extend cities into outer space and under the sea.

If you like Freeciv, you will love CCP. Engaging game play is improved with enhanced graphics, sound, and animation. English, French, German, Italian, and Spanish versions are available.

NOTE Freeciv is dependent on the Open Sound System for audio support. The Open Sound home page (www.opensound.com/osshw.html) has a list of supported sound cards, mostly older devices. If you do not have a card that's on the list, you may be unable to enjoy the audio.

The CCP demo comes with an excellent tutorial to start you out. If you have never played a civilization game before, the tutorial is a great way to start. Figure 23-7 shows an example scene from the Civilization: Call to Power for Linux demo.

FIGURE 23-7

Civilization: Call to Power features excellent graphics and network play.

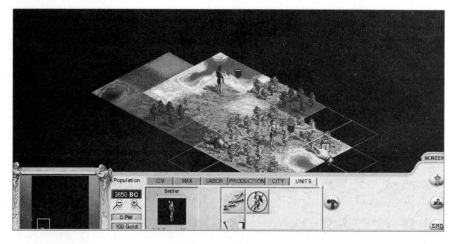

Myth II: Soulblighter

If you like knights and dwarves and storming castles, Myth II: Soulblighter for Linux might be for you. In Myth II, you are given a mission and some troops with various skills. From there, you need strategy and the desire to shed lots of virtual blood to meet your goal.

Myth II was created by Bungie Software (www.bungie.com) and ported to Linux by Loki Entertainment Software (www.lokigames.com). The Loki port of the popular Myth game includes improved graphics and new scenarios. A demo version is available that runs well in most distributions (particularly Fedora/Red Hat). You can get it via the Demo Launcher described earlier. You need at least a modest Pentium 133 MHz, 32MB RAM, 80MB swap space, and 100MB of free disk space. You also need network hardware for multiuser network play (network card or dial-up), and a sound card if you want audio. Figure 23-8 shows a screen in Myth II.

FIGURE 23-8

Use warriors, archers, and dwarves to battle in Myth II.

Heretic II

Based on the Quake engine, Heretic II sets you on a path to rid the world of a deadly, magical plague. As the main character, Corvus, you explore dungeons, swamps, and cities to uncover and stop the plague. The graphics are rich, and the game play is quite engaging.

You will experience some crashing problems with Heretic II out-of-the-box. Be sure to check for the update to Heretic II at www.updates.lokigames.com, which should fix most of the problems.

Neverwinter Nights

BioWare (www.bioware.com) dipped its foot into Linux gaming waters with a Linux client for its wildly popular Neverwinter Nights game. Neverwinter Nights is a classic role-playing game in the swords-and-sorcery mold. You can develop your character and go adventuring, or play online with others via a LAN or over the Internet. You can even build your own worlds and host adventures as the Dungeon Master. Neverwinter Nights is licensed by Wizards of the Coast to use Dungeons & Dragons rules and material.

Of course, to use the Neverwinter Nights Linux client, you must purchase the game from BioWare. You must also have access to certain files from a Windows installation of the game. Keep in mind that getting Neverwinter Nights running is not a simple process. Important installation instructions and downloadable files are located at http://nwn.bioware.com/downloads/linuxclient.html. This site includes additional information about expansion packs and updates. If you want the Neverwinter Nights experience on your Linux system to be pleasant, I highly recommend reading the instructions thoroughly. And you will need patience in addition to a high-bandwidth Internet connection. Depending on the version of Neverwinter Nights to which you have access, you may need to download up to 1.2GB of files.

Summary

With the addition of hot titles such as Unreal Tournament 2004, StarWars: Empire at War, and EverQuest 2 to the list of playable titles, Linux continues to grow as a gaming platform. You can spend plenty of late nights gaming on Linux. Old UNIX games that have made their way to Linux include a variety of basic X Window–based games. There are card games, strategy games, and some action games for those less inclined to spend 36 hours playing Doom 3.

On the commercial front, Civilization: Call to Power for Linux and Myth II are available to use on your Linux system. Unfortunately, these will probably disappear because Loki Software (which ported those applications to Linux) went out of business. Fortunately, the future of high-end Linux gaming seems to be in the hands of TransGaming Technologies, which has created Cedega from previous WINE technology to allow Windows games to run in Linux.

Commercial games that run natively in Linux are also available. These include games from id Software, such as Quake III Arena and Return to Castle Wolfenstein.

Part V

Running Servers

Chapter 24

Running a Linux, Apache, MySQL, and PHP (LAMP) Server

With the growing availability of broadband Internet connections and a popular desire to run personal Web sites and Web logs (blogs), an increasing number of people are setting up Web application servers on their home Internet connections. Web applications are also finding more popularity in business environments because Web applications reduce the number of programs that need to be maintained on workstations.

One popular variety of Web application server is known as a *LAMP server* because it brings together Linux, Apache, MySQL, and PHP. LAMP servers combine components from several open source projects to form a fast, reliable, and economical platform for other readily available applications.

This chapter helps you install and configure your own LAMP server. It begins with an introduction to the various components, guides you through the installation and configuration, and finishes with the installation of a sample Web application.

The examples in this chapter are based on a system running Debian GNU/Linux but conceptually should work on other distributions, if you take into account that other Linux systems use different ways to install the software and start and stop services. Descriptions of how to set up LAMP configuration files, however, should work across multiple Linux distributions with only slight modifications. You can find more information about Debian in Chapter 9.

Components of a LAMP Server

You're probably familiar with Linux by this point, so this section focuses on the other three components—Apache, MySQL, and PHP—and the functions they serve within a LAMP system.

Apache

Within a LAMP server, Apache HTTPD (also known as the Apache HTTP Server) provides the service with which the client Web browsers communicate. The daemon runs in the background on your server and waits for requests from clients. Web browsers connect to the HTTP daemon and send requests, which the daemon interprets, sending back the appropriate data. Apache HTTPD includes an interface that allows modules to tie into the process to handle specific portions of a request. Among other things, modules are available to handle the processing of scripting languages such as Perl or PHP within Web documents and to add encryption to connections between clients and the server.

Apache began as a collection of patches and improvements to the HTTP daemon developed at the National Center for Supercomputing Applications (NCSA) at the University of Illinois, Urbana-Champaign. The NCSA HTTP daemon was the most popular HTTP server at the time, but had started to show its age after its author, Rob McCool, left NCSA in mid-1994.

 Another project that came from NCSA is Mosaic. Most modern Web browsers can trace their origins to Mosaic.

In early 1995, a group of developers formed the Apache Group and began making extensive modifications to the NCSA HTTPD code base. Apache soon replaced NCSA HTTPD as the most popular Web server, a title it still holds today.

The Apache Group later formed the Apache Software Foundation (ASF) to promote the development of Apache and other free software. With the start of new projects at ASF, the Apache server became known as Apache HTTPD, although the two terms are still used interchangeably. Current ASF projects include Jakarta (open source Java solutions), MyFaces (a Web application framework), and SpamAssassin (an e-mail filtering program).

MySQL

MySQL is an open source DBMS (database management system) that has become popular among Webmasters because of its speed, stability, and features. MySQL consists of a server that handles storage and access to data, and clients to handle interfacing with and managing the server. Client libraries are also included, and they can be used by third-party programs, such as PHP, to connect to the server.

In a LAMP server, MySQL is used for storing data appropriate to the Web applications that are being used. Common uses include data such as usernames and passwords, entries in a journal, and data files.

 If you are not sure how a database works, refer to the sidebar "How MySQL Databases Are Structured" later in this chapter.

MySQL was originally developed by Michael (Monty) Widenius of TcX (Sweden). In 1994, TcX needed a backend database for Web applications and decided to use one supporting SQL, a standardized and widely recognized language for interacting with databases.

TcX investigated the free databases that were available at the time, plus some commercial databases, but could not find a system that supported the features it needed and could handle its large databases at the same time. Because it already had experience writing database programs, TcX decided that the best way to get what it wanted was to develop a new system that supported SQL.

In 1995, TcX released the source code for MySQL on the Internet. MySQL was not an open source program at that time (because of some of the restrictions in its license), but it still began to see widespread use. MySQL was later released under the GNU General Public License (GPL).

PHP

PHP is a programming language that was developed specifically for use in Web scripts. It is preferred by many developers because it's designed to be embedded within HTML documents, making it simpler to manage Web content and scripts within a single file.

PHP originated as a set of Perl scripts by Rasmus Lerdorf called PHP/FI (Personal Home Page/Forms Interpreter). Over time, more features were implemented, and Rasmus rewrote PHP/FI in C.

In late 1997, Andi Gutmans and Zeev Suraski began working on a complete rewrite of PHP/FI. As the language evolved and more features were implemented, Gutmans and Suraski decided that it would be appropriate to rename the project to more accurately reflect these features. The name PHP Hypertext Preprocessor (PHP) was chosen, with Lerdorf's approval, to maintain familiarity for users of PHP/FI.

The core features of PHP are included within the PHP code itself, and additional features are implemented in the form of extensions. The latest version of PHP is 5, but several implementations still include the libapache-mod-php4 (PHP 4) package, and PHP 6 is in development. Among the major changes offered in PHP 5 is enhanced security. This release improved the security features that have always been in PHP and fixed some possible holes. This made the language even more stable. Additional information about each release, and what it offers, can be found at `www.php.net/`.

Setting Up Your LAMP Server

Before proceeding through the examples in this section, be sure that your Linux operating system is installed and configured. The specific instructions in this section were tested on a Debian GNU/Linux system. If you try this on a different Linux system, understand that such things as software packaging, the location of startup scripts and configuration files, and other features may be different.

When you install your Linux system, you typically choose whether to install a set of software packages that are appropriate for a workstation or a server. You may choose to set up a server on a system that has been configured using the layout and software packages intended for a workstation. However, that's not recommended unless you are providing services for only a very small number of users whom you know well and trust. In fact, many systems administrators don't even like to have the X Window System and other GUI components installed on a server.

Installing Apache

The next step toward a functioning LAMP server is to install the Apache HTTP server, which can be found in the apache package. Use APT to retrieve and install the package:

```
# apt-get install apache
```

During the configuration process, you are asked whether you want to enable the suexec mechanism. The suexec feature increases the security of CGI applications and is generally recommended. You can change your selection later using debconf to reconfigure the apache package. More information about debconf can be found in Chapter 9.

> **NOTE** As of this writing, the latest version of Apache is 2.2.6. The installation process in this chapter installs Apache version 1.3, and all the configuration examples here have been tested against it. If you would rather install Apache 2.x, it is available in the apache2-mpm-prefork package and uses libapache2-mod-php4. The numbering can be confusing when it comes to Apache. Many of the updates to the HTTPD server are bug and security fix releases, and the core releases continue to be available. As of this writing, Apache HTTP Server 1.3.39 and 2.0.61 legacy releases are also currently available.

The server should automatically start once the installation is finished, which means that you're now ready to install PHP.

Installing PHP

Now you're ready to install and test the PHP module in Apache. This is the most common method for installing PHP, but it introduces some security concerns on multiuser systems because all PHP scripts are run as the same user as the Apache daemon. Be sure to read the Security section of the PHP manual at http://php.net/manual/en/security.php before granting other users access to manipulate PHP files on your server.

The PHP Apache module is contained in the php5 or php4 package, which is installed using APT. The following lines download and install the Apache php4 module and the MySQL extensions, configure Apache to load the module automatically, and instruct Apache to reload its configuration:

```
# apt-get install libapache-mod-php4 php4-mysql php4-gd
# apache-modconf apache enable mod_php4
Replacing config file /etc/apache/modules.conf with new version
# apachectl restart
```

The version numbers will change based upon what you are installing. For example, with PHP 5 and Apache 2, use:

```
# apt-get install libapache2-mod-php5 php5-mysql php5-gd
```

Don't worry if the second line does not print out a message as this example shows. That simply means that the module has already been configured.

NOTE Just as the numbering and versions of Apache can sometimes be confusing, similar thoughts can be expressed about PHP. As of this writing, there are active development versions in both 5.*x* and 4.4.*x* (and PHP 6 is under development). Even though PHP 5 has been out for a while, the PHP Group has committed to releasing security and security-related updates for PHP 4 through most of 2008.

At this point, Apache should be ready to process HTTP requests, complete with processing of PHP files. To test it, create a file named /var/www/info.php containing a call to the phpinfo() function:

```
# cat > /var/www/info.php
<?php
    phpinfo();
?>
^D
# chmod 644 /var/www/info.php
```

The ^D means that you should press Ctrl+D on your keyboard. This tells the cat command that you are at the end of the input. Now try opening the page by going to http://localhost/info.php. You should see a page full of information about your Apache and PHP installation, as shown in Figure 24-1.

FIGURE 24-1

The PHP information page

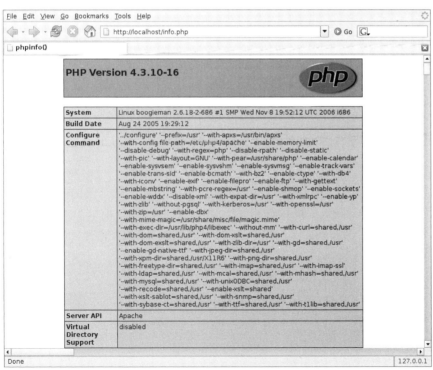

If, instead of an information page, you are prompted to download the file, check the appropriate PHP installation section (earlier in the chapter) to verify that all the steps were completed successfully.

After everything is tested and working, you should remove the `info.php` file so that it can't be used by potential attackers to gather specifics about your system:

```
# rm -f /var/www/info.php
```

Installing MySQL

The MySQL database system is divided into three main packages: the server, clients, and client libraries. The server is contained within the mysql-server package and requires the other two to function. APT is aware of this, which means the packages will be installed automatically when you install mysql-server:

```
# apt-get install mysql-server
```

> **NOTE** Make sure the hostname settings have been configured as described in Chapter 9 before installing the mysql-server package. Failure to do so could result in an error that causes the installation to fail.

The installation scripts in the mysql-server package provide you with a couple of notices and ask whether you want to remove databases when purging the mysql-server package. "No" is the safest option because it reduces the chance of accidentally losing your data. You also are asked whether you want the MySQL server to start on boot. You should probably say "Yes" here.

Access to databases within MySQL is managed based on account information stored within the mysql database. As with UNIX systems, the superuser account is named `root`. The default installation does not set a password on this account, and it creates an anonymous account and a test database that should be removed unless you are certain that you need them:

```
# mysql -u root mysql
Welcome to the MySQL monitor.  Commands end with ; or \g.
Your MySQL connection id is 3 to server version: 4.0.24 Debian-10-log
Type 'help;' or '\h' for help.  Type '\c' to clear the buffer.
mysql> UPDATE user SET Password=PASSWORD('newpassword')
    -> WHERE User='root';
Query OK, 2 rows affected (0.00 sec)
Rows matched: 2  Changed: 2  Warnings: 0
mysql> DELETE FROM user WHERE User = '';
Query OK, 2 rows affected (0.00 sec)
mysql> FLUSH PRIVILEGES;
Query OK, 0 rows affected (0.00 sec)
mysql> DROP DATABASE test;
Query OK, 0 rows affected (0.00 sec)
mysql> \q
Bye
```

The UPDATE command, as used in this example, changes the password for the MySQL root account (replace newpassword with the password you want to use), the DELETE command removes the anonymous user, and the FLUSH command tells the running MySQL server to reload the list of user accounts from the database. Finally, the DROP command removes the test database.

How MySQL Databases Are Structured

For those who aren't familiar with how a database system is structured, here's a quick introduction:

- *Databases* are the basic organizational block in a database system. Most database systems (including MySQL) are designed to support multiple databases from a single server. This allows separate databases to be created for different users or different functions.

- *Tables* are found within a database. A table is very much like a spreadsheet in that it has *rows* and *columns*. Columns define the different types of data that every entry can or must have, and every entry takes the form of a row. A database can hold multiple tables, allowing you to have many different data sets within a single database.

Operating Your LAMP Server

With the components of your LAMP server installed and running, you are ready to configure Apache and try it out. For this example, Apache is set up to serve content for your own domain using a feature called *virtual hosting*, after which you'll see how to install the Coppermine Photo Gallery program, which enables you to create an online photo gallery on your LAMP server.

Editing Your Apache Configuration Files

The configuration files for Apache HTTPD are incredibly flexible, meaning that you can configure the server to behave in almost any manner you want. This flexibility comes at the cost of increased complexity in the form of a large number of configuration options (called *directives*), but in practice there are only a few directives with which you'll need to be familiar.

NOTE See http://httpd.apache.org/docs/ **for a complete list of directives supported by Apache.**

In Debian, the Apache configuration is stored in text files read by the Apache server, beginning with /etc/apache/httpd.conf. Configuration is read from start to finish, with most directives being processed in the order in which they are read.

Additional files may also be read based on the AccessConfig, ResourceConfig, and Include directives. On modern installations, the AccessConfig and ResourceConfig options point to empty files, and the traditional contents of those files have been moved to the main httpd.conf file.

The `Include` directive is distinct from `AccessConfig` and `ResourceConfig` in that it can appear more than once and can include more than one file at a time. Files referenced by `Include` directives are processed as if their contents appeared at the location of the relevant `Include` statement. `Include` can point to a single file, to a directory in which all files are read, or to a wildcard that specifies a specific set of files within a directory.

> **NOTE**   Subdirectories are also processed when `Include` points to a directory.

The scope of many configuration directives can be altered based on context. In other words, some parameters may be set on a global level and then changed for a specific file, directory, or virtual host. Other directives are always global in nature, such as those specifying which IP addresses the server listens on, and some are valid only when applied to a specific location.

Locations are configured in the form of a start tag containing the location type and a resource location, followed by the configuration options for that location, and finishing with an end tag. This form is often called a *configuration block,* and looks very similar to HTML. A special type of configuration block, known as a *location block,* is used to override settings for specific files or directories. These blocks take the following form:

```
<locationtag specifier>
(options specific to objects matching the specifier go within this block)
</locationtag>
```

Different types of location tags exist and are selected based on the type of resource location that is being specified. The specifier that is included in the start tag is handled based on the type of location tag. The ones you generally use and encounter are `Directory`, `Files`, and `Location`.

> **NOTE**   In this chapter, `Location` refers specifically to the third type of tag, and *location* refers generically to any of the three.

- `Directory` tags are used to specify a path based on the location on the file system. For instance, `<Directory />` refers to the root directory on the computer. Directories inherit settings from directories above them, with the most specific `Directory` block overriding less specific ones, regardless of the order in which they appear in the configuration files.

- `Files` tags are used to specify files by name. `Files` tags can be contained within `Directory` blocks to limit them to files under that directory. Settings within a `Files` block will override the ones in `Directory` blocks.

- `Location` tags are used to specify the URI used to access a file or directory. This is different from `Directory` in that it relates to the address contained within the request and not to the real location of the file on the drive. `Location` tags are processed last and override the settings in `Directory` and `Files` blocks.

Match versions of these tags — `DirectoryMatch`, `FilesMatch`, and `LocationMatch` — have the same function but can contain regular expressions in the resource specification. `FilesMatch` and `LocationMatch` blocks are processed at the same time as `Files` and `Location`, respectively. `DirectoryMatch` blocks are processed after `Directory` blocks.

Apache can also be configured to process configuration options contained within files with the name specified in the `AccessFileName` directive (which is generally set to `.htaccess`). Directives in access configuration files are applied to all objects under the directory they contain, including sub-directories and their contents. Access configuration files are processed at the same time as `Directory` blocks, using a similar "most specific match" order.

> **NOTE** Access control files are useful for allowing users to change specific settings without having access to the server configuration files. The configuration directives permitted within an access configuration file are determined by the `AllowOverride` setting on the directory in which they are contained. Some directives do not make sense at that level and generally result in a "server internal error" message when trying to access the URI. The `AllowOverride` option is covered in detail at `http://httpd.apache.org/docs/mod/core.html#allowoverride`.

Three directives commonly found in location blocks and access control files are `DirectoryIndex`, `Options`, and `ErrorDocument`:

- `DirectoryIndex` tells Apache which file to load when the URI contains a directory but not a filename. This directive doesn't work in `Files` blocks.

- `Options` is used to adjust how Apache handles files within a directory. The `ExecCGI` option tells Apache that files in that directory can be run as CGI scripts, and the `Includes` option tells Apache that server-side includes (SSI) are permitted. Also commonly used is the `Indexes` option, which tells Apache to generate a list of files if one of the filenames found in the `DirectoryIndex` setting is missing. An absolute list of options can be specified, or the list of options can be modified by adding + or - in front of an option name. See `http://httpd.apache.org/docs/mod/core.html#options` for more information.

- `ErrorDocument` directives can be used to specify which file to send in the event of an error. The directive must specify an error code and the full URI for the error document. Possible error codes include 403 (access denied), 404 (file not found), and 500 (server internal error). You can find more information about the `ErrorDocument` directive at `http://httpd.apache.org/docs/mod/core.html#errordocument`.

Another common use for location blocks and access control files is to limit access to a resource. The `Allow` directive can be used to permit access to matching hosts, and the `Deny` directive can be used to forbid it. Both of these options can occur more than once within a block and are handled based on the `Order` setting. Setting `Order` to `Deny,Allow` permits access to any host that is not listed in a `Deny` directive. A setting of `Allow,Deny` denies access to any host not allowed in an `Allow` directive.

Like most other options, the most specific `Allow` or `Deny` option for a host is used, meaning that you can `Deny` access to a range and `Allow` access to subsets of that range. By adding the `Satisfy` option and some additional parameters, you can add password authentication. For more information about access control, see `http://httpd.apache.org/docs/mod/mod_access.html`.

Location blocks (in the generic sense) can be enclosed within a `VirtualHost` block. Virtual hosts, which are described in greater detail in the next section, are a convenient (and almost essential) tool for altering server behavior based on the server address or name that a request is directed to. Most global configuration options are applied to virtual hosts but can be overridden by directives within the `VirtualHost` block.

Adding a Virtual Host to Apache

Apache supports the creation of separate Web sites within a single server to keep content separate. Individual sites are configured in the form of virtual hosts, which also are useful when only a single site will be used. Here's how to configure a virtual host:

Create a file named /etc/apache/conf.d/vhosts.conf using this template:

```
NameVirtualHost *:80
<VirtualHost *:80>
    ServerName       www.example.org
    ServerAlias      web.example.org
    DocumentRoot     /home/username/public_html/
    User             username
    Group            groupname
    DirectoryIndex   index.php index.html index.htm
</VirtualHost>
```

The NameVirtualHost line tells Apache to determine which virtual host to serve documents from based on the hostname provided by the HTTP client. The *:80 specification means that requests to port 80 on any IP address will be treated in this manner.

Similarly, the *:80 specification in the VirtualHost block indicates what address and port this virtual host applies to. The port is optional for both the NameVirtualHost and VirtualHost specifications but should always be used to prevent interference with SSL virtual hosts.

The ServerName and ServerAlias lines tell Apache which names this virtual host should be recognized as, so replace them with names appropriate to your site. You can leave out the ServerAlias line if you do not have any alternate names for the server, and you can specify more than one name per ServerAlias line or have multiple ServerAlias lines if you have several alternate names.

The DocumentRoot line specifies where the Web documents for this site are stored. If you plan to have more than one site per user, you will need to modify this layout appropriately. Replace username with the name of the account that is administrating the Web site. For this example, each Web site is required to be administered by a different user account.

The User and Group lines are used by suexec to determine which account to run scripts as. The groupname parameter should be changed to username's primary group. In most modern installations, this is the same as the username. These two lines must be left out if you aren't using suexec.

When you are done, use apachectl to check the configuration and then do a graceful restart:

```
# apachectl configtest
Syntax OK
# apachectl graceful
```

 **NOTE** Unless you have already created it, you will receive a warning about public_html **not existing. Run** mkdir ~/public_html **as the user that owns the Web site in order to create it.**

Additional virtual hosts can be added by repeating the `VirtualHost` block and repeating the configuration test (`configtest`) and reload (`graceful`) steps.

> **NOTE** You may want to place individual virtual hosts in separate files for convenience. However, you should be careful to keep your primary virtual host in a file that will be read before the others, because the first virtual host receives requests for site names that don't match any in your configuration. In a commercial Web-hosting environment, it is common to make a special default virtual host that contains an error message indicating that no site by that name has been configured.

User Content and the userdir Setting

In situations in which you do not have the ability to set up a virtual host for every user that you want to provide Web space for, you can easily make use of the mod_userdir module in Apache. With this module enabled (which it is by default), the `public_html` directory under every user's home directory is available to the Web at `http://servername/~username/`. For example, a user named `wtucker` on `www.example.com` stores Web content in `/home/wtucker/public_html`. That content would be available from `http://www.example.com/~wtucker`.

Installing a Web Application: Coppermine Photo Gallery

Once your LAMP server is operational, you can begin installing or creating applications to run on it. One such application is Coppermine Photo Gallery (CPG), the installation of which is demonstrated in this section. CPG is a Web-based photo gallery management system written in PHP. Through its Web interface, you can upload pictures to your own photo galleries, which will be available on the Web through your LAMP server.

You can install CPG under a virtual host or under a user's home directory on your main host. A single server can easily support many CPG installations using either of these methods.

To install CPG on the Debian system described in this chapter, follow these steps:

1. Install the unzip and imagemagick programs. Unzip is used to unpack the CPG program after downloading, and imagemagick is used to resize images and create thumbnails:

```
# apt-get install unzip imagemagick
```

2. Create a MySQL database for CPG. You can use a database name other than cpg if you wish. The database username (the part before `@'localhost'` in the GRANT statement) and the database name do not need to match. Be sure to replace *mypassword* with something different:

```
# mysql -u root -p
Enter password:
Welcome to the MySQL monitor.  Commands end with ; or \g.
Your MySQL connection id is 8 to server version:
4.0.24_Debian-10-log
```

```
Type 'help;' or '\h' for help.  Type '\c' to clear the
buffer.
mysql> CREATE DATABASE cpg;
Query OK, 1 row affected (0.00 sec)
mysql> GRANT ALL PRIVILEGES ON cpg.*
TO 'cpg'@'localhost' IDENTIFIED BY 'mypassword';
Query OK, 0 rows affected (0.00 sec)
mysql> \q
Bye
```

3. Log in as the user that will own the CPG installation and download the latest version from the Internet:

```
$ mkdir -p ~/public_html
$ cd ~/public_html
$ wget http://dl.sourceforge.net/sourceforge/coppermine/cpg1.4.10.zip
--19:30:46--  http://dl.sourceforge.net/coppermine/cpg1.4.10.zip
          => `cpg1.4.10.zip'
Resolving dl.sourceforge.net... 64.74.207.41, 66.35.250.221,...
Connecting to dl.sourceforge.net[64.74.207.41]:80... connected.
HTTP request sent, awaiting response...200 OK
Length: 3,214,893 [application/zip]
100%[================>] 2,924,274      58.02K/s    ETA 00:00
`cpg1.4.10.zip'
```

4. Unpack the archive:

```
$ unzip cpg1.4.10.zip
Archive:  cpg1.4.10.zip
  inflating: cpg1410/addfav.php
  inflating: cpg1410/xp_publish.php
[...]
  inflating: cpg1410/zipdownload.php
```

5. Rename the freshly unpacked cpg directory, and then set the permissions so that files can be uploaded from PHP:

```
$ mv cpg1410 photos
$ cd photos
$ chmod 777 include
$ find albums -type d | xargs chmod 777
```

6. Go to a Web browser on any machine that can reach your LAMP server over the network and open the install.php script under your coppermine directory.

   ▪ If you're installing CPG under a user directory under your main host, the URL is http://*servername*/~*username*/photos/install.php.

   ▪ If you're installing CPG under a virtual host, the URL is http://*virtualhostname*/photos/install.php.

7. Configure CPG to work with your installation by filling in the following fields and selecting Let's Go!:

■ **Username and Password** — The administrative login and password that you will use to administer CPG.

■ **Email Address** — The administrator's (your) e-mail address.

■ **MySQL Host** — The server name that CGP will connect to for the database. In this case, you want to use `localhost`.

■ **MySQL Database Name** — The name of the database that you created in Step 2. (In the example, I used `cpg`.)

■ **MySQL Username and Password** — The username and password that you created in Step 2 for accessing the database. (In the example, I used `cpg` and `mypassword`, respectively.)

■ **MySQL table prefix** — The prefix for the tables that will be used by CPG. The default value (`cpg133_`) is fine.

■ **ImageMagick path** — The directory containing the imagemagick binary. On Debian systems, this is `/usr/bin`.

8. You're now done installing CPG. At this point you can click Let's Continue to see the default Coppermine Photo Gallery page. You can use this CPG Web interface to create photo galleries and upload photos. Figure 24-2 shows a sample gallery.

FIGURE 24-2

A sample Coppermine photo gallery

While a complete description of the dozens of features of the Coppermine Photo Gallery is beyond the scope of this example, here are a few tips if you want to continue setting up a working photo gallery. To begin, go to the home page of the photo gallery you just created (`http://server/` `~user/photos`) and log in with the administrative user and password you created. Then do the following:

- **Add an album** — Click the Albums button and then click New. Type a name for the album and select Apply modifications. Then select Continue as instructed.

- **Upload files** — Click the Upload file link at the top of the page. From the Upload file page, add either the full paths to filenames (File Uploads) or Web addresses (URI/URL Uploads) of the images you want to install. Then click Continue. If the uploads were successful, click Continue again.

  At this point, you can add information to be associated with each image you just uploaded. Select the Album each will go into, a file title, and a description, and then select Continue. After you have added information for all your uploaded images, click Continue again to return to the main photo gallery. There you can see your images sorted by album, as random files, or by latest additions.

If you installed Coppermine on a public server, you can give the Web address of that server to your friends and family and they can begin viewing your photo albums. There is a lot you can do to customize your Coppermine Photo Gallery. You can begin by going through the settings on the Configuration page (click the Config link to get there). Click the Users or Groups link to create user or group accounts that give special access to upload or modify the content of your gallery.

Troubleshooting

In any complex environment, you occasionally run into problems. This section includes tips for isolating and resolving the most common errors that you may encounter.

NOTE   This section refers to the Apache HTTPD binary as `apache`, **which is what it is named on Debian systems. However, in most other distributions, the binary is named** `httpd`. **On different systems, you may need to substitute** *httpd* **for** *apache* **when it appears by itself, although not for commands such as** `apachectl`.

Configuration Errors

You may occasionally run into configuration errors or script problems that prevent Apache from starting or that prevent specific files from being accessible. Most of these problems can be isolated and resolved using two Apache-provided tools: the `apachectl` program and the system error log.

When encountering a problem, first use the `apachectl` program with the `configtest` parameter to test the configuration. In fact, it's a good idea to develop the habit of running this every time you make a configuration change:

```
# apachectl configtest
Syntax OK
# apachectl graceful
/usr/sbin/apachectl graceful: httpd gracefully restarted
```

In the event of a syntax error, apachectl indicates where the error occurs and also does its best to give a hint about the nature of the problem. You can then use the graceful restart option (apachectl graceful) to instruct Apache to reload its configuration without disconnecting any active clients.

NOTE The graceful **restart option in** apachectl **automatically tests the configuration before sending the reload signal to** apache, **but it is still a good idea to get in the habit of running the manual configuration test after making any configuration changes.**

Some configuration problems pass the syntax tests performed by apachectl, but then result in the HTTP daemon exiting immediately after reloading its configuration. If this happens, use the tail command to check Apache's error log for useful information. On Debian systems, the error log is in /var/log/apache/error.log. On other systems, the location can be found by looking for the ErrorLog directive in your Apache configuration.

An error message that you might encounter looks something like this:

```
[crit] (98)Address already in use: make_sock: could not bind to port 80
```

This error often indicates that something else is bound to port 80 (not very common unless you have attempted to install another Web server), that another Apache process is already running (apachectl usually catches this), or that you have told Apache to bind the same IP address and port combination in more than one place.

You can use the netstat command to view the list of programs (including Apache) with TCP ports in the LISTEN state:

```
# netstat -nltp
Active Internet connections (only servers)
Proto  Local Address  Foreign Address  State   PID/Program name
tcp    0.0.0.0:80     0.0.0.0:*        LISTEN  2105/apache
```

The output from netstat (which was shortened to fit here) indicates that an instance of the apache process with a process ID of 2105 is listening (as indicated by the LISTEN state) for connections to any local IP address (indicated by 0.0.0.0) on port 80 (the standard HTTP port). If a different program is listening to port 80, it is shown there. You can use the kill command to terminate the process, but if it is something other than apache (or httpd), you should also find out why it is running.

If you don't see any other processes listening on port 80, it could be that you have accidentally told Apache to listen on the same IP address and port combination in more than one place. There are three configuration directives that can be used for this: BindAddress, Port, and Listen:

- BindAddress: Enables you to specify a single IP address to listen on, or you can specify all IP addresses using the * wildcard. You should never have more than one BindAddress statement in your configuration file.

663

- `Port`: Specifies which TCP port to listen on but does not enable you to specify the IP address. `Port` is generally not used more than once in the configuration.
- `Listen`: Enables you to specify both an IP address and a port to bind to. The IP address can be in the form of a wildcard, and you can have multiple `Listen` statements in your configuration file.

Generally, it is a good idea to use only one type of these directives to avoid confusion. Of the three, `Listen` is the most flexible, so it is probably the one you want to use the most. A common error when using `Listen` is to specify a port on all IP addresses (`*:80`) as well as that same port on a specific IP address (`1.2.3.4:80`), which results in the error from `make_sock`.

Configuration errors relating to SSL (discussed later in this chapter) commonly result in Apache's not starting properly. Make sure all key and certificate files exist and that they are in the proper format (use `openssl` to examine them, as shown later in this chapter).

For other error messages, try doing a Web search to see if somebody else has encountered the problem. In most cases, you can find a solution within the first few matches.

If you aren't getting enough information in the `ErrorLog`, you can configure it to log more information using the `LogLevel` directive. The options available for this directive, in increasing order of verbosity, are `emerg`, `alert`, `crit`, `error`, `warn`, `notice`, `info`, and `debug`. Select only one of these. Any message that is at least as important as the `LogLevel` you select will be stored in the `ErrorLog`. On a typical server, this is set to `warn`. You should not set it to any lower than `crit`, and you should avoid leaving it set to `debug` because that can slow down the server and result in a very large `ErrorLog`.

As a last resort, you can also try running `apache` manually to check for crashes or other error messages:

```
# /usr/sbin/apache -d /etc/apache -F ; echo $?
```

The `-d` flag tells `apache` where to look for its configuration file, and the `-F` flag tells it to run in the foreground. The semicolon separates this command from the `echo` command, which displays the return code (`$?`) from Apache after it exits. In the event that `apache` crashes during this step, you can use tools such as `gdb` and `strace` to trace the problem.

Access Forbidden and Server Internal Errors

Two common types of errors that you may encounter when attempting to view specific pages on your server are permission errors and server internal errors. Both types of errors can usually be isolated using the information in the error log. After making any of the changes described in the following list to attempt to solve one of these problems, try the request again and then check the error log to see if the message has changed (for example, to show that the operation completed successfully).

NOTE "File not found" errors can be checked in the same way as access forbidden and server internal errors. You may sometimes find that Apache is not looking where you think it is for a specific file. Generally, the entire path to the file shows up in the error log. Make sure you are accessing the correct virtual host, and check for any `Alias` settings that might be directing your location to a place you don't expect.

- **File permissions** — A "file permissions prevent access" error indicates that the `apache` process is running as a user that is unable to open the requested file. Make sure that the account has execute permissions on the directory and every directory above it, as well as read permissions on the files themselves. Read permissions on a directory are also necessary if you want Apache to generate an index of files. See the manual page for `chmod` for more information about how to view and change permissions.

NOTE Read permissions are not necessary for compiled binaries, such as those written in C or C++, but can be safely added unless there is a need to keep the contents of the program secret.

- **Access denied** — A "client denied by server configuration" error indicates that Apache was configured to deny access to the object. Check the configuration files for `<Location>` and `<Directory>` sections that might affect the file you are trying to access. Remember that settings applied to a path are also applied to any paths below it. You can override these by changing the permissions only for the more specific path to which you want to allow access.

- **Index not found** — The "Directory index forbidden by rule" error indicates that Apache could not find an index file with a name specified in the `DirectoryIndex` directive and was configured to not create an index containing a list of files in a directory. Make sure your index page, if you have one, has one of the names specified in the relevant `DirectoryIndex` directive, or add an `Options Indexes` line to the appropriate `<Directory>` or `<Location>` section for that object.

- **Script crashed** — "Premature end of script headers" errors can indicate that a script is crashing before it finishes. Sometimes, the errors that caused this also show up in the error log. When you're using `suexec` or `suPHP`, this error may also be caused by a file ownership or permissions error. These errors are indicated in `/var/log/apache/suexec.log` or `/var/log/apache/suphp.log`.

Securing Your Web Traffic with SSL/TLS

You want to add security for your server, including your own certificates. Your data is important, and so is your capability to pass it along your network or the Internet to others. Networks just aren't secure enough by themselves to protect your communications. This section examines ways in which you can help guard your communications.

Electronic commerce applications such as online shopping and banking are generally encrypted using either the Secure Socket Layer (SSL) or Transport Layer Security (TLS) specifications. TLS is based on version 3.0 of the SSL specifications, so they are very similar in nature. Because of this similarity — and because SSL is older — the SSL acronym is often used to refer to either variety. For Web connections, the SSL connection is established first, and then normal HTTP communication is "tunneled" through it.

> **NOTE** Because SSL negotiation takes place before any HTTP communication, name-based virtual hosting (which occurs at the HTTP layer) does not work with SSL. As a consequence, every SSL virtual host you configure needs to have a unique IP address.

During connection establishment between an SSL client and an SSL server, asymmetric (public key) cryptography is used to verify identities and establish the session parameters and the session key. A symmetric encryption algorithm such as DES or RC4 is then used with the negotiated key to encrypt the data transmitted during the session. The use of asymmetric encryption during the handshaking phase allows safe communication without the use of a preshared key, and the symmetric encryption is faster and more practical for use on the session data.

For the client to verify the identity of the server, the server must have a previously generated private key, as well as a certificate containing the public key and information about the server. This certificate must be verifiable using a public key that is known to the client.

Certificates are generally digitally signed by a third-party certificate authority (CA) that has verified the identity of the requester and the validity of the request to have the certificate signed. In most cases, the CA is a company that has made arrangements with the Web browser vendor to have its own certificate installed and trusted by default client installations. The CA then charges the server operator for its services.

Commercial certificate authorities vary in price, features, and browser support, but remember that price is not always an indication of quality. Some popular CAs include InstantSSL (`www.instantssl.com`), Thawte (`www.thawte.com`), and VeriSign (`www.verisign.com`).

You also have the option of creating self-signed certificates, although these should be used only for testing or when a very small number of people will be accessing your server and you do not plan to have certificates on multiple machines. Directions for generating a self-signed certificate are included in the following section.

The last option is to run your own certificate authority. This is probably practical only if you have a small number of expected users and the means to distribute your CA certificate to them (including assisting them with installing it in their browsers). The process for creating a CA is too elaborate to cover in this book but is a worthwhile alternative to generating self-signed certificates. You can find guides on running your own CA at `http://sial.org/howto/openssl/ca/`.

The following procedure describes how to generate and use SSL keys with the LAMP server (running on a Debian GNU/Linux system) configured in this chapter. For a general discussion of SSL keys and procedures specific to Fedora and other Red Hat Linux systems, refer to Chapter 6.

Generating Your Keys

To begin setting up SSL, use the `openssl` command, which is part of the OpenSSL package, to generate your public and private key:

1. Use APT to verify that OpenSSL is installed. If it is not present, APT downloads and installs it automatically:

```
# apt-get install openssl
```

2. Generate a 1024-bit RSA private key and save it to a file:

```
# mkdir /etc/apache/ssl.key/
# cd /etc/apache/ssl.key/
# openssl genrsa -out server.key 1024
# chmod 600 server.key
```

> **NOTE** You can use a filename other than `server.key` and should do so if you plan to have more than one SSL host on your machine (which requires more than one IP address). Just make sure you specify the correct filename in the Apache configuration later.

In higher-security environments, it is a good idea to encrypt the key by adding the `-des3` argument after the `genrsa` argument on the `openssl` command line:

```
# openssl genrsa -des3 -out server.key 1024
```

3. You are asked for a passphrase, which is needed every time you start Apache.

> **CAUTION** Do not lose this passphrase because it cannot be easily recovered.

4. If you plan to have your certificate signed by a CA (including one that you run yourself), generate a public key and a certificate signing request (CSR):

```
# mkdir ../ssl.csr/
# cd ../ssl.csr/
# openssl req -new -key ../ssl.key/server.key -out server.csr
Country Name (2 letter code) [AU]:US
State or Province Name (full name) [Some-State]:Washington
Locality Name (eg, city) []:Bellingham
Organization Name (eg, company) [Internet Widgits Pty
Ltd]:Example Company, LTD.
Organizational Unit Name (eg, section) []:Network
Operations
Common Name (eg, YOUR name) []:secure.example.org
```

```
Email Address []:dom@example.org
Please enter the following 'extra' attributes
to be sent with your certificate request
A challenge password []:
An optional company name []:
```

The Common Name should match the name that clients will use to access your server. Be sure to get the other details right if you plan to have the CSR signed by a third-party CA.

5. When using a third-party CA, submit the CSR to it and then place the certificate it provides you into /etc/apache/ssl.crt/server.crt (or a different file, as desired).

6. If you don't plan to have your certificate signed, or if you want to test your configuration, generate a self-signed certificate and save it in a file named server.crt:

```
# mkdir ../ssl.crt/
# cd ../ssl.crt/
# openssl req new -x509 -nodes -sha1 -days 365 -key
../ssl.key/server.key -out server.crt
Country Name (2 letter code) [AU]:.
State or Province Name (full name) [Some-State]:.
Locality Name (eg, city) []:.
Organization Name (eg, company) [Internet Widgits Pty
Ltd]:TEST USE ONLY
Organizational Unit Name (eg, section) []:TEST USE ONLY
Common Name (eg, YOUR name) []:secure.example.org
Email Address []:dom@example.org
```

Configuring Apache to Support SSL/TLS

Once your keys have been generated, you need to install the mod_ssl Apache module, which adds SSL/TLS support to Apache, and then configure it using the appropriate configuration directives. Here's how:

1. SSL and TLS support can be added to Apache by installing the mod_ssl package:

```
# apt-get install libapache-mod-ssl
# apache-modconf apache enable mod_ssl
Replacing config file /etc/apache/modules.conf with new version
```

2. Add an SSL-enabled virtual host to your Apache configuration files. Using the earlier virtual host as an example, your configuration will look something like this:

```
Listen *:443
<VirtualHost *:443>
    ServerName      secure.example.org
```

```
        DocumentRoot      /home/username/public_html/
        User              username
        Group             groupname
        DirectoryIndex    index.php index.html index.htm
        SSLEngine         On
        SSLCertificateKeyFile /etc/apache/ssl.key/server.key
        SSLCertificateFile /etc/apache/ssl.crt/server.crt
        SSLCACertificateFile /etc/apache/ssl.crt/ca.crt
</VirtualHost>
```

This example uses a wildcard for the IP address in the `VirtualHost` declaration, which saves you from having to modify your configuration file in the event that your IP address changes but also prevents you from having multiple SSL virtual hosts. In the event that you do need to support more than one SSL virtual host, replace * with the specific IP address that you assign to that host.

> **NOTE**   See the "Troubleshooting" section earlier in the chapter for more information about the `Listen` **directive.**

A CA generally provides you with a certificate file to place in `ca.crt` and sometimes also provides you with a separate file that you will need to reference using a `SSLCertificateChainFile` directive. The mod_ssl package also includes `/etc/apache/ssl.crt/ca-bundle.crt`, which contains the certificates from most of the well-known certificate authorities and can be referenced as long as the appropriate CA certificate is included. When running your own CA, point this directive to a file containing the public key from that CA. Omit this line when using a self-signed certificate.

3. Test the Apache configuration and then perform a full restart:

```
# apachectl configtest
Syntax OK.
# apachectl stop
# apachectl start
```

4. Browse to `https://servername/` and verify the SSL configuration. When using a self-signed certificate, or one signed by a CA, you are asked whether you want to accept the certificate.

> **NOTE**   Another option is the LAMPP project (`www.xampp.org`), which is an all-in-one LAMP server with PERL support. It is a really good quick-and-dirty way to get a LAMPP server running. It is also good for testing pages before publishing when you have only one machine.

Summary

Combining Linux with an Apache Web server, MySQL database, and PHP scripting content (referred to as a LAMP server) makes it possible for you to configure your own full-featured Web server. The instructions in this chapter shows you how to set up Apache to do virtual hosting, add content to a MySQL database, and allow PHP scripting in the content on your server. For added security, this chapter describes how to add your own certificates and troubleshoot problems that might arise with your server.

Chapter 25

Running a Mail Server

E lectronic mail hardly requires an introduction. Communications made through the original forms of e-mail helped shape the Internet. Widespread availability of access to e-mail and enhancements such as MIME (Multipurpose Internet Mail Extensions, which allow for inclusion of attachments and alternate message formats) have helped to make e-mail the most popular application on the Internet.

With a Linux system and a suitable Internet connection, you can easily set up your own mail server for personal or business use. This chapter includes a description of how Internet mail works at the protocol level, and then guides you through the process of setting up a mail server, complete with spam and virus filtering. In the final section, you learn how to secure network communications between clients and your mail server through the use of SSL/TLS (Secure Sockets Layer and Transport Layer Security) protocols.

The examples in this chapter are based on a Debian GNU/Linux system. (See Chapter 9 for more information about Debian.) However, much of the knowledge you gain from setting up a mail server in Debian applies to other Linux systems as well.

Internet E-Mail's Inner Workings

E-mail messages are generated either by an automated process, such as a form processor on a Web page or an automated notification system, or by an MUA (mail user agent) controlled by an end user. Messages are delivered through one of two methods to the software performing the MTA (mail transfer agent) function on a server:

- **SMTP** — The Simple Mail Transfer Protocol is a network-based protocol that allows for transmission of messages between systems.

- **Local IPC** — Inter-process communications are often used instead of SMTP when transferring a message between programs within a system.

Upon receiving a message, the MTA places it in a queue to be processed by an MDA (mail delivery agent). Mail delivery agents come in two varieties:

- **Local MDAs** — Deliver messages to mailboxes on the local server. Simple versions copy messages directly to a specified mailbox, while complex implementations can alter messages or delivery parameters based on user-specified rules.

- **Remote MDAs** — Deliver messages over the network to remote servers. Full remote MDAs use DNS (the Domain Name System) to determine the mail exchanger hosts for recipient addresses and deliver to the best one available for each. Simple remote MDAs (sometimes called "null clients") forward messages to a central server to continue the delivery process. Most remote MDAs are capable of either method and will act as configured by the administrator that performed the configuration.

NOTE   You will often see the term MTA used in reference to the software that performs both MTA and MDA functions. This is a carry-over from older designs that did not separate the functions and is still fairly accurate given the fact that most mail server implementations include a minimum of an MTA, remote MDA, and basic local MDA.

When a message reaches its destination server, it is written to the user's mailbox by the local MDA. From that point, the message may be viewed by the user using one of three methods:

- **Direct access to the mailbox** — An MUA (mail user agent) with access to the mailbox file, directly or through a network file system, can read messages from the disk and display them for the user. This is generally a console or Web mail application running on the server.

- **Downloaded to a workstation for local viewing** — Most mail users use POP3 (Post Office Protocol, version 3) to download messages to their local computers and view them in applications such as Evolution or Balsa. By default, messages are removed from the server during this process (similar to when you get your "snail mail" from the mailbox).

- **Accessed interactively over the network** — Most clients also support viewing messages while they are still on the server, through IMAP (Internet Message Access Protocol). Unlike POP3, this protocol enables users to access multiple folders on their servers and also allows them to access their messages from anywhere. However, this also creates a heavier burden on the server because it must process (and store) everything that the user decides to keep. Most Web mail applications use IMAP as their backend protocol for accessing mailboxes; this eliminates the need for direct access to the mail files and makes it easier to split functions between systems.

About the System and the Software Used

The mail server configuration described in this chapter is based on the Exim mail transfer agent. Along with Exim, several other components are added for managing the server and checking e-mail contents for spam and viruses:

- **Exim** (`www.exim.org/`) — An MTA written and designed by Philip Hazel at the University of Cambridge, with contributions from many people around the world. The version referred to in this chapter includes the Exiscan-ACL patch (`http://duncanthrax.net/exiscan-acl/`) from Tom Kistner. This patch allows content scanning from within Exim. Because this patch is integrated with Exim, its features are considered part of Exim for the purposes of this chapter.

- **Maildrop** (`www.courier-mta.org/maildrop/`) — A local MDA that is part of the Courier MTA package, but is also available as a standalone program. It is used in this configuration to allow the use of advanced features, such as mailbox quotas and server-side message sorting.

- **Courier IMAP** and **POP** (`www.courier-mta.org/imap/`) — Like Maildrop, these are parts of the Courier MTA that are also available separately. They were chosen for their easy installation, good performance, and compatibility with the Maildir-format mail directories.

- **ClamAV** (`www.clamav.net`) — An open source virus scanner that detects more than 20,000 viruses, worms, and Trojans. It uses a virus pattern database to identify viruses and includes a program named freshclam that handles updating the database automatically. Like SpamAssassin, ClamAV includes a daemon (clamd), a client (clamdscan), and a second command-line tool that does not use the daemon (clamscan).

- **SpamAssassin** (`http://spamassassin.apache.org/`) — A spam-filtering program written in Perl. It uses a large set of rules to help determine how "spammy" a message looks and assigns a score based on the total of the rule values. For performance reasons, SpamAssassin uses a background daemon called spamd to perform message analysis. Access to this daemon is performed through the spamc client. A `spamassassin` command that performs the analysis without using spamd is also installed but is not used by either of the example configurations in this chapter.

Preparing Your System

You will need a few common items for the mail server configuration covered in this chapter, starting with the proper hardware. A personal mail server can easily run on a Pentium-class computer, although you may notice occasional slowdowns while incoming messages are being scanned. Disk space requirements depend mostly on how much mail you want to have room for, so plan on having a few gigabytes for the operating system (which will leave you plenty of extra, just in case), plus the amount of mail you want to store.

The operating system should be installed with only the basic set of packages before you begin these examples. Some general information about the installation is provided in Chapter 9. Although the software described in this chapter works even if you aren't running Debian, the installation methods will not. If you don't have a spare system to act as a dedicated mail server, you can still use it as your workstation, although this is obviously recommended only for personal use.

Your network settings should also be properly configured before you begin installing the mail software. The exact requirements depend on the method by which mail will be delivered to your server:

- **Direct delivery** is the method used by most traditional mail servers. DNS records tell remote servers that any mail addressed to your domain should be sent to your server via SMTP.

- **Retrieval from a mail host** is also possible using an MRA (mail retrieval agent) such as Fetchmail. This option can be used when you have a mailbox under a shared domain but want to access the mail on your own server. This can also be done in combination with direct delivery if you have both your own domain and mailboxes under shared domains.

 Configuration of Fetchmail is explained in the "Configuring Mail Clients" section of this chapter.

Configuring DNS for Direct Delivery

For direct delivery to function, the SMTP service (TCP port 25) must be accessible to the outside world through a fixed name in DNS. This name will be in the form of an A (Address) record. A records allow DNS resolver processes to determine the IP address associated with a specific name and are used by most of the common protocols on the Internet. A typical DNS A record looks something like this:

```
bigserver.example.org    IN    A    10.0.12.16
```

The first parameter, bigserver.example.org, is the label, and the second parameter is the class (IN for Internet, which is where most DNS records are found). The A indicates the type, and the final parameter is the IP address associated with the label.

Once you have your A record, you can direct mail to your server using an MX (Mail eXchanger) record. The A and MX records do not need to be part of the same domain, which allows for much greater flexibility. Here is a sample MX record:

```
widgets.test.    IN    MX    0    bigserver.example.org.
```

This MX record indicates that mail for any address@widgets.test should be sent through the server bigserver.example.org. The 0 indicates the numeric priority for this MX record. When more than one MX record exists for a given label, the MX with the lowest priority is tried first. If a temporary error is encountered, the next highest priority mail server is tried, and so on until the list is exhausted. At that point, the sending server will keep trying periodically until the message times out (generally five days). If multiple MX records exist with the same priority, they are tried in a random order.

 **Most mail servers will also fall back on the IP address listed in the A record for a label in the event that no MX records exist. However, it is considered bad practice to rely on this.**

In some cases, it may be complicated to establish an A record because your IP address frequently changes. Obviously, this is not suitable for commercial purposes, but there is a workaround that is acceptably reliable for personal use. This is achieved through dynamic DNS services that are available (often at no charge) through a number of different companies. A list of these companies is maintained at `http://dmoz.org/Computers/Software/Internet/Servers/Address_Management/Dynamic_DNS_Services/`. Two of the most popular are:

- **ZoneEdit** (`www.zonedit.com/`) — Supported by the ez-ipupdate package.
- **No-IP** (`www.no-ip.com/`) — Supported by the no-ip package.

 **The ez-ipupdate package supports both of these, plus a number of others. View the package description (`apt-cache show ez-ipupdate`) for more information.**

Most of these services will provide you with a hostname under a shared domain at no charge and can also provide a similar service for your own domain for a reasonable fee.

Configuring for Retrieval from a Mail Host

The configuration requirements when retrieving mail from a mail host are pretty limited. Your server should be ready to accept mail addressed to `localhost` and should generally have a name that is unique to it. In the event that a message sent to one of your mailboxes is rejected, the server will need to have a valid host name by which to identify itself when sending out the DSN (Delivery Status Notification).

You must be able to access the server from clients, although you may need to do so only from clients within your network. In either case, you should be familiar with the information about DNS and A records in the previous section.

Installing and Configuring the Mail Server Software

Once you have finished with the prerequisites, you will be ready to begin the software installation. The software installation and configuration have been divided into two sections. The first section covers the installation of Exim and Courier. The second section covers the installation of ClamAV and SpamAssassin and configuring Exim to use them to filter incoming mail.

Installing Exim and Courier

Installing and configuring Exim and Courier are very straightforward thanks to the quality of the packages that come with Debian. Chances are, if you have a new Debian system, it already has a version of Exim installed. However, you'll want to use a specific version of Exim that contains features for content scanning. Here are the installation steps:

1. Start by installing this particular Exim package:

    ```
    # apt-get install exim4-daemon-heavy
    ```

2. You need to change a few of the configuration options from the defaults. Run the following command:

    ```
    # dpkg-reconfigure --priority=medium exim4-config
    ```

    You are asked a number of questions. Here's how to answer them:

    - **Split configuration into small files:** Yes.
    - **General type:** Select "Mail sent by smarthost; received via SMTP or fetchmail" if you need to send all of your outgoing mail through a server at your Internet service provider. Otherwise, select "Internet site; mail is sent and received directly using SMTP."
    - **Mail name:** Enter the name of your mail server here.
    - **IP addresses:** Clear this box (or leave it empty if it is already so) so that Exim will listen on all local IP addresses.
    - **Destinations to accept mail for:** Enter any domains that your server will be accepting mail for. Be sure to separate them with colons, and not commas or spaces.
    - **Domains to relay for:** Enter the names of any domains that your machine will relay mail for, meaning that it can receive mail from them but then passes it on. In most cases, you will not want to enter anything here.
    - **Machines to relay for:** Enter the IP address ranges of any client machines that you want your server to accept mail from. Another (safer) option is to leave this empty and require clients to authenticate using SMTP authentication. SMTP authentication is best performed over an encrypted connection, so this process is described in the security section at the end of this chapter.
    - **Keep DNS queries to a minimum:** No.

3. This configuration uses Maildrop for local mail delivery. Maildrop can deliver messages to the Maildir-style folders that Courier is expecting, and can also handle basic sorting and filtering (as described in the "Configuring Mail Clients" section). This package is not installed by default, so install it as follows:

    ```
    # apt-get install maildrop
    ```

4. Create Maildir mail directories for every user already on the system. This step must be performed for every user that is already on the system, and must be run as the user because running this command as root will result in Maildrop being unable to write to the folders:

```
$ maildirmake.maildrop $HOME/Maildir
$ maildirmake.maildrop -f Trash $HOME/Maildir
```

5. Create mail directories under /etc/skel. The contents of /etc/skel will be copied to the home directories of any new accounts that you create after the setup is completed:

```
# maildirmake.maildrop /etc/skel/Maildir
# maildirmake.maildrop -f Trash /etc/skel/Maildir
```

6. Configure Maildrop to deliver to the Maildir folders instead of mbox files stored in /var/spool/mail. Use your favorite text editor to edit /etc/maildroprc and add this line at the end of the file:

```
DEFAULT="$HOME/Maildir/"
```

7. Exim needs to be configured to deliver messages using Maildrop. Use your preferred text editor to open /etc/exim4/update-exim4.conf.conf and add the following line at the end of the file:

```
dc_localdelivery='maildrop_pipe'
```

8. Tell Exim to load the most recent configuration change:

```
# invoke-rc.d exim4 reload
```

9. Install Courier IMAP and Courier POP:

```
# apt-get install courier-imap courier-pop
```

Select "no" when asked whether or not the installer should create directories for Web-based administration.

Your system should now be capable of receiving messages. You should also be able to connect to your server using a mail client such as Thunderbird or Evolution. This is a good time to test mail delivery, even if you're planning to follow the directions in the next section to enable virus and spam filters later. More information about configuring a mail client to connect to your server can be found in the section "Configuring Mail Clients" later in this chapter.

Installing ClamAV and SpamAssassin

Installing and configuring the virus and spam filtering mechanisms is more involved than installing Exim and Courier, but should still go smoothly as long as you follow the steps carefully. Keep in mind, however, that this will add a lot of complexity to the system, so it is a good idea to make sure the Exim mail server is working first so that you don't have as many things to check if the system doesn't work as expected.

> **NOTE**   The version of ClamAV included with Debian starting with version 3.1 (aka "Sarge") uses an older virus-scanning engine. Because the updated engine is not likely to make it into an update any time soon because of the Debian upgrade policies, a group of Debian developers has created special sets of the ClamAV packages that are designed for easy installation on Sarge. For more information about how to use these packages instead of the stock versions, see `http://volatile .debian.net/`. You may choose to do this from the start, or to add the appropriate URIs to your APT configuration later and do an upgrade. In either case, the configuration process detailed in this section will be about the same. You can also upgrade the database routinely using `clamav-freshclam`, `clamav-getfiles` to generate new `clamav-data` packages.

Here's how to install ClamAV and SpamAssassin, and then configure Exim to use them for scanning messages:

1. Install the ClamAV and SpamAssassin packages:

    ```
    # apt-get install clamav-daemon clamav-testfiles \
      spamassassin spamc
    ```

    You'll be asked a number of questions about how ClamAV should be configured. Here's how to answer them:

    - **Virus update method** — This is the method that freshclam (part of ClamAV) will use to download updated virus databases. The recommended option is to run freshclam as a daemon.

    - **Local database mirror site** — This is the site that freshclam will retrieve the virus information updates from. The second part of the site is the two-letter country code. Select your country code or that of a nearby country if yours isn't available.

    - **HTTP proxy information** — Do not enter anything here unless you are required to use a proxy server to access Web servers. If your connection is suitable for running a mail server, then you probably don't need to use a proxy server.

    - **Notify clamd after updates** — Select "yes" here.

2. Add the clamav user to the Debian-exim group and restart the ClamAV daemon. This allows the ClamAV daemon access to read the files in Exim's mail queue:

    ```
    # gpasswd -a clamav Debian-exim
    # invoke-rc.d clamav-daemon restart
    ```

3. Replace the report template used by SpamAssassin with one that will fit more easily in a message header. Use a text editor to add these lines to the end of /etc/spamassassin/local.cf:

```
clear_report_template
report _YESNO_, score=_SCORE_, required=_REQD_, summary=
report _SUMMARY_
```

4. Configure the SpamAssassin background daemon to run automatically and to not attempt to create preference files for users. Change the following options in /etc/default/spamassassin:

```
ENABLED=1
OPTIONS="--max-children 5"
```

5. Start the SpamAssassin daemon:

```
# invoke-rc.d spamassassin start
```

6. Create the entries that will be included in Exim's ACL (Access Control List) for scanning message data. Use a text editor to create a file named /etc/exim4/acl_check_data_local that contains the following:

```
deny message = $malware_name detected in message
     demime = *
     malware = *
warn message = X-Spam-Score: $spam_score ($spam_bar)
     condition = ${if <{$message_size}{80k}{1}{0}}
     spam = nobody:true/defer_ok
warn message = X-Spam-Status: $spam_report
     condition = ${if <{$message_size}{80k}{1}{0}}
     spam = nobody:true/defer_ok
deny message = Spam score too high ($spam_score)
     condition = ${if <{$message_size}{80k}{1}{0}}
     spam = nobody:true/defer_ok
     condition = ${if >{$spam_score_int}{120}{1}{0}}
```

The first block rejects messages that contain viruses or other malware, and the second and third add headers to messages indicating whether or not SpamAssassin considers them spam. The final block checks $spam_score_int (the spam score multiplied by 10) and rejects the message if it is greater than 120.

The /defer_ok in the last three blocks tells Exim that it is okay to continue processing in the event that the SpamAssassin daemon could not be contacted. You can remove it if you would prefer to have the server return a temporary failure code in such cases. You can also add /defer_ok to the end of the malware = * line if you want processing to continue in the event that a message cannot be scanned by ClamAV.

7. Tell Exim which virus scanner to use and how to connect to SpamAssassin. Use a text editor to create a file named `/etc/exim4/conf.d/main/10_exim4-exiscan_acl_options` that contains the following:

```
av_scanner = clamd:/var/run/clamav/clamd.ctl
spamd_address = 127.0.0.1 783
CHECK_DATA_LOCAL_ACL_FILE = CONFDIR/acl_check_data_local
```

8. Tell Exim to load the new configuration:

```
# invoke-rc.d exim4 reload
```

All messages transmitted through your server should now be checked for viruses using ClamAV. Additionally, messages less than 80 kilobytes will also be checked using SpamAssassin. This is a good time to test the configuration again. Fixes for the problems that you are most likely to encounter can be found in the next section.

Testing and Troubleshooting

This section contains some generic troubleshooting tips, plus specific information about some common errors and how to fix them.

Checking Logs

All logging information for Exim is written to three log files that can be found in `/var/log/exim4`. The first of these, `mainlog`, contains log entries for all events, including normal events such as message deliveries. The second, `rejectlog`, contains entries for rejected messages. The third, `paniclog`, contains information about configuration or other errors, and is usually empty unless a serious problem has occurred. Every entry in these files generally starts with a timestamp.

Entries in the `mainlog` will often include a string of 15 characters, such as `1E9PTu-0003jN-QY`. This is the message identifier for the message that the log entry is related to. Immediately after the message identifier there will generally be a two-character string. Table 25-1 details what those strings mean.

Entries associated with a message that has not been accepted into the queue will not have the message identifier or two-character flags. Some samples of these types of entries are included in the next section.

Logging information for the Courier IMAP and POP daemons is saved to `/var/log/mail.log`. Normal entries include `LOGIN` and `LOGOUT` messages. `DISCONNECTED` messages generally indicate that a connection was broken before a normal logout was performed.

TABLE 25-1

Exim Log File Messages

Symbol	Description	Explanation
<=	Message arrival	These entries show messages coming into Exim, generally through SMTP or local IPC.
=>	Message delivery	These entries show message deliveries, whether they are to a local mailbox or to a remote host using SMTP or some other transport.
->	Additional addresses in message delivery	These entries show delivery to additional addresses for messages that have already been delivered to another recipient (and logged with an => entry).
**	Delivery failure	These entries show permanent delivery errors. Errors such as these indicate that the message has been removed from the mail queue and in most cases a DSN (Delivery Status Notification) has been generated and sent to the original message sender.
==	Delivery deferral	These entries show temporary delivery problems. The system will continue to retry sending these until delivery succeeds, or a permanent failure occurs as a result of a retry timeout.

NOTE The tail utility is useful for watching for new entries to a log. Use the -f switch to instruct tail to watch for new entries and display them to the screen as they are written to the log. For example: `tail -f /var/log/exim4/mainlog`.

Common Errors (and How to Fix Them)

There are two common types of problems that you will encounter with your server: messages being rejected or not delivered by Exim and login failures when connecting to Courier.

Messages Rejected by Exim

The first places to check when messages are rejected by Exim are the `mainlog` and `rejectlog` files. Here are examples of some common errors and tips for fixing them:

- **Relaying Denied** — The following error indicates that the client sending the message is not recognized as a client by Exim and that the recipient domain is not in the list of local or relay domains:

```
H=sample.client [10.0.12.16] F=<sender@example.org> rejected
RCPT <rcpt@remotesite.example.org>: relay not permitted
```

If the client IP address will not change frequently or is in part of a trusted range of IP addresses, you can add them by running the following:

```
# dpkg-reconfigure --priority=medium exim4-config
```

The same command can also be used to add the recipient domain as a local or relay domain.

CAUTION Do not add client IP ranges unless you trust all of the users that can connect from those addresses. Likewise, do not add a domain as a relay domain unless you know the owner of the domain and have made arrangements to relay mail for them. Doing either of these incorrectly could open your server up as a relay that can be used by spammers to attack other sites.

If the client IP address is likely to change frequently and is not part of a trusted range, you should either configure the client to use a mail server that is local to it or configure SMTP authentication in Exim. More information about enabling SMTP authentication can be found on your server in `/usr/share/doc/exim4-base/README.SMTP-AUTH` and `/etc/exim4/conf.d/auth/30_exim4-config_examples`.

NOTE The Courier authdaemon examples in `30_exim4-config_examples` can be enabled, allowing Exim to use that facility for authentication and negating the need to set up a different mechanism. In order for it to work, however, you will need to add the Debian-exim user to the daemon group (`gpasswd -a Debian-exim daemon`) and restart Exim.

- **ClamAV Misconfiguration** — The following error indicates that the ClamAV daemon could not read the temporary message file:

```
1E9PDq-0003Lo-BY malware acl condition: clamd: ClamAV
returned /var/spool/exim4/scan/1E9PDq-0003Lo-BY:
  Access denied. ERROR
```

Make sure you added clamav to the Debian-exim group and restarted ClamAV, as shown in the installation section.

- **ClamAV Unavailable** — This error usually indicates that the ClamAV daemon is not running:

```
1E9PGL-0003MX-38 malware acl condition: clamd: unable to
connect to UNIX socket /var/run/clamav/clamd.ctl
    (No such file or directory)
```

Start it using `invoke-rc.d clamav-daemon start`. You can also use the clamdscan program to test the daemon, as follows:

```
# clamdscan /usr/share/clamav-testfiles/clam.exe
/usr/share/clamav-testfiles/clam.exe: ClamAV-Test-File FOUND
----------- SCAN SUMMARY -----------
Infected files: 1
Time: 0.001 sec (0 m 0 s)
```

Messages Not Delivered by Exim

In some cases, messages will be accepted by the server but will not be deliverable. Some of these errors are considered temporary failures and will not generate a bounced message until the retry timer runs out. The error that you are most likely to see will look something like this in the mainlog file:

```
1E9PTu-0003jN-QY == user@example.org R=local_user T=maildrop_pipe defer (0):
Child process of maildrop_pipe transport returned 75 (could mean temporary
error) from command: /usr/bin/maildrop
```

This error indicates that Exim attempted to pass the message to Maildrop, but Maildrop returned an error code. The most likely cause is a missing Maildir directory, or a Maildir directory that is owned by the wrong user. The next section shows how to detect and fix these problems.

Login Failures When Connecting to Courier

Aside from genuine password errors (which can be remedied by entering the correct password in the mail client), there are also a few other conditions that can result in login failures. Some of these conditions will also result in temporary delivery problems. A normal login failure will result in a log entry that looks similar to this:

```
courierpop3login: LOGIN FAILED, ip-[::ffff:1.2.3.4]
```

In this case, a user from IP 1.2.3.4 entered the wrong username or password.

Several of the other errors that may occur will not be logged to the mail log, which means that you may have to test them by connecting manually to the POP3 service (from the mail server, or from a remote machine) and sending a valid username and password. This example shows how to connect to the POP3 service from a shell prompt on the mail server:

```
$ telnet localhost 110
Trying 127.0.0.1...
Connected to localhost.localdomain.
Escape character is '^]'.
+OK Hello there.
USER username
+OK Password required.
PASS password
```

The response you receive from the server should be similar to one of the following:

- **+OK logged in** — This is a normal response and should mean that there are no problems with the service.

- **-ERR Maildir: No such file or directory** — This error indicates that the user's account does not have a Maildir directory. Use the `maildirmake` command to create it, as shown in the section "Installing Exim and Courier."

- **-ERR Maildir: Permission denied** — This error indicates that the user's Maildir directory cannot be read or belongs to the wrong user. To remedy this, run this command as root:

```
# chown -R username:groupname ~username/Maildir
```

Be sure to replace *username* and *groupname* with the login name and primary group of the user. In a stock Debian system, the primary group name will be the same as the username.

- **-ERR Login failed** — If you're certain that you are using the correct username and password, it could be that the Courier authdaemon service is not running. Try to start (or restart) it using this command:

```
# invoke-rc.d courier-authdaemon restart
```

Configuring Mail Clients

Any mail client with support for POP3 or IMAP should be able to access mail from your server. Just use the name of your server in the mail server settings, and follow the troubleshooting steps in the previous section if something doesn't work.

CROSS-REF   You can find more information about mail clients for Linux in Chapter 22.

Configuring Fetchmail

Fetchmail is an MRA (mail retrieval agent) that you can use to pull mail from a remote account to your new server. It is configured in the `$HOME/.fetchmailrc` file and is very easy to set up. To pull mail to your server, log in as the user that the mail should go to, and then configure and run it from there.

NOTE   Run Fetchmail as the user for whom the mail is being retrieved. You should never run it as root. If you're doing a complex setup in which you retrieve mail from a single mailbox that needs to be sorted for multiple users, see the fetchmail man page for information about multidrop mailboxes.

A `.fetchmailrc` file can be as simple as this:

```
poll mailserver.yourisp.example protocol pop3 username "foo"
```

If you have more than one mail server, you can add it as an additional line. If the server from which you are pulling mail supports IMAP, you can use `imap` instead of `pop3`. Other options that you can have are `password=your password` and `ssl`. Storing the password in the file enables you to run Fetchmail without entering a password, and the `ssl` option tells Fetchmail to use an SSL/TLS connection to the server.

> **NOTE** Your `.fetchmailrc` file should not be readable by others, and Fetchmail will generally complain if it is. To set the permissions so that only you can read it, run `chmod 0600 $HOME/.fetchmailrc/`.

Running Fetchmail is as simple as typing

```
$ fetchmail
```

If you want to have Fetchmail run in the background, you can use the `--daemon` (or `-d`) flag with a parameter telling it how often (in seconds) to poll the servers:

```
$ fetchmail --daemon 300
```

To have Fetchmail automatically start when the system boots, add this to your `crontab` file:

```
@reboot    /usr/bin/fetchmail --daemon 300
```

> **NOTE** Fetchmail cannot prompt for passwords when run in this manner, which means that you must store the passwords in `.fetchmailrc` for this to work.

If you haven't configured a `crontab` file before, setting it up can be as easy as entering the following three commands:

```
$ cat > mycron
@reboot    /usr/bin/fetchmail --daemon 300
<Ctrl+D>
$ crontab mycron
```

Configuring Web-Based Mail

If you're running an IMAP server, you can offer Web-based access by installing SquirrelMail (`http://squirrelmail.org/`, also found in the squirrelmail package). Start by configuring your system as a LAMP server (see Chapter 24), and then install and configure the appropriate package.

Securing Communications with SSL/TLS

Because communication between mail clients and the server often contains sensitive information such as passwords, it is usually desirable to enable SSL/TLS encryption. Here's how to enable SSL/TLS in Exim and Courier:

1. Install the Courier daemons with SSL/TLS support:

```
# apt-get install courier-imap-ssl courier-pop-ssl
```

2. Third-party CA certificates are provided on the ca-certificates package. This will be referenced in the configuration, so install it, too:

```
# apt-get install ca-certificates
```

Debconf asks you whether you want to trust the CA certificates by default. In most cases, you want to select Yes.

3. If you are going to be using a certificate from a CA that is not already recognized (this is generally only true if you are running your own CA), place the CA public certificate in its own file in /etc/ssl/certs/ and update the certificate database:

```
# update-ca-certificates
```

4. Generate the private key and certificate signing request, as described in Chapter 24. The best location for these files is in /etc/ssl/private/. Here's an example:

```
# cd /etc/exim4
# openssl genrsa -out mail.key 1024
# chmod 640 mail.key
# openssl req -new -key mail.key -out mail.csr
# chown root:Debian-exim mail.key
```

5. Get your CSR (Certificate Signing Request) signed and place the certificate in /etc/mail/private/mail.crt. Or, to use a self-signed certificate, do the following:

```
# cd /etc/exim4
# openssl req -new -x509 -nodes -sha1 \
  -days 365 -key mail.key -out mail.crt
# chmod 640 mail.crt
# chown root:Debian-exim mail.crt
```

CAUTION Some remote servers will refuse to send messages to your server if your certificate is not signed by a CA that they recognize. Also, make sure the common name (cn) attribute on your certificate matches the name of the server in DNS.

6. Concatenate the private key and certificate into a single file for Courier:

```
# cd /etc/courier
# cat /etc/exim4/mail.key /etc/exim4/mail.crt > mail.pem
# chmod 600 mail.pem
```

7. Enable SSL/TLS in the Courier IMAP and POP daemons by editing both /etc/courier/imapd-ssl and /etc/courier/pop3d-ssl, and by replacing the values for TLS_CERTFILE and TLS_TRUSTCERTS with the following:

```
TLS_CERTFILE=/etc/courier/mail.pem
TLS_TRUSTCERTS=/etc/ssl/certs/ca-certificates.pem
```

8. Tell Exim where it can find the private key and certificate, and enable TLS. Create a file named `/etc/exim4/conf.d/main/12_exim4-config_local_tlsoptions` containing the following:

```
MAIN_TLS_CERTIFICATE = CONFDIR/mail.crt
MAIN_TLS_PRIVATEKEY = CONFDIR/mail.key
MAIN_TLS_ENABLE = 1
```

9. Restart Exim:

```
# invoke-rc.d exim4 restart
```

Your server should now support SSL/TLS when communicating with SMTP, POP, and IMAP clients.

Summary

Using Linux and a good Internet connection, you can set up and maintain your own mail server. Preparing your computer to become a mail server includes configuring your network connection, setting up delivery and retrieval methods, and adding required software packages.

This chapter describes how to install, configure, and troubleshoot the Exim MTA. Exim can be used in tandem with spam filtering software (such as SpamAssassin) and virus scanning software (such as ClamAV). Methods for securing your mail server include configuring support for SSL/TLS encryption.

Chapter 26

Running a Print Server

Sharing printers is a good way to save money and make your printing more efficient. Very few people need to print all the time, but when they do want to print something, they usually need it quickly. Setting up a print server can save money by eliminating the need for a printer at every workstation. Some of those savings can be used to buy printers that can output more pages per minute or have higher-quality output.

You can attach printers to your Linux system to make them available to users of that system (standalone printing) or to other computers on the network as a shared printer. You can also configure your Linux printer as a remote CUPS or Samba printer. With Samba, you are emulating Windows printing services, which is pretty useful given the abundance of Windows client systems.

This chapter describes configuring and using printers on Linux systems with various desktop environments in use. Some of the details may vary from one distribution to another, but the information included here should work well for the more commonly used distributions. This chapter focuses on the Common UNIX Printing Service (CUPS), which is the recommended print service for the majority of Linux installations. Examples in this chapter use the Printer Configuration options in the GNOME and K Desktop environments.

Once a local printer is configured, print commands such as lpr are available for carrying out the actual printing. Commands also exist for querying print queues (lpq), manipulating print queues (lpc), and removing print queues (lprm). A local printer can also be shared as a print server for users on other computers on your network.

Common UNIX Printing Service

CUPS has become the standard for printing from Linux and other UNIX-like operating systems. It was designed to meet today's needs for standardized printer definitions and sharing on IP-based networks (as most computer networks are today). Nearly every Linux distribution today comes with CUPS as its printing service. Here are some of the service's features:

- **IPP** — CUPS is based on the Internet Printing Protocol (www.pwg.org/ipp), a standard that was created to simplify how printers can be shared over IP networks. In the IPP model, printer servers and clients who want to print can exchange information about the model and features of a printer using HTTP (that is, Web content) protocol. A server can also broadcast the availability of a printer so a printing client can easily find a list of locally available printers.

- **Drivers** — CUPS also standardized how printer drivers are created. The idea was to have a common format that could be used by printer manufacturers so that a driver could work across all different types of UNIX systems. That way, a manufacturer had to create the driver only once to work for Linux, Mac OS X, and a variety of UNIX derivatives.

- **Printer classes** — You can use printer classes to create multiple print server entries that point to the same printer or one print server entry that points to multiple printers. In the first case, multiple entries can each allow different options (such as pointing to a particular paper tray or printing with certain character sizes or margins). In the second case, you can have a pool of printers so that printing is distributed, decreasing the occurrence of congested print queues often caused by a malfunctioning printer or a printer that is dealing with very large documents.

- **UNIX print commands** — To integrate into Linux and other UNIX environments, CUPS offers versions of standard commands for printing and managing printers that have been traditionally offered with UNIX systems.

Many Linux distributions come with simplified methods of configuring CUPS printers. Here are a few examples:

- In Fedora and other Red Hat Linux systems, the Printer Configuration window (system-config-printer command) enables you to configure printers that use the CUPS facility.

- In Ubuntu, select System ➪ Administration ➪ Printing to open the Printers window that lets you add, delete, and manage printers.

- In SUSE, the YaST facility includes a printer configuration module. From the YaST Control Center, select Hardware ➪ Printer.

For distributions that don't have their own printer configuration tools, you can configure CUPS in several ways, using tools that aren't specific to a Linux distribution. Here are a couple of ways:

- **Configuring CUPS from a browser** — CUPS offers a Web-based interface for adding and managing printers. You can access this service by typing **localhost:631** from a Web browser on the computer running the CUPS service. (See the section "Using Web-Based CUPS Administration," later in this chapter.) The KDE desktop comes with a tool for managing CUPS server features. To launch the KDE CUPS Server Configuration window, type **/usr/bin/cupsdconf** from a Terminal window.

■ **Configuring CUPS manually** — You also can configure CUPS manually (that is, edit the configuration files and start the cupsd daemon manually). Configuration files for CUPS are contained in the /etc/cups directory. In particular, you might be interested in the cupsd.conf file, which identifies permission, authentication, and other information for the printer daemon, and printers.conf, which identifies addresses and options for configured printers. Use the classes.conf file to define local printer classes.

> **COMING FROM WINDOWS** You can print to CUPS from non-UNIX systems as well. For example, you can use a PostScript printer driver to print directly from Windows XP to your CUPS server. You can use CUPS without modification by configuring the XP computer with a PostScript driver that uses http://printservername:631printers/targetPrinter as its printing port.

To use CUPS, you need to have it installed. Most Linux distributions let you choose to add CUPS during the initial system install or will simply add CUPS by default. If CUPS was not added when you first installed your Linux distribution, check your original installation medium (DVD or CD) to see if it is there for you to install now. Fedora, Slackware, Ubuntu, SUSE, and many other Linux distributions have CUPS on the first CD or DVD of their installation sets.

Setting Up Printers

While it is usually best to use the printer administration tools specifically built for your distribution, many Linux systems simply rely on the tools that come with the CUPS software package. This section explores how to use CUPS Web-based administration tools that come with every Linux distribution and then examines the printer configuration tool system-config-printer, which comes with Fedora and Red Hat Enterprise Linux systems to enable you to set up printers.

Using Web-Based CUPS Administration

CUPS offers its own Web-based administrative tool for adding, deleting, and modifying printer configurations on your computer. The CUPS print service (using the cupsd daemon) listens on port 631 to provide access to the CUPS Web-based administrative interface.

If CUPS is already running on your computer, you can immediately use CUPS Web-based administration from your Web browser. To see if CUPS is running and start setting up your printers, open a Web browser on the local computer and type the following into its location box:

```
http://localhost:631/admin
```

A prompt for a valid login name and password may appear. If so, type the root login name and the root user's password, and then click OK. A screen similar to the one shown in Figure 26-1 appears.

FIGURE 26-1

CUPS provides a Web-based administration tool.

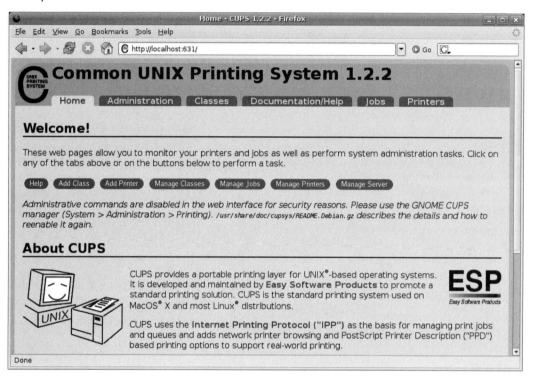

By default, Web-based CUPS administration is available only from the local host. To access Web-based CUPS administration from another computer, you must change the /admin section in the /etc/cups/cupsd.conf file. As recommended in the text of this file, you should limit access to CUPS administration from the Web. The following example includes an Allow line to permit access from a host at IP address 10.0.0.5. (You must also change the Listen 127.0.0.1:631 line to listen outside your local host, as described a bit later.)

```
<Location /admin>
AuthType Basic
AuthClass System
Order Deny, Allow
Deny from All
Allow From 127.0.0.1
Allow From 10.0.0.5
</Location>
```

From the computer at address 10.0.0.5, you would type the following (substituting the CUPS server's name or IP address for *localhost*):

    http://localhost:631/admin

When prompted, enter the root username and password.

Now, with the Admin screen displayed, here's how to set up a printer:

1. Click the Add Printer button. The Add New Printer screen appears.

2. Type a Name, Location, and Description for the printer and click Continue.

3. Select the device to which the printer is connected. The printer can be connected locally to a parallel, SCSI, serial, or USB port directly on the computer. Alternatively, you can select a network connection type for Apple printers (appSocket/HP JetDirect), Internet Printing Protocol (http or ipp), or a Windows printer (using SAMBA or SMB).

4. If prompted for more information, you may need to further describe the connection to the printer. For example, you may need to enter the baud rate and parity for a serial port, or you might be asked for the network address for an IPP or Samba printer.

5. Select the make of the print driver (if you don't see the manufacturer of your printer listed, choose PostScript for a PostScript printer or HP for a PCL printer). For the make you choose, you will be able to select a specific model.

6. If the printer is added successfully, the next page you see shows a link to the description of that printer. Click that link. From the new printer page, you can print a test page or modify the printer configuration.

After you are able to print from CUPS, you can return to the CUPS Web-based administration page and do further work with your printers. Here are a few examples of what you can do:

- **List print jobs** — Click Jobs to see what print jobs are currently active from any of the printers configured for this server. Click Show Completed Jobs to see information about jobs that are already printed.

- **Create a printer class** — Click Classes; then click Add Class and identify a name and location for a printer class. Click Continue. Then, from the list of Printers configured on your server, select the ones to go into this class.

- **View printers** — You can click the Printers link from the top of any of the CUPS Web-based administration pages to view the printers you have configured. For each printer that appears, you can click Stop Printer (to stop the printer from printing but still accept print jobs for the queue), Reject Jobs (to not accept any further print jobs for the moment), or Print Test Page (to print a page). Figure 26-2 shows the Printers page.

FIGURE 26-2

Print test pages or temporarily stop printing from the Printers page.

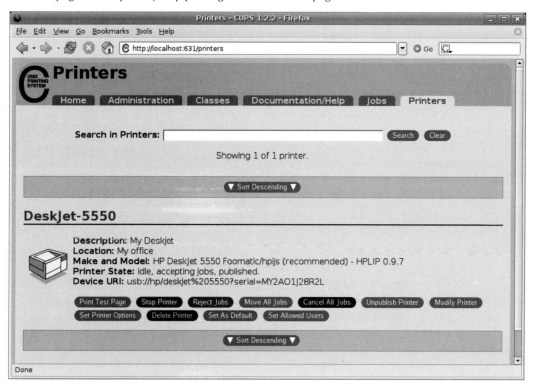

Using the Red Hat Printer Configuration Window

If you are using Fedora, RHEL, or other Red Hat–sponsored systems, you can use the Printer Configuration window to set up your printers. In fact, I recommend that you use it instead of CUPS Web administration because the resulting printer configuration files are tailored to work with Red Hat systems.

To install a printer from your GNOME desktop in Fedora, open the Printer Configuration window by selecting System ⇨ Administration ⇨ Printing (with Fedora 8, select System ⇨ Printing) or as root user by typing **system-config-printer**. This tool lets you add and delete printers and edit printer properties. It also lets you send test pages to those printers to make sure they are working properly.

The key here is that you are configuring printers that are managed by your print daemon (cupsd for the CUPS service). After a printer is configured, users on your local system can use it. You can refer to the section "Configuring Print Servers" to learn how to make the server available to users from other computers on your network.

The printers that you set up can be connected directly to your computer (as on a parallel port) or to another computer on the network (for example, from another UNIX system or Windows system).

Configuring Local Printers in Fedora

Add a local printer (in other words, a printer connected directly to your computer) with the Printer Configuration window using the following procedure. (See the sidebar "Choosing a Printer" if you don't yet have a printer.)

TIP   Connect your printer before starting this procedure. This enables the printer software to autodetect the printer's location and to immediately test the printer when you have finished adding it.

Choosing a Printer

The PostScript language is the preferred format for Linux and UNIX printing and has been for many years. Every major word-processing product that runs on Fedora, SUSE, Debian, and UNIX systems supports PostScript printing, so a printer that natively supports PostScript printing is sure to work in Linux.

If you get a PostScript printer and it is not explicitly shown in the list of supported printers, simply select the PostScript filter when you install the printer locally. No special drivers are needed. Your next best option is to choose a printer that supports PCL. In either case, make sure that PostScript or PCL is implemented in the printer hardware and not in the Windows driver.

Avoid printers that are referred to as *Winprinters*. These printers use nonstandard printing interfaces (those other than PostScript or PCL). Support for these low-end printers is hit or miss. For example, some low-end HP DeskJet printers use the pnm2ppa driver to print documents in Printing Performance Architecture (PPA) format. Some Lexmark printers use the pbm217k driver to print. Although drivers are available for many of these Winprinters, many of them are not fully supported.

Ghostscript may also support your printer; if it does, you can use it to do your printing. Ghostscript (found at www.ghostscript.com) is a free PostScript-interpreter program. It can convert PostScript content to output that can be interpreted by a variety of printers. Both GNU and Aladdin Ghostscript drivers are available. Although the latest Aladdin drivers are not immediately released under the GPL, you can use older Aladdin drivers that are licensed under the GNU.

You'll find an excellent list of printers supported in Linux at www.linux-foundation.org/en/OpenPrinting (select the Printers link). I strongly recommend that you visit that site before you purchase a printer to work with Linux. In addition to showing supported printers, the site has a page describing how to choose a printer for use with Linux (www.linux-foundation.org/en/OpenPrinting/Database/SuggestedPrinters).

Adding a Local Printer in Fedora

To add a local printer from Fedora, follow these steps:

1. Select System ➪ Administration ➪ Printing from the Desktop menu (System ➪ Printing in Fedora 8) or type the following as root user from a Terminal window:

```
# system-config-printer &
```

   The Printer Configuration window appears, as shown in Figure 26-3.

2. Click New Printer. A New Printer window appears.

3. Add the following information:

   ■ **Printer Name** — Add the name you want to give to identify the printer. The name must begin with a letter, but after the initial letter, it can contain a combination of letters, numbers, dashes (-), and underscores (_). For example, an HP printer on a computer named maple could be named hp-maple.

   ■ **Description** — Add a few words describing the printer, such as its features (an HP LaserJet 2100M with PCL and PS support).

   ■ **Location** — Add some words that describe the printer's location (for example, "In Room 205 under the coffeepot").

4. Click Forward. The Select Connection window appears.

FIGURE 26-3

Add printers connected locally or remotely with the Printer Configuration window.

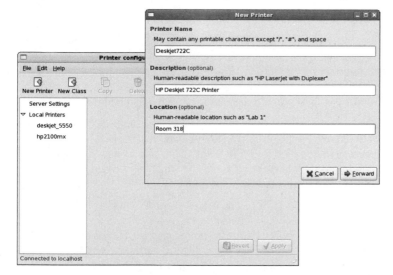

5. If the printer you want to configure is detected, simply select it. If it is not detected, choose the device to which the printer is connected (LPT #1 and Serial Port #1 are the first parallel and serial ports, respectively) and click Forward. (Refer to the next procedure for information on selecting remote printers.)

6. Either select to choose a print driver from the database (and select the manufacturer) or select to Provide PPD File (and choose that driver). Click Forward to choose the specific driver to use for your printer (you may have several choices).

COMING FROM WINDOWS If you have a printer that works in Windows, but doesn't work in Linux, refer back to the disk (probably a CD) that was included with the printer. Choose Provide PPD File, and then look for the PPD file on that disk to test that printer driver with Linux.

7. Click the model of your printer in the Models box, and then choose a driver for your printer.

TIP If your printer doesn't appear on the list but supports PCL (HP's Printer Control Language), try selecting one of the HP printers (such as HP LaserJet). If your printer supports PostScript, select PostScript printer from the list. Selecting Raw Print Queue enables you to send documents to the printer that are already formatted for that printer type.

8. Click the Printer, Driver, or PPD button. In many cases, you'll see good information from the Linux Printing Database about how your printer is configured and how to tune it further. Click Forward to continue.

9. If the information looks correct, click Apply to create the entry for your printer.

   The printer appears in the main Printer Configuration window. If you want the printer to be your default printer, click the Make Default Printer button. As you add other printers, you can change the default printer by selecting the one you want and clicking the Make Default Printer button.

10. Printing should be working at this point. To make sure, select the printer you just added from the left column. Then click the Print Test Page button. (If you want to share this printer with other computers on your network, refer to the section "Configuring Print Servers" later in this chapter.)

Editing a Local Printer in Fedora

After selecting the printer you want to configure, choose from the following tabs to change its configuration:

■ **Settings** — The Description, Location, Device URI, and Make and Model information you created earlier are displayed on this tab. In addition to the original options added, the following describes how to change other options:

   ▪ **State** — Select check boxes to indicate whether or not the printer will print jobs that are in the queue (Enabled), accept new jobs for printing (Accepting Jobs), or be available to be shared with other computers that can communicate with your computer (Shared).

697

- Make Default Printer — Select this button to choose the printer as the default printer.

- **Policies**. Click the Policies tab. From this tab, you can set the following items:

  - Banner — Add banner pages at the beginning or end of a job. This is good practice for a printer that is shared by many people. The banner page helps you sort who gets which print job. The standard banner page shows the ID of the print job, the title of the file, the user that requested the print job, and any billing information associated with it.

  - Policies — In case of error, the stop-printer selection causes all printing to that printer to stop. You can also select to have the job discarded (abort-job) or retried (retry-job) in the event of an error condition.

- **Access control**. If your printer is a shared printer, you can select this tab to create a list that either allows users access to the printer (with all others denied) or denies users access to the printer (with all others allowed).

- **Printer Options**. Click Printer Options to set defaults for options related to the printer driver. The available options are different for different printers. Many of these options can be overridden when someone prints a document. Here are a few of the options you might want to set:

  - Watermark — Several Watermark settings are available to enable you to add and change watermarks on your printed pages. By default, Watermark and Overlay are off (None). By selecting Watermark (behind the text) or Overlay (over the text), you can set the other Watermark settings to determine how watermarks and overlays are done. Watermarks can go on every page (All) or only the first page (First Only).

    Select Watermark Text to choose what words are used for the watermark or overlay (Draft, Copy, Confidential, Final, and so on). You can then select the font type, size, style, and intensity of the watermark or overlay.

  - Resolution Enhancement — You can use the printer's current settings or choose to turn resolution enhancement on or off.

  - Page Size — The default is U.S. letter size, but you can also ask the printer to print legal size, envelopes, ISO A4 standard, or several other page sizes.

  - Media Source — Choose which tray to print from. Select Tray 1 to insert pages manually.

  - Levels of Gray — Choose to use the printer's current levels of gray or have enhanced or standard gray levels turned on.

  - Resolution — Select the default printing resolution (such as 300, 600, or 1,200 dots per inch). Higher resolutions result in better quality but take longer to print.

  - EconoMode — Either use the printer's current setting or choose a mode where you save toner or one where you have the highest possible quality.

Click Apply when you are satisfied with the changes you made to the local printer.

 **For a description of other driver options, refer to the CUPS Software User Manual** (`/usr/share/doc/cups-*/sum.html`) **under the Standard Printer Options heading.**

Configuring Remote Printers in Fedora

To use a printer that is available on your network, you must identify that printer to your Linux system. Supported remote printer connections include Networked CUPS (IPP) printers, Networked UNIX (LPD) printers, Networked Windows (SMB) printers, NetWare printers, and JetDirect printers. (Of course, both CUPS and UNIX print servers can be run from Linux systems as well as other UNIX systems.)

In each case, you need a network connection from your Linux system to the servers to which those printers are connected. To use a remote printer requires that someone set up that printer on the remote server computer. See the section "Configuring Print Servers" later in this chapter for information on how to do that on your Linux server.

Use the Printer Configuration window to configure each of the remote printer types:

1. From the Desktop menu, select System ➪ Administration ➪ Printing (in Fedora 8, select System ➪ Printing).

2. Click New Printer. The New Printer window appears.

3. Add a Printer Name, Description, and Location (as described previously) and click Forward. The Select Connection window appears.

4. Depending on the type of ports you have on your computer, select one of the following:

   - **LPT #1** — For a printer connected to your parallel port.
   - **Serial Port #1** — For a printer connected to your serial port.
   - **AppleSocket/HP JetDirect** — For a JetDirect printer.
   - **Internet Printing Protocol (IPP)** — For a CUPS or other IPP printer.
   - **LPD/LPR Host or Printer** — For a UNIX printer.
   - **Windows Printer via SAMBA** — For a Windows system printer.

Continue with the steps in whichever of the following sections is appropriate.

Adding a Remote CUPS Printer

If you chose to add a CUPS (IPP) printer from the Printer Configuration window, you must add the following information to the window that appears:

- **Hostname** — Hostname of the computer to which the printer is attached (or otherwise accessible). This can be an IP address or TCP/IP hostname for the computer. (The TCP/IP name is accessible from your `/etc/hosts` file or through a DNS name server.)

■ **Printer name** — Printer name on the remote CUPS print server. CUPS supports printer instances, which allows each printer to have several sets of options. If the remote CUPS printer is configured this way, you are able to choose a particular path to a printer, such as `hp/300dpi` or `hp/1200dpi`. A slash character separates the print queue name from the printer instance.

Complete the rest of the procedure as you would for a local printer (see the section "Adding a Local Printer in Fedora" earlier in this chapter).

Adding a Remote UNIX Printer

If you chose to add a UNIX printer (LPD/LPR) from the Printer Configuration window, you must add the following information to the window that appears:

■ **Host name** — Hostname of the computer to which the printer is attached (or otherwise accessible). This is the IP address or TCP/IP name for the computer (the TCP/IP name is accessible from your `/etc/hosts` file or through a DNS name server).

■ **Printer name** — Printer name on the remote UNIX computer.

Complete the rest of the procedure as you would for a local printer (see the "Adding a Local Printer in Fedora" section earlier in this chapter).

TIP If the print job you send to test the printer is rejected, the print server computer may not have allowed you access to the printer. Ask the remote computer's administrator to add your hostname to the `/etc/lpd.perms` file. (Type **lpq -P***printer* to see the status of your print job.)

Adding a Windows (SMB) Printer

Enabling your computer to access an SMB printer (the Windows printing service) involves adding an entry for the printer in the Select Connection window.

When you choose to add a Windows printer to the Printer Configuration window (Windows Printer via SAMBA), you are presented with a list of computers on your network that have been detected as offering SMB services (file and/or printing service). At that point, here is how you can configure the printer:

1. Select the server or group (click the arrow next to its name so that it points down).
2. Select the printer from the list of available printers shown.
3. Fill in the username and password needed to access the SMB printer. Click Verify to check that you can authenticate to the server.
4. Click Forward to continue.

Alternatively, you can identify a server that does not appear on the list of servers. Type the information needed to create an SMB URI that contains the following information:

■ **Workgroup** — The workgroup name assigned to the SMB server. Using the workgroup name isn't necessary in all cases.

- **Server** — NetBIOS name or IP address for the computer, which may or may not be the same as its TCP/IP name. To translate this name into the address needed to reach the SMB host, Samba checks several places where the name may be assigned to an IP address. Samba checks the following (in the order shown) until it finds a match: the local /etc/hosts file, the local /etc/lmhosts file, a WINS server on the network, and responses to broadcasts on each local network interface to resolve the name.

- **Share** — Name under which the printer is shared with the remote computer. It may be different from the name by which local users of the SMB printer know the printer.

- **User** — Username is required by the SMB server system to give you access to the SMB printer. A username is not necessary if you are authenticating the printer based on share-level rather than user-level access control. With share-level access, you can add a password for each shared printer or file system.

- **Password** — Password associated with the SMB username or the shared resource, depending on the kind of access control being used.

> **CAUTION**
> When you enter a User and Password for SMB, that information is stored unencrypted in the /etc/cups/printers.conf file. Be sure that the file remains readable only by root.

The following is an example of the SMB URI you could add to the SMB:// box:

```
jjones:my9passswd@FSTREET/NS1/hp
```

The URI shown here identifies the username (jjones), the user's password (my9passswd), the workgroup (FSTREET), the server (NS1), and the printer queue name (hp).

Complete the rest of the procedure as you would for a local printer (see the section "Adding a Local Printer in Fedora" earlier in this chapter).

If everything is set up properly, you can use the standard lpr command to print the file to the printer. Using this example, employ the following form for printing:

```
$ cat file1.ps | lpr -P NS1-PS
```

> **TIP**
> If you are receiving failure messages, make sure that the computer to which you are printing is accessible. For the preceding NS1-PS printer example, you can type **smbclient -L NS1 -U jjones**. Then type the password (my9passswd, in this case). If you get a positive name query response after you enter a password, you should see a list of shared printers and files from that server. Check the names, and try printing again.

Working with CUPS Printing

Tools such as CUPS Web-based Administration and the Fedora Printer Configuration window effectively hide the underlying CUPS facility. There may be times, however, when you want to work directly with the tools and configuration files that come with CUPS. The following sections describe how to use some special CUPS features.

Configuring the CUPS Server (cupsd.conf)

The cupsd daemon process listens for requests to your CUPS print server and responds to those requests based on settings in the /etc/cups/cupsd.conf file. The configuration variables in the cupsd.conf file are in the same form as those in the Apache configuration file (httpd.conf).

Red Hat's Printer Configuration window adds access information to the cupsd.conf file. For other Linux systems, you may need to configure the cupsd.conf file manually. You can step through the cupsd.conf file to further tune your CUPS server. Let's take a look at some of the settings in the cupsd.conf file.

No classification is set by default. With the classification set to topsecret, you can have Top Secret displayed on all pages that go through the print server:

```
Classification topsecret
```

Other classifications you can substitute for topsecret include classified, confidential, secret, and unclassified.

The ServerCertificate and ServerKey lines (commented out by default) can be set up to indicate where the certificate and key are stored, respectively:

```
ServerCertificate /etc/cups/ssl/server.crt
ServerKey /etc/cups/ssl/server.key
```

Activate these two lines if you want to do encrypted connections. Then add your certificate and key to the files noted.

The term *browsing* refers to the act of broadcasting information about your printer on your local network and listening for other print servers' information. Browsing is on by default only for the local host (@LOCAL). You can allow CUPS browser information (BrowseAllow) for additional selected addresses. Browsing information is broadcast, by default, on address 255.255.255.255. Here's how these defaults appear in the cupsd.conf file:

```
Browsing On
BrowseProtocols cups
BrowseOrder Deny,Allow
BrowseAllow from @LOCAL
BrowseAddress 255.255.255.255
Listen *:631
```

To enable Web-based CUPS administration, the cupsd daemon listens on port 631 for all network interfaces to your computer based on this entry: Listen *:631.

By turning on BrowseRelay (it's off by default), you can allow CUPS browse information to be passed among two or more networks. The source-address and destination-address can be individual IP addresses or can represent network numbers:

```
BrowseRelay source-address destination-address
```

This is a good way to enable users on several connected LANs to discover and use printers on other nearby LANs.

You can allow or deny access to different features of the CUPS server. An access definition for a CUPS printer (created from the Printer Configuration window) might appear as follows:

```
<Location /printers/ns1-hp1>
Order Deny,Allow
Deny From All
Allow From 127.0.0.1
AuthType None
</Location>
```

Here, printing to the ns1-hp1 printer is allowed only for users on the local host (127.0.0.1). No password is needed (AuthType None). To allow access to the administration tool, CUPS must be configured to prompt for a password (AuthType Basic).

Starting the CUPS Server

For Linux systems that use SystemV-style startup scripts (such as Fedora, RHEL, and SUSE), starting and shutting down the CUPS print service is pretty easy. Use the chkconfig command to turn on CUPS so it starts at each reboot. Run the cups startup script to have the CUPS service start immediately. Type the following as root user:

```
# chkconfig cupsd on
# /etc/init.d/cups start
```

If the CUPS service was already running, you should use restart instead of start. Using the restart option is also a good way to reread any configuration options you may have changed in the cupsd.conf file.

Other Linux systems vary in how they start up the CUPS service. For example, in Slackware, you can turn on CUPS printing permanently by simply making the rc.cups script executable and then turn it on immediately by executing it (typing the following as root user):

```
# chmod 755 /etc/rc.d/rc.cups
# /etc/rc.d/rc.cups start
```

In Gentoo Linux, you use the add option of the rc-update command to have the CUPS service start at each reboot and run the cupsd runlevel script to start it immediately. For example, type the following as root user:

```
# rc-update add cupsd default
# /etc/init.d/cupsd start
```

Most Linux systems have similar ways of starting the CUPS service. You may need to poke around to see how CUPS starts on the distribution you are using.

Configuring CUPS Printer Options Manually

If your Linux distribution doesn't have a graphical means of configuring CUPS, you can edit configuration files directly. For example, when a new printer is created from the Printer Configuration window, it is defined in the /etc/cups/printers.conf file. Here is what a printer entry looks like:

```
</Printer hp>
<DefaultPrinter printer>
Info HP LaserJet 2100M
Location HP LaserJet 2100M in hall closet
DeviceURI parallel:/dev/lp0
State Idle
Accepting Yes
Shared Yes
JobSheets none none
QuotaPeriod 0
PageLimit 0
KLimit 0
</Printer>
```

This is an example of a local printer that serves as the default printer for the local system. The most interesting information relates to DeviceURI, which shows that the printer is connected to parallel port /dev/lp0. The state is Idle (ready to accept printer jobs), and the Accepting value is Yes (the printer is accepting print jobs by default).

The DeviceURI has several ways to identify the device name of a printer, reflecting where the printer is connected. Here are some examples listed in the printers.conf file:

```
DeviceURI parallel:/dev/plp
DeviceURI serial:/dev/ttyd1?baud=38400+size=8+parity=none+flow=soft
DeviceURI scsi:/dev/scsi/sc1d6l0
DeviceURI socket://hostname:port
DeviceURI tftp://hostname/path
DeviceURI ftp://hostname/path
DeviceURI http://hostname[:port]/path
DeviceURI ipp://hostname/path
DeviceURI smb://hostname/printer
```

The first three examples show the form for local printers (parallel, serial, and scsi). The other examples are for remote hosts. In each case, *hostname* can be the host's name or IP address. Port numbers or paths identify the locations of each printer on the host.

TIP If you find that you are not able to print because a particular printer driver is not supported in CUPS, you can set up your printer to accept jobs in raw mode. This can work well if you are printing from Windows clients that have the correct print drivers installed. To enable raw printing in CUPS, uncomment the following line in the /etc/cups/mime.types file in Linux:

```
application/octet-stream
```

And uncomment the following line in the /etc/cups/mime.convs file:

```
application/octet-stream application/vnd.cups-raw 0 -
```

After that, you can print files as raw data to your printers without using the -oraw option to print commands.

Using Printing Commands

To remain backward-compatible with older UNIX and Linux printing facilities, CUPS supports many of the old commands for working with printing. Most command-line printing with CUPS can be performed with the lpr command. Word-processing applications such as StarOffice, OpenOffice, and AbiWord are set up to use this facility for printing.

You can use the Printer Configuration window to define the filters needed for each printer so that the text can be formatted properly. Options to the lpr command can add filters to properly process the text. Other commands for managing printed documents include lpq (for viewing the contents of print queues), lprm (for removing print jobs from the queue), and lpc (for controlling printers).

Printing with lpr

You can use the lpr command to print documents to both local and remote printers. Document files can be either added to the end of the lpr command line or directed to the lpr command using a pipe (|). Here's an example of a simple lpr command:

```
$ lpr doc1.ps
```

When you specify just a document file with lpr, output is directed to the default printer. As an individual user, you can change the default printer by setting the value of the PRINTER variable. Typically, you add the PRINTER variable to one of your startup files, such as $HOME/.bashrc. Adding the following line to your .bashrc file, for example, sets your default printer to lp3:

```
export PRINTER=lp3
```

To override the default printer, specify a particular printer on the lpr command line. The following example uses the -P option to select a different printer:

```
$ lpr -P canyonps doc1.ps
```

The lpr command has a variety of options that enable lpr to interpret and format several different types of documents. These include -# *num*, where *num* is replaced by the number of copies to print (from 1 to 100) and -l (which causes a document to be sent in raw mode, presuming that the document has already been formatted). To learn more options to lpr, type **man lpr**.

Listing Printer Status with lpc

Use the lpc command to list the status of your printers. Here is an example:

```
$ lpc status
hp:
                printer is on device 'parallel' speed -1
                queuing is enabled
                printing is disabled
                no entries
                daemon present
deskjet_5550:
                printer is on device '/dev/null' speed -1
                queuing is enabled
                printing is disabled
                no entries
                daemon present
```

This output shows two active printers. The first (hp) is connected to your parallel port. The second (deskjet_5550) is a network printer (shown as /dev/null). The hp printer is currently disabled (offline), although the queue is enabled so people can continue to send jobs to the printer.

Removing Print Jobs with lprm

Users can remove their own print jobs from the queue with the lprm command. Used alone on the command line, lprm removes all the user's print jobs from the default printer. To remove jobs from a specific printer, use the -P option, as follows:

```
$ lprm -P lp0
```

To remove all print jobs for the current user, type the following:

```
$ lprm -
```

The root user can remove all the print jobs for a specific user by indicating that user on the lprm command line. For example, to remove all print jobs for the user named mike, the root user types the following:

```
$ lprm mike
```

To remove an individual print job from the queue, indicate its job number on the lprm command line. To find the job number, type the **lpq** command. Here's what the output of that command may look like:

```
$ lpq
printer is ready and printing
Rank    Owner            Job Files              Total Size Time
active  root             133 /home/jake/pr1        467
2       root             197 /home/jake/mydoc    23948
```

The output shows two printable jobs waiting in the queue. (The printer is ready and printing the job listed as active.) Under the Job column, you can see the job number associated with each document. To remove the first print job, type the following:

```
# lprm 133
```

Configuring Print Servers

You've configured a printer so that you and the other users on your computer can print to it. Now you want to share that printer with other people in your home, school, or office. Basically, that means configuring the printer as a print server.

The printers configured on your Linux system can be shared in different ways with other computers on your network. Not only can your computer act as a Linux print server (by configuring CUPS); it can look to client computers such as an SMB print server. After a local printer is attached to your Linux system and your computer is connected to your local network, you can use the procedures in this section to share the printer with client computers using a Linux (UNIX) or SMB interface.

Configuring a Shared CUPS Printer

Making the local printer added to your Linux computer available to other computers on your network is fairly easy. If a TCP/IP network connection exists between the computers sharing the printer, you simply grant permission to all hosts, individual hosts, or users from remote hosts to access your computer's printing service.

To manually configure a printer entry in the /etc/cups/cupsd.conf file to accept print jobs from all other computers, add an Allow from All line. The following example from a cupsd.conf entry earlier in this chapter demonstrates what the new entry would look like:

```
<Location /printers/ns1-hp1>
Order Deny,Allow
Deny From All
Allow From 127.0.0.1
AuthType None
Allow from All
</Location>
```

Instead of `Allow from All`, you can allow a particular network (for example, `10.0.0.0/255.255.255.0`), network interface (`Allow from @IF(eth0)`), or individual IP address (`Allow from 10.0.0.1`).

On Fedora systems, it's best to set up your printer as a shared printer using the Printer Configuration window. Here's how:

1. From the Desktop menu, select System ➪ Administration ➪ Printing (System ➪ Printing in Fedora 8). The Printer Configuration window appears.

2. Click the name of the printer you want to share. (If the printer is not yet configured, refer to the section "Setting Up Printers" earlier in this chapter.)

3. Select the Shared box on the Settings tab so that a check mark appears in the box.

4. If you want to restrict access to the printer to selected users, select the Access Control tab and choose one of the following options:

   ▪ **Allow Printing for Everyone Except These Users** — With this selected, all users are allowed access to the printer. By typing usernames into the Users box and clicking Add, you exclude selected users.

   ▪ **Deny Printing for Everyone Except These Users** — With this selected, all users are excluded from using the printer. Type user names into the Users box and click Add to allow access to the printer for only those names you enter.

Now you can configure other computers to use your printer, as described in the section "Setting Up Printers." If you try to print from another computer and it doesn't work, here are a few troubleshooting tips:

- **Open your firewall.** If you have a restrictive firewall, it may not permit printing. You must enable access to port 513 (UDP and TCP) and possibly port 631 to allow access to printing on your computer. See Chapter 17 for information on configuring your firewall.

- **Enable LPD-style printing.** Certain applications may require an older LPD-style printing service to print on your shared printer. To enable LPD-style printing on your CUPS server, you must turn on the cups-lpd service. Most Linux distributions that include CUPS should also include cups-lpd. In Fedora and other Red Hat systems, type **chkconfig cups-lpd on** as root user. Then restart the xinetd daemon (`service xinetd restart`).

- **Check names and addresses.** Make sure that you entered your computer's name and print queue properly when you configured it on the other computer. Try using the IP address instead of the hostname. (If that works, it indicates a DNS name resolution problem.) Running a tool such as ethereal enables you to see where the transaction fails.

Access changes to your shared printer are made in the `/etc/cups/cupsd.conf` file.

Configuring a Shared Samba Printer

Your Linux printers can be configured as shared SMB printers. To share your printer as though it were a Samba (SMB) printer, simply configure basic Samba server settings as described in Chapter 27. All your printers should be shared on your local network by default. The next section shows what the resulting settings look like and how you might want to change them.

Understanding smb.conf for Printing

When you configure Samba, the /etc/samba/smb.conf file is constructed to enable all of your configured printers to be shared. Here are a few lines from the smb.conf file that relate to printer sharing:

```
printcap name = /etc/printcap
load printers = yes
printing = cups
encrypt passwords = yes
smb passwd file = /etc/samba/smbpasswd
unix password sync = Yes
[printers]
        comment = All Printers
        path = /var/spool/samba
        browseable = yes
        writeable = no
        printable = yes
```

These example settings are the result of configuring Samba from the Samba Server Configuration window in Fedora. The lines show that printers from /etc/printcap were loaded and that the CUPS service is being used. Password encryption is on, and the /etc/samba/smbpasswd file stores the encrypted passwords. Because password sync is on, each user's Samba password is synchronized with the user's local UNIX password.

The last few lines are the actual printers' definition. The last line shows that users can print to all printers (printable = yes).

Setting Up SMB Clients

Chances are good that if you are configuring a Samba printer on your Linux computer, you want to share it with Windows clients. If Samba is set up properly on your computer and the client computers can reach you over the network, their finding and using your printer should be fairly straightforward.

The first place a client computer looks for your shared Samba printer is in Network Neighborhood (or My Network Places, for Windows 2000). From the Windows 9x desktop, double-click the Network Neighborhood icon. (From Windows 2000 or XP, double-click the My Network Places icon.) With Windows Vista, you open the Network icon. The name of your host computer (the NetBIOS name, which is probably also your TCP/IP name) appears on the screen or within a work-group folder on the screen. Open the icon that represents your computer. The window that opens shows your shared printers and folders.

If your computer's icon doesn't appear in Network Neighborhood or My Network Places, try using the Search window. From Windows XP, choose Start ⇨ Search ⇨ Computer or People ⇨ A Computer on the Network. Type your computer's name into the Computer Name box and click Search. Double-click your computer in the Search window results panel. A window displaying the shared printers and folders from your computer appears (see Figure 26-4).

FIGURE 26-4

You can search for your computer's printers.

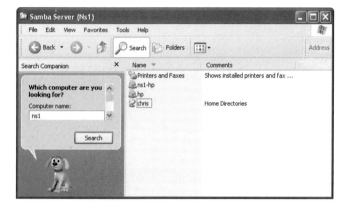

After your shared printer appears in the window, configure a pointer to that printer by opening (double-clicking) the printer icon. A message tells you that you must set up the printer before you can use it. Click Yes to proceed to configure the printer for local use. The Add Printer Wizard appears. Answer the questions that ask you how you intend to use the printer, and add the appropriate drivers. When you are done, the printer appears in your printer window.

Another way to configure an SMB printer from a Windows XP operating system is to go to Start ⇨ Printers and Faxes. In the Printers and Faxes window that appears, click the Add a Printer icon in the upper-left portion of the window, and then select Network Printer from the first window. From there you can browse and/or configure your SMB printer.

Summary

Providing networked printing services is an essential efficiency on today's business network. With the use of a few network-attached devices, you can focus your printer spending on a few high-quality devices that multiple users can share instead of numerous lower-cost devices. In addition, a centrally located printer can make it easier to maintain the printer, while still enabling everyone to get his or her printing jobs done.

The default printing service in nearly every major Linux distribution today is the Common UNIX Printing Service (CUPS). Any Linux system that includes CUPS offers the CUPS Web-based administrative interface for configuring CUPS printing. It also offers configuration files in the /etc/cups directory for configuring printers and the CUPS service (cupsd daemon).

In Fedora systems, you can configure your printer with the Printer Configuration windows available in both K Desktop and GNOME environments. A variety of drivers makes it possible to print to different kinds of printers, as well as to printers that are connected to computers on the network.

You can set up your computer as a Linux print server, and you can also have your computer emulate an SMB (Windows) print server. After your network is configured properly and a local printer is installed, sharing that printer over the network as a UNIX or SMB print server is not very complicated.

Chapter 27

Running a File Server

Most networked computers are on the network in the first place so that users can share information. Some users need to collectively edit documents for a project, share access to spreadsheets and forms used in the daily operation of a company, or perform any number of similar file-sharing activities. It also can be efficient for groups of people on a computer network to share common applications and directories of information needed to do their jobs. By far the best way to accomplish the centralized sharing of data is through a file server.

A centralized file server can be backed up, preserving all stored data in one fell swoop. It can focus on the tasks of getting files to end users, rather than running user applications that can use client resources. And a centralized file server can be used to control access to information—security settings can dictate who can access what.

Linux systems include support for each of the most common file server protocols in use today. Among the most common file server types in use today are the Network File System (NFS), which has always been the file-sharing protocol of choice for Linux and other UNIX systems, and Samba (Server Message Block, or SMB, protocol), which is often used by networks with many Windows and OS/2 computers.

COMING FROM WINDOWS Samba allows you to share files with Windows PCs on your network, as well as access Windows file and print servers, making your Linux box fit in better with Windows-centric organizations.

This chapter describes how to set up file servers and clients associated with NFS and Samba.

> **TIP** When selecting file services to provide, keep in mind that less is more. If your clients and servers support multiple-file access capabilities (both NFS and SMB, for example), pick the service that lends itself to making the task less complicated. In many cases, NFS is supported by clients and servers regardless of the operating system that they use. It's rare that you would need to enable more than one of the file services discussed in this chapter.

Setting Up an NFS File Server

Instead of representing storage devices as drive letters (A, B, C, and so on), as they are in Microsoft operating systems, Linux systems connect file systems from multiple hard disks, floppy disks, CD-ROMs, and other local devices invisibly to form a single Linux file system. The Network File System (NFS) facility enables you to extend your Linux file system in the same way, to connect file systems on other computers to your local directory structure.

An NFS file server provides an easy way to share large amounts of data among the users and computers in an organization. An administrator of a Linux system that is configured to share its file systems using NFS has to perform the following tasks to set up NFS:

1. **Set up the network.** If a LAN or other network link is already connecting the computers on which you want to use NFS, you already have the network you need.

2. **Choose what to share on the server.** Decide which file systems on your Linux NFS server to make available to other computers. You can choose any point in the file system and make all files and directories below that point accessible to other computers.

3. **Set up security on the server.** You can use several different security features to suit the level of security with which you are comfortable. Mount-level security lets you restrict the computers that can mount a resource and, for those allowed to mount it, lets you specify whether it can be mounted read/write or read-only. With user-level security, you map users from the client systems to users on the NFS server so that they can rely on standard Linux read/write/execute permissions, file ownership, and group permissions to access and protect files. Linux systems that support Security Enhanced Linux (SELinux), such as Fedora and Red Hat Enterprise Linux, offer another means of offering or restricting shared NFS files and directories.

4. **Mount the file system on the client.** Each client computer that is allowed access to the server's NFS shared file system can mount it anywhere the client chooses. For example, you may mount a file system from a computer called maple on the `/mnt/maple` directory in your local file system. After it is mounted, you can view the contents of that directory by typing **ls /mnt/maple**. Then you can use the `cd` command below the `/mnt/maple` mount point to see the files and directories it contains.

Figure 27-1 illustrates a Linux file server using NFS to share (export) a file system and a client computer mounting the file system to make it available to its local users.

FIGURE 27-1

NFS can make selected file systems available to other computers.

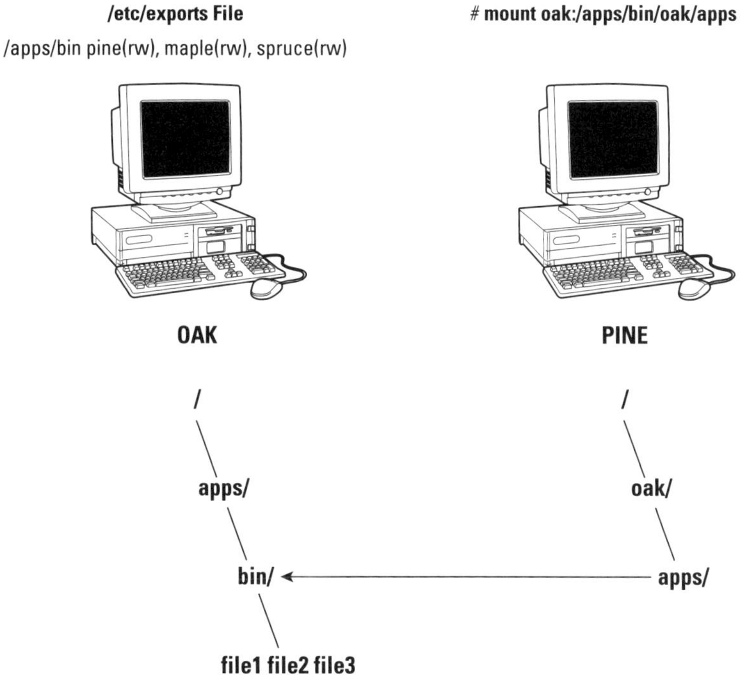

In this example, a computer named oak makes its /apps/bin directory available to clients on the network (pine, maple, and spruce) by adding an entry to the /etc/exports file. The client computer (pine) sees that the resource is available and mounts the resource on its local file system at the mount point /oak/apps, after which any files, directories, or subdirectories from /apps/bin on oak are available to users on pine (given proper permissions).

Although it is often used as a file server (or other type of server), Linux is a general-purpose operating system, so any Linux system can share file systems (export) as a server or use another computer's file systems (mount) as a client. Contrast this with dedicated file servers, such as NetWare, which can only share files with client computers (such as Windows workstations) and never act as a client.

NOTE A file system is usually a structure of files and directories that exists on a single device (such as a hard disk partition or CD-ROM). A Linux file system refers to the entire directory structure (which may include file systems from several disks or NFS resources), beginning from root (/) on a single computer. A shared directory in NFS may represent all or part of a computer's file system, which can be attached (from the shared directory down the directory tree) to another computer's file system.

Getting NFS

While nearly every Linux system supports NFS client and server features, NFS is not always installed by default. You'll need different packages for different Linux systems to install NFS. Here are some examples:

- **Fedora and other Red Hat Linux systems** — You need to install the nfs-utils package to use Fedora as an NFS server. There is also a graphical NFS Configuration tool that requires you to install the system-config-nfs package. NFS client features are in the base operating system. To turn on the nfs service, type the following:

```
# service nfs start
# chkconfig nfs on
```

- **Debian** — To act as an NFS client, the nfs-common and portmap packages are required; for an NFS server, the nfs-kernel-server package must be added. The following apt-get command line (if you are connected to the Internet) installs them all. Then, after you add an exported file system to the /etc/exports file (as described later), you can start the nfs-common and nfs-kernel-server scripts, as shown here:

```
# apt-get install nfs-common portmap nfs-kernel-server
# /etc/init.d/nfs-kernel-server start
# /etc/init.d/nfs-common start
```

- **Gentoo** — With Gentoo, NFS file system and NFS server support must be configured into the kernel to use NFS server features. Installing the nfs-utils package (emerge nfs-utils) should get the required packages. To start the service, run rc-update and start the service immediately:

```
# emerge nfs-utils
# rc-update add portmap default
# rc-update add nfs default
# /etc/init.d/nfs start
```

The commands (mount, exportfs, and so on) and files (/etc/exports, /etc/fstab, and so on) for actually configuring NFS are the same on every Linux system I've encountered. So once you have NFS installed and running, just follow the instructions in this chapter to start using NFS.

Sharing NFS File Systems

To share an NFS file system from your Linux system, you need to export it from the server system. Exporting is done in Linux by adding entries into the /etc/exports file. Each entry identifies a directory in your local file system that you want to share with other computers. The entry also identifies the other computers that can share the resource (or opens it to all computers) and includes other options that reflect permissions associated with the directory.

Remember that when you share a directory, you are sharing all files and subdirectories below that directory as well (by default). So, you need to be sure that you want to share everything in that directory structure. There are still ways to restrict access within that directory structure, and those are discussed later in this chapter.

Configuring the /etc/exports File

To make a directory from your Linux system available to other systems, you need to export that directory. Exporting is done on a permanent basis by adding information about an exported directory to the /etc/exports file.

The format of the /etc/exports file is

```
Directory    Host(Options)    # Comments
```

where *Directory* is the name of the directory that you want to share, and *Host* indicates the host computer to which the sharing of this directory is restricted. *Options* can include a variety of options to define the security measures attached to the shared directory for the host. (You can repeat *Host/Option* pairs.) *Comments* are any optional comments you want to add (following the # sign).

As root user, you can use any text editor to configure /etc/exports to modify shared directory entries or add new ones. Here's an example of an /etc/exports file:

```
/cal    *.linuxtoys.net(rw)                  # Company events
/pub    (ro,insecure,all_squash)             # Public dir
/home   maple(rw,squash uids=0-99) spruce(rw,squash uids=0-99)
```

The /cal entry represents a directory that contains information about events related to the company. It is made accessible to everyone with accounts to any computers in the company's domain (*.linuxtoys.net). Users can write files to the directory as well as read them (indicated by the rw option). The comment (# Company events) simply serves to remind you of what the directory contains.

The /pub entry represents a public directory. It allows any computer and user to read files from the directory (indicated by the ro option) but not to write files. The insecure option enables any computer, even one that doesn't use a secure NFS port, to access the directory. The all_squash option causes all users (UIDs) and groups (GIDs) to be mapped to the nfsnobody user, giving them minimal permission to files and directories.

The /home entry enables a set of users to have the same /home directory on different computers. Say, for example, that you are sharing /home from a computer named oak. The computers named maple and spruce could each mount that directory on their own /home directories. If you gave all users the same username/UIDs on all machines, you could have the same /home/user directory available for each user, regardless of which computer they are logged into. The uids=0-99 entry is used to exclude any administrative login from another computer from changing any files in the shared directory.

These are just examples; you can share any directories that you choose, including the entire file system (/). Of course, there are security implications of sharing the whole file system or sensitive parts of it (such as /etc). Security options that you can add to your /etc/exports file are described throughout the sections that follow.

Hostnames in /etc/exports

You can indicate in the /etc/exports file which host computers can have access to your shared directory. If you want to associate multiple hostnames or IP addresses with a particular shared directory, be sure to have a space before each hostname. However, add no spaces between a hostname and its options. For example:

```
/usr/local maple(rw) spruce(ro,root_squash)
```

Notice that there is a space after (rw) but none after maple. Here are ways to identify hosts:

- **Individual host** — Enter one or more TCP/IP hostnames or IP addresses. If the host is in your local domain, you can simply indicate the hostname. Otherwise, use the full host.domain format. These are valid ways to indicate individual host computers:

```
maple
maple.handsonhistory.com
10.0.0.11
```

- **IP network** — Allow access to all hosts from a particular network address by indicating a network number and its netmask, separated by a slash (/). Here are valid ways to designate network numbers:

```
10.0.0.0/255.0.0.0
172.16.0.0/255.255.0.0
192.168.18.0/255.255.255.0
```

- **TCP/IP domain** — Using wildcards, you can include all or some host computers from a particular domain level. Here are some valid uses of the asterisk and question mark wildcards:

```
*.handsonhistory.com
*craft.handsonhistory.com
???.handsonhistory.com
```

The first example matches all hosts in the handsonhistory.com domain. The second example matches woodcraft, basketcraft, or any other hostnames ending in craft in the handsonhistory.com domain. The final example matches any three-letter hostnames in the domain.

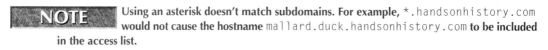

NOTE   Using an asterisk doesn't match subdomains. For example, *.handsonhistory.com would not cause the hostname mallard.duck.handsonhistory.com to be included in the access list.

- **NIS groups** — You can allow access to hosts contained in an NIS group. To indicate an NIS group, precede the group name with an at (@) sign (for example, @group).

Access Options in /etc/exports

You don't have to just give away your files and directories when you export a directory with NFS. In the options part of each entry in /etc/exports, you can add options that allow or limit access by setting as read/write permission. These options, which are passed to NFS, are as follows:

- ro — Client can mount this exported file system read-only. The default is to mount the file system as read/write.

- rw — Explicitly asks that a shared directory be shared with read/write permissions. (If the client chooses, it can still mount the directory read-only.)

User Mapping Options in /etc/exports

In addition to options that define how permissions are handled generally, you can use options to set the permissions that specific users have to NFS shared file systems.

One method that simplifies this process is to assign each user with multiple user accounts the same username and UID on each machine. This makes it easier to map users so that they have the same permissions on a mounted file system that they do on files stored on their local hard disks. If that method is not convenient, user IDs can be mapped in many other ways. Here are some methods of setting user permissions and the /etc/exports option that you use for each method:

- **root user** — The client's root user is generally mapped into the nfsnobody username (UID 65534). This prevents a client computer's root user from being able to change all files and directories in the shared file system. If you want the client's root user to have root permission on the server, use the no_root_squash option.

 There may be other administrative users, in addition to root, that you want to squash. I recommend squashing UIDs 0–99 as follows: squash_uids=0-99.

- **nfsnobody user/group** — By using the nfsnobody username and group name, you essentially create a user/group with permissions that do not allow access to files that belong to any real users on the server, unless those users open permission to everyone. However, files created by the nfsnobody user or group are available to anyone assigned as the nfsnobody user or group. To set all remote users to the nfsnobody user/group, use the all_squash option.

  The nfsnobody user is assigned to UIDs and GIDs of 65534 to prevent the ID from running into a valid user or group ID. Using the anonuid or anongid option, you can change the nfsnobody user or group, respectively. For example, anonuid=175 sets all anonymous users to UID 175, and anongid=300 sets the GID to 300. (Only the number is displayed when you list file permissions unless you add entries with names to /etc/password and /etc/group for the new UIDs and GIDs.)

- **User mapping** — If a user has login accounts for a set of computers (and has the same ID), NFS, by default, maps that ID. This means that if the user named mike (UID 110) on maple has an account on pine (mike, UID 110), he can use his own remotely mounted files on either computer from either computer.

If a client user who is not set up on the server creates a file on the mounted NFS directory, the file is assigned to the remote client's UID and GID. (An `ls -l` on the server shows the UID of the owner.) Use the `map_static` option to identify a file that contains user mappings.

> **TIP** The `exports` man page describes the `map_static` option, which enables you to create a file that contains new ID mappings so that you can remap client IDs into different IDs on the server.

Exporting the Shared File Systems

After you have added entries to your `/etc/exports` file, run the `exportfs` command to have those directories exported (made available to other computers on the network). Reboot your computer or restart the NFS service, and the `exportfs` command runs automatically to export your directories. If you want to export them immediately, run `exportfs` from the command line (as root).

> **TIP** It's a good idea to run the `exportfs` command after you change the exports file. If any errors are in the file, `exportfs` identifies them for you.

Here's an example of the `exportfs` command:

```
# /usr/sbin/exportfs -a -v
exporting maple:/pub
exporting spruce:/pub
exporting maple:/home
exporting spruce:/home
exporting *:/mnt/win
```

The `-a` option indicates that all directories listed in `/etc/exports` should be exported. The `-v` option says to print verbose output. In this example, the `/pub` and `/home` directories from the local server are immediately available for mounting by those client computers that are named (maple and spruce). The `/mnt/win` directory is available to all client computers.

Running the `exportfs` command temporarily makes your exported NFS directories available. To have your NFS directories available on an ongoing basis (that is, every time your system reboots), you need to set your `nfs` startup scripts to run at boot time. This is described in the next section.

Starting the NFS Daemons

If NFS has been disabled on your system (or is not active by default), you need to start the service. Different Linux distributions have different ways of turning on the NFS service, as you saw in the section "Getting NFS" earlier in the chapter. This section explores how the service is turned on in Fedora and other Red Hat Linux systems.

In Fedora, you can use the `chkconfig` command to turn on the NFS service so that your files are exported and the nfsd daemons are running when your system boots. There are two startup scripts you want to turn on for the service to work properly. The NFS service exports file systems (from /etc/exports) and starts the nfsd daemon that listens for service requests. The nfslock service starts the lockd daemon, which helps allow file locking to prevent multiple simultaneous use of critical files over the network.

To turn on the NFS service, type the following as root user:

```
# chkconfig nfs on
# chkconfig nfslock on
```

The next time you start your computer, the NFS service will start automatically, and your exported directories will be available. If you want to start the service immediately, without waiting for a reboot, type the following:

```
# /etc/init.d/nfs start
# /etc/init.d/nfslock start
```

The NFS service should now be running and ready to share directories with other computers on your network.

Using NFS File Systems

After a server exports a directory over the network using NFS, a client computer connects that directory to its own file system using the mount command. That's the same command used to mount file systems from local hard disks, CDs, and floppies, but with slightly different options.

mount can automatically mount NFS directories added to the /etc/fstab file, just as it does with local disks. NFS directories can also be added to the /etc/fstab file in such a way that they are not automatically mounted (so you can mount them manually when you choose). With a noauto option, an NFS directory listed in /etc/fstab is inactive until the mount command is used, after the system is up and running, to mount the file system.

Manually Mounting an NFS File System

If you know that the directory from a computer on your network has been exported (that is, made available for mounting), you can mount that directory manually using the mount command. This is a good way to make sure that it is available and working before you set it up to mount permanently. Here is an example of mounting the /tmp directory from a computer named maple on your local computer:

```
# mkdir /mnt/maple
# mount maple:/tmp /mnt/maple
```

The first command (mkdir) creates the mount point directory (/mnt is a common place to put temporarily mounted disks and NFS file systems). The mount command identifies the remote computer and shared file system separated by a colon (maple:/tmp), and the local mount point directory (/mnt/maple) follows.

NOTE If the mount fails, make sure the NFS service is running on the server and that the server's firewall rules don't deny access to the service. From the server, type **ps ax | grep nfsd** to see a list of nfsd server processes. If you don't see the list, try to start your NFS daemons as described in the previous section. To view your firewall rules, type **iptables -L** (see Chapter 18 for a description of firewalls). By default, the nfsd daemon listens for NFS requests on port number 2049. Your firewall must accept udp requests on ports 2049 (nfs) and 111 (rpc).

To ensure that the mount occurred, type **mount**. This command lists all mounted disks and NFS file systems. Here is an example of the mount command and its output (with file systems not pertinent to this discussion edited out):

```
# mount
/dev/sda3 on / type ext3 (rw)
...
...
...
maple:/tmp on /mnt/maple type nfs (rw,addr=10.0.0.11)
```

The output from the mount command shows the mounted disk partitions, special file systems, and NFS file systems. The first output line shows the hard disk (/dev/sda3), mounted on the root file system (/), with read/write permission (rw), with a file system type of ext3 (the standard Linux file system type). The just-mounted NFS file system is the /tmp directory from maple (maple:/tmp). It is mounted on /mnt/maple and its mount type is nfs. The file system was mounted as read/write (rw), and the IP address of maple is 10.0.0.11 (addr=10.0.0.11).

This is a simple example of using mount with NFS. The mount is temporary and is not remounted when you reboot your computer. You can also add options for NFS mounts:

- -a — Mount all file systems in /etc/fstab (except those indicated as noauto).

- -f — This goes through the motions of (fakes) mounting the file systems on the command line (or in /etc/fstab). Used with the -v option, -f is useful for seeing what mount would do before it actually does it.

- -F — When used with -a, you tell mount to fork off a new incarnation of mount for each file system listed to be mounted in the /etc/fstab file. An advantage of using this option, as it relates to NFS shared directories, is that other file systems can be mounted if an NFS file system isn't immediately available. This option should not be used, however, if the order of mounting is important (for example, if you needed to mount /mnt/pcs and then /mnt/pcs/arctic).

- -r — Mounts the file system as read-only.

- -w — Mounts the file system as read/write. (For this to work, the shared file system must have been exported with read/write permission.)

The next section describes how to make the mount more permanent (using the /etc/fstab file) and how to select various options for NFS mounts.

Automatically Mounting an NFS File System

To set up an NFS file system to mount automatically each time you start your Linux system, you need to add an entry for that NFS file system to the /etc/fstab file. That file contains information about all different kinds of mounted (and available to be mounted) file systems for your system.

Here's the format for adding an NFS file system to your local system:

```
host:directory    mountpoint    nfs    options    0    0
```

The first item (host:directory) identifies the NFS server computer and shared directory. mountpoint is the local mount point on which the NFS directory is mounted. It's followed by the file system type (nfs). Any options related to the mount appear next in a comma-separated list. (The last two zeros configure the system to not dump the contents of the file system and not run fsck on the file system.)

The following are examples of NFS entries in /etc/fstab:

```
maple:/tmp    /mnt/maple nfs    rsize=8192,wsize=8192  0 0
oak:/apps     /oak/apps  nfs    noauto,ro             0 0
```

In the first example, the remote directory /tmp from the computer named maple (maple:/tmp) is mounted on the local directory /mnt/maple (the local directory must already exist). The file system type is nfs, and read (rsize) and write (wsize) buffer sizes (discussed in the section "Using mount Options" later in this chapter) are set at 8192 to speed data transfer associated with this connection. In the second example, the remote directory is /apps on the computer named oak. It is set up as an NFS file system (nfs) that can be mounted on the /oak/apps directory locally. This file system is not mounted automatically (noauto), however, and can be mounted only as read-only (ro) using the mount command after the system is already running.

> **TIP** The default is to mount an NFS file system as read/write. However, the default for exporting a file system is read-only. If you are unable to write to an NFS file system, check that it was exported as read/write from the server.

Mounting noauto File Systems

Your /etc/fstab file may also contain devices for other file systems that are not mounted automatically. For example, you might have multiple disk partitions on your hard disk or an NFS shared file system that you might want to mount only occasionally. A noauto file system can be mounted manually. The advantage is that when you type the mount command, you can type less information and have the rest filled in by the contents of the /etc/fstab file. So, for example, you could type:

```
# mount /oak/apps
```

With this command, mount knows to check the /etc/fstab file to get the file system to mount (oak:/apps), the file system type (nfs), and the options to use with the mount (in this case ro for read-only). Instead of typing the local mount point (/oak/apps), you could have typed the remote file system name (oak:/apps) and had other information filled in.

> **TIP** When naming mount points, including the name of the remote NFS server in that name can help you remember where the files are actually being stored. This may not be possible if you are sharing home directories (/home) or mail directories (/var/spool/mail). For example, you might mount a file system from a machine called duck on the directory /mnt/duck.

Using mount Options

You can add several mount options to the /etc/fstab file (or to a mount command line itself) to influence how the file system is mounted. When you add options to /etc/fstab, they must be separated by commas. For example, here the noauto, ro, and hard options are used when oak:/apps is mounted:

```
oak:/apps    /oak/apps  nfs    noauto,ro,hard    0 0
```

The following are some options that are valuable for mounting NFS file systems:

- hard — If this option is used and the NFS server disconnects or goes down while a process is waiting to access it, the process will hang until the server comes back up. This is helpful if it is critical that the data you are working with not get out of sync with the programs that are accessing it. (This is the default behavior.)

- soft — If the NFS server disconnects or goes down, a process trying to access data from the server will time out after a set period of time when this option is on. An input/output error is delivered to the process trying to access the NFS server.

- rsize — The number of bytes of data read at a time from an NFS server. The default is 1024. Using a larger number (such as 8192) will get you better performance on a network that is fast (such as a LAN) and is relatively error-free (that is, one that doesn't have a lot of noise or collisions).

- wsize — The number of bytes of data written at a time to an NFS server. The default is 1,024. Performance issues are the same as with the rsize option.

- timeo=# — Sets the time after an RPC timeout occurs that a second transmission is made, where # represents a number in tenths of a second. The default value is seven-tenths of a second. Each successive timeout causes the timeout value to be doubled (up to 60 seconds maximum). Increase this value if you believe that timeouts are occurring because of slow response from the server or a slow network.

- retrans=# — Sets the number of minor timeouts and retransmissions that need to happen before a major timeout occurs.

- retry=# — Sets how many minutes to continue to retry failed mount requests, where # is replaced by the number of minutes to retry. The default is 10,000 minutes (which is about one week).

- bg — If the first mount attempt times out, try all subsequent mounts in the background. This option is very valuable if you are mounting a slow or sporadically available NFS file system. By placing mount requests in the background, your system can continue to mount other file systems instead of waiting for the current one to complete.

NOTE If a nested mount point is missing, a timeout to allow for the needed mount point to be added occurs. For example, if you mount /usr/trip and /usr/trip/extra as NFS file systems and /usr/trip is not yet mounted when /usr/trip/extra tries to mount, /usr/trip/extra will time out. If you're lucky, /usr/trip comes up and /usr/trip/extra mounts on the next retry.

- fg — If the first mount attempt times out, try subsequent mounts in the foreground. This is the default behavior. Use this option if it is imperative that the mount be successful before continuing (for example, if you are mounting /usr).

Any of the options that don't require a value can have no appended to it to have the opposite effect. For example, nobg indicates that the mount should not be done in the background.

Using autofs to Mount NFS File Systems on Demand

Recent improvements to auto-detecting and mounting removable devices have meant that you can simply insert or plug in those devices to have them detected, mounted, and displayed. However, to make the process of detecting and mounting remote NFS file systems more automatic, you still need to use a facility such as autofs (short for automatically mounted file systems).

The autofs facility will mount network file systems on demand when someone tries to use the file systems. With the autofs facility configured and turned on, you can cause any NFS shared directories to mount on demand. To use the autofs facility, you need to have the autofs package installed. (For Fedora, you can type yum install autofs or for Debian type apt-get install autofs to install the package from the network.)

With autofs enabled, if you know the hostname and directory being shared by another host computer, simply change (cd) to the autofs mount directory (/net by default). This causes the shared resource to be automatically mounted and made accessible to you.

The following steps explain how to turn on the autofs facility:

1. As root user from a Terminal window, open the /etc/auto.master file and look for the following line:

```
/net    -hosts
```

   This causes the /net directory to act as the mount point for the NFS shared directories you want to access on the network. (If there is a comment character at the beginning of that line, remove it.)

2. Start the autofs service by typing the following as root user:

```
# /etc/init.d/autofs start
```

3. On a Fedora system, set up the autofs service to restart every time you boot your system:

```
# chkconfig autofs on
```

Believe it or not, that's all you have to do. If you have a network connection to the NFS servers from which you want to share directories, try to access a shared NFS directory. For example, if you know that the /usr/local/share directory is being shared from the computer on your network named shuttle, you can do the following:

```
$ cd /net/shuttle
```

If that computer has any shared directories that are available to you, you can successfully change to that directory.

You also can type the following:

```
$ ls
usr
```

You should be able to see that the usr directory is part of the path to a shared directory. If there were shared directories from other top-level directories (such as /var or /tmp), you would see those as well. Of course, seeing any of those directories depends on how security is set up on the server.

Try going straight to the shared directory as well. For example:

```
$ cd /net/shuttle/usr/local/share
$ ls
info man music television
```

At this point, the ls command should reveal the contents of the /usr/local/share directory on the computer named shuttle. What you can do with that content depends on how it was configured for sharing by the server.

This can be a bit disconcerting because you won't see any files or directories until you actually try to use them, such as changing to a network-mounted directory. The ls command, for example, won't show anything under a network-mounted directory until the directory is mounted, which may lead to a sometimes-it's-there-and-sometimes-it's-not impression. Just change to a network-mounted directory, or access a file on such a directory, and autofs will take care of the rest.

Unmounting NFS File Systems

After an NFS file system is mounted, unmounting it is simple. You use the umount command with either the local mount point or the remote file system name. For example, here are two ways you could unmount maple:/tmp from the local directory /mnt/maple:

```
# umount maple:/tmp
# umount /mnt/maple
```

Either form works. If maple:/tmp is mounted automatically (from a listing in /etc/fstab), the directory will be remounted the next time you boot Linux. If it was a temporary mount (or listed as noauto in /etc/fstab), it won't be remounted at boot time.

 **The command is** umount, **not** unmount. **This is easy to get wrong.**

If you get the message device is busy when you try to unmount a file system, it means the unmount failed because the file system is being accessed. Most likely, one of the directories in the NFS file system is the current directory for your shell (or the shell of someone else on your system). The other possibility is that a command is holding a file open in the NFS file system (such as a text editor). Check your Terminal windows and other shells, and cd out of the directory if you are in it, or just close the Terminal windows.

If an NFS file system won't unmount, you can force it (umount -f /mnt/maple) or unmount and clean up later (umount -l /mnt/maple). The -l option is usually the better choice because a forced unmount can disrupt a file modification that is in progress.

Other Cool Things to Do with NFS

You can share some directories to make it convenient for a user to work from any of several different Linux computers on your network. Some examples of useful directories to share are:

- /var/spool/mail — By sharing this directory from your mail server and mounting it on the same directory on other computers on your network, you can enable users to access their mail from any of those other computers. This saves users from having to download messages to their current computers or from having to log in to the server just to get mail. There is only one mailbox for each user, no matter from where it is accessed.

- /home — This is a similar concept to sharing mail, except that all users have access to their home directories from any of the NFS clients. Again, you would mount /home on the same mount point on each client computer. When the user logs in, he or she has access to all of the startup files and data files contained in his or her /home/user directory.

 **If your users rely on a shared** /home **directory, you should make sure that the NFS server that exports the directory is fairly reliable. If** /home **isn't available, the user may not have the startup files to log in correctly, or any of the data files needed to get work done. One workaround is to have a minimal set of startup files (.bashrc, .Xdefaults, and so on) available in the user's home directory when the NFS directory is not mounted. This enables the user to log in properly at those times.**

- /project — Although you don't have to use this name, a common practice among users on a project is to share a directory structure containing files that people on the project need to share so that everyone can work on original files and keep copies of the latest versions in one place. (Of course, a better way to manage a project is with CVS or some other version control–type software, but this is a poor person's way to do it.)

- /var/log — An administrator can keep track of log files from several different computers by mounting the /var/log file on the administrator's computer. (Each server may need to export the directory to enable root to be mapped between the computers for this to work.) If there are problems with a computer, the administrator can then easily view the shared log files live.

If you are working exclusively with Linux and other UNIX systems, NFS is probably your best choice for sharing file systems. You can mount NFS shares on a Windows client, but only if you have NFS client software for Windows, something most organizations do not have. If your network consists primarily of Microsoft Windows computers or a combination of systems, you may want to look into using Samba for file sharing.

Setting Up a Samba File Server

Samba is a software package that comes with Fedora and Red Hat Enterprise Linux systems and many other Linux systems. (You can obtain the Samba software package from www.samba.org if it is not included with your distribution.) Samba enables you to share file systems and printers on a network with computers that use the Server Message Block (SMB) or Common Internet File System (CIFS) protocol. SMB is the Microsoft protocol that is delivered with Windows operating systems for sharing files and printers. CIFS is an open, cross-platform protocol that is based on SMB. Samba contains free implementations of SMB and CIFS.

NOTE In Windows file and printer sharing, SMB is sometimes referred to as CIFS (Common Internet File System), which is an Internet standard network file system definition based on SMB, or NetBIOS, which was the original SMB communication protocol.

The Samba software package contains a variety of daemon processes, administrative tools, user tools, and configuration files. To do basic Samba configuration, start with the Samba Server Configuration window, which provides a graphical interface for configuring the server and setting directories to share.

Most of the Samba configuration you do ends up in the /etc/samba/smb.conf file. If you need to access features that are not available through the Samba Server Configuration window, you can edit /etc/samba/smb.conf by hand or use SWAT, a Web-based interface, to configure Samba.

Daemon processes consist of smbd (the SMB daemon) and nmbd (the NetBIOS name server). The smbd daemon makes the file-sharing and printing services you add to your Linux system available to Windows client computers. The Samba package supports the following client computers:

- Windows 9x
- Windows NT
- Windows ME
- Windows 2000
- Windows XP
- Windows Vista
- Windows for Workgroups
- MS Client 3.0 for DOS
- OS/2
- Dave for Macintosh computers

- Mac OS X
- Samba for Linux

NOTE Mac OS X Server ships with Samba, so you can use a Macintosh system as a server. This chapter, however, discusses using a Linux system as a server. You can then have Macintosh, Windows, or Linux client computers. In addition, Mac OS X ships with both client and server software for Samba.

As for administrative tools for Samba, you have several shell commands at your disposal: `testparm` and `testprns`, with which you can check your configuration files; `smbstatus`, which tells you what computers are currently connected to your shared resources; and the `nmblookup` command, with which you can query computers.

Samba uses the NetBIOS service to share resources with SMB clients, but the underlying network must be configured for TCP/IP. Although other SMB hosts can use TCP/IP, NetBEUI, and IPX/SPX to transport data, Samba for Linux supports only TCP/IP. Messages are carried between host computers with TCP/IP and are then handled by NetBIOS.

Getting and Installing Samba

You can get Samba software in different ways, depending on your Linux distribution. Here are a few examples:

- **Debian** — To use Samba in Debian, you must install the samba and smbclient packages using `apt-get`. Then start the Samba service by running the appropriate scripts from the `/etc/init.d` directory, as follows:

```
# apt get install samba samba-common smbclient swat
# /etc/init.d/samba start
# /etc/init.d/smb-client start
```

- **Gentoo** — With Gentoo, you need to have configured net-fs support into the kernel to use Samba server features. Installing the net-fs package (`emerge net-fs`) should get the required packages. To start the service, run `rc-update` and start the service immediately:

```
# emerge samba
# rc-update add samba default
# /etc/init.d/samba start
```

- **Fedora and other Red Hat Linux systems** — You need to install the samba, samba-client, samba-common, and optionally, the system-config-samba and samba-swat packages to use Samba in Fedora. You can then start Samba using the `service` and `chkconfig` commands as follows:

```
# service smb start
# chkconfig smb on
```

The commands and configuration files are the same on most Linux systems using Samba. The Samba project itself comes with a Web-based interface for administering Samba called Samba Web

Administration Tool (SWAT). For someone setting up Samba for the first time, SWAT is a good way to get it up and running.

> **NOTE** If your Linux installation does not have help documents for Samba available, consult the documentation on the Samba project home page (www.samba.org). Also, check the extensive help information that comes with SWAT.

Configuring Samba with SWAT

In addition to offering an extensive interface to Samba options, SWAT comes with an excellent help facility. And if you need to administer Samba from another computer, SWAT can be configured to be remotely accessible and secured by requiring an administrative login and password.

Turning on the SWAT Service

Before you can use SWAT, you must do some configuration. The first thing you must do is turn on the SWAT service, which is done differently in different Linux distributions.

Here's how to set up SWAT in Fedora and other Red Hat Linux systems:

1. Turn on the SWAT service by typing the following, as root user, from a Terminal window:

```
# chkconfig swat on
```

2. Pick up the change to the service by restarting the xinetd startup script as follows:

```
# service xinetd restart
```

Linux distributions such as Debian, Slackware, and Gentoo turn on the SWAT service from the inetd superserver daemon. After SWAT is installed, you simply remove the comment character from in front of the swat line in the /etc/inetd.conf file (as root user, using any text editor) and restart the daemon. Here's an example of what the swat line looks like in Debian:

```
swat   stream    tcp   nowait.400   root   /usr/sbin/tcpd   /usr/sbin/swat
```

With the SWAT service ready to be activated, restart the inetd daemon so it rereads the inetd.conf file. To do that in Debian, type the following as root user:

```
# /etc/init.d/inetd restart
```

The init.d script and xinetd services are the two ways that SWAT services are generally started in Linux. So if you are using a Linux distribution other than Fedora or Debian, look in the /etc/inetd.conf file or /etc/xinetd.d directory (which is used automatically in Fedora), for the location of your SWAT service.

When you have finished this procedure, a daemon process will be listening on your network interfaces for requests to connect to your SWAT service. You can now use the SWAT program, described in the next section, to configure Samba.

Starting with SWAT

You can run the SWAT program by typing the following URL in your local browser:

```
http://localhost:901/
```

Enter the root username and password when the browser prompts you. The SWAT window (see Figure 27-2) appears.

Use SWAT from your browser to manage your Samba configuration.

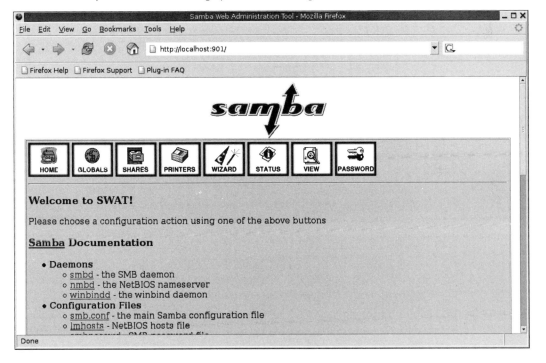

> **TIP**   Instead of running SWAT from your local browser, you can run it from another computer on the network by substituting the server computer's name for localhost. (To allow computers besides localhost to access the swat service on Fedora systems, you must change or remove the `only_from = 127.0.0.1` line from the `/etc/xinetd.d/swat` file and restart the xinetd service.)

The following sections explain how to use SWAT to create your configuration entries (in `/etc/samba/smb.conf`) and to work with that configuration.

> **CAUTION**   Any time you use a GUI to change a plain-text configuration file (as you do with SWAT), you may lose some of the information that you put in by hand. In this case, SWAT deletes comment lines and rearranges other entries. To protect changes you have made manually, make a backup copy of your /etc/samba/smb.conf file before you edit it with SWAT.

Creating Global Samba Settings in SWAT

A group of global settings affects how file and print sharing are generally accomplished on a Samba server. These settings appear under the [global] heading in the /etc/samba/smb.conf file. To view and edit global variables, click the GLOBALS button on the SWAT window.

Seven types of options are available: base, security, logging, tuning, printing, browse, and WINs.

> **NOTE**   Each option relates to the exact parameters used in the /etc/samba/smb.conf file. You can refer to the smb.conf man page (type **man smb.conf**) to get more information on these parameters.

Base Options

The following options relate to basic information associated with your Samba server:

- **Workgroup** — The name of the workgroup associated with the group of SMB hosts. By default, the value for this field is WORKGROUP.

- **Realm** — If you are using kerberos authentication, this value indicates the kerberos realm to use. Typically, that is reflected by the hostname of the server providing the service.

- **NetBIOS name** — The name assigned to this Samba server. You can use the same name as your DNS hostname or make it blank, in which case the DNS hostname is used automatically. Your DNS hostname is filled in for you by default.

- **NetBIOS alias** — Enables you to set a way of referring to a host computer (an alias) that is different from the host's TCP/IP DNS name.

- **Server string** — A string of text identifying the server. This name appears in places such as the printer comment box. By default, it says Samba and the version number.

- **Interfaces** — Enables you to set up more than one network interface and let Samba browse several different subnetworks. The form of this field can be IP Address/Subnetwork Mask. Or, you could identify a network interface (such as eth0 for the first Ethernet card on your computer). For example, a Class C network address may appear as:

  192.168.24.11/255.255.255.0

Security Options

Of the security options settings, the first (Security) is the most important one to get right. It defines the type of security used to give access to the shared file systems and printers to the client computers. (To see some of the fields described here, you need to click the Advanced view.)

- **Security** — Sets how password and user information is transferred to the Samba server from the client computer. As noted earlier, it's important to get this value right. Samba versions 2.0 and later have a different default value for security (`security=user`) than the earlier versions of Samba do (`security=share`). If you are coming from an earlier version of Samba and clients are failing to access your server, this setting is a good place to start. Here are your options:

- **user** — The most common type of security used to share files and printers among Windows 95/98/2000/NT/XP clients. It is the default set with Samba in the current release. This setting is appropriate if users are doing a lot of file sharing (as opposed to a Samba server used mostly as a print server). It requires that a user provide a username/password before using the server. The easiest way to get this method working is to give a Linux user account to every client user who will use the Samba server, therefore providing basically the same file permissions to a user account through Samba as the same user would get if he or she were logged in directly to Linux.

- **share** — The `share` value for security works best for just print sharing or for providing file access that is more public (guest sharing). A client doesn't need to provide a valid username and password to access the server. However, the user typically has a guest level of permission to access and change files. See the sidebar "Assigning Guest Accounts" in this chapter for further information.

- **server** — From the client's point of view, this is the same as `user` security in that the client still has to provide a valid username/password combination to use the Samba server at all. The difference is on the server side. With `server` security, the username/password is sent to another SMB server for validation. If that fails, Samba tries to validate the client using `user` security.

- **domain** — From the client's point of view, this is the same as `user` security. This setting is used only if the Samba server has been added to a Windows NT domain (using the `smbpasswd` command). When a client tries to connect to the Samba server in this mode, its username and password are sent to a Windows NT Primary or Backup Domain controller. This is accomplished the same way that a Windows NT server would perform validation. Valid Linux user accounts must still be set up.

- **Encrypt passwords** — Controls whether encrypted passwords can be negotiated with the client. This is on (`Yes`) by default. For domain security, this value must be `Yes`. Later versions of Windows NT (4.0 SP3 or later) and Windows 98 and Windows 2000 expect encrypted passwords to be on.

- **Update encrypted** — Allows users who log in with a plain-text password to automatically have their passwords updated to encrypted passwords when they log in. Normally, this option is off. Turn it on when you want an installation using plain-text passwords to have everyone updated to encrypted password authentication. It saves users the trouble of running the `smbpasswd` command directly from the server. After everyone is updated, this feature can be turned off. When this option is on, the Encrypt passwords option should be set to `No`.

- **Obey PAM restrictions** — Turn this on (`Yes`) if you want to use PAM for account and session management. Even if activated, PAM is not used if the encrypted passwords feature is turned on (`encrypt passwords = yes`). (PAM stands for Pluggable Authentication Modules and is used for authenticating host computers and users.)

- **PAM password change** — Indicates to use the PAM password change control flag for Samba. If this is on (Yes), SMB clients will use PAM instead of the program listed in the Password Program value for changing SMB passwords.

- **Passwd program** — Indicates which password program to use to change Linux user passwords. By default, /usr/bin/passwd is used, with the current username (%u) inserted.

- **Passwd chat** — Sets the chat that goes on between the Samba daemon (smbd) and the Linux password program (/usr/bin/passwd by default) when smbd tries to synchronize SMB passwords with Linux user passwords.

- **UNIX password sync** — With this on (Yes), Samba tries to update a user's Linux user password with his or her SMB password when the SMB password is changed. To do this, SMB runs the passwd command as the root user. This is on by default.

- **Guest account** — Specifies the username for the guest account. When a service is specified as Guest OK, the name entered here is used to access that service. The account is usually the nobody username.

> **TIP**   Make sure that the guest account is a valid user. (The default of **nobody** should already be set up to work.) With an invalid user as the guest account, the **IPC$** connection that lists the shared resources fails.

- **Username map** — Identifies the file that contains a mapping of client usernames to the Samba server. By default, this file is /etc/samba/smbusers.

- **Hosts allow** — Contains a list of one or more hosts that are allowed to use your computer's Samba services. By default, users from any computer can connect to the Samba server (of course, they still have to provide valid usernames and passwords). Generally, you use this option to allow connections from specific computers (such as 10.0.0.1) or computer networks (such as 10.0.0.) that are excluded by the Hosts deny option.

- **Hosts deny** — Contains a list of one or more hosts from which users are not allowed to use your computer's Samba services. You can make this option fairly restrictive, and then add the specific hosts and networks you want to use the Samba server. By default, no hosts are denied.

Logging Options

The following options help define how logging is done on your Samba server:

- **Log level** — Sets the debug level used when logging Samba activity. Raise the level from the default (0) to log more Samba activity.

- **Log file** — Defines the location of the Samba smb log file. By default, Samba log files are contained in /var/log/samba (with filenames log.nmbd, log.smbd, and smb.log). In this option, the %m is replaced by smb to set the smb log file as /var/log/samba/smb.log.

- **Max log size** — Sets the maximum amount of space, in kilobytes, that the log files can consume. By default, the value is set to 0 (no limit).

Assigning Guest Accounts

Samba always assigns the permissions level of a valid user on the Linux system to clients who use the server. In the case of share security, the user is assigned a guest account (the nobody user account by default).

If the guest account value isn't set, Samba goes through a fairly complex set of rules to determine which user account to use. The result is that it can be hard to ensure which user permissions will be assigned in each case. That's why user security is recommended if you want to provide more specific user access to your Samba server.

Performance Options

The Socket Options option lets you pass options to the protocols Samba uses to communicate. The following options are set by default: TCP_NODELAY, SO_RCVBUF=8192, and SO_SNDBUF=8192. The first option disables Nagle's algorithm, which is used to manage the transmission of TCP/IP packets. The other two options set the maximum size of the sockets receive buffer and the sockets send buffer to 8192, respectively. These options are set to improve performance (reportedly up to 10 times faster than without setting these options). In general, you shouldn't change these options.

Printing Options

The printing options are used to define how printer status information is presented. For the overwhelming majority of Linux systems, the printing value is set to cups. You can use printing styles from other types of operating systems, such as UNIX System V (sysv), AIX (aix), HP UNIX (hpux), and Berkeley UNIX (bsd), to name a few. LPRng (lprng), offered by many UNIX systems, is also included. Other printing options enable you to redefine the location of basic printing commands (lpq, lprm, and so on) and printing files (such as the name of the printcap file).

Browse Options

A browse list is a list of computers that are available on the network to SMB services. Clients use this list to find computers that are on their own LAN and also computers in their workgroups that may be on other reachable networks.

In Samba, browsing is configured by options described later in this section and implemented by the nmbd daemon. If you are using Samba for a workgroup within a single LAN, you probably don't need to concern yourself with the browsing options. However, if you are using Samba to provide services across several physical subnetworks, you might want to consider configuring Samba as a domain master browser. Here are some points to think about:

- Samba can be configured as a master browser, which allows it to gather lists of computers from local browse masters to form a wide-area server list. (Browse masters keep track of available shared directories and printers on the network of Samba systems and broadcast information about those resources as necessary.)

- If Samba is acting as a domain master browser, Samba should use a WINS server to help browse clients resolve the names from this list.

- Samba can be used as a WINS server, although it can also rely on other types of operating systems to provide that service.

- There should be only one domain master browser for each workgroup. Don't use Samba as a domain master for a workgroup with the same name as an NT domain.

If you are working in an environment that has a mix of Samba and Windows NT servers, use an NT server as your WINS server. If Samba is your only file server, choose a single Samba server (nmbd daemon) to supply the WINS services.

> **NOTE** A WINS server is basically a name server for NetBIOS names. It provides the same service that a DNS server does with TCP/IP domain names: It can translate names into addresses. A WINS server is particularly useful for allowing computers to communicate with SMB across multiple subnetworks where information is not being broadcast across the subnetworks' boundaries.

To configure the browsing feature in Samba, you must have the workgroup named properly (described earlier in this section). Here are the global options related to SMB browsing:

- **OS level** — Set a value to control whether your Samba server (nmbd daemon) may become the local master browser for your workgroup. Raising this setting increases the Samba server's chance to control the browser list for the workgroup in the local broadcast area.

  If the value is 0, a Windows machine will probably be selected. A value of 60 ensures that the Samba server is chosen over an NT server. The default is 20.

- **Preferred master** — Set this to Yes if you want to force selection of a master browser and give the Samba server a better chance of being selected. (Setting Domain Master to Yes along with this option ensures that the Samba server will be selected.) This is set to Auto by default, which causes Samba to try to detect the current master browser before taking that responsibility.

- **Local master** — Set this to Yes if you want the Samba server to become the local browser master. (This is not a guarantee, but gives it a chance.) Set the value to No if you do not want your Samba server selected as the local master. Local Master is Auto by default.

- **Domain master** — Set this to Yes if you want the Samba server (nmbd daemon) to identify itself as the domain master browser for its workgroup. This list will then allow client computers assigned to the workgroup to use SMB-shared files and printers from subnetworks that are outside their own subnetwork. This is set to No by default.

> **NOTE** If browsing isn't working, check the nmbd log file (/var/log/samba/log.nmbd). To get more detail, increase the debug information level to 2 or 3 (described earlier in this section) and restart Samba. The log can tell you if your Samba server is the master browser and, if so, which computers are on its list.

WINS Options

Use the WINS options if you want to have a particular WINS server provide the name-to-address translation of NetBIOS names used by SMB clients:

- **WINS server** — If there is a WINS server on your network that you want to use to resolve the NetBIOS names for your workgroup, enter that server's IP address here. Again, you probably want to use a WINS server if your workgroup extends outside the local subnetwork.

- **WINS support** — Set this value to Yes if you want your Samba server to act as a WINS server. (It's No by default.) Again, this is not needed if all the computers in your workgroup are on the same subnetwork. Only one computer on your network should be assigned as the WINS server.

In addition to the values described here, you can access dozens more options by clicking the Advanced View button. When you have filled in all the fields you need, click Commit Changes on the screen to have the changes written to the /etc/samba/smb.conf file.

Configuring Shared Directories with SWAT

To make your shared directory available to others, add an entry to the SWAT window. To use SWAT to set up Samba to share directories, do the following:

> **NOTE** You may see one or more security warnings during the course of this procedure. These messages warn you that someone can potentially view the data you are sending to SWAT. If you are working on your local host or on a private LAN, the risk is minimal.

1. From the main SWAT window, click the SHARES button.

2. Type the name of the directory that you want to share in the Create Share box, and then click Create Share.

3. Add any of these options:

   - **Comment** — A few words to describe the shared directory (optional).

   - **Path** — The path name of the directory you are sharing.

   - **invalid users** — Lets you add a list of users who are not allowed to log in to the Samba service. Besides identifying usernames directly (from your /etc/passwd file), invalid users can be identified by Linux group or NIS netgroup, by adding a + or & in front of the name, respectively. Precede the name with @ to have Samba first check your NIS netgroup, then the Linux group for the name.

   - **valid users** — Add names here to identify which Linux user accounts can access the Samba service. As with invalid users, names can be preceeded with +, &, or @ characters.

   - **admin users** — Lets you identify users who have administrative privilege on a particular share. This is available with security = share type of security only.

- **Read list** — Add users to whom you want to grant only read access to shares (even if a share is available with read-write access). This is available with the `security = share` type of security only.

- **Write list** — Add users to whom you want to grant write access to shares, even if the share is available to all others with read-only access. This is available with the `security = share` type of security only.

- **Guest account** — If `Guest ok` is selected, the username that is defined here is assigned to users accessing the file system. No password will be required to access the share. The `nobody` user account (used only by users who access your computer remotely) is the default name used. (The FTP user is also a recommended value.)

- **Read only** — If `Yes`, files can only be read from this file system, but no remote user can save or modify files on the file system. Select `No` if you want users to be allowed to save files to this directory over the network.

- **Guest ok** — Select `Yes` to enable guest users access to this directory without requiring a password.

- **Hosts allow** — Add the names of the computers that will be allowed to access this file system. Separate hostnames by commas, spaces, or tabs. Here are some valid ways of entering hostnames:

  - **localhost** — Allows access to the local host.

  - **192.168.12.125** — IP address. Enter an individual IP address.

  - **192.168.12.** — Enter a network address to include all hosts on a network. (Be sure to put a dot at the end of the network number or it won't work!)

  - **pcren, pcstimpy** — Enables access to individual hosts by name.

  - **EXCEPT** *host* — If you are allowing access to a group of hosts (such as by entering a network address), use `EXCEPT` to specifically deny access from one host from that group.

- **Hosts deny** — Denies access to specific computers by placing their names here. By default, no particular computers are excluded. Enter hostnames in the same forms you used for `Hosts allow`.

- **Browseable** — Indicates whether you can view this directory on the list of shared directories. This is on (`Yes`) by default.

- **Available** — Enables you to leave this entry intact but turns off the service. This is useful if you want to close access to a directory temporarily. This is on (`Yes`) by default. Select `No` to turn it off.

4. Select Commit Changes.

At this point, the shared file systems should be available to the Samba client computers (Windows 9x, Windows NT, Windows 2000, OS/2, Linux, and so on) that have access to your Linux Samba server. Before you try that, however, you can check your Samba configuration.

Checking Your Samba Setup with SWAT

From the SWAT window, select the STATUS button.

From this window, you can restart your smbd and nmbd processes. Likewise, you can see lists of active connections, active shares, and open files. (The preferred way to start the smbd and nmbd daemons is to set up the smb service to start automatically. Type **chkconfig smb on** to set the service to start at boot time.)

Working with Samba Files and Commands

Although you can set up Samba through the Samba Server Configuration window or SWAT, many administrators prefer to edit the /etc/samba/smb.conf directly. As root user, you can view the contents of this file and make needed changes. If you selected user security (as recommended), you will also be interested in the smbusers and smbpasswd files (in the /etc/samba directory). These files, as well as commands such as testparm and smbstatus, are described in the following sections.

Editing the smb.conf File

Changes you make using the Samba Server Configuration window or SWAT Web interface are reflected in your /etc/samba/smb.conf file. Here's an example of a smb.conf file (with comments removed):

```
[global]
workgroup = ESTREET
server string = Samba Server on Maple
hosts allow = 192.168.0.
printcap name = /etc/printcap
load printers = yes
printing = cups
log file = /var/log/samba/%m.log
max log size = 0
smb passwd file = /etc/samba/smbpasswd
security = user
encrypt passwords = Yes
unix password sync = Yes
passwd program = /usr/bin/passwd %u
passwd chat = *New*password* %n\n *Retype*new*password* %n\n *passwd:
        *all*authentication*tokens*updated*successfully*
pam password change = yes
```

739

```
        obey pam restrictions = yes
        socket options = TCP_NODELAY SO_RCVBUF=8192 SO_SNDBUF=8192
        username map = /etc/samba/smbusers
        dns proxy = no
        [homes]
        comment = Home Directories
        browseable = no
        writable = yes
        valid users = %S
        create mode = 0664
        directory mode = 0775
        [printers]
        comment = All Printers
        path = /var/spool/samba
        browseable = no
        guest ok = no
        writable = no
        printable = yes
```

I won't go through every line of this example, but here are some observations. In the [global] section, the workgroup is set to ESTREEI, the server is identified as the Samba Server on Maple, and only computers that are on the local network (192.168.0.) are allowed access to the Samba service. You must change the local network to match your network.

Definitions for the local printers that will be shared are taken from the /etc/printcap file, the printers are loaded (yes), and the CUPS printing service is used.

Separate log files for each host trying to use the service are created in /var/log/samba/%m.log (with %m automatically replaced with each hostname). There is no limit to log file size (0).

This example uses the user-level security (security = user), which allows a user to log in once and then easily access the printers and the user's home directory on the Linux system. Password encryption is on (encrypt passwords = yes) because most Windows systems have password encryption on by default. Passwords are stored in the /etc/samba/smbpasswd file on your Linux system.

The dns proxy = no option prevents Linux from looking up system names on the DNS server (used for TCP/IP lookups).

The [homes] section enables each user to access his or her Linux home directory from a Windows system on the LAN. The user will be able to write to the home directory. However, other users will not be able see or share this directory. The [printers] section enables all users to print to any printer configured on the local Linux system.

Adding Samba Users

Performing user-style Samba security means assigning a Linux user account to each person using the Linux file systems and printers from his or her Windows workstation. (You could assign users to a guest account instead, but in this example, all users have their own accounts.) Then you need to add SMB passwords for each user. For example, here is how you would add a user whose Windows workstation login is chuckp:

1. Type the following as root user from a Terminal window to add a Linux user account:

```
# useradd -m chuckp
```

2. Add a Linux password for the new user as follows:

```
# passwd chuckp
Changing password for user chuckp
New UNIX password: ********
Retype new UNIX password: ********
```

3. Repeat the previous steps to add user accounts for all users from Windows workstations on your LAN that you want to give access to your Linux system.

4. Type the following command to create the Samba password file (smbpasswd) on Fedora Linux systems:

```
# cat /etc/passwd | /usr/bin/mksmbpasswd.sh > /etc/samba/smbpasswd
```

In Debian systems, use the /usr/sbin/mksmbpasswd command instead of mksmbpasswd.sh.

5. Add an SMB password for the user as follows:

```
# smbpasswd chuckp
New SMB password: **********
Retype new SMB password: **********
```

6. Repeat this step for each user. Later, each user can log in to Linux and rerun the passwd and smbpasswd commands to set private passwords.

> **NOTE** In the most recent version of Samba, options are available in the smb.conf file that cause SMB and Linux passwords to be synchronized automatically. See descriptions of the passwd program, passwd chat, and UNIX password sync options in the SWAT section of this chapter.

Starting the Samba Service

When you have your Samba configuration the way you would like it, restart the Samba server as described earlier in the "Getting and Installing Samba" section. You can now check SMB clients on the network to see if they can access your Samba server.

Testing Your Samba Permissions

You can run several commands from a shell to work with Samba. One is the testparm command, which you can use to check the access permissions you have set up. It lists global parameters that are set, along with any shared directories or printers.

Checking the Status of Shared Directories

The `smbstatus` command enables you to view who is currently using Samba shared resources offered from your Linux system. The following is an example of the output from `smbstatus`:

```
# smbstatus
Samba version 3.0.24-12.fc7
PID      Username       Group          Machine
-------------------------------------------------------------------
25770    chris          chris          booker        (10.0.0.50)
25833    chris          chris          10.0.0.50     (10.0.0.50)
Service      pid    machine        Connected at
-------------------------------------------------------------------
IPC$         25729  booker         Sun Apr 22 12:06:29 2007
mytmp        25770  booker         Sun Apr 22 12:16:03 2007
mytmp        25833  10.0.0.50      Sun Apr 22 12:25:52 2007
IPC$         25730  booker         Sun Apr 22 12:06:29 2007
Locked files:
Pid   Uid DenyMode  Access   R/W Oplock SharePath   Name   Time
-------------------------------------------------------------------

25833 501 DENY_NONE 0x12019f RDWR NONE  /tmp .b.txt.swp Sun Apr 22 12:26:18 2007
```

This output shows that from your Linux Samba server, the `mytmp` service (which is a share of the `/tmp` directory) is currently open by the computer named booker. PID 25833 is the process number of the smbd daemon on the Linux server that is handling the service. The file that is open is the `/tmp/.b.txt.swap` file, which happened to be opened by a `vi` command. It has read/write access.

Using Samba Shared Directories

Once you have configured your Samba server, you can try using the shared directories from a client computer on your network. The following sections describe how to use your Samba server from another Linux system or from various Windows systems.

Using Samba from Nautilus

To connect to a Samba share from a Nautilus file manager, use the Open Location box by clicking File ➪ Open Location. Then type **smb:** into your Nautilus file manager Location box.

A list of SMB workgroups on your network appears in the window. You can select a workgroup, choose a server, and then select a resource to use. This should work for shares requiring no password.

The Nautilus interface seems to be a bit buggy when you need to enter passwords. It also requires you to either send clear-text passwords or type the username and password into your location box. For example, to get to my home directory (`/home/chris`) through Nautilus, I can type my username, password, server name, and share name as follows:

```
smb://chris:my72mgb@arc/chris
```

Mounting Samba Directories in Linux

Linux can view your Samba shared directories as it does any other medium (hard disk, NFS shares, CD-ROM, and so on). Use mount to mount a Samba shared file system so that it is permanently connected to your Linux file system.

Here's an example of the mount command in which a home directory (/home/chris) from a computer named toys on a local directory (/mnt/toys) is mounted. The command is typed, as root user, from a Terminal window:

```
# mkdir /mnt/toys
# mount -t smbfs -o username=chris,password=a72mg //toys/chris /mnt/toys
```

The file system type for a Samba share is smbfs (-t smbfs). The username (chris) and password (a72mg) are passed as options (-o). The remote share of the home directory on toys is //toys/chris. The local mount point is /mnt/toys. At this point, you can access the contents of /home/chris on toys as you would any file or directory locally. You will have the same permission to access and change the contents of that directory (and its subdirectories) as you would if you were the user chris using those contents directly from toys.

To mount the Samba shared directory permanently, add an entry to your /etc/fstab file. For the example just described, you'd add the following line (as root user):

```
//toys/chris    /mnt/toys    smbfs    username=chris,password=a72mg
```

Troubleshooting Your Samba Server

A lot can go wrong with a Samba server. If your Samba server isn't working properly, the descriptions in this section should help you pinpoint the problem.

Basic Networking in Place?

You can't share anything with other computers without a network. Before computers can share directories and printers from Samba, they must be able to communicate on your LAN.

Your Samba server can use the TCP/IP name as the NetBIOS name (used by Window networks for file and printer sharing), or a separate NetBIOS name can be set in the smb.conf file. It is critical, however, that the broadcast address be the same as the broadcast address for all clients communicating with your Samba server. To see your broadcast address, type the following (as root user):

```
# ifconfig -a
eth0      Link encap:Ethernet   HWadd 00:D1:B3:75:A5:1B
          inet addr:10.0.0.1  Bcast:10.0.0.255  Mask:255.255.255.0
```

The important information is the broadcast address (Bcast:10.0.0.255), which is determined by the netmask (Mask:255.255.255.0). If the broadcast address isn't the same for the Samba server and the clients on the LAN, the clients cannot see that the Samba server has directories or printers to share.

Samba Service Running?

A basic troubleshooting check is to see if the service is running. Try the `smbclient` command from your Linux system to see that everything is running and being shared as you expect it to be. The `smbclient` command is a great tool for getting information about a Samba server and even accessing shared directories from both Linux and Windows computers. While logged in as root or any user who has access to your Samba server, type the following:

```
$ smbclient -L localhost
Password: **********
Domain=[ESTREET] OS=[Unix] Server=[Samba 3.0.3-4]
  Sharename      Type      Comment
  ---------      ----      -------
  homes          Disk      Home Directories
  IPC$           IPC       IPC Service (Samba Server)
  ADMIN$         Disk      IPC Service (Samba Server)
  hp-ns1         Printer
Domain=[ESTREET] OS=[Unix] Server=[Samba 3.0.8-4]
  Server              Comment
  ---------           -------
  PINE                Samba Server
  MAPLE               Windows XP
  NS1                 Samba Server
  Workgroup           Master
  ---------           -------
  ESTREET             PINE
```

The Samba server is running on the local computer in this example. Shared directories and printers, as well as servers in the workgroup, appear here. If the Samba server is not running, you see `Connection refused` messages, and you need to start the Samba service as described earlier in this chapter.

Firewall Open?

If the Samba server is running, it should begin broadcasting its availability on your LAN. If you try to access the server from a Windows or Linux client on your LAN but get a `Connection refused` error, the problem may be that the firewall on your Linux Samba server is denying access to the NetBIOS service.

CROSS-REF   Chapter 18 covers firewalls.

If you have a secure LAN, you can type the following (as root user) to flush your firewall filtering rules temporarily:

```
# iptables -F
```

Try to connect to the Samba server from a Windows or Linux client. If you find that you can connect to the server, turn the firewall back on:

```
# /etc/init.d/iptables restart
```

You then need to open access to ports 137, 138, and 139 in your firewall so that the Samba server can accept connections for services. (See Chapter 18 for information about modifying your firewalls.)

User Passwords Working?

Try accessing a shared Samba directory as a particular user (from the local host or other Linux system on your LAN). You can use the smbclient command to do this. Here is an example:

```
# smbclient //localhost/tmp -U chris
added interface ip=10.0.0.1 bcast=10.0.0.255 nmask=255.255.255.0
Password: *******
Domain=[ESTREET] OS=[Unix] Server=[Samba 2.2.7a]
smb: \>
```

In this example, smbclient connects to the directory share named tmp as the Samba user named chris. If the password is accepted, you should see information about the server and a smb:\> prompt. If you cannot access the same shared directory from a Windows client, it's quite possible that the client is passing an improper username and password. Part of the problem may be that the Windows client is not providing encrypted passwords.

For certain Windows clients, using encrypted passwords requires that you change a Windows registry for the machine. One way to change the registry is with the Windows regedit command. Registry changes required for different Windows systems are contained within the /usr/share/doc/samba-*/docs/Registry directory.

> **TIP** The smbclient command, used here to list server information and test passwords, can also be used to browse the shared directory and copy files after you are connected. After you see the smb:\> prompt, type **help** to see the available commands. The interface is similar to any ftp client, such as sftp.

If your particular problem has not been addressed in this troubleshooting section, please refer to the user documentation that accompanies the Samba project. On Fedora systems, look in the /usr/share/doc/samba-*/htmldocs directory for some excellent documentation you can read from your Web browser. In particular, refer to the Samba-HOWTO-Collection/diagnosis.html file for help with troubleshooting.

Summary

By providing centralized file servers, an organization can efficiently share information and applications with people within the organization, with customers, or with anyone around the world. Several different technologies are available for making your Linux computer into a file-serving powerhouse.

The Network File System (NFS) protocol was one of the first file server technologies available. It is particularly well suited for sharing file systems among Linux and other UNIX systems. NFS uses standard `mount` and `umount` commands to connect file systems to the directory structures of client computers.

The Samba software package that comes with many Linux distributions (or can be easily installed if it doesn't) contains protocols and utilities for sharing files and printers among Windows and OS/2 operating systems. It uses SMB protocols that are included with all Microsoft Windows systems and therefore provides a convenient method of sharing resources on LANs containing many Windows systems.

Part VI

Programming in Linux

Chapter 28

Programming Environments and Interfaces

You can slice and dice the topic of Linux programming environments and interfaces in a variety of ways. For example, a list of the programming languages known to have compilers that target or run on Linux easily runs to three single-spaced, typewritten pages. You could also examine the literally hundreds of programming libraries that exist for Linux. Alternatively, you can organize the discussion by dividing everything into three categories: graphically oriented interfaces, command-line interfaces, and other environments.

To some readers, a "programming environment" means a graphical, point-and-click integrated development environment (IDE) like that provided by Borland's Kylix or IBM's Eclipse. Yet another way to approach the subject is to look at Linux's development support for certain academic and computing subjects, such as graphics, databases, mathematics, engineering, chemistry, text processing, physics, biology, astronomy, networking, and parallel computing.

Unfortunately, there's no single definitive taxonomy on which everyone agrees, so this chapter takes the easy way out and divides things into environments and interfaces. For the purposes of this chapter, a *programming environment* refers to the setting in which programming takes place and the *accoutrement* with which someone performs programming tasks.

Understanding Programming Environments

Conventionally understood, a programming environment is either graphically oriented or command line–oriented. However, the Linux programming environment also consists of the services and capabilities provided by the system itself — that is, by the kernel and the core system components. Whether you use a mouse-driven IDE or a text editor and `make`, Linux imposes certain requirements and provides a number of capabilities that determine what the code you write in an IDE or text editor must do and can do.

In this chapter, the term *programming interface* refers to the rules or methods followed to accomplish a particular task. As with programming environments, programming interfaces are usually thought of as graphical or command line:

- **Graphical interface** — Uses the X Window System, or X, to receive and process user input and display information.
- **Command-line interface** — A strictly text-based affair that does not require a windowing system to run.

For example, Firefox, a Web browser, has a graphical interface; it won't work if X isn't running. Pine, a popular e-mail client, has a command-line interface; it works whether X is running or not.

There is a third type of interface, however, an *application programming interface*, or API. An API provides a structured method to write a program that performs a certain task. For example, to write a program that plays sounds, you use the sound API; to write a program that communicates over a TCP/IP network, you use the socket API. Neither playing a sound nor communicating over a TCP/IP network necessarily requires a graphical or command-line interface; both graphical and command-line programs can play sounds or use TCP/IP, provided they use the proper API.

Using Linux Programming Environments

Linux boasts arguably the richest programming environment of any operating system currently available. As mentioned earlier, this chapter uses the term "programming environment" to describe the tools used to write computer programs on a Linux system and to refer to underlying services that make programming on a Linux system possible (or, perhaps, worthwhile).

This section looks first at the fundamental services and capabilities that inform and constrain programming on a Linux system. Next, you examine a few of the most popular graphical IDEs for creating programs on a Linux system. The section closes with a look at some of the command-line tools used for writing programs.

NOTE A number of tools are available that simplify cross-platform programming. One such tool is SlickEdit. This interface runs on 8 platforms, supports 40 languages and emulates 13 editors. More information on it can be found at `www.slickedit.com`.

As you will discover, some of the graphical IDEs provide comfortable editors for writing code, drawing dialog boxes, and navigating the file system, but use the command-line tools to do the work of compiling the code, hiding the command-line tools beneath an attractive interface.

The Linux Development Environment

The Linux development environment consists of the services and capabilities provided by the kernel and core system components, including libraries of prebuilt functions that ship with each Linux distribution. These services and capabilities both define and limit how to write programs that run on a Linux system.

Consider files and the file system. Linux, like the UNIX systems on which it is modeled, is built on the key idiom that "everything is a file." This is a powerful metaphor and model that dramatically simplifies writing application programs to communicate with all sorts of devices. How? You can use the same function, the `write()` system call, to write data to a text file; to send data to a printer; to send keystrokes to an application; and, if you had one, to tell your network-connected coffee pot to brew another pot of coffee.

The file metaphor works this way because Linux treats all devices, such as modems, monitors, CD-ROM drives, disc drives, keyboards, mice, and printers, as if they were files. Device drivers, which are part of the kernel, sit between a device and the user and application trying to access it. A device driver translates an application's `write()` call into a form that the device can understand.

So, if an application uses the `write()` system call to write data to a text file on an ext3 file system, the ext3 driver writes the necessary bytes to a file on the disk, but if the application later uses the `write()` system call to write that same data to a printer, the printer driver transmits that data out the parallel port (or across the network) to the printer in a manner that the printer can understand and interpret. This is one way in which the Linux development environment informs, or defines, writing programs on a Linux system.

The catch? If the device you want to use doesn't have a driver (also called a kernel module), you can't use the `write()` call to do anything with that device. You simply do not have a way to communicate with the device. This is how the Linux development environment constrains programming on a Linux system.

What, then, in addition to the file idiom already discussed, are the key features of Linux that characterize its development environment? In no particular order:

- The process model
- CPU and memory protection
- The security model
- Preemptive multitasking
- Its multiuser design
- Interprocess communication
- The building blocks approach

Let's take a closer look at each of these features.

The Process Model

The process model is the way that Linux creates and manages running processes. Provided that a process has the necessary privileges, it can create (or spawn) other processes, referred to as child processes. The parent process can also exchange data with child processes. Of course, the capability to create child processes is not unique to Linux, but the particular way in which Linux does so is characteristic of all UNIX-like systems.

When a process calls the fork() system call, it creates an exact copy of itself. After being created by the fork() call, the child process typically calls one of a family of functions collectively known as exec(), providing a program to execute and any options or arguments to that program. Listing 28-1 illustrates the fork()/exec() process in a short program in the C language.

> **NOTE** Actually, the child process created when a process calls a fork(), isn't an *exact* duplicate of the parent. The process ID (PID) of the child process is different, as is the parent PID (PPID); any file locks held by the parent are reset, and any signals pending for the parent are cleared in the child.

LISTING 28-1

Simple fork() and exec() Sequence

```
/*
 * forkexec.c - illustrate simple fork/exec usage
 */
#include <stdio.h>
#include <unistd.h>
#include <sys/types.h>
#include <sys/wait.h>

int main(int argc, char *argv[])
{
        pid_t child;
        int status;

        child = fork();
        if (child == 0) {
                printf("in child\n");
                execl("/bin/ls", "/bin/ls", NULL);
        } else {
                printf("in parent\n");
                waitpid(child, &status, 0);
        }

        return 0;
}
```

Don't worry about what all the code means. The key points to understand are:

- The `child = fork()` statement creates a new (child) process.
- The code between `if (child == 0)` and the `else` statements is executed in the child process. In particular, the child uses the `execl()` function call to execute the `/bin/ls` program, which creates a directory listing of the current directory.
- The `waitpid()` statement is executed in the parent process, which means that the parent process will wait for the child process to terminate before continuing execution.

You can compile this program with the following command (if you have the GCC compiler installed):

```
$ gcc forkexec.c -o forkexec
```

and then execute it like this:

```
$ ./forkexec
in parent
in child
28.doc  a.out  forkexec  forkexec.c
```

Your output might be slightly different. The point to take away from this example is that Linux makes it very easy to create new processes programmatically. Because it is so easy, it is a common and powerful programming technique and a characteristic of the Linux programming model. Linux is hardly alone in providing a mechanism by which one program can start another, but the `fork()/exec()` technique is unique to Linux (and the UNIX systems on which Linux is based).

CPU and Memory Protection

Another fundamental component of programming on Linux systems is that the operating system itself, which consists of the Linux kernel, is almost entirely insulated from all application programs. The kernel runs in a protected CPU mode known variously as ring 0, kernel mode, or, more prosaically, kernel space. User programs such as Web browsers, e-mail clients, graphics programs, and games run outside of kernel mode in what is colloquially referred to as *user space*.

The distinction between kernel space and user space is important. The kernel has raw, uncontrolled access to system resources such as the CPU, RAM, and attached peripherals. The kernel mediates all access from user space programs to system resources, funneling it through the *system call*, or syscall, interface. The syscall interface carefully checks the data passed in from user programs before passing that data on to other parts of the kernel. As a result of this careful gatekeeping, it is extremely rare for even the most poorly written user space program to crash the kernel.

The strict division between kernel and user space code is what contributes to Linux's reliability and stability and why you hardly ever see the familiar Windows "Blue Screen of Death" on a Linux system (except in a screensaver).

In addition to the distinction between kernel and user mode code, the kernel and user programs have their own distinct memory regions. Each process, each instance of a running program, has a virtual memory space, known more formally as the process address space, of 4GB (under most 32-bit processor architectures, as 4GB is 2^{32}, or two raised to the thirty-second power). Under most circumstances, the kernel gets 1GB of this space, while user space gets the other 3GB. (There are other options for the layout of memory in Linux — this is just the most common.)

User space programs are not permitted to access kernel memory directly. As with CPU and peripheral protection, the motivation for strict memory partitioning is to prevent ill-behaved (or even deliberately malicious) programs from modifying kernel data structures, which can create system instability or even crash the system.

The distinction between kernel and user space is another fundamental feature of the Linux development environment that gives developers considerable flexibility to write almost any code they want with reasonable assurance that if their program crashes, it won't also crash the system. At the same time, the syscall interface that serves as the gateway between user mode code and kernel mode code enables user mode programs to access kernel features and services in a safe, controlled manner.

Moreover, the kernel can perform tasks that ordinarily might be executed by user space programs without needing a different programming model. For example, if you implement some sort of user space functionality, such as providing a basic HTTP server, in the kernel, the same syscall interface makes it possible to interact with the HTTP server; there is no need to use a new or different programming interface.

On the downside, the sharp delineation between kernel and user space creates some disadvantages for normal users. For example, unlike Microsoft Windows, user space programs do not have direct access to hardware devices. For user space programs to access a sound card, for example, the system administrator must take steps to permit this sort of access. However, this is a small inconvenience compared to the increased stability for which Linux systems are known.

The Security Model

As you learned earlier in this book, all users are not created equal. Some users, such as the root user, are effectively omnipotent and can do anything on a system. Most users have more limited access. The user (and group) IDs of these less privileged users control what programs they can execute and the files they can access. The same restrictions apply to the development environment. For example, if you write a program, you might not be able to access a certain feature, such as locking memory with the mmap() system call, unless your program runs with root permissions.

If your program creates files, the default file permissions are controlled by the umask of the user executing the program and/or a umask that you might specifically set at runtime using the umask() system call. Naturally, your program cannot create, delete, or modify files or directories if it doesn't have the necessary privileges. The Linux development environment also makes it possible for a program to drop or add privileges at runtime by calling functions that change its UID or GID.

The impact of the Linux security model on programming is two-fold. First, the same rules and restrictions that affect running programs and other elements of normal system usage also affect the process of creating programs and what those programs can do. This effect is no more than the logical consequence of the Linux security model itself. Programmatically, however, you have more ways, or perhaps more finely grained ways, to interact with the security subsystem than you do as a normal user of the system.

The second effect of the Linux security model for programmers is that writing a program imposes significant burdens on programmers to program securely. An e-mail program, for example, that stores usernames and passwords in a text file that is unencrypted and/or readable by any user (oftentimes called world-readable) is just as insecure as a program that fails to check user input for buffer overflow.

To use a subtler example, when faced with a problem that seems to require root privileges, such as access to a sound card, the initial impulse is usually to run the program as root. However, there are often user space solutions that can accomplish the same goal and that do not require root access. In the case of writing programs that access a sound card, for example, the ALSA (Advanced Linux Sound Architecture) libraries give application programmers access to a rich interface for emitting squeaks and squawks without needing to rely on running a program as the root user.

Preemptive Multitasking

Perhaps the easiest way to express the preemptive multitasking characteristic of programming in a Linux environment is simply to say that you don't own the CPU; it only seems as if you do.

In imprecise terms, the CPU (actually, the CPU scheduler, which is part of the kernel) allocates a quantum of time (on the order of 50 milliseconds) to execute your program, then preempts it (interrupts or suspends it) to spend another 50-millisecond quantum executing another program. It then preempts the second program to execute the third, and so on until the scheduler returns to your program, when (under normal circumstances) the round robin starts again.

The context switch between programs happens so rapidly that you have the illusion that your program is running all the time.

Task preemption happens automatically and unavoidably; very few processes escape preemption. What you might not realize, however, is that a process can voluntarily yield its quantum of CPU time. That is, while a process cannot request additional CPU time, it can voluntarily give it up. The implication of this for a developer is that you can delay executing certain blocks of code if they are either non-critical or rely on input from other processes that are still running. The function that makes this possible is named `sched_yield()`.

Multitasking, while a boon for computer users, poses (at least) three potential problems for programmers: deadlocks, livelocks, and races:

- **Deadlocks** — A deadlock occurs when two or more processes are unable to proceed because each is waiting for one of the others to do something. Deadlocks can happen in several ways. For example, suppose an e-mail client is communicating with a mail server, waiting for the server to send a message. A deadlock occurs if the mail server is waiting for input from the e-mail client before sending the message. This type of deadlock is sometimes referred to as a deadly embrace. A starvation deadlock occurs when one or more low-priority processes never get time on the CPU because they are crowded out by higher-priority processes. A third common type of deadlock occurs when two processes are trying to send data to each other but can't because the input buffer on each process is so busy trying to send data that it never reads any data sent by the other process. This type of deadlock is colorfully referred to as constipation.

- **Livelocks** — A livelock occurs when a task or process, usually a server process, is unable to finish because its clients continue to create more work for it to do before the server can clear its queue. The difference between a livelock and a deadlock is that a deadlocked process doesn't have any work queued; it is blocked or waiting for something to happen. A livelocked process, on the other hand, has too much work to do and never empties its work queue.

- **Races** — A race occurs when the result of a computation depends on the order in which two events occur. Say, for example, that two processes are accessing a file. The first process writes data to the file, and the second process reads data from the file to calculate and display a summary value. If the reader process reads the file after the writer completes, the reader calculates and returns the correct value. If the reader process reads the file before the writer completes, the reader will calculate and return an incorrect summary value.

The likelihood of deadlocks, livelocks, or races occurring increases dramatically on multitasking (and multiuser) systems because the number of processes that are potentially competing for access to a finite number of resources is greater. Good design, careful analysis, and the judicious use of locks, semaphores, and other mutual exclusion (or mutex) mechanisms that mediate access to shared resources, can prevent or reduce their occurrence.

Multiuser by Design

Linux is multiuser by design, an element of the Linux development model that has far-reaching consequences for developers. A program cannot assume, for example, that it has sole access to any resource such as a file, memory, peripheral devices, or CPU time; multiple programs might be attempting to print simultaneously or trying to allocate memory.

Similarly, a program cannot be written with the assumption that only one copy of the program is running at a time. So, if you are writing a program that creates temporary working files in /tmp, you need to ensure that the temporary files created by Bubba's copy of the program are distinct from the temporary files created by Mary Beth's instance of the program. If you don't, hilarity will ensue (if not hilarity, at least confusion and consternation).

Another common need is for programs to honor per-user configurations. At start-up time, a program might apply reasonable global defaults and then read a user's configuration file to apply, say, a custom color scheme.

There are also a number of per-user settings, such as environment variables, that programs need to know how to accommodate. For example, the $MAIL environment variable identifies where the user's mail spool file is kept, and the $VISUAL environment variable defines the user's preferred full screen editor (which all true Linux users know is vi). The $PRINTER environment variable stores the name of the user's default printer and, of course, $HOME identifies the user's home directory.

In a pervasively multiuser system such as Linux, programs and programmers must always take into account that most resources a program might want to use are usually shared. Likewise, they must also take into account that most real-world usage scenarios (more formally known as *use cases*) assume that multiple instances of the program are running at the same time.

Interprocess Communication

Interprocess communication (IPC) enables programs to share data and resources with a minimum amount of overhead and is used extensively on all Linux systems. It is especially common with daemons and server processes that spawn child processes to handle client connections. IPC comes in three varieties: shared memory, semaphores, and message queues.

- **Shared memory** — Shared memory is just what the name suggests: a region or segment of memory specifically set aside for use by multiple processes. Because shared memory is never paged out to disk, it is an extremely fast way for two processes to exchange data.

- **Semaphores** — Semaphores, briefly mentioned in the "Preemptive Multitasking" section, serve as flags that indicate a condition controlling the behavior of processes. For example, one process can set a semaphore to indicate a specific file is in use. Before other processes attempt to access that file, they check the semaphore's status and don't (or shouldn't) attempt to access the file if the flag is set.

- **Message queues** — Message queues are first-in-first-out (FIFO) data structures that make it possible for processes to exchange short messages in a structured, orderly manner.

> **NOTE** Message queues are not necessarily accessed in FIFO data structures. System V UNIX-style message queues are, but POSIX message queues enable readers to pull messages out of a queue in an arbitrary order.

Shared memory, semaphores, and message queues are idiomatic in the Linux development environment. They solve three distinct domains of problems that arise when multiple processes need to exchange data or share resources without having to resort to slow disk files or network connections. All of which is to say that you don't always need IPC, but it sure is nice to have when you do need it.

The Building Blocks Philosophy

The building blocks philosophy that characterizes the Linux development is best expressed as a short series of rules or principles:

- Do one thing very well.

- Whenever possible, accept input data from standard input and send output data to standard output.

- Keep individual programs as self-contained as possible.

- Remember that someone will use your program in ways you didn't intend and for purposes that you never imagined.

The first rule simply means that programs should not try to be all things to all people: a text editor doesn't need to be able to send e-mail messages and a drawing program doesn't also need to be able to function as a Web browser. Although it is less true today than it used to be, the best Linux programs don't have every imaginable feature (also known as *featuritis*). Rather, developers spend time perfecting the program's intended purpose and making it possible for programs to interoperate.

The second rule allows you to create chains of commands, each of which uses the output of the previous command as its input. A typical use of this behavior is a command pipeline, as in the following rather contrived example:

```
$ cat /etc/passwd | cut -f 5 -d: | tr [:lower:] [:upper:] | sort | head -5
```

The first part of the command pipeline, `cat /etc/passwd`, writes the contents of the `/etc/passwd` file to standard output. The second part, `cut -f 5 -d:`, cuts out the fifth field of its standard input (the contents of `/etc/passwd`), using the colon character (`:`) as the field delimiter (the fifth field of `/etc/passwd` is the GECOS or name field).

The third part, `tr [:lower:] [:upper:]`, translates all lowercase characters in the standard input to uppercase characters. The next element, `sort`, performs an alphabetic sort on the first letter of its input before sending the sorted list to standard output. The final component, `head -5`, displays only the first five lines of its standard input to standard out. The output of this pipeline might resemble the following:

```
ADM
BIN
DAEMON
GAMES
LP
```

The following command pipeline should prove more useful: it e-mails the current uptime and load average to the root user:

```
$ uptime | mailx -s "System Usage" root
```

The third rule, keeping programs self-contained, is related to the second. The concept behind it is that programs intended for use in command pipelines should make no assumptions about what their input might look like or do any massaging of the output.

Consider the `cut` command shown in the first command pipeline. It takes arbitrarily formatted input and allows the user to specify on what piece of data to operate (the fifth field in the example, where fields are colon-delimited) and then just displays the requested data on standard output. `cut` doesn't do any post-processing of the output, allowing the user to do with it as he or she pleases, probably using another tool.

The fourth rule is really more a philosophical observation in that you can't really predict all the ways in which your program might be put to use. Indeed, as S.C. Johnson once noted, "A successful [software] tool is one that was used to do something undreamed of by its author."

The point is that the Linux toolkit, for both developers and end users, is full of small tools and utilities that are building block programs routinely used to create larger programs and tools that, together, perform complex tasks that no single program can do, or can do efficiently. Another element of the building blocks approach is that it enables tasks to be performed in batch mode, without active user intervention or participation. This building block philosophy is another characteristic feature of the Linux development environment, one that can make your life a lot simpler once you grok the idea. It also helps you to stand on the shoulders of those who have come before because you can build on existing building blocks instead of having to create everything anew.

Graphical Programming Environments

If you are sitting in front of a Linux system, chances are pretty good that:

- It is running some version of the X Window System.
- There are several terminal (or shell) windows (terminal emulators) running on top of X's graphical interface.
- One or more natively graphical programs are also running, such as a Web browser.

Linux programming environments can be divided into two broad categories: graphical IDEs and discrete collections of command line–based tools. Developers and users coming from a predominantly Windows background will be familiar with IDEs; the 800-pound gorilla in the Windows world is Microsoft's Visual Studio product.

This section looks at some of the full-featured graphical IDEs that collect and merge all the constituent components necessary for the development task, such as an editor, compiler, linker, debugger, class browser, and project manager, in a single, unified interface. The examples discussed include the open source Eclipse environment, KDE environment, and Code Crusader environment.

Eclipse: The Universal Tool Platform

Eclipse is a large, Java-based development platform. In principle and in practice, Eclipse is a universal IDE that is used to create applications as diverse as Web sites, C, C++, and Java programs, and even plug-ins that extend Eclipse itself. Eclipse is amply capable of handling every aspect of Linux development in an astonishing variety of languages. Figure 28-1 shows Eclipse with the "Hello, World" example program, written in Java, on the screen.

FIGURE 28-1

The Eclipse IDE

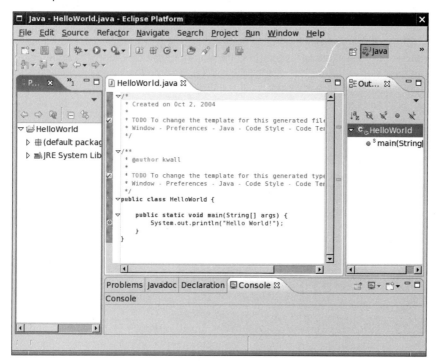

Figure 28-1 illustrates a number of characteristics typical of IDEs. The project view on the left side of the screen provides a project file browser that enables you to see at a glance the contents of the programming project. You can see the primary project folder, HelloWorld, and some of the associated files necessary to support Java projects, such as the default package for Java projects and a folder containing the necessary JRE (Java Runtime Environment) files.

The code editor view in the center of the screen shows the code for the `HelloWorld.java` program. Although it isn't visible in the black-and-white figure produced for this book, the code editor performs on-the-fly syntax highlighting using color and font-style changes. Java keywords are purple; plain comments appear in green; javadoc-style comments appear in a pale blue; strings are colored blue; and normal code is black. This is all quite customizable to your liking as well.

The right side of Eclipse displays another feature common among IDEs: a class browser. Class browsers enable developers to see the structure of their programs from the point of view of the code modules that make up the program rather than as mere files in a directory. This feature is not terribly useful for a small program such as `HelloWorld.java`, but larger programs that consist of dozens of classes or code modules are much easier to navigate using a code or class browser.

The bottom of the screen shows various information and status windows. For example, the Problems view shows problems that might have occurred while compiling the program. Eclipse, like many other IDEs, allows you to double-click on an error in the Problems view to jump right to the error in the associated code file (see Figure 28-2).

FIGURE 28-2

Eclipse's Problems view

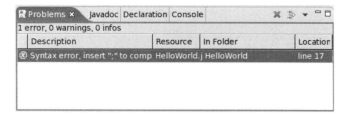

The Javadoc view, which is unique to the Eclipse Java development plug-in, enables you to view the output of Javadoc, a tool that creates documentation from specially formatted Java source code comments. The Declaration view works in combination with the class browser to show you the complete declaration of methods and data types. The Console view shows the actual output of the Java program.

While much of Eclipse was designed to support developing applications in the Java language, plug-ins provide support for C, C++, Perl, Python, and other languages.

 For more information about Eclipse, including download information, visit the Eclipse home page at www.eclipse.org/.

KDevelop: KDE's IDE

KDevelop, another open source IDE licensed under the GPL, was originally created to provide an IDE that interoperated seamlessly with KDE and the Qt framework (a large C++ application framework) on which KDE is based. Over the years, however, KDevelop has evolved into an attractive, feature-rich development environment supporting a number of languages other than C++. Today, KDevelop is a general-purpose IDE, although it works best when used to create Qt-based applications written in C++. Figure 28-3 shows a representative screenshot of KDevelop.

If you compare KDevelop's appearance to Eclipse's appearance, you will see that both have the same types of components. In Figure 28-3, the class browser is located on the left side of the screen, the project window is located in the upper-right portion of the screen, and KDevelop's version of the Declaration view is displayed in the lower-right portion of the screen.

FIGURE 28-3

The KDevelop IDE

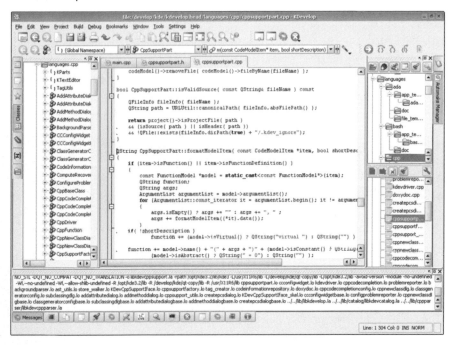

The log view that occupies the bottom of the KDevelop interface in Figure 28-3 shows the compilation process. As with Eclipse, KDevelop's toolbars and menus are stuffed with buttons and menu items that cater to the needs of developers, just as a word processor is customized with buttons and menu items specific to the task of writing and formatting documents.

> **NOTE** For more information about KDevelop, including download information, visit the KDevelop home page at `http://kdevelop.kde.org/`. The language status support page (`www.kdevelop.org/HEAD/doc/api/html/LangSupportStatus.html`) shows the current status of programming languages supported.

Code Crusader

Code Crusader is a commercially available and supported IDE written in C++ and specifically targeted at the Linux developer; it is not available for Windows. You can use Code Crusader to write Java, FORTAN, C++, and, of course, C programs. Unlike the IDEs discussed so far, Code Crusader does not include a built-in debugger. Rather, New Planet Software, developer of Code Crusader, makes its debugger application, Code Medic, available separately (although you can buy the two together as an IDE bundle). Figure 28-4 shows Code Crusader with the `forkexec.c` program from Listing 28-1 open in an editor window.

FIGURE 28-4

The Code Crusader IDE

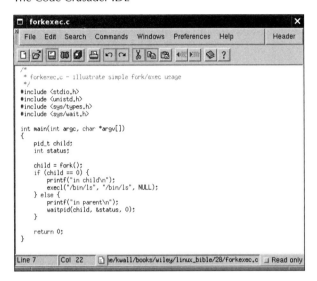

As you can see in Figure 28-4, Code Crusader has a much simpler, cleaner interface than the other IDEs mentioned so far. Another significant difference between Code Crusader and the larger IDEs such as Eclipse and KDevelop is that each IDE component, such as the project browser, the class browser, editor windows, and the log viewer, opens in its own, independent window rather than being part of a single-document interface (SDI).

Having multiple windows is more consistent with traditional Linux and UNIX windowing conventions, but developers coming from a Windows background might find Code Crusader's multiple-document interface (MDI) a little jarring at first. On the other hand, programmers who prefer a leaner, cleaner interface might prefer Code Crusader to the rather overstuffed-looking interfaces that Eclipse and KDevelop offer.

 For more information about Code Crusader, including download information, visit the Code Crusader home page at www.newplanetsoftware.com/jcc/.

There are many more IDEs than the three discussed in this section. Some are less mature or still in beta stage. Others are special-purpose IDEs, such as the Quanta HTML editor, or the GLADE interface designer for GNOME. If Eclipse, KDevelop, and Code Crusader don't appeal to you, a quick search at Freshmeat (use http://freshmeat.net/browse/65/ to get right to the IDE category) or SourceForge (http://sourceforge.net/softwaremap/trove_list.php?form_cat=65 takes you straight to the IDE category) should turn up many options from which to choose. As of this writing, the Freshmeat IDE category has 181 entries and the SourceForge IDE category has 748 entries; there's something available for everyone. This is Linux, after all, so you are free to choose the IDE that appeals to you the most. As you'll learn in the next subsection, however, not everyone wants (or needs) a GUI IDE.

The Command-Line Programming Environment

The Linux command-line programming environment or CLI (command-line interface) stands in sharp contrast to the GUI IDEs described in the previous section. It often shocks developers who have only a Windows development background and who aren't accustomed to using a CLI.

To be fair, it must be intimidating to find yourself in front of a command prompt without anything to double-click to start and not the faintest clue how to proceed. That said, while a CLI might seem Spartan to the newcomer, programming at the command line is surprisingly powerful and allows you to mix and match best-of-breed tools in a way that most IDEs cannot begin to approach. The CLI programming environment can match the environment provided by GUIs feature for feature, with the single exception of the graphical interface itself.

The inconvenience, if inconvenience it is, arises from the fact that the CLI programming environment relies on separate tools. For example, assuming you are working in the X Window System, you might be running one or more text editors, such as vi, pico, nano, joe, or emacs, each in its own terminal window. You might use another terminal window for compiling your program, either by invoking the compiler gcc (the GNU compiler collection) directly, or by using the make utility. In still another window you might be running a debugger such as gdb (the GNU debugger). If you are unfamiliar with the library you are using, you might have a Web browser open to view some sort of online documentation, or you might be using a program such as xman that displays Linux manual (man) pages in a graphical format.

It is not a given, however, that graphical IDEs are better than using discrete tools. Rather, it is a matter of which model developers feel most comfortable using, which method makes developers the most productive, and which approach best fits each developer's personal working style. Many long-time UNIX and Linux developers feel more comfortable with and work more productively using command-line tools: vi or emacs for writing and editing code, gcc and make for compilation, and gdb and kgdb for debugging.

In any event, the lines are not so sharply drawn. emacs, for example, has the facility to invoke both compilation and debugging facilities, has an extremely rich code-editing interface (syntax highlighting and automatic indentation, for example), and also supports other code development features. emacs also includes features such as source code control, symbol and class browsing, and built-in support for at least three different online help facilities.

If you prefer vi, it can be also be configured to support symbol and class browsing using the ctags program, has basic syntax highlighting (depending on the implementation), and can also work with the error messages produced by failed compilation.

Perhaps the GUI versus CLI debate boils down to this distinction: CLI-oriented programming environments give developers direct access to the tools and utilities they need, don't consume system resources to draw an attractive GUI, and don't provide so-called point-and-click programming. GUI-oriented programming environments hide the tools and utilities underneath a consistent, unified interface; provide a convenient dash board or instrument panel for access to the necessary programming tools; and let developers take advantage of some of the conveniences associated with graphical environments.

Linux Programming Interfaces

As defined at the beginning of this chapter, a programming interface refers to the rules or methods followed to accomplish a particular task. Like programming environments, programming interfaces are usually thought of as either graphical or command line.

Graphical interfaces use the X Window System to receive and process user input and display information. Command-line interfaces, sometimes referred to as text-mode user interfaces (TUIs), are strictly text-based and do not require a windowing system to run. Thanks to the X Window System, however, you can also execute CLI-based programs in terminal emulators running on top of X.

There also is a third type of interface: an *application programming interface*, or *API*. This section of the chapter looks at the ncurses library used to create text-mode user interfaces, examines some of the popular graphical interfaces in use today, and describes a small set of the most popular APIs used by Linux programmers.

Creating Command-Line Interfaces

There are three primary means of creating programs that interact with users at the command line. Two use libraries of screen manipulation routines, S-Lang and ncurses, to create TUIs, and the third just uses standard input and standard output, conventionally known as stdin and stdout, respectively. Using stdin and stdout is trivially simple. Input and output occur one line at a time; users type input using the keyboard or pipe input in from a file, and output is displayed to the screen or redirected to a file. Listing 28-2 shows such a program, readkey.c.

LISTING 28-2

Reading and Writing to stdin and stdout

```
/*
 * readkey.c - reads characters from stdin
 */
#include <stdio.h>

int main(int argc, char *argv[])
{
        int c, i = 0;

        /* read characters until newline read */
        printf("INPUT: ");
        while ((c = getchar()) != '\n') {
                ++i;
                putchar(c);
        }
        printf("\ncharacters read: %d\n", i + 1);

        return 0;

}
```

In this program, the ++i syntax is used to increment the variable i by one each time through the `while` loop.

To compile this program, use the following command:

```
$ gcc readkey.c -o readkey
```

In the preceding code listing, `readkey.c` reads input from stdin until it encounters a newline (which is generated when you press the Enter key). Then it displays the text entered and the number of characters read (the count includes the newline) and exits.

Here's how it works:

```
$ ./readkey
INPUT: There are three primary means of creating programs that interact with
users at the command line
There are three primary means of creating programs that interact with users at
the command line
characters read: 96
```

The text wraps oddly because of this book's formatting constraints. You can also feed `readkey.c` input from stdin using the `cat` command:

```
$ cat /etc/passwd | ./readkey
INPUT: root:x:0:0::/root:/bin/bash
characters read: 28
```

In this case, you see only the first line of `/etc/passwd` because each line of the file ends with a newline. It should be clear that programmatically interacting with the command line is simple, but not terribly user-friendly or attractive.

Creating Text-Mode User Interfaces with ncurses

Screen manipulation libraries such as S-Lang and ncurses create more attractive programs, but, as you might expect, the tradeoff for a nicer looking interface is more complicated code. ncurses, which stands for *new curses*, is free re-implementation of the classic curses UNIX screen-handling library. The term *curses* derives from the phrase *cursor optimization*, which succinctly describes what the curses library does: compute the fastest way to redraw a text-mode screen and place the cursor in the proper location.

ncurses provides a simple, high-level interface for screen control and manipulation. It also contains powerful routines for handling keyboard and mouse input, creating and managing multiple windows, and using menus, forms, and panels. ncurses works by generalizing the interface between an application program and the screen or terminal on which it is running.

Given the literally hundreds of varieties of terminals, screens, and terminal emulation programs available, and the different features they possess (not to mention the different commands to use these features and capabilities), UNIX programmers quickly developed a way to abstract screen manipulation. Rather than write a lot of extra code to take into account the different terminal types, ncurses provides a uniform and generalized interface for the programmer. The ncurses API insulates the programmer from the underlying hardware and the differences between terminals.

ncurses gives to character-based applications many of the same features found in graphical X Window applications — multiple windows, forms, menus, and panels. ncurses windows can be managed independently, may contain the same or different text, can scroll or not scroll, and be visible or hidden. Forms enable the programmer to create easy-to-use data entry and display windows, simplifying what is usually a difficult and application-specific coding task. Panels extend ncurses' capability to deal with overlapping and stacked windows. Menus provide, well, menus, again with a simpler, generalized programming interface. The ncurses library even provides support for mouse input.

To give you an idea of how ncurses works and what is involved in writing code to use it, Listing 28-3 shows the `readkey.c` program (now named `nreadkey.c`) introduced in Listing 28-2, adapted here to work with ncurses.

LISTING 28-3

Reading Input and Writing Output with ncurses

```
/*
 * nreadkey.c - reads characters from stdin
 */
#include <stdio.h>
#include <curses.h>

int main(int argc, char *argv[])
{
        int c, i = 0;
        int maxx, maxy;
        int y, x;

        /* start ncurses */
        initscr();

        /* draw a purty border */
        box(stdscr, ACS_VLINE, ACS_HLINE);
        mvwaddstr(stdscr, 1, 1, "INPUT: ");
        refresh();

        /* read characters until newline read */
        noecho();
        while ((c = getch()) != '\n') {
                ++i;
                getyx(stdscr, y, x);
                /* at the right margin */
                if (x == 79) {
                        mvaddch(y + 1, 1, c);
                } else {
                        waddch(stdscr, c);
                }
```

continued

LISTING 28-3   *(continued)*

```
            refresh();
    }
    echo();
    refresh();

    /* print the character count */
    getmaxyx(stdscr, maxy, maxx);
    mvwprintw(stdscr, maxy - 2, 1, "characters read: %d\n", i);
    curs_set(0);
    refresh();

    /* time to look at the screen */
    sleep(3);

    /* shutdown ncurses */
    endwin();

    return 0;

}
```

One of the first things you notice is that nreadkey.c is about twice as long as readkey.c. The additional code addresses the need to set up the screen, position the cursor, and so forth. To see if the additional code is worth it, compile nreadkey.c using the following command:

```
$ gcc nreadkey.c -lncurses -o nreadkey
```

To run the program, type **./nreadkey**. Figure 28-5 shows the result after typing the same text as typed for readkey.c earlier.

FIGURE 28-5

An ncurses-based TUI

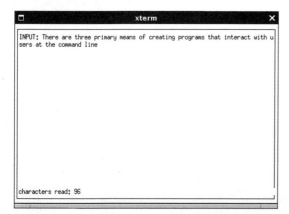

Ncurses-based programs can also read input piped from stdin. Figure 28-6 shows the results of the command `cat /etc/passwd | ./nreadkey`.

FIGURE 28-6

Displaying input piped to an ncurses-based program

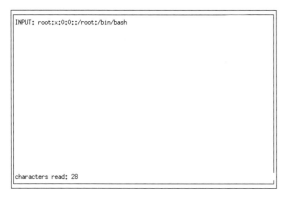

```
INPUT: root:x:0:0::/root:/bin/bash




characters read: 28
```

As you saw with the command pipeline used with the `readkey.c` program (shown in Listing 28-2), the input is truncated at the end of the first line because each line in `/etc/passwd` ends with the newline character, and `readkey.c` uses the newline character to signal the end of input.

 For more information about ncurses, including download information, visit the ncurses Web page at `http://dickey.his.com/ncurses/ncurses.html`.

Creating Text-Mode User Interfaces with S-Lang

S-Lang, created by John Davis, is an alternative to ncurses for creating TUIs. In addition to providing screen manipulation and cursor control routines, S-Lang also consists of an embeddable S-Lang interpreter, a large library of built-in (intrinsic) routines that simplify certain parts of programming, and a variety of predefined data types and data structures. Listing 28-4 shows the same program as Listing 28-3, with appropriate updates to reflect use of S-Lang instead of ncurses.

LISTING 28-4

Reading Input and Writing Output with S-Lang

```
/*
 * sreadkey.c - simple S-Lang-based UI
 */
#include <stdio.h>
#include <string.h>
#include <slang/slang.h>
```

continued

LISTING 28-3   *(continued)*

```
int main(int argc, char *argv[])
{
        int i = 0;
        unsigned int ch;

        /* start s-lang */
        SLtt_get_terminfo();
        SLang_init_tty(-1, 0, 1);
        SLsmg_init_smg();

        /* draw a purty border */
        SLsmg_draw_box(0, 0, 24, 80);
        SLsmg_gotorc(1, 1);
        SLsmg_write_nchars("INPUT: ", 7);
        SLsmg_refresh();

        /* read characters until newline read */
        while(1) {
                ++i;
                ch = SLang_getkey();
                if (ch == 13)
                        break;
                if (SLsmg_get_column() == 79)
                        SLsmg_gotorc(2, 1);
                SLsmg_write_char(ch);
                SLsmg_refresh();
        }

        /* print the character count */
        SLsmg_gotorc(22, 1);
        SLsmg_write_nchars("characters read: ", 17);
        SLsmg_printf("%d", i);
        SLsmg_refresh();

        /* time to look at the screen */
        sleep(3);

        /* shutdown s-lang */
        SLsmg_reset_smg();
        SLang_reset_tty();

        return 0;

}
```

To compile this program use the following command:

```
$ gcc sreadkey.c -lslang -o sreadkey
```

You will need the slang, slang-devel, ncurses, and ncurses-devel packages to compile and run this program.

To run the program, type **./sreadkey**. Figure 28-7 shows the result after typing the same text as typed for `readkey.c` earlier.

FIGURE 28-7

An S-Lang–based TUI

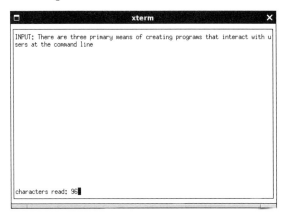

As you can see from Figure 28-7, the basic appearance and functionality of `sreadkey.c` is the same as `nreadkey.c`. The differences between the two, which have to do with the TUI framework used to create `sreadkey.c`, are invisible to the user. S-Lang–based programs can also read input piped from stdin.

From a developer's perspective, there are significant differences between ncurses and S-Lang in program structure and the actual library usage, but the output is almost identical.

 For more information about S-Lang, including download information, visit the S-Lang Web page at `www.s-lang.org`.

Creating Graphical Interfaces

When it comes to creating GUIs, Linux programmers have more options available than they do for creating TUIs. Probably the most popular and certainly the best-known toolkits used to create graphical applications are Qt and GTK+. Qt is the C++ application framework that powers KDE, the K Desktop Environment. GTK+ is the toolkit underneath GNOME, the GNU Network Object Model Environment. GTK+ is written largely in C, but it has language bindings available for many other programming languages, such as Perl, C++, and Python, so you can use GTK+ features in many programming environments. Because of the limited space available, this chapter does not show examples of Qt and GTK+ applications.

NOTE For more information about GTK+, visit the GTK+ Web site at `www.gtk.org`. You can find information about the Qt framework at `http://troll.no/`.

Although Qt and GTK+ are the big hammers of Linux graphical development, there are many other toolkits, frameworks, and libraries that you can use to develop GUI-based applications for Linux. The following list, arranged alphabetically, describes some of the available toolkits. Most of these toolkits and frameworks describe widget sets, which are implemented in one or more programming libraries. *Widget* is the term applied to a user interface abstraction, such as a scrollbar or a button, created using the toolkit.

- **Athena** — The Athena library was one of the earliest (think ancient) widget libraries available for the X Window System. It is a thin layer of abstraction on top of raw Xlib calls that makes it slightly less painful to create scrollbars, text entry boxes, and other typical GUI elements. It is part of the standard X11 distribution.

- **3D Athena Toolkit** — The 3D Athena Toolkit is a 3D version of the original Athena toolkit. It gives Athena a 3D look and is a considerable visual improvement over plain vanilla Athena. The 3D Athena toolkit, although no longer widely used, is still available on the Web at `http://directory.fsf.org/graphics/3d/xaw3d.html`.

- **FLTK** — FLTK, which is pronounced "full tick," is an acronym for the Fast Light Toolkit. FLTK is a GUI for X, Mac OS X, and Microsoft Windows. Written in C++, FLTK makes it possible to write GUIs that look almost identical regardless of the platform on which the GUI runs. FLTK also supports OpenGL graphics. You can find more information about FLTK on the Web at `www.fltk.org`.

- **XForms** — XForms is a GUI toolkit based on Xlib. It isn't highly configurable like the other GUI toolkits discussed in this section, but its simplicity makes XForms easier to use than the other graphical toolkits. It comes with a GUI builder that makes it fast and easy to get working applications up and running. More information about XForms can be found on the Web at `http://savannah.nongnu.org/projects/xforms/`.

- **OpenGL** — OpenGL is the industry-standard 3D graphics toolkit. It provides the most realistic and lifelike graphics currently available for the X Window System. It is generally available as part of XFree86. More information about OpenGL is available on the Web at `www.opengl.org`.

- **Motif** — Motif was one of the first widget or interface toolkits available for the X Window System that combined both an interface toolkit and a window manager. Originally available only as a commercial product, it is now available in an open source version as OpenMotif from the MotifZone at `www.openmotif.org`.

- **Xlib** — Xlib is shorthand for the X library, a low-level, C-based interface to the raw X Window System protocol. If you want to write as close to the X graphics core as possible, you write Xlib-based programs. Indeed, most window managers, widget libraries, and GUI toolkits are written using Xlib. While using straight Xlib gives you the best performance, it is extremely code-intensive. Xlib is an essential ingredient of the standard X distribution. You can learn more about Xlib from the HTML manual page, available on the Web at `www.the-labs.com/X11/XLib-Manual`.

- **Xt** — Xt Intrinsics are a very thin layer of functions and data structures on top of Xlib. Xt Intrinsics create an object-oriented interface that C programs can use to create graphical elements. Without other widget sets, the Intrinsics are not especially useful. Xt, like Xlib, is a part of the standard X distribution and is not available separately.

Application Programming Interfaces

Application programming interfaces, or APIs, provide programmers with libraries of code for performing certain tasks. There are many APIs, probably as many as there are types of programming problems that need to be solved. The ncurses library, for example, provides an API that you can use to create text-mode user interfaces. In turn, ncurses works by using either the terminfo or termcap API to perform the actual screen updates in a manner consistent with the underlying type of display device in use.

Developers keep having to perform a specific type of programming task, such as updating a database, communicating over a network, getting sound out of a sound card, or performing complicated mathematical calculations. As a result, there is at least one database API, socket API, sound API, or mathematical API already in existence that they can use to simplify those tasks.

NOTE This section discusses APIs for use in C and C++ programming. You can also make use of these libraries in other programming languages, but you may need to write software to adapt to the C-based API. For example, Perl, Python, and Java all have a means to call on C functions or APIs, but you will need to write the code needed to adapt the actual C library to your programming language.

APIs consist of three components:

- **Header file** — Declares the interface (the function calls, macros, and data structures) that developers can use in their own programs.

- **One or more library files** — Implement(s) the interfaces declared in the header files and against which programs must be linked.

- **API documentation** — Describes how to use the API and often provides example code. The documentation might be provided in manual pages, text files, HTML files, GNU TeXinfo files, or some combination of all of these formats.

Table 28-1 describes many popular or widely used APIs, but the list provided here is far from complete.

TABLE 28-1

Common Linux APIs

API	Category	Description
aalib	ASCII art	AA-lib is a library that outputs graphics as ASCII art. For an amazing demonstration of AA-lib's capabilities, look into BB Demo or the screenshot gallery links at the AA-project homepage: `http://aa-project.sourceforge.net/index.html`.
arts	Sound	The analog realtime synthesizer (aRts) is KDE's core sound system, designed to create and process sound using small specialized modules. These modules might create a waveform, play samples, filter data, add signals, perform effects (such as delay, flanger, or chorus), or output the data to the soundcard.
atk	Accessibility	ATK is a library of accessibility functions used by GNOME.
audiofile	Audio	audiofile, used by the esound daemon (Enlightened Sound Daemon), is a library for processing various audio file formats. You can also use it to develop your own audio file–based applications.
db-4	Database	The Berkeley Database (Berkeley DB) library enables developers to create applications with database support.
expat	XML	Expat is a stream-oriented C library for parsing XML. It is used by Python, GNOME, Xft2, and other applications.
gdbm	Database	The GNU Database Manager (GDBM) is a set of database routines that work similarly to the standard UNIX dbm routines.
gdk_pixbuf	2-D Graphics	GdkPixbuf is an API for loading, scaling, compositing, and animating images. GdkPixBuf is required by many GTK+ programs.
glib	General	GLib is a general purpose API of C language routines. The library includes support for features such as lists, trees, hashes, memory allocation, and many other things. GLib is required by almost every GTK+ application.
glut	3-D Graphics	The GL Utility Toolkit (GLUT) is a 3D graphics library based on the OpenGL API. It provides a higher-level interface for creation of OpenGL-based graphics.
gmp	Mathematics	The GNU Multiple Precision (GMP) API implements a library for arbitrary precision arithmetic, such as operations on signed integers, rational numbers, and floating-point numbers.
gnet	Network	GNet is an object-oriented library of network routines. Written in C and based on GLib, GNet is used by gnomeicu and Pan.

TABLE 28-1	(continued)	
API	**Category**	**Description**
imlib	Graphics	ImLib (image library) is an image loading and rendering API designed to simplify and speed up the process of loading images and obtaining X Window System.
libao	Audio	libao is a cross-platform audio library used by other libraries and programs that use audio, including ogg123, GAIM, and the Ogg Vorbis libraries.
libart_lgpl	2-D Graphics	Libart is a library for high-performance 2D graphics used by KDE and GNOME.
libexif	Graphics	This library provides an API allowing programs to read, parse, edit, and save Exchangeable Image File Format (EXIF) data in image files. EXIF is a format used to store extra information in images, such as the JPEG files produced by digital cameras.
libglade	Graphics	The GLADE library, used heavily in GNOME programs, allows programs to load user interfaces from definitions stored in external files. This allows the interface to be changed without recompiling the program.
libid3tag	Audio	libid3tag is a library for reading ID3 tags. ID3 tags allow extra information to be embedded in audio files.
libieee1284	Hardware	libieee1284 enables applications that need to communicate with (or at least identify) devices that are attached via IEEE1284-compliant parallel ports, such as scanners.
libjpeg	Graphics	The JPEG library provides a rich API for manipulating JPEG-format images, including reading, writing, converting, compressing, and decompressing images.
libmad	Audio	libmad provides a high-quality MPEG audio decoder API. libmad provides full 24-bit PCM output, so applications using this API can produce high-quality audio.
libmng	Graphics	libmng implements the Multiple-image Network Graphics (MNG) API. MNG provides multi-image animation capabilities similar to animated GIFs, but free of patent encumbrances.
libogg	Audio	Libogg is a library for reading and writing ogg format bitstreams. libogg is needed to use the Ogg Vorbis audio format.
libpng	Graphics	The Portable Network Graphics (PNG) standard is an extensible file format for the lossless, portable, well-compressed storage of images. PNG provides a patent-free replacement for GIF. (As of this writing, the GIF compression patent should have expired.)
libtermcap	Hardware	libtermcap implements the GNU termcap library API, a library of C functions that enable programs to send control strings to terminals in a way that is independent of the terminal type.

continued

TABLE 28-1	(continued)	
API	**Category**	**Description**
libtiff	2-D Graphics	The TIFF library provides an API for working with images stored in the Tag Image File Format (TIFF), a widely used format for storing high-quality, high-resolution images.
libungif	2-D Graphics	libungif provides an API unencumbered by patents for loading and saving images in GIF format.
libusb	Hardware	libusb allows user space application access to USB devices.
libvorbis	Audio	This library supports the Vorbis General Audio Compression Codec, commonly known as Ogg Vorbis. Ogg Vorbis is an open, patent- and royalty-free, general-purpose compressed audio format for audio and music.
libwmf	Graphics	libwmf provides an API for interpreting, displaying, and converting metafile images to standard image formats such as PNG, JPEG, PS, EPS, and SVG.
libxml2	XML	libxml2 is the XML parser library used by GNOME and KDE.
libxslt	XML	libxslt provides XSLT support for libxml2. XSLT is a language used to transform XML documents into other formats.
orbit	CORBA	ORBit is a high-performance Common Object Request Broker Architecture (CORBA) object request broker (ORB). ORBit allows programs to send requests and receive replies from other programs, regardless of the locations of the two programs. GNOME uses ORBit heavily.
pango	Text layout	Pango is a library for layout and rendering of text, with an emphasis on internationalization. Pango forms the core of text and font handling in GTK+-2.0.
pcre	Regular expressions	The Perl-compatible regular expression (PCRE) library implements an API for regular expression pattern matching that uses the same syntax and semantics as Perl 5. The PCRE library is used by many programs.
pilot-link	PalmOS	pilot-link implements a library for communicating with Palm handheld devices and with other devices that adhere to the PalmOS interface standard. gnome-pilot and KPilot use pilot-link.
popt	General	popt is a C library for parsing command-line parameters. popt was heavily influenced by the `getopt()` and `getopt_long()` functions, but improves on them by allowing more powerful argument expansion and allowing command-line arguments to be aliased via configuration files.
sdl	Multimedia	The Simple DirectMedia Layer (SDL) provides a generic, cross-platform API for low-level access to audio, keyboards, mice, joysticks, 3D hardware via OpenGL, and 2D framebuffers. This is a popular API for many Linux games (see `www.libsdl.org`).

TABLE 28-1	*(continued)*	
API	**Category**	**Description**
t1lib	Graphics	t1lib provides an API for generating character and string glyphs from Adobe Type 1 fonts.
taglib	Audio	TagLib is a library for reading and editing the meta-data stored in ID3v1 and ID3v2 (MP3 files) and Ogg Vorbis comments and ID3 tags (Ogg Vorbis files).
zlib	Data compression	zlib provides a general-purpose, thread-safe data compression library that implements the data formats defined by RFC1950, RFC1951, and RFC1952 (see www.ietf.org/rfc.html to find any of the RFCs just mentioned).

As you can see, a wide variety of APIs exist for performing an equally wide variety of programming tasks. Chances are pretty good that if you need to perform some sort of programming task, someone has written a library that you can use to do it.

Summary

The phrase "Linux programming environments and interfaces" is shorthand that masks a rich set of features.

This chapter looked at both graphical programming IDEs and the less visually attractive but just as powerful command-line or text-mode programming environments. You also learned some of the characteristics of Linux and of Linux systems that define and shape programming and programs on, and for, Linux.

The second part of the chapter looked at the variety of programming interfaces, and the methods available for getting particular programming tasks done. You learned that you can create text-mode or command-line interfaces and that you can choose from a variety of graphical interfaces for structuring user interaction with your program. Finally, you took a fast-paced look at some of the many APIs that make it possible to do a variety of things, such as manipulate or create images or interact with a database.

Chapter 29

Programming Tools and Utilities

The preceding chapter, "Programming Environments and Interfaces," provided a high-level view of Linux programming, focusing on the overall development environment and introducing the idioms that give programming on a Linux system its distinctive character. This chapter goes into greater detail and describes some of the tools and toys found on a typical Linux development system.

The goal of this chapter is not to turn you into a developer in 30 pages or less, but simply to explore some of the variety of tools developers use so you will at least know what they are and what they do. You'll also learn how to use some of the programs and utilities.

IN THIS CHAPTER

Using the GCC compiler

Automating builds with make

Examining library utilities

Exploring source code control

Debugging with GDB

The Well-Stocked Toolkit

Whether you prefer a graphical development environment or the classic command-line environment, you need a good set of tools if you want to write, compile, and debug programs for Linux. The good news is that Linux has plenty of editors, compilers, and debuggers from which to choose. The bad news is that Linux has plenty of editors, compilers, and debuggers from which to choose.

The range of programming tool options is good news for developers because they can pick the best and most appropriate tools for the development task at hand. The proliferation of choices is bad news for system administrators who need to install and maintain the tools and for people who evaluate the tools. Too many choices make choosing the right one a difficult task.

This chapter discusses the most popular programs and utilities of their types. In most cases, alternatives (and sometimes multiple alternatives) exist, but I cover only one to keep the discussion simple. (I try to mention the others just so you're familiar with their names.)

What constitutes a well-stocked Linux development toolkit? The basics include an editor to write the code, one or more compilers to turn source code into binaries, and a debugger to track down the inevitable bugs. Most people have a favorite editor, and you'd have a difficult time trying to persuade them to try a new one. Most editors support some set of programming-related functionality (some more than others, to be sure). There are too many to cover in this space, so suffice it to say: You'll need an editor.

Perhaps the most popular console editors are vi and emacs. vi is a commercial editor, being part of the commercial UNIX offerings, so what you can actually get is usually a clone such as vim, elvis, or (my own personal favorite) nvi (*new* vi). I prefer nvi because it is a port of vi from BSD UNIX to Linux. Other popular editors include pico (the Pine mail client editor made available as a separate program), jed, joe, jove, and nano. If you prefer graphical editors, gedit in GNOME and kedit in KDE also provide basic programming support, as does nedit, a Linux and UNIX-based programmer's editor.

CROSS-REF   Chapter 2 has a short tutorial on using the vi editor, as well as short descriptions of several other popular open source text editors.

When it comes to compilers, GCC is the compiler of choice, or, if you will, the choice of the GNU generation, so this chapter discusses only GCC. Other compilers are available for Linux, such as Intel's C and C++ compiler and a very powerful (and expensive) offering from the Portland Compiler Group. Similarly, GDB, the GNU debugger, is the only debugger described in this chapter.

In Chapter 28, you examined the role that programming interfaces play in simplifying the development task. Interfaces usually include one or more libraries that implement the functionality that interfaces define. Because you need to be able to work with programming libraries, utilities for creating, examining, and manipulating libraries also occupy the well-stocked programming toolkit.

To this list, most developers would add a build automation tool, such as make, because most non-trivial projects need some sort of utility that handles building and rebuilding complicated, multi-file projects with a minimum of effort and time.

Another challenge for large projects is tracking source code changes and maintaining a record of what code changed, when it changed, how it changed, and who changed it. This task is the province of source code control systems, and this chapter looks at two: RCS and CVS.

Using the GCC Compiler

The GNU Compiler Collection (GCC) is by far the most dominant compiler (rather, the most dominant *collection* of compilers) used on Linux systems. It compiles programs written in C, C++, Objective-C, Fortran, Java, and Ada. This chapter focuses on the C compiler.

GCC gives programmers extensive control over the compilation process. That process includes up to four stages: preprocessing, compilation, assembly, and linking. You can stop the process after any of these stages to examine the compiler's output at that stage. GCC can also handle the various C dialects, such as ANSI C or traditional (Kernighan and Ritchie) C. You can control the amount and type of debugging information, if any, to embed in the resulting binary. And like most compilers, GCC also performs code optimization.

The gcc command invokes the C compiler. To use it, provide it the name of a C source file and use its -o option to specify the name of the output file. gcc will preprocess, compile, assemble, and link the program, generating an executable, often called a binary. Here's the simplest syntax:

```
gcc infile.c [-o outfile]
```

infile.c is a C source code file, and -o says to name the output file outfile. The [] characters indicate optional arguments throughout this book. If the name of the output file is not specified, gcc names the output file a.out by default. Not all steps need to be handled by the gcc program itself, as gcc can hand off processing tasks such as linking to ld, the GNU linker.

The following example uses gcc to create the hello program from the source file hello.c. First, the source code:

```
/*
 * hello.c - canonical hello world program
 */
#include <stdio.h>
int main(int argc, char *argv[])
{
        printf("Hello, Linux programming world!\n");
        return 0;
}
```

Now, to compile and run this program, type the following:

```
$ gcc hello.c -o hello
```

If all goes well, gcc does its job silently and returns to the shell prompt. It compiles and links the source file hello.c (gcc hello.c), creating a binary named hello, as specified using the -o hello argument.

If you run the program, here's the output you get:

```
$ ./hello
Hello, Linux programming world!
```

CAUTION The command that executed the hello program specifically included the current directory, denoted with a . because having the current directory in your path is a security risk. That is, instead of a $PATH environment variable that resembles /bin:/usr/bin:/usr/local/bin:., it should be /bin:/usr/bin:/usr/local/bin so that a cracker cannot put a dangerous command in your current directory that happens to match the name of the more benign command you really want to execute.

With GCC (and any other C compiler), the preprocessing stage handles constructs such as the `#include <stdio.h>` as well as `#define` macros. Once these are handled, normal processing begins.

GCC relies on file extensions to determine what kind of source code file it is — that is, in which programming language the source code is written. Table 29-1 lists the most common extensions and how GCC interprets them.

TABLE 29-1

GCC's Filenaming Conventions

Extension	Type
`.a`, `.so`	Compiled library code
`.c`	C language source code
`.C`, `.cc`	C++ language source code (these may also have .cpp, .cxx, .CPP,.cp, or .c++ as an extension)
`.i`	Preprocessed C source code
`.ii`	Preprocessed C++ source code
`.m`	Objective-C source code
`.o`	Compiled object code
`.S`, `.s`	Assembly language source code

Compiling Multiple Source Code Files

Most non-trivial programs consist of multiple source files, and each source file must be compiled to object code before the final link step. To do so, pass `gcc` the name of each source code file it has to compile. GCC handles the rest. The `gcc` invocation might resemble the following:

```
$ gcc file1.c file2.c file3.c -o progname
```

`gcc` would create `file1.o`, `file2.o`, and `file3.o` and then link them all together to create `progname`. As an alternative, you can use `gcc`'s `-c` option on each file individually, which creates object files from each file. Then in a second step, you link the object files together to create an executable. Thus, the single command just shown becomes:

```
$ gcc -c file1.c
$ gcc -c file2.c
$ gcc -c file3.c
$ gcc file1.o file2.o file3.o -o progname
```

One reason to do this is to avoid recompiling files that haven't changed. If you change the source code only in `file3.c`, for example, you don't need to recompile `file1.c` and `file2.c` to recreate `progname`. Another reason to compile source code files individually before linking them to create the executable is to avoid long-running compilation. Compiling multiple files in a single `gcc` invocation can take a while if one of the source code modules is really lengthy.

Let's take a look at an example that creates a single binary executable from multiple source code files. The example program named `newhello` comprises a C source code file, `main.c` (see Listing 29-1); a header file, `msg.h` (see Listing 29-2); and another C source code file, `msg.c` (see Listing 29-3).

LISTING 29-1

Main Program for newhello

```
/*
 * main.c   driver program
 */
#include <stdio.h>
#include "msg.h"
int main(int argc, char *argv[])
{
        char msg_hi[] = { "Hi there, programmer!" };
        char msg_bye[] = { "Goodbye, programmer!" };
        printf("%s\n", msg_hi);
        prmsg(msg_bye);
        return 0;
}
```

LISTING 29-2

Header file for newhello Helper Function

```
/*
 * msg.h - header for msg.c
 */
#ifndef MSG_H_
#define MSG_H_
void prmsg(char *msg);
#endif /* MSG_H_ */
```

LISTING 29-3

Definitions for newhello Helper Function

```
/*
 * msg.c - function declared in msg.h
 */
#include <stdio.h>
#include "msg.h"
void prmsg(char *msg)
{
        printf("%s\n", msg);
}
```

The command to compile these programs to create newhello is

```
$ gcc msg.c main.c -o newhello
```

The gcc command finds the header file msg.h in the current directory and automatically includes that file during the preprocessing stage. The stdio.h file resides in a location known to the gcc command, so this file also gets included. You can add directories to search for such files, called *include* files, with the -I command-line option.

To create the object files individually, you might use the following commands:

```
$ gcc -c msg.c
$ gcc -c main.c
```

Then, to create newhello from the object files, use the following command:

```
$ gcc msg.o main.o -o newhello
```

When you run this program, the output is:

```
$ ./newhello
Hi there, programmer!
Goodbye, programmer!
```

Before it creates the newhello binary, gcc creates object files for each source file. Typing long commands such as this does become tedious, however. The section "Automating Builds with make" later in this chapter shows you how to avoid having to type long, involved command lines.

GCC Command-Line Options

The list of command-line options GCC accepts runs to several pages, so Table 29-2 describes only the most common ones. (Type **man gcc** to see a more complete list of options available with GCC.)

TABLE 29-2

GCC Command-Line Options

Option	Description
-ansi	Supports the ANSI/ISO C standard, turning off GNU extensions that conflict with the standard.
-c	Compiles without linking, resulting in an object file but not an executable binary.
-Dfoo=bar	Defines a preprocessor macro foo with a value of bar on the command line.
-g	Includes standard debugging information in the binary.
-ggdb	Includes lots of debugging information in the binary that only the GNU debugger (GDB) can understand.
-Idirname	Prepends dirname to the list of directories searched for include files.
-Ldirname	Prepends dirname to the list of directories searched for library files. By default, gcc links against shared libraries.
-lfoo	Links against libfoo.
-MM	Outputs a make-compatible dependency list.
-o file	Creates the output file file (not necessary when compiling object code). If file is not specified, the default is a.out.
-O	Optimizes the compiled code.
-On	Specifies an optimization level n, 0<=n<=3.
-pedntic	Emits all warnings required by the ANSI/ISO C standard.
-pedantic-errors	Emits all errors required by the ANSI/ISO C standard.
-static	Links against static libraries.
-traditional	Supports the Kernighan and Ritchie C syntax. (If you don't understand what this means, don't worry about it.)
-v	Shows the commands used in each step of compilation.
-W	Suppresses all warning messages.
-Wall	Emits all generally useful warnings that gcc can provide. Specific warnings can also be flagged using -Wwarning, where warning is replaced by a string identifying an item for which you want to list warnings.
-werror	Converts all warnings into errors, stopping the compilation.

As mentioned earlier, -o file tells GCC to place output in the file file regardless of the output being produced. If you do not specify -o, for an input file named file.suffix, the defaults are to name the executable a.out, the object file file.o, and the assembly language file file.s. Preprocessor output goes to stdout.

Automating Builds with make

The make utility is a tool to control the process of building and rebuilding software. make automates what software gets built, how it gets built, and when it gets built, freeing programmers to concentrate on writing code. It also saves a lot of typing because it contains logic that invokes GCC compiler-appropriate options and arguments. Furthermore, it helps you to avoid errors in typing all the complicated commands to build an application; instead, you just type one or two `make` commands. Use this section to familiarize yourself with the look and layout of makefiles.

For all but the simplest software projects, make is essential. In the first place, projects composed of multiple source files require long, complex compiler invocations. make simplifies this by storing these difficult command lines in the makefile, a text file that contains all of the commands required to build software projects.

make is convenient for both the developer and the users who want to build a program. As developers make changes to a program, whether to add new features or incorporate bug fixes, make makes it possible to rebuild the program with a single, short command. make is convenient for users because they don't have to read reams of documentation explaining in excruciating, mind-numbing detail how to build a program. Rather, they can simply be told to type **make** followed by **make test** followed by **make install**. Most users appreciate the convenience of simple build instructions.

Finally, make speeds up the edit-compile-debug process. It minimizes rebuild times because it is smart enough to determine which files have changed, and recompiles only files that have changed.

So, how does make accomplish its magical feats? By using a makefile, which contains rules that tell make what to build and how to build it. A rule consists of the following:

- **Target:** The "thing" make ultimately tries to create
- **Dependencies:** A list of one or more dependencies (usually files) required to build the target
- **Commands:** A list of commands to execute to create the target from the specified dependencies

Makefiles constitute a database of dependency information for the programs they build and automatically verify that all of the files necessary for building a program are available.

When invoked, GNU make looks for a file named `GNUmakefile`, `makefile`, or `Makefile`, in that order. For some reason, most developers use the last form, `Makefile`. Makefile rules have the general form

```
target : dependency dependency [...]
        command
        command
        [...]
```

In this syntax, *target* is usually the file, such as a binary or object file, to create. *dependency* is a list of one or more files required as input to create *target*. Each *command* is a step such as a compiler invocation or a shell command that is necessary to create target. Unless specified otherwise, make does all of its work in the current working directory.

> **CAUTION** The first character in a *command* must be the tab character; eight spaces will not suffice. This often catches people unaware, and can be a problem if your preferred editor "helpfully" translates tabs to eight spaces. If you try to use spaces instead of a tab, make displays the message Missing separator and stops.

Listing 29-4 shows a sample makefile for building a text editor imaginatively named editor.

LISTING 29-4

A Sample Makefile

```
editor : editor.o screen.o keyboard.o
        gcc -o editor editor.o screen.o keyboard.o
editor.o : editor.c
        gcc -c editor.c
screen.o : screen.c
        gcc -c screen.c
keyboard.o : keyboard.c
        gcc -c keyboard.c
clean :
        rm -f *.o core *~
realclean : clean
        rm -f editor
```

To compile editor, you simply type **make** in the directory that contains the makefile. It's that simple.

This example makefile has six rules. The first defines how to create the target named editor. The first target in every makefile is the default target (unless you specifically define one using the .DEFAULT directive, which is not covered in this chapter). The default target is the one that make builds if no target is specified as an argument to make. editor has three dependencies: editor.o, screen.o, and keyboard.o; these three files must exist to build editor. The second line in the first rule is the command that make must execute to create editor: gcc -o editor editor.o screen.o keyboard.o. It builds the executable from the three object files: editor.o, screen.o, and keyboard.o.

The next three rules tell make how to build the individual object files. Each rule consists of one object file target (editor.o, screen.o, keyboard.o); one source code file dependency (editor.c, screen.c, keyboard.c); and a rule that defines how to build that target.

The fifth rule defines a target named clean with no dependencies. When a target has no dependencies, its commands are executed whenever the target is invoked. In this case, clean deletes the constituent object files (*.o), plus any core files (core) as well as any emacs backup files (*~) from previous builds.

The sixth rule defines a target named realclean. It uses the fifth rule as one of its dependencies. This causes make to build the clean target and then to remove the editor binary.

Here is where make's value becomes evident. Ordinarily, if you tried to build editor using the command from the second line, gcc would complain loudly and ceremoniously quit if the dependencies did not exist. make, on the other hand, after determining that editor requires these files, first verifies that they exist and, if they don't, executes the commands to create them.

After creating the dependencies, make returns to the first rule to create the editor executable. Of course, if the dependencies for the components editor.c, screen.c, or keyboard.c don't exist, make gives up because it lacks targets named, in this case, editor.c, screen.c, and keyboard.c (that is, no rules are defined in the makefile for creating editor.c, screen.c, and keyboard.c).

All well and good, you are probably thinking, but how does make know when to build or rebuild a file? The answer is simple: If a specified target does not exist in a place where make can find it, make builds or rebuilds it. If the target does exist, make compares the timestamp on the target to the timestamp on the dependencies. If one or more of the dependencies is newer than the target, make rebuilds that target, assuming that the newer dependency implies some code change that must be incorporated into the target.

 **You can force make to think that a file has changed by using the** touch **command. The** touch **command changes the modified date for a file without altering the file's contents.**

Library Utilities

Programming libraries are collections of code that can be reused across multiple software projects. Libraries are a classic example of software development's ardent goal: code reuse. They collect frequently used programming routines and utility code into a single location.

The standard C libraries, for example, contain hundreds of frequently used routines, such as the output function printf() and the input function getchar() that would be wearisome to rewrite each time you create a new program. Beyond code reuse and programmer convenience, however, libraries provide a great deal of thoroughly debugged and well-tested utility code, such as routines for network programming, graphics handling, data manipulation, and system calls.

You need to know the tools at your disposal for creating, maintaining, and managing programming libraries. There are two types of libraries: static and shared:

- **Static libraries:** Static libraries are specially formatted files that contain object files, called modules or members, of reusable, precompiled code. They are stored in a special format along with a table or map that links symbol names to the members in which the symbols are defined. The map speeds up compilation and linking. Static libraries are typically named with the extension .a, which stands for archive.

- **Shared libraries:** Like static libraries, shared libraries are files that contain other object files or pointers to other object files. They are called shared libraries because the code they contain is not linked into programs when the programs are compiled. Rather, the dynamic linker/loader links shared library code into programs at runtime.

Shared libraries have several advantages over static libraries. First, they require fewer system resources. They use less disk space because shared library code is not compiled into each binary but linked and loaded from a single location dynamically at runtime. They use less system memory because the kernel shares the memory the library occupies among all the programs that use the library.

Second, shared libraries are slightly faster because they need to be loaded into memory only once. Finally, shared libraries simplify code and system maintenance. As bugs are fixed or features added, users need only obtain the updated library and install it. With static libraries, each program that uses the library must be recompiled.

NOTE There can be advantages to static libraries as well, if you want to build an application that does not depend on anything on the host system, or special-purpose commands where you are not sure of the deployment environment. In general, however, shared libraries are recommended.

The dynamic linker/loader, ld.so, links symbol names to the appropriate shared library in which they are defined at runtime. Shared libraries have a special name, the *soname*, that consists of the library name and the major version number. The full name of the C library on one of my systems, for example, is libc-2.3.4.so. The library name is libc.so; the major version number is 2; the minor version number is 3; and the release or patch level is 4. For historical reasons, the C library's soname is libc.so.6. Minor version numbers and patch level numbers change as bugs are fixed, but the soname remains the same and newer versions are usually compatible with older versions.

I emphasize the soname because applications link against it. How does linking work? The ldconfig utility creates a symbolic link from the actual library (for example, libc-2.3.2.so) to the soname (for example, libc.so.6), and stores this information in /etc/ld.so.cache. At runtime, ld.so scans the cache file, finds the required soname and, because of the symbolic link, loads the actual library into memory and links application function calls to the appropriate symbols in the loaded library.

The nm Command

The nm command lists all of the symbols encoded in an object or binary file. It's used to see what function calls a program makes or to see if a library or object file provides a needed function. nm has the following syntax:

```
nm [options] file
```

nm lists the symbols stored in *file*, which must be a static library or archive file, as described in the preceding section. *options* control nm's behavior. Symbols are things like functions referenced in the code, global variables from other libraries, and so on. You can use the nm command as a tool when you have to track down a missing symbol needed by a program.

Table 29-3 describes useful options for nm.

nm Command-Line Options

Option	Description
-C	Converts symbol names into user-level names. This is especially useful for making C++ function names readable.
-l	Uses debugging information to print the line number where each symbol is defined, or the relocation entry if the symbol is undefined.
-s	When used on archive (.a) files, prints the index that maps symbol names to the modules or members in which the symbol is defined.
-u	Displays only undefined symbols, symbols defined externally to the file being examined.

Here's an example that uses nm to show some of the symbols in /usr/lib/libdl.a:

```
$ nm /usr/lib/libdl.a | head
dlopen.o:
00000040 T __dlopen_check
         U _dl_open
         U _dlerror_run
00000040 W dlopen
00000000 t dlopen_doit
dlclose.o:
         U _dl_close
```

The ar Command

ar creates, modifies, or extracts archives. It is most commonly used to create static libraries, which are files that contain one or more object files. ar also creates and maintains a table that cross-references symbol names to the members in which they are defined. The ar command has the following syntax:

```
ar {dmpqrtx} [options] [member] archive file [...]
```

ar creates the archive named *archive* from the file(s) listed in file. At least one of d, m, p, q, r, t, and x is required. You will usually use r. Table 29-4 lists the most commonly used ar options.

TABLE 29-4

ar Command-Line Options

Option	Description
-c	Suppresses the warning ar would normally emit if the archive doesn't already exist.
-q	Adds files to the end of archive without checking for replacements.
-r	Inserts files into archive, replacing any existing members whose name matches that being added. New members are added at the end of the archive.
-s	Creates or updates the map linking symbols to the member in which they are defined.

TIP Given an archive created with the ar command, you can speed up access to the archive by creating an index to the archive. ranlib does precisely this, storing the index in the archive file itself. ranlib's syntax is:

```
ranlib [-v|-V] file
```

This generates a symbol map in *file*. It is equivalent to ar -s *file*.

The ldd Command

While nm lists the symbols defined in an object file, unless you know what library defines which functions, it is not terribly helpful. That is ldd's job. It lists the shared libraries that a program requires to run. Its syntax is:

```
ldd [options] file
```

ldd prints the names of the shared libraries that *file* requires. Two of ldd's most useful options are -d, which reports any missing functions, and -r, which reports missing functions *and* missing data objects. For example, the following ldd reports that the mail client mutt (which may or may not be installed on your system) requires eight shared libraries.

```
$ ldd /usr/bin/mutt
        libncursesw.so.5 => /lib/libncursesw.so.5 (0x40021000)
        libssl.so.0 => /usr/lib/libssl.so.0 (0x40066000)
        libcrypto.so.0 => /usr/lib/libcrypto.so.0 (0x40097000)
        libc.so.6 => /lib/libc.so.6 (0x40195000)
        libgpm.so.1 => /lib/libgpm.so.1 (0x402c5000)
        libdl.so.2 => /lib/libdl.so.2 (0x402cb000)
        /lib/ld-linux.so.2 => /lib/ld-linux.so.2 (0x40000000)
        libncurses.so.5 => /lib/libncurses.so.5 (0x402ce000)
```

The output might be different on your system.

The ldconfig Command

ldconfig determines the runtime links required by shared libraries that are located in /usr/lib and /lib, specified in libs on the command line, and stored in /etc/ld.so.conf. It works in conjunction with ld.so, the dynamic linker/loader, to create and maintain links to the most current versions of shared libraries available on a system. It has the following syntax:

```
ldconfig [options] [libs]
```

Running ldconfig with no arguments simply updates the cache file, /etc/ld.so.cache. options control ldconfig's behavior. The -v option tells ldconfig to be verbose as it updates the cache. The -p option says to print without updating the current list of shared libraries about which ld.so knows. To see what ldconfig is doing when updating the cache, the -v option will print out a display of directories and symlinks ldconfig has found.

Environment Variables and Configuration Files

The dynamic linker/loader ld.so uses a number of environment variables to customize and control its behavior. These variables include:

- $LD_LIBRARY_PATH: This variable contains a colon-separated list of directories in which to search for shared libraries at runtime. It is similar to the $PATH environment variable.

- $LD_PRELOAD: This variable is a whitespace-separated list of additional, user-specified shared libraries to load before all other libraries. It is used selectively to override functions in other shared libraries.

ld.so also uses two configuration files whose purposes parallel those environment variables:

- /etc/ld.so.conf: Contains a list of directories that the linker/loader should search for shared libraries in addition to the standard directories, /usr/lib and /lib, as well as /lib64 on 64-bit architecture systems.

- /etc/ld.so.preload: Contains a disk-based version of the $LD_PRELOAD environment variable, including a whitespace-separated list of shared libraries to be loaded prior to executing a program.

You can use $LD_PRELOAD to override installed versions of a library with a specific version; this is often useful when you are testing a new (or different) library version but don't want to install the replacement library on your system. In general, use the environment variables only while you create your programs. Don't depend on these environment variables in production, as they have created security issues in the past, so you may not be able to control the values of the variables.

Source Code Control

Version control is an automated process for keeping track of and managing changes made to source code files. Why bother? Because:

- One day you *will* make that one fatal edit to a source file, delete its predecessor, and forget exactly which line or lines of code you "fixed."

- Simultaneously keeping track of the current release, the next release, and eight bug fixes manually *will* become mind-numbing and confusing.

- Frantically searching for the backup tape because one of your colleagues overwrote a source file for the fifth time *will* drive you over the edge.

- One day, over your morning latte, you will say to yourself, "Version control, it's the Right Thing to Do."

Source Code Control Using RCS

The Revision Control System (RCS) is a common solution to the version control problem. RCS, which is maintained by the GNU project, is available on almost all UNIX systems, not just on Linux. Two alternatives to RCS are the Concurrent Version System (CVS), which also is maintained by the GNU project, and the Source Code Control System (SCCS), a proprietary product.

Before you proceed, however, Table 29-5 lists a few terms that will be used throughout the chapter. Because they are used so frequently, I want to make sure you understand their meaning insofar as RCS and version control in general are concerned.

TABLE 29-5

Version Control Terms

Term	Description
Lock	A working file retrieved for editing such that no one else can edit it simultaneously. A working file is locked by the first user against edits by other users.
RCS file	Any file located in an RCS directory, controlled by RCS, and accessed using RCS commands. An RCS file contains all versions of a particular file. Typically, an RCS file has a , v extension.
Revision	A specific, numbered version of a source file. Revisions begin with 1.1 and increase incrementally, unless forced to use a specific revision number.
Working file	One or more files retrieved from the RCS source code repository (the RCS directory) into the current working directory and available for editing.

RCS manages multiple versions of files, usually but not necessarily source code files. It automates file version storage and retrieval, change logging, access control, release management, and revision identification and merging. As an added bonus, RCS minimizes disk space requirements because it tracks only file changes.

One of RCS's attractions is its simplicity. With only a few commands, you can accomplish a great deal.

Checking Files In and Out

You can accomplish a lot with RCS using only two commands (ci and co) and a directory named RCS. ci stands for "check in," which means storing a working file in the RCS directory; co means "check out" and refers to retrieving an RCS file from the RCS repository.

To get started, you need to create an RCS directory. All RCS commands will use this directory, if it is present in your current working directory. The RCS directory is also called the *repository*. When you check a file in, RCS asks for a description of the file, copies it to the RCS directory, and deletes the original. "Deletes the original"? Ack! Don't worry, you can retrieve it with the check out command, co.

Here's how to create an RCS directory:

```
$ mkdir RCS
```

Next, create the following source file (naming it howdy.c) in the same directory in which you created the RCS directory.

```
/*
 * $Id$
 * howdy.c - Sample to demonstrate RCS Usage
 */
#include <stdio.h>
int main(void)
{
    fprintf(stdout,  Howdy, Linux programmer!");
    return EXIT_SUCCESS;
}
```

Now, use the command ci howdy.c to check the file into the repository:

```
$ ci howdy.c
RCS/howdy.c,v  <-- howdy.c
enter description, terminated with single '.' or end of file:
NOTE: This is NOT the log message!
>> Simple program to illustrate RCS usage
>> .
initial revision: 1.1
done
```

With the file safely checked into the repository, you can check it out and modify it. To check a file out for editing, use the `co` command. Here's an example:

```
$ co -l howdy.c
RCS/howdy.c,v  -->  howdy.c
revision 1.1 (locked)
done
```

The working file you just checked out is editable. If you do not want to edit it, omit the `-l` option.

Making Changes to Repository Files

To see version control in action, make a change to the working file. If you haven't already done so, check out and lock the `howdy.c` file. Change anything you want, but I recommend adding `\n` to the end of `fprintf()`'s string argument because Linux (and UNIX), unlike DOS and Windows, does not automatically add a newline to the end of console output.

Next, check the file back in, and RCS will increment the revision number to 1.2, ask for a description of the change you made, incorporate the changes you made into the RCS file, and (annoyingly) delete the original. To prevent deletion of your working files during check-in operations, use the `-l` or `-u` option with `ci`. Here's an example:

```
$ ci -l howdy.c
RCS/howdy.c,v  <--  howdy.c
new revision: 1.2; previous revision: 1.1
enter log message, terminated with single '.' or end of file:
>> Added newline
>> .
done
```

The messages shown in the preceding code may differ depending on whether you modified the file or did not lock the file during check out.

When used with `ci`, both the `-l` and `-u` options cause an implied check-out of the file after the check-in procedure completes. `-l` locks the file so you can continue to edit it, whereas `-u` checks out an unlocked or read-only working file.

Additional Command-Line Options

In addition to `-l` and `-u`, `ci` and `co` accept two other very useful options: `-r` (for revision) and `-f` (force). Use `-r` to tell RCS which file revision you want to manipulate. RCS assumes you want to work with the most recent revision; `-r` overrides this default. The `-f` option forces RCS to overwrite the current working file. By default, RCS aborts a check-out operation if a working file of the same name already exists in your working directory. So if you really botch your working file, use the `-f` option with `co` to get a fresh start.

RCS's command-line options are cumulative, as you might expect, and RCS does a good job of disallowing incompatible options. To check out and lock a specific revision of `howdy.c`, you would use a command such as `co -l -r2.1 howdy.c`. Similarly, `ci -u -r3 howdy.c` checks in `howdy.c`, assigns it revision number 3.1, and deposits a read-only revision 3.1 working file back into your current working directory.

The following example creates revision 2.1 of `howdy.c`. Make sure you have checked out and changed `howdy.c` somehow before executing this command.

```
$ ci -r2 howdy.c
RCS/howdy.c,v  <--  howdy.c
new revision: 2.1; previous revision: 1.2
enter log message, terminated with single '.' or end of file:
>> Added something
>> .
done
```

This command is equivalent to `ci -r2.1 howdy.c`.

The next example checks out revision 1.2 of `howdy.c`, disregarding the presence of higher-numbered revisions in the working directory.

```
$ co -r1.2 howdy.c
RCS/howdy.c,v  -->  howdy.c
revision 1.2
done
```

The handy command shown next discards all of the changes you've made to version 1.2 (above) and lets you start over with a known good source file.

```
$ co -l -f howdy.c
RCS/howdy.c,v  -->  howdy.c
revision 2.1 (locked)
done
```

When used with `ci`, `-f` forces RCS to check in a file even if it has not changed.

Source Code Control with CVS

You may have noticed that RCS has some shortcomings that make it inadequate for use on large projects. First, without some sophisticated wrapper scripts to provide the directory handling machinery, RCS doesn't work very well with a single, centralized repository. And you need such a repository for a programming team with more than a few members.

An RCS repository is always the current directory unless you exert yourself to use a directory located elsewhere. More pertinent for Linux and other open source projects, RCS is utterly unsuitable for distributed development because it doesn't support network protocols. (That is, it doesn't work over the Internet.)

Furthermore, RCS suffers from programmers forgetting commands. If you forget to check out a file with a certain option, you may regret it later. Even if you work alone, you may find CVS a better option.

The Concurrent Versions System (CVS) supports both centralized repositories and network-based access. It is well-suited for use by multiple programmers, and a single CVS repository can support multiple projects. To keep the discussion simple, however, the example in this chapter deals only with a repository accessed locally. The following steps resemble the process described earlier for RCS, but they are slightly more involved and obviously use CVS concepts:

1. Create a CVS repository:

```
$ mkdir /space/cvs
$ export CVSROOT=/space/cvs
$ cvs init
```

The first command creates a directory named /space/cvs in which to establish the repository. The second command defines the environment variable $CVSROOT with this directory. Defining $CVSROOT makes using CVS much simpler. The third command initializes the repository, which creates some administrative directories CVS needs to work properly.

2. Create a top-level working directory in which to store your various projects and then change into this directory:

```
$ mkdir projects
$ cd projects
```

3. Check out a copy of the CVS root directory into the directory you just created:

```
$ cvs -d $CVSROOT co -l .
cvs checkout: Updating .
```

The -d option tells cvs the name of the directory containing the CVS repository ($CVSROOT, or /space/cvs); co means check out (just as with RCS); the -l option, which stands for local, means to work only in the current directory rather than recursing through subdirectories; and the . specifies the current directory.

4. Create a directory to hold a project and add it to the repository:

```
$ mkdir newhello
$ cvs add newhello
Directory /space/cvs/newhello added to the repository
```

5. Change into the new directory, copy your project files into it (fill in the `your_new_hello_code` with the name of the directory where you have the actual source code files for the new project), and then add those files (and any directories that might be present) to the repository:

```
$ cd newhello
$ cp /your_new_hello_code/* .
$ cvs add *c *h
cvs add: scheduling file `hello.c' for addition
cvs add: scheduling file `msg.c' for addition
cvs add: scheduling file `main.c' for addition
cvs add: scheduling file `showit.c' for addition
cvs add: use 'cvs commit' to add these files permanently
```

6. Do as the instructions recommend: Execute the command `cvs commit` to make the added files and directories permanent. You'll first see a screen (which is actually a vi editor session) asking you to enter a log message. If you don't want to enter a log message, press Esc, and type **ZZ** to save and exit. After you close the vi session, the output you see should resemble the following:

```
$ cvs commit
cvs commit: Examining .
RCS file: /space/cvs/newhello/hello.c,v
done
Checking in hello.c;
/space/cvs/newhello/hello.c,v  <--  hello.c
initial revision: 1.1
done
RCS file: /space/cvs/newhello/msg.c,v
done
Checking in msg.c;
/space/cvs/newhello/msg.c,v  <--  msg.c
initial revision: 1.1
done
RCS file: /space/cvs/newhello/showit.c,v
done
Checking in main.c;
/space/cvs/newhello/main.c,v  <--  main.c
initial revision: 1.1
done
```

Notice that CVS uses RCS filenaming conventions to work with files in the repository. This is because CVS was built on top of RCS and retains compatibility with the basic RCS feature set.

CVS handles checking files in and out slightly differently than RCS. When checking a file out, it isn't necessary to specifically request a lock to get a writable copy of the file. To work on a file, you do need to use the `checkout` or `co` command:

```
$ cd projects
$ cvs -d /space/cvs co newhello
cvs checkout newhello
U newhello/hello.c
U newhello/msg.c
U newhello/main.c
```

The checkout command used in this example specifies the path to the repository using the -d option. This is unnecessary if you set the $CVSROOT environment variable. After you have made changes to files such as main.c, you can check them in using the cvs commit command (commit is comparable to RCS's ci command):

```
$ cd projects/newhello
$ cvs commit .
cvs commit: Examining .
[editor session]
Checking in main.c;
/space/cvs/newhello/main.c,v <--  main.c
new revision: 1.2; previous revision: 1.1
done
```

When you check in a modified file, CVS opens an editor session to enable you to enter a log message that describes the changes you made. The editor used is the editor defined in the $EDITOR environment variable or compiled-in default (usually the vi text editor) if $EDITOR is undefined. This example did not use the -d option because the $CVSROOT environment variable is set.

To check out a specific version, or revision, of a file, use the -r option following the checkout or co command, followed by a revision number. For example, to check out revision 1.1 of the main.c file, use the following command.

```
$ cvs checkout -r 1.1 main.c
U main.c
```

To see the differences between two revisions, use the diff command, using the -r m.n, where m.n indicates the revision number you want to check. If you specify -r only once, the indicated version will be compared against the working file (using the diff option). If you specify -r twice, the two versions will be compared against each other. The following example compares revision 1.2 of showit.c to the current working revision (the revision currently in the working directory):

```
$ cvs diff -r 1.2 main.c
Index: main.c
===================================================================
RCS file: /space/cvs/newhello/main.c,v
retrieving revision 1.2
retrieving revision 1.3
diff -r1.2 -r1.3
9,10c9,10
<         char msg_hi[] = { "Hi there, programmer!" };
<         char msg_bye[] = { "Goodbye, programmer!" };
---
```

```
>          char msg_hi[] = { "Hi there, programmer!\n" };
>          char msg_bye[] = { "Goodbye, programmer!\n" };
12c12
<          printf("%s\n", msg_hi);
---
>          printf("%s", msg_hi);
```

The diff output is easier to understand than you might expect. Lines that begin with < appear in the first file (revision 1.2 of main.c) but not in the second (revision 1.3 of main.c). Similarly, lines beginning with > appear in the second file, but not in the first. Each section of diff output begins with an alphanumeric sequence such as 9,10c9,10 or 12c12.

The numeric values of the diff output indicate the lines in the first and second files to which an operation must be applied to get the second file from the first. The operation to perform (such as inserting, deleting, or changing lines) is specified by the alphabetic character. So, for example, the sequence 9,10c9,10 means that if you want to create the second file from the first, you have to change (c) lines 9 and 10 of the first file to lines 9 and 10 of the second file.

Finally, if you totally botch all of your changes to your working files and want to revert to the most recent versions, use the update command It updates the specified directory with the most recent versions stored in the repository, as shown in the following example.

```
$ cd ~/projects/newhello
$ cvs update .
cvs update: Updating .
U showit.c
U msg.c
U hello.c
```

There's much more to CVS than the few examples presented here. For additional information, visit the CVS home page on the Web at www.nongnu.org/cvs.

While CVS improves a lot on the limitations of RCS, CVS has its own limitations. SVN, or Subversion, is a newer source code control system that aims to solve many of the limitations of CVS. See subversion.tigris.org for more on SVN.

Debugging with GNU Debugger

Software is buggy, and some programs have more bugs than other programs. While debugging sessions will never be aggravation-free, the advanced features of GNU Debugger (GDB) lighten the load and enable you to be more productive in squashing bugs. A debugger runs a program in a special mode that allows you to view the inner workings of the programs, especially the value of variables at a given point in the code. The theory is that by exposing the inner workings of the program, you can more easily determine what is not correct in the program's source code — that is, where the bug is located.

Time and effort invested in learning GDB is well spent if you can track down and fix a serious bug in just a few minutes. GDB can make this happen. Most of what you will need to accomplish with GDB can be done with a surprisingly small set of commands. The rest of this chapter explores GDB features and shows you enough GDB commands to get you going.

Effective debugging requires that your source code be compiled with the `-g` option to create a binary with an extended symbol table. For example, the following command

```
$ gcc -g file1 file2 -o prog
```

causes *prog* to be created with debugging symbols in its symbol table. If you want, you can use GCC's `-ggdb` option to generate still more (GDB-specific) debugging information. However, to work most effectively, this option requires that you have access to the source code for every library against which you link. While this can be very useful in certain situations, it can also be expensive in terms of disk space. In most cases, you can get by with the plain `-g` option.

Starting GDB

To start a debugging session, simply type **gdb** *progname*, replacing ***progname*** with the name of the program you want to debug. Using a core file is optional but will enhance GDB's debugging capabilities. Of course, you'll need a program on which to try out GDB debugging, so Listing 29-5 provides one: debugme.c.

LISTING 29-5

A Buggy Program

```c
/*
 * debugme.c - poorly written program to debug
 */
#include <stdio.h>
#define BIGNUM 5000
#define SZ 100
void index_to_the_moon(int ary[]);
int main(int argc, char *argv[])
{
        int intary[100];
        index_to_the_moon(intary);
        return 0;
}
void index_to_the_moon(int ary[])
{
        int i;
        for (i = 0; i < BIGNUM; ++i)
                ary[i] = i;
}
```

Compile this program using the command `gcc -g debugme.c -o debugme`. Then, execute the program using the command `./debugme`.

```
$ ./debugme
Segmentation fault (core dumped)
$ file core
core: ELF 32-big LSB core file Intel 80386, version 1 (SYSV
), SVR4-style, SVR4-stylee, from 'debugme'
```

On most systems, when you execute `./debugme`, it immediately causes a segmentation fault and dumps core, as shown in the output listing.

> **NOTE**   A *core dump* refers to an application failing and copying all data stored in memory for the application into a file named `core` in the current directory. That file can be used to help debug a problem with the application. The file output may be called `core`, or have a numeric extension, such as `core.12345` (usually the process ID of the program that died).

If you don't see the `core dumped` message, try executing the shell command `ulimit -c unlimited`, which allows programs to drop a memory dump in their current working directory.

The program has a bug, so you need to debug it. The first step is to start GDB, using the program name, `debugme`, and the core file, `core`, as arguments:

```
$ gdb debugme core
```

After GDB initializes, the screen should resemble Figure 29-1.

FIGURE 29-1

GDB's startup screen

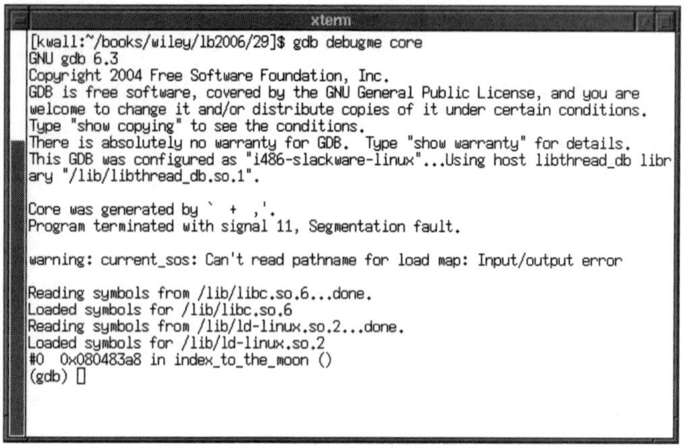

```
xterm
[kwall:~/books/wiley/lb2006/29]$ gdb debugme core
GNU gdb 6.3
Copyright 2004 Free Software Foundation, Inc.
GDB is free software, covered by the GNU General Public License, and you are
welcome to change it and/or distribute copies of it under certain conditions.
Type "show copying" to see the conditions.
There is absolutely no warranty for GDB.  Type "show warranty" for details.
This GDB was configured as "i486-slackware-linux"...Using host libthread_db libr
ary "/lib/libthread_db.so.1".

Core was generated by ` + ,'.
Program terminated with signal 11, Segmentation fault.

warning: current_sos: Can't read pathname for load map: Input/output error

Reading symbols from /lib/libc.so.6...done.
Loaded symbols for /lib/libc.so.6
Reading symbols from /lib/ld-linux.so.2...done.
Loaded symbols for /lib/ld-linux.so.2
#0  0x080483a8 in index_to_the_moon ()
(gdb) []
```

As you can see near the middle of the figure, GDB displays the name of the executable that created the core file: `` ` + ,' ``. Obviously, the displayed name is wrong; it should be debugme. The odd characters and the incorrect program name would give an experienced developer an immediate clue that the program has a significant memory bug. The next line in the figure, the text that reads Program terminated with signal 11, Segmentation fault, explains why the program terminated. A segmentation fault occurs anytime a program attempts to access memory that doesn't explicitly belong to it. GDB also helpfully displays the function it was executing, index_to_the_moon.

> **TIP** If you don't like the licensing messages (they annoy me), use the `-q` (or `--quiet`) option when you start GDB to suppress them. Another useful command-line option is `-d dirname`, where `dirname` is the name of a directory, which tells gdb where to find source code (it looks in the current working directory by default).

After you load the program and its core dump into the debugger, run the program in the debugger. To do so, type the command run at the GDB command prompt, (gdb), as the following example shows:

```
(gdb) run
Starting program: /home/kwall/code/debugme
Program received signal SIGSEGV, Segmentation fault.
0x0804483db in index_to_the_moon (ary=0xbffff4b0) at debugme.c:24
24                    ary[i] = i;
```

This short output listing shows that the segmentation fault occurred in the function index_to_the_moon at line 24 of debugme.c. Notice the last line of the output; GDB displays the line of code, prefixed with the line number (24), where the segmentation fault occurred. It also shows the memory address (in hexadecimal format) at which the fault occurred: 0xbffff4b0.

You can pass any arguments to the run command that your program would ordinarily accept. GDB also creates a full shell environment in which to run the program. Ordinarily, GDB uses the value of the environment variable $SHELL to create the simulated environment. If you want, however, you can use GDB's set and unset commands to set or unset arguments and environment variables before you use the run command to run the program in the debugger.

To set command-line arguments to pass to the program, type **set args *arg1 arg2***, where ***arg1*** and ***arg2*** (or any number of arguments) are options and arguments the program being debugged expects. Use **set environment *env1 env2*** to set environment variables (again, ***env1*** and ***env2*** are placeholders for the environment variables you want to set or unset).

Inspecting Code in the Debugger

What is happening in the function index_to_the_moon that's causing the error? You can execute the backtrace (or bt or back) command to generate the function tree that led to the segmentation fault. The backtrace doesn't usually show you *what* the problem is, but it does show you more precisely *where* the problem occurred. Here's how the function trace for the example looks on my system:

```
(gdb) backtrace
#0  0x080483db index_to_the_moon (ary=0x7ffffc90) at debugme.c:24
#1  0x080483a6 in main (argc=104,argv=0x69) at debugme.c:15
```

A backtrace shows the chain of function calls that resulted in the error. The backtrace starts with the most recently called function — index_to_the_moon() in this case — which resides at the hexadecimal memory address shown in the second column of the display (0x0800483db). The function index_to_the_moon() was called by the main() function. As you can see from the output, the most recently called function was index_to_the_moon(), so, somewhere in the function, the segmentation fault occurred. Incidentally, the backtrace also shows that index_to_the_moon() was called from line 15 of the main() function in debugme.c.

> **TIP**   It's not necessary to type complete command names while using GDB. Any sufficiently unique abbreviation works. For example, back suffices for backtrace.

It would be helpful, however, to have some idea of the context in which the offending line(s) of code exist. For this purpose, use the list command, which takes the general form, list [*m*, *n*], where *m* and *n* are the starting and ending line numbers you want displayed. For example:

```
(gdb) list 10,24
```

would display code lines 10 through 24.

A bare list command displays 10 lines of code, including the line where the error was first detected, as illustrated here:

```
(gdb) list
15              index_to_the_moon(intary);
16
17              exit(EXIT_SUCCESS);
18      }
19
20      void index_to_the_moon(int ary[])
21      {
22              int i;
23              for (i = 0; i < BIGNUM; ++I {
24                      ary[i] = i;
```

Examining Data

One of GDB's most useful features is its ability to display both the type and the value of almost any expression, variable, or array in the program being debugged. It can print the value of any legal expression in the language in which your program is written. The command is, predictably enough, print. Here are a couple of print commands and their results:

```
(gdb) print i
$1 = 724
(gdb) print ary[i]
Cannot access memory at address 0xc0000000.
```

This example continues the earlier examples of debugging debugme.c because you are still trying to identify where and why debug me crashed. Although in this example, the program crashed at the point when the counter variable i equaled 724 (the expression $1 refers to an entry in GDB's value history, explained in a moment), where it crashes on your system depends on several variables. Those variables could include the system's memory layout, the process's memory space (especially the kernel's stack space), the amount of available memory on your system, and other factors.

The result of the second command (print ary[i]) makes it pretty clear that the program does not have access to the memory location specified, although it does have legal access to the preceding one.

The expression $1 is an alias that refers to an entry in GDB's value history. GDB creates value history entries for each command you type that produces computed results. The alias numbers increment sequentially each time you execute a command that produces some sort of computed output. As a result, you can access these computed values using aliases rather than retyping the command. For example, the command $1-5 produces the following:

```
(gdb) print $1-5
$2 = 719
```

Notice that the alias incremented to $2. If you later need to use the value 719, you can use the alias $2. The value history is reset each time you start GDB and the values are not accessible outside of GDB.

You are not limited to using discrete values because gdb can display the addresses of data stored in an arbitrary region of memory. For example, to print the first 10 memory locations associated with ary, use the following command:

```
(gdb) print ary@10
$3 = {0xbffffc90, 0x40015580, 0x400115800, 0x0, 0x1, 0x2, 0c3, 0x4, 0x5}
```

The notation @10 means to print the 10 values that begin at ary. Say, on the other hand, that you want to print the five values stored in ary beginning with the first element. The command for this would be as follows:

```
(gdb) print ary[1]@5
$4 = {1, 2, 3, 4, 5}
```

Why go to the trouble of printing variable or array values? Although it isn't necessary in this particular example because you know where the trouble occurs, it is often necessary to see the value of a variable at a particular point in a program's execution so you can monitor what is happening to variables. It's pretty clear in this case that the index_to_the_moon() function is suspect, but depending on experience, some people may not see the exact problem within the function.

In the case of arrays, a command that prints the values in an array, such as print ary[1]@5 in the preceding example, enables you to confirm at a glance that the values are what you expect them to be. If the values don't match up with your expectations, however, that is a clue that some code is altering the array in a way you didn't intend. As a result, you can focus your bug hunting on a specific section of code.

GDB also can tell you the types of variables using the whatis command. GDB's whatis command is comparable to the man -f command, which searches the whatis database of system commands for short descriptions of those system commands (the manual page whatis database is totally separate from the whatis command used by GDB). While man's whatis database works on system commands, GDB's whatis command describes the types of variables and other data structures used in a program.

```
(gdb) whatis i
type = int
(gdb) whatis ary
type = int *
(gdb) whatis index_to_the_moon
type = void (int *)
```

This feature may seem rather useless because, of course, you know the types of all the variables in your program (yeah, right!). But, you will change your mind the first time you have to debug someone else's code or have to fix a multi-file project for which you haven't seen the source files for a couple of months. The whatis command can also help you track down bugs that result from assigning an inappropriate value to a variable.

Setting Breakpoints

As you debug problematic code, it is often useful to halt execution at some point. Perhaps you want to stop execution before the code enters a section that is known to have problems. In other cases, you can set breakpoints so you can look at the values of certain variables at a given point in the execution flow. In still other situations, you might find it useful to stop execution so you can step through the code one instruction at a time.

GDB enables you to set breakpoints on several different kinds of code constructs, including line numbers and function names, and enables you to set conditional breakpoints, where the code stops only if a certain condition is met. To set a breakpoint on a line number, use the following syntax:

```
(gdb) break linenum
```

To stop execution when the code enters a function, use the following:

```
(gdb) break funcname
```

In either case, GDB halts execution before executing the specified line number or entering the specified function. You can then use `print` to display variable values, for example, or use `list` to review the code that is about to be executed. If you have a multi-file project and want to halt execution on a line of code or in a function that is not in the current source file, use the following forms:

```
(gdb) break filename:linenum
(gdb) break filename:funcname
```

Conditional breakpoints are usually more useful. They enable you to temporarily halt program execution if or when a particular condition is met. The correct syntax for setting conditional breakpoints is as follows:

```
(gdb) break linenum if expr
(gdb) break funcname if expr
```

In the preceding code, `expr` can be any expression that evaluates to true (non-zero). For example, the following `break` command stops execution at line 24 of `debugme` when the variable i equals 15:

```
(gdb) break 24 if i == 15
Breakpoint 1 at 0x80483cb: file debugme.c, line 24.
(gdb) run
Starting program: /home/kwall/code/debugme
Breakpoint 1, index_to_the_moon (ary=0xbffff4b0) at debugme.c:24
24                      ary[i] = i;
```

> **TIP** Verify the line numbers as seen by gdb. In this case, gdb has line 24 as the assignment of `ary[i]` to the value of `i`, as shown in the preceding code. Use the gdb `list` command to verify the line numbers used by gdb.

Stopping when i equals 15 is an arbitrary choice to demonstrate conditional breaks. As you can see, gdb stopped on line 24. A quick `print` command confirms that it stopped when the value of i reached the requested value:

```
(gdb) print i
$1 = 15
```

To resume executing after hitting a breakpoint, type **continue**. If you have set many breakpoints and have lost track of what has been set and which ones have been triggered, you can use the `info breakpoints` command to refresh your memory.

Working with Source Code

Locating a specific variable or function in a multi-file project is a breeze with GDB, provided you use the `-d` switch to tell it where to find additional source code files. This is a particularly helpful option when not all of your source code is located in your current working directory or in the program's compilation directory (which GCC recorded in its symbol table).

To specify one or more additional directories containing source code, start GDB using one or more -d dirname options, as this example illustrates:

```
$ gdb -d /source/project1 -d /oldsource/project1 -d /home/
bubba/src killerapp
```

To locate the next occurrence of a particular string in the current file, use the search string command. Use reverse-search string to find the previous occurrence of string. If you want to find the previous occurrence of the word "return" in debugme.c (refer to Listing 29-5), for example, use the command reverse-search return. GDB obliges and displays the text:

```
(gdb) reverse-search return
17                 return ret;
```

The search and reverse-search commands are especially helpful in large source files that have dozens or hundreds of lines. One common use of the reverse-search command is to find the file and/or line in which a variable is first used or in which it is defined. The search command similarly enables you to locate with relative ease each location in which a program symbol (variable, macro, or function) is used, perhaps to find the use that changes a variable unexpectedly or the place where a function is called when it shouldn't be.

Summary

This chapter took you on a whirlwind tour of a few of the most common programs and utilities used by Linux programmers. You learned how to use GCC to compile programs, how to use make to automate compiling programs, and how to find information about programming libraries using programs such as ldd, nm, and ldconfig. You also learned enough about the source code control systems RCS and CVS to be comfortable with the terminology and how to use their most basic features. Finally, you learned how to use the GNU debugger (GDB) to figure out why, or at least where, a program fails.

Appendix A

Media

The DVD and CD that accompany *Linux Bible 2008 Edition* contain a variety of Linux systems that you can use. Some of these Linux systems can be booted and run live, while others can be used to install a Linux system permanently to hard disk. Some can do both.

Most of the Linux systems included here are slightly remastered versions of official live and installation CDs that come from different Linux projects. Changes made to those CDs were made exclusively to allow each to be booted from a single boot screen on the DVD or CD. Once you have selected a Linux to start up, however, it should behave exactly like the original CD from the selected Linux project.

General information on running live or installing the various Linux distributions on the CD and DVD is in Chapter 7. Specific instructions for using and installing each Linux distribution are contained in the other chapters in Part III (see Chapters 8 through 19).

CAUTION The software contained on the CD and DVD is covered under the GNU Public License (GPL) or other licenses included on the medium for each software distribution. Use the software on the DVD and CD (as you would any GPL software) at your own risk. Refer to README, RELEASE-NOTES, and any licensing files delivered with each distribution, and be sure that you agree with the terms they spell out before using the software.

Finding Linux Distributions on the DVD

The following sections describe the nine Linux distributions on the DVD that accompanies this book. Eight of these nine distributions are immediately bootable from the DVD, although some are made to run as live CDs and others are used to install to hard disk. The ninth distribution, Freespire, is included in the form of an ISO image that you can copy from the DVD to burn to a separate CD.

Fedora Linux

The DVD that comes with this book includes a large portion of the Fedora 8 distribution that normally comes on a single DVD. This is the recommended Linux distribution for trying out most of the procedures in this book. You can install Fedora directly from the DVD without having to create CDs from the DVD to install separately.

Because so much of the Fedora 8 Linux distribution is included, you have access to a broad range of software packages (more than 1,900), allowing you to get a feel for using Linux as a desktop, server, or programmer's workstation. To begin installing Fedora to your hard disk, insert the DVD into your PC's DVD drive, reboot, and type the following from the boot prompt:

```
boot: linux
```

Details on installing and using Fedora are in Chapter 8.

NOTE If you find that you like Fedora, consider getting *Fedora 8 and Red Hat Enterprise Linux Bible* (Wiley Publishing, 2008) to learn more about that distribution. While some of the material overlaps with this book's, you will get more complete coverage of installation and different kinds of servers available with Fedora 8.

KNOPPIX Linux

The KNOPPIX 5.1.1 live CD Linux distribution is configured to boot by default from the DVD that comes with this book. KNOPPIX is the most popular bootable Linux and offers some unique features to set it apart from other bootable Linux distributions.

To boot KNOPPIX directly from the DVD, insert the DVD into your PC's DVD drive, reboot, and type the following from the boot prompt:

```
boot: knoppix
```

Information on using KNOPPIX and configuring it in various ways is in Chapter 11.

Slackware 12

The DVD that comes with this book contains the first CD image of the Slackware 12 distribution. Slackware is the oldest surviving Linux system and continues to have a loyal following among

Linux enthusiasts. To begin installing Slackware to your hard disk, insert the DVD into your PC's DVD drive, reboot, and type the following from the boot prompt:

```
boot: slack
```

Chapter 14 tells you how to install Slackware on your computer from this book's DVD or an official Slackware CD. Chapter 3 describes how to configure a simple window manager for Slackware.

Ubuntu 7.10

The Ubuntu 7.10 (Gutsy Gibbon) installation and live CD are contained on the DVD that comes with this book. That image can be used to run live, and then install, a minimal desktop system. Further software installation can be done from the Internet, after the basic install is done.

To boot the Ubuntu live CD image from the DVD that comes with this book, insert the DVD into your PC's DVD drive, reboot, and type the following from the boot prompt:

```
boot: ubuntu
```

Your computer will boot a live CD version of Ubuntu that is intended to be used as a desktop system. An icon on the desktop lets you install the contents of the CD image to your computer's hard disk. The procedure for booting and installing Ubuntu 7.10 is in Chapter 17.

Mandriva

The Mandriva One 2008.0 live CD is contained on the DVD that comes with this book. This live CD contains a desktop-oriented Mandriva distribution that can be booted live, and then used to install the contents of the Mandriva One live CD to hard disk.

To start Mandriva One from the DVD, insert the DVD into your computer's DVD drive, reboot the computer, and type the following at the boot prompt:

```
boot: mandriva
```

You can run and install Mandriva One as described in Chapter 16. You can also refer to Chapter 16 for information about other versions of Mandriva.

BackTrack 2 Linux Security Suite

BackTrack 2 is a live CD that contains a set of tools for testing, repairing, and otherwise securing Linux systems, Windows systems, and networks. Use the BackTrack menu on the main menu of this live CD to select from dozens of security-related tools. BackTrack is discussed in Chapter 19.

To boot the BackTrack live CD image from the DVD that comes with this book, insert the DVD into your PC's DVD drive, reboot, and type the following from the boot prompt:

```
boot: back
```

Gentoo 2007.1 Linux

The Gentoo minimal install CD image is included on the DVD that comes with this book. With the Gentoo CD, you can install a minimal Linux system, to which you can add any of the nearly 7,000 software packages that are available with Gentoo. Those packages can be obtained over a network connection or from a local CD, DVD, or hard disk. (A procedure for installing from the minimal Gentoo install CD is described in Chapter 13.) This same minimal install CD is included on the CD that comes with this book. To boot the Gentoo minimal CD from the DVD that comes with this book, insert the DVD into your PC's DVD drive, reboot, and type the following from the boot prompt:

```
boot: gentoo
```

Refer to Chapter 13 for information on using Gentoo. Procedures described in that chapter let you either install a desktop system from binary packages or build much of the Gentoo operating system from scratch, specifically for your computer hardware, downloading needed packages from the Internet.

Freespire 2.0

Freespire is the free, community-driven Linux system that is sponsored by Linspire, Inc. (makers of the Linspire commercial desktop Linux system). The Freespire 2.0 CD is included on the DVD that comes with this book. The Freespire CD can be run in several different ways. You can either run it as a live CD or start an installer to install the contents of that CD to your computer's hard disk. Freespire also lets you launch the gparted utility from the boot prompt so that you can change your computer's hard disk partitions before installing Freespire.

Instead of booting the Freespire CD directly from the DVD that comes with this book, you need to burn the ISO image included on that DVD to a separate CD. Here's how to do that:

1. Insert the DVD that comes with this book into your computer's DVD drive.

2. From the Freespire folder on the DVD, copy the freespire_2.0.3.iso to your computer's hard disk.

3. Eject the DVD and insert a blank CD into the DVD drive (which presumably can be used to burn CDs).

At this point, refer to the "Creating Linux CDs" section later in this appendix for information on burning the CD image to a physical CD.

openSUSE Linux

The openSUSE Linux 10.3 installation CD lets you install the SUSE Linux operating system to your hard drive from software downloaded over the network. SUSE Linux is developed and supported by Novell, which offers SUSE as part of a wider range of enterprise-ready Linux and NetWare software. openSUSE is the Novell-sponsored, community-supported free Linux.

To begin installing openSUSE to your hard disk, insert the CD into your PC's CD drive, reboot, and type the following from the boot prompt:

```
boot: suse
```

To install openSUSE from this CD, follow the installation instructions in Chapter 10.

Finding Linux Distributions on the CD

The CD that comes with this book boots directly to a variety of smaller live and install CDs. The live/install CDs included on this CD include Debian (network install), Gentoo (network install), Damn Small Linux (live/install), and INSERT (security CD), System Rescue CD, SLAX, and Puppy Linux live CDs. Coyote Linux is contained on a tar/gzip that you copy to a hard disk and build into a floppy Linux distribution from instructions in Chapter 18.

Debian GNU/Linux

The network install ISO image of the Debian GNU/Linux distribution is contained on the CD. Debian offers thoroughly tested releases that many Linux consultants and experts use because of Debian's excellent software packaging and stability. Debian is used as the sample distribution for creating a Web server (LAMP) and mail server, as described in Chapters 24 and 25, respectively.

You can start a Debian installation directly from the CD that comes with this book. With a basic install done from the CD, to add the components you need for a desktop or server system, you need to have a connection to the Internet.

To begin installing Debian to your hard disk, insert the CD into your PC's CD drive, reboot, and type the following from the boot prompt:

```
boot: debian
```

The procedure for installing Debian is included in Chapter 9.

Gentoo Minimal 2007 Linux

The Gentoo minimal install CD image is included on the CD that comes with this book. This image allows you to have a working, minimal Gentoo system without going on the Internet.

To boot the Gentoo minimal CD image from the CD that comes with this book, insert the CD into your PC's DVD drive, reboot, and type the following from the boot prompt:

```
boot: gentoo
```

Refer to Chapter 13 for information on installing Gentoo on your computer.

Damn Small Linux

Damn Small Linux is set up to boot directly from the CD that accompanies this book. This distribution illustrates how a useful desktop Linux distribution, which includes full network connectivity and some useful productivity applications, can fit in a very small space.

To run Damn Small Linux live, insert the CD into your PC's CD drive, reboot, and type the following from the boot prompt:

```
boot: dsl
```

See Chapter 19 for information on using Damn Small Linux.

Inside Security Rescue Toolkit

Inside Security Rescue Toolkit (INSERT) is a small, bootable Linux distribution that contains a variety of useful tools for checking, repairing, and recovering computers and networks. INSERT is small enough to fit on a bootable business card CD or mini-CD. While many of its tools are text-based, INSERT includes a simple graphical interface (using X and FluxBox window manager) and a few graphical tools.

To run INSERT live, insert the CD into your PC's CD drive, reboot, and type the following from the boot prompt:

```
boot: insert
```

Refer to Chapter 19 for descriptions of what's inside INSERT.

System Rescue CD

Like INSERT, System Rescue CD is a bootable Linux that includes a variety of tools for checking and fixing your installed computer systems. It includes tools for managing and fixing file systems, checking for viruses, monitoring the network, and checking whether a machine has been cracked. The System Rescue CD image can be booted directly from the CD that comes with this book.

To run System Rescue CD live, insert the CD into your PC's CD drive, reboot, and type the following from the boot prompt:

```
boot: rescuecd
```

Refer to Chapter 19 for further information about System Rescue CD.

Coyote Linux

Although not considered a major Linux distribution, Coyote Linux is an excellent illustration of a useful Linux distribution that fits on a floppy disk (1.4MB). You can copy the tar file of Coyote Linux on the CD that comes with this book to a Linux system, configure Coyote Linux to suit your needs, and copy the resulting boot image to floppy disk.

See Chapter 18 for information on how to configure and use Coyote Linux as a firewall.

SLAX

The SLAX Popcorn bootable CD image is included on the CD that comes with this book. This live CD contains a well-stocked desktop Linux system. SLAX is described in Chapter 19.

To run SLAX live, insert the CD into your PC's CD drive, reboot, and type the following from the boot prompt:

```
boot: slax
```

Puppy Linux

This mini live CD contains a desktop Linux system that can be used for creating documents, playing multimedia content, accessing the Internet, and many other functions. This distribution contains many features for configuring your desktop and saving your features across reboots. Puppy Linux is described in Chapter 19.

To run Puppy Linux live, insert the CD into your PC's CD drive, reboot, and type the following from the boot prompt:

```
boot: puppy
```

Linux Distributions Not on the DVD or CD

Not all of the Linux distributions featured in this book are included on the DVD or CD. Some of these did not encourage free redistribution of their products, while others were simply too large to include in their entirety and were not available on a single install CD or bootable live CD.

The following Linux distributions described in the book are not on the CD or DVD. The link after each distribution's name indicates the Internet site where you can find out how to purchase or otherwise obtain it.

- Yellow Dog Linux (www.terrasoftsolutions.com/store)
- Linspire (www.linspire.com/products_linspire_whatis.php)
- Red Hat Enterprise Linux (www.redhat.com/rhel/)

Some of these distributions have downloadable versions available on the Internet. I recommend that you try a Linux distribution site such as DistroWatch.com (www.distrowatch.com) to see if there is a free version of any of these distributions to try out.

If you decide to download or otherwise obtain ISO images of a Linux distribution, the following section describes how to burn those images to a physical CD.

Creating Linux CDs

You can use several tools to create bootable CDs for either installing or just running Linux from CD images on the DVD or CD. Before you begin, you need to have the following:

- **DVD or CD ISO images** — Download the ISO images you want to burn to a physical DVD or CD. (For Freespire only, you can copy the CD image to your hard disk from the DVD that comes with this book.)
- **Blank DVDs/CDs** — You need blank DVDs or CDs to burn the images to.
- **CD burner** — You need a drive that is capable of burning CDs or DVDs, depending on which you are burning.

Here's how to create bootable Linux CDs from a running Linux system (such as Fedora):

1. Download the ISO images you want to your computer's hard drive. (You'll need between 50MB and 700MB of hard disk space, depending on the size of the CD image you choose. Single-layer DVD images are usually under 4.7GB.)

2. Open a CD/DVD burning application. For this procedure, I recommend K3B CD/DVD Burning Facility (www.k3b.org). In Fedora, select the Applications menu and choose Sound & Video ⇨ K3b (or type **k3b** from a Terminal window). The K3b - CD Kreator window appears.

 K3b may not be installed on your Linux system by default. For Fedora, install K3b by typing **yum install k3b** as root user from a Terminal window.

3. From the K3b window, select Tools ⇨ Burn CD ISO Image to burn a CD image or Tools ⇨ Burn DVD ISO Image to burn a DVD image. You are asked to choose an image file.

4. Browse to the image you just downloaded or copied to hard disk and select it. Once the image you want is selected, the Burn CD Image window appears, as does a checksum on the image. (Often, you can compare the checksum number that appears against the number in an md5 file from the download directory where you got the live CD to be sure that the CD image was not corrupted.) Figure A-1 shows the Burn CD Image window ready to burn an image of Damn Small Linux.

5. Insert a blank CD into the CD burner drive, which may be a combination with your DVD drive. (If a CD/DVD Creator window pops up, you can just close it.)

6. Check the settings in the Burn CD Image window (often the defaults are fine, but you may want to slow down the speed if you get some bad burns). You can also select the Simulate check box to test the burn before actually writing to the CD. Click Start to continue.

7. When the CD is done burning, eject it (or it may eject automatically) and mark it appropriately (information such as the distribution name, version number, and date).

FIGURE A-1

Use K3b to burn your installation CDs.

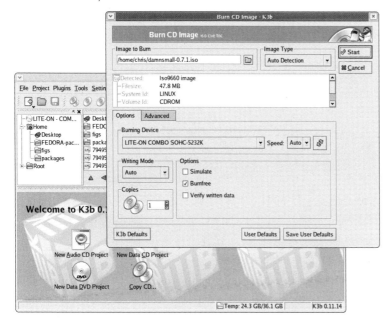

Now you're ready to begin installing (or booting) the Linux distribution you just burned. Refer to Chapter 7 for general information on installing Linux. Then go to the chapter that covers your particular distribution to find its specific installation procedure.

If you don't have Linux installed or K3b available at the moment, you can burn CDs from any CD-burning application you have available. There's a nice overview of CD installation tools and how to use them to burn CDs at the Gentoo Web site (www.gentoo.org/doc/en/faq.xml). It describes disk-burning tools that are available on Windows, Mac OS X, and Linux systems.

If you have no GUI, or don't mind working from the shell, you can use the cdrecord command to burn the ISOs. With a blank CD inserted and the ISO image you want to burn in the current directory, here's a simple command line for burning a CD image to CD using cdrecord:

```
# cdrecord -v whatever.iso
```

See the cdrecord man page (man cdrecord) to see other options available with the cdrecord command.

NOTE The growisofs command is another useful tool for burning CD and DVD ISO images. See the growisofs man page for further information.

Getting Source Code

To offer as many Linux distributions on the limited media available with the book, we have included only binary versions of the software and no source code. However, every distribution included with the book offers the source code used to build it in a form that can be downloaded from the Internet.

The following list contains links to where you can get the source code for all of the Linux distributions included with this book. In some cases, you need to choose a convenient mirror site from which to download the source code:

- **BackTrack:** `www.remote-exploit.org/backtrack_download.html`
- **Fedora:** `http://fedoraproject.org/wiki/Distribution/Download`
- **Freespire:** `http://wiki.freespire.org/index.php/Download_Freespire`
- **Gentoo:** `www.gentoo.org/main/en/where.xml`
- **KNOPPIX:** `www.knopper.net/knoppix-mirrors/index-en.html`
- **Mandriva:** `www.mandriva.com/en/download/mandrivaone`
- **Slackware:** `www.slackware.org/getslack`
- **Ubuntu:** `www.ubuntu.com/getubuntu/download`
- **Coyote:** `http://sourceforge.net/project/showfiles.php?group_id=63552`
- **Damn Small Linux:** `www.damnsmalllinux.org/download.html`
- **Debian:** `www.debian.org/CD/netinst`
- **INSERT:** `http://sourceforge.net/projects/insert`
- **Puppy:** `www.puppylinux.org/user/downloads.php`
- **SLAX:** `www.slax.org/download.php`
- **SUSE:** `http://download.opensuse.org/distribution`
- **SystemRescueCd:** `http://sourceforge.net/project/showfiles.php?group_id=85811`

Because links to Linux download sites change all the time, if the source code is not readily available from the links shown, try contacting the projects directly to find out where downloadable source code currently resides.

Appendix B

Entering the
Linux Community

Using and playing with Linux is great fun. Connecting up with others who share your joy in Linux can make the whole Linux experience that much better. Some of the ways you can connect to the Linux community include:

- Joining a Linux User Group (LUG)
- Contributing to an open source project
- Asking or answering questions at online Linux forums
- Connecting to a Linux IRC chat room

Activity in the Linux and the open source communities has grown so dramatically in recent years that many diverse outlets exist for learning and getting to know other Linux enthusiasts. This appendix contains a variety of resources that you can use to help you expand your knowledge and activity in Linux and its growing communities.

If you find that Linux is something you enjoy and want to help to flourish in the future, there are a variety of ways in which you can become a Linux advocate. Some ways of getting information on Linux advocacy information are included later in this appendix.

General Linux Sites

While Slashdot.org is probably the news site that most Linux enthusiasts keep track of and participate in, there are many other places to look for Linux and open source news as well.

- **Slashdot** (`slashdot.org`) — Probably the top news site for open source devotees. People submit links to news articles, book reviews, and interviews related to technology, science, politics, or other "news for nerds." Then everyone piles on with their own commentaries. Having your book or project "slash-dotted" means you have made the big time — although you are as likely to get crushed as you are to get praised.

- **Digg** (`http://digg.com/linux_unix`) — Some say that Digg.com has become more popular than Slashdot for providing articles relating to Linux. You can vote on which articles are most interesting to you.

- **Groklaw** (`www.groklaw.net`) — The place to look for information regarding legal issues surrounding open source software.

- **Linux Today** (`www.linuxtoday.com`) — This site gathers news that is of particular interest to software developers and IT managers.

- **LWN.net** (`www.lwn.net`) — Produces a weekly newsletter covering a range of Linux topics.

- **Newsforge** (`www.newsforge.com`) — Bills itself as the "Online Newspaper for Linux and Open Source." Contains many original articles, as well as links to up-to-the-minute open source stories from other locations on the Web.

- **LinuxInsider** (`www.linuxinsider.com`) — Covers news articles related to Linux issues around the world.

- **Linux at Wikipedia** (`http://en.wikipedia.org/wiki/Linux`) — Contains an excellent write-up of what Linux is, and includes other Wikipedia links to related topics, companies, and issues. Also, provides a good understanding of Linux history and relationships.

- **Linux.com** (`www.linux.com`) — Provides Linux information, news, tips, articles, and reference material.

- **CertCities.com** (`http://certcities.com/certs/linux_unix/columns/`) — Regularly publishes articles on Linux and UNIX.

If you need help or have questions about Linux, here are a few sites to try:

- **Linux Questions** (`www.linuxquestions.org`) — In addition to offering forums on different Linux distributions, this is a great place to ask questions related to hardware compatibility, security, and networking. The site also has some good tutorials, as well as reviews of books and Linux distributions.

- **Google Linux** (`www.google.com/linux`) — Search for Linux-specific information from this part of the Google search site.

- **Linux Forums** (`www.linuxforums.org`) — Contains active forums on your favorite distributions and has active IRC channels as well.

- **The Linux Documentation Project** (`www.tldp.org`) — Offers a wide range of HOWTOs, guides, FAQs, man pages, and other documentation related to Linux.

- **Linux Help** (`www.linuxhelp.net`) — Offers forums, news, and current information about the Linux kernel. Also contains information about finding Linux mailing lists, newsgroups, and user groups.

- **Linux Online** (`www.linux.org`) — Provides a central source of information related to Linux distributions, documentation, books, and people.

- **Linux Kernel Archives** (`www.kernel.org`) — The primary site for Linux kernel development. You can get the latest stable or testing versions of the Linux kernel. Not the first place to start with Linux, but I thought you'd want to know it's there.

Linux Distributions

Every major Linux distribution has a Web site that provides information about how to get it and use it. If you haven't chosen a distribution yet, here are some sites that can help you evaluate, find, and get a Linux distribution that interests you:

- **Distrowatch** (`distrowatch.com`) — Contains information about a few hundred different Linux distributions. The site provides an easy way to find out about different distributions, and then simply connect to the distribution's home page, download site, or related forums.

- **LWN.net Linux Distributions** (`lwn.net/Distributions`) — If you want to read succinct descriptions of more than 400 Linux distributions on one page, this is the place to go.

Here are key sites associated with Linux distributions covered in this book:

- **Fedora** (`http://fedoraproject.org`) — Community-driven Linux, supported by Red Hat. Look to Livna.org (`rpm.livna.org`) for downloads of add-on software for Fedora. FedoraForum.org is a popular Forum site for Fedora.

- **Red Hat Enterprise Linux** (`www.redhat.com`) — Check the main Red Hat Web site for information on commercial Linux products.

- **Debian GNU/Linux** (`www.debian.org`) — Get news, documentation, support, and download information about Debian. Try the Debian news site (`www.us.debian.org/News/`) for the latest news articles on Debian.

- **Ubuntu Linux** (`www.ubuntu.com`) — Learn about the Ubuntu Linux distribution, community, and related products from this official Ubuntu site. From the Ubuntu Wiki (`https://wiki.ubuntu.com`), find links to documentation, HOWTOs, community sites, events, and releases.

- **SUSE** (`www.novell.com/linux/`) — Get product and support information from this project's site. The Novell site also provides information about Novell's own Linux offerings and details of its recent alliance with Microsoft.

- **openSUSE** (`www.opensuse.org`) — Get information and downloads, connect to mailing lists and forums, and participate in the community-supported version of SUSE.

- **KNOPPIX** (`www.knopper.net/knoppix/index-en.html`) — The official KNOPPIX page on its creator's (Klaus Knopper's) Web site. An active KNOPPIX forum is available from `www.knoppix.net/forum/`.

- **Yellow Dog** (`www.terrasoftsolutions.com/products/ydl`) — From this site, sponsored by Terra Soft Solutions, you can purchase Yellow Dog Linux on CDs or get it pre-installed on Mac hardware. The `YDL.net` site offers some extra services for Yellow Dog Linux users, such as personal e-mail accounts and Web space.

- **Gentoo** (`www.gentoo.org`) — The center for the very active Gentoo community. The site contains a wealth of information about Gentoo and plenty of forums and IRC channels in which to participate. You'll find a solid and growing documentation set to back up the distribution and tons of software packages to try (in the thousands).

- **Slackware** (`www.slackware.org`) — Check the changelogs at this site to get a feel for the latest Slackware developments. Try LinuxPackages (`www.linuxpackages.net`) for a broader range of information about Slackware.

- **Linspire** (`www.linspire.com`) — Purchase a computer running Linspire from this site, or just buy the boxed set. Linspire offers a Live CD version you can try out for free.

- **Mandriva** (`www.mandrivalinux.com`) — Formed from the merger of Mandrake Linux and Connectiva Linux, the Mandriva Linux Web site gives visitors a variety of Linux products, services, and support.

Companies and Groups Supporting Linux

Some companies and organizations make important contributions to Linux and open source software without producing their own Linux distribution. Here are some of the most prominent ones:

- **SourceForge** (`web.sourceforge.com`) — It maintains the open source development site Freshmeat (`freshmeat.net`) as well as SourceForge (`www.sourceforge.net`). It also maintains information technology sites, such as Slashdot (`slashdot.org`), NewsForge (`www.newsforge.com`), Linux.com (`www.linux.com`), and IT Manager's Journal (`www.itmanagersjournal.com`).

- **IBM** (`www.ibm.com/linux`) — Because IBM has taken on the lion's share of lawsuits against Linux and done a lot to further Linux, especially in the enterprise area, it deserves a mention here. There are many good resources for Linux at IBM's Web site, including some excellent white papers covering Linux in business.

- **Ibiblio** (`www.ibiblio.org`) — Contains a massive archive of Linux software and documentation (`www.ibiblio.org/pub/linux`).

Major Linux Projects

As you know by now, the name Linux comes from the Linux kernel created by Linus Torvalds. The desktop, application, server, and other software needed to create a full Linux system are added from other open source projects. The following is a list of some of the major open source software organizations that usually have software included with Linux:

- **Free Software Foundation** (www.fsf.org) — Supports the GNU project, which produces much of the software outside the kernel that is associated with Linux. In particular, open source versions of nearly every early UNIX command have been implemented by the GNU project.

- **Apache Software Foundation** (www.apache.org) — Produces the Apache (HTTP) Web server. It also manages related projects, such as SpamAssassin (spam filtering software) and a variety of modules for serving special Web content (perl, SSL, PHP, and so on).

- **K Desktop Environment** (www.kde.org) — Develops KDE, one of the two leading desktop environments used with Linux.

- **GNOME** (www.gnome.org) — Develops the other leading Linux desktop environment (used as the default desktop for Red Hat Linux systems).

- **X.Org** (www.x.org) and **XFree86** (www.xfree86.org) — These two organizations provide different implementations of the X Window System graphical desktop framework software.

- **Internet Systems Consortium** (www.isc.org) — Develops several major open source software projects related to the Internet. These include Bind (domain name system server), INN (InterNetNews news server), and DHCP (dynamic host configuration protocol).

Linux User Groups

A good way to learn more about Linux and become more a part of the Linux community is to hook up with a Linux User Group (LUG). LUGs tend to come and go, so you might have to do some work to track one down in your area. Here are some places to start your search:

- **Google** (www.google.com/linux) — I found both of the LUGs I've been associated with by using Google to search for the word "Linux" and the city closest to where I was living.

- **Linux Meetup Groups** (linux.meetup.com) — Enter your ZIP code to search for the nearest LUG in your area.

- **Linux Online** (www.linux.org/groups) — Offers a large, international list of Linux User Groups. Select your country to see a list of available groups.

If there is no Linux User Group in your area, you might consider starting one. To get information on what LUGs are all about and some suggestions about starting one, refer to the Linux User Group HOWTO (www.tldp.org/HOWTO/User-Group-HOWTO.html).

Advocating Linux

There are lots of ways you can help advocate Linux in the world. Here are links to a few sites that can help you advocate Linux:

- **Advocating Linux** (`http://liw.iki.fi/liw/texts/advocating-linux.html`)— Discusses ways to promote the use of Linux (as well as some approaches to avoid).
- **25 Reasons** (`www.linfo.org/reasons_to_convert.html`)— Contains a list of 25 reasons to convert to Linux.
- **The Linux Advocate** (`www.thelinuxadvocate.com/`)— This blog discusses pressing issues related to using and advocating Linux.
- **Linux Advocacy Group** (`www.faqs.org/faqs/linux/advocacy`)— The FAQ available from this site describes the comp.os.linux.advocacy news group. From that news group, you can communicate with others who are interested in Linux. The group's charter is "For discussion of the benefits of Linux compared to other operating systems."

This book itself can be a useful tool for Linux advocacy. Besides getting a flavor for the different Linux distributions, and many of the major ways to use Linux, you can also directly boot up several different Linux distributions from the CD and DVD that come with this book so you can show people how Linux works.

Index

H

Y

Z

GNU General Public License

Version 2, June 1991

Copyright © 1989, 1991 Free Software Foundation, Inc.

59 Temple Place - Suite 330, Boston, MA 02111-1307, USA

Preamble

The licenses for most software are designed to take away your freedom to share and change it. By contrast, the GNU General Public License is intended to guarantee your freedom to share and change free software — to make sure the software is free for all its users. This General Public License applies to most of the Free Software Foundation's software and to any other program whose authors commit to using it. (Some other Free Software Foundation software is covered by the GNU Library General Public License instead.) You can apply it to your programs, too.

When we speak of free software, we are referring to freedom, not price. Our General Public Licenses are designed to make sure that you have the freedom to distribute copies of free software (and charge for this service if you wish), that you receive source code or can get it if you want it, that you can change the software or use pieces of it in new free programs; and that you know you can do these things.

To protect your rights, we need to make restrictions that forbid anyone to deny you these rights or to ask you to surrender the rights. These restrictions translate to certain responsibilities for you if you distribute copies of the software, or if you modify it.

For example, if you distribute copies of such a program, whether gratis or for a fee, you must give the recipients all the rights that you have. You must make sure that they, too, receive or can get the source code. And you must show them these terms so they know their rights.

We protect your rights with two steps: (1) copyright the software, and (2) offer you this license which gives you legal permission to copy, distribute and/or modify the software.

Also, for each author's protection and ours, we want to make certain that everyone understands that there is no warranty for this free software. If the software is modified by someone else and passed on, we want its recipients to know that what they have is not the original, so that any problems introduced by others will not reflect on the original authors' reputations.

Finally, any free program is threatened constantly by software patents. We wish to avoid the danger that redistributors of a free program will individually obtain patent licenses, in effect making the program proprietary. To prevent this, we have made it clear that any patent must be licensed for everyone's free use or not licensed at all.

The precise terms and conditions for copying, distribution and modification follow.

Terms and Conditions for Copying, Distribution and Modification

0. This License applies to any program or other work which contains a notice placed by the copyright holder saying it may be distributed under the terms of this General Public License. The "Program", below, refers to any such program or work, and a "work based on the Program" means either the

Program or any derivative work under copyright law: that is to say, a work containing the Program or a portion of it, either verbatim or with modifications and/or translated into another language. (Hereinafter, translation is included without limitation in the term "modification".) Each licensee is addressed as "you".

Activities other than copying, distribution and modification are not covered by this License; they are outside its scope. The act of running the Program is not restricted, and the output from the Program is covered only if its contents constitute a work based on the Program (independent of having been made by running the Program). Whether that is true depends on what the Program does.

1. You may copy and distribute verbatim copies of the Program's source code as you receive it, in any medium, provided that you conspicuously and appropriately publish on each copy an appropriate copyright notice and disclaimer of warranty; keep intact all the notices that refer to this License and to the absence of any warranty; and give any other recipients of the Program a copy of this License along with the Program.

   You may charge a fee for the physical act of transferring a copy, and you may at your option offer warranty protection in exchange for a fee.

2. You may modify your copy or copies of the Program or any portion of it, thus forming a work based on the Program, and copy and distribute such modifications or work under the terms of Section 1 above, provided that you also meet all of these conditions:

   a) You must cause the modified files to carry prominent notices stating that you changed the files and the date of any change.

   b) You must cause any work that you distribute or publish, that in whole or in part contains or is derived from the Program or any part thereof, to be licensed as a whole at no charge to all third parties under the terms of this License.

   c) If the modified program normally reads commands interactively when run, you must cause it, when started running for such interactive use in the most ordinary way, to print or display an announcement including an appropriate copyright notice and a notice that there is no warranty (or else, saying that you provide a warranty) and that users may redistribute the program under these conditions, and telling the user how to view a copy of this License. (Exception: if the Program itself is interactive but does not normally print such an announcement, your work based on the Program is not required to print an announcement.)

   These requirements apply to the modified work as a whole. If identifiable sections of that work are not derived from the Program, and can be reasonably considered independent and separate works in themselves, then this License, and its terms, do not apply to those sections when you distribute them as separate works. But when you distribute the same sections as part of a whole which is a work based on the Program, the distribution of the whole must be on the terms of this License, whose permissions for other licensees extend to the entire whole, and thus to each and every part regardless of who wrote it.

   Thus, it is not the intent of this section to claim rights or contest your rights to work written entirely by you; rather, the intent is to exercise the right to control the distribution of derivative or collective works based on the Program.

   In addition, mere aggregation of another work not based on the Program with the Program (or with a work based on the Program) on a volume of a storage or distribution medium does not bring the other work under the scope of this License.

3. You may copy and distribute the Program (or a work based on it, under Section 2) in object code or executable form under the terms of Sections 1 and 2 above provided that you also do one of the following:

   a) Accompany it with the complete corresponding machine-readable source code, which must be distributed under the terms of Sections 1 and 2 above on a medium customarily used for software interchange; or,

b) Accompany it with a written offer, valid for at least three years, to give any third party, for a charge no more than your cost of physically performing source distribution, a complete machine-readable copy of the corresponding source code, to be distributed under the terms of Sections 1 and 2 above on a medium customarily used for software interchange; or,

c) Accompany it with the information you received as to the offer to distribute corresponding source code. (This alternative is allowed only for noncommercial distribution and only if you received the program in object code or executable form with such an offer, in accord with Subsection b above.)

The source code for a work means the preferred form of the work for making modifications to it. For an executable work, complete source code means all the source code for all modules it contains, plus any associated interface definition files, plus the scripts used to control compilation and installation of the executable. However, as a special exception, the source code distributed need not include anything that is normally distributed (in either source or binary form) with the major components (compiler, kernel, and so on) of the operating system on which the executable runs, unless that component itself accompanies the executable.

If distribution of executable or object code is made by offering access to copy from a designated place, then offering equivalent access to copy the source code from the same place counts as distribution of the source code, even though third parties are not compelled to copy the source along with the object code.

4. You may not copy, modify, sublicense, or distribute the Program except as expressly provided under this License. Any attempt otherwise to copy, modify, sublicense or distribute the Program is void, and will automatically terminate your rights under this License. However, parties who have received copies, or rights, from you under this License will not have their licenses terminated so long as such parties remain in full compliance.

5. You are not required to accept this License, since you have not signed it. However, nothing else grants you permission to modify or distribute the Program or its derivative works. These actions are prohibited by law if you do not accept this License. Therefore, by modifying or distributing the Program (or any work based on the Program), you indicate your acceptance of this License to do so, and all its terms and conditions for copying, distributing or modifying the Program or works based on it.

6. Each time you redistribute the Program (or any work based on the Program), the recipient automatically receives a license from the original licensor to copy, distribute or modify the Program subject to these terms and conditions. You may not impose any further restrictions on the recipients' exercise of the rights granted herein. You are not responsible for enforcing compliance by third parties to this License.

7. If, as a consequence of a court judgment or allegation of patent infringement or for any other reason (not limited to patent issues), conditions are imposed on you (whether by court order, agreement or otherwise) that contradict the conditions of this License, they do not excuse you from the conditions of this License. If you cannot distribute so as to satisfy simultaneously your obligations under this License and any other pertinent obligations, then as a consequence you may not distribute the Program at all. For example, if a patent license would not permit royalty-free redistribution of the Program by all those who receive copies directly or indirectly through you, then the only way you could satisfy both it and this License would be to refrain entirely from distribution of the Program.

If any portion of this section is held invalid or unenforceable under any particular circumstance, the balance of the section is intended to apply and the section as a whole is intended to apply in other circumstances.

It is not the purpose of this section to induce you to infringe any patents or other property right claims or to contest validity of any such claims; this section has the sole purpose of protecting the integrity of the free software distribution system, which is implemented by public license practices. Many people have made generous contributions to the wide range of software distributed through that system in reliance on consistent application of that system; it is up to the author/donor to decide if he or she is willing to distribute software through any other system and a licensee cannot impose that choice.

This section is intended to make thoroughly clear what is believed to be a consequence of the rest of this License.

8. If the distribution and/or use of the Program is restricted in certain countries either by patents or by copyrighted interfaces, the original copyright holder who places the Program under this License may add an explicit geographical distribution limitation excluding those countries, so that distribution is permitted only in or among countries not thus excluded. In such case, this License incorporates the limitation as if written in the body of this License.

9. The Free Software Foundation may publish revised and/or new versions of the General Public License from time to time. Such new versions will be similar in spirit to the present version, but may differ in detail to address new problems or concerns.

    Each version is given a distinguishing version number. If the Program specifies a version number of this License which applies to it and "any later version", you have the option of following the terms and conditions either of that version or of any later version published by the Free Software Foundation. If the Program does not specify a version number of this License, you may choose any version ever published by the Free Software Foundation.

10. If you wish to incorporate parts of the Program into other free programs whose distribution conditions are different, write to the author to ask for permission. For software which is copyrighted by the Free Software Foundation, write to the Free Software Foundation; we sometimes make exceptions for this. Our decision will be guided by the two goals of preserving the free status of all derivatives of our free software and of promoting the sharing and reuse of software generally.

NO WARRANTY

11. BECAUSE THE PROGRAM IS LICENSED FREE OF CHARGE, THERE IS NO WARRANTY FOR THE PROGRAM, TO THE EXTENT PERMITTED BY APPLICABLE LAW. EXCEPT WHEN OTHERWISE STATED IN WRITING THE COPYRIGHT HOLDERS AND/OR OTHER PARTIES PROVIDE THE PROGRAM "AS IS" WITHOUT WARRANTY OF ANY KIND, EITHER EXPRESSED OR IMPLIED, INCLUDING, BUT NOT LIMITED TO, THE IMPLIED WARRANTIES OF MERCHANTABILITY AND FITNESS FOR A PARTICULAR PURPOSE. THE ENTIRE RISK AS TO THE QUALITY AND PERFORMANCE OF THE PROGRAM IS WITH YOU. SHOULD THE PROGRAM PROVE DEFECTIVE, YOU ASSUME THE COST OF ALL NECESSARY SERVICING, REPAIR OR CORRECTION.

12. IN NO EVENT UNLESS REQUIRED BY APPLICABLE LAW OR AGREED TO IN WRITING WILL ANY COPYRIGHT HOLDER, OR ANY OTHER PARTY WHO MAY MODIFY AND/OR REDISTRIBUTE THE PROGRAM AS PERMITTED ABOVE, BE LIABLE TO YOU FOR DAMAGES, INCLUDING ANY GENERAL, SPECIAL, INCIDENTAL OR CONSEQUENTIAL DAMAGES ARISING OUT OF THE USE OR INABILITY TO USE THE PROGRAM (INCLUDING BUT NOT LIMITED TO LOSS OF DATA OR DATA BEING RENDERED INACCURATE OR LOSSES SUSTAINED BY YOU OR THIRD PARTIES OR A FAILURE OF THE PROGRAM TO OPERATE WITH ANY OTHER PROGRAMS), EVEN IF SUCH HOLDER OR OTHER PARTY HAS BEEN ADVISED OF THE POSSIBILITY OF SUCH DAMAGES.

END OF TERMS AND CONDITIONS